Economics of Terrorism and Counter-Terrorism Measures

Satya P. Das

Economics of Terrorism and Counter-Terrorism Measures

History, Theory, and Evidence

Springer

Satya P. Das
Department of Economics
University of South Florida
Tampa, FL, USA

ISBN 978-3-030-96576-1 ISBN 978-3-030-96577-8 (eBook)
https://doi.org/10.1007/978-3-030-96577-8

This Springer imprint is published by the registered company Springer Nature Switzerland AG
The registered company address is: Gewerbestrasse 11, 6330 Cham, Switzerland

To ....

Parents
Rajashree, Sanghamitra,
Sidhartha, Sanjay,
Arpita, Sumeet, and Arup

Preface

The book grew out of an upper-undergraduate class, Economics of War and Terror (later titled Economics of War, Terror and Conflict), that I taught at the University of Illinois at Urbana-Champaign during 2015–2018. I clearly remember when Martin Perry, Chairman of the Department of Economics, wrote to me in 2014 that he would like me to teach this course as a visiting professor. I was excited at the prospect of teaching such an offbeat-topic course, but apprehensive too. I knew that Walter Enders and Todd Sandler had published a book, entitled *The Political Economy of Terrorism*, which I hadn't read but had heard about. I wasn't sure if this book will work for the course. Another well-respected textbook on terrorism by Jonathan White, *Terrorism and Homeland Security*, came to my knowledge later. In any case, I was more familiar with research papers on terrorism (and virtually nothing on war) published in professional journals and had no idea about how one could frame the main ideas of frontline research papers that are technically demanding in terms of tools that a junior or a senior undergraduate student would grasp. But, somehow, I had the inner confidence that I will be able to figure this out on my own. Essentially, that happened. As I taught the course repeatedly over the semesters, the slides got better, I discovered many other pieces of research in and outside of economics, and the proportion of lectures on terrorism in the total number of lectures on terrorism, war, and conflict grew.

Apart from my own enthusiasm, two things kept me going. First, it is the students. At the semester end, some of them would come up to me and say that it was a difficult course—unlike what they had anticipated in the beginning—and yet they enjoyed it. Some even went to the extent of expressing that it was one of the best courses they took at UIUC. This was immensely gratifying. I had taught undergraduate courses in economics in the USA several decades ago, but my evaluation in this course turned out to be the best in my long teaching career. (For a change, no one complained about my "foreign" accent in the course evaluation forms.) I found the undergraduate students at UIUC smart, enthusiastic, and receptive. Second, it is the appreciation and support I received from Martin Perry. On almost every occasion where he would introduce me to someone, he would say that I was teaching this course and it was quite popular. He even mentioned that when he introduced me as a visiting faculty in the graduation ceremony at the end of the 2016–2017 academic year. I am grateful to Martin Perry.

The idea of writing this book naturally came during the last semester of teaching at UIUC. I had many slides on different aspects of terrorism. I needed to convert them into regular text—at least that is what I had initially thought. But, as I pondered over the content, I quickly realized that a book on the economics of terrorism must go far beyond what I was able to cover in a semester-long course. It has taken me much longer to finish the book than what I had anticipated. Being semi-retired and enjoying the sunshine and warm weather of Florida played an important role.

I thank the reviewers for their useful and encouraging comments. I am especially grateful to Lorraine Klimowich, the commissioning editor of Springer Nature, who was supportive right from the word "go."

I am especially indebted to my wife, Rajashree, for her patience. My spending of hours and days in planning and writing chapters has already deprived us of some precious time together, especially when both of us are in our golden years of life and platinum jubilee is around the corner.

Tampa, FL, USA Satya P. Das
January 2022

Contents

Abbreviations

2SLS: Two-stage least squares

ABT: Ansarullah Bangla Team
AeH: Ahl-e-Hadith
ALF: Animal Liberation Front
AML: Anti-money laundering
AML/CFT: Anti-money laundering and combating financing of terrorism
AMLID: Anti-Money Laundering International Database
ANO: Abu Nidal Organization
APG: Asia Pacific Group
AQAP: al-Qaida in the Arabian Peninsula
AQI: al-Qaeda in Iraq
AQIM: al-Qaeda in the Islamic Maghreb
AQIS: al-Qaeda in the Indian Subcontinent
AR: Auto-regressive
ARMA: Auto-regressive moving average
ASALA: Armenian Secret Army for the Liberation of Armenia
ATS: American Terrorism Study
ATUS: American Time Use Survey
AUC: United Self-Defence Forces of Colombia

BAAD: Big, Allied and Dangerous
BHPS: British Household Panel Survey
BRFSS: Behavioral Risk Factor Surveillance System

CBRN: Chemical, Biological, Radioactive and Nuclear
CDD: Customer Due Diligence
CFATF: Caribbean Financial Action Task Force
CFT: Combating Financing of Terror
CIRA: Continuity IRA
COIN: Counter-insurgency
CPI(M): Communist Party of India (Marxist)
CPOST: Chicago Project on Security & Threats
CPP: Communist Party of Philippines
CSP: Coalition to Save the Preserves
CT: Counter-Terrorism
CTITF: Counter-Terrorism Implementation Task Force

Daesh: al-Dawla al-Islamiya fi al-Iraq wa al-Sham
DEA: Drug Enforcement Administration
DiD: Difference-in-Differences
DNFBP: Designated and non-financial businesses and profession
DOD: Department of Defense
DOTS: Data on Terrorist Subjects
DPKO: Department of Peace Keeping Operations
DUP: Democratic Unionist Party

EAG: Euro Asian Group
ECDB: Extremist Crime Database
EDD: Enhanced Due Diligence
EIJ: Egyptian Islamic Jihad

ELF: Earth Liberation Front
ELN: Ejército de Liberación Nacional
EOKA: Ethnikí Orgánosis Kipriakoú Agónos
ERP: Ejército Revolucionario del Pueblo
ESAAMLG: Eastern and Southern Africa Anti-Money Laundering Group
ETA: Euskadi Ta Askatasun
ETIM: East Turkestan Islamic Movement
ETLO: East Turkistan Liberation Organization
EU TFTS: EU TFTS: European Terrorist Finance Tracking System

FALN: Fuerzas Armadas de Liberacion Nacional
FARC: Fuerzas Armadas Revolutionarias de Colombia
FATA: Federally Administered Tribal Area
FATF: Financial Action Task Force
FBA: Fenian Brotherhood of America
FDI: Foreign Direct Investment
FDN: Nicaraguan Democratic Force
FinCEN: Financial Crimes Enforcement Network
FIND: Fixed INTERPOL Network Database
FIU: Financial Intelligence Unit
FLN: Front de Libération Nationale
FMLN: Farabundo Marti National Liberation Front
FPL: Fuerzas Populares de Liberación Farabundo Martí
FSLN: Sandinista National Liberation Front or Frente Sandinista de Liberación Nacional
FTF: Foreign Terrorist Fighter
FTO: Foreign Terrorist Organization

GAFILAT: Financial Action Task Force of Latin America
GAFISUD: Financial Action Task Force on Money Laundering in South America
GAL: Anti-Terrorist Liberation Groups
GHQ: General Health Questionnaire
GIABA: Inter-Governmental Action Group Against Money Laundering in West Africa
GLS: Generalized least squares
GPI: Global Peace Database
GPML: Global Programme against Money Laundering
GSPC: Salafist Group for Preaching and Combat
GTD: Global Terrorism Database
GTI: Global Terrorism Index

HDP: People's Democratic Party
HLFRD: Holy Land Foundation for Relief and Development
HN: Haqqani Network
HNLC: Hynniewtrep National Council
HTS: Hayat Tahrir al-Sham
HuJI-B: Harkat-ul-Jihad-al Islami Bangladesh

I&I: Intelligence and infiltration
IAI: Islamic Army of Iraq
IBC: Iso-Benefit Curve
ICD: Implantable cardioverter-defibrillator
ICU: Islamic Courts Union
IDC: Iso-Damage Curve
IDF: Israel Defense Forces
IEC: Israeli Electric Corporation
IED: Improved Explosive Device
IEP: Institute for Peace and Economics
IEWG: Information Exchange on Money Laundering/Terrorist Financing Working Group
IG: Egyptian Islamic Group
IM: Indian Mujahideen
IMF: International Monetary Fund
IMoLIN: International Money Laundering Information Network
IMU: Islamic Movement of Uzbekistan

INL: Bureau of International Narcotics and Law Enforcement Affairs
INLA: Irish National Liberation Army
INTERPOL: International Criminal Police Organization
IPKF: Indian Peace Keeping Force
IPLO: Irish People's Liberation Organization
IRA: Irish Republic Army
IRB: Irish Republic Brotherhood
IRGC: Islamic Revolutionary Guard Corps
IS: Islamic State
ISCAP: Islamic State Central Africa Province
ISGS: Islamic State in the Greater Sahara
ISI: Islamic State of Iraq
ISI-Pakistan: Inter-Services Intelligence
ISIL: Islamic State of Iraq and Levant
ISIS: Islamic State of Syria and Iraq
ISIS-DRC: Islamic State of Iraq and Syria âĂŞ Democratic Republic of the Congo
ISIS-Egypt: Islamic State in Egypt
ISIS-K: ISIS-Khorakan
ISIS-Libya: Islamic State in Libya
ISIS-Mozambique: Islamic State of Iraq and Syria âĂŞ Mozambique
ISVG: Institute for the Study of Violent Groups
ISWAP: Islamic State in West Africa Province
ITERATE: International Terrorism Attributes of Terrorist Events
IVC: International Verification Commission

J&K: Jammu & Kashmir
JaK: Jund al-Khilafah
JCAG: Justice Commandos of the Armenian Genocide
JDL: Jewish Defense League
JeM: Jaish-e-Mohammad
JI: Jemaah Islamiyah
JKLF: Jammu & Kashmir Liberation Front
JMB: Jamaat-ul-Mujahideen Bangladesh
JRA: Japanese Red Army
JTIC: Jane's Terrorism & Insurgency Centre
JuD: Jamaat-ud-Dawa

KCP: Kangleipak Communist Party
KDPI: Kurdistan Democratic Party - Iran
KFR: Kidnapping for Ransom
KH: Kata'ib Hezbollah
KKK: Ku Klax Klan
KLO: Kamtapur Liberation Organization
KOF: Konjunkturforschungsstelle
KYC: Know Your Customer
KYKL: Kanglei Yawol Kanna Lup

LCB: Lebanese Canadian Bank
LeT: Lashkar-e-Taiba
LRA: Lord's Resistance Army
LTTE: Liberation Tigers of Tamil Eelam

MA: Moving average
MAR: Mean-adjusted return
MAR: Minorities at Risk
MAS: Muerte a Secuestradores
MB: Muslim Brotherhood
MC: Marginal cost
MDI: Markaz-ad-Dawa-wal-Irshad
MENA: Middle East and North Africa
MIND: Mobile INTERPOL Network Database
MIPT: Memorial Institute for the Prevention of Terrorism
MIRA: Armed Revolutionary Independence Movement
MKAR: Market-Adjusted Return
MML: Milli Muslim League
MNJTF: Multinational Joint Task Force
MNPF: Manipur Naga People's Front

MRTA: Tupac Amaru Revolutionary Movement
MSB: Money Service Business
MSCWG: Membership, Support, and Compliance Working Group

NFDI: Net Foreign Direct Investment
NGO: Non-Government Organization
NLFT: National Liberation Front of Twipra
NNC: Naga National Council
NORAID: Northern Aid Committee
NPA: New People's Army
NPO: Non-Profit Organization
NSU: National Social Underground
NTJ: National Thowheeth Jama'ath
NuFAD: Nuclear Facilities Attack Database
NWLF: New World Liberation Front

OAS/CICAD: Organization of American States - Inter-American Drug Abuse Control Commission
OCO: Overseas Contingency Operations
OECD: Organization of Economic Cooperation and Development
OIR: Operation Inherent Resolve
OIRA: Official IRA
OIRA: Original IRA
OLS: Ordinary least squares
OPEC: Organization of Petrol Exporting Countries
OPTEMPO: Operational tempo

PA: Palestinian Authority
PCC: Colombian Community Party
PCPSR: Palestinian Center for Policy and Survey Research
PCS: Partido Comunista Salvadoreño
PDCK: People's Democratic Council of Karbi Longri
PEP: Politically exposed persons
PFLP: Popular Front for the Liberation of Palestine
PFLP-GC: Popular Front for the Liberation of Palestine - General Command
PHS: Population and Housing Survey
PIJ: Palestinian Islamic Jihad
PIRA: Provisional IRA
PIRUS: Profiles of Individual Radicalization in the United States
PJAK: Partiya Jiyana Azadi Kurdistan
PKK: Kurdistan Workers Party
PLAM: People's Liberation Army
PLC: Palestinian Legislative Council
PLO: Palestine Liberation Organization
POICN: Profiles of Incidents involving CBRN and Non-State Actors
PP: People's Party
PPF: Production Possibility Frontier
PPP: Purchasing Power Parity
PPT-US: Profiles of Perpetrators of Terrorism in the United States
PRI: Political Rights Index
PRTC: Partido Revolucionario de los Trabajadores Centroamericanos
PSOE: Spanish Socialist Workers Party
PTSD: Post Traumatic Stress Disorder
PUP: Progressive Unionist Party

RAF: Red Army Faction
RAR: Risk-adjusted return
RAW: Research and Analysis Wing
RBA: Risk-Based Approach
RDD: Regression Discontinuity Design
RDWTI: RAND Database of Worldwide Terrorism Incidents
RIHS: Revival of Islamic Heritage Society
RIRA: Real IRA
RN: Resistencia Nacional
ROYG: Republic of Yemen Government
RSRSBCM: Riyadus-Salikhin Reconnaissance and Sabotage Battalion of Chechen Martyrs
RUC: Royal Ulster Constabulary
RZ: Revolutionäre Zellen

SAM: Surface to Air Missiles
SANIP: Syria, Afghanistan, Nigeria, Iraq and Pakistan
SATP: South Asia Terrorism Portal
SD: Security-deterrence
SDD: Simplified Due Diligence
SDF: Syrian Democratic Forces
SDLP: Social Democratic and Labour Party
SDR: Special Drawing Rights
SIMI: Students Islamic Movement of India
SLA: South Lebanon Army
SMB: Social marginal benefit
SMC: Social marginal cost
SOCOM: Special Operations Command
SPIR: Special Purpose Islamic Regiment
STaR: Smooth transition regression
START: Study of Terrorism and Responses to Terrorism
STC: Southern Transition Council
SUR: Seemingly Unrelated Regression
SWB: Subjective well-being
SWIFT: Society for Worldwide Interbank Financial Telecommunication

TAJK: Tehreek-e-Azaadi Jammu and Kashmir
TEL: Terrorist Exclusion List
TEVUS: Terrorism and Extreme Violence in the United States
TFS: Counter Threat Finance and Sanctions
TFTC: Terrorist Financing Targeting Center
TFTP: Terrorist Finance Tracking Program
TIM: Tanzim Islahul Muslimeen
TKB: Terrorism Knowledge Base
TMT: Türk Mukavemet Teşkilati
TOPs: Terrorist Organization Profiles
TTP: Tehreek-e-Taliban
TUF: Tamil United Front
TULF: Tamil United Liberation Front
TWEED: Terrorism in Western Europe: Events Data

UBO: Ultimate beneficial owner
UDA: Ulster Defence Association
UDP: Ulster Democratic Party
UFF: Ulster Freedom Fighters
ULFA: United Liberation Front of Assam
ULFA-I: United Liberation Front of Assam - Independent
UNCTC: UN Counter-Terrorism Centre
UNOCT: UN Office of Counter-Terrorism
UNODC: UN Office on Drugs and Crime
UP: Patriotic Union
USAID: U.S. Agency for International Development
UUP: Ulster Unionist Party
UVF: Ulster Volunteer Force

VAR: Vector Auto-Regression (Auto-Regressive)
VAT: Value-added tax

WITS: Worldwide Incidents Tracking System
WMD: Weapons of Mass Destruction
WoT: War on Terror

YPJ: Yekîneyên Parastina Jin

Part I
Introduction

Chapter 1

Introduction

1.1 What This Book Is About and My Goals

THIS book presents a systematic study of terrorism from the standpoint of economic analysis, pitched at an upper-undergraduate economics level. However, the contents of some chapters are general and descriptive enough to arouse interest among students and colleagues in economics, political science, and other social sciences as well as those interested in security studies especially terrorism and the general public.

As said in the Preface, the book is an outcome of my research in the field of terrorism and teaching of it at the University of Illinois at Urbana-Champaign over three years. Around 2005 when I initiated my research on terrorism, many of my colleagues were intrigued. They would ask me what I meant by "researching"—as an economist—on a subject like terrorism: tackling terrorism is like a war, what do economists have to say, really? Some thought the economics of terrorism referred "only" to how terrorism is funded. I still face such questions and perceptions now, but much less so than earlier, since, by now, there already exists a huge body of research in economics and other social disciplines on terrorism.

My goals in writing this book are as follows. First and foremost, almost all of us have some opinion on the problem of terrorism, since this has affected all of us one way or another. How true are our beliefs on various aspects of terrorism? One of my objectives is to dispel common myths and demystify terrorism, so-to-speak, by presenting data and deducing data-based conclusions. Indeed, some facts may surprise you. I put such facts and their implications in a text box: ***Is That So?*** For instance, Islamic fundamentalism is *not* the prime motivation behind the majority of lone-wolf attacks in the USA in recent years (see *Is that So?* No. 1.5). In addition to *Is that So?*, the text also contains *Supplement Break* boxes, presenting relevant information as supplementary material.

S. P. Das, *Economics of Terrorism and Counter-Terrorism Measures*,
https://doi.org/10.1007/978-3-030-96577-8_1

Second, there is a considerable emphasis on analytics, relying on various methodologies, both theoretical and empirical, used in economics and other social sciences. I illustrate and/or develop many of these tools and techniques from scratch. It is my intention that students, professionals, and even casual researchers can learn some of the tools in the process of gaining knowledge on terrorism that can be potentially applied outside of the issue of terrorism.

Third, an obvious question of paramount importance is, how can we contain, reduce, or hopefully eliminate terrorism? More conventionally put, how we can win the war on terror (WoT)? To answer this question, we need to deeply understand how counter-terrorism (CT) measures work. Fighting terrorism is not just a war game with unlimited supplies of arms and resources. CT measures are costly both directly and indirectly. For instance, the direct cost of security measures against terror attacks would include paying for personnel, equipment, etc. that is financed by the taxpayers. There are serious indirect costs in terms of loss of privacy and civil liberty. Using armed forces overseas to fight terrorists and terror organizations will not just burden the national treasury but also entail potential collateral damage in terms of civilian lives lost and properties damaged, not to mention, coffins coming home from overseas. For liberal democracies like the USA and other Western nations, lives lost and properties damaged in other countries because of their military interventions do carry costs in terms of international relations and goodwill.

In sum, choosing the kind and level of measures to counter terror is not just a result of available technology and military might, but, to a large extent, an economic decision, because resources needed for these measures and some of their side effects are costly. Hence understanding through an economics lens the mechanisms behind how various CT measures may work is immensely useful. The book contains theoretical models that aim to illustrate the economic mechanisms of different types of CT measures as well as a vast array of empirical studies and regularities. All this may, hopefully, help us to devise more effective CT measures than otherwise.

Fourth, while the content of the book is of general interest, I wish to appeal particularly to students and young professionals who have begun, or are going to assume positions of, decision making in their careers. I hope that the material of this book would help them in dealing with the global menace of terrorism.

Understanding the analytical contents requires knowledge of basic micro, first-order conditions of utility or profit maximization, statistical concepts of hypothesis testing and regression etc. In helping the reader recapitulate micro theory concepts used in the book, General Appendix A provides an exposition of the concept of compensating surplus and elements of the basic game theory. In some chapters, we discuss in depth the empirical results in the literature as well as the underlying statistical/econometric methodologies. General Appendix B lays out the notions of hypothesis testing, regression, and more advanced statistical/econometric methods, so that the reader understands or at least can have an intuitive feel of how the results are derived and what they mean with some degree of inner comfort.

The treatment of the concepts covered in the two General Appendix chapters is minimal, far from being a substitute of independently learning micro theory, statistics, and econometrics. Yet, their contents are intuitive and self-contained in a way. This is consistent with one of the objectives of the book: to help learn techniques and concepts in the process of understanding the analytical results pertaining to terrorism.

1.2 On the Current Chapter

This chapter has many sections. In Sect. 1.3, it is argued why terrorist behavior may be characterized as rational, i.e., how it responds to incentives. Therefore, the study of terrorism falls squarely in the domain of economic analysis. In Sect. 1.4 we define terrorism and learn its attributes as a distinct form of violence. Long-term objectives of some terror organizations are outlined, and, differences and similarities between terrorism, freedom fighting, insurgency, and civil war are briefly described. Section 1.5 notes that terror attacks use different modes and tactics. Domestic and transnational terrorism are distinguished and compared in Sect. 1.6.

A global perspective on terrorism in terms of its impact on different countries and magnitude of deaths from terrorism is presented in Sect. 1.7. Section 1.8 lists the major international organizations in recent decades and where they are based. How the USA officially designates foreign terror organizations, and, a list of domestic terror organizations that have operated on the US soil are introduced in Sects. 1.9 and 1.10, respectively.

Because almost all violent or ultra-violent terror organizations in recent times are Islamic and many of them practice and promote Islamic fundamentalism, it is important to understand the history and different strands of Islam and related concepts. These are outlined in Sect. 1.11. Section 1.12 briefly describes women participation in terror organizations. The role of internet in terrorism is evaluated in Sect. 1.13.

Analyzing CT measures is a prime goal of this book. A pre-requisite for understanding how these measures differ from each other and work is a functional classification of such measures. This is articulated in Sect. 1.14. The root or fundamental causes of terrorism and the respective preventive measures are introduced in Sect. 1.15. Section 1.16 briefly lays out different parts and the constituent chapters of this book. Terrorism being a vast subject, any book on it is bound to be selective. Section 1.17 spells out what is not covered in the text. All chapters, including the current chapter, close with a "bulleted" take-away section.

1.3 Rationality, Economics, and Terrorism

Any economic analysis of terrorism presupposes a basic question: What do we mean by an "economic analysis" of terrorism? Put differently, how can "economic" principles, based on rationality, be useful in understanding the seemingly irrational behavior such as killing a group of people by willingly sacrificing one's own life? Are not the terrorists utterly irrational?

It is however important to bear in mind that what "we" may consider as irrational or crazy behavior by someone else can very well be her/his conscious decision that weighs benefits and costs. No suicide bomber would ever carry a dozen of bombs in a small boat by himself, drive into an empty sea, and blow himself up: Terrorists calculate potential benefit from their perspective and undertake calculated risks. The benefit from engaging in terror may lie in geo-political gains that can be facilitated by target countries, whereas terror is used as a means to coerce these countries to grant their demand. Or the terrorists may derive benefits or "utility" from hurting or causing damage to some other population/countries out of hatred or revenge. They choose their specific targets or location of attack depending on how hard it is to penetrate. In other words, they calculate costs of executing an attack. By definition, calculated risk-taking is an economic decision making. In 1995 M. Al Zahar, a Hamas Leader, is quoted in *Al Quds* (East Jerusalem), saying that "we must examine the costs and benefits of continued armed operations."[1] To put it another way, terrorists respond to incentives—like rational entities—whereas incentives are affected by counter-terror measures. For instance, in early 1970s when metal detectors were first introduced at airports for pre-board screening of passengers and carry-on luggage, it dramatically reduced skyjacking attempts that were earlier happening in relatively large numbers. In short, terrorists compare their sense of benefits to costs and respond to incentives.

Shapiro (2013) reports that Osama Bin Laden even offered a financial incentive of $2400 for his new recruits to voluntarily leave the group. The idea was to screen out those who were not deeply committed to the cause: Only those who value of the cause more than $2400 will remain. This is a purely economic decision at play.[2]

We have our first *Is That So* clip:

Is That So? 1.1: Terrorists and Terror Organizations as Rational Entities

Terrorists and terror organizations respond to incentive, hence can be regarded as rational entities, from their own behavioral perspective.

It is also pertinent to recognize that a country's choice of CT measures reflects economic decision making. It is *not* true that a government would go to any arbitrary extent to subdue or eliminate terrorists and terror organizations regardless of costs. As a purely hypothetical yet relevant example, the USA would not—and should not—use nukes to destroy terrorist bases in a foreign land—because the collateral damage of such an action would be unthinkable and unacceptable to a liberal democracy, leaving alone the cost of lost goodwill. Similarly, it would not deploy a massive military force along with more conventional hardware to fight terrorists—since that would cost a large number of American lives and burden the tax payers too heavily. It is natural to suppose that a rational state would decide the type and the extent of counter-terror measures by weighing costs and benefits.

---

[1] Hamas is a Palestinian terror group.

[2] Interestingly, Shapiro (2013) narrates that Zappos, an online shoe company, offered an incentive of $2000 for newly trained recruits to leave the company for parallel reasons.

Hence terrorism rightfully belongs to the domain of economics. Economic analyses can potentially help us to design effective measures to curb the problem—and hopefully win the war on terror.

9/11 attacks were of course the game changer that led to massive interest in the study of terrorism. A vast amount of empirical and theoretical research by economists as well as political scientists, mathematicians, and psychologists has followed since. Terrorism is well beyond the limited realm of military tactics to kill or capture terrorists.

1.4 What Is Terrorism?

1.4.1 Various Definitions

How is terrorism different from other forms of conflict or violence? Lines are partially blurred—e.g., what we may call terror activities may be seen by others as freedom struggle—yet discernible. Richards (2015) presents a detailed study of the definition of terrorism. He defines it as the use of violence or force with the primary purpose of generating a psychological impact beyond the immediate victims for a political motive. According to Global Terrorism Index, an annual publication by the Institute for Economics and Peace (IEP)—a global think-tank headquartered in Sydney, founded by an IT entrepreneur and philanthropist Steve Killelea— terrorism is "the threatened or actual use of illegal force and violence by a non-state actor to attain a political, economic, religious, or social goal through fear, coercion, or intimidation." I prefer the characterization by the US Department of Defense:

Definition of Terrorism

Terrorism is "the calculated use of unlawful violence or threat of unlawful violence to inculcate fear, intended to coerce or to intimidate governments or societies in the pursuit of goals that are generally political, religious, or ideological."

This will be our definition of terrorism.

1.4.2 Attributes

Although individual definitions differ, they are similar. Terrorism, as a form of violence, has these attributes.

[a] Like guerrilla warfare, *there are no rules of engagement*. Targeted victims could be civilians and non-combatants as well as political figures, armed forces, and their facilities.

[b] As an immediate or a short-term goal, *generating public fear, i.e., a fear impact beyond the immediate victims*, is what separates terrorism from other forms of violence like guerrilla war. Compared to other forms of violence like homicide, terrorism entails what economists call a *negative externality*, meaning an adverse

effect passed on to others or public in general.[3] The very act of terrorist violence and damage, although local, creates a negative externality of generating a sense of insecurity and fear in the minds of the public. While the chances of being harmed by terrorism may be negligible or small, terrorism can have "huge and enduring effects on human behavior" (Becker and Rubinstein, 2011).

[c] The short-term goal of spreading fear and insecurity can be equivalently thought of as a means to force the authorities (whose population is being targeted) to grant some political, religious, or ideological goals. *The ultimate target or enemy is some government, authority, or a group of states.*

[d] Violence is perpetrated by *non-state actors* or *sub-national groups*. If a state is sponsoring or financing terror groups, it is a situation of *state-sponsored terrorism.* Libya was accused of state-sponsored terrorism after the downing of Pan Am Flight 103 over Lockerbie, Scotland, back in 1988. The US Department of State brands some nations as terror sponsors. As of January 2021, the list had four countries as sponsors of terrorism: Syria (since 1979), Iran (since 1984), North Korea (from 2017), and Cuba (from 2021). If a government or a state applies terror tactics to its own citizens (like Stalin did), it is *state terror*, *not* typically counted as a terror event, because it does not involve non-state actors.

In brief, terrorism is defined by the following ingredients:

① Non-state or sub-state actors or groups.

② Use of violence with no rules of engagement, targeting general public, government officials, or armed forces to create fear as a short-term goal or means.

③ Some political, religious, or ideological motives in the long run.

Supplements Break 1.1 briefly discusses how the fear psychosis due to terror attacks differs from the usual post-traumatic stress disorder (PTSD).

It is worth emphasizing that our definition of terrorism is devoid of any normative content or value judgment. Armed struggle for freedom of a country or a region can be a noble cause, but as long as this is carried out by non-state groups, by our definition and for analytical purposes, it falls into the category of terrorism. This is discussed in more detail in Sect. 1.4.5.[4]

To keep terrorism in perspective, certain forms of violence and usage of the term terrorism are *not* terrorism in terms of our definition. Consider for instance the American Revolution. Although there were some guerrilla operations, rebels did not kill British citizen randomly or mass murders were not used to intimidate the British. It was mostly a regular warfare between two armies. Thus, it was not terrorism. During WWII, the American forces dropped atom bombs in two cities in Japan, causing massive horror, diseases, and devastation. Yet this is not regarded as terrorism, because no non-state actors were involved and there was no long-term

[3] Infections like flu or covid from others is an example of negative externality. Another example will be carbon emission by one country significantly affecting the global environment.

[4] It may be noted that, apart from fear resulting from terror attacks, terrorist groups use kidnapping for ransom (KFR) and extortion to finance themselves. These activities also create fear among the general public.

Supplement Break 1.1: Fear Effects of Terrorism and Post-Traumatic Stress Disorder (PTSD)

From a psychological viewpoint, Sinclair and Antonius (2012) argue that fear effects of terrorism experienced by direct or potential victims are somewhat different from individual experience of traumatic event like a road accident, accidental victims of domestic violence, a soldier's experience in a war etc. The psychological effect of terrorism has two distinct characteristics, compared to the standard PTSD. One is that terrorism is not as accidental as other forms of extreme events since the public knows that there are groups out there who would strive to unleash future attacks. Hence there is a sense of *anticipatory fear* more than that associated with, say, road accident. Anticipatory fear can have short-run as well as long-run deleterious psychological effects. Second, since terrorism typically affects a group of people and appears prominently in the media, people outside the epicenter also feel psychological distress.

Numerous studies exist that assess the psychological effects over time of *9/11* attacks, and major terror events that have occurred elsewhere. They will be discussed in Chap. 6.

political or ideological objectives on the part of the USA, other than to defeat an enemy in a conventional, inter-state war.

1.4.3 Long-Term Objectives of Some Terror Organizations

Terrorism differs from other forms of violence like homicide in that there are some long-term political, social, or ideological objectives of the perpetrators. Here are some examples.

The Irish Republican Army (IRA) has fought with the British since the 1920s with the objective of constituting the entire island of Ireland as a united Irish republic. An ethnic group within a country may be using terror in order to gain statehood or greater civilian and political autonomy. Sri Lankan tigers engaged in terrorism intermittently from early 1980s to 2009 and demanded more civil rights. From 1982 to 2011, the Sudanese People Liberation Army demanded greater regional autonomy, more voice in national affairs, and a greater share in the economic development.[5] Hamas seeks to secure a separate Palestinian–Islamic state. Taliban's long-term objective was to establish an Islamic theocracy in Afghanistan (and it may materialize in the very near future).

The original stated objective of al-Qaeda was political: the removal of foreign soldiers and equipment from the Arabian peninsula. But later it became ideological: spread of Islam and rejection of Western values.

Harkat ul-Jihad al-Islami of Bangladesh, al-Jihad in Egypt, and Jemaah Islamiyah (JI) that operates in Southeast Asia aim to create a pan-Islamic state out of Indonesia, Malaysia, Singapore, Southern Philippines, and Southern Thailand.

Most prominently, the Islamic State of Iraq and Syria (ISIS), the Islamic State of Iraq and Levant (ISIL), or simply the Islamic State (IS) envisioned all parts of the world that were once under Sunni Islamic domination to be ruled by one or more caliphates. It includes Iraq, the Levant (Syria, Lebanon, Palestine, Israel, and

[5] In 2011, it became the regular army of Southern Sudan as a separate country.

Jordan), Northern Africa, the Indian subcontinent, some parts of central Asia as well as parts of Spain and Portugal.

1.4.4 Three Players in a "Terrorist Act"

In the theatrical parlance, terrorism is enacted by three players:

1. Perpetrator(s).
2. Victims.
3. An audience.

Terrorists or terrorist organizations are the perpetrators. Victims may be civilians, officials, politicians, or passive military. The audience could be a province, country, or a group of countries. The entire world was an audience for terror events like *9/11* and 2008 Mumbai attacks.[6]

1.4.5 Terrorism, Freedom Fighting, Insurgency, and Civil War

If the objective of a sub-national organization causing public fear by means of violence is political freedom or independence from a foreign power, then calling it a terror organization and its members terrorists arouses serious normative concerns. The IRA in Ireland sought independence from the British. Sri Lankan Tigers initially sought independence from Sri Lanka, and, later moderated its objective to gaining more rights and autonomy. Hamas in Gaza and West Bank seeks a separate homeland for the Palestinians. Are these groups then terrorists or freedom fighters? It depends on whom you ask. While the members and their sympathizers would regard them freedom fighters or liberators, the governments brand them as terrorists and fight them.

From our analytical perspective, we take a positive, not a normative, view of terrorism. According to our definition of terrorism, nationalist groups will be considered as terror organizations— insofar as (a) they are sub-national and (b) their acts of violence engender fear in conducting normal life and business. In essence, it is the tactics used that may equate or differentiate between nationalist groups and terror groups.

Similarly, insurgency and terrorism may or may not coincide. An insurgency is a challenge to an existing government for control of all or some territory, or to force political concessions. Insofar as insurgent groups are non-state actors and have political objectives they are similar to terror groups. But if the insurgency involves targeting government forces without killing the public and thereby without generating public fear for safety it is not terrorism. But if it aims to influence the government by acts of terror against the public or passive military, it is terrorism. Hence an insurgent group can be a terror group and vice versa, but not necessarily. It is the method used to achieve the political objective that distinguishes between insurgency and terrorism.

Civil war (or intra-state war) is different from terrorism. It involves a limited number of groups vying with each other by engaging in warfare in order to gain

[6] The latter involved twelve coordinated shooting and bombing attacks carried out by terrorists belonging to Lashkar-e-Taiba (LeT), a terror organization based in Pakistan. (The ordeal went on for four days claiming the lives of 164 people and injuring 308).

political control over a country or a vast region. Furthermore, "civil wars must surpass some threshold of deaths, which is not true for terrorism" (Gaibulloev & Sandler, 2019).[7] It is the conflict between large groups and the scale of violence that differentiate between terrorism, insurgency, or nationalist movement on one hand and civil war on the other.[8]

1.5 Modes/Tactics of Terror Attack

Terrorists have employed several modes of attack with varying combinations, such as bombing, suicide bombing, hijacking, suicide hijacking (like *9/11*), shooting out with police, and hostage-taking, among many others. An elaborate list of twenty five types of terror attacks is given in Enders and Sandler (2012, Table 3.2). The most common method used is bombing and explosion—because of its logistic simplicity, compared to other tactics.

Economic principles can help us to understand the mode of attacks. For instance, a relatively secured facility or a "hardened target" is more likely to encourage suicide attack since its chance of success in killing is greater, compared to a conventional tactics like gun fire or bombing.

1.6 Domestic Versus Transnational Terrorism

The perpetrators may or may not belong to the same region or country as the majority of victims. ***Transnational terrorism*** refers to terrorist incidents where the perpetrators' main residence is different from where the terror act is carried out. Otherwise, if terror acts are committed by own residents, it is termed as ***domestic terrorism***.

There are many prominent transnational terrorist events. *9/11* is the most (in)famous, of course. There were nearly 3000 victims including the hijackers, and, the victims belonged to sixty two nationalities including the USA. Among the nineteen hijackers, fifteen were from Saudi Arabia, two from United Arab Emirates, and one from Egypt. 2002 Bali bombings are another example where 202 people from more than twenty two countries were killed. Two terror organizations were involved: Jemaah Islamiyah, a Southeast Asian militant group, and al-Qeada.

---

[7] The threshold number is, typically, 1000 within a year.

[8] It is possible but not necessary that a nationalist movement leads to a civil war. This could happen when rival nationalist groups fight for power when a foreign power or a dominant regime vacates and a power vacuum sets in. Historians think that if India and Pakistan were not created as two nations when the British left India, a civil war was inevitable. Many believe that when the US occupation granted sovereignty to an appointed Iraqi government in 2004, headed by Ayad Allawi, unanimously elected by the Governing Council as the interim prime minister, Iraq plunged into a civil war or civil-war-cum insurgency, although the USA never termed it as civil war (Fearon, 2007). In early 2004, a revered Shiite shrine in Samarra was bombed. That led to a "chain of revenge killings." A month after the bombing, Ayad Allawi said, "If this is not civil war, then God knows what civil war is" (Wong, 2006).

Incidences of domestic terrorism galore. Here are a few examples. Timothy McVeigh's attack of Federal buildings in Oklahoma in 1995 is an example in the USA. In the 2015 San Bernardino (California) shooting killed fourteen people where the perpetrators were citizens or permanent residents of the USA. It was somewhat different from the 1995 Oklahoma incidence in that, unlike Timothy McVeigh, the perpetrators were radicalized and suspected to be inspired by ISIS. It was still described as domestic terrorism, although a separate classification for such inspired attacks may emerge in the future. An attack on February 5, 2012 by Taliban on police in Kandahar, Afghanistan, claimed ten lives. On December 15, 2015, five were killed in Somalia by al-Shabaab, a terror group based in Somalia.

While instances of transnational terrorism very often attract the headlines news, the incidences of domestic terrorism far outnumber those of transnational terrorism. According to Enders et al. (2011), over 1970–2007, the ratio of domestic to transnational terrorism events globally was around 3.60.

According to a large and open-source database on terrorism, namely, GTD, to be described further in Chap. 3), the same ratio over the period 1970–2019 is about 12.54. Many graphs, tables, and numbers in this book rely on the GTD version released in early 2021.[9]

Furthermore, there is a huge difference between a group of five countries that are worst affected by terrorism, namely, Syria, Afghanistan, Nigeria, Iraq, and Pakistan (we shall call these countries SANIP) and the rest of the world. In SANIP, the domestic to transnational terror events ratio is 129, which is way higher than that for all countries. It reveals that for the worst affected countries, terrorism is much more a domestic problem than international.

Is That So? 1.2: Number of Domestic Terror Attacks vis-à-vis International Terror Attacks

Although incidences of transnational terrorism often hug the limelight, domestic terrorism far outnumbers transnational terrorism in terms of number of events.

Are domestic and transnational terrorism correlated? One may think not, since the underlying reasons behind domestic terrorism may be country-specific and idiosyncratic, whereas transnational terrorism may be driven by common factors. Actually, they are positively and strongly correlated. Globally, the correlation coefficient is about 87% (GTD, annual data from 1970–2019). Since in SANIP, transnational terrorism is rather minuscule compared to domestic terrorism, the correlation is positive but weaker, around 40%. Enders and Sandler (2012, Chapter 3) argue that are at least two reasons for a positive correlation between domestic and transnational terrorism. First, there are copycat effects: A successful incidence of domestic or transnational terrorist event encourages terror attempts that are transnational or domestic respectively. Second, domestic terrorism may spill over to transnational terrorism as the terrorists increasingly seek to attract global attention for their cause.

[9] We should note that this database does not include the year 1993 because of data inconsistency issues.

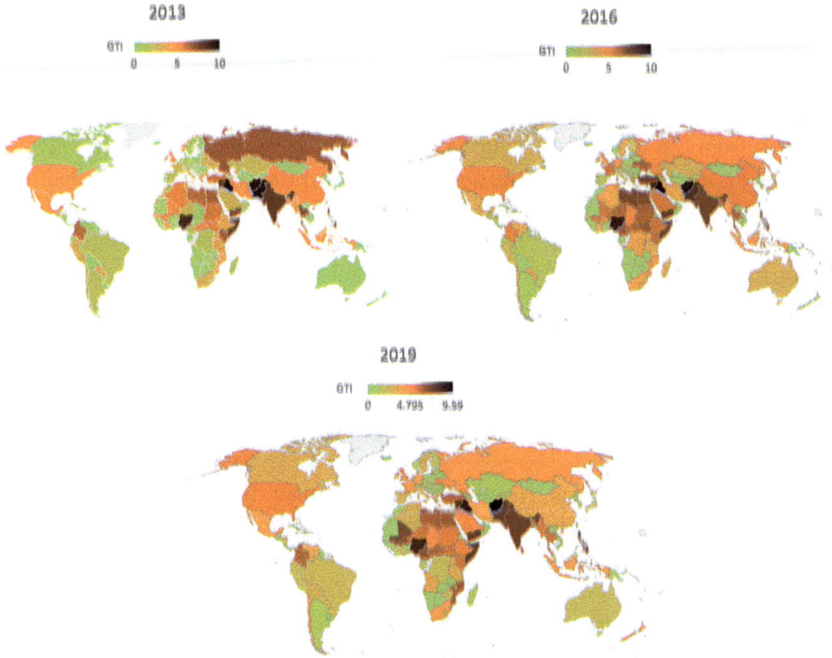

Fig. 1.1: Global terrorism index (GTI) for 2013, 2015, and 2019. *Sources*: Institute for Economics & Peace (2014b, 2017, 2019); prepared by Bing ©Australian Bureau of Statistics, GeoNames, Microsoft, Tom Tom, Wikipedia; permission to reproduce from IEP is thankfully acknowledged

1.7 Global Terrorism: A Preliminary Look

1.7.1 Overall Impact of Terrorism across Countries

How global is the terrorism problem? How are the different countries impacted by terrorism? IEP has been publishing indices of terrorism impact for various countries since 2012. Called the Global Terrorism Index (GTI), it ranges from zero to ten and is computed annually by using the total number of terror incidents occurring in a country and their severity in terms of fatalities (death), injuries, and the value of the property damage.[10]

Figure 1.1 depicts the GTI maps that color-code countries according to how severely they were afflicted by terrorism in 2013, 2015, and 2019. We observe some patterns from Fig. 1.1 and the data:
[a] There is a wide variation in the impact of terrorism across countries. In 2010s, five countries—Syria, Afghanistan, Nigeria, Iraq, and Pakistan (SANIP)—have borne the brunt of the terror attacks and their GTIs are at least eight out of ten. Among SANIP countries, Iraq scores the highest (=10) in 2013 and 2015, whereas Afghanistan's score is the highest in 2019 (=9.59).

Is That So? 1.3: Countries Most Affected by Terrorism in the Post 9/11 Era

In the post 9/11 era, the top five countries most severely affected by terrorism are: Syria, Afghanistan, Nigeria, Iraq, and Pakistan.

Although not in top 5, countries like Somalia, Yemen, India, and Philippines have faced high incidence of terror consistently from 2013 to 2019.
[b] Between 2013 and 2015 terrorism made inroads into the African continent.
[c] Terror attacks remain widespread. In 2013, 2015, and 2019 respectively, 95, 108, and 99 countries witnessed at least one terror attack on their soil.
[d] In general, the richer countries have experienced less terror incidents than the poorer nations.
[e] Figure 1.1 does not exhibit who the perpetrators or the targets are. An attack could be domestic (i.e., perpetrators are local), yet foreign nationals may be the main victims. Indeed, there are many attacks in poorer terrorism-prone countries, in which main targets are the nationals from richer nations. Terrorism is thus a grave concern for both developed and developing countries.

1.7.2 Deaths from Terrorism

How many die from terrorism? Figure 1.2 displays the global figures from 1970 to 2019. Since 2000, while the number of deaths from terrorism increased rather dramatically between 2000 and 2014, it has (thankfully) declined afterwards.

Figure 1.3 offers a perspective on how lethal terror attacks are. It may surprise some of you that 51% of terror attacks do *not* involve any death, and the average number of deaths per terror attack is about 2.41. It is important to know that among all forms of terror attacks, suicide attacks are most lethal. These attacks began to happen in the early 1980s. Figure 1.3 also illustrates the contrast between kill distributions associated with all attacks and suicide attacks only. This is why Robert Pape of University of Chicago, who has extensively studied suicide attacks, calls them the lung cancer of terrorism.

[10] GTI is prepared in consultation with the Global Peace Index(GPI) expert panels and derived from data on terror incidents from GTD. The GPI attaches the weights equal to 1, 3, 0.5, and 2, respectively, to the number of incidents, fatalities, injuries, and the measure of property damage.

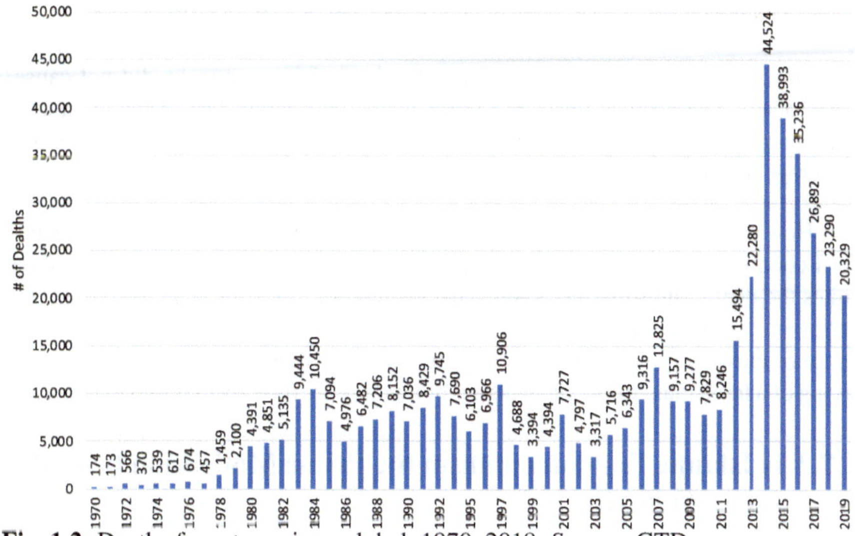

Fig. 1.2: Deaths from terrorism: global, 1970–2019. *Source*: GTD

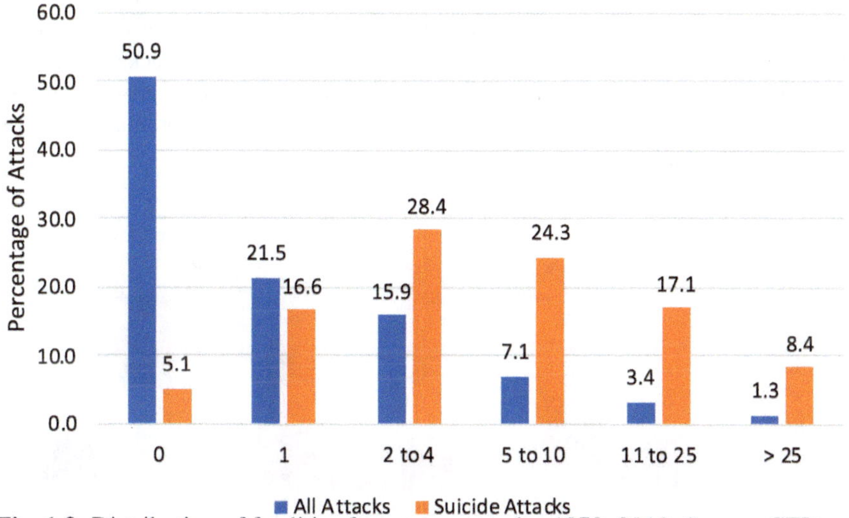

Fig. 1.3: Distribution of fatalities from terror attacks, 1970–2019. *Source*: GTD

Is That So? 1.4: Lethality of Suicide Terror Attacks

During the period 1970–2019, a little over half of terror attacks did not cause any death. The average death per terror attack was about 2.41. Suicide attacks are more lethal than other forms of terror attacks. In the period 1981–2019, the average death from suicide attacks was about 10.22.

How do deaths from terrorism compare with other forms of violence? Institute for Economics & Peace (2016b) notes that the global homicide rate is about fifteen times the death rate from terrorism. That should not, however, lead us to think that terrorism is not a major issue. It is because, unlike homicide, terrorism creates a sense of mass fear, insecurity, and anxiety that affects mental health and day-to-day living of a large mass of people whether or not they are directly exposed to terrorism.

1.7.3 Is Islamic Fundamentalism the Prime Motivation behind Lone-Wolf Attacks?

Most major terror attacks in the twenty-first century thus far have been perpetrated by Islamic fundamentalist groups. In recent years, lone-wolf terror attacks have become more frequent in the USA and Europe. It is presumed that most of them are inspired by Islamic fundamentalism. However, if lone-wolf attacks in the USA in 2010s are any guide, Fig. 1.4 indicates that Islamic fundamentalism is *not* the principal cause. Political factors, individual issues, and white supremacist motives are more important.

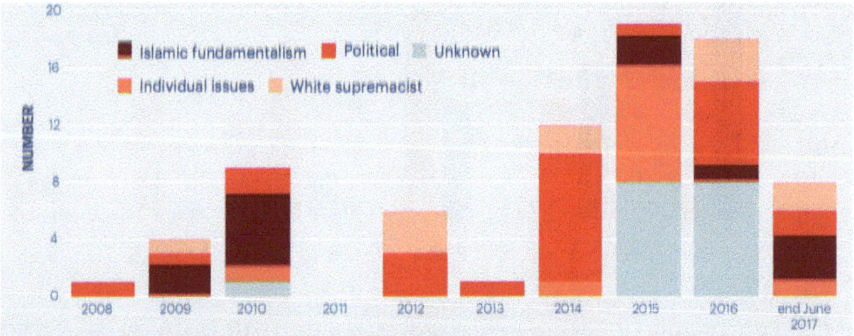

Fig. 1.4: Lone Wolf attacks in the USA, 2008-June 2017. *Source*: (Institute for Economics & Peace, 2017, Figure 4.7); permission to reproduce from IEP is thankfully acknowledged

Is That So? 1.5: Motivations Behind Lone-Wolf Terror Attacks in the USA in Recent Years

Political factors, individual issues, and white supremacy, not Islamic fundamentalism, are the dominant motivations behind lone-wolf attacks in the USA in recent years.

1.8 Major International Terror Organizations

Name	Full name or meaning of the name	Region(s)
	Non-Secular	
al-Qaeda	The Base	Middle East; highly decentralized; has affiliates in different countries
al-Shabaab	The Youth	Somalia, Kenya, Uganda
Boko Haram	Western Education is Sin	Nigeria, Cameroon
Hamas	Zeal	Gaza strip and West Bank
Hezbollah	Party of God	Lebanon and Syria
ISIS/ISIL	Islamic State of Iraq and Syria/Islamic State of Iraq and Levant	Syria and Iraq; has affiliates in many countries
Jabhat Fateh al Sham (previously) Jabhat al-Nusra	Front for the Conquest of Syria/the Levant	Syria
Jemaah Islamiyah	Islamic Congregation	Indonesia and South East Asia
Lashkar-e-Taiba	Army of the Righteous	Pakistan and India
Taliban	Students	Afghanistan; has affiliates in Pakistan
	Secular	
FARC	Fuerzas Armadas Revolucionarias de Colombia (Revolutionary Armed Forces of Colombia)	Colombia
LTTE	Liberation Tigers of Tamil Ealam	Sri Lanka
PIRA	The Provisional Irish Republican Army	Northern Ireland, Ireland, United Kingdom
PKK	Kurdistan Workers' Party	Iraq, Syria, Turkey

Table 1.1: Major International Terror Organizations and Region(s) of their operations

Which are the major terror organizations around the world in recent times? Table 1.1 records the names, their meaning and the areas of their base and operation under two categories: secular or non-secular. Unlike what many think, not all major terror groups are fundamentalist (or non-secular). Notice that Taliban means "students" in *Pashto*, a language spoken in parts of Afghanistan and Pakistan. It is because the Taliban originated with a group of seminary students.

It is important to note that the present al-Qaeda is *not* a single organization—which it was, prior to *9/11*. Post-*9/11* crackdown on al-Qaeda led its leaders to flee and hide and the original al-Qaeda disintegrated. However, as we will learn in Chap. 2, several regional al-Qaeda groups emerged in its place, pledging allegiance to the original al-Qaeda's mission and in return receiving the "blessings" and moral support from the original al-Qaeda's leaders, namely, Osama Bin Laden till his death in 2011 and Ayman al-Zawahiri, the post-Bin-Laden leader of the original al-Qaeda who is presumably alive as of 2021. These affiliates include al-Qaeda in the Islamic Maghreb, AQIM (in Libya, Algeria, Ivory Coast, Mali, Nigeria, Tunisia, and Burkina Faso), al-Qaeda in the Arabian Peninsula, AQAP, (in Yemen and Saudi Arabia) and al-Qaeda in the Indian Peninsula, AQIS, (in India, Pakistan, and Bangladesh). Al-Shabaab in Somalia and Boko Haram in Nigeria have also declared their allegiance to al-Qaeda.

We will discuss these and other organizations in detail in Chap. 2.

1.9 US Listing of Foreign Terrorist Organizations and their State Sponsors

Major countries like the USA, the UK, Canada, EU, Australia, and others have their own official list of terror organizations inside and outside of their borders. The US government has three such lists, each having its own procedures and mechanisms to deal with terrorism in terms of punishing terrorists and their sympathizers in different ways.

Foreign Terror Organizations (FTOs) This list is prepared by the US Secretary of State in accordance with the Immigration and Nationality Act of 1965 and based on whether a foreign organization engages in terror activities as defined by the USA. The list in the State Department's website as March 16, 2021, has 70 names. Some previously designated terror organizations become unlisted if they cease to exist or be active. All names in Table 1.1 appear in this list, except Taliban. In Chap. 2 we will learn why this is so.

Terrorist Exclusion List (TEL) More fully, it is The Patriot Act Terrorist Exclusion List, created by the US Secretary of State under the USA Patriot Act of 2001 in consultation with or at the request of the Attorney General. A TEL designation allows the Department of Homeland Security to restrict or exclude entry into the USA (and deportation) of individuals deemed to be associated with these organizations. The current list has 57 entries (based on access to the website of the US Department of State on March 16, 2021).

Executive Order 13224 An Executive Order passed by George W. Bush on September 23, 2001 and renewed every year since then; it arms the US government with an important legal tool to curb terrorist funding. Ninety nine individuals and entities are designated by the Department of State under this executive order as of March 16, 2021.

These listings apart, the US government has a list of designated state sponsors of terrorism, which allows the USA to (legally) impose unilateral sanctions and apply pressure to bring about changes in the behavior and policies of these states. As of March 2021, this list had four countries: Syria (since 1979), Iran (since 1984), Sudan (since 1993), and North Korea (since 2017). This designation is based on an evaluation of repeated support for acts of international terrorism.

1.10 Terror Organizations in the USA

There are extremist/terror organizations based in the USA too, e.g., Ku Klax Klan, Animal Liberation Front, Earth Liberation Front, and The Justice Department (see Miller, 2016). All these groups however have not been active at the same time, and, the scales of their attacks are much smaller than the major transnational terror organizations. The objectives of the US based terror and/or extreme organizations are also markedly different from their foreign counterparts. Some of them will be discussed in detail in Chap. 2.

1.11 Different Strands of Islam and Sharia Law

The most dangerous terror organizations in the first two decades of the twenty-first century happen to be Islamic. Out of fourteen listed in Table 1.1, eleven are Islamic. Members of some Islamic terror organizations murder people in the name of religion, e.g., ISIS. They are jihadists. One should note that the original meaning of jihad is *not* killing people of other faith in the name of Islam. It means an inner spiritual struggle against greed, vice, sin, etc. or simply inner purification. See *Is that So* 1.6 below.

Is That So? 1.6: Original Meaning of Jihad

Jihad originally means an internal spiritual struggle toward faith and overcoming vices and sins, rather than killing to preserve or spread Islam.

Boys, sometimes girls too, were named "Jihad" because of its true pious meaning. No more—thanks to Bin Laden, who, almost single-handedly, transformed its meaning. Jihadism now means something external: a collective struggle or a holy war to preserve—and spread—the Islam by killing the *infidels*, meaning the non-believers, who are from other religions or even other Muslims that do not practice Islam in its extreme form.

All this might create a perception that Islam is monolithic and generally violent. On the contrary, there are several strands of Islam in terms of beliefs and jurisprudence. Furthermore, while some jihadists even kill Muslims from other sects or who do not adhere to extreme—often distorted—versions of Islam, many Muslim sects do *not* preach or practice violence. It is important to understand the origin and the nature of different strands of Islam and Islamic taxes in order to better understand the behavior—and funding—of different Islamic terror groups.[11]

1.11.1 Two Main Sects: Sunnies and Shi'ites

The passing away of Prophet Mohammed in 632 AD was followed by a split among the followers of the Islamic faith. One group—who later came to be known as Shi'ites—believed that the leader should be a direct descendant of Prophet Mohammed. Their choice was Mohammed's cousin and son-in-law Ali (his full name was Ali ibn Abi Talib). The other group—later to be known as Sunnis—held that the leader should be chosen by consensus on the ground that Prophet Mohammed emphasized the role of community in individual lives. Initially, the difference between the two faiths was not severe. Immediately upon Mohammed's demise, his friend Abu Bakr was chosen as the first "caliph" (the leader of the Muslim community at large). After his death, he was succeeded by Umar in 634 AD. The Arabs expanded during his leadership, defeating Byzantines and the Persians. Umar was killed by a Persian captive in 644 AD and another friend of Mohammed, Uthman, became the third caliph. While the Arabs continued to expand, Uthman was alleged to have consolidated his family wealth at the expense of the larger Islamic community. He was assassinated in 656 AD and succeeded by Ali (preferred by the Shi'ites). Ali was the caliph from 656 AD to 661 AD, during which period the Muslim leadership went through a turmoil. Ali, although chosen as the caliph, did not command a strong support due to the cleavage among the Muslim leaders. He used the armed force against the Uthman's family and yet sought peace with him. Like the previous two caliphs, Ali was killed, and, subsequently, the family of Uthman headed the Islamic movement and ruled the first Arab empire. The followers of Ali did not give up however. There was a battle at Karbala (in present-day Iraq) in 680 between Umayyads—the descendants of Uthman's family—and Hussain who was invited by the followers of Ali. Hussain was killed, but, the battle of Karbala was momentous for Shi'ites. A deep rift developed between the two groups, leading to two dominant sects within the Islamic religion. Sunnis believed that these four leaders were the "Rightly Guided Caliphs" or the true successors of Mohammed, whereas Shi'ites held Ali as the only true leader.

How are the Sunni and Shi'ite populations distributed across Islamic countries?

Is That So? 1.7: Distribution of Sunni's and Shi'tes in Different Islamic Countries

More than 80% of the world's 1.5 billion Muslim population is Sunni. They are the majority in all Islamic countries, except three. Iran and Bahrain are the only countries where the vast majority of population is Shi'ite (90% and 85%, respectively). In Iraq, the population share of Shi'ites is about 67%.[12]

---

[11] For a detailed description of radical Islam and global terrorism, see Mohanty (2012), among others.

[12] In Lebanon, among multiple religions, both Sunni and Shi'ite are a majority, each about 27% of the population.

Furthermore,

Is That So? 1.8: Number of Muslim-Majority Countries

There are about fifty Muslim majority countries. Indonesia is the largest Muslim population country, followed by Pakistan and India (although India is a Hindu-majority country).

1.11.2 Strands within Sunni and Shi'ite Muslims

Within Sunnis and Shi'ites, there are different schools of jurisprudence, called ***mazhabs*** ("way to act"), based on the recorded saying and deeds of Prophet Mohammed, reasoning, and juridical consensus. They are shown respectively in panel (a) and panel (b) of Fig. 1.5: Hanafi, Maleki, Safii, and Habali for Sunnis and Twelvers, Ismailis, Zaydis, and others for Shi'ias.

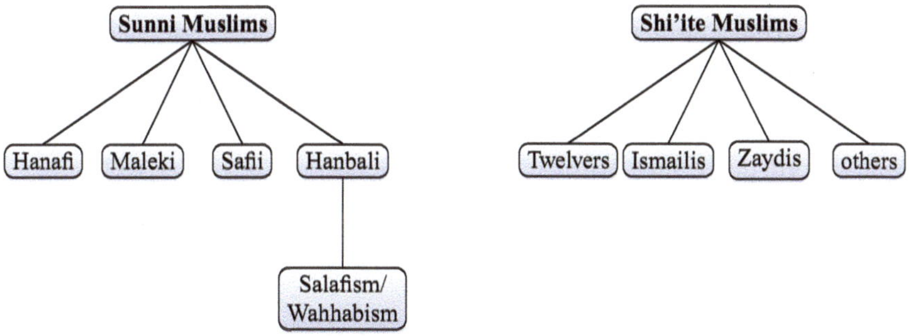

Fig. 1.5: Different schools of islamic jurisprudence

Unlike the difference between Sunnis and Shi'ites—which are two different sects—the belief systems across the schools of thought in each sect are the same. Hence, these are *not* different sects within Sunnis or Shi'ites. As an example, for Sunnis, there are subtle differences in the methods of prayer among the four schools, yet the differences are not so great as to require separate prayers by the followers of each school.

All major Islamic terror groups except for Hezbollah and Kata'ib Hezbollah are Sunni. We briefly touch upon different strands for Sunnis only here, while the chapter appendix describes the strands of both sects in greater detail.

Among the Sunnis, the Hanafi school of jurisprudence is the oldest and the most liberal (Hasan, 2012). The Hanbali school is the most rigid. Salafism falls within the Hanbali school, and it differentiates itself in terms of the religious practices it emphasizes. There are three strands within Salafism: (a) *purists* or quietists who are the largest, non-violent, and do not believe in participating in politics, thought to be a diversion that encourages deviancy, (b) *politicos* or *Harakis*, the second largest, who emphasize political participation and (c) *jihadists* are the minority, who harbor an ideological goals to be achieved by means of violence (Wiktorowicz, 2006). While the jihadists constitute the minority, the most violent terror organizations in recent times, e.g., al-Qaeda and ISIS, belong to this strand.

Wahhabism is a form of Salafism, originating in the eighteenth century in central Arabia, currently Saudi Arabia. Because it falls within Salafism, it holds many of the same ideals. It embodies a puritanical form of Islam and stresses the oneness of God (*tawhid*). It rejects Islamic school of thought that do not conform to the narrowly interpretations of the Quran, the *Sunna*, and *hadith*. Wahhabism questions the legitimacy of interpretations that are more accepting of what they see as illegitimate practices—like visiting tombs, shrines, and graves or adopting foreign dress. It is very hostile to Shi'ia Islam, which it views as a heretical sect.

The differences between Salafism and Wahhabism are nuanced yet important. First, Wahhabism is Salafism of the kind (a) or (b) described, but not (c), i.e., it does *not* advocate violence. Second, Wahhabists are loyal to the royal Saudi family, whereas Salafists are, in general, not.

Beginning in the 1970s, the Saudi government spent billions of its newfound oil wealth on promoting Wahhabism abroad through building and funding schools, mosques, and other institutions. This has resulted in many Muslims around the world adopting more conservative values than what was there prior to the 1970s. Furthermore, after the Iranian 1979 Revolution, Saudi's mission to spread Wahhabism has intensified as it competes with Iran's drives to spread Shi'ite Islam.

It is worth noting that

Is That So? 1.9: Salafism and Wahhabism

In the post 9/11 era, the fundamentalist Sunni Islamic terror groups are followers of Salafism and Wahhabism.

Figure 1.6 shows the geographical distribution of Islamic sects and schools around the world.

1.11.3 Sharia Law and Islamic Taxes

Because of the spread of Islamic fundamentalism and its practice by Islamic extremist groups, most of us have now heard of and know something about the Sharia Law. The term "Sharia" means God's immutable divine law. There are four sources of Sharia: the Quran, *sunnah* (authentic hadith), *qiyas* (analogical reasoning), and *ijma* (juridical consensus). The five dominant schools of jurisprudence, four belonging to Sunni Islam and Jafari for the Twlever Shi'ites are regarded as different schools of the Sharia law.

There are several taxes sanctioned by the Islamic Law. Two of them, *zakht* and *ushr*, respectively protection and extortion taxes, are prominent in terms of their use by Islamic terror organizations. Imposed on Muslims only, *zakht* is a 2.5% tax earmarked for donation to the poor and needy Muslims. As we shall see in Chap. 2, various terror organizations have charged fees from households and business

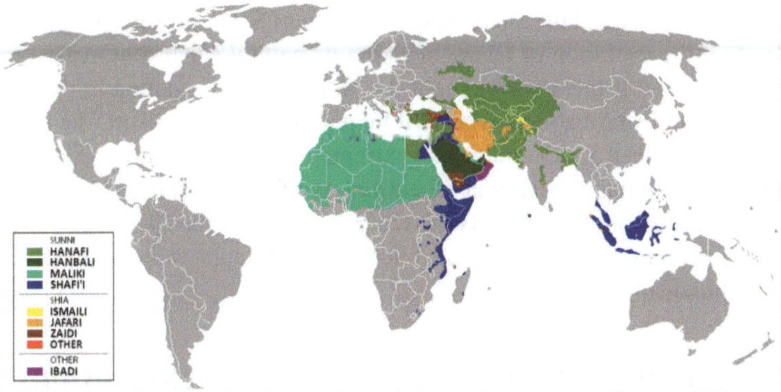

Fig. 1.6: Geographic distribution of islamic population according to different schools of islam. *Source:* Map is attributed to Peaceworld111—Own work, CC BY-SA 4.0, https://commons.wikimedia.org/w/index.php?curid=37809704

organizations in the name of *zakht*, which far exceed 2.5%. *Ushr* (literally meaning one tenth) is a 10% tax on harvests. There is a 5% tax on use of water from wells, which is also called *ushr*.

1.11.4 How are Different Sects and Schools Related to Islamic Terrorism?

Many members of al-Qaeda groups, al-Nusra and ISIS are Sunni and they belong to the jihadist minority among the Salafists. This partly explains why these groups practice and promote extreme versions of Islam. State-sponsored terrorism is correlated with the religious affinity of a terror organization. Hezbollah, a Shi'ite group based in southern Lebanon, is heavily funded by Iran, a Shi'ite-dominated Muslim country.[13]

It is important to note that in the course of aggressively promoting Wahhabism, Saudi Arabia has been commonly accused of supporting Sunni terror groups. But remember that even though Wahhabism branched out from Salafism, it is non-violent. This is why Saudi Arabia vehemently refutes the allegation that it supports terror organizations like al-Qaeda or ISIS. It is publicly opposed to these organizations and partners with the USA in the fight against terror. At the same time, organizations like ISIS obtain funds from people linked with donations from individuals and non-government funded organizations in Saudi Arabia for the sake of financing social work and spreading Wahhabism. It is alleged that mosques and radical schools funded by Saudi money also encourage young individuals toward extremism and terrorism. Thomas Hegghammer, a Norwegian terrorism expert who has advised the

[13] It is interesting to note that Hamas, a Sunni Muslim group and which operates mostly from Gaza strip, receives financial support from Iran too, although not to the extent of Hezbollah. But this is because Hamas fights Israel, a sworn enemy of Iran.

US government, has said the most important effect of Saudi proselytizing might have been to stunt the evolution of Islam, blocking its natural expansion to a diverse and globalized world. "If there was going to be an Islamic reformation in the twentieth century, the Saudis probably prevented it by pumping out literalism," he said.

The link between Saudi Arabia and extreme terror organizations remains highly debatable. On one hand there is no direct link between any terror organization and Saudi Arabia, but, on the other, its proactive support for the spread of Wahhabism through contributions to mosques and schools is thought to be conducive to the growth of jihadism.

1.12 Women Participation in Terror Organizations

One might think that terror acts and organizations belong to the world of men only. Not true. Women participation is significant in many terror organizations—especially those which are leftist and/or have political objectives.[14] It is because they tend to be more gender equal than those whose ideologies are ethnic and religion-based only. Some terror-group leaders are women.

The very first terror organization, *Narodnaya Volya* in Russia in the late nineteenth century, had women members. Nechaev, in his *Revolutionary Catechism*, considered women as "priceless assets." In one of the earliest instances in the post WWII era, in 1956, an Algerian woman named Zohra Drif and the wife of a leader of the National Liberation Front that carried out violence in order to secure Algeria's independence from France, planted a bomb in a milk cafe killing and wounding French soldiers. Because of this act, she is considered as the heroine of the Algerian War of Independence.

Margherita Cagol held No. 2 position in the Italian Red Brigade next to her husband/boyfriend Renato Curcio, the founder. As a member of the Popular Front for the Liberation of Palestine, Leila Khalel, was the first woman plane hijacker, who took part in two hijackings, one in 1969 and the other in 1970. The Japanese Red Army was founded by Fusako Shigenobu, a woman.

Nelly Avila Moreno was one of the most vicious and ruthless leaders of FARC in Colombia. Her guerrilla alias was Karine and she was considered a female Rambo. In Ireland, many members of the Provisional IRA (PIRA) were women. About 1/3 members of Tamil Tigers in Sri Lanka were women, known as *Freedom Birds*. Rajiv Gandhi, a former prime minister of India, was killed in 1991 by a baby-faced female Tamil Tiger, Thenmozhi Rajaratnam, nicknamed Dhanu, in the state of Tamil Nadu, India. Chechen terrorists who were killed by Russian forces after they took nearly 800 as hostages in a theater in Moscow in 2002 had women members strapped with bomb vests, whom the Russian media called the *Black Widows*. More generally, *Black Widows* were the suicide bombers and the wives of Chechen men who died during the insurgency in Chechnya.

---

[14] Bin Laden dedicated his book, *Military Studies in the Jihad against the Tyrants*, to protecting Muslim women; but they had little role to play in his terror plans.

The Kurdistan Workers Party, PKK, designated as a terror organization by the USA, the E.U., and Turkey, aggressively pushes gender equality. Its militia has a separate women protection unit, YPJ (Yekîneyên Parastina Jin in Kurdish). The Syrian Democratic Force, which is backed by the USA and which took a major role in liberating Raqqa in Syria from the occupation of ISIS in 2017 was led a YPJ woman, Rojda Felat.

Even ISIS with its extremely ideological goal attracted women. In a lecture, Sarah Lyons-Padilla, a cultural psychologist, presented an instance of a tweet by a woman recruit of ISIS from the West, which reads as follows.

> Born+Raised in West,
> Ive never felt more safe+protected thn n #IS
> Even w/ all the strikes crazy drivers +
> impending World War.

Is That So? 1.10: Women Participation in Terrorism

All terrorists are not men. There are prominent women terrorists. Rajiv Gandhi, a former prime minister of of India, was killed by a woman terrorist belonging to LTTE. The PKK actively promotes women participation and leadership.

1.13 Internet and Terrorism

Barring completely isolated lone-wolf terror attacks, other forms of terror attacks critically depend on communication and coordination, training, spreading of ideas, etc. Despite many virtues of internet, there is no doubt that it aids terror. There are several, sometimes overlapping, categories of a terror organization's functions that are facilitated by the internet, e.g., propaganda aimed to radicalize and incite terrorism, recruitment, financing, training, planning, execution, and cyber attacks.

Terror organizations and their sympathizers host websites, use social media accounts like Facebook and Twitter, chat rooms, and, apps like WhatsApp and email. They release videos either from a website or by making them viral, the origin of which is difficult to trace. For example, before being dissolved in 2009, LTTE maintained a website, `http://www.eelamwebsite.com`. Organizations like al-Qaeda and ISIS do not have their own exclusive websites; but they hack into existing websites to broadcast their propaganda videos. The contents of ISIS-related websites were brutal, containing videos of bombings, beheadings, and even children carrying out executions. As ISIS began to lose its occupied territories, it started to deliberately use children for propaganda in order to radicalize youth and glorify gruesome murder and violence in the minds of the youth.

An avid user of Twitter, ISIS's Twitter activities peaked in 2016, when the media company hosting Twitter had to shut down about 125,000 accounts linked to ISIS. According to CNN, Twitter suspended 377,000 accounts in the second half of 2016 only that were suspected to have links with terror. Twitter is used by other organizations too. An extraordinary event occurred in 2013, when al-Shabaab live-twitted its attack on a mall in Nairobi, Kenya. Through Twitter it informed the world about the reason of the attack and gave live updates of its actions in the mall. When that account was suspended, live commentary resumed some hours later under a different name. This terror attack resulted in 67 deaths and more than 175 injuries. Al-Shabaab also uses Facebook and YouTube for its propaganda. The Ku Klax Klan (KKK) of the USA uses Twitter too to spread its white supremacist messages.

Al-Qaeda and ISIS published web magazines periodically containing interviews with prominent members, material spreading extreme versions of Islam and glorifying their causes, how-to-do instructions (making bombs, blowing up a train, etc.) as well as material for recruitment. AQAP's magazine was called *Inspire*, published first in 2010. ISIS had two magazines, *Dabiq* first published in 2014 and *Rumiyah* in 2016 an abridged version of *Dabiq*.[15]

Potential recruits for terrorist organizations are targeted carefully through the internet. Initial contact is a very important step in the recruiting process. Recruiters reach out in various ways through the internet—like a friend request on Facebook, follower on Twitter, online video games, apps like WhatsApp, and direct messaging.

Communication is important for organizing and executing terrorist acts. Terror groups have used ***steganography***—hidden files, messages, images, or videos in another file, message, image, or video—to hide their own communications and break the code to steal information from security forces. Terrorists use email too. Rather than using personal communication devices, they prefer cybercafes so that tracing of individuals becomes difficult. They use other ways to avoid the danger of unsecured email. For instance, a group of members uses the same email id and shares the same password to get into a particular email account. One member can draft an email but not send it and others can improvise or add and not send it. The final draft is read by all and then deleted. This is not recorded because it is never sent.[16]

Terrorist groups also engage in cyber attacks that disrupt the proper functioning of the infrastructure of targets through hacking computer systems and infecting them with viruses and malware. Internet banking is used by terrorists and terror organizations to transfer funds, details of which will be studied in Chap. 4.

While internet is weaponized by terrorists, it is used against them too. Security forces of various countries monitor suspected websites and chat rooms and gain valuable intelligence. *Anonymous* is an internet "hacktivist" group, whom supporters call "freedom fighters" and "digital Robin Hoods," and, critics label as "cyber terrorists." In 2013 *Anonymous* raised a cyber war against the KKK and took control of its twitter account, calling it "Operation KKK" and pledging to take down any material they post online. The group released details of hundreds of alleged sympathizers of KKK on the internet.

---

[15] These magazines were colorful and could compete with *Time* and *Newsweek* in terms of the professional quality of production. Compared to al-Qaeda's *Inspire*, ISIS magazines stressed less on how-to manuals and more on propaganda and radicalization.

[16] There is an instance where a Colombian terror group was charged for arms trafficking partly on the basis of its email (White, 2017).

1.14 Counter-Terrorism Measures

The main purpose behind learning about terror organizations is to effectively design policies and measures to deal with them. Much of the book is devoted to how CT measures are expected to work.

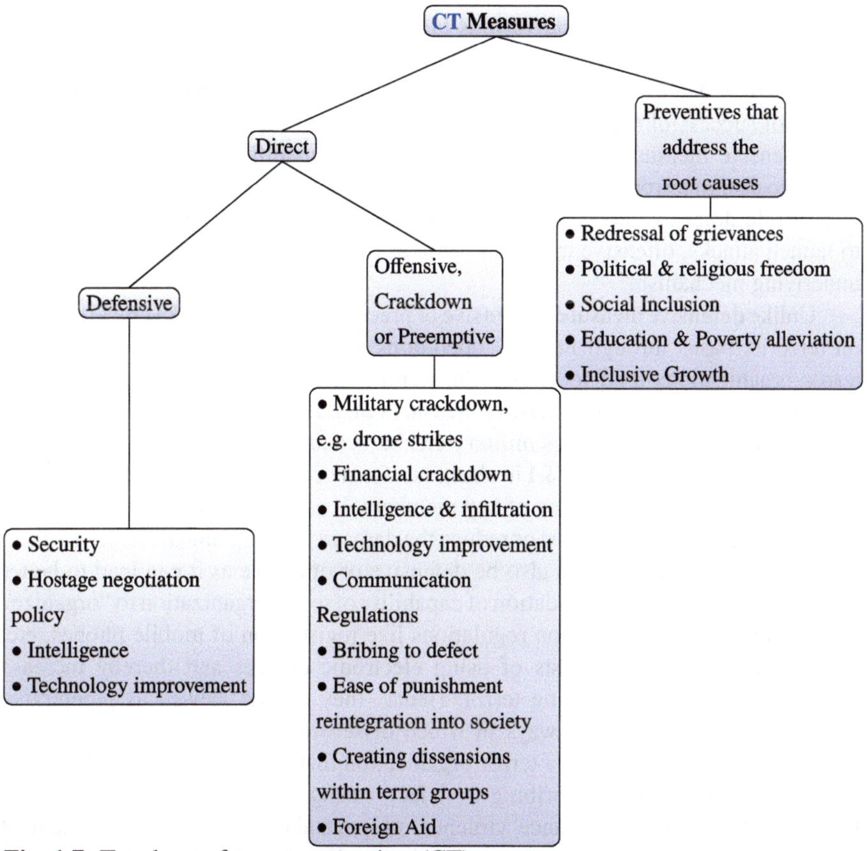

Fig. 1.7: Typology of counter-terrorism (CT) measures

1.14.1 A Classification

A typology of CT measures is displayed in Fig. 1.7. They are divided into two groups, direct and preventive. Direct measures tend to suppress or crush the problem without addressing the underlying root cause. In turn, these are classified into two categories: defensive and offensive.

Defensive measures include various security procedures that countries use at the airports, train stations, and various facilities. Many countries have passed laws barring the officials to negotiate with terrorists in hostage situations. This can be interpreted as defensive measures in that they serve as deterrence by reducing the chance of successful negotiation from the viewpoint of the kidnappers.

Offensive measures are those that reduce the capability of terrorists or terror groups to design terror attacks with the help of manpower, equipment, and infrastructure. While defensive measures are directly protective and also act as a deterrence to launch attacks, offensive measures serve as a deterrence too, but with a different underlying mechanism.

Unlike defensive measures, offensive or preemptive measures like cracking down on terrorist bases through military operations and chocking the flow of funds to terror organizations tend to reduce the terror organization's capability to launch attacks. In economic terms, *offensive measures increase a terror organization's cost of "producing" terror.* Besides military crackdown and combating terror financing, intelligence, and infiltration, I&I in short, is a form of preemptive measures in that it leads to apprehension or killing of key members. It can be defensive as well insofar as critical information can avert or reduce the damage from a planned terrorist attack. Investment in technology can also be defensive or offensive as it can lead to better security procedures or a degradation of capability of terror organization to "organize" a terror attack. Communication regulations like registration of mobile phones, etc. tend to increase security costs of using electronic devices and thereby increase the marginal cost of producing terror. Hence, they can be viewed as preemptive measures. There are several ways in which dissensions or disagreements may be planted or aggravated within a terror organization that can weaken and induce it to implode. Examples include bribing to defect, easing punishment for reintegration to those who wants to renounce violence, propaganda of corruption by financial intermediaries within a terrorist group, and spreading misinformation or confusing information about the intentions of a target country toward fulfilling the demand of a terror group. Some of these are "benevolent" CT measures, not really offensive literally, but they increase the cost of holding the organization together, equivalent to an increase in the cost of producing terrorism (Frey & Luechinger, 2003). In this sense they are preemptive. Terrorism-targeted foreign aid can also be seen as a preemptive measure in that the task of containing a terror organization or a group of terror organizations is delegated to another country.

Throughout the book we shall call defensive measures as ***security-deterrence*** (SD) and offensive or crackdown measures as ***preemption***. Both SD and preemptive measures can be viewed as strategies toward winning the war on terror (WoT) in the standard sense of what we mean by winning a war.

Direct measures are obviously important and necessary, but, as said earlier, do not address the underlying cause behind why some groups of people choose terrorism in the first place. In the terminology of medical science, direct measures are the cures or procedures to treat a disease. On the other hand, other non-violent interventions like political and diplomatic solutions, political and religious freedom, and poverty alleviation programs, etc. that address the long-run objectives or the root causes of terror are the preventive measures, parallel to prevention of a disease. These are elucidated in greater detail in the following section.

1.15 Root, Breeding and Propagating Factors and Preventive Measures

While greatly essential and many times successful, counter-terror measures like security, preemption, intelligence, etc. tend to *suppress* the problem of terrorism. They are not preventive and do not address the root causes of the problem. It is often invoked that a long-term solution of terrorism requires addressing the "root causes of terrorism." In principle, this is incontrovertible, a truism. However, the problem is that according to some, poverty and lack of education are "the" root cause of terrorism. Others may feel that it is the lack of political and religious freedom or something else, instead. It will thus be useful to have some clarity on the *basis* on which we may regard something as a root cause of terrorism.

One such basis is the lack of fulfillment of what the terrorists or terror organizations *want*—like withdrawal of foreign troops from the territory of a country or a political objective such as a separate state. For instance, Palestinian groups want a homeland for the Palestine people, IRA aims for the autonomy of the entire island of Ireland, and, Taliban's main objective, besides establishing a theocracy in Afghanistan, was to achieve withdrawal of foreign forces from Afghanistan. The key characteristic of such demands or wants is that they are arguably justifiable or legitimate. Hence the corresponding intervention would entail meeting such demands—partially at least.[17]

What about ideological objectives like the establishment of Caliphate over a region of the world by ISIS, shunning Western education and values by Boko Haram or returning to the rules government by the Old Testament by the Lord's Resistance Army in central Africa? These are a very different category of wants. This is where fundamentalist interpretation of religion and terrorism become inseparable. Such wants are highly concerning, unjustified, and unacceptable from the perspective of the culture of liberal democracy. Acceding to them is not an option. In economic terms, *accepting the political demands by non-state actors have finite costs, whereas meeting ideological demands is infinitely costly.*

In order to tackle the untenable wants or even the first category of "legitimate" demands, we may go one step deeper and ask what kind of deprivation or dissatisfaction in the first place leads to these wants. If we think that some sort of cultural

[17] These concessions would be typically granted, if at all, in the form of some quid pro quo resulting from negotiations.

or religious deprivation or a lack of religious freedom is an underlying cause, then these are the root causes of terrorism too. More generally, we can say that lack of political, civil, and religious freedom or rights are root causes of terrorism in the sense that they breed an inner urge or compulsion to engage in violence in order to attain them—be it political or ideological. In the same vein, lack of governance, deficient public services, social exclusion, economic deprivation due to lack of education and other factors, and, extreme economic inequality may also be regarded as root causes of terrorism as they engender a sense of frustration, which, in turn, gives rise to these wants as a form of achievement to strive for.

In relatively recent times, home-grown terrorism has become an issue in western countries. Significant number of citizens and permanent residents of these countries, typically young Muslims, have been enticed by violent terror organizations like al-Qaeda affiliates and ISIS. They have been inspired with or without traveling to where these organizations operate from. Here, the root causes are different from demanding a separate state, lack of civil rights, or religious freedom. As the research by Lyons-Padilla et al. (2015) suggests, it is not religious fundamentalism per se but economic and social exclusion in the "host" country that drives some young Muslims toward religious fundamentalism and propensity to join or be inspired by extremist and violent groups.

Apart from root causes, the *environment* that is conducive for terrorism to grow and propagate can also be construed as fundamental factors behind terrorism. Some extraneous comparison may clarify this. We all know that mosquitoes are the root cause of malaria. Hence killing them by chemical spray addresses the root cause of malaria. However, at the same time, cleaning swamps and standing water in which mosquitoes breed and grow is an equally important preventive. In some situations the propagation mechanism can be as important as the root cause of a disease. Think of the Covid-19 pandemic that created unprecedented havoc in the entire world in 2020 and the first half of 2021. While the virus is the root cause and a vaccine is the ultimate preventive, social distancing and mask wearing are important practices to deter the propagation of the infection rate until a vast majority of us is vaccinated. Furthermore, reduced immune system is the environment in which a virus can be potentially dangerous and fatal.

Returning to terrorism, a reduced immune system is akin to a conflict-ridden region or country devoid of normal law and order that enables terrorist organizations to form and flourish. We may thus regard ongoing conflicts as a fundamental cause of terrorism. It has also been argued that globalization or more precisely unfettered free movement of people across countries is a fundamental factor behind terrorism to have become a global problem—which is similar to the argument that an absence of social distancing is a main factor of the rapid spread of the coronavirus until most of the population is vaccinated.

Our preceding discussion leads to Table 1.2 that summarizes plausible root, fundamental and propagating causes of terrorism, and the corresponding preventive or long-run measures of addressing them. The critical difference between measures that address the root causes and the standard direct CT measures is that the former

Root, Breeding and Propagating Factors		*Corresponding Measures*
Lack of fulfillment of legitimate or justifiable grievances	→	Redressing legitimate grievances
Political, civil and religious restrictions	→	Fostering political and religious freedom and civil liberty
Lack of education, poverty and non-inclusive growth	→	Social sector development & inclusive growth
Gross Inequality	→	More equitable distribution of income and wealth
Economic and social exclusion	→	Economic and social inclusion
Pre-existing internal conflict	→	Cession of internal conflict
Globalization	→	Increased scrutiny of people's background in granting visa or for international travel

Table 1.2: Root causes of terrorism and corresponding measures

category of measures are non-violent, holistic, and they tend to reduce the incentives to engage in terrorism *voluntarily*.

1.16 Plan of the Book

This book is organized in five parts.

Part I Introduction It contains three chapters, including the current chapter. Chapter 2 traces history of modern terrorism, supposed to have begun in the second half of the nineteenth century and organized broadly in terms of four waves *a la* Rapoport (2004). It features narratives of scores (around sixty) terror organizations in different era including their origin, objective, progress, activities, and finance, as well as extreme but not exactly terror groups like Ku Klax Klan in the USA and National Social Underground in Germany.

Systematic data on terror incidents around the world is available beginning with the year 1970 in various degrees of detail. Chapter 3 enlists various available data sources on terror incidents and generates time trends and patterns of various attributes of terrorism from 1970 onward.

Part II Financing, Costs, and Consequences of Terrorism It has three chapters. Chapter 4 provides an assessment of costs of planning and executing terror attacks, and, how terror organizations are financed. That is, it discusses the financing side of organizing or "producing" terror. (Curbing of terror finance as a counter-terrorism measure is discussed later in Chap. 10.) Chapter 5 outlines the economic costs resulting from terrorism. It is organized into three parts: (a) economic costs of two major terrorist events, namely, 9/11 in the USA in 2001 and train bombings in the Spain in 2004 in terms of the opportunity cost of deaths and injuries, the cost of damaged properties and infrastructure and its adverse effect on activities measured by loss of national output or GDP, (b) country- and year-wise estimated economic costs of terrorism computed by the IEP and (c) costs of counter-terror measures. Chapter 6 traces the economic and psychological-physical health consequences of terrorism as well as how terrorism affects economic behavior. For example, how much impact does terrorism exert on GDPs, the growth rate of GDPs, foreign direct investment, and financial markets? How was mental health of residents in the USA and elsewhere affected by *9/11* attacks?

Part III Organization and Behavior of Terror Groups This part consists of only one chapter, that is, Chap. 7, which portrays a terrorist group as a firm. It cites examples of rivalry and cooperation among terrorist organizations—as do firms in the marketplace. They are also studied as networks. Firms in a market economy face various internal-organization issues arising out of the necessity to engage in delegation of tasks. Terrorist "firms" experience similar issues and these are compounded by the fact that they are illegal entities and its members constantly face physical safety issues from government forces as well as own people. Just as business firms have a limited lifetime, so do terrorist groups. These issues are the subject matter of Chap. 7.

Part IV Fighting the War on Terror: How Counter-Terror Measures Work This part focuses on "conventional" CT measures. Chapter 8 deals with the economic choice of security as a primary defensive measure against terrorism. The costs of security include resource costs like those of security and law enforcement personnel, equipment, travel, etc. as well as the implicit costs of the loss of civil liberty. Channels through which security reduces the adverse effect of terror are discerned.

The economic choice of offensive measures in terms of preemptive strikes on the personnel, equipment, and infrastructure of terror organizations is modeled and analyzed in Chap. 9. Many argue that such offensive tactics are the only means that can hand us a win over the WoT by taking the war to the door of the enemy. This chapter presents a definition of winning or losing the WoT and shows theoretically that, under some plausible assumptions, it is *impossible* to win the war through offensive measures only. This impossibility result should not be misinterpreted to imply that it is futile to use force against terrorists. The point is that such preemptive measures, while essential, may not be enough and need to be coupled with conciliatory measures. Curbing flow of funds to finance terror is an offensive measure similar to preemptive strikes, except that it does not cause collateral damage. Chapter 10, mostly descriptive, outlines various measures introduced by different countries and international bodies to curb terror financing.

While Chaps. 8 through 10 analyze defensive and offensive counter-terror tools separately, the interaction between these two generic measures and how they should both respond to an increase in terrorism are discussed in Chap. 11. It also analyzes intelligence and infiltration as means to weaken terror networks.

Terrorist organizations use kidnapping and hostage-taking, which (a) spread the fear of terrorism as well as (b) help them build resources through ransom payments and release of their personnel who have been already in custody by governments. Security provision of high-value or high-target individuals and leaders reduces the damage from this kind of terrorism. In this respect, our analysis of security in Chap. 8 applies to kidnapping and hostage-taking. However, to deal with terrorists demanding ransom or return of some of their members, governments typically use a different type of measure, namely, no-negotiation legislations. The underlying idea is to deter kidnapping and hostage-taking through a policy commitment. Of course, if such an event has already occurred, i.e., *ex post*, this policy may not be sensible. Countries that have such legislations *have to* and *do* engage in back-channel negotiations. Thus, the desirability of such legislations has been intensely debated. Using the concept of sequential games, Chap. 12 illustrates how such a no-negotiation policy is supposed to work. It also outlines the ongoing debate on the efficacy of such legislations and reviews empirical studies on various aspects of hostage-taking phenomena.

Part V Addressing Fundamental Cause of Terrorism It begins with Chap. 13—a continuation of Chap. 9 in the sense that it shows how grievance redress together with preemptive measures can yield better outcome than can the reliance of preemptive measures only. Chapter 14 explores the link between religion and terrorism, an object of highly charged debates and a contentious issue.

Chapter 15 is the concluding chapter. In earlier chapters we analyze how terrorists and terrorist organizations behave and how they may respond to counter-terrorism measures set by defending states. Different models of terrorism emphasize different scenarios and provide us various insights as to how counter-terror measures may work from a cost–benefit, economic perspective. Against this background, Chap. 15 addresses the important "So What?" question: *all said and done, what are underlying causes of terrorism in reality?* It delves into the empirical evidence on various root, breeding, and spreading causes of terrorism that have been advocated. The list includes foreign occupation, poverty, lack of education, lack of political and religious freedom, income and wealth inequality, lack of social and economic inclusion, pre-existing conflicts, and globalization. Equipped with evidence-backed plausible causes, an understanding of terrorist behavior and economic mechanisms behind various types of counter-terrorism measures, we will, hopefully, be able to tackle the global menace of terrorism more effectively.

The book also features two general appendices, namely, General Appendix A and General Appendix B, on many of the theoretical and empirical concepts that are used in various chapters. They can be read on their own.

1.17 Aspects of Terrorism Not Covered in the Book

The word "terrorism" has become so popular that it is used to dramatize any act of "threatening." It is not our aim to cover terrorism in all of its different literal interpretations. It is even not possible—and, in my opinion, not desirable—to include in a book all aspects of terrorism as a general threat or a means of violence, lest it should lose focus and be burdensome to the reader.

There are three important aspects of terrorism, which are outside the scope of this book, namely, cyber terrorism, the criminology approach to the understanding of terrorism, and negotiations with a terrorist organization toward a permanent solution.

Cyber Terrorism What does *cyber terrorism* mean? According to FBI of the USA, cyber terrorism as any "premeditated, politically motivated attack against information, computer systems, computer programs and data which results in violence against noncombatant targets by sub-national groups or clandestine agents." The important distinction with our "standard" definition of terrorism introduced earlier is that the violence is not direct. There are no organized cyber terrorist groups like, for example, al-Qaeda, Taliban or IRA. Cyber terrorism is an increasing menace no doubt, but its subject matter deserves a separate treatment of its own.

Criminological Analysis of Terrorism This is based on the (natural) premise that terrorism is a criminal act and thus belongs to criminology as a discipline. It focuses on motivation and surrounding socio-economic circumstances that drive an individual or a group of individuals to terrorism. Within its purview, there are particular theories. The strain theory of terrorism focuses on the major causes of terrorism, which we will discuss in Chap. 15. The social-learning theory analyzes how social interaction drives individuals to terrorism and terror groups. It includes situational approach to and victimization theory of terrorism also (LaFree & Freilich, 2017). However, in the criminology approach to terrorism, the postulated behavior of individuals is based on rationality or bounded rationality (Fisher & Dugan, 2019). Hence economic considerations do play a role. The difference lies in the emphasis: the processes behind how individuals become terrorists versus dealing with terrorists and terror groups from a cost–benefit standpoint.

Negotiations with Terrorist Group toward a Long-Term Permanent Solution A comprehensive, holistic approach toward solving a nation- or region-specific terrorism problem typically involves negotiation that includes acceding to demand of a terrorist group at least partially. Theoretical analysis of such negotiations is outside the scope of this book however, although Chap. 2 presents the description of some actual negotiation processes. Chapter 12 deals with negotiation with terrorists in a hostage situation. But this is quite different from negotiating for a long-term solution. Chapter 13 analyzes unilateral concessions to a terrorist group by a state, which anticipates, so-to-speak, negotiations on mutual commitments to actions.

1.18 Take-Aways

- Terrorists and terror organizations respond to incentive, hence can be regarded as rational entities from their own behavioral perspective and amenable to economic analysis.

- As a form of violence, terrorism is characterized by three ingredients: (a) non-state or sub-state actors or groups, (b) use of violence with no rules of engagement, targeting general public, government officials, or passive armed forces to create fear as a short-term goal or means, and, (c) some political, religious, or ideological motives in the long run.
- Terrorism may or may not be sponsored by an official state. By definition, the use of violence by a state to "terrorize" population is not typically counted as acts of terrorism (although it may qualify as terror in the common sense of the word).
- While incidences of international or transnational terrorism often hug the limelight, domestic terrorism incidences far outnumber international terrorism incidences.
- In the post 9/11 era, the countries most severely affected by terrorism are: Syria, Afghanistan, Nigeria, Iraq, and Pakistan.
- Over the period 1970–2019, about half of terror attacks do not cause any death. The average death per terror attack is about 2.41. Suicide attacks are more lethal than other forms of terror attacks. During 1982–2016, the average death from suicide attacks is about 10.22.
- Political factors, not Islamic fundamentalism, are the most dominating motivation behind lone-wolf attacks in the USA in recent years.
- More than 80% of the world's 1.5 billion Muslim population is Sunni. They are the majority in all Islamic countries, except three. Iran and Bahrain are the only countries where the vast majority of population is Shi'ite (90% and 85%, respectively). In Iraq, the population share of Shi'ites is about 67%.
- There are about fifty Muslim majority countries. Indonesia is the largest Muslim population country, followed by Pakistan and India (although India is a Hindu-majority country).
- In the post 9/11 era, the fundamentalist Islamic terror groups are followers of Salafism and Wahhabism.
- There are prominent women terrorists. The former prime minister of of India was killed by a woman terrorist belonging to LTTE. The PKK actively promotes women participation and leadership.
- We may classify various CT measures into two categories: direct and preventive. Direct CT measures can be further divided into defensive and office measures, as illustrated in Fig. 1.7.
- Preventive CT measures include redressing legitimate grievances, fostering political and religious freedom and civil liberty, inclusive growth, economic and social inclusion, etc. These are summarized in Table 1.2.
- The book does not cover cyber terrorism, the criminology approach to terrorism or an analysis of negotiation and settlement with a terrorist organization for long-lasting solution like a treaty.

Appendix to Chapter 1

1.A Details on Islam Religion

1.A.1 Strands within Sunnis

Within Sunni beliefs, the four major schools are derived from (a) Quran, (b) ***Sunnah***, meaning "tradition" or the "way" in Arabic and which translates into "the way of the Prophet" or the Prophet's daily application of the principles based on "ahadith," plural of ***hadith***, meaning the recorded saying or deeds of Prophet Mohammed collected over his lifetime, (c) *qiyas* (analogical reasoning), and (d) *ijma* (juridical consensus).

Hanafi, Maleki, Safii, and Hanbali Schools Hanafis are the followers of the *fiqh* (interpretation) of Imam Nauman Ibn Bashir Abu Hanifa. As said in the main text, the Hanafi school of jurisprudence is the oldest and the most liberal of the four (Hasan, 2012). The Hanafis see Quran, the *Sunnah*, the *ijma* (consensus), and *qiyas* (deduction from analogy) as the sources of law. The Hanafi *mazhab* is prevalent in Turkey, Central Asia, the Balkans, Iraq, Syria, Lebanon, Jordan, Afghanistan, Pakistan, India, and Bangladesh.

The Maleki *mazhab*, named after Anas bin Malik, is the second oldest of the four. The Malikis lay great emphasis on *istadlal*—juristic deduction. It is practiced mostly in North and West Africa, Mauritania, Kuwait, and Bahrain.

Named after Mohammed Ibn Idrees Al-Shafi, Safii is the third in sequence. Safiis (also written as Shafis) emphasize *ijma* (consensus). Imam Al-Shafi compiled all the *hadiths* of the earlier two *mazhabs* and attempted to categorize them into authentic, strong, weak, etc., while discarding all the weak *hadith* and keeping the rest: This laid the foundations of this school. The Safiis are widely spread, prevalent in Egypt, Sudan, Ethiopia, Somalia, parts of Yemen, Indonesia, and Malaysia and constituting about 15% of Muslims globally.[18]

The Hanbali school, the last of the four, is based on the *fiqh* of the Iraqi scholar Ahmad ibn Hanbal, and, was institutionalized by his students. It is most rigid of the four schools and follows the *Sunnah* almost literally. It is prevalent in Saudi Arabia, Qatar, parts of Oman, and the U.A.E.

Salafism and Wahhabism Within the Hanbali school, Salafism comes from the word *Salaf*, meaning predecessors or forebears, referring to the earlier generations of Muslims, presumed to be very devout. As a reformist movement, it originated in the thirteenth century to rid Islam of corruptive leaders. It surfaced again in Egypt in the late nineteenth century as a response to European colonialism. It embraces the puritanical and narrow interpretations of Islam and Quran, and, rejects religious innovations and alternative interpretations.

An offshoot of Salafism, Wahhabism is based on the teaching of Mohammad ibn Abd al-Wahhab, a Sunni preacher who sought to revive Islam in its original principles and rejected

[18] One difference in practice between Saffi and Hanafi traditions is that, in order to marry, in the Safii tradition, women need a *wali* (custodian or protector) as a minimum, while they would need a witness as a minimum in the Hanafi tradition. Another is that the *Asr* prayer (afternoon prayer) time is calculated an hour earlier in Safii than in Hanafi school.

many common Muslim practices. The movement around his teachings became prominent because of its alliance with the Saud family and its leader, Muhammad ibn Saud. Wahhabs would give religious legitimacy to Saudi expansionism and political rule, while the Saudis would adopt and support Wahhab's ideology. This implicit understanding has been held for more than 300 years and dominates in the Arabian Peninsula till today.

1.A.2 Strands within Shi'ites

There are several schools of thought. The predominant one is ***Twelver Shi'ism***, pervasive in Iran, Iraq, Lebanon, and Bahrain, and the believers constitute about 80% of all Shi'ites around the world. It is also called ***Ashna Asari***. Twelvers accept a line of twelve infallible imams descendent from Ali and believe them to have been divinely appointed from birth.[19] The twelve imams are viewed as harbors of the faith and the designated interpreters of law and theology. Twelvers believe that the twelfth and last of these imams, Imam Al Mahdi, "disappeared" in the late ninth century. The "hidden imam" is expected to return to lead the community. The Twelvers follow the jurisprudence of the sixth imam: Imam Jafar-us-Sadiq. It is called the ***Jafari*** jurisprudence.[20]

Ismailis or ***Sevener*** Shi'ites are the second largest among the Shi'ite schools. Although most Shi'ites agree on the basic premise that Ali was the first rightful imam, they disagree on his successors. This group recognizes only the first seven imams (the seventh was named Ismail, hence the names "Ismaili" and "Sevener"). Ismailis are scattered throughout the world but are prominent in Afghanistan, India, and Pakistan. There are also Ismaili communities in East and South Africa.[21]

The ***Zaydis***, who acknowledge the first five imams but differ over the identity of the fifth, are a minority within Shi'ite Islam, mostly found in Yemen.[22] The Zaydis reject the concepts of the imams' infallibility and of a "hidden imam." The Zaydis follow Zayd ibn Ali's teachings for Islamic jurisprudence (which is somewhat close to Hanafi Sunni Islam).[23]

These Shi'ite schools are depicted in the right panel of Fig. 1.5.

1.A.3 Other Sects

Besides Sunni and Shi'ia, there are two other sects within the Muslim religion, broadly interpreted. A very small minority, known as *Ibadi*s, follows Mohammed as the Prophet but they are neither Sunni nor Shi'ia, although sometimes misrepresented as a Sunni sect. Most *Ibadi*s live in Oman, East Africa, Algeria, Libya, and Tunisia. They believe strongly in the existence of a just Muslim society and argue that religious leaders should be chosen by community leaders for their knowledge and piety, without regard to race or lineage.

There is another group called *Ahmadiya*, who are not the true followers of Prophet Mohammed. Instead, they follow Mirza Ghulam Ahmad Khadiani who lived in the nineteenth century. Of British–India origin, this is the most recent sect of Muslims in a broader sense. Many traditional Muslims do not consider *Ahmadiayas* as real Muslims.[24]

---

[19] These imams are: Hazrat Ali, Imam Hasan, Imam Hussain, Imam Zainul Abideen, Imam Al-Baqir, Imam Jafar-us-Sadiq, Imam Musa Al-Kazim, Imam Ar-Riza, Imam Al-Jawwad, Imam Al-Naqi, Imam Al-Askari, and Imam Al Mahdi.

[20] The Akbaris and Usulis are subgroups within the Twelvers.

[21] Nizaris, Khojas, Mustalians, and Dawoodi Bohras are subgroups of Ismailis.

[22] They constitute about 40% Muslims in Yemen.

[23] There are other, very minor, subgroups of Shi'ite faith.

[24] A Physics Nobel laureate, Abdus Salam, from Pakistan, is a prominent scholar from this community.

1.A.4 Sufism

Outsiders to Islam often consider Sufism as a distinct sect of Islam. It is however best described as a dimension of Islam that cuts across different sects of Islam. It is Islamic mysticism. Sufis emphasize inward search for God, learning from teachers, not so much from books, and, disregard materialism. They do not believe in religion playing an active role in political affairs.

Through the centuries the Sufis have contributed hugely to Islamic literature, e.g., Rumi, Omar Khayyám, and Al-Ghazali. This literature cherishes pluralism and tolerance, and, has been quoted by Western philosophers, writers, and theologians. But this is precisely the reason why the Islamic extremists are antagonistic toward sufism.

A sufi shrine in the Sindh province of Pakistan was attacked in 2017 killing dozens of people and the Islamic State claimed its ownership. In the same year militants stormed a Sufi mosque on the Sinai Peninsula, killing at least 305 people in what officials have called the worst terrorist attack in Egypt's modern history.

Questions

1.1 "Terrorists are insane. To assume that they are rational and apply economic principles to understand terrorism is foolish." Defend or refute.

1.2 "Economics of terrorism is primarily concerned with how terrorist activities may be financed and how we may limit the flow of funds for such activities." Defend or refute.

1.3 American military involvement in Afghanistan and Iraq has led to many civilian deaths. Can we equate this with acts of terrorism? Why or why not?

1.4 Why are suicide attacks considered the lung cancer of terrorism?

1.5 "Most terror attacks in the post *9/11* era have occurred in five countries. Hence, it is not appropriate to say that terrorism is a global problem." Defend or refute.

1.6 "Most of the victims of terror attacks by Islamic terror groups are Muslim." Defend or refute.

1.7 How can we differentiate between defensive and offensive measures in dealing with terrorism in terms of economic concepts?

1.8 Articulate the differences between direct and preventive measures in dealing with terrorism.

Chapter 2

Origin, Objective, and History of Terrorism and Terrorist Organizations

2.1 Introduction

Because *9/11* attacks occurred in the beginning of the twenty-first century and terrorism is on the prime time news ever since, one may think that, historically speaking, terrorism is a relatively recent phenomenon. Not so. In this chapter, we trace the history of terrorism and the evolution of various terror organizations since the mid/late nineteenth century.[1] The list of terror organizations mentioned or reviewed in this chapter is long, albeit, by no means exhaustive. Besides their origin, we discuss, depending on the available information, their sources of finance, organizational structure, tactics of terror used—and their dissolution. Different methods of terror financing in general will be covered in Chap. 4. It is sufficient to take note here that terror groups raise funds through both illegal and legal means. Since terror organizations are non-state actors, the available information on them varies widely. Hence, there is a considerable variation in our depiction of the finance of terror organizations individually.

Understanding the dynamics of terrorism and terrorist groups should help us to better interpret terrorism as an evolutionary process, not as accidental episodes of history. We will learn the uniqueness of each of them: Terrorist organizations are *not* just clones of one other. While there are similarities, major terror organizations differ significantly among themselves.[2] Understanding the differences as well as how they position themselves in the socio-political structure is a pre-requisite for effectively dealing with them. In accordance with our definition of terrorism in Chap. 1, we desist from normative considerations in describing terror groups.

We begin with the origin of terrorism in Sect. 2.2. In Sect. 2.3, we introduce four broad "waves" of "modern terrorism" since its inception. This provides a broad conceptual framework within which to place and study various terror organizations.

---

[1] For more detailed accounts of the history of terrorism and various terror organizations, the reader may refer to Law (2009).

[2] There are books and chapters dedicated to particular terror organizations, e.g., Marcus (2007) on PKK, Berman (2009) on Taliban, Hamas and Hezbollah, Rashid (2010) on Taliban, and McCants (2015) on ISIS.

S. P. Das, *Economics of Terrorism and Counter-Terrorism Measures*,
https://doi.org/10.1007/978-3-030-96577-8_2

The first three waves are covered in Sects. 2.4, 2.5, and 2.6, respectively. Some major terror organizations in the post-World War II era have overlapped between the third wave and the fourth wave. They are described in Sect. 2.7. The fourth and the final is the religious wave, which includes the fundamentalist terror organizations in the modern era. They are detailed in Sect. 2.8. Section 2.9 outlines various terror groups and their activities in Russia, Central Asia, China, South and South-East Asia as well as the USA. Finally, there are extreme organizations such as Ku Klux Klan (KKK) in the USA and the National Social Underground (NSU) in Germany, which do not fit into our definition of terrorism as a form of violence. They are briefly reviewed in Sect. 2.10.

2.2 Origin of Terrorism

Terrorism can be traced back to the Zealot struggle in the first century (Enders & Sandler, 2012 and Martin, 2018). Zealots, a radical political group of Jews, wanted to drive the Romans out of the Judaea province (currently in Israel). They resented the Romans as well as other Jews who sought reconciliation with the Romans. *Sicarii*, a splinter group of Zealots, attacked and killed Romans and their sympathizers with daggers and was particularly active during 66–73 A.D.

Moving fast forward, when and where did "modern" terrorism begin? Ironically, the precursor to modern terrorism coincides with the birth of liberal democracy in France. Shortly after the French Revolution and the birth of the first French Republic in 1792, the Revolutionary government itself launched a massive campaign to punish those who opposed the Revolution, namely, the nobles, the priests, and the commodity hoarders. Within a year—between September 1793 and July 1794, called by some historians as the *Reign of Terror* (in French *La Terreur*)—more than 300,000 were arrested, 17,000 were executed, and about 10,000 died in prison. Guillotine was the common method of execution.

However, from our perspective, this was not terrorism. It was, literally speaking, "state terrorism," not even state-sponsored terrorism: there was no sub-national group that actually killed individuals and enjoyed the support of the French state. Moreover, there was no long-term objective in this act of violence: atrocities were just tools of punishment. At the same time, it was the first instance since the eighteen century where a mass of people were targeted and killed within a state, and this did not happen in the course of warfare with countries.

2.3 Modern Terrorism: Four Waves

Modern terrorism featuring sub-national groups that unleashed terror began in Russia in the late nineteenth century. In an insightful and influential paper, Rapoport (2004) has grouped modern terrorism since that period into four waves:

1. Anarchism
2. Anti-Colonial
3. New Left
4. Religious

The basic tenets of Rapoport's analysis are the following. Terrorism is a part of the modern culture. Different ideologies have shaped different waves. Each wave reflects its dominant, but not the only, feature. When a wave's energy cannot stimulate new organizations, it loses steam. In each wave, some kind of societal cause or revolution is the overriding aim, and, this is interpreted differently in different waves. Furthermore, some organizations (such as IRA) have outlived their original wave and have morphed into the mold of a new wave.

While all major terror groups do not fall into this stylized pattern, Rapoport's classification is a useful way to organize and categorize the phenomenon of terrorism nearly over the last hundred fifty years.[3]

In this chapter, the history of terrorism and the evolution of terror organizations are organized within Rapoport's broad conceptual framework, while details and specifics—which we emphasize—are consistent with Shughart II (2006). Walls (2017) provides a nice broad summary of Rapoport's four waves, which is reproduced in Table 2.1, barring two changes noted in the footnote. These features will be discerned in the course of our description.

2.4 Anarchism, the First Wave

Anarchism emerged in Europe in the mid-nineteenth century from the oppression by authoritarian rules and the power of the elite. Known as the father of anarchism, Pierre-Joseph Proudhon in France was the first self-portrayed anarchist. In 1849, he proclaimed that "Whoever lays his hand on me to govern me is a usurper and tyrant, and I declare him my enemy." The anarchists wanted a government-less state. Following Proudhon's footsteps emerged a group of social radicals in Russia—Mikhail Bakunin, Sergey Nechaev, and Peter Kropotkin, among others. Proudhon and Bakunin did not engage in or encourage violence: they were writers, philosophers, and activists. Proudhon actually believed that social revolution can be achieved by peaceful means, and he favored workers' associations and cooperatives.[4] Proudhon and Karl Marx corresponded with each other but parted ways later. Bakunin was more proactive yet peaceful, whereas Sergey Nechaev and Peter Kropotkin were inclined toward violence.

[3] In his review of the post-World War II history of terrorism, Shughart II (2006) follows Rapoport's framework while adding an important point that post-war terrorism—whether it belongs to the anti-colonial, new left and the religious wave—owes its origin to the political marginalization of ethnic and religious groups meted out by the colonial powers in the late nineteenth century and the early twentieth century. In addition, Shughart II (2006) describes terrorism in different regions of the world in more detail than does Rapoport.

[4] In 1873, Spanish anarchists led a workers' strike demanding an eight-hour working day.

Wave	*Catalyst*	*Goals*	*Targets*	*Tactics*	*Reasons for decline*
Anarchist, 1870s–1910s	Slow political reforms and declining legitimacy of monarchy	Revolution, eliminate government oppression	Heads of state	Assassinations by using dynamite, bank robberies	Aggressive state opposition, beginning of World War I
Nationalist, 1920s–1960s	Versailles Peace Treaty, increased desire for self-determination	Eliminate colonial rule, create new states	Police and military	Guerrilla style hit-and-run attacks	Achieved goals, colonial rulers withdrew from territories
New Left, 1960s–1980s	Rise of Soviet Union*	Eliminate the capitalist system	Governments, increased focus on the USA	Hijacking, kidnapping, assassinations	End of cold war
Religious, 1979–2020s (predicted)	Iranian Revolution, new Islamic century, Soviet Invasion of Afghanistan	Creation of global Islamic caliphate	Own government, armed forces and citizens of different faiths; the USA; the UK; Israel; Europe; mass transport systems; public venues†	Suicide bombings, aircrafts, and vehicles are weapons	Unknown

*: This is different from Rapoport, instead of Vietnam war and cold war tensions, we have "rise of the Soviet Union"

†: "Own government & citizens of different faiths" are my own addition.

Table 2.1: Summary of four waves by Walls (2017). Permission to reproduce from the author is thankfully acknowledged

2.4.1 Narodnaya Volya

Drawing inspiration from these leaders, a group of people in Europe became branded as anarchists, who attempted to kill prominent government officials and dignitaries. The first recorded *organized* group came into existence in Russia by the name of Narodnaya Volya, meaning People's Will.

Influenced by a book, *Catechism of a Revolutionist* written in 1869 by Sergey Nechaev, in which Mikhail Bakunin had a major contribution, a group named *Land and Liberty* formed itself in 1876. It advocated the demise of the state and land ownership by peasants. The group split into two factions in 1879: one militant and the other supporting socialist propaganda. Led by Andrey I. Zhelyabov and Sofiya L. Perovskaya, the militant faction formed Narodnaya Volya, a small group. Its most spectacular act was the assassination of Czar Alexander II by a bomb. Alexander III, who succeeded Alexander II, suppressed and repressed those favoring reforms that included Narodnaya Volya's members and sympathizers. It attempted to kill Alexander III too but failed. Although the assassination of Alexander II was spectacular, Narodnaya Volya did not bring about significant changes in Russian polity or society. However, its ideas attracted wide support in Russia and, later, outside Russia, and, its tactics were honed by subsequent terror organizations.

2.4.2 Spread of Anarchism and the Philosophy of Narodnaya Volya[5]

Narodnaya Volya's philosophy was a precursor of Russian revolutions in 1905 and 1917. Although Lenin was critical of its view of a Utopian state, he admired the group's selfless resistance to the czarism and its reliance on secrecy and centralization of authority. The group marked the birth of modern terrorism, since it was the first organized sub-national group that carried out terror attacks.

Is That So? 2.1: First "Modern" Terror Organization

Modern terrorism began in Russia in the late nineteenth century with a group called *Narodnaya Volya.*

Modern terrorism that began in Russia in 1880s spread, within a decade, to Western Europe, the Balkans, and Asia. The anarchists killed several heads of state. The French President Sadi Carnot was a victim in 1894, and the Spanish Prime Minister Antonio Canovas was killed in 1897, followed by Empress Elizabeth in Austria and King Umberto of Italy in 1898 and 1900, respectively. These assassinations led Bismarck of Germany to comment that "... anarchist crime was an infectious disease, in which vanity and the lust of fame often played a part." The 1890s were called the ***Golden Age of Assassinations***.

The idea of anarchism in Europe had found its way to the USA. On September 6, 1901 (almost exactly 100 years before *9/11* attacks), President McKinley was assassinated in Buffalo, New York, by Leon Czolgosz, believed to be an anarchist.[6]

Back in Russia, the defeat of Russia in its war with Japan in 1905 led to a massive public uprising. The Russian Revolution of 1905 was punctuated by workers' demonstrations, social and political unrest, and mutiny by the Russian navy. The revolt spread to Poland, Finland, and the Balkan region. The czar, Nicholas II, replaced autocracy by constitutional monarchy. At the same time, the Revolution was repressed by the government. However, these events laid the foundation for the much bigger Bolshevik Revolution of 1917. Both its leaders—Vladimir Lenin and Leon Trotsky—used the tactics of bombing and assassination against the Russian government and political machinery emulating the footsteps of Narodnaya Volya.

---

[5] The material sources are von Borcke (1982), Martin (2018, Chapter 1) and Encyclopedia Britannica.

[6] Interestingly, McKinley's successor Theodore Roosevelt called for the wiping out of terrorism everywhere: "Anarchy is a crime against the whole human race, and all mankind should band together against the Anarchist. His crimes should made a crime against the law of nations.... declared by treaties among all civilized powers." One hundred years after, President George W. Bush declared that "war (that) would not end until every terrorist group of global reach has been found, stopped, and defeated."

As observed keenly by Rapoport (2004), anarchism was facilitated by two factors. First, it was based on a doctrine. Second, this doctrine as well as the tactics rapidly traveled with the help of massive improvements in transport and communications. Even in the initial stage of anarchism, Proudhon and the Russian anarchists traveled extensively, promoting their ideas and missions.

2.5 Anti-Colonial, the Second Wave

Anarchism was succeeded by an anti-colonial wave starting in 1920s, which lasted for about forty years. In this wave, there was a fusion of terrorism and nationalism. Rapoport attributes the advent of this era to the famous Versailles Peace Treaty of 1919 that concluded World War I. In the treaty, the victors applied the principle of self-determination to break up the empires of the defeated states mostly in Europe, which, according to Rapoport, became the seeds of movement against the victors' own colonies.[7] The uprising against the British can be explained in the light of this thesis. With the exception of India, violence was a common method used against the colonial masters.[8] Furthermore, as a former British colony and the new emerging global heavyweight, the USA pressed for the abolition of colonial empires.

Compared to the first era of terrorism, the objectives, targets, and tactics changed. Political independence was the objective. Instead of high-profile political dignitaries, the police and troops became the targets. Note that those engaged in terror to seek independence could be seen both as terrorists and as freedom fighters. However, the definition of terrorism we adopted in Chap. 1 does not distinguish between terrorists and violent freedom fighters.

We now study the major terror groups of this era.

2.5.1 The Original IRA (OIRA)—First Generation[9]

The Irish Republican Army (IRA) of Ireland is a unique organization that spanned not one but three waves: second, third, and fourth. We describe its evolution in terms of four generations. The first "generation" began its activities during and after World War I. The second generation began to shape in the early 1920s, and it lasted till late 1960s, and, during this period, the IRA underwent major organizational changes. It overlapped between the second and third waves of terrorism. By the end of late 1960s, the third wave had already set in, and the third generation overlapped between the third and fourth waves of terrorism, while the fourth generation, the latest, began in late 1990s.

We cover the first and second generations of IRA here. Its third and fourth generations will be described in Sects. 2.7.1 and 2.7.2.

[7] He wrote that "Whether the victors fully understood the implications of their decisions or not, they undermined the legitimacy of their own empires."

[8] Violence was also adopted by patriotic groups in India, but it did not succeed.

[9] See White (2017, Chapter 1).

The origin of IRA can be traced to the nineteenth century Fenian Brotherhood of America (FBA) in the USA whose aim was to establish an Irish Republic in North America. That failed obviously, and FBA was dissolved in 1880s. However, it had gained an international reputation and formed a natural alliance with the Irish Republic Brotherhood (IRB), a small revolutionary group in Ireland already in existence since 1850s, whose objective was to secure a republic of Ireland, independent from the British. In the Easter Week of 1916, IRB launched its first initiative against the British, known as the ***Easter Rising*** or the ***Easter Rebellion***. IRB was defeated, however.

Following the unsuccessful Easter Rising, the IRB brought various other paramilitary Irish groups, including the Irish Volunteers, the Irish Citizen Army, and the Hibernian Rifles, under one banner. A name and its abbreviation popularized by the FBA earlier were adopted and announced in 1917: the Irish Republican Army (IRA). It was not a terror organization initially and, further, was allied with a political party, Sinn Féin (meaning "We Ourselves") that was established in 1905 with the same objective: an independent Irish republic.

In the 1918 general election, Sinn Féin secured the majority of seats. Following its election manifesto, the Irish Assembly—Dáil Éireann—declared independence of the "Irish people," without a mention of independence of all thirty two counties, and IRA was officially declared as the army of the newly proclaimed Irish Republic. This group became known as the ***Original IRA*** or ***OIRA***. The declaration of independence led to war with England, known as the Irish War of Independence. It lasted from 1919 to 1921. The OIRA fought against the British forces by using guerrilla tactics.[10] The Irish War for Independence ended with the Anglo-Irish Treaty in 1921, which partitioned Ireland into a Catholic Irish Free State and a Protestant Northern Ireland, which became a British province, Ulster. See Fig. 2.1, where Ulster is the Northern part of Island, still a part of the UK till date.

2.5.2 Anti-Treaty IRA or the "Irregulars"—the Second Generation[11]

Started in the anti-colonist era, this generation of IRA lived into the next wave, the wave of the new left. The Anglo-Irish treaty led to a split within the OIRA: one group supporting and the other opposing it. By 1922, Ireland had plunged into a civil war, with the anti-treaty faction of OIRA, called ***the Irregulars*** wanting a fully independent country for the Irish island. The civil war ended in 1923 with the defeat of the Irregulars. However, they neither surrendered nor disbanded and moved

[10] OIRA was led by Cathal Brugha, Richard Mulcahy, and Eoin O'Duffy as the chiefs of staff. However, it was Michael Collins, an elected member of Sinn Féin, who became most famous for his leadership of the republican military campaign against Britain—although nominally he was the Director of Intelligence of IRA. He directed a group of gunmen targeting to assassinate British agents. This culminated with the killing of fourteen British officers in Dublin in 1920. The British forces retaliated by opening fire at a Gaelic football game, killing twelve.

[11] See Encyclopedia Britannica.

Fig. 2.1: Map of Ireland. *Source*: Google map

on with their goal of a united Irish Republic, reminding its goal to the successive governments and committing violence off and on.

Following the civil war, the Irregulars' membership dwindled rapidly throughout the 1920s. But it surged to more than 10,000 during the 1930s, thanks to the Great Depression. In course of time, the Irregulars—to be called IRA henceforth—were declared illegal twice, in 1931 and 1936. In the political arena, the Irish Free State adopted a republican constitution in 1937 that made southern Ireland a full republic (a country), except the name. This marginalized the IRA, and it turned its focus to Northern Ireland, which was under the control of the British. It also carried out bombings in England before and during World War II. At one point, it sought assistance from Adolf Hitler to help remove the British from Ireland (The Telegraph, 2001).

Post-World War II and particularly after the withdrawal of Ireland from the British Commonwealth in 1949, the IRA pitched for the unification of Southern and Northern Ireland. In the mid-1950s, it deployed guerrilla tactics against the British, yielding no results, however. From 1962 onward, the IRA reshaped into a Marxist political-revolutionary group. The distinction between the IRA and the Sinn Féin began to shrink, while Sinn Féin abandoned the old policy of ***abstentionism*** and sought to work toward Irish unity through political involvement.[12]

The transformation from a paramilitary force into a socialist political group alienated the radicals, who thought that the IRA had become a group of "thinkers,"

[12] Abstentionism refers to participation in the election process but not in the deliberative process in the legislature. In Ireland, the abstentionists boycotted the Irish parliament because of their opposition to England's jurisdiction over Northern Ireland.

not "doers." By the mid-1960s, the IRA was financially weak and fractured, unable to garner the support of the Catholics in different parts of Northern Ireland.

Just when the IRA was about to eclipse, the tides turned in the late 1960s when the Catholics in Northern Ireland launched a civil rights campaign against discrimination in voting, housing, and employment by the dominant Protestant government and population. There were extremists colluding with the unionists who supported being part of England. The extremists had the tacit support of the mostly Protestant police force. Major attacks were led from both sides. The IRA attempted to defend the besieged Catholic communities in the province.

However, the widespread use of violence led to an internal conflict and a division within the IRA. Following a Sinn Féin conference in 1969, the IRA split into Official IRA (OIRA)—different from the Original IRA, referred to as OIRA also—and Provisional IRA (PIRA). The two differed on whether or not to use violence and also on abstentionism. The Officials, mostly Marxists, preferred parliamentary tactics, whereas the Provisionals or "Provos" embraced violence—terrorism—to push the British out of Ireland.

The emergence of PIRA or Provos marked the onset of the Third Generation of IRA, which will be described later in Sect. 2.7.1.

2.5.3 Israel and Palestine: Haganah, Irgun Zvai Leumi, and Lehi[13]

Violence or terrorism to secure colonial independence was witnessed in other parts of the world too. In the Israeli–Palestine region, terrorism in the Zionist struggle for homeland was directed toward the British, who occupied the region (see Fig. 2.2). There were three major Jewish paramilitary groups: Haganah (meaning Defense), Irgun Zvai Leumi (which meant National Military Organization, shortly addressed as Irgun), and Lehi (meant Fighters for the Freedom of Israel). All three aimed at an independent Israeli state.

Haganah It was the first major Zionist military organization. Surfacing in 1920, its initial objective was not to drive out the British but protect the Jewish settlements from the revolts of Palestinian Arabs. Relatively moderate in violence, it conformed to the Jewish practice of *Havlagah*, meaning self-restraint. There was however a bloody Arab uprising from 1936 to 1939, which was primarily aimed at the British but manifested the distrust and hatred between Arabs and the Jews. This led to fights between the two communities. After this, Haganah changed its strategy from defending from "within the fences" to offense initiatives outside the domain of Jewish settlements. It began to develop a mobile warfare doctrine. During World War II, Haganah assisted the British against the Nazis who oppressed the Jews. But after the war, it turned against the British. It focused on illegal immigration of Jews as well as attacking British ships and radar installations used to deter immigrants from entering the country.

[13] See Hoffman (1985), White (2017, Chapter 8) and Encyclopedia Britannica.

Fig. 2.2: Palestine Region under the British, 1920–1922. *Source*: "British Mandate of Palestine: Map," The Land of Israel/Palestine: image database, accessed November 15, 2021, https://ancient-world-project.nes.lsa.umich.edu/image-database/items/show/251

Haganah had branches outside Palestine, including the USA, Europe, and Morocco, where its members trained immigrant jews including Holocaust survivors before they migrated to Israel. The Haganah members outside Palestine procured arms from the USA and Europe and sent them to Palestine. It also had its own clandestine weapons factories, named TAAS (Ta'asiya Zvai'it). More than forty in number, they produced guns, bullets, and explosives.

After the Israeli independence in 1948, Haganah merged with the Israeli army. Politically, it was aligned to a merged group of parties, named Mapai. David Ben Gurion, the first prime minister of Israel, was the leader of Mapai. Three subsequent prime ministers, namely, Moshe Sharett, Levi Eshkol, and Golda Meir, also belonged to Mapai, which later evolved into the Labor Party of Israel.

Irgun Zvai Leumi An offshoot of Haganah, this group operated between 1931 and 1948. In 1929, there was clash between Arabs and Jews in which sixty Jews were killed and another sixty died from sporadic violence. This prompted a split in Haganah and the birth of Irgun. Unlike Haganah, it was violent right from its inception. It was opposed to the British and carried out bombing and assassinations against the British before and after World War II, while during the war it supported the British. It was violently anti-Arab too. In 1948, it was led by Menachem Begin, who later became the Prime Minister of Israel. Like Haganah, Irgun members merged with the Israeli military. Politically, Irgun is the predecessor of the right-wing party "Herut" (meaning Freedom) that later became Likud.

Lehi This was a breakaway group from Irgun, founded in 1940. It was led by Avraham Stern, and the group was called the "Stern Gang" by the British. It parted ways with the Irgun as Irgun adopted the Haganah's policy of supporting the British during World War II. Vehemently anti-British, it repeatedly attacked British personnel and even sought assistance from the Axis powers. The British police killed Stern in 1942 and arrested other leaders later. But its activities continued. In 1944 in Cairo, it assassinated Lord Moyne, the British minister of State for the Middle East. Lehi attacked British airfields and aircrafts, and other strategic installations. However, unlike Haganah or Irgun, it had no political party to carry on and be assimilated into Israel political system or military after its independence in 1948.

In sum:

Is That So? 2.2: Groups in Israel

There were three major Jewish paramilitary groups working toward the independence of Israel as well as fighting with Arabs: Haganah, Irgun Zvai Leumi (an offshoot of Haganah), and Lehi (a splinter group of Irgun). After Israel's independence, Haganah and Irgun merged into Israel army and polity, whereas Lehi simply disbanded.

All the three groups were heavily engaged in protecting the Jewish people and settlement from Arabs. However, unlike against the British, their conflicts with Arabs cannot be strictly interpreted as terrorism, since the ultimate enemy, in this context, is not a state. The objective was to live peacefully along Arabs within one state or as neighboring countries.

These groups applied and refined the methods of Michael Collins of IRA, relying upon bombing and assassinations. Interestingly, the tactics of Jewish terrorism found its way to the Third Generation of IRA that would use similar tactics against the British after 1969.

Fig. 2.3: Map of Cyprus. *Source*: Google map

2.5.4 Cyprus: Ethnikí Orgánosis Kipriakoú Agónos (EOKA)[14]

The island of Cyprus came under the British rule in 1878. Cyprus insurgency against the British occurred between 1956 and 1959, starting with an underground movement of the Greek Cyprots, organized under EOKA—Ethnikí Orgánosis Kipriakoú Agónos—the National Organization of Cypriot Fighters. EOKA used the tactics of the Jewish extreme groups like sabotaging military installations, ambushing military convoys and patrols, and assassinating British soldiers and local informers. During 1956–1959, EOKA reportedly killed 371 British service men (*BBC News*, November 23, 2009). More than 30,000 British troops were assigned to combat the organization. Many EOKA members were brutally tortured and/or hanged by the British.

While EOKA primarily targeted British interests, Cypriots of the Turkish origin who were serving the British security forces became their targets too. It is argued that right after the EOKA campaign began, the British successfully turned the Cyprus issue from a colonial problem to a Greek–Turkish issue.

As distrust between EOKA and the Turkish minority population in Cyprus mounted, a Turkish group, named, Türk Mukavemet Teşkilati (TMT)—Turkish Resistance Organization—was formed in 1957 with its goal of opposing *Enosis*, the notion of Greek communities living outside Greece to become a Greek State. In 1958, encounters between EOKA and TMT claimed the lives of 55 Turkish Cypriots and 60 Greek Cypriots. After its independence from the British in 1960, the Constitution of Cyprus provided for a Greek Cypriot president, a Turkish Cypriot vice president, and a civil service with 70% Greek and 30% Turkish Cypriots. But mutual suspicion between the Greek majority and the Turkish minority grew over time, and the post-independent Cyprus plunged into a civil war. Frightened, the Turkish Cypriots asked help from Turkey, which invaded the island in 1974. Turkish military is present till date in the northern part of the country, while the southern part of Cyprus is populated mostly by Greeks. The international community regards the Turkish troops in Cyprus as "occupation," while Turkey maintains that it is legal and necessary.

The dotted lines from west to east in Fig. 2.3 mark the UN buffer zone, the south and north of which are the Greek–Cypriot controlled area and Turkish–Cypriot controlled area, respectively.

2.5.5 Algeria: Front de Libération Nationale (FLN)[15]

Another prominent region of terrorism and struggle for independence was Algeria (see Fig. 2.4). The fight was against the French. The Algerian War of Independence dates back to 1945 when a march for independence turned into a massacre as the protesters killed more than one hundred European settlers. In retaliation, the French army killed thousands of Algerians. This became known as the Sétif massacre. At the center of the Algerian struggle for independence was a group named Front de Libération Nationale, FLN.

[14] See Novo (2010), White (2017, Chapter 7) and Encyclopedia Britannica.

[15] See Encyclopedia Britannica.

Fig. 2.4: Map of Algeria. *Source*: Google map

In 1954, a paramilitary group of people, hiding from authorities, formed FLN. Beginning with a five-man leadership, the group was active between 1954 and 1962 and, like EOKA, applied the method of the Jewish terror groups. In 1956, it focused on Algiers, the capital city.

A unique feature of FLN was the active participation of women. They supported the men who were fighting by providing food, safe houses, clean clothes, and medical services. A famous incidence in 1956 involved a young woman, Zohra Drif, who, because of her lighter complexion, passed as a French, crossed curfew areas and planted a bomb in a milk bar cafe, killing three members of French army and critically wounding many.[16] This invited reprisal by the French military, which tortured and repressed FLN members. But it only hardened FLN's resolve. The Muslim majority in Algeria started to turn against the French rule because of its repressive measures. By staging attacks in Algiers where many foreign nationals and journalists were present, FLN was able to internationalize its cause. It is estimated that during 1954–1962 FLN killed more than 16,000 Algerian civilians and was involved in the disappearance of more than 13,000. However, in general, Algerians and other Muslim nations regarded the FLN members as heroes who were able to beat the French, the occupiers, to secure independence for Algeria.

2.6 The New Left, the Third Wave

This era was inspired by the Soviet communist system and the success of USSR. as a world power alongside the USA. As an alternative to the capitalist system, communism was appealing to the young generation at the time, who aspired to

[16] As of 2021, she lived in Algeria.

bring a change toward a fairer society along with an equally efficient economy. They believed that violence was the way to achieve it, much like the Bolshevik revolution. The Vietnam debacle of the USA fed the belief that the present system was vulnerable. Leftist–extremist groups started to emerge in "the Third World as well as in the Western heartland itself" (Rapoport, 2004), e.g., American Weather Underground in the USA, the French Action Directe in France, the West German Red Army Faction (RAF), the Italian Red Brigades (Brigate Rosse) and the Japanese Red Army, FARC in Colombia, Shining Path in Peru, and so on.

There is however a notable difference between leftwing extreme groups in advanced countries and those in Latin America. The former aimed to weaken and topple the current system but did not go out to directly help the poor and downtrodden, whereas their Latin American counterparts were insurgents and at the same time offered social services to the poor rural population.

2.6.1 American Weather Underground[17]

It started with a group of students at the University of Michigan—Ann Arbor. The group was active between 1969 and 1977. According to a document released in 1974, its aim was to overthrow the American imperialism. It tried to bomb the US Capitol in 1971 as a retaliation "against US invasion of Laos." Its next target was the Pentagon. As a retaliation against US actions in Hanoi, on May 19, 1972—the day marked the birthday of Ho Chi Minh of the-then North Vietnam—it placed a bomb in a women's bathroom in the Air Force wing of the Pentagon, which caused flooding and loss of some classified information. The organization started to disintegrate after the USA withdrew from Vietnam.[18]

2.6.2 Action Directe, France[19]

This radical-left group, active between 1979 and 1987, carried out violent attacks on the Jewish population in France as well as attempted assassination of business, political, and military figures. In the beginning, its ideology resembled some combination of anarchism and Maoism, but it became more radical over time. It executed about fifty attacks, including the killing of General René Audran in 1985 and Georges Besse, the Chairman of Renault in 1987. In 1985, it allied with the West German Red Army Faction. It ceased to exist in 1987 when four of its prominent members were arrested. (They were later sentenced to life imprisonment.)

---

[17] See Encyclopedia Britannica and Eckstein (2016).

[18] A Robert Redford starer, *The Company You Keep*, revolves around a story line involving the members of the American Weather Underground.

[19] See Dartnell (1995) and Encyclopedia Britannica.

2.6.3 Red Army Faction (RAF), West Germany[20]

Known also as Baader-Meinhof Group or Gang, it was a major radical-left-wing organization. Unlike the American Weather Underground or the French Action Directe, it was active for three decades, 1960s to 1990s. Branding the USA as an imperialist power and equating the West German government as Nazis, it originated from the radical German university protest movements in the 1960s. At the height of its popularity, about 25% of the youth in West Germany expressed sympathy for the group. Many condemned their tactics but understood their resentment with the "new order." Throughout 1970s and 1980s, RAF killed political and business figures as well as targeted US armed forces stationed in West Germany, hoping that its activities would spark revolutionary changes. However, the fatalities it caused among the US forces numbered less than ten, and the US forces were never alarmed by it. Altogether it murdered less than forty. RAF lost its appeal after the break-up of the Soviet union and the unification of Germany. Finally, it ceased to exist in the 1990s. Interestingly, in 2015, there was an armed robbery in Brenan, which was believed to be the handiwork of three fugitives from the disbanded RAF. However, it was not considered to be a revival of RAF. The reason behind this robbery was thought to be fugitive survival rather an act of terrorism.

2.6.4 Revolutionäre Zellen (RZ)

Less well-known than RAF, Revolutionäre Zellen (RZ) was another violent West German leftist organization, which described itself as an urban guerrilla group. Inside Germany, it actually carried out more attacks and crimes than did RAF. It came to limelight for its 1976 hijacking of an Air France flight from Athens to Entebbe, Uganda, in collaboration with the Popular Front for the Liberation of Palestine (PFLP). The group ceased to exist with the unification of Germany.

2.6.5 The Italian Red Brigades[21]

Like the American Weather Underground and Red Army Faction, the Red Brigades started in an educational institution: the University of Trento. A study group led by Renato Curcio to analyze and emulate Karl Marx, Mao Zedong (China), and Che Guevara (from Argentina) formed the Red Brigades. It was constituted in 1970 with Curcio as its leader, along with his girlfriend, Margherita Cagol, and Alberto Franceschini. Initially, it committed petty crimes like arson and vandalism but later engaged itself in kidnapping for ransom (KFR) to fund its activities. It targeted prominent business leaders and high-profile government officials. In 1974, it abducted the Italian prosecutor Mario Sossi, asking in return the release of eight of its members who were earlier arrested. Its most infamous act of terror was the kidnapping and murder in 1978 of Aldo Moro, a prominent member of the Christian Democratic Party. However, it was condemned by some of its own members. In 1979, the Red

[20] See Stefanik (2009) and Encyclopedia Britannica.

[21] See Sundquist (2010) and Encyclopedia Britannica.

Brigades shot and killed Guido Rossa, a prominent union official, who had reported some Red Brigades members for distributing propaganda. This act of terror proved very costly to the organization in terms of losing popularity and support from factory workers. In course of its lifetime, the Red Brigades committed more than 14,000 acts of violence. Its activities began to wane in 1980 as its members got arrested. By the end of 1982, nearly 200 bases of Red Brigades were uncovered and destroyed by the Italian police. It became divided and was finally disbanded in the mid-1980s.

2.6.6 The Japanese Red Army (JRA)[22]

It was founded sometime between 1969 and 1971 by Fusako Shigenobu in Lebanon, while she was working with PFLP, the Popular Front for the Liberation of Palestine, and a Palestinian terror organization (see Sect. 2.7.6).[23] The group was sometimes referred to as Arab-JRA. JRA undertook several major terrorist operations, including the hijacking of a Japan Air Lines airplane in 1973, a massacre at Tel Aviv's Lod Airport (1972), and the seizure and occupation of embassies in various countries. In 1971–72, the organization underwent severe infighting leading to the execution of fourteen of its militants by fellow Japanese Red Army members. These killings shocked the Japanese public and were followed by successful government prosecutions of many of the perpetrators. Although the Japanese Red Army remained quite small, its terrorist activities continued into the 1990s. Its leader Shigenobu was on the run in the Middle East, until arrested in Osaka in 2000. Interestingly, she conceded that she had misjudged the Japanese tolerance of violence.

We now turn to violent leftist groups in Latin and Central America.

2.6.7 Revolutionary Armed Forces of Colombia (FARC)[24]

2.6.7.1 Narrative

The oldest and the largest of terror groups in Latin America, the Revolutionary Armed Forces of Columbia (FARC), started in 1964 as a military wing of the Colombian Marxist–Leninist Communist Party.[25] This party, a peasant force, tried to promote anti-imperialism and agrarianism, believed in a redistribution of wealth from the rich to the poor and abhorred the presence of multinational firms and foreign governments influencing Colombia, especially the USA.

The FARC funded itself from kidnappings and the drug trade (cocaine) and its provision of social services—to be elaborated later—attracted a large number of recruits seeking to escape poverty. The 1970s were a period of growth for the FARC. It grew from roughly 500 fighters to an estimated 3000 by the early 1980s.

---

[22] See Box and McCormack (2004) and Encyclopedia Britannica.

[23] JRA's native name is "Rengo Sekigun."

[24] See Encyclopedia Britannica, Leech (2011), Stanford University (2015d) and White (2017, Chapter 10).

[25] Its native name is Fuerzas Armadas Revolucionarias de Colombia.

In 1982, the first peace talk took place between FARC and the Colombian government, leading to an agreement in 1984 at La Uribe, called the Uribe accord. It stipulated the Government's commitment toward agrarian reforms, improvement in education, health, housing, and employment in rural Colombia. The Uribe accord led, in 1985, to FARC and other left-wing groups, including the Colombian Community Party (PCC), to form a political party, Patriotic Union (Unión Patriótica) or UP briefly, which participated in elections beginning in 1986 and won a large fraction of the votes. Unfortunately, the Uribe peace accord lasted for three years only, because the right-wing paramilitary groups started to target and kill the members of UP. Supported by the wealthy landowners, politicians, Colombian army, and the US corporations, these groups also aimed against the guerrillas of FARC and killed many innocent civilians on the suspicion of their affiliation with FARC or UP. The most prominent of these groups was Muerte a Secuestradores (Death to Kidnappers) (MAS).

By 1988, hundreds of UP leaders, including its Presidential candidate Jaime Pardo, were assassinated. From 1988 to 1992, between 4000 and 6000 UP members, including another presidential candidate, Bernardo Jaramillo, were murdered. These murders and disappearances severely dented UP's growth. Many of its members fled the country. Political violence decimated the party, and it virtually disappeared by 2002.

Despite the peace accord in the 1980s, the FARC's violent tactics and kidnappings continued as the group believed that political reforms made by the government were grossly inadequate. In 1997, the older right-wing paramilitary forces merged into a newer right-wing group, the United Self-Defence Forces of Colombia (AUC). Colombia continued to be gripped by violence. A second peace attempt ensued in 1998, when President Andrés Pastrana demilitarized a 16,000 square miles (42,000 square km) area in southern Colombia, effectively ceding territorial control to FARC. However, FARC and the government could not agree on the terms of international verification of the demilitarized zone. The National Liberation Army (ELN), the next largest leftist group in Colombia, demanded its own demilitarized zone but was declined. Negotiations began in early 1999 but fizzled away quickly because of disagreements and continued use of terrorism. In April of the same year, ELN hijacked a domestic flight with 46 passengers and crew on board.[26]

The FARC's increasing influence in the country, extreme kidnapping records, and involvement in the drug trade invited both domestic and international response. In 1999, a quarter of the Colombian population protested in cities throughout the country, in the "No Más" (meaning "no more") protests against FARC and violence.

The USA has been long involved in Colombian affairs. In 1999, it stepped up measures with a new project, Plan Colombia, aiming to disarm FARC, ELN as well as the AUC, and eliminate the cocaine trade. The success of Plan Colombia is debatable. While the USA claimed that it was able to largely disarm these groups, cocaine production fell drastically, and thus it was a success, and other studies have argued otherwise.

---

[26] The plane landed on a clandestine runway, some hostages were released, and about 35 people were held as hostage for one year.

In 2002, Álvaro Uribe Vélez became the president on the platform that he would aggressively combat the guerrilla forces. During the election season, the FARC kidnapped the presidential candidate Ingrid Betancourt, and this intensified the political motivation to combat the FARC. It also hijacked an airliner and kidnapped a Colombian senator on board. After this incidence, President Uribe remilitarized the territory. He also launched an anti-guerrilla program that professionalized the army and took advantage of paramilitary assistance by the USA, while embracing support from the USA's Plan Colombia. By the end of 2002, FARC's military and political initiatives dwindled because of mounting pressure from the Colombian military. Uribe continued intensive policing and military operations against the FARC over the subsequent years, as a result of which the FARC's was weakened, and the number of attacks and kidnappings by the organization declined considerably.

Meanwhile, the FARC rejected many proposals by the Colombian government and the international community that called for the return of Ingrid Betancourt and other hostages. In 2008, a military operation that involved infiltration into FARC secured her release along with fourteen others. In the same year, the FARC suffered severe reversals. Colombian troops crossed the border into Ecuador to raid a FARC encampment. The FARC's leader and one of the organization's founders, Manuel Marulanda Vélez, nicknamed Tirofijo ("Sureshot"), died of a heart attack. Alfonso Cano (nom de guerre of Guillermo Saenz Vargas), who served as the head of the organization's underground political arm, the Clandestine Communist Party of Colombia (founded in 2000), became the FARC's new leader in 2008. In 2010, FARC's leadership suffered another jolt when one of its principal leaders, best known as "Mono Jojoy" (but also known as Jorge Briceño or Luis Suárez), was killed in a military air strike. FARC's activities continued to diminish, except that in 2011 it launched several deadly attacks. But in the same year, it lost Cano in a raid by the Colombian forces. In 2012, the FARC finally announced that it would relinquish KFR, and it unilaterally freed the last members of the army and police forces it held. However, nothing was said about its many civilian hostages. By 2014, the FARCs had about 7000 fighters who rarely battled with police or military. That year it also entered a peace negotiation with the government. The peace process between the FARC's and the Colombian government is detailed in the *Supplement Break* 2.1.

Supplement Break 2.1: FARC and the Peace Accord

It is Uribe's crackdown on FARC, experts agree, that forced FARC to the negotiating table in 2012. Talks began in Oslo and continued in Havana. The governments of Chile, Cuba, Norway, and Venezuela acted as hosts, mediators, and observers. Five principles were set for the negotiations: (1) illegal crop eradication, (2) members' reintegration with civilian life, (3) future political participation of FARC's members, (4) transitional justice and reparations, and (5) rebel disarmament and implementation of the peace deal.

Agreements on three of the five points were reached, after which the government of Colombia suspended the talks in November 2014, when a high-ranking army officer along with two others were kidnapped. Talks resumed when the FARC released him a few weeks later. In December 2014, the FARC initiated a unilateral cease fire, and, soon after, President Santos (who came to power in 2010) directed negotiators in Havana to open discussions on a bilateral ceasefire (which he had previously refused to consider until a final agreement had been reached). In March 2015, Santos ordered a halt to the bombing of FARC camps. While clashes between the government troops and the guerrillas soon resumed because of idiosyncratic reasons, both parties remained committed to negotiations.

Mid-2015 saw a return to ceasefire by both the FARC and the government. September 2015 was momentous as Santos and FARC representatives announced a pledge toward a final peace agreement. In mid-2016, a permanent ceasefire agreement was signed in Havana in the presence of the UN Secretary General and Presidents of Cuba, Chile, and Venezuela. It stipulated that FARC fighters would turn in their weapons within 180 days under the monitoring of the UN officials. A historic peace agreement followed in September 2016.

However, the very next month the peace agreement was narrowly rejected by a referendum in Colombia, the general perception being that the treaty was too lenient on FARC. Nevertheless, the government and the FARC both announced that they would maintain the ceasefire as they prepared to return to the negotiating table.[a] In November 2016, a renegotiated accord was ratified by the House of Representatives and the Senate.[b] The process of relinquishing the weapons held by the FARC guerrillas proceeded peacefully. By August 2017, the FARC had turned over the last of its accessible weapons to UN representatives, bringing the total of decommissioned weapons to over 8100 guns and about 1.3 million cartridges. This action of FARC led the Colombian government to declare an official end to its conflict with the FARC, and, FARC began its transition into a political party.

As a part of the agreement, the Colombian government pledged to spend billions of dollars in rural areas, which many Colombians, including the rebels, say, was long neglected. Many hoped that the investments, which experts said could cost between $80 and $90 billion over the next ten years, would create economic alternatives to the drug trade. Furthermore, the Colombian government rolled out more than 80 special laws and 1000 programs to implement the terms of the peace deal that include rural electrification projects, job retraining, and income support schemes for former militia members, and tax incentives for companies that build public infrastructure. The government has reportedly given former FARC members key roles in its vast campaign to remove land mines.

---

[a] Despite the defeat of the referendum, Nobel peace prize was accorded to President Santos. While the Nobel committee did acknowledge the defeat of the referendum, it hoped that the prize would give him "the strength to succeed. . . ."

[b] The new accord stipulated, for example, that FARC would declare and surrender all its assets that will be used to compensate the victims of the conflict, and the guerrillas convicted of war crimes would serve stricter jail terms. The new accord was not put to another referendum.

Is That So? 2.3: FARC in Colombia

FARC (*Fuerzas Armadas Revolucionarias de Colombia*), a left-wing terror organization in Colombia, is the oldest and the largest terror groups in Latin America. It started in the 1960s and dissolved in 2016–2017 through a peace accord.

The Colombian conflict over the four/five decades reportedly claimed over 200,000 lives. The estimated number of land mines in Colombia is the second largest in history, next to Afghanistan.

2.6.7.2 Funding

At the very initial stage, FARC presumably received support from Russia and Cuba, but this is unknown. Over years, its principal funding sources were drugs, KFR, extortion, and, toward the end of its existence, mining.

KFR and Extortion In the initial years, FARC financed itself almost entirely by KFR targeting the elites and politicians. Although later it tapped coca production to bolster its finance, it continued with KFR for financial motives and as a bargaining tool to secure the release of its arrested members.

As an example, when Betancourt was released in 2008 after six years of captivity, the Colombian government claimed that she was secured after a highly successful military operation without a shot being fired. But according to Swiss ratio, FARC was paid $20 million to release Betancourt (Siddiqui, 2008).[27]

Coca Production In the late 1970s, the FARC began to tax the farmers of coca leaves that produce cocaine to fund its activities, a practice that powered its rapid growth throughout the 1980s. While, in the beginning, FARC was opposed to coca because of its exploitation by free-market oriented traffickers, the initial revenues were attractive, which convinced the leadership to protect coca farmers and charge them a *gramaje* (farm tax). In the Seventh "Guerrilla Conference" in 1982, the FARC leaders formally supported the coca cultivation—a monumental decision that would have long-lasting implications for Colombian history.

On one hand, drug production enriched the FARC, but, on the other, harmed FARC's reputation. Reports on the FARC by the Colombian government, the USA, and news sources quickly started referring to the group as a drug cartel and its leaders as drug traffickers—while the FARC steadfastly maintained that it only taxed the production, not in the business of transport or sale of coca leaves.

Mining Unlike the past, in the final stages in the 2010s, the FARC tapped mining of gold, tungsten, wolfram, and tantalum, which overtook drugs as the main source of its funding. It taxed machinery that entered its territory for mining. The estimated profits from gold mining are more than five times those from cocaine trafficking

[27] It is noteworthy that after the peace deal and dissolution of FARC, in 2016 its (former) members have apologized for the "great pain" they caused by kidnapping thousands of people.

(Stanford University, 2015d). According to Reuters (2015), recapturing 63 mines in 2015 from the control of FARC deprived it of earnings to a tune of $9 million per month.

While FARC's size and terror activities declined through the 2010s, it continued to remain strong financially. Zehorai (2014) listed FARC among the top ten "richest" terror organizations as of 2014 with an annual turnover estimated at $600 million.

2.6.7.3 Public Services

FARC provided services to the rural population such as establishing local clinics, organizing public works, constructing infrastructure, and providing means of transportation. It also took over other roles of the state by dispensing justice and stipulating laws regarding the carrying of arms, working hours, fishing, hunting, consuming liquor, prostitution, drug abuse, etc. Indeed, in many municipalities, the FARC was the sole provider of essential public services (see Self (2007) and Felbab-Brown et al. (2018)).

2.6.7.4 Current Status of Violence in Colombia

More than four years have elapsed between the Colombian peace accord and the time of writing of this chapter. How is the peace accord working? According to Casey (2019), two and half years after the accord, 3000 militants returned to fighting. Infrastructure building promises stipulated in the Accord remained unfulfilled. President Iván Duque has reportedly voiced skepticism over the success of the accord. Land use for coca leaf production remains high. A similar assessment was reached by Grattan (2020).

These are signs of concern. The Colombian government must address the fundamental, long-term issues of rural development and ways to wean farmers away from coca production. It does not mean that the peace accord has proved unsuccessful. The level of violence in Colombia is certainly much lower compared to the previous decades.

2.6.8 The National Liberation Army (ELN), Colombia

This group (whose native name is Ejército de Liberación Nacional) originated in the 1960s as did FARC. It was the second largest armed group in Colombia and more politically motivated than FARC. For a long time, it stayed out of protecting drug production on ideological grounds—and got involved with it much later. The ELN reached the height of its power in the late 1990s, when it carried out hundreds of kidnappings and hit infrastructure such as oil pipelines (Stanford University, 2015c). In 2013, the estimated size of its guerrilla forces stood between 1380 and 3000 (Wikipedia, accessed on November 6, 2018). ELN and FARC had an ambiguous relationship. They cooperated in some parts of the country, while elsewhere they clashed directly.

Peace talks with ELN began in 2017 but has been suspended since 2019. The government has demanded unilateral ceasefire and renunciation of violence by ELN as a pre-condition for the resumption of talks. But ELN has rejected this. It is speculated that peace talks may resume during the Biden administration (Acosta, 2020).

2.6.9 Shining Path, Peru[28]

2.6.9.1 Narrative

Named also by its native name "Sendero Luminoso" and considered as one of the most dangerous terror organizations ever, this radical Maoist group originated in Peru in 1970 (see Peru's map in Fig. 2.5). It did not accept the orthodox Marxist theory and regarded the teaching of its own founder, Abimael Guzmán, a former philosophy professor, to be the highest evolution of the Marxist thought. Guzmán's preachings were considered a hybrid of Marxism, Maoism, and native Indian traditionalism. Shining Path's main goal was to destroy the existing Peruvian political institutions and replace them with a communist peasant revolutionary regime.

Fig. 2.5: Map of Peru. *Source*: Google map

It began its terror campaigns against the government in 1980 when it attacked polling stations and destroyed ballot boxes on the eve of the country's first national election over a decade. On one hand, Guzmán attempted to create a military based on rural population, and on the other, it tried to combine "Mao Zedong's ruthless

[28] See White (2017) and Martin (2018) for more detailed accounts.

revolutionary zeal with guerrilla philosophy of Che Guevara" (White, 2017).[29] The group waged widespread terror. Anyone unwilling to join or support the group was presumed to be an enemy. The group's methods were brutal, including stoning victims to death, or placing them in boiling water. It attacked the security forces and other representatives of the state, and massacred peasant communities perceived as being opposed to their struggle. The group killed about 70,000 people over two decades (Martin, 2018). Interestingly, the Shining Path encouraged feminism. Till her death in 1988, Augusta La Torre, the first wife of Guzmán, was the second-in-command of the group.

The Peruvian government's crackdown of the Shining Path commenced around 1990. The government forces attacked its bases and imprisoned and tortured the group members and its sympathizers. Guzmán was captured in 1992 and imprisoned for life.[30] The group withered after Guzmán's capture. 5500 members sought the government amnesty. The Peruvian government claimed that Shining Path was finished. However, it perpetrated terror attacks and hostage-taking in 2000s and even in 2010s, albeit at a much lower scale and frequency. After almost each crackdown, the Peruvian government would declare the demise of the organization. For instance, White (2017, Chapter 10) narrates a hostage-taking incidence in 2012, which was crushed by Peruvian forces and after which the President of Peru declared the decimation of Shining Path. But this was followed by an attack only three weeks later. In 2015, the Peruvian government admitted that the organization has not been "exterminated" (BBC News, 2015a). However, it is no longer a major terror organization by any criterion and remains a pale shadow of what it used to be in 1980s and 1990s.

2.6.9.2 Funding

Like the Colombian terror groups, the Shining Path's main source of finance was the taxing of coca production, which supported its members, carrying out attacks as well as public services like water supply, sewage, transportation, and street cleanup, whenever it took over a village. The Shining Path also provided a system of law and order, hitherto missing, albeit a brutal one.

Is That So? 2.4: Shining Path in Peru

Shining Path is one of the most dangerous terror organizations ever. It was a radical Maoist group that originated in Peru in 1970. During 1970s and 1980s, it killed about 70,000 people.

[29] Che Guevara was a well-known Argentine Marxist revolutionary (as well as a scholar and physician).

[30] At the time of his capture, he was sheltered by a ballet dancer, Maritza Garrido Lecca, who hailed from a well-off family. It remains a mystery why she would shelter Guzmán. She was incarcerated in 1992 and released recently in 2017 (BBC News, 2017a).

2.6.10 Tupac Amaru Revolutionary Movement (MRTA), Peru[31]

Founded in 1983 and named after the eighteenth century Indian revolutionary Túpac Amaru II who revolted against the Spanish, MRTA was another Marxist–Leninist group in Peru. Highly trained, well armed, and specialized in urban terrorism, the group followed the philosophy of Fidel Castro. Its well-educated leaders came largely from the middle and upper-middle classes. Members included students, professors and other intellectuals, labor leaders, lawyers, and reporters. The rural force of MRTA was also recruited from the peasantry.

By 1990, MRTA was estimated to have about 1000 hard-core members, with another several thousand supporters and sympathizers. However, the group was less violent than Shining Path, having some respect for democracy and human rights. MRTA supported its activities largely through bank robberies, kidnappings, and extortion.

MRTA was strongly opposed to American officials and commercial presence in the region.[32] Between 1983 when it began terrorist operations and 1992, the organization had hit US targets over a hundred times. Its targets included US official facilities and personnel, Mormon churches, and American commercial establishments and their customers, both Peruvian and foreign.

In 1992, its leader Víctor Polay Campos was captured and imprisoned. But its most well-known act of terror occurred afterward in 1996, when fourteen MRTA members took over the Japanese Ambassador's residence in Lima during a diplomatic reception, capturing nearly four hundred hostages and seeking in return its jailed comrades. The government forces stormed the residence, rescuing all but one of the remaining hostages, and killing all the guerrillas. The MRTA has not conducted a significant terrorist attack ever since.

2.6.11 Tupamaros, Uruguay[33]

The Tupamaros, also named after Túpac Amaru II, were a Marxist guerrilla group that operated in Uruguay from the early 1960s to the mid-1980s. Its native name was Movimento de Liberacion National. Unlike many other Latin American countries, Uruguay was a prosperous country in the first half of the twentieth century, and people of Uruguay were considered as the most contented citizens (Woodruff, 2008). Economic decline started to set in by the late 1950s because of global economic competition. Upon this background, the group came into existence in 1963 under the leadership of Raúl Sendic, a labor organizer. In 1965, Tupamaros had about fifty members. As Uruguay was very urban and about half of its population lived

[31] See Martin (2018, Chapter 7).

[32] Directors of the Kentucky Fried Chicken restaurant chain in Lima received "almost daily" demands from the MRTA during January and February 1991 for "war taxes," and one director left the country to avoid being kidnapped.

[33] See White (2017, Chapter 11) and Encyclopedia Britannica for a detailed account of this terror organization.

in Montevideo, the capital city, Tupamaros was mostly confined to this city. Urban terrorism was its hallmark.

In the initial years, it was not dangerous. It rubbed banks and business and distributed food and necessities to the poor. Toward late 1960s, it began to turn violent. It engaged in intimidating the security forces and political kidnapping. Those taken were held in a secret "People's Prison." All this was shocking to the nation. The organization also carried out bombings against foreign establishments, particularly those of the USA and Brazil. In 1970, it kidnapped and killed Dan Mitrione, who worked for the US agency for International Development and was alleged to be a CIA agent. In 1971, it kidnapped the British ambassador, Geoffrey Jackson, and held him for eight months. Reportedly, he persuaded his captors that keeping him as a prisoner would not yield any results (Reuters, 1987).

The group's success was brief. By 1971, people were turned away from leftist ideas and voted against the leftists. By the time the military coup occurred in 1973, Tupamaros was severely damaged by government troops. About 300 of its members were killed and another 3000 arrested. After democracy returned to Uruguay in mid-1980s, most of those who were jailed, including Sendic, were released under a general amnesty. Tupamaros was reorganized as a political party. José Alberto Mujica Cordano, the President of Uruguay from 2010 to 2015, was a member of the Tupamaros.

A highly organized group, Tupamaros, was confined to Uruguay without any outside support. In fact, its structure and tactics were emulated by left-wing groups in Europe and the USA.

2.6.12 Farabundo Marti National Liberation Front (FMLN)[34]

Also known as Frente Farabundo Marti de Liberacion Nacional-Frente Democratico Revolucionario, it was a left-wing political party in El Salvador, which, in 1980, grew out of a coalition of five guerrilla organizations: the Fuerzas Populares de Liberación Farabundo Martí (FPL), Ejército Revolucionario del Pueblo (ERP), the Resistencia Nacional (RN), the Partido Comunista Salvadoreño (PCS) and the Partido Revolucionario de los Trabajadores Centroamericanos (PRTC). The FMLN was one of the main participants in the Salvadoran Civil War that span 1980 to 1992. During the course of the civil war, its paramilitary units carried out armed struggle mostly against the government troops (trained and supported by the USA). In 1989, the FMLN mounted major attacks in 1989 on a number of urban centers, including San Salvador, the capital city. This caught the national army by surprise. However, after weeks of intense fighting and aerial bombardment by the Salvadoran Air Force, the guerrilla units were forced out of San Salvador.

The Global Terrorism Database (GTD) reports over 3000 deaths from military attacks by FMLN.[35] Following the peace accord reached in 1992, all armed units of FMLN were dissolved, and it became a political party.

---

[34] See Encyclopedia Britannica.

[35] GTD will described in some detail in Chap. 3.

2.6.13 Naxalites: India

A violent leftist uprising started in a village named Naxalbari in the state of West Bengal, India, in 1967. It gathered momentum and spread across the states of West Bengal, Odisha, and Andhra Pradesh and soon transformed into an insurgency. Led by two communist party leaders, Kanu Sanyal and Charu Majumdar, landless peasants, mostly lower-caste and tribals, as well as students and leftist scholars joined this movement, demanding land ownership and better wages from wealthy upper-caste landlords. It became known as Naxal or Naxalite movement, and the members were called Naxalites (sometime Maoists).[36] Naxalism is based on the belief that the Indian government and the bureaucracy are grossly apathetic toward the well-being of the poor in tribal areas, and, policy measures and institutions work toward impoverishing, rather than uplifting, them. In 1971, over 3650 class-based attacks were reported, and more than 850 people were reportedly killed (Lynch III, 2016). However, in 1972, the violent suppression by the state and paramilitary forces subdued the Naxals. By 1973, the main cadres of the Naxalites had been eliminated: either killed or incarcerated. The general election in India in 1977, following the lifting of the Emergency regime, installed a United Front government at the center, which allowed the release of Naxalite leaders and activists. The 1977 to 1994 period marks the second phase of the Naxalite movement, during which its presence was concentrated in forest and tribal areas along the borders between Odisha, Andhra Pradesh, and in some parts of Maharashtra province. The second wave Naxalite insurgents kidnapped landlords and forced them to confess to crimes, apologize to villagers, and repay forced bribes.[37]

From the mid-1990s to the early 2000s, the Naxalite/Maoist insurgency remained largely out of the public view. But the movement remained alive. The period from 2004 onward marks the third phase during which the movement actually spread to a vast territory covering parts of Bihar, Odisha, Jharkhand, Maharashtra, and Andhra Pradesh. The stretch of regions is sometimes referred to as *red corridor*. A map of the red corridor comparing between 2007 and 2018 is shown in Fig. 2.6.

The Maoists organized their bases in inaccessible and neglected forest areas, whose inhabitants (mainly tribals) had been denied their basic rights like minimum wages (e.g., for tobacco leaf pickers in Andhra Pradesh) and had been exposed to violence by feudal landlords, private contractors, forest guards, and the police. In their base areas, the Maoists carried out land reforms, established schools, and provided health facilities, thus acting as a surrogate government—described as *janata sarkar*, or people's government.[38]

The government of India has followed a strategy of military intervention against the Naxalite movement, despite repeated warnings by its own agencies that what is

---

[36] There were two communist parties at the time. The Naxalite movement was led by the Communist Party of India (Marxist), CPI(M) in brief.

[37] The second phase was led by a charismatic Communist revolutionary, Kondapalli Seetharamaiah.

[38] Difference phases are described in more detail in Lynch III (2016); also see Banerjee (2017).

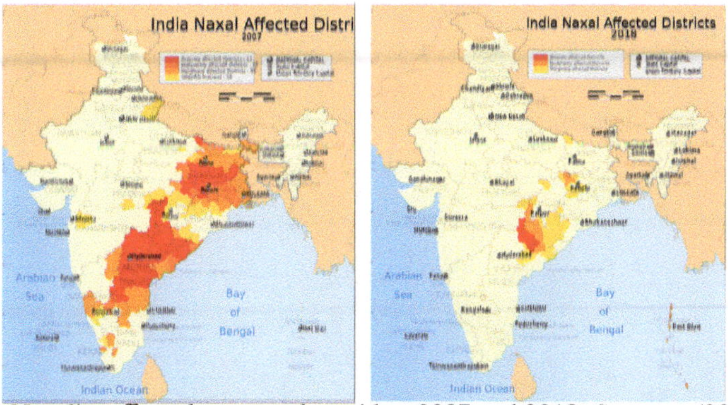

Fig. 2.6: Naxalite affected areas, red corridor: 2007 and 2018. *Sources*: (2007) By w:user:Planemad—Own work International Borders: University of Texas map library—India Political map 2001Disputed Borders: University of Texas map library—China–India Borders—Eastern Sector 1988 & Western Sector 1988—Kashmir Region 2004—Kashmir Maps. State and District boundaries: Census of India—2001 Census State Maps—Survey of India Maps. Other sources: US Army Map Service, Survey of India Map Explorer, Columbia University Map specific sources: CNN-IBNNaxal affected areas in India, CC BY-SA 3.0, https://commons.wikimedia.org/w/index.php?curid=1848951; (2018) By Ganesha811—Own work, CC BY-SA 4.0, https://commons.wikimedia.org/w/index.php?curid=111662194

fundamentally required is redressing the economic and social inequities (Banerjee, 2017).[39]

2.6.14 Khmer Rouge*

Khmer Rouge started way back in 1951 in Cambodia as an anti-colonial group with a Marxist–Leninist orientation against the French occupation.[40] It means Red Khmer in French, where Khmer refers to Cambodia. For nearly twenty years, the party's members were engaged in clandestine activities—without much success—based in jungle and mountain areas against the government of Prince Norodom Sihanouk. But, after a right-wing military coup toppled Sihanouk in 1970, the Khmer Rouge entered into a political coalition with him and began to attract growing support in the Cambodian country side, a trend that was accelerated by the destructive US bombing campaigns over Cambodia in the early 1970s. By this time the Khmer Rouge was also

[39] In relatively recent news, Naxalites killed one soldier and four civilians in the state of Chhattisgarh in November 2018 (*Times of India*, November 8, 2018). According to *Indian Express*, May 1, 2019, the Naxalites killed 15 security personnel by improvised explosive device, IEDexplodes and sets fire on 30 vehicles on the same day. In March 2021, two soldiers were killed, and three civilians were injured by IED in the state of Jharkhand.

[40] Figure 2.7 provides a map of Cambodia.

Fig. 2.7: Map of Cambodia. *Source*: Google map

receiving substantial aid from North Vietnam, which had withheld its support during the years of Sihanouk's rule. In a civil war that continued for nearly five years from 1970, the Khmer Rouge gradually expanded its areas of control in the Cambodian country side. Finally, in 1975, its forces mounted a victorious attack on the capital city of Phnom Penh and established a national government to rule Cambodia. The military leader of the Khmer Rouge, Pol Pot, became the Prime Minister.[41] Khmer Rouge wanted to implement the idea of the Chinese cultural revolution and build a classless society. Its rule over the next four years was punctuated by some of the worst excesses of any Marxist government in the twentieth century. During its rule, an estimated 1.5 million (possibly up to 2 million) Cambodians died, and many of the country's professional and technical class were exterminated (Encyclopedia Britannica). Khmer Rouge sets up *killing fields* where people were killed and buried (BBC News, 2018). Under Pol Pot's regime, the Khmer Rouge tried to take Cambodia virtually back to the Middle Ages, forcing millions of people from the cities to work on communal farms in the country side.

The Khmer Rouge government was overthrown in 1979 by Vietnamese troops. The party retreated to remote areas of the country, where they remained active for a while but gradually withered. As Cambodia began the process of reopening to the international community, the full horrors of the regime came to light.[42]

[41] Pol Pot taught French literature, geography, and history in a private school but was simultaneously planning for a revolution.

[42] Pol Pot was denounced by his former comrades in a show trial in July 1997 and sentenced to house arrest in his jungle home. But less than a year later he was dead, denying the millions of

We note that Khmer Rouge is *not* typically described as a terror organization (and that is why this subsection is marked with an asterisk), because its atrocities were committed when it was in power, not when it was a sub-national group.

Is That So? 2.5: Khmer Rouge in Cambodia

Although not exactly a terror organization according to our definition (since the group committed its atrocities while in "official" power), it is the most ruthless group in Asia to date. It killed between one to two million people. Sculls of (some) Khmer Rouge victims are on display for tourists in Cambodia.

2.6.15 The New People's Army (NPA): The Philippines[43]

Fig. 2.8: Map of Philippines. *Source*: Google map

2.6.15.1 Narrative

Still an active group since 1969, NPA, is the military wing of the Communist Party of the Philippines (CPP) founded in 1968.[44] Together, they are called CPP—NPA. NPA was established by Jose Maria Sison, a Maoist-oriented student activist. In 1969, Sison joined hands with a communist armed group leader Bernabé Buscayno, and NPA was born with Buscayno as its first commander.

The CPP-NPA aims to overthrow the Philippine government and form a new state led by the working class and expel the American influence from the Philippines.

people who were affected by this brutal regime the chance to bring him to justice. The UN helped establish a tribunal to try surviving Khmer Rouge leaders, beginning work in 2009. Three Khmer Rouge leaders have been sentenced.

[43] Most of the information is based on White (2017) and Stanford University (2015b).

[44] Figure 2.8 provides a map of Philippines.

Most of its power base is in Luzon, although it has made inroads into Manila and Mindanao. It is the "longest-running communist insurgency in the world" (White, 2017).

The group began in Luzon with less than hundred members and a small number of rifles. In 1970, Sison outlined the CPP-NPA's guiding principles in a book titled *Philippine Society and Revolution*. By the 1980s, CPP-NPA's membership had scaled 25,000. But since then, it has continued to slide. In the 1990s, there were about 10,000 members, and in recent years, it has about 7000 members.[45]

Soon after its formation in 1969, the Philippine government launched a large military offensive against it, decimating its small central group of fighters. But the organization survived. It initially focused on its own growth and strengthening its support among the peasantry. In 1972, the CPP-NPA received its first shipment of weapons from the Chinese government, which had been supporting the group rhetorically earlier. But in 1976, the CPP-NPA lost the Chinese government's support when the Philippines and China normalized their relations after years of severed ties following ascendancy of the Chinese Communist Party to power in 1949. In the same year, the Philippine government captured and jailed many important CPP-NPA members, including Buscayno. Sison was captured in 1977.[46] Despite the removal of key figures, the CPP-NPA was able to spread beyond Luzon to Visayas and Mindanao, the Philippines's other major regions. At the time, the Philippine military was fighting the CPP-NPA as well as the Muslim separatist rebels in the south, prioritizing the latter. CPP-NPA-related violence reached its zenith in 1985 with 1282 military and police deaths, 1362 civilian deaths, and 2134 CPP-NPA deaths.

A cyclical pattern of negotiations and violence continued through 1990s and 2000s. In mid-2000s, the Philippine forces massively increased their operations against the organization. At the same time, the Philippine government has been under the human rights violations watch by the UN due to extrajudicial means, like fake encounters, by which many CPP-NPA members were killed by the Philippine military.

As White (2017) notes, two factors have kept CPP-NPA active till today: the structure of political power in Philippines and the unequal distribution of wealth.

2.6.15.2 Funding

From 1969 until the normalization of Philippine–Chinese relations in 1976, the CPP-NPA received support, weapons, and funds from China. The CPP-NPA also sought support, weapons, funds, and training from like-minded groups overseas, e.g., the Japanese Red Army and the Maoist factions of the Palestine Liberation Organization (PLO). External funding was limited, however. The main source of the CPP-NPA's funding was the *revolutionary taxes*, a form of extortion of local merchants and business establishments. In early 2000, its annual turnover was around $30 million,

[45] CPP-NPA has many female members, recruited as guerrillas from a very young age. Their whole life is controlled by CPP-NPA. Dubbed "Amazonas" for the mythic race of Greek female warriors, they are not permitted to develop romantic relationships without the permission of the male leaders.

[46] Both leaders were released later in the mid-1980s by Corazon Aquino.

raised mostly from these taxes (White, 2017). The CPP-NPA also raises funds by "selling" campaign permits to political candidates who wish to campaign in areas under its controls.

2.7 Secular Terror Groups Overlapping between the Third and Fourth Wave Era

As said earlier, Rapoport's four waves are defined in terms of the dominant spirit (long-term objective) of the majority of terror organizations in an era. But there are major terror groups whose objectives are somewhat different from the mainstream goals defining the era in which these groups operated. More specifically, during the Religious (Fourth) Wave, some major groups are secular, i.e., they do not adhere to or preach religious orthodoxy, and their long-term goals are not ideological. Examples include IRA, which continued its demand for an Irish homeland. The Euskadi Ta Askatasuna (ETA) demanded autonomy in the Basque country bordering between Spain and France. Many Arab groups have sought a Palestinian homeland. LTTE aimed to establish a homeland for Tamils in the Sri Lankan island. The Nicaraguan Democratic Force (FDN)'s objective was to oust a leftist regime in the 1980s. We set out here to discuss these groups.

2.7.1 The Provisional IRA (PIRA)—Third Generation[47]

2.7.1.1 Narrative

Continuing the thread from the second generation of IRA in Sect. 2.5.2, by 1969, Northern Ireland was bled by street violence arising from bitter sectarian division. On one side, there were the ***nationalists*** or the ***republicans*** who envisioned a politically unified Ireland. On the other, there were the ***unionists*** or the ***loyalists*** who supported British authority over Northern Ireland. The Provisional IRA (PIRA) and the Irish National Liberation Army (INLA) were the Catholic nationalists, whereas Ulster Volunteer Force (UVF) and Ulster Defence Association (UDA) represented the unionists, who were protestants. The British security forces were called in, and they were supported by the Royal Ulster Constabulary (RUC). They undertook a dual role of a policing and a counter-insurgency (COIN), but primarily against the republicans, although there were some incidents of collusion between the British security forces and the loyalists.

Despite the presence of British forces, conflicts escalated steadily. The post 1969 years became known as the period of the ***Troubles***, a clever nomenclature that did not name or blame any particular organization. The early years of the Troubles were the bloodiest. Violence aside, the Troubles era was marked by mass protests and acts of civil disobedience, segregation, and the creation of no-go areas.

[47] Our description is based on, among other sources, White (2017, Chapter 6) Encyclopedia Britannica and the BBC History.

Beginning in 1970, the Provisional IRA (PIRA) or the Provos carried out a guerrilla campaign including assassinations and ambushes against the British security forces, as well as a bombing infrastructure, commercial establishments, and political figures. The Provos called their campaign the "Long War," and they borrowed their tactics from Jewish terrorists in the 1940s and Algerian groups in 1950s. On the other side, the loyalists targeted republicans/nationalists, and attacked the wider catholic community in what they claimed was retaliation.

By 1972, the situation had deteriorated so badly that it prompted British government to suspend the Northern Ireland parliament and impose direct rule. During the same year however, the British government secretly reached out to PIRA, which was routinely referred to as "the" IRA, for a peace talk. But the latter's insistence on nothing short of a new Irish republic was unacceptable. In 1973, the Provos expanded their attacks to mainland Britain and eventually to continental Europe. It was estimated that, between 1969 and 1994, the IRA killed about 1800 people, including nearly 600 civilians.

In 1973, another peace effort, called Sunningdale Agreement, found its way in the form of a power-sharing deal negotiated among unionists, nationalists, and others. But it was fragile and violence erupted on the streets soon after this agreement. A subsequent IRA truce in 1975 also floundered. Despite tough security measures deployed by the British government, violence continued unabated.

The situation looked hopeless in the mid-1970s. The whole of Northern Ireland was shocked when in West Belfast three children were killed and their mother injured by a speeding car in 1976. The driver was an IRA member who was fatally wounded in a chase by the British Army. The children's aunt made an impassioned plea for peace, and a massive support led to the formation of a group called the Peace People. This attracted worldwide attention. The group marched for peace in Belfast and other towns.[48] Ten thousand people showed up in London's Trafalgar Square to hear folk singer Joan Baez sing "We Shall Overcome." But, Northern Ireland, already deeply divided, was not ready for peace. Unionists believed the IRA was the problem, and peace would be restored if it went away. For nationalists and republicans, the problem was the British rule and the unionists' failure to compromise and share power on equal terms.

Reconciliation finally began to take roots in mid-1980s, and the historic Good Friday Agreement was signed in 1998. Situations leading to this watershed event and beyond are described in detail in the *Supplemental Break 2.2*.

2.7.1.2 Funding

Against a powerful adversary like the British government, PIRA had to raise a massive funding and maintain a military as well as its political wing Sinn Féin in order to fulfill its objectives. Depending on the source of information, its annual budget before 1990s ranged from £6.5 million and £15 million, whereas its annual budget in 1993 was estimated at around £5.3 million (Kiser, 2005). A lion's share

---

[48] The Peace People did win the Nobel Peace Prize in 1976, but their reputation diminished over disputes about the money.

Supplement Break 2.2: IRA and the Peace Accord

A historic peace accord was signed over the Good Friday week of 1998 by the Irish Republic, the British government and eight political parties of Northern Ireland, including Sinn Féin, the Ulster Unionist Party, the Social Democratic and Labour Party (SDLP), and the Alliance Party. The only major political group opposing it was the Democratic Unionist Party (DUP). The accord is widely known as the ***Good Friday Agreement*** or the ***Belfast Agreement***.[a] Coming to effect in 1999, the Good Friday Agreement stipulated renunciation of arms and a return to the self-government of Northern Ireland by a power-sharing arrangement.

What led to this historic agreement? Following over a decade and half long of violence in Northern Ireland and IRA's terrorist attacks against the British in Britain and elsewhere since 1969, an Anglo-Irish Agreement was reached in 1985 that gave the Irish government an advisory role in Northern Ireland affairs, with an implicit political acknowledgment by the British that a united Ireland is a possibility with the consent of the people. Obviously, it did not please the unionists. Republicans welcomed it, and even the hard-liners within the republicans were intrigued. However, the hard-liners in PIRA felt short-changed in that it was a far cry from a united Ireland. They broke away, and their faction came to be known as ***Continuity IRA*** (CIRA)). Both PIRA and CIRA claimed to present the original IRA (and were illegal). However, overall, the late 1980s witnessed a desire for peace by the stakeholders.

In addition, there was a back-channel talk facilitated by the Roman Catholic clergymen between the SDLP leader John Hume and the Sinn Féin leader Gerry Adams about how to end the violence and reach a political settlement. In 1990, the British took an unprecedented step of contacting and negotiating with Sinn Féin. The British and Irish governments signed what is called the Downing Street Declaration in 1993, laying out the principles on how a settlement could be achieved. Unionists were nervous, but the republicans saw a political path toward a unified Ireland.

There was a "surprise" in 1994, when the PIRA called a ceasefire, which was reciprocated by unionist paramilitary groups. However, CIRA was not in support and started a campaign of violence against the British Army in Northern Ireland.

At the same time, Irish American politicians in the USA weighed in. President Bill Clinton made an influential visit to Belfast in 1995. However, the IRA ceasefire broke down in 1996 over the failure to make progress through the talks. It took another year for the ceasefire to be restored. This paved the way toward the most inclusive talks ever held on Northern Ireland's future. They were chaired by Clinton's ally and senator George Mitchell, who stipulated six principles to be endorsed by all concerned parties. These were called the ***Mitchell Principles***.[b]

The principles called for peaceful means. Mitchell recommended that all parties sign up to these principles and that some decommissioning could take place during the talks. However, this was not enough to prevent sliding back to violence. As luck would have it, Tony Blair's Labor government coming to power in 1997 was transformational, as he was committed to the peace process and had the advantage of having no political baggage. An agreement was designed in the 1997.[c] While PIRA agreed to a ceasefire, it was opposed by a group within PIRA, which broke away and came to be known as Real IRA (RIRA) in the late 1997. The unionists were divided too on how to proceed. The extreme groups among the unionists feared that the negotiations might weaken Northern Ireland's place within the UK. In the beginning of 1998, the prospects for peace in Northern Ireland looked dim. However, the moderate unionist group, UUP, remained in the talks. The Sinn Féin was committed, so was Tony Blair and the USA weighed in further. All this led to the Good Friday Agreement. It was made up of two interrelated documents: (a) a *Multi-Party Agreement* by most of Northern Ireland's political parties and (b) an international agreement between the British and Irish governments, the *British-Irish*

Agreement.[d] Decommissioning of arms and subsequent release of prisoners were called for in return. The Republic of Ireland removed its territorial claims to the whole island of Ireland. In 1998, the agreement was approved by voters across the island of Ireland in two referendums.[e]

The years following 1998 remained turbulent and uncertain. The Northern Ireland Assembly was established but periodically replaced by direct rule from London, largely over concerns about continued paramilitary activity by Real IRA and ultra-unionists. The republicans were not strongly opposed to it as long as it was not hostile to the Catholics in northern Ireland. It took until 2005 for the IRA to decommission. In 2006, an agreement was reached between the British and Irish governments and the political parties in Ireland, called ***The St. Andrews Agreement*** of 2006. DUP and Sinn Féin agreed to a power-sharing arrangement. Direct rule from London can be imposed only through an emergency legislation in the British parliament, not, as earlier, by triggering a section of the Northern Ireland Act. Ian Paisley of DUP and Martin McGuinness, an ex-IRA, were the First and Deputy First Minister.[f]

In the decade to follow, Northern Ireland experienced relative political stability—thanks to the power-sharing arrangement. However, in 2017, the power-sharing arrangement broke down as the relationship between DUP and Sinn Féin deteriorated because of opposite stands on Northern Ireland's position on the USA, same-sex marriage, abortion, dealing with the legacy of the Troubles era, etc. However, in January 2020, a deal was reached on power-sharing.

---

[a] It was caricatured as the Sunningdale for slow learners by the SDLP deputy leader Seamus Mallon, because the treaty was somewhat similar to the Sunningdale Agreement of 1973 that had failed.

[b] They were (1) democratic and exclusively peaceful means of resolving political issues; (2) total disarmament of all paramilitary organizations; (3) agreeing that such disarmament must be verifiable to the satisfaction of an independent commission; (4) to renounce for themselves, and to oppose any effort by others, to use force, or threaten to use force, to influence the course or the outcome of all party negotiations; (5) abiding by the terms of any agreement reached in all party negotiations and resorting to democratic and exclusively peaceful methods in trying to alter any aspect of that outcome with which they may disagree; and (6) urging that "punishment" killings and beatings stop and to take effective steps to prevent such actions.

[c] The path toward this agreement was not without problems. For instance, in February 1996, the IRA released a statement announcing the end of its ceasefire, and an hour later a massive explosion rocked Canary Wharf, killing two people.

[d] The agreement contained a complex series of provisions relating to a number of areas including: (i) the status and system of government of Northern Ireland within the United Kingdom (Strand 1); (ii) the relationship between Northern Ireland and the Republic of Ireland (Strand 2); and (iii) the relationship between the Republic of Ireland and the United Kingdom (Strand 3).

[e] In Northern Ireland, voters were asked in the Northern Ireland Good Friday Agreement referendum, 1998, whether they support the multi-party agreement. In the Republic of Ireland, voters were asked whether they would allow the state to sign the agreement and allow necessary constitutional changes (Nineteenth Amendment of the Constitution of Ireland) to facilitate it.

[f] Once sworn enemies, they suddenly worked together in the same office and were nicknamed "the Chuckle Brothers" as a result of their good rapport.

of PIRA's budget came from the Irish diaspora in North America, Europe, and Australia.

External Charity PIRA appealed to Irish diaspora through its newspaper, *An Phoblacht*. Northern Aid Committee (NORAID) based in New York played an indispensable role, collecting donations from the Irish diaspora and the Irish–American activities. During the 1970s and the 1980s, it funded between $3 million and $5 million for "the cause" (Clarke, 2015).[49]

Own Business PIRA members owned private security firms, taxicab services, construction firms, and restaurants and used the proceeds to finance PIRA activities. Many became "business men with terrorist interests" (Clarke, 2015).

KFR As examples, in 1979, PIRA kidnapped Ben Dunne, a wealthy owner of retail store chain and reportedly netted £750,000. Interestingly, in 1983, it kidnapped a famous race horse, named Shergar. According to New York Times, a ransom of £2 million was asked but was never paid. It was a sensational news, and prize money was declared for sharing information to police. However, Shergar was never seen again (Clarke, 2015).

Other Sources Armed robbery provided a consistent flow of funds in the 1980s. In 1983 and 1984, there were 359 and 622 armed robberies reported in Northern Ireland, totaling $6 million and $1.2 million, respectively, a significant fraction of which was attributed to PIRA. PIRA also used smuggling and trafficking that involved pigs, cattle, and other livestock.[50] PIRA also profited from smuggling and arbitrage of fuel across southern and northern Ireland by exploiting price differences. It would collect around £500 per truckload of fuel (Adams, 1986 and Kiser, 2005).

PIRA took advantage of value-added tax or VAT and would provide counterfeit goods for cash that would avoid the VAT. It is reported that PIRA even acquired properties in Eastern Europe and Turkey that would produce counterfeit goods to be sold in North Ireland for profit (Clarke, 2015).

---

[49] PIRA had developed a relationship with Libya's Mohammed Qaddafi, an ardent opponent of the British. It is estimated that in the early 1970s it received about $3.5 million from him (Clarke, 2015). From the 1968 to mid-80s, the total estimated amount received from Qaddafi was $20 million (Kiser, 2005).

[50] More specifically, the European Economic Community provided various incentives to southern Ireland to export their produce to the UK, which includes northern Ireland. Many PIRA operatives posing as farmers would export pigs, livestock, and grain from southern to northern Ireland. From northern Ireland, they would be smuggled back to southern Ireland to be exported again to northern Ireland. British intelligence estimated that PIRA gained about £8000 per week in the mid-1980s through these schemes (Kiser, 2005).

Is That So? 2.6: IRA and the "Troubles" Era

The 1970s and 1980s mark the deadliest period in the history of IRA. It is called the period of "Troubles." The group's activities abated substantially since the Good Friday Agreement (also known as Belfast Agreement) in 1998.

2.7.2 Real IRA—the Fourth Generation[51]

2.7.2.1 Narrative

We noted in *Supplemental Break 2.2* that the Real IRA opposed the Good Friday accord and came into existence as a splinter group of the Provisional IRA in 1997. Four months after the signing of this agreement, a car bombing by RIRA killed 29 people, making it the deadliest single attack in the 30-year history of the Troubles. This was widely condemned. The US president Bill Clinton visited Omagh three weeks after the bombing, inspecting the damage and speaking with the victims. The RIRA offered apology saying that it targeted commercial properties, not civilians. It declared its own ceasefire and its leaders were arrested.

RIRA has been held responsible for a number of attacks in central London, such as an RPG rocket assault on the central headquarters of MI6 (British intelligence organization) in 2000 and the car bomb explosion in front of the headquarters of the BBC in 2001. The murder of two British soldiers in 2009, the first to be killed in Ireland since the peace agreement, was also the work of this group.

In 2013, it was thought to have less than 100 members (Nugent, 2013). Very much unlike the Provisional IRA in the Troubles era, the Real IRA has engaged in terror attacks only sporadically. Northern Ireland has remained calm since the Good Friday Agreement in 1998. Yet, according to the British government, the Real IRA poses a substantial potential threat to peace in Northern Ireland.

2.7.2.2 Funding

As will be noted in Table 4.2 in Chap. 4, the RIRA was one of the richest terror organizations as of 2018. According to Zehorai (2014, 2018), its main funding sources are smuggling and illegal trade, aid, and donations. It oversees a global network of smuggling and illegal trade in various goods—from electronics and oil barrels to cigarettes and tobacco.[52]

---

[51] See Encyclopedia Britannica and Zehorai (2014, 2018).

[52] Some years ago an Irish–American businessman was arrested for smuggling 350 thousand cartons of cigarettes from Panama to Ireland, worth £3.6 million. This arrest revealed the main arteries of the organization's funding.

A special report produced by the international accounting firm KPMG (Klynveld Peat Marwick Goerdeler) suggests that the illegal cigarette trade on the black market in Britain was among the largest in Europe. In 2016, approximately 5.55 billion cigarettes were sold illegally—with a black-market value of around $1.1 billion annually. A significant fraction of it accrued to RIRA (Zehorai, 2018).

Apart from illegal trade in tobacco, the RIRA obtained significant royalties from its pirate network of falsified alcohol and fuel products as well as protection fees it collected in those areas under its influence.

Another important source of the organization's finance is a part of the Irish–American population who remain opposed to the peace agreement.

2.7.3 The Euskadi Ta Askatasuna (ETA)[53]

Active from 1959 to 2011, ETA was a terror group in País Vasco (Basque Country) in Spain.[54] The Basque Country has two parts: the Northern part that is in France, called *Iparralde*, and considered to be the Basque fatherland, and, the Southern part, *Hegoalde*, in Spain.[55] *Hegoalde* has two main regions: the Basque Autonomous Community with Vitoria-Gasteiz as capital and the Chartered Community of Navarre whose capital is Pamplona. Thus, the Basque Country consists of two Spanish regions and French region. Its language is Euskera, which is older than Latin, and "language isolate" meaning that it is not related to any other language. The Basque Country's culture and traditions are quite different from Spanish or French, while it is highly industrialized.

In the entire span of the conflict, ETA killed more than 850 (including 300 civilians at least) and injuring 2600. At various points of time, it was classified as a terrorist organization by Spain, France, the UK, the USA, Canada, and the EU.

ETA started as a leftist, nationalist, student resistance movement in the Spanish part of the Basque country, vehemently opposed to General Franco's repressive military regime that suppressed this part of the Basque Country. Its goal was to achieve independence. The conflict was between ETA and Spain mostly, whereas that between ETA and the French army was relatively minor.

ETA began its violence in 1959 through car bombings and assassinations. As Spanish repression escalated in the 1970s, so did the activities of ETA. It engaged in Marighella style assassinations and robbery (White, 2017).[56] It is most well-known for assassinating Spain's Prime Minister Blanco, a right-hand man of General Franco, in 1973. Inadvertently, Blanco's murder played a role in Spain's transition from dictatorship to democracy.

---

53 See Encyclopedia Britannica, Reuters (2011), Bothen (2014), White (2017, Chapter 6), and Minder (2018).

54 Its native name translates to "Basque Homeland and Liberty."

55 Figure 2.9 is a map of the Basque Country.

56 Marighella was a Brazilian writer, who wrote a mini-manual on urban guerrilla warfare.

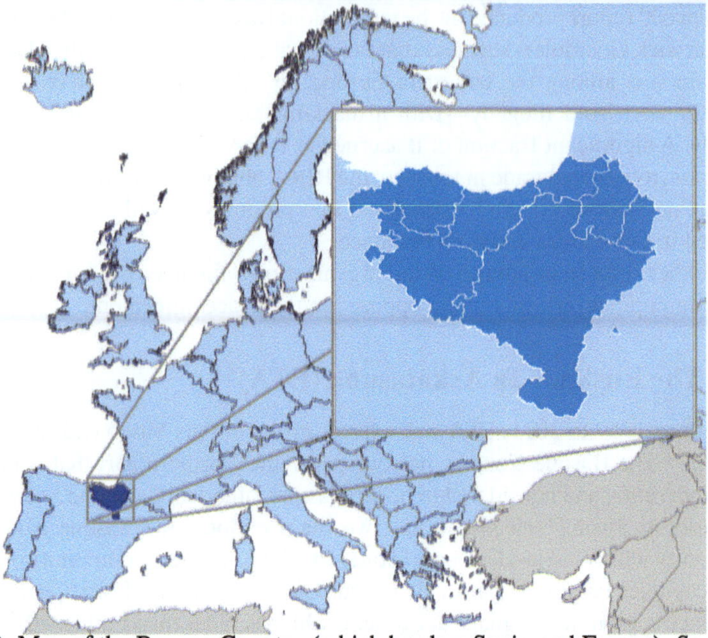

Fig. 2.9: Map of the Basque Country (which borders Spain and France). *Source*: By Zorion (User:Zorion)—Own work, CC BY-SA 3.0, https://commons.wikimedia.org/w/index.php?curid=12399081

The violence of ETA continued through the seventies, peaking in 1980. By that time sub-national death squads had emerged. Branded as Anti-Terrorist Liberation Groups (GAL), these groups tortured and killed suspected terrorists (ETA members) and their sympathizers. Their activities peaked in the mid-80s. This is when the Spanish and French authorities switched gear. They did not support the GAL and at the same time led joint operations against ETA.[57] This led to the arrest and imprisonment of 500 members, including the majority of the leaders. The Spanish government also opened up and allowed self-policing, political involvement, and cultural expressions in the region. Because of these politico-social measures combined with military crackdown, ETA attacks became less frequent. Its leaders were captured in early 1990s. Sensing, for the first time, the distinct possibility of military defeat, it shifted its targets from Spanish security forces to politicians, local authorities, businessmen, academics, and journalists. In particular, the kidnapping and killing in 1997 of a young counselor from the center-right People's Party (PP), Miguel Ángel Blanco, prompted an outrage across Spain and proved to be a turning point. A new strand

[57] However, in a ruling the Spanish Supreme Court noted that GAL received money from the Spanish Interior Ministry.

of more overtly anti-terrorist and anti-Basque nationalist (constitutionalist) activism rose to the fore.[58]

Train bombings in Madrid in 2004 had a bearing on ETA. The PP, which was the Spain's ruling party and had won the election on the platform of a hard-line approach toward ETA, quickly blamed ETA for these bombings and doubled down on it despite evidences that these bombings were the handiwork of Islamic terrorists. The Spanish electorate probably sensed that it was lied to. In the next election, PP was voted out, and the Spanish Socialist Workers Party (PSOE) came to power under the leadership of José Luis Rodríguez Zapatero.

Unlike the PP, Zapatero actively sought a dialogue with ETA and obtained the approval of the Spanish parliament in 2005.[59] A ceasefire was negotiated in 2006 in which ETA announced its first "permanent ceasefire." But, the "permanent" ceasefire did not last long. ETA carried out a bomb blast in late 2006 in the parking lot of Madrid's new airport killing two. This was heavily criticized by Spain and the Basque nationalists. Four years of unprecedented police pressure ensued, with the help of France, that ended in the captures of many ETA members. ETA was mortally weakened, lacking significant domestic or international support and suffering from internal dissent. The political wing had already distanced itself from ETA. According to polls in 2010, an outright rejection of ETA reached 62%, the highest in its history.

The situation was ripen for reconciliation. There was no bilateral talk between ETA and the Spanish government, but indirect peace talks between ETA, the Spanish government and the nationalist left, a non-violent political party in Basque Country in favor of more autonomy, took place, facilitated by international efforts. An International Verification Commission (IVC), originally consisting of six prominent members, was set up in 2011. In the same year, an international conference was held in San Sebastián, where international leaders including, among others, Kofi Annan, the General Secretary of the UN at the time and Harlem Brundtland, the former prime minister of Norway, issued a declaration for ETA to end all violence. Three days after the conference, ETA declared a "definitive end to its armed activity." This was confirmed by Spanish and French security forces soon after. In 2017, ETA revealed the locations of its weapons caches and declared itself to be completely disarmed.[60]

---

[58] Two prominent ones were Foro de Ermua (Ermua Forum)—named after the Basque town represented by Blanco—and Basta Ya! (meaning Enough is Enough!).

[59] Numerous attempts were made earlier toward ceasefires, which were consistently violated by ETA and last only for a few months. In 2004, Spain succeeded in capturing a senior ETA member Mikel Antza as well as important documents and a stockpile of weapons possessed by ETA. As a result, the group was further weakened.

[60] Also see Abadie and Gardeazabal (2003) for a narrative of ETA's terror activities.

2.7.4 Kurdistan Workers' Party (PKK) and Other Kurdish Groups[61]

Fig. 2.10: Kurdish inhabitation. *Source*: downloaded from Wikipedia on November 14, 2021. "The following maps were produced by the US Central Intelligence Agency, unless otherwise indicated." "Boundary representation is not necessarily authoritative." Perry-Castañeda Library Map Collection at The University of Texas at Austin [1] http://www.lib.utexas.edu/maps/middle_east_and_asia/kurdish_lands_92.jpg linked from Perry-Castañeda Library Map Collection at The University of Texas at Austin, Public Domain, https://commons.wikimedia.org/w/index.php?curid=1656189

2.7.4.1 Narrative

The Kurdish population is the fourth largest ethnic group in the Middle East and the largest ethnic group without a homeland. It is one of the indigenous peoples of the Mesopotamian plains and the highlands in what are now south-eastern Turkey, north-eastern Syria, northern Iraq, north-western Iran, and south-western Armenia; see Fig. 2.10. The Kurdish adheres to different religions and creeds, while the majority are Sunni Muslims.

[61] See Encyclopedia Britannica and Hakeymez (2017).

Within the Kurdish population, the Kurdish Workers' Party (PKK), also known as Kongra-Gel, was formed in 1970s with a Marxist–Leninist leaning.[62] In 1984, it launched an armed struggle against the Turkish government, calling for an independent Kurdish state. During the 1980s and 1990s, PKK attacks and reprisals by the Turkish government led to a state of virtual war in eastern Turkey. In the 1990s, Turkish troops also attacked PKK bases in the so-called safe havens of Iraqi Kurdistan in northern Iraq. In 1999, its leader, Abdullah Öcalan, was captured and imprisoned, after which its activities were curtailed. However, it regrouped itself in 2004 and resumed violence. The PKK is listed as a terrorist organization by Turkey, the EU, and the USA.

Although a Sunni group, PKK's distinguishing feature is that it is highly secular. It does not believe in strict rituals or anything close to the Sharia law. And, it aggressively promotes women participation (see below).

Peace talks between the Turkish government and PKK leaders began in 2009 and continued till 2011 without much success. By this time, PKK's objective/demand had changed from an independent state to an autonomous state within Turkey that guarantees Kurdish cultural and linguistic rights. While the peace talks were underway, Turkish authorities continued to arrest members of legal Kurdish parties, usually on charges of having belonged to terrorist groups. This led to increased violence after the talks, reaching its highest level in more than a decade.

Under pressure from the EU, another round of peace talks began in 2012 between the Turkish government headed by President Erdoğan and PKK's leader Öcalan in prison. It continued for nearly three years, during which there was ceasefire and little violence. But it collapsed in 2015 with each side blaming the other, and hostilities resumed. Erdoğan urged the Turkish parliament to strip politicians with links to PKK of immunity from prosecution, so that they can be put on trial if there are allegations of links with hostile groups. This was clearly aimed against his opponents and paved the way for the trial of pro-Kurdish legislators. The bill toward suspension of immunity was initiated by his own party, Adalet ve Kalkınma Partisi (Justice and Development Party or AK party, and it got passed in 2016. As soon as the 2015 peace talks were over, the Turkish military started to bomb PKK bases in the south-eastern province of Sirnak. In mid-2016, a PKK car bomb in Cizre killed 11 policemen and injured 78. Between the end of peace talks in 2015 and the end of the year 2016, hundreds died in Turkey's Kurdish majority region. At the time of writing this chapter (late 2021), PKK remains active. Over more than thirty six years of conflict between Turkish authority and PKK have claimed more than 40,000 Turkish and Kurdish lives. This includes 5291 deaths from PKK attacks since their beginning in 1984 till 2019, according to GTD, and fatalities associated with military operations by Turkish forces against PKK, other groups and the Kurdish population.

Erdoğan insists that the Kurds already enjoy full Turkish citizenship in a "democratic Turkey" and are full-fledged Turkish nationals. At the same time, he has pushed a hard-line approach toward PKK.[63] In early 2021, Erdoğan has moved toward ban-

---

[62] Partiya Karkeren Kurdistan is its full native name.

[63] Erdoğan has stated that military operation will continue "until the very last rebel is killed."

ning a main opposition party, namely, the Peoples' Democratic Party (HDP) on the ground that HDP is an offshoot of PKK, which is outlawed (Prashad and Tonak, 2021).

2.7.4.2 Funding

PKK receives its funding from expatriate Kurds living in Europe, who also provide logistic support. It also has raised funds from narcotic trading, including heroin from Afghanistan, Iran, and Pakistan—labeled as ***Golden Crescent***—to different parts of England and continental Europe; see The Mackenzie Institute (2016a) and Freedman and Levitt (2009). 80% of drugs in Europe is reportedly linked to PKK (Freeman, 2011).

2.7.4.3 Social Services: Rights of Women

PKK proactively promotes safety and rights of women, which may be broadly interpreted as social service.[64] PKK ensures that nearly every wing under its control is equally represented by both sexes, except for women institutions where all top administrators must be women. Women are given rights to divorce and keep children and house.

Is That So? 2.7: PKK or the Kurdistan Workers' Party

An Islamic group spread over Turkey, Iraq, Syria, and Armenia, PKK is secular, and it aggressively promotes the rights of women and women leadership.

2.7.4.4 Kurdish Population Outside of Turkey

In Iraq, there are seven million Kurds (roughly 15% of the population). Since 1991, they have consolidated autonomous rule under American protection and now enjoy, effectively, the status of an independent state.

In Syria, there are about two million Kurds (9% of Syrian population), who were largely inactive politically under the Assad regimes. But, in 2010s the civil war enables them to establish a semi-autonomous region—which Erdoğan resents, fearing that it could prompt Turkish Kurds to seek more autonomy. The Syrian Kurdish forces, called Syrian Democratic Forces or SDF, had the support of US military to counter ISIS and were in fact instrumental in liberating Raqqa from the hands of ISIS. Turkey was, of course, opposed to the alliance between SDF and the US military.

---

[64] Norland (2018) narrates an incident where an Arab man, along with men witnesses, approached a Women's House, an official place, to complain against his former wife for return of gold he had given as bride price. After arguments and counter arguments, the woman administrators decided that the former wife should not only keep gold but also is entitled for household furniture from the complainant. The Arab man started to lose temper and shout. The administrator warned him that if he gets unruly, she will call the police. The man not only had to pay to the woman, but also was sent to the court for prosecution for two weeks of beating and abusing his former wife.

The unanticipated and abrupt departure of US forces from northern Syria in 2019 paved the way for Turkey to push into Syria.[65] It created a safe zone across the Turkey–Syria border with a dual purpose of sheltering Syrian refugees and fighting with SDF forces so as to keep the border free from them.[66]

There are eight million Kurds in Iran, nearly 10% of Iran's population, who officially enjoy political representation but have historically experienced socio-political discrimination. The oldest organization representing the aspirations of the Kurdish population in Iran is the Kurdistan Democratic Party—Iran (KDPI), established in 1946. KDPI started out as a leftist political party in Iran. Soon after its inception, it declared the Mahabad region in Iran as an independent Kurdish state. This movement was crushed by the Shah of Iran, and KDPI went underground in the mid-1950s. Since then, it has continued its insurgency against Iran.[67]

2.7.5 Palestine Liberation Organization (PLO) and Fatah[68]

2.7.5.1 Narrative

Middle East has been the home to many terror groups. Palestine Liberation Organization (PLO) is the first among them (although since the 1990s it is no more considered a terror group). It is a conglomerate of various Palestinian parties, created in 1964 by the Arab League of Nations toward the common goal, at that time, of establishing a Palestine State in place of Israel.[69] Thus, initially, PLO did not recognize Israel as a legitimate country and engaged in armed struggle against it to reclaim its territory as the land for the Palestine. This changed in 1974, soon after the Yom Kippur War in October 1973, when it expressed to consider Gaza Strip, West Bank, and East Jerusalem only as a Palestinian state in a transitory phase and decided to downscale its arms engagement against Israel. Finally in 1993, it signed an agreement with Israel, the ***Oslo Accord***, in accordance with which it recognized the separate existence of Israel and abandoned its campaign of arms struggle against Israel. Since then, its aim is to establish—through diplomacy and negotiations—a Palestinian state consisting of Gaza Strip, West Bank, and East Jerusalem with East Jerusalem as its capital as per the ***1967 borders***, which refer to borders of Israel

[65] SDF says that it was "stabbed in the back" by the USA (BBC News, 2019).

[66] In the absence of the USA, Russia is the main power broker in the region as of 2020. An agreement between Russia and Turkey stipulates that the safe zone will be patrolled by Russian and allied Syrian forces, so as to keep the border free from fighting between Turkey and the Kurdish forces.

[67] There are other Kurdish insurgent groups too, e.g., Partiya Jiyana Azadi Kurdistan (Party for a Free Life in Kurdistan) or PJAK. The origin of PJAK is unclear. According to the Washington Institute for Near East Policy, a think-tank in Washington D.C., it is an offshoot of PKK since the early 2000s. Nearly half of its members are presumably women, and they are among the fiercest fighters. The main target of KDPI and PJAK is the Iranian Revolutionary Guard. Both groups are presumably active. For instance, Reuters (2019) reports drones and missile strikes by the Revolutionary Guards on the location of these groups in mid-2019.

[68] See Encyclopedia Britannica, www.history.com, Tahhan (2017), and Robinson (2018).

[69] As of 2021, the Arab League has 22 members. Its original members were Egypt, Iraq, Jordan, and Lebanon.

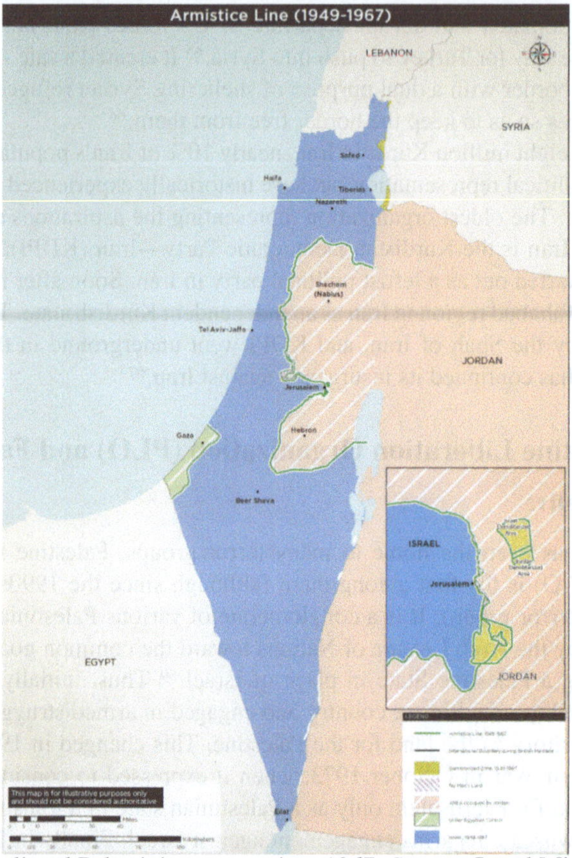

Fig. 2.11: Israeli and Palestinian occupation, 1967. *Source*: Israel Ministry of Foreign Affairs

stipulated prior to the 1967 War; see Fig. 2.11 wherein Israel and Palestine areas are, respectively, heavily colored and stripped. In other words, a ***a two-state solution*** for the Israel–Palestine issue is its long-term objective. From 1993, it has ceased to be treated as a terror organization.

In the beginning, from 1964 to 1967, PLO was "chaired" by Ahmad Shuqairi, who was succeeded by Yahya Hammuda for a brief period. In 1969, Yāsir Arafāt was elected as the Chairman of PLO, and he remained in this office till his death in 2004. Since then and as of 2021, Mahmoud Abbas is PLO's Chairman.

Fatah, an inverted acronym of Harakat al-Taḥrīr al-Waṭanī al-Filasṭīnī meaning "Palestine National Liberation Movement," is the dominant political-cum-military group or party within PLO and is synonymous with PLO since 1969 when its head Yāsir Arafāt became PLO's Chairman. Its aim is same as that of PLO—a separate state for the Palestinians—and it is a *secular* Sunni Muslim organization. From 1964–1965 till late 1980s, it waged guerrilla warfare against Israel. In 1969 alone, it carried out over 2000 guerrilla attacks against Israel. As noted above, its arms struggle began to decline from the early/mid-seventies and was formally abandoned in 1993.

Origin of Fatah and Its Merger with PLO

Fatah predates PLO. It came into existence in the 1950s under the leadership of Arafāt. As of 1963 its base was in Syria, where the Syrian army trained its forces and provided military equipment. Fatah, then, had about 200 members. Its first major guerrilla attack, back in 1964, attempted to blow up the pipes of Israel's National Water Carrier at Ain Bone on the west bank of the Jordan River. In the process, Syria exerted control over Fatah, while Fatah strove to maintain its autonomy. With the creation of PLO, Fatah became a part of it but was small.[70] After the disastrous Six-Day War in 1967, Fatah, however, was remarkably able to keep up its raids on Israel. In 1967, it was allotted 33 of 105 seats in the PLO's Executive Committee. Arafāt skillfully led a defensive battle at Karamah on the west bank of the Jordan in 1968, which was seen as a moral victory against the Israeli army.[71] Since this operation, money rolled into the PLO's coffers from Libya, Saudi Arabia, Kuwait, Qatar, and other oil-rich Arab states. Volunteer terrorists arrived in large numbers at the PLO training camps that spread from Algeria to Iraq. Fatah membership exceeded 15,000. Arafāt became "Mr. Palestine" and Fatah became synonymous with PLO.

PLO/Fatah: From 1968 to Oslo Accord in 1993

Following Karamah, Arafāt moved his Headquarters from Syria to Jordan, so the PLO could raid Israel's newly occupied territories on the West Bank. King Hussein of Jordan did not really support Arafāt and his undisciplined PLO/Fatah terrorists in his kingdom, but their high popularity in the Arab world forced him to be hospitable. Arafāt and his troops arrogantly took advantage of their popularity. By 1969 when Arafāt became the elected Chairman of PLO, Fatah was the largest and best-funded of all the Palestinian organizations and had taken over effective control of PLO. In 1969–70, the UN recognized that the people of Palestine are entitled to equal rights and self-determination in accordance with the Charter of the UN.

In Jordan, the PLO members repeatedly clashed with Jordanian security forces between 1968 and 1970. In 1970, the PFLP faction of the Palestinian terrorists hijacked several jetliners and Arafāt refused to control or punish them. (We will learn about PFLP in Sect. 2.7.6.) It was painfully obvious to King Hussein that Arafāt could not control his unruly "army" of terrorists. During the same year, Jordan's army led assaults on Fatah and PLO, known as *Black September*, which drove Fatah and PLO out of Jordan and into Lebanon. This humiliation led to a

[70] It is believed that an apprehension by President Nasser of Egypt about Syrian dominance through Fatah in the Israel–Palestine conflict led him to create PLO in 1964.

[71] Israel intention was to conduct a hit-and-run raid on the Palestinians in Jordan with tank and an infantry unit, not wage an attack on Jordan itself. But as soon as the Israeli tanks crossed the border to Jordan, Jordan responded with a counter-attack with its tanks. Since the objective was not to provoke a conflict with Jordan, Israeli tanks disengaged, and, as a result, its infantry had to retreat.

breakaway militant group from Fatah that called itself the ***Black September***; see Sect. 2.7.7.

PLO's strategy toward achieving its goal shifted in 1974. For the first time, it opened itself to political and diplomatic channels alongside arms struggle and accepted a two-state solution at least on an interim basis. It called for a cessation of attacks outside Israel. It was probably a result of a realization following the failure of the armies of Egypt and Syria to defeat Israel in the Yom Kippur War in October 1973.[72] In exchange, it sought the approval of the international community for its claim toward the legitimate representative of the Palestinians. This came rather quickly. In 1974, the Arab League recognized PLO as the "sole legitimate representative of the Palestinian people" and offered it a full membership of the League. Immediately thereafter, the UN recognized the right of the Palestinians to independence and self-determination and granted PLO the status of a non-member national-movement observer status. Arafāt addressed the UN General Assembly in the same year.[73]

Oslo Accord Onward

As noted, in 1993, Israel and the Fatah-led PLO signed the Oslo Accord, according to which Fatah/PLO recognized Israel's right to existence and eschewed violence against it. In return, Israel accepted PLO as the lawful representative of the Palestine people, and both sides agreed for the establishment of a Palestinian Authority (PA), a semi-autonomous government body that would assume the responsibility of governing Gaza strip and West Bank until a deal is reached with Israel.

PA was established in 1994 with an administrative structure and security forces, and Gaza city became Fatah's headquarters. Elections were held in PA-administered areas in 1996. Arafāt won the presidency, and Fatah captured a majority of seats within the Palestinian Legislative Council (PLC). Following Arafāt' death in 2005, Mahmoud Abbas, one of the original members of Fatah, became the elected PA president.

Dramatic events occurred in 2006, when elections were held for the PLC, and Fatah unexpectedly lost to a "freedom-fighting" terror/militant group, Hamas (see Sect. 2.8.10), which had a political wing, but, unlike Fatah, was hostile toward Israel and took recourse to violence and terrorism to achieve the same objective of a Palestinian independent state. Administrative corruption and incompetence were behind Fatah's loss. Although the two groups eventually formed a coalition government with Fatah as a "junior partner," it was tenuous and violence escalated between Hamas and Fatah forces in the Gaza Strip, leading Abbas to dissolve the Hamas-led government

[72] This fundamental shift did not please all factions within PLO.

[73] In 1982 PLO/Fatah was pushed out of Lebanon after the Israeli invasion of Southern Lebanon. Syrian forces were fighting the Israel Defense Forces (IDF), and at that time, there was no cordiality between Syria and Arafāt. Hence, if Israel won, it would expel PLO/Fatah, and if Syria gained the upper hand, they would have installed their forces instead of PLO/Fatah. It was bad news for PLO/Fatah in either case, and it left Lebanon and moved to Tunis, Tunisia. Opposing factions developed within Fatah during 1983, leading to an internal leadership struggle. However, by early 1990s, Arafāt was at the helm of Fatah again.

and declare a state of emergency in 2007. But, thereafter, Fatah exerted very little influence in the Gaza Strip and was effectively pushed out.[74] Since then and until 2017, Hamas was in control of Gaza. Nonetheless, Fatah/PLO is recognized by the international community including Israel and remains central to Israeli–Palestinian peace negotiations. With the help of Egypt's mediation, Hamas and Fatah officials reached a reconciliation agreement in 2011. An interim government was formed. After months of negotiation over the leadership of the interim government, the two parties announced in 2012 that they had selected Abbas as the interim prime minister.

In 2012, PLO gained a non-member Observer State status in the UN—an upgrade from a non-member national-movement observer status granted back in 1974 and one step away from a full-fledged state membership. Being a non-member observer state, Palestine has the same status in the UN as does the Vatican, and as Austria before it became a full-fledged member way back in 1955.[75] The USA was opposed to it since the non-member observer status granted to PLO put pressure on Israel.

As will be discussed in detail under "Funding" of Hamas in Sect. 2.8.10, the economic fortune of Hamas started to decline after 2014. By 2017, it was considerably weakened, leading it to "concede" to Fatah/PA. Hamas and Fatah declared a treaty in 2017 signed in Egypt that ended their decade-long animosity. Hamas agreed to transfer administrative powers in Gaza to a Fatah-backed government. The deal included 3000 members of the West Bank-based PA's police force redeployed to Gaza (on the top of Hamas's own police force of around 20,000). Till the time of writing this section, the deal was not implemented.[76]

Although since 1993 Fatah/PLO is not considered or designated as a terror organization, it has provided indirect support to violence or terrorism against Israel. For instance, it supported the Second Intifada during 2000–2005 in terms of contributing to the "Fund for Families of Martyrs and the Injured," which provided financial support for the families whose members were killed or injured while being engaged in conflict with Israel (Levitt, 2015).

[74] The autonomous part of the West Bank continued to remain in the control of Fatah and PA.

[75] Apart from being closer, in principle, toward being a full member, the new status means that Palestinians now have access to the International Criminal Court. Potentially, it enables PLO to bring charges, for example, against Israeli generals for "war crimes" committed toward Palestine people. In turn, this may embitter Israeli–Palestinian relations.

[76] Several stumbling blocks remain. One is with regard to the weapons possessed by the military wing of Hamas in Gaza, which includes an arsenal of rockets. Hamas has refused to hand over its security forces, contending that weapons should stay with the military groups under it (thinking that it is only way Israel will be compelled at some time in the future to grant full independence to the Palestinian people), whereas PA, the peace partner of Israel, insists that weapons should be handed over to it. Abu Amer (2018) reports that there is an international pressure for a truce between Hamas and Israel, which is not viewed favorably by Fatah/PLO, since Gaza and West Bank will be treated independently and it will be effectively sidelined from any control or administration of Hamas.

2.7.5.2 Funding[77]

Often regarded as the first "state within state," Fatah/PLO had an extensive network of funding.[78] In the 1980s, its operating annual budget was around $400 million. In 1993, its estimated wealth was between 10 and 14 billion dollars.

Originally, it was funded by wealthy Palestinians who fled from Israel to Lebanon. Over years, there were four main "legal" sources of funds: (a) Arab States, (b) wealthy Palestinians, international government organizations, non-government organizations (NGOs) and charities, (c) income from investments, and (d) a Palestinian Liberation Tax Fund. The Arab states contributed funds to help PLO for its cause and also because of extortion as it threatened attack on vulnerable Arab leaders. Between 1973 and 1986, it received in the range of $100 to $300 million dollars from Arab countries with the most from Libya.[79] External state support to PLO started to dwindle in the late 1980s and almost dried up by 1990. Arafāt's increasing assertion of independence was believed to be the underlying cause.

Palestine Liberation Tax Fund was financed by a "donation" between 3.5 and 7% of income by Palestinian expatriates.[80] PLO also used illegal and criminal means to raise funds like extortion, kidnapping, smuggling, and counterfeit currency. But these acts were typically committed by low rank members, "not always sanctioned by PLO leadership" (Kiser, 2005).

2.7.6 Popular Front for the Liberation of Palestine (PFLP) and PFLP-GC[81]

The PFLP is a secular Palestinian revolutionary socialist organization founded in 1967 by George Habash (a Palestinian Christian) that blended Marxist–Leninist ideology and Arab nationalism. It is the second largest faction in PLO. While Fatah attempted to build support for the Palestinian cause from Arab countries, the PFLP saw it as inertia among the Middle East leaders. It took a harder line on Palestinian aspirations, opposing the moderate stance of Fatah. It did not recognize and was against any negotiations with Israel. Instead of seeking help and assistance from Arab nations, it sought the backing from the Soviet Union and China.

By early 1968, the PFLP had trained between one and three thousand guerrillas. It gained notoriety in the late 1960s and early 1970s for a series of armed attacks and especially aircraft hijackings, targeting Israeli *and* non-Israeli population. In fact, PFLP was the pioneer in aircraft hijackings-cum-hostage-taking. In 1968, it executed the first major, highly visible successful plane hijacking in history—heralding the

---

[77] Most of the materials below are based on Kiser (2005).

[78] It is reported that in 1981 it had so much cash that it loaned $12 million to the government of Nicaragua.

[79] Libya's contribution started to dry up from 1983 due to pressure from the USA.

[80] It is reported that in Algeria and Libya, the "due" amount was even deducted before the Palestinian workers received their paychecks.

[81] See Encyclopedia Britannica and BBC News (2014).

birth of Post World II modern terrorism in terms of tactics. Details are given in *Supplement Break* 2.3.

Is That So? 2.8: Birth of Post-World War II Modern Terrorism

The plane hijacking by PFLP (Popular Front for the Liberation of Palestine) in 1968 marked the birth of Post-World War II modern terrorism in terms of tactics.

This incidence set off a wave of hijackings by the group. In 1969, it hijacked a TWA flight from Rome to Tel Aviv with the help of two hijackers including Leila Khaled, the first woman hijacker in history.[82]

Supplement Break 2.3: The 1968 Hijacking of an El Al Flight and Birth of Post-War Modern Terrorism in terms of Tactics

Hijacking a plane and taking hostages, i.e., using a plane as a weapon, began with PFLP terrorists in 1968. An Israeli El Al Flight en route from Rome to Tel Aviv was diverted at gun point to Algiers by three members of PFLP. One of them actually took part in flying the plane. Soon after it arrived in Algiers, the terrorists talked to Algerian authorities, who impounded the plane. They immediately freed 23 non-Israeli passengers and five days later released Israeli women and children. But it held twelve Israeli men and ten crew members as hostages for nearly forty days—"a long time." This forced Israel to negotiate, contrary to its official no-negotiation policy. All hostages were released. $7.5 million was reportedly paid as ransom by the French government. Hijackers were flown to a safe haven. Sixteen Arab prisoners from the 1967 Arab–Israeli war were released.

It was at the center of international attention for the entire period and thus a watershed event. It showed that such an operation can be pulled off and inspired future skyjackings. Modern terrorism in terms of this tactic was born with this incident.

Ironically, while PFLP successfully executed the first ever major plane hijacking-cum-hostage-taking operation, another such attempt in 1976 by some of its members and supporters ended in a spectacular failure. An Air France flight from Tel Aviv to Paris via Athens was hijacked shortly after takeoff from Athens by an armed group of three men and a woman calling itself the Che Guevara cell of the Haifa section of the PFLP.[83] PFLP assumed the responsibility of this hijacking and later denied. The hijackers demanded the release of forty Palestinian terrorists held by Israel and ten others in other countries. The plane was flown to Entebbe in Uganda, where out of 248 passengers, all non-Israeli passport holders were released, leaving 106 Israeli passengers as hostages. After a stand-off, the Israeli commando dramatically raided and rescued nearly 102 hostages. See *Supplemental Break* 2.4 for more detail.

The collapse of the Soviet Union during the late 1980s undermined the PFLP, and the group lost ground to Islamist movements, particularly Hamas. Attempting

[82] Later, Leila Khaled took part in another hijacking, this time as a member of *Black September*.

[83] Two of three men were Palestinians. The leader of the hijackers and the woman were Wilfried Böse and Brigitte Kuhlmann of West Germany, who were the founding members of Revolutionäre Zellen (RZ) and associated with the PFLP network.

Supplement Break 2.4: Operation Entebbe, Operation Thunderbolt, or Operation Jonathan, 1976

Based on information provided by the Israeli intelligence agency Mossad, this was launched by Israel Defense Forces (IDF). Three Israeli transport planes carrying 100 commandos flew during the night over 4000 km. At the Entebbe airport, the operation lasted about one and half hours. Out of 106 hostages, 102 were rescued, three were killed, and one died in the hospital later. Five Israeli commanders were wounded. Most heartbreaking, the only commando killed was its leader, Yonatan Netanyahu, the older brother of Benjamin Netanyahu, the former prime minister of Israel. All hijackers and forty five Ugandan soldiers were killed. Soviet-build MIG aircrafts of the Uganda's air force stationed at the airport were destroyed. The military code name of this mission was Operation Thunderbolt.

What is not widely known is the critical help rendered by Kenya. On their journey back, Kenya allowed the planes to be refueled at the Nairobi airport and had arranged for immediate medical care for the passengers (*New York Times*, July 10, 1976). As the *Times of Israel*, July 4, 2016, reported, the airport lounge was turned into a makeshift hospital, equipped with operating tables, anesthetic equipment, and oxygen canisters. Kenyan troops and members of the General Services Unit mobilized quickly and secured the airport area for providing aid to passengers and refueling of the aircraft.[a]

Later, the operation was named Operation Jonathan in the memory of its commander. Operation Jonathan goes down in history as one of the most audacious and successful counter-terror rescue mission.[b]

[a] The-then Uganda's dictator Idi Amin was humiliated and enraged by the success of the Operation Entebbe and the cooperation by Kenya. Dozens of Kenyans living in Uganda were reported murdered in retaliation. Warships were dispatched by the USA to the Kenyan coast as a deterrence to Uganda.

[b] David (2016) is a well-regarded book on the Operation Thunderbolt, written by the British military historian and broadcaster Saul David. There are a few movies based on Operation Entebbe, *7 Days in Entebbe*, 2018 being the latest at the time of writing this chapter.

to bolster its position after the 1993 Oslo peace accord, the PFLP added its weight behind a disparate group of Palestinian organizations opposed to the deal. It boycotted Palestinian elections in 1996, but three years later "accepted" the Palestine Authority and sought to join Arafāt's administration.[84]

PFLP is designated as a terror group by the USA, Canada, Australia, and the EU.

It is important to note that PFLP is different from ***PFLP-GC*** (GC for General Command). A spin-off from PFLP in 1968, PFLP-GC, is based in Syria. In the 1970s and 1980s, it was involved in the Palestinian insurgency in south Lebanon and launched a number of attacks against Israeli soldiers and civilians including the Avivim school bus massacre (1970), the bombing of Swissair Flight 330 (1970), the Kiryat Shmona massacre (1974), and the Night of the Gliders (1987). Since the late

[84] The group's deputy secretary general and former military wing commander, Abu Ali Mustafa, was allowed by the Israel authorities to return to the West Bank from Syria.

1980s, it has been mostly inactive. However, in the Syrian Civil War in 2010s, it fought on the side of the Syrian government.[85]

2.7.7 Black September[86]

Black September (Aylūl Aswad) emerged in 1971 as an extremist militant breakaway faction of Fatah, primarily but not only targeting Israel. Soon after it was formed, it killed Jordan's prime minister in 1971, following the PLO eviction from Jordan earlier in the year. It was implicated in several acts of terrorism in 1972, the most infamous one being the murder of eleven Israeli athletes during the Olympic games in Munich, West Germany. In retaliation, Israel ordered its national intelligence agency, the Mossad, to kill senior Black September and PLO operatives. The Mossad conducted several operations, including the 1973 killing of three Black September members in Beirut.[87]

In 1974, Black September was dissolved by Fatah, possibly as a response to the pressure placed on Black September by the Mossad. Most of its members were reassigned to other Palestinian groups.

2.7.8 Abu Nidal Organization (ANO)[88]

Just when Black September was fading away, another splinter group from PLO emerged in 1974, named after its leader Abu Nidal, meaning "Father of Struggle" (his real name was Sabri al-Banna). It started in Iraq and later moved to Libya. In the mid-1980s, it was regarded as the most dangerous terror organization in the world. Abu Nidal long argued that the PLO membership should not be confined to Palestinians but open to all Arabs. After the 1973 Yom Kippur war when the invading Arab armies were defeated heavily by Israel, and, Fatah and PLO expressed a more conciliatory approach to Israel, Abu Nidal continued his pan-Arab ideal of one state, in alliance with Iraq, Libya, and Syria. ANO carried out attacks in nearly twenty countries. Its targets included PLO, Arab states, and moderate Palestinians who were partially accommodative of Israel. Toward his goal of establishing a pan-Arab empire in the Middle East, he thought the war should go beyond the Middle East.

It is estimated that ANO killed and injured about 900. Many of its attacks were spectacular, like attempted assassination of the Israeli ambassador to Britain in 1982, the murder of the Jordanian ambassadors to India, Italy, and Spain, simultaneous attack on Vienna and Rome airports in 1985 and downing Pan Am Flight 103 in 1986. It shot twenty-one worshipers in an Istanbul synagogue in 1986.

ANO enjoyed support of Iraq (1974–1983), Syria (1981–1987), and Libya (1987–1992). Finally, through diplomatic and other pressures like economic sanctions, the USA induced Libya and Syria to withdraw their support to this group.

---

[85] Its paramilitary wing is called the Jihad Jibril Brigades.

[86] See Encyclopedia Britannica, www.history.com and Spencer (2010).

[87] These operations were code-named Wrath of God and Spring of Youth.

[88] See Ibrahim (1989), Randal (1990), The Guardian (2002), and The Mackenzie Institute (2015a).

ANO had created a lot of enemies of its own too. By 1992–1993, it had weakened considerably. Abu Nidal is believed to have died of gunshot wound about ten years later in 2002.

ANO operated under different names like al-Fatah Revolutionary Council, Arab Revolutionary Brigades, Black September (not the Black September discussed earlier), Black June, and Revolutionary Organization of Socialist Muslims.

The group was designated as a terrorist organization by the USA, the UK, Israel, and the EU. Also note that

Is That So? 2.9: Abu Nidal Organization in the Middle East

Abu Nidal Organization (ANO) is considered as the predecessor of al-Qaeda in many ways. Its demise in early 1990s synced with the rise of al-Qaeda.

2.7.9 Al-Aqsa Martyrs Brigades

A secular group, it emerged as an armed offshoot of Fatah in the West Bank in 2000 after the start of the Second Intifada.[89] This is why the Second Intifada is also known as al-Aqsa Intifada. In 2002, it carried out a major suicide bombing in Jerusalem, after which it was enlisted as a foreign terror organization by the USA.[90] In 2004, the group negotiated a ceasefire with Israel but resumed attacks when Hamas won Palestinian elections in 2006. It operates to a lesser degree in Gaza. Unlike Hezbollah (see Sect. 2.8.11) or Hamas, the group recognizes Israel but claims to primarily aim toward Israeli incursions and attacks in Palestinian areas. It was reportedly active as of late 2010s. For instance, in 2017, it claimed responsibility for launching rockets from Gaza to southern Israel. The leadership of this brigade or its closeness to Fatah is unclear (Encyclopedia Britannica).

2.7.10 Liberation Tigers of Tamil Eelam (LTTE): Tamil Tigers

2.7.10.1 Narrative[91]

There are two primary ethnic groups in Sri Lanka. Sinhalese are the majority (about 75% of the population according to 2012 census) and predominantly Theravāda Buddhist by religion, whereas Tamils, Hindu by religion, constitute a minority group (about 18% of the population). Tensions between these groups started following Sri Lanka's independence from the British in 1948.[92] Tamils felt marginalized and disenfranchised, and there were sporadic clash between the two groups over the years. As Sri Lanka passed various legislations amounting to Sinhalese domination in bureaucracy and educational institutions—which the Sinhalese thought was

[89] The First and the Second Intifadas are described in Sect. 2.8.10.

[90] As a result, Arafāt's reputation as a partner in the peace process was dented.

[91] The following material is based on Encyclopedia Britannica, Chalk (1999, 2003), Al Jazeera (2009), Stanford University (2015a), Clarke (2015), and Haelig (2017).

[92] Officially, Sri Lanka remained as the Dominion of Ceylon till 1972, after which it became a Republic.

theirs rightfully—the resentment brewed among the Tamils. Various Tamil groups merged in 1972 to form Tamil United Front (TUF). By the mid-1970s, their demand crystallized into a separate Tamil state (country). TUF was renamed Tamil United Liberation Front (TULF), and it contested election in 1977 on the mandate of a separate Tamil State, Eelam (a Tamil native name for Sri Lanka), consisting of north-eastern regions of the island.

While TULF attempted to attain its objective through the political medium, various extra-constitutional Tamil groups emerged on the premises that Eelam can be achieved through violence—similar to IRA and Palestinian groups. One of them was LTTE, formed in 1976 under the leadership of Velupillai Prabhakaran. Over time, LTTE became the dominant Tamil insurgent group. Initially, LTTE and other Tamil groups carried out sporadic attacks on police and politicians. A major communal riot in 1983 created an unprecedented cleavage, leading to a large number of Tamils in Sinhalese dominated areas migrating to the north-eastern areas and abroad. The "Eelam war," so-to-speak, began in 1983 and continued till 2009.[93]

Following Haelig (2017), the Eelam war can be summarized into four phases and intermittent interventions and peace talks. 1983 to 1987 can be construed as Phase I. Starting from the ambush in 1983, by 1985 LTTE had taken control of most of the Jaffna peninsula. It is speculated that during Phase I, LTTE received military supplies and training from the CIA counterpart of India, the Research and Analysis Wing (RAW).

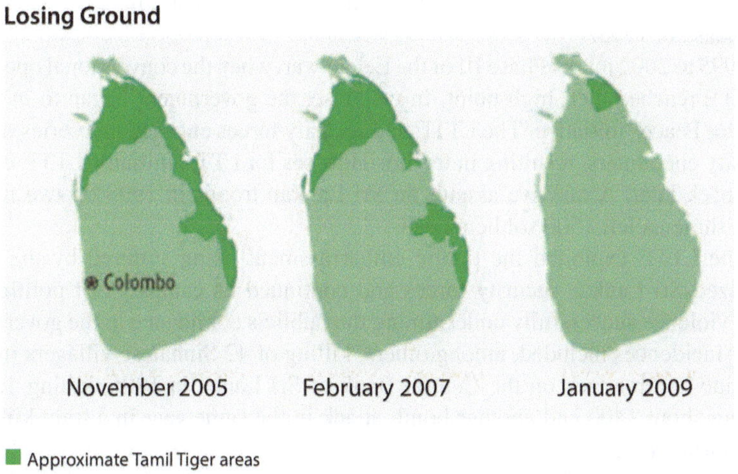

Fig. 2.12: Areas controlled by LTTE over time. *Source*: Ministry of Defense, Sri Lanka

It was during this period that the LTTE relied most heavily on low-intensity guerrilla tactics as it continued to build up its capabilities and refine its terror

[93] Before 1983, the LTTE membership was around forty only (Joshi, 1996).

operations. Neither the Sri Lankan Government nor the LTTE was prepared for high-intensity military engagement with one another. Also, the Sri Lankan Government did not engage in any civil-society based efforts to thwart the Tamil insurgency. The LTTE began to form its naval arm, the Sea Tigers. During Eelam War I, Sea Tigers were largely used to harass Sri Lankan navy units along the coastline and transport LTTE resources between short distances.

In 1987 India and Sri Lanka signed an accord to bring the conflict to a closure and an Indian Peace Keeping Force (IPKF) marched on to the island to end the hostilities and supervise a surrender of arms by the Tamil militants. Diplomat efforts were also underway to negotiate a ceasefire. However, unanticipated conflicts broke out between the peace-keepers and the LTTE, which forced the Indian forces to pull out of Sri Lanka in 1989.[94]

The Eelam war resumed. The period 1990–1995 can called Phase II, during which the LTTE began its transformation into a conventional military force. It began to challenge the government control over parts of the island. It was also during this period that the LTTE began to utilize terrorism and political violence as an operational strategy—mainly relying on suicide bombers targeting soft civilian and military constellations. The LTTE developed a separate branch focused entirely on terrorism and political violence: The ***Black Tigers***. Taking the cue from Hezbollah in Lebanon, the Black Tigers revolutionized the tactic of suicide bombing and utilized it to a great effect throughout the remainder of the conflict. Suicide bombing claimed the lives of Sri Lankan Deputy Defense Minister Ranjan Wijeratne, the former Prime Minister of India Rajiv Gandhi in 1991, and, the Sri Lankan President Ranasinghe Premadasa in 1993.

1995 to 2002 marks Phase III of the Eelam war, when the conventional operations of LTTE reached their high point. In response, the government began to mount its "War for Peace" initiative. The LTTE and security forces engaged in a series of high-intensity encounters, resulting in territorial losses for LTTE initially. LTTE claimed them back later. A massive assault on Sri Lankan troops in 1998 on two military establishments left 1500 soldiers dead.

The LTTE exploited the public embarrassment being suffered by the poorly organized Sri Lankan security forces and continued its campaign of political and urban violence successfully undermining the public's confidence in the government. Terror incidences included, among others, killing of 42 Sinhalese villagers in 1995, a suicide bomb attack on the Central Bank of Sri Lanka in 1996, killing 100 and injuring about 1400 and another bomb attack in the same year in a train killing 80 and injuring 450.

Despite the significant success, with its limited size of fighters (about 20,000), LTTE could not however sustain itself in the face of much greater resources and manpower of the Sri Lankan government. Eelam War III ended in a strategic stalemate that saw the LTTE manpower and resource base drastically curtailed. Indiscriminate

---

[94] Another possible reason behind the withdrawal of Indian forces is its own fear of potential secessionist demand, should LTTE succeed. Indian military intervention against LTTE later became the reason behind the spectacular assassination of Rajiv Gandhi by the LTTE.

killing led to a decline in the support for LTTE, especially among the Tamilian diaspora in North America and Europe who were the group's major financiers.

By 2002 the Tigers had dropped their demands for a separate homeland in exchange for a power-sharing deal with the government. A ceasefire was negotiated, and Norway and some other countries agreed to monitor the ceasefire. But in 2003 the LTTE pulled itself out of the negotiation, saying they were being marginalized. Suicide bombing campaign was resumed.

The period 2006–2009 was the last phase, Phase IV. In 2006 Sri Lankan government mounted an all-out offensive against the LTTE. By 2009, the LTTE was defeated decisively, and its leader Prabhakaran was killed. As described by White (2017), in the closing stage, the Sri Lankan forces devised a novel strategy of creating no-fire zones: Tamils who would move to these areas will be secured; otherwise, they would be targeted and risk injury or death. The strategy was a tactical success. Figure 2.12 depicts LTTE's loss of territory over Phase IV.

An estimated 70,000 people were killed during the conflict between the LTTE and the Sri Lankan government. Indeed,

Is That So? 2.10: LTTE in Sri Lanka

In the pre 9/11 era, LTTE of Sri Lanka was the leader of all terror organizations in terms of suicide attacks.

2.7.10.2 Organization and Capabilities

The LTTE consisted of a highly developed military wing and a secondary political wing. The military wing had several units, e.g., naval (Sea Pigeons and Sea Tigers), airborne, intelligence, and suicide mission (The Black Tigers). Sea Tigers were the largest wing of LTTE. LTTE soldiers ("Tigers"), especially the Black Tigers, went through rigorous training and were personally vetted by Prabhakaran.

Until 1987, LTTE was mostly dependent on India's RAW for its arms and explosives. After India's exit from Sri Lanka, LTTE diversified its sources of arms procurement. The procurement network was run by LTTE's office of overseas purchases, also known as the KP department.[95] Under the KP department, Sea Pigeons was a shipping network with a fleet of ten to twelve deep-sea vessels, all equipped with sophisticated radar systems and INMARASAT communications technology. The vessels sailed under the flags of Panama, Honduras, and Liberia. Most of the time, these ships would carry legitimate products such as tea, rice, paddy, hardware, etc., but they were also used to transport explosives, ammunitions, and drugs. The attached personnel with Sea Pigeons were the Sea Tigers. The shipping network operated from Hong Kong in the east to the Arabian peninsula in the west.

LTTE's defensive arsenal included rocket propelled grenades, light anti-tank weapons, surface to air missiles (SAMs), indigenously produced Pasilan 2000 rockets. As the first known use of SAMs by an insurgent group, LTTE shot down two

[95] "KP" was a short hand for an alias Kumaran Pathmanathan, whose real name was Tharmalingam Shanmugam.

cargo planes of Sri Lankan air force in 1995 killing 97 people. According to Peter Chalk, the Tigers acquired US Stinger-class missiles from PKK in 1996 and used this to shoot down a Sri Lankan civilian aircraft *Lionare* in 1996 (Bonner (1998) and (Clarke, 2015, Chapter 3)). Captured weapons from the Sri Lankan army constituted approximately 60–70% of the LTTE's arsenal. Additional high-tech weaponry was purchased using overseas funds.

2.7.10.3 Funding

In the initial years, LTTE engaged in armed robbery and theft to finance itself, but over time, these means were used less.

Diaspora From early 1980s onward, LTTE funded itself mostly from external sources: the Tamil diaspora in Canada, Europe, the USA, India, and Australia. The background is that after the 1983 ethnic conflict, thousands of Tamilians fled Sri Lanka to these destinations and they provided funds to LTTE. The main financial management body of the LTTE was the Aiyanna Group, responsible for monitoring financial flows and revenues, including donations from overseas Tamil communities and LTTE supporters. Even shortly before LTTE ceased its activities in 2009, the overseas Sri Lankans sent an estimated $2.8 million to the LTTE (Stanford University, 2015a).[96,97]

In many instances, funds from diaspora were used in legitimate businesses, e.g., open restaurants in Tamil Nadu, Paris, London, Toronto, or Cambodia), the proceeds from which was utilized by the LTTE.

From the mid-1990s onward, 80–90% of the LTTE's funds came from abroad. In some years, LTTE received, per month, $800,000 from Canada, $500,000 from Scandinavia, $400,000 from UK, and $250,000 from the USA. (Chalk, 1999). In certain years, the LTTE had an annual budget of around $200–$300 million.

Drugs Smuggling The Sri Lankan Ministry of Defense reported that the LTTE was actively involved in the illicit drug trade and smuggled heroin from Burma and other Southeast Asian countries to Western Europe. Being equally distant from two regions of Asia where the bulk of the world's heroine is produced, the Golden

[96] According to Human Rights Watch (2006), for many years, the LTTE pressured members of the Tamil community to contribute funds for its operations. In late 2005 and early 2006, as armed conflicts escalated in Sri Lanka's northern and eastern regions, threatening the four-year-old ceasefire between the government and the LTTE, the LTTE launched a massive fund-raising drive in Canada and parts of Europe, pressurizing individuals and business owners in the Tamil diaspora to contribute funds for the "final war." In Canada, families were typically pressed for between CAN$2500 and CAN$5000, while some businesses were asked for nearly CAN$100,000. Members of the Tamil community in the UK, France, Norway, and other European countries were asked for similar amounts.

[97] Individuals who refused were sometimes threatened. Some were told that if they did not pay the requested sum, they would not be able to return to Sri Lanka to visit family members. Others were warned they would be "dealt with" or "taught a lesson." After refusing to pay over CAN$20,000, one Toronto business owner said LTTE representatives made threats against his wife and children.

Triangle (a name given by CIA) covering parts of Thailand, Myanmar and Laos and the Golden Crescent over Pakistan, Afghanistan and Iran, LTTE was involved in drug procurement and distribution. With the help of its naval division—Sea Pigeons (the vessels) and Sea Tigers (the personnel associated with these vessels)—LTTE channeled the heroin produced in the Golden Triangle and Golden Crescent to other parts. Colombo was a trans-shipment point for heroine shipment to Europe and the USA.[98] Tamil groups in Europe linked to LTTE took part in drug trafficking too.[99]

Other Criminal Activities The LTTE also secured a significant amount of funds from other criminal activities, including piracy and human and arms smuggling. The Sri Lankan Ministry of Defense reported that the LTTE hijacked several ships in the waters just outside Sri Lanka, such as the Irish Mona (2005), the Athena (2007), Princess Kash (1998), and MV Farah III (2007). The LTTE also controlled the majority of smuggling of Tamil people to Western countries.[100] The LTTE was also known to levy an "exit tax" for individuals trying to leave Tamil-controlled areas (Clarke, 2015).

Internal Funding LTTE had limited capacity to raise funds internally. Around 20% of the LTTE's funding came from internal sources, including extortion, taxation, and payments for protection. One of the main sources of internal revenues for the LTTE were custom duties on merchandise passing through areas controlled by the LTTE. These customs duties ranged from 10 to 30% of the cost of the items. The LTTE also engaged in commercial ventures, but with little success. LTTE invested funds in stocks and money markets. Essentially, it used the contributions as seed money to start and grow businesses. It also bought and sold gold to make capital gains (Stanford University, 2015a). The LTTE raised funds through fraud too.[101]

2.7.10.4 Other Aspects

The LTTE was suspected of having links with a number of Islamist groups, such as the Moro Islamic Liberation Front in the Philippines and the Taliban in Afghanistan.

---

[98] LTTE allegedly linked up with a crime boss, Dawood Ibrahim, in Pakistan to engage in drug trafficking.

[99] The evidence of LTTE involvement in drugs first surfaced in Italy in the mid-1980s when a group of Tamils with LTTE link were arrested. In fact, the Italian police busted several Tamil and LTTE related groups throughout the eighties. About 20% of all heroine seized in Switzerland in the 1980s had a "Tamil connection" (Clarke, 2015).

[100] The estimated cost was $10,000–40,000 for a Sri Lankan Tamil to reach Canada illegally. According to a Sri Lankan government report, human trafficking raised about U$340 million for the LTTE, which involved a hauling of 17,000 people to eleven different countries (Xinhua News Agency, 2000).

[101] In 1999 the Royal Canadian police reported that Tamil gangs involved in fraud in banks and casinos in Toronto were transferring the proceeds to LTTE in Sri Lanka. Some credit card frauds in the UK were associated with LTTE-linked individuals and so were some social security frauds in France. KFR was not used much, although there is one instance in 2006 when it kidnapped three teenagers.

These links were, however, largely restricted to arms transfers and other commercial activities.

LTTE was declared as a terror organization by the USA in the 1990s. Although violent, LTTE was a secular group. About 1/3 of its membership were women, called ***freedom birds***. Before its demise in 2009, it ran a news service called Eelam Website, `http://www.eelamwebsite.com`.

Although the LTTE was officially disbanded in 2009 after the death of its leader Prabhakaran, a US State Department report in August 2011 claimed that the LTTE's international network of financial support continued to exist, and its overseas divisions continued to acquire weapons after 2009 (Stanford University, 2015a). There are speculations that LTTE might still be in the process of regrouping.

2.7.11 Nicaraguan Democratic Force (FDN) and the Nicaraguan Resistance

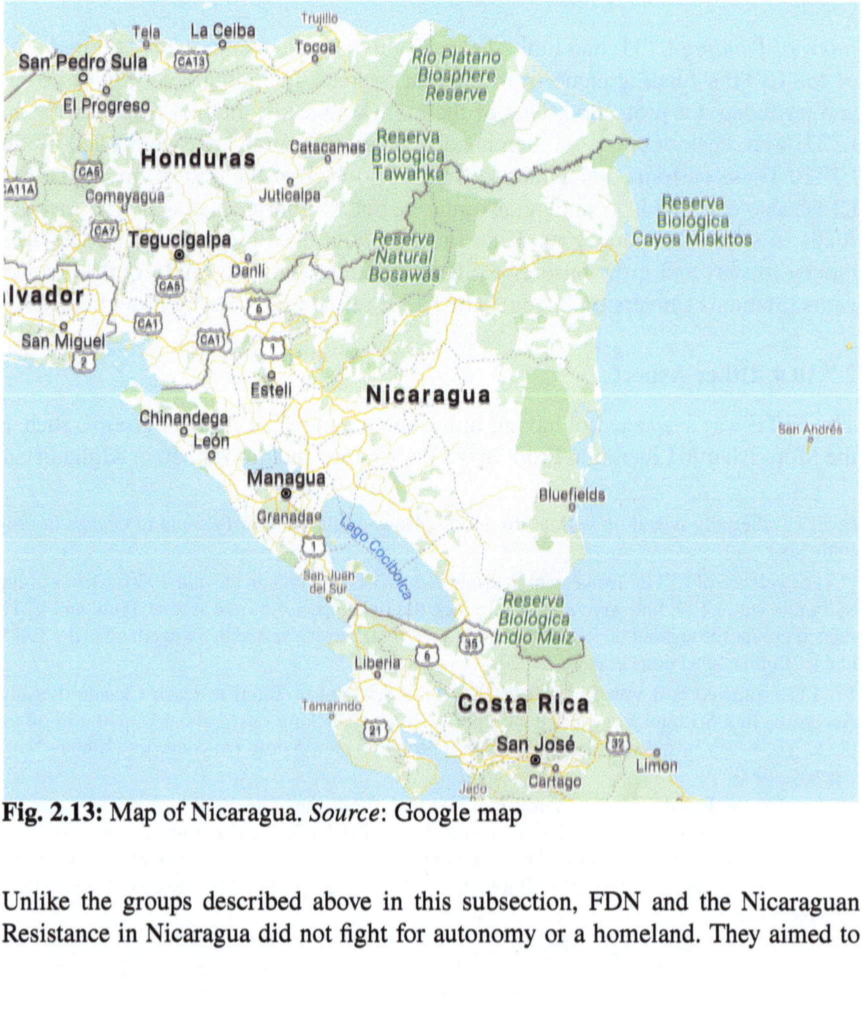

Fig. 2.13: Map of Nicaragua. *Source*: Google map

Unlike the groups described above in this subsection, FDN and the Nicaraguan Resistance in Nicaragua did not fight for autonomy or a homeland. They aimed to overthrow the left-wing Sandinista Junta in Nicaragua. A number of armed groups based in Honduras unified to form FDN in the early 1980s. It was one of the earliest "Contra" groups—right-wing groups supported by the USA in their effort to bring down the Sandinista regime under Daniel Ortega, which had strong ties with the Soviet Union and Cuba.[102,103]

Although the government forces were FDN's prime enemy, it aimed at civilians too and used terrorist tactics. Over a span of five years, 1983–1987, it was responsible for over six thousand deaths. In 1987 it merged with Nicaraguan Resistance, a grand alliance of opposition forces. The last reported violent activity by the Nicaraguan Resistance took place in 1990. During 1987–1990, it carried out more than two hundred attacks, claiming more than five hundred lives.[104]

2.8 Religious, the Fourth Wave

This is Rapoport's "modern" era of terrorism, a religious wave because many terror organizations in recent times have preached and practiced religious extremism: they are not secular. For instance, al-Qaeda, Taliban and ISIS force adherence to radical versions of Islam.

It is important to differentiate between practicing religious orthodoxy and killing in the name of religion with an ideological motive. One must note that (a) all terror organizations that practice extreme versions of Islam do *not* kill in the name of Islam and (b) there are also major Islamic terror organizations in modern times that are actually secular. We must also understand the similarities and differences between religion-based terror organizations, without which misconceptions are bound to arise, leading to ineffective policy measures. Here are some important facts on how religious orthodoxy, terror organizations, and modern terrorism over the last few decades are interlinked.

[a] Almost any religion has different sects, some of which may be considered orthodox, extreme, or fundamentalist. But *most orthodox sects are non-violent*. See Chap. 14 for further discussion.

[b] Fundamentalist terror organizations like al-Qaeda and ISIS preach Islamic extremism *and* kill in the name of Islam. The second part, that is, killing in the name of Islam, has been distorted as jihadism, thanks to Osama Bin Laden.

However, the principal objective of some other non-secular, fundamentalist organizations like Hamas in Gaza and West Bank, Hezbollah in Lebanon or even Taliban in Afghanistan is *not* to kill in the name of religion or carry out jihad. Hamas aims to secure a Palestinian homeland, Hezbollah an Islamic state in Lebanon and Taliban an Islamic theocracy within Afghanistan. In other words, *some terror groups adhere to the extreme versions of the religion but do not harbor an ideological/religious goal to be imposed on followers of other faiths or cultures. Put differently, they do not target* per se *to kill the* infidels *in the name of jihad.* Thus:

---

102 "Contra" means counter revolution.

103 Figure 2.13 is a map of Nicaragua.

104 Daniel Ortega's party, the Sandinista National Liberation Front or FSLN, was voted out of power by a national election held in 1990. Interestingly, he is the President of Nicaragua since 2007.

Is That So? 2.11: Muslim Fundamentalism and Jihadism

While related to each other, Muslim fundamentalism and jihadism do not fully coincide.

[c] While most non-secular terror organizations in recent times are Islamic, *terror has been used by factions in religions other than Islam, albeit in lesser scale.* Examples are "Khalistani" Sikh group in Punjab, India, committing murders in early 1980s, a Jewish terror group (The Jewish Underground)'s attempt to blow up Islamic shrine, Temple Mount, in Jerusalem in 1984, and Aum Shinrikyo's (a group that combined Buddhist, Hindu, and Christian believes) release of nerve gas in 1995 on a Tokyo subway killing 12 and injuring about 3000.
[d] *There are major terror organizations in this era that are secular*, e.g., IRA in Ireland, FARC in Columbia, LTTE in Sri Lanka, and the PKK. The aim of these organizations, already described in Sect. 2.7, is political.
[e] There are right-wing extreme organizations such as Ku Klux Klan in the USA, which are non-secular, yet do not exactly fit the definition of a terror organization in that their ultimate target is not a government or some national authority. But they engage themselves in practicing and promoting racially motivated violence.
[f] While they are *international* terror groups such as al-Qaeda and ISIS that most often hug the media limelight:

Is That So? 2.12: Majority of Terror Organizations are not International

The majority of terror or extreme organizations is domestic or regional, i.e., not international.

The examples are Hamas (in West Bank and Gaza), Hezbollah (Lebanon), Taliban (Afghanistan with some presence in Pakistan, IRA (Ireland), FARC (Colombia), LTTE (Sri Lanka), and KKK in the USA.

Figure 2.14 presents an organizational chart distinguishing different groups in modern times. It is only first group to the left whose aim is jihadism.

2.8.1 Beginning of the Fourth Wave

Islamic fundamentalism, not jihadism, was triggered by two events in 1979, the Iranian Revolution and the attack on the Grand Mosque of Mecca signifying the beginning of a new Islamic century. Jihadism took roots later, during and after the Russian occupation of Afghanistan. These three events are believed to have coalesced to mark the advent and evolution of the new religious wave of terrorism (Rapoport, 2004).

Is That So? 2.13: Birth of the Religious Wave

The religious wave of terror and jihadism was born with three events: the Iranian Revolution, the attack on the Grand Mosque of Mecca in 1979, and the Russian occupation of Afghanistan, 1979–1989.

2.8.1.1 The Iranian Revolution

Socio-political oppression by the Shah of Iran gave birth to the rise of the religious leader Ayatollah Khomeini. Back from his exile in France, he was welcomed by a massive crowd in Tehran in early 1979. He declared Iran as an Islamic Republic.[105] Western culture was denounced. The US embassy was seized, and sixty six Americans were taken hostage in November 1979. The hostage crisis lasted till January 1980, when Ronald Reagan took the office as the President of the USA. This monumental event marked the beginning of religious extremism in modern times.

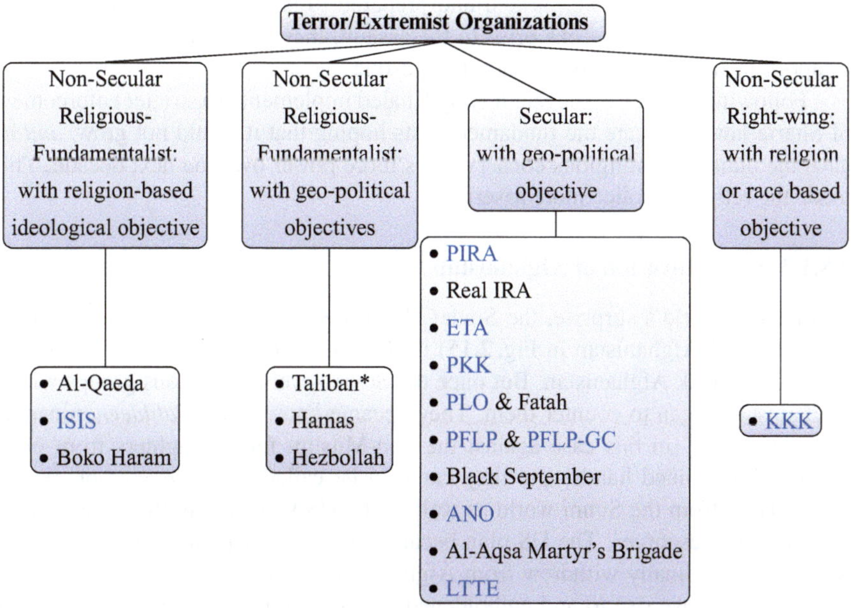

Fig. 2.14: Terror/extremist organizations and their types in the fourth-religious era of terrorism

2.8.1.2 Attack on the Grand Mosque of Mecca

The year 1979 also marked a new Islamic century. In the tradition of the *mujaddid*, a person is believed to appear at the turn of every century of the Islamic calendar to revive Islam, cleanse it of extraneous elements, and restore it to its pristine purity. According to the Islamic calendar, the first day of the year 1400 was November 20, 1979. On the same day, there was a massive assault on the Grand Mosque in Mecca by nearly 500 Islamic extremists, led by Juhayman al-Otaybi, a member of an influential family in Najd and a former member of the Saudi National Guard.

[105] Iran continues to be an Islamic Republic till today.

He declared his accompanying brother-in-law Mohammed Abdullah al-Qahtani to be the *Mahdi* (or the redeemer) who arrives on the Earth several years before the Judgment Day. His followers embellished the fact that Al-Qahtani's name and his father's name are identical to Prophet Mohammed's name and that of his father. They developed a saying, "His and his father's names were the same as Mohammed's and his father's, and he had come to Makkah from the north," to justify their belief. The siege and battle lasted more than two weeks and resulted in 255 deaths inside the mosque, besides 127 military personnel who were killed. Total casualties, including wounded, exceeded 1000. Al-Otaybi was captured after the battle, and Al-Qahtani was killed during the recapturing of the mosque.

The militants were well armed and prepared to lay siege to the mosque for a long time. In days and weeks prior to the assault, they had gradually stashed their weapons in small chambers beneath the Mosque.

Following the attack, the Saudi King Khaled implemented a stricter enforcement of Sharia law to placate the fundamentalists hoping that it would not grow, *and* he gave the ulama and religious conservatives more power over the next decade. This made the religious police more assertive.

2.8.1.3 Soviet Invasion of Afghanistan

To much of world's surprise, the Soviet Union invaded Afghanistan in December 1979 (map of Afghanistan in Fig. 2.15).[106] Historians differ on why Soviet Union decided to attack Afghanistan. But once the Soviets were in, various groups within Afghanistan began to counter them. They became known as *mujahideen*, meaning "holy warriors," in this case against the non-Muslim forces. Fighters from other Arab nations joined hands, and they came to be called *Arab Afghans* or *Afghan Arabs*. Help from the Sunni world as well as the USA. poured in the form of arms and financial resources. The US plan became known as "Operation Cyclone." The Russian forces finally withdrew from Afghanistan in 1989. The "victory" over the Soviet Union gave rise to and emboldened Islamic groups in the region extending into central Asian countries that were part of the Soviet Union, namely, Azerbaijan, Chechnya, Kyrgyzstan, Tajikistan, and Uzbekistan. In general, the Muslim groups gathered the confidence that a super power *can* be defeated.

Another important element came into play during the Soviet occupation of Afghanistan: the preachings of Abdullah Yusuf Azzam, a Palestine Sunni Islam scholar and theologist, who had considerable influence on Osama Bin Laden. Azzam grew up with a hatred toward Israel and was educated with Islamic law and philosophy. He was deeply convinced that the whole of Islam population was under threat—from within who do not practice Islam in its extreme form and from the outsiders who have dominated Muslims and have military presence in their land for too long. After the Soviets entered Afghanistan, Azzam was one of the first eminent Arabs who moved to Afghanistan to join the mujahideens. There he met Osama Bin Laden, who was then in his twenties and helping mujahideens too. Deeply impacted

[106] On hearing the news, President Carter's national security advisor, Zbigniew Brzezinski, was said to have jubilantly exclaimed "Now we can give the Soviets their Vietnam."

Fig. 2.15: Map of Afghanistan. *Source*: Google map

by Azzam's thinking, Bin Laden redefined and propagated the word "jihad."[107] Jihadism was "born" in the late 1980s out of the inner confidence to beat a super power and Azzam's philosophy. Azzam is regarded as the father of jihadism.

2.8.2 Major Terror Organizations During the Fourth Wave: Two Groups

We can divide the major terror organizations in the fourth wave into two groups: those that are fundamentalists or non-secular and which defined this wave, and those that are secular. Secular groups, e.g., FARC, IRA, LTTE, and PKK, that do not "belong" to this wave but has been active during the era have already been described. We focus here on the first group, which include familiar names like al-Qaeda, ISIS, Boko Haram, and Taliban.

2.8.3 Al-Qaeda and Its Affiliates

2.8.3.1 Main Al-Qaeda[108]

Of all terror organizations in modern times, al-Qaeda is the most widely known, thanks to its ownership of the deadliest terror attack till date: "the" *9/11*. As explained by White (2017), the origin of al-Qaeda can be traced to the cold war days when the USA partnered with Saudi Arabia to contain Russia and communism. Saudi Arabia, a conservative Muslim country, was opposed to the Soviet Union because of its atheistic socialism. Although, unlike Saudi Arabia, the USA is secular, the partnership had a common goal. When the Soviets attacked Afghanistan, both the USA and Saudi Arabia decided to strike back. Both funded the war and arms. Ammunition

[107] In an interview in 2018 with Martin Chulov of *The Guardian*, Bin Laden's mother confirms that Bin Laden, who was in his 20s then, was brainwashed by Azzam and converted to jihadism in Afghanistan when he fought against the Soviets.

[108] See Encyclopedia Britannica, Rollins (2011) and White (2017, Chapter 11).

was supplied to the mujahideen groups with the help of the USA and its allies. The USA operated in Afghanistan in proxy via the Pakistani intelligence agency, the Inter-Services Intelligence (ISI-Pakistan). When the Soviets left Afghanistan in 1989, the USA rejoiced the victory. But, its abandonment, so-to-speak, of Afghanistan created a vacuum.

In the words of White (2017), the mujahideens came to believe that the supreme power of God was siding with them to beat the Satan. Overcoming Russia, together with Azzam's view, coalesced into a goal of (global) jihad. A group of Arabs met in Peshawar, Pakistan, in 1989 to form the al-Qaeda, meaning the Base. The group comprised upper-middle-class, educated Muslims from prominent Saudi and Egyptian families, including Osama Bin Laden, whom the group chose as their leader and who could help finance initial operations using his personal wealth.[109]

The group formed a goal of defending a perceived threat to the global Muslim community from its enemies. Thus global jihad became the aim of al-Qaeda, and Bin Laden used this word to rally the Muslims. As noted earlier, he was influenced by Abdullah Yusuf Azzam, also a co-founder of al-Qaeda and another terror group based in Pakistan, Lashkar-e-Taiba. An Egyptian-born, third individual, Ayman al-Zawahiri, a medical surgeon by profession, who later became the leader of Egyptian jihad, was instrumental in designing a grand model of al-Qaeda and its structure. Azzam was killed in 1989 by a car bomb in Peshawar, Pakistan.[110] As a result, Osama Bin Laden and Ayman al-Zawahiri became the undisputed leaders of al-Qaeda.[111]

After al-Qaeda was formed, Bin Laden moved back to his native country, Saudi Arabia, along with Afghans who got absorbed in the construction business. His agents also started to buy real estate in militantly islamist Sudan. Bin Laden and al-Qaeda's first target was the Saudi government establishment, on the grounds that it allowed the American army and ammunition to stay in Saudi Arabia after the Gulf war. A terror attack on an American base in Saudi Arabia would come to pass a few years later.

Subsequently, Bin Laden and al-Qaeda started to base their operations from the militantly Islamist Sudan. One of the earlier terror attacks by al-Qaeda was a bomb explosion in Yemen in 1992 in a hotel where American troops were housed en route to a peacekeeping mission in Somalia. (The peacekeeping mission's objective was to help out a humanitarian crisis, but al-Qaeda suspected that it was a move by the USA to dominate another Muslim populated region or country.) No American troops were killed however, but two Australian tourists lost their lives. They trained and armed the Somali rebels who killed 18 American servicemen in Mogadishu in 1993. Al-Qaeda was linked to the first attack on World Trade Center in 1993. It bombed a US National Guard training center in Riyadh in 1995. In 1996 it used a truck bomb that destroyed the Khobar Towers, an American military residence in Dhahran, Saudi Arabia.

---

[109] Some analysts believe that Bin Laden acquired training from the CIA to fight against the Soviets.

[110] Who was instrumental in setting the car bomb is not clear.

[111] Ayman al-Zawahiri is reportedly alive (as of 2021).

In the same year (1996), Osama Bin Laden moved al Qaeda's base from Sudan to the mountains of Afghanistan where the group could run training camps and was afforded protection by the local Taliban. The new trainees were taught by highly trained war savvy fighters, many of whom were experienced mujahideen fighters. The volunteers were tightly organized and chosen for specific assignments based on their skills, connections, and nationality.[112]

In 1998, al-Qaeda launched two major attacks simultaneously: at the US embassy in Nairobi, Kenya, that claimed 253 lives and injured 4500 and at Dar-es-Salaam, Tanzania, killing 11 and injuring 85. In 2000, its suicide bombers attacked, with the help of a small boat, the USS Cole, a US navy guided-missile destroyer, parked in Aden, Yemen, killing thirteen American sailors. This is regarded as the precursor of the *9/11* attacks. Then came the mayhem on September 11, 2001.

These attacks were masterminded by Osama Bin Laden from his base in Afghanistan and executed through various cells in Asia, Europe, and North America. Having owned the most destructive terror attacks of *9/11*, al-Qaeda earned its reputation as the most dangerous terror organization in the very early twenty first century. At the same time, it became the No. 1 adversary of the US and other western countries. High visibility became its own enemy. Its members were on the run after the *9/11* attacks.

As the US and allied troops moved into Afghanistan, it was no more al-Qaeda's safe haven. Its main physical presence was pushed to the tribal areas of Pakistan. It launched a few major terror attacks after *9/11*, none of which were remotely close to magnitude of the *9/11* attacks. For instance, in 2003 it carried out a series of bombings in residential compounds in Riyadh killing 39 people. Back in 2002 bomb explosions in Bali killed more than 200 people, and they were carried out by a regional terror organization, Jemaah Islamiyah (JI), which was supported by al-Qaeda.

Train bombing in Madrid in 2004 that claimed the lives of nearly 200 was praised by al-Qaeda but no direct link with it was established. In 2005, a series of bombs detonated in London killed 52 and injured more than 700. But no link with al-Qaeda was found. However, both these terror incidents are believed to be *al-Qaeda inspired.*

While the al-Qaeda bases in Afghanistan were flushed out, a different organizational structure began to take shape. On one hand, Bin Laden remained as the leader of al-Qaeda until his death in Pakistan in the hands of the US Navy SEAL in 2011. A few weeks after his death, Ayman al-Zawahiri became the new leader of al-Qaeda. He is believed to be living somewhere in the border areas between Afghanistan and Pakistan as of 2021. Zawahiri has been one of the al-Qaeda's most prominent spokesmen, appearing in dozens of videos and audiotapes since 2003. The last one appeared in back in 2014, when he called for an Islamist resurgence in India. But,

[112] All participants were given a several-thousand-page manual, the *Encyclopedia of Jihad.* After the extensive training, some members stayed in the area to help prepare and train new recruits, while others were dispatched to the countries where the fighting was underway giving them immediate opportunities to carry out missions. Many trained al-Qaeda operatives were sent back to their homelands to form sleeper cells and await further instructions. Many were sent to Asia and Europe to set up more global networks, the USA being its prized target.

thanks to the coordinated efforts of the USA and its allies, this original strand of al-Qaeda now remains more like an idea rather than an active terror organization.

However, it is the war with Iraq that led to the emergence of al-Qaeda *affiliates* in different regions, who were bound by the spirit of the original al-Qaeda, that is, global jihad, but otherwise on their own. They would only obtain their recognition, blessings, and sometimes directives from Bin Laden till he was alive and from Ayman al-Zawahiri afterward.

2.8.3.2 Al-Qaeda of Iraq and Birth of ISIS[113]

The first and the most notorious of such affiliates was the ***al-Qaeda in Iraq (AQI)***, formed in 2004 by the Jordanian jihadist Abu Musab al-Zarqawi.[114] He actually demanded and obtained Bin Laden's approval of him being the leader of Al Qaeda's "franchise" in Iraq. AQI carried out deadly attacks on the US forces, Iraqi Shi'ite population as well as Iraqi government institutions.[115]

Before Zarqawi was killed by the US forces in 2006, he helped al-Qaeda acquire its second affiliate in 2006, ***al-Qaeda in the Islamic Maghreb (AQIM)***. His death weakened AQI. Abu Ayyub al-Masri, an Egyptian bomb-maker trained in Afghanistan, then took over AQI's mantle. It is Masri who convinced several other groups to merge into his, and, Islamic State of Iraq (ISI) was born. Masri chose Abu Umar al-Baghdadi, an Iraqi, as the head of the ISI. The group also continued to be called AQI.

However, the foreign elements in the leadership and membership of AQI continued to alienate local Iraqis. By 2007, local concerns forced Abu Umar al-Baghdadi to issue a public statement claiming that only 200 foreign fighters were members of AQI. It is true that AQI was Iraqi in majority in 2006, but in 2007 coalition forces captured records of 700 foreign nationals joining AQI and its affiliates between August 2006 and August 2007 alone. However, foreign fighters were on the decline, with fewer coming each month than earlier in the insurgency. In any case, Baghdadi's declaration was not enough to assuage many Iraqis.

The local resistance to AQI led to the *Anbar Awakening*, a movement of Sunnis in Anbar Province to cooperate with the US forces against the insurgency. This paved the way for increased US and Iraqi security operations and diminished AQI's capacity by the end of 2007. AQI was unable to enforce its extreme interpretations of Islamic law in the areas where it operated and struggled to maintain territory.

By early 2008, the coalition forces and local security personnel had killed 2400 AQI members and taken 8800 as prisoners. By spring 2009, the USA was funding around 100,000 local Sunnis to fight AQI. The local fighters carried out a campaign against the group, assassinating members and warning others not to work with the group. By mid-2010, AQI had lost stable communication with al-Qaeda leadership,

[113] See Encyclopedia Britannica, Byman (2013) and Stanford University (2017a).

[114] Al-Zarqawi had served in Afghanistan to fight the Russian forces. He reportedly became a fundamentalist and embraced the notion of jihadism during his stay in Afghanistan (Martin, 2018).

[115] Many Iraqi Sunnis actually criticized AQI for its foreign components, its attempts to impose its own radical brand of Islam on Iraqis, killing Shi'ites and its use of extreme violence.

and 36 of AQI's 42 leaders had been killed or captured. Both Masri and Baghdadi were killed in a joint US-Iraqi raid in 2010. Abu Bakr al-Baghdadi (not to be confused with the deceased, Abu Umar al-Baghdadi) then assumed control. Through 2011, the coalition forces continued to coordinate efforts with tribal security forces, killing the majority of AQI's leadership and leaving it in disarray.

Fig. 2.16: Map of Iraq and Syria. *Source*: Google map

However, ISI/AQI began rising from its ashes as the coalition forces withdrew in late 2011. In 2012 and 2013, Baghdadi led two separate terror campaigns in Iraq: in 2012, the "Breaking Walls" campaign targeted the Maliki government and prioritized freeing members from prison; in 2013, the "Soldier's Harvest" campaign shifted the target to Iraqi security forces. The Iraqi government's lack of inclusiveness and security failures expedited AQI's return to prominence. In late 2012, Sunnis in Iraq began protesting against Maliki's poor governance in the Anbar province. When Iraqi security forces invaded the protest camps, Sunni attacks against Shi'ite targets increased. In 2013 a local uprising drove the Iraqi security forces out of much of Anbar Province, paving the way for AQI's expansion.

Meanwhile, AQI used the ongoing Syrian Civil War—which began in 2011—as a training ground and tool for expansion. In 2013, Baghdadi moved into Syria and changed the group's name to the Islamic State in Iraq and Syria (ISIS). Figure 2.16 depicts a map of Iraq and Syria. He also claimed that AQI had created Jabhat al-Nusra (al-Nusra) in Syria and that the two groups were now merged. However, both the al-Nusra leadership and Ayman al-Zawahiri, the post-Bin-Laden leader of al-Qaeda, disputed the merger.

Zawahiri dictated that ISIS should limit its operations to Iraq, but this was publicly rejected by Abu Bakr Baghdadi. ISIS continued to operate in Syria, often clashing with other Islamist groups and ignoring calls for mediation. Attempts at reconciliation with al-Qaeda leadership failed, and al-Qaeda officially severed its link with ISIS in early 2014.

2.8.3.3 Al-Qaeda in the Islamic Maghreb (AQIM)

AQIM is a militant group in North Africa, which operated in Algeria, Côte d'Ivoire, Libya, Mali, Niger, Mauritania, and Tunisia (see Fig. 2.17). It evolved out of the Salafist Group for Preaching and Combat (GSPC), a violent militant group in Algeria fighting its government during the country's civil war between 1991 and 2002. It vowed its allegiance to al-Qaeda in 2006 and formally became AQIM in 2007. In 2007, it carried out simultaneous bombing on the regional UN Headquarters and the Algerian Constitutional Court in Algiers, claiming 33 lives. It then started to expand into other North African countries with the aim of establishing an Islamic Caliphate covering North Africa. It has lost its strength since 2013 but is still active.

Fig. 2.17: Map of North Africa. *Source*: Google map

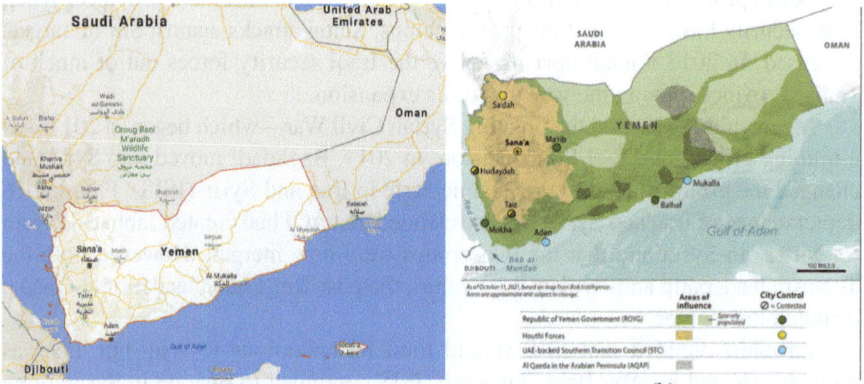

(a) (b)

Fig. 2.18: Saudi Arabia and Yemen (**a**) Map of Yemen (**b**) Control of Yemen as of November 2021. (**a**) *Source*: Google map; (**b**) *Source*: Congressional Research Service (2021)

2.8.3.4 Al-Qaida in the Arabian Peninsula (AQAP)

In 2009, al-Qaeda named its branch in Yemen and Saudi Arabia as ***al-Qaida in the Arabian Peninsula*** (AQAP).[116] Designated as a foreign terror organization by the USA in 2010, AQAP is considered to be the most active al-Qaeda branch outside of Afghanistan and Pakistan. It aims to control oil fields, overthrow Saudi and Yemeni governments, and form an Islamic caliphate. In 2012, the CIA detected and foiled AQAP's plan to load sophisticated bombs aboard an airliner scheduled to fly to the USA (Shane & Schmit, 2012). According to CNN Library (2018), it had about four thousand members in 2018. Hundreds have been killed in the two countries from its attacks. Like other terror groups, it has provided public services including security to the local population, sustaining its support base.

Its leader Nasser al-Wuhayshi was killed in 2015 by an air raid. In 2017, the US forces raided AQAP's bases in Yemen, following which Qasim al-Rimi, the-then leader succeeding al-Wuhayshi, released an audio message taunting President Donald Trump. A US-led counter-terrorism operation killed Qasim al-Rimi in early 2020. His successor is Khalid Batarfi, "a poetry-reciting veteran al-Qaeda operative often shown in videos offering religious guidance on good parenting and other subjects," according to Raghavan (2020).

The civil war in Yemen, described in the *Supplemental Break* 2.5, has been advantageous for AQAP to operate and mount attacks. The dark stripes in Fig. 2.18 (b) indicate the areas of control or influence by AQAP as of November 2021. At the same time it competes with the Islamic State over territory, influence, and recruitment. Overall, however, it is much weakened in 2020–21 compared to a decade ago.[117]

2.8.3.5 Deaths from al-Qaeda and its Affiliates

How deadly have been al-Qaeda and its affiliates? Figure 2.19 graphs the trend of deaths due to al-Qaeda and its affiliates, relative to ISIL, Boko Haram, Taliban, and al-Shabaab. While these four organizations will be discussed later, note the trend of al-Qaeda related deaths. As crackdown on al-Qaeda began on a massive scale, there is a huge decline in the death toll following *9/11*. But there was an increasing trend after *9/11* as it regrouped around its affiliates. The affiliates of al-Qaeda remain violent However, they are not as deadly as the other four Islamic groups depicted in Fig. 2.19.

---

[116] See the map of Yemen in Fig. 2.18.

[117] Other lesser known suspected al-Qaeda affiliates are Jund al-Islam, al-Mourabitoun, Ajnad Misr, Ansar al-Islam (not to be confused with Ansar al-Islam that operates in Iraq and Syria) in Egypt and Hurras al-Din in Syria.

Supplement Break 2.5: Yemeni Civil War

Arab Spring uprising is the origin of the Yemeni civil war. In 2011, it compelled President Ali Abdullah Saleh, who was dictatorial, to transfer power to his deputy, Abdrabbuh Mansour Hadi. But Hadi was unable to deal with multiple problems facing Yemen like unemployment, corruption, insurgency by Houthis in Southern Yemen and loyalty of security personnel to the former President Saleh.

Houthis are Zaydi Shi'ite Muslims, a minority group in the Shi'ite population (see Chap. 1), who live in Yemen from the ninth century. The Houthi movement (called "Ansar Allah," meaning "Supporters of God") began in the 1990s under the charismatic leadership of Hussein al Houthi with the objective of countering Saleh and his corrupt and oppressive regime, supported by the USA and the Saudi Arabia. American invasion of Iraq in 2003 radicalized the Houthis.

Hadi's weekness in dealing with issues facing Yemen led Houthis to take control of areas in and around Saada province. Dissatisfied with the Hadi regime, Yemenis including Sunni Muslims began to support Houthis in the mid-2010s. Ironically, they joined hands with the forces to loyal to Saleh (who was their erstwhile enemy) and took over Sanaa, the capital city of Yemen. Amidst massive unpopularity, Hadi was seen as a stooge of Saudi Arabia. Civilian air traffic between Sanaa and Tehran was opened. Iran was willing to supply cheap oil to Yemen. Rumors of more Iranian influenced flourished. The Houthis tool control of the main port at Hudaydah, and they were marching toward Aden, the capital of the south and the largest port on the Indian Ocean. Greater potential involvement and influence by Iran in its "backyard" disturbed Saudi Arabia, who, in 2015, decided to go to war in support of Hadi and stem the Houthi-Saleh alliance from partnering with Iran and consolidating its control of Yemen. The Saudi war was supported by the USA, UAE, and Bahrain.[a] Saudi Arabia's initial announcement of involvement in Yemen for a short while did not come to pass.

Yemen became embroiled in a full-fledged civil war with four main parties: Yemeni government, ROYG (Republic of Yemen Government) with Hadi as the leader, albeit, weak, along with Houthis, Saudi Arabia, and UAE. Later on, UAE parted ways with Saudi Arabia as well as ROYG. In the southern part surrounding Aden, it supported a cessionist group STC (Southern Transition Council), and in other parts of the south side of Yemen, it supported non-cessionist forces opposed to both ROYG and Houthis. Saudi Arabia was in full support of ROYG.

All sides, purportedly, committed war crimes. Humanitarian disaster in the forms of displacement, starvation, and disease for the common people gripped Yemen. In a major twist in 2017, Saleh broke with Houthis and signaled Saudi Arabia for partnership. But, within days of his flipping over to Saudi Arabia, the Iran-backed Houthi militants killed Saleh and his supporters in an urban battle. Apparently, Saudis had no plans to rescue or assist Saleh and their scheme to win the war began to collapse. According to Ridel (2017), the war was costing Saudi Arabia about $5 to $6 billion per month.

In March 2018, Houthi forces targeted Riyadh with missile attacks, killing an Egyptian national and wounding two others. In mid-2019, the Houthis launched cruise missiles at Abha International Airport and killed a Syrian civilian and wounded 47 others. In September 2019, Saudi Arabia's eastern oil fields of Abqaiq and Khurais were attacked by air, disrupting nearly half the kingdom's oil production—representing around 5% of the global oil output. The Houthis claimed responsibility but Saudi Arabia and the US accused Iran of carrying out the attacks. In mid-2020, there was a drone and missile attack on Riyadh, which was intercepted by the Saudi-led coalition. With the help of American weaponry, the coalition kept on attacking Houthi bases. In the meanwhile, the Houthis could not be dislodged from the capital city of Sanaa as well as Saada and north-western

Yemen. They also sieged the city of Taiz, from where ballistic missiles and drone strikes on Saudi Arabia were launched. President Hadi continued to remain in Saudi Arabia. In 2019, both US Congress and Senate passed a resolution to end US support to Saudi Arabia. This was vetoed by President Trump, and the Senate failed override the veto. Areas of control by the different parties as of October 2020 are shown in Fig. 2.18b.

In early 2021, the Saudi coalition blocked the entry of petroleum products into al-Hudaydah Port for two months. Attacks and counter-attacks by Houthis and Saudis continued till March 2021. Soon after Joe Biden took the office of the Presidency, the Biden administration first froze arms sales to Saudi Arabia and the UAE and in February 2021, officially stopped US support to the Saudi coalition. Apparently, diplomatic channels of ending the Yemeni civil war were being explored by the USA as of March 2021 and in the same month, and the Saudi government proposed a ceasefire that includes reopening Sanaa airport, and allowing fuel and food imports through al-Hudaydah port.

At the time of writing this chapter (end of 2021), political settlement in Yemen remains a far cry. According to Congressional Research Service (2021), 145,000 Yemenis have lost their lives over the period 2015–2021. The humanitarian crisis is deep with no end in sight.

[a] Oman and Pakistan were not supportive of the war.

2.8.3.6 International Spread of al-Qaeda and Its Affiliates

The spread of al-Qaeda and its affiliates is illustrated in Fig. 2.20. We see that despite the crackdown on the main al-Qaeda in the aftermath of *9/11*, it grews internationally. It is because of the growth of its affiliates. In 2011, the attacks by al-Qaeda and its affiliates spanned ten countries. However, since then, its global presence is diminishing. Country-wise distribution of the number of attacks for each year in the 2000s and 2010s is presented in Table 2.2. Note that throughout the 2010s, al-Qaeda was most active in Yemen—represented by AQAP.

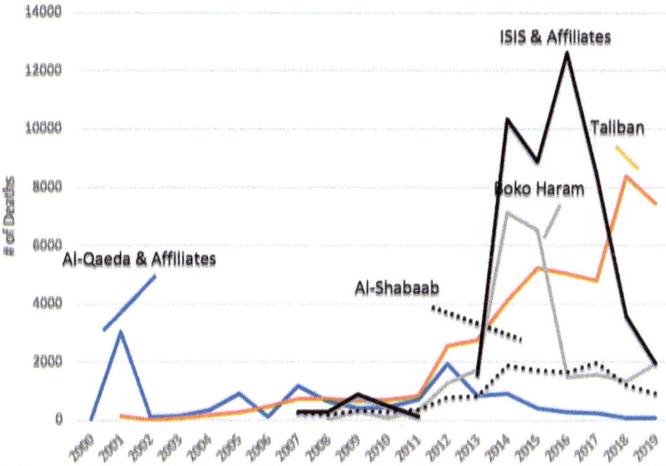

Fig. 2.19: Deaths from attacks by four major terror groups in 2000s and 2010s. *Source*: GTD

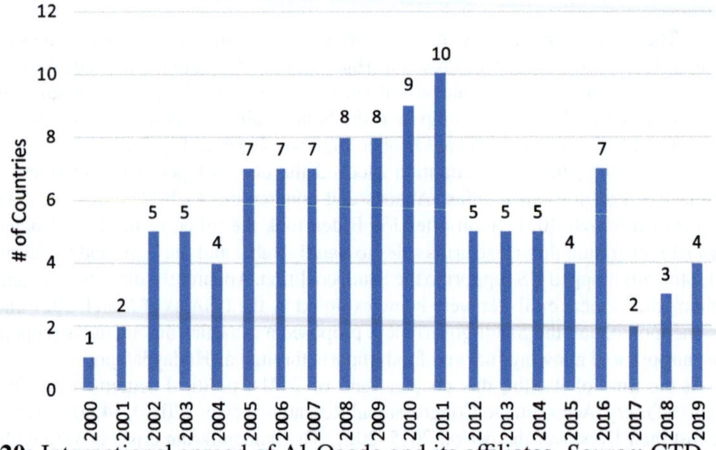

Fig. 2.20: International spread of Al-Qaeda and its affiliates. *Source*: GTD

2000 Attacks		**2001 Attacks**		**2002 Attacks**		**2003 Attacks**		**2004 Attacks**	
Yemen	2	France	1	Afghanistan	7	Afghanistan	11	Iraq	6
		United States	4	International	1	Iraq	1	Pakistan	6
				Kenya	2	Pakistan	1	Saudi Arabia	6
			5	Pakistan	3	Saudi Arabia	6	Spain	6
				Tunisia	1	Turkey	2		
2005 Attacks		**2006 Attacks**		**2007 Attacks**		**2008 Attacks**		**2009 Attacks**	
Afghanistan	1	Afghanistan	1	Algeria	68	Algeria	42	Algeria	23
Iraq	65	Bangladesh	2	Iraq	41	Iraq	42	Iraq	22
Jordan	3	Iraq	5	Morocco	1	Mauritania	1	Mali	3
Pakistan	1	Lebanon	1	Pakistan	3	Niger	2	Mauritania	4
Sweden	1	Pakistan	1	UK	1	Pakistan	3	Niger	2
UK	8	Saudi Arabia	1	West Bank & Gaza Strip	1	Tunisia	2	Saudi Arabia	1
Yemen	1	Somalia	1	Yemen	1	Turkey	1	USA	1
						Yemen	8	Yemen	3
2010 Attacks		**2011 Attacks**		**2012 Attacks**		**2013 Attacks**		**2014 Attacks**	
Algeria	13	Algeria	7	Algeria	8	Algeria	8	Algeria	3
Iraq	37	Iraq	29	Iraq	304	Iraq	82	Mali	11
Mali	1	Mali	3	Nigeria	1	Libya	1	Saudi Arabia	2
Mauritania	1	Mauritania	3	Saudi Arabia	1	Mali	6	Tunisia	1
Niger	2	Morocco	1	*Yemen*	*198*	*Yemen*	*142*	*Yemen*	*294*
Pakistan	1	Niger	2						
UAE	1	Pakistan	1						
UK	1	Syria	2						
Yemen	*46*	Tunisia	2						
		Yemen	*75*						
2015 Attacks		**2016 Attacks**		**2017 Attacks**		**2018 Attacks**		**2019 Attacks**	
Algeria	5	Algeria	1	Mali	1	Algeria	1	Mali	1
France	1	Burkina Faso	4	*Yemen*	*53*	Mali	1	Saudi Arabia	1
Mali	10	Ivory Coast	1			*Yemen*	*25*	United States	1
Yemen	*138*	Libya	1					*Yemen*	*24*
		Mali	16						
		Niger	1						
		Yemen	*88*						

Table 2.2: Country-wise distribution of attacks by Al-Qaeda & its affiliates, 2000–2019. *Source*: GTD

2.8.3.7 Funding of al-Qaeda[118]

There is no evidence of external *state* support to al-Qaeda, except that it came into existence because of mujahideens in Afghanistan who were funded by Saudi Arabia and the USA among other countries. There is a clear difference in the pattern of financing for al-Qaeda before *9/11* and al-Qaeda affiliates after *9/11*.

Pre 9/11 It is speculated that in its initial years al-Qaeda was significantly funded by Osama Bin Laden, who was a son of a Saudi billionaire. In a video released in 2011 following the killing of Bin Laden, al-Zawahiri, the next and current leader of al-Qaeda, eulogized Bin Laden and talked about his initial financial support to al-Qaeda. This remains verified however, except that Bin Laden received about $1 million per year from his family business (Kiser, 2005). Contrary to what some believe, *9/11* was financed by fund-raising, not personal fortunes of Bin Laden (9/11 Commission Report, 2004).

Charity and businesses were a source of finance for al-Qaeda in the *9/11* era.[119] As described by Clarke (2015), in Sudan, al-Qaeda was able to earn money through a range of legal businesses, including construction, manufacturing, currency trading, import–export companies, and agriculture. At one point, it was believed that Bin Laden owned 80 companies scattered throughout the globe. Several of these businesses were located in Yemen.[120]

Al-Barakaat is a network of companies founded in Mogadishu, Somalia with headquarters in Dubai. This conglomerate was used by al-Qaeda in as many as forty different countries, with services as diverse as telecommunications, construction, money remittance, and other banking services. Al-Barakaat managed, invested, and distributed funds for al-Qaeda, while simultaneously functioning as a source of financing and cash transfers for Bin Laden. On an annual basis, it is believed that this al-Qaeda front dealt with more than $140 million in transmitted payments, while skimming fees to the tune of 2–5%, a service that generated millions of dollars for al-Qaeda (Clarke, 2015).

Apart from charities and business, there is evidence of al-Qaeda acquiring money through online fraud (Clarke, 2015). In Italy, tax fraud generated funding

[118] This section draws heavily from Clarke (2015).

[119] Charities such as al-Haramain (based in Saudi Arabia), the Global Relief Foundation, and others were knowingly associated with al-Qaeda, whereas a Kuwait-based charity, Revival of Islamic Heritage Society (RIHS), got unwittingly linked with al-Qaeda: most donors were unaware that al-Qaeda operatives were working in RIHS (Kiser, 2005). Al-Haramain was accused of supporting not only al-Qaeda but also other jihadist groups like Lashkar-e-Taiba (LeT) in Pakistan and a Somali group, al Itihaad al Islamia, which was aligned with al-Qaeda. Some of RIHS's subsidiaries were later shut down by the governments of the countries where these subsidiaries operated. Funding terrorism was not the sole purpose of any of these charity organizations: they were known for social and religious work as well.

[120] Al-Qaeda's network of businesses and shell corporations around the world also included Wadi al-Aqiq, the Laden International firm, Hijra Construction, the Themar al-Mubaraka Company, Khalifa Trading Industries among many others. Al Taqwa, with offices in Switzerland, Liechtenstein, Italy, and the Caribbean, helped al-Qaeda launder money while also providing important indirect investment services for Bin Laden and company.

for al-Qaeda-linked militants. The 1993 attack on the World Trade Center was funded with money stolen through credit card and other low-level frauds, as was the December 1999 "Millennium Plot" to attack the Los Angeles International Airport, a case in which the plotters committed check fraud, credit card fraud, and identity theft. Kiser (2005) notes that in African countries including Sierra Leonne, Liberia, and the DRC, al-Qaeda profited from the sale of gold, gemstones, tanzanite, and the so-called conflict diamonds or blood diamonds. Douglas Farah, an American journalist, estimates that al-Qaeda invested approximately $50 million in the West African illicit diamond market.

Post 9/11 Following *9/11*, charity organizations and businesses that were advertently and inadvertently linked with terror came under intense scrutiny. As rational entities, al-Qaeda and other terror groups diverted to illegal means of raising money, especially KFR.

Throughout the Maghreb, a sparsely populated stretch of arid desert territory in Northwest Africa, AQIM continuously kidnapped Europeans and exchanged them for hefty ransom from Germany, Switzerland, Austria, Sweden, The Netherlands, France, and Spain. According to Callimachi (2014), AQIM received an estimated amount close to $100 million between 2008 and 2014 by KFR.

AQAP has also relied on KFR that constitutes at least 50% of the group's operating budget. Local Yemenis have worked on commission for AQAP for abducting foreigners in the capital city, Sanaa. Indeed, KFR became such a central tactic of these groups that AQAP, AQIM, and al-Shabaab in Somalia have coordinated efforts through the establishment of a common kidnapping protocol. These groups have closely worked with local criminal gangs who conduct the actual kidnapping and then exchange the hostages for a commission.

Altogether, according to July 2014, investigative report by the *New York Times*, al-Qaeda, and its affiliates raised at least $125 million from KFR between 2008 and 2013 with $66 million in 2013 alone.

AQIM has been linked to Colombian cocaine traffickers in a quid pro quo that brought cash to the terrorists while providing the drug traffickers with access (and in some cases, heavily armed escorts) across the desert region between Mauritania, Mali, and Algeria, where narcotics transit through en route to the European market. AQIM has earned a significant amount of money from trafficking tobacco, cocaine, and synthetic drugs between Spain and Algeria.

As international banking transfers inevitably came under greater scrutiny after *9/11*, al-Qaeda began relying more on moving funds through Hawala, to be described in Chap. 4. It worked through extended families, tribes, clans, and sub-clans. Mules were reportedly used to move bulk cash, valuable commodities (gemstones, precious metals), and other valuable items.[121]

---

[121] Al-Qaeda members also used armed robbery and theft to raise funds. There is evidence that an al-Qaeda cell in France robbed ATMs, while a separate French cell attempted to rob a cash distribution center by blowing a hole in the wall of the building as it attempted (and failed) to steal €4 million. Al-Qaeda cells have also been known to be linked with credit card theft. Stolen

2.8.4 ISIS, ISIL, or IS

In 2010s, ISIS was the most familiar and dangerous name in the realm of terrorism—just as al-Qaeda was after the *9/11* attacks. Notice in Fig. 2.19 that ISIS was the deadliest terror organization in the 2010s till 2017. Most of its killings took place in Syria and Iraq.

While the origin of ISIS goes back to the US occupation of Iraq, it bursts into international infamy only as late as 2014, with its swift expansion of controlled territory and exhibition of brutal, gruesome killing in the name of jihad. Interestingly, its decline was as steep as its rise. By the end of 2017, it lost almost all the territories it had gained, while its manpower shrank considerably.

As described earlier, the withdrawal of coalition forces from Iraq created a vacuum that brought ISI/AQI from its brink to its prominence, and AQI morphed into ISI and next to ISIS. ISIS fought against the governments of both Iraq and Syria, tribal groups and militias in Iraq, the Kurdish peshmerga (military force of the Kurdish regional government in Iraq), and various rebel groups in Syria.[122]

Abu Bakr al-Baghdadi, a secretive figure, was its leader since 2010. In 2014 the group changed its name again, this time, to Islamic State (IS) and declared Baghdadi as the caliphate. He died in Syria by suicide in 2019 while being attacked by the US forces.[123]

Many Middle Eastern and European nations call ISIS "Daesh," an acronym of *al-Dawla al-Islamiya fi al-Iraq wa al-Sham.* IS resents this name, since depending on its conjugation in Arabic, it can connote "to trample down and crush" or "a bigot who imposes his view on others."[124]

Is That So? 2.14: Origin of the Islamic State

Al-Qaeda of Iraq morphed into the Islamic State of Iraq that in turn became ISIS or ISIL. In 2014 its name was changed to Islamic State (IS).

2.8.4.1 Territorial Gains and Losses

ISIS began to occupy large territories in January of 2014, when it first defeated Iraqi forces and took control of Fallujah and Raqqa. In the mid-2014, it acquired Mosul in Iraq, and Dier Azzor and Palmyra, Syria. By November 2014, the group's territorial gains slowed because it began to encounter non-Sunni towns, whose populations were more resistant to its occupation than Sunni-majority towns. In Syria, ISIS continued to face hostile militant groups as well as the Assad regime. In Iraq, both the government forces and the Shi'ite militias continued their campaign against ISIS. In the north, ISIS faced the Kurdish peshmerga. Tribesmen, both Sunni and Shi'ite,

credit cards have been used to purchase items such as GPS, night vision goggles, sleeping bags, telephones, knives, tents, and other supplies for jihadists operating in Iraq.

[122] Peshmerga (meaning "Those who face death") is a Kurdish fighter group in the Kurdistan region of Iraq.

[123] The raid on his hideout was code-named Operation Kayla Mueller.

[124] In 2014, it threatened to cut out the tongue of anyone who called them Daesh in public.

also made gains against ISIS in Iraq. Finally, the US-led coalition of airstrikes limited the group's mobility and took out oil wells and refineries run by the group, decreasing its revenue stream. However, the group maintained a hold on much of its territory. ISIS's occupation was the largest in former half of 2015; see Fig. 2.21.

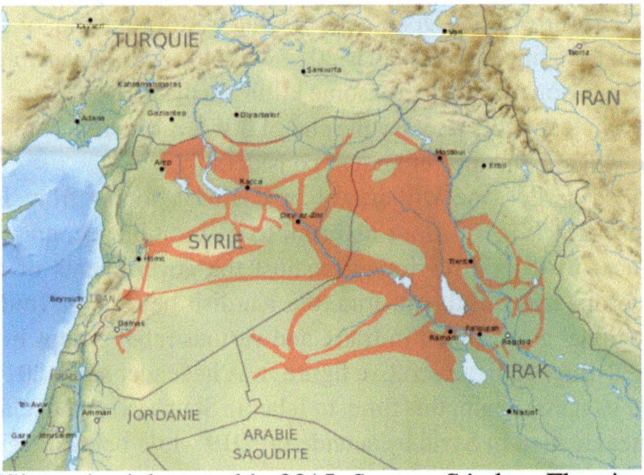

Fig. 2.21: ISIS's territorial control in 2015. *Source:* Sémhur, Flappierfh—own work from near East topographic map-blank.svg by Sémhur, data from the New York Times, CC BY-SA 4.0, https://commons.wikimedia.org/w/index.php?curid=45246616

Since then, it started to lose more than it could gain. Losing territories started in early 2015. It was driven out of the Syrian border town of Kobane after more than four months of fighting led by Kurdish forces backed by coalition air strikes. In March 2015, Iraq announced the "liberation" of Tikrit. Amidst these losses, ISIS captured Ramadi, Iraq, the capital of Anbar province, in May 2015. But in June 2015, the Kurdish forces recaptured Tal Abyad in northern Syria, a turning point for the Syrian Kurds (Salith, 2015). Iraqi forces were able to enter Ramadi in February 2016. Syrian rebels retook Raqqa in November 2016.

The recapture of Mosul started in October 2016. East Mosul was "liberated" in January 2017. The Iraqi army attacked West Mosul in February 2017. In March 2017, the Russian-backed Syrian forces repossessed Palmyra, and in May 2017, the US-backed forces captured Tabqa. Abadi, the prime minister of Iraq, announced the total control of Mosul in June 2017. Iraqi forces recaptured Hawija in October 2017.[125] In October 2017, Raqqa was liberated by the Syrian Democratic forces, an alliance of Kurdish and Arab forces backed by the USA. The Syrian government forces reclaimed Dier Azzor in November 2017. By the end of 2017, ISIS lost 95% of its territories it held in late 2014 and early 2015 (Wilson Center, 2019).

[125] Whereas in the beginning of 2015, ISIS was in control of about 35,060 square miles, by the middle of 2017, it was reduced to 13,980 square miles—roughly the size of Maryland (Jamieson, 2017).

Is That So? 2.15: Rise and Fall of ISIS

In terms of atrocities and territorial gain, ISIS rose meteorically in 2014. Its fall in 2016 and 2017 was equally dramatic.

2.8.4.2 Outside of Iraq and Syria

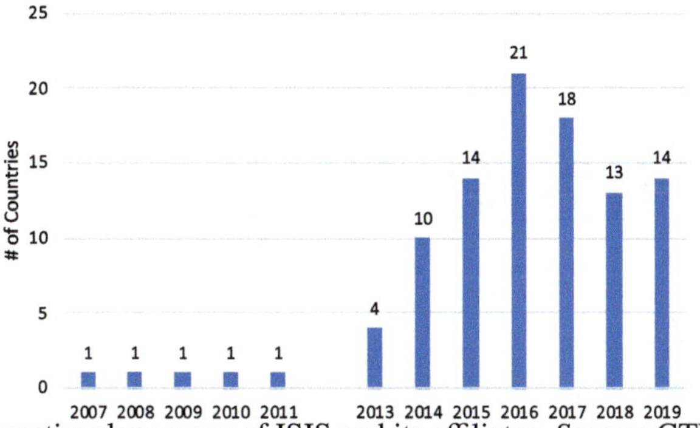

Fig. 2.22: International presence of ISIS and its affiliates. *Source*: GTD. No information available for the year 2012

While ISIS was making advances in Iraq and Syria, its presence outside of these countries expanded as well. In 2015, the ISIS took advantage of domestic instability in Libya to establish a stronghold within the nation. Despite Egypt's reprisal with airstrikes after the video release of the beheading of twenty-one Egyptian Coptic Christians on a Libyan beach, the ISIS presence in Libya continued to expand. In February 2016, the Pentagon estimated that the number of ISIS fighters in Libya doubled to 5000 since fall 2015. However, by the end of 2016, the Libyan forces were able to push back. Yet ISIS continued to threaten Libya's oil reserves and gained access to neighboring states, such as Tunisia.

Figure 2.22 shows the rapidly growing international presence of ISIS and its affiliates from 2013 to 2016 and its decline since then. Mark that during 2007–2011 it was in its previous incarnation, Islamic State of Iraq or ISI, which was confined to Iraq. Affiliates of ISIS will be more specifically discussed in Sect. 2.8.4.6. Country-wise break-up of attacks by ISIS and its affiliates is shown in Table 2.3. Most of their attacks occurred in Iraq and Syria. Yet there are major attacks linked to ISIS outside of these countries.[126]

---

[126] In January 2015, the organization attacked a luxury hotel in Tripoli, killing eight people. A month later, it released a video showing the beheading of twenty-one Egyptian Coptic Christians on a Libyan beach. The government of Egypt responded with airstrikes, killing sixty four ISIS fighters in coastal Libya.

2007 Attacks		2008 Attacks		2009 Attacks		2010 Attacks		2011 Attacks		2013 Attacks	
Iraq	18	Iraq	20	Iraq	57	Iraq	46	Iraq	4	Iraq	341
										Syria	33
										Tunisia	1
										Turkey	2

2014 Attacks		2015 Attacks		2016 Attacks		2017 Attacks		2018 Attacks		2019 Attacks	
Belgium	1	Afghanistan	59	Afghanistan	57	Afghanistan	126	Afghanistan	115	Afghanistan	61
Egypt	3	Bahrain	2	Bangladesh	21	Australia	1	Burkina Faso	8	Bangladesh	7
Iraq	***1101***	Bangladesh	10	Belgium	2	Bangladesh	4	Egypt	1	Burkina Faso	4
Israel	1	Egypt	6	Burkina Faso	2	Egypt	10	India	6	India	2
Lebanon	24	France	9	Egypt	7	India	5	***Iraq***	***654***	***Iraq***	***349***
Libya	2	***Iraq***	***996***	Georgia	1	Iran	2	Malaysia	1	Lebanon	3
Pakistan	2	Jordan	1	Germany	1	***Iraq***	***1194***	Mali	17	Mali	8
Saudi Arabia	1	Lebanon	12	Indonesia	1	Kyrgyzstan	1	Niger	1	Niger	7
Syria	***114***	Pakistan	19	***Iraq***	***1222***	Lebanon	8	Pakistan	24	Pakistan	8
Turkey	4	Saudi Arabia	7	Jordan	5	Mali	2	Philippines	3	Philippines	5
		Somalia	1	Lebanon	7	Niger	3	***Syria***	***70***	Sri Lanka	8
		Syria	***179***	Malaysia	1	Pakistan	44	Tajikistan	2	***Syria***	***86***
		Turkey	12	Niger	2	Philippines	18	Tunisia	1	Tajikistan	2
		West Bank and Gaza Strip	2	Pakistan	31	Russia	3			Tunisia	3
				Philippines	8	***Syria***	***121***				
				Russia	2	Turkey	7				
				Saudi Arabia	6	United Kingdom	2				
				Syria	***152***	West Bank and Gaza Strip	1				
				Tunisia	4						
				Turkey	57						
				Yemen	1						

Table 2.3: Country-wise distribution of attacks by ISIS & its affiliates, 2007–2019. *Source:* GTD. No information available for the year 2012

ISIS brought down a Russian plane over the Sinai Peninsula in late 2015, killing all 224 people on board. In response, Russia increased its troops in Syria to an estimated 3000–6000 until March 2016 when President Putin announced a partial withdrawal. In November 2015, eleven members of the ISIS killed 130 civilians and injured 100 more in a series of attacks in Paris: gunmen and suicide bombers attacked a concert hall, a soccer stadium, restaurants, and bars. Within days, nine of the ISIS operatives were killed; the final operative was captured in Brussels in early 2016. According to French President Hollandaise, the attacks were planned in Syria and organized in Belgium. Following the attack by ISIS on Paris, US-led coalition airstrikes significantly increased. From November 2015 to January 2016, it is estimated that the coalition forces killed about 6400 ISIS members, including several prominent leaders such as Abd al-Rahman Mustafa al-Qaduli, a top military commander, and Abu Umar al-Shishani, Minister of War. In early 2016, ISIS coordinated three suicide attacks in Belgium: two at Brussels' Zaventem Airport and one at a metro station. The attacks claimed 32 lives and injured more than 300. Following the Brussels bombings, Belgian authorities arrested four men in connection with the attacks, including Mohammad Abrini and Osama Krayem, both of whom were linked to the November 2015 Paris attacks. In mid-2017, an ISIS operative detonated a bomb at an Ariana Grande pop concert in Manchester, UK, which killed 23 civilians and wounded 250.

In addition to direct involvement, ISIS has "inspired" several attacks worldwide. In December 2015, a married couple of Pakistani origin attacked a holiday party in San Bernardino, California. The couple pledged allegiance to Baghdadi on Facebook and were gunned down in a shootout with law enforcement officials following the attack. Additionally, in mid-2016, a gunman, Omar Mateen, called 911 and pledged allegiance to ISIS while conducting an attack on a posh nightclub in Orlando, Florida.[127]

2.8.4.3 Foreign Recruits

The rise of ISIS in the mid-2010s attracted a large number of volunteers from other countries. According to World Bank (2016), they came from nearly all continents. Saudi Arabia, Tunisia, Morocco, Turkey, and Egypt are the top five countries of origin of recruits to Daesh. Among the non-Muslim majority countries, Russia, France, and Germany topped list for the largest numbers of Daesh's foreign workforce.

2.8.4.4 Governance and Social Services

If you think that a merciless organization like ISIS that beheaded its prisoners could not be doing anything "good," you are mistaken. In its hey days of expansion and brutality, it provided governance and social services in the areas under its control (Caris and Reynolds, 2014). While it charged *zakht*, an Islamic tax, it established outreach centers, ran a system of courts and punishments, administered utility ser-

[127] He was killed after a three-hour stand-off with Florida police.

vices like electricity and sewage, and worked toward education of the population.[128] In areas affected by conflict, ISIS provided security and jobs and distributed food and medical supplies.[129] Interestingly, as Rosen (2015) notes further, there were unusual clashes between ISIS members and humanitarian groups. Both wanted to reach out to people but for very different reasons. ISIS wanted to spread the image that it was not about just violence and killing (Rosen, 2015).

ISIS also ran buses between Syria to Mosul, Iraq (where it publicly killed captives and trained children for guerrilla war.) The streets of ISIS-occupied areas were, in general, clean, and garbage collection was one of ISIS's top priorities (Perper, 2018).

2.8.4.5 Funding

In the height of its power and violence in 2014 and 2015, ISIS was unarguably the wealthiest terror organization having a turnover of $2 to 3 billion annually. (Zehorai (2014) and others). However, unlike Sri Lankan Tigers, Hezbollah, or Hamas, ISIS did not enjoy the financial support of the Syrian or Iraqi diaspora (possibly due to intense scrutiny of funds movement). There is also no direct evidence of financial support from the governments of oil-rich Sunni Arab countries like Saudi Arabia, Kuwait, or Qatar. However, there is a prevailing view that the contributions of private individuals and organizations in these countries toward the spread of Wahhabi School of Thought—which advocates stringent religious practices—within the Sunni faith helped spread Islamic extremism and indirectly helped organizations like ISIS.

There are three main sources of ISIS's revenues: ① oil and gas, ② taxes and fees, and, ③ looting, confiscation, and fines. There are also accounts of ISIS engaging in KFR, human trafficking, etc., bringing relatively a small amount of funds. Revenue estimates of ISIS greatly vary over the sources of information.

Oil and Gas This was ISIS's principal source of revenue during 2014–2015. By occupying vast areas of Iraq and Syria, ISIS took control of many oil and gas fields. It controlled about 60% of the oil reserves in Syria and was able to get its hand on seven major oil and gas reserves in Iraq, including Iraq's largest oil refinery. It used the existing oil smuggling network since the time of economic sanction imposed on Iraq under Saddam Hussein. ISIS sold tens of thousands of barrels every day in the black market.[130] Although sold at a discount of 40% to 75% from the market rate, ISIS pocketed around $3 million every day—more than a billion dollars annually (Zehorai, 2014). This was just from oil.[131]

---

[128] Hubbard (2015) writes, "[ISIS members] have fixed power lines, dug sewage systems, and painted sidewalks. In Raqqa, they search markets and slaughterhouses for expired food and sick animals."

[129] Some members carried relief bags with a label "IS Department of Relief."

[130] ISIS would sell oil to independent dealers. In turn, these independent dealers would supply oil to the refineries, dealers further in the chain, or local oil markets (Äijälä, 2016).

[131] There are other studies such as Heißner et al. (2017), which place the oil revenues to be significantly less than ISIS's revenues from looting, confiscations, and fines.

Why did not the USA simply bomb refineries controlled by ISIS and the convoy routes that carry oil? In fact, the first bombing of US and allied forces on ISIS controlled oil fields occurred—and that too in a limited scale—as late as November 2015. One theory of not bombing the oil fields is that it might take a long time and a lot of resources to rebuild them. The reason behind not bombing oil transport routes in Iraq was the expected collateral damage as convoys passed through densely populated country sides and villages. Massive collateral damage could seriously impair diplomatic and political efforts to bring stability and peace in the region.

Taxes and Fees[132] In the occupied regions, ISIS taxed people's income, grain, and livestock. It charged invoices for water and electricity consumption and even collected car registration fees. These were collected as *zakht*. While *zakht* is normally 2.5%, ISIS charged around 10% on individual income and capital, rationalizing on the grounds of living in an age of war. On top of that, it collected business tax of 10–15%, sales tax of 2%. Cash withdrawals from banks were charged 5%, and pharmaceutical drugs were taxed at 10–35%. The most profitable source of *zakht* was agriculture, particularly the harvest of wheat, barley, and cotton. Iraqi farmers paid their taxes to ISIS collectors in grain and livestock, while Syrian agriculturists paid *zakht* in cash calculated from market prices. In 2015, ISIS was able to collect approximately over $20 million from these sources.

Another lucrative source of *zakht* came from transport and trade. Around 600 trailer trucks queued every day on Turkey's border ready to deliver groceries, such as rice and cooking oil, to Syria. According to several traders, it was more profitable to pay *zakht* to ISIS than bribes to Assad's militia. Trucks driving into ISIS territory paid tariffs that amounted approximately $140 million dollars per year to ISIS. ISIS's profits from taxation and extortion reached nearly tens of millions of dollars per month, around $400 million per year (Äijälä, 2016).

Looting and Confiscation It is alleged that ISIS funded itself from looting. During every occupation, its activists looted many items in their path—from banks and armories, food and supplies to the museums and ancient sites. But there is little evidence behind some of the reported activities. One prominent example—which is still highly disputed—is the heist of Mosul's central bank in 2014 that allegedly netted around $425 million for ISIS. Although the looting was broadly reported in media, many scholars have accused this theory as false.[133]

---

132 See Äijälä (2016).

133 For instance, according to Iraqi bankers in Financial Times, the robbery never took place, and the money stayed inside the safe deposits. Moreover, the incident had no eyewitnesses, and ISIS itself has never bragged about it (Äijälä, 2016).

Other Sources ISIS also used KFR. The numbers are generally concealed, as the payments are usually made in cash and they came from private businesses or families. In one instance in 2014, a Scandinavian company gave $70,000 dollars to ISIS in order to save the life of one of its employees. It is highly speculated that France paid a ransom of $18 million to secure the release of four of its citizens, although France has always denied it (Äijälä, 2016).[134] In 2014, various governments paid a total of approximately $125 million to release citizens kidnapped by the organization (Zehorai, 2014).

It is reported that ISIS was involved in human trafficking, especially of Yazidi women. ISIS ran a campaign of enslaving solely Yazidi females in its online propaganda magazine, partly because ISIS wanted to oppress Yazidis. [135,136]

According to some estimates, there were about 3000–5000 females enslaved by ISIS. Some were sold to non-ISIS Middle Easterners for thousands of dollars and to ISIS's "soldiers" for $40 to $160 (Äijälä, 2016). There is evidence, albeit weak, that ISIS was involved in selling human organs of its prisoners. In 2015, American forces revealed a genuine gold mine of information on its invasion in Syria. Among the data uncovered, they found a certification, which gives religious permission to take organs form live "apostates," for the sake of saving the life of a Muslim. The commanding states that the operation was legitimate even if it was fatal for the captive. "The apostate's life and organs do not have to be respected and may be taken with impunity." But there is no estimates of revenues for ISIS from this source (Äijälä, 2016).

Beginning 2014, ISIS started to release propaganda videos displaying its destruction of historical sites in Syria and Iraq—in its bid to erase symbols of pre-Islamic past. It is reported that the historic and cultural artifacts were put up for sale. One estimate of proceeds from such sale stands around $2 million annually (Äijälä, 2016).

[134] In August 2014, ISIS broadcasted its beheading of the captured US journalist James Foley to show what happens to those who do not cooperate with ISIS. Foley's case was unique in many ways. The requested ransom on him was $125 million, which far exceeded the average amount. Why did ISIS kill him and not get any ransom? The theory is that such execution signals a commitment so that, in the future, the concerned parties will be highly pressed to pay the ransom.

[135] ISIS's hostility toward Yazidis stemmed from Yazidis' practice of religion by oral tradition instead of a written scripture, whereas religion or ways of life without scriptures are generally frowned upon by Islamic fundamentalists. By some interpretations, under Islamic rules, Jews and Christians are regarded as "people of the book" and thus could live among Muslims provided they pay a protection fee known as *dhimma*.

[136] The Yezidis follow an ancient religion that borrows elements of many faiths. They believe in one god and seven angels. But this belief is passed down orally, with no sacred book like the Bible or Quran. This made Yazidis worse than Christians and Jews, in the eyes of ISIS.

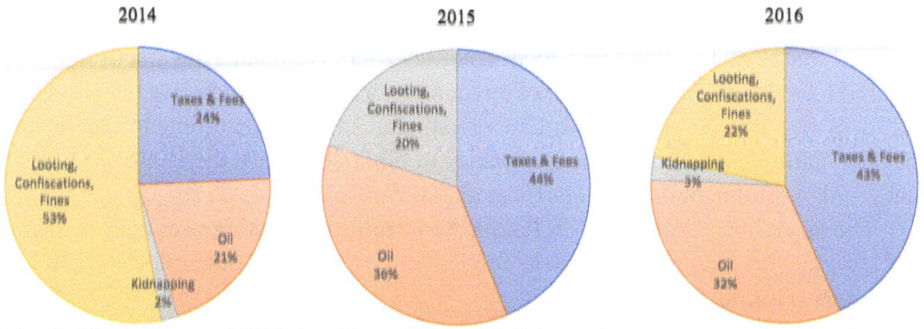

Fig. 2.23: Sources of ISIS funding, 2014–2016, based on average estimates for each year. *Source*: Heißner et al. (2017)

Funds over Time As ISIS began to lose territory, money from oil began to dry up. Another contributing factor to the decline in funds from oil was the fall in world oil prices. Indeed, the price of oil collapsed, plunging from $110 per barrel in the beginning of 2014, to less than $30 per barrel in 2016, further slashing the organization's funds. Taxes, ransom, protection fees, and antiquities became important components of wealth-building (Zehorai, 2014). Figure 2.23 graphs ISIS's funding composition during 2014–2016 according to Heißner et al. (2017).

2.8.4.6 ISIS in Subsequent Years

According to the *US News*, December 27, 2017, while "In January, about 35,000 Islamic State group fighters were in Iraq and Syria controlling more than 17,000 square miles—an area roughly the size of Pennsylvania. Now, between 1000 and 3000 extremists are occupying less than 2000 square miles, according to officials at the US military headquarters in Baghdad overseeing the war." In March 2019, ISIS in Syria, reportedly confined to its last enclave, Baghouz, was flushed out by US-led forces. One school of thought is that ISIS is a spent force in Syria and Iraq. Others believe that many members and sympathizers are still present in these countries and are just biding time at the moment.

From 2015 onward, ISIS has moved to or has been more active in other countries. The civil war in Yemen has enabled ISIS to operate in Yemen. Indeed, there is a contest between al-Qaeda and ISIS to control territory (Raghavan, 2019). The Economist July 14, 2018 reported increasing ISIS presence in Nigeria, Niger, and Pakistan.

The *ISIS movement*, so-to-speak, has appeared in Philippines (Beech and Gutierrez, 2019) as well as in Bangladesh, Sri Lanka, West Africa (ISWAP), greater Sahara (ISGS), Libya (ISIS-Libya), Egypt (ISIS-Egypt), Congo (ISIS-DRC), central Africa (ISCAP), and Mozambique (ISIS-Mozambique). In Sri Lanka, a coordinated series of attacks on the Eastern Sunday of 2019 in three churches and three luxury hotels in Colombo claimed nearly 300 lives and injured 500.[137] Sri Lankan authorities believed that it was planned by a local Islamic group, National Thowheeth Jama'ath (NTJ). However, there is no record of terror attacks by this outfit before these attacks. NTJ was engaged in petty crimes like vandalism. According to some media reports and suspicion by law enforcement agencies in other countries, the Islamic State had some link with this massacre (Harris et al., 2019).

The IS claimed an ambush on Palma, Mozambiques, lasting over days in March 2021, which left thousands homeless and leaving the area and dozens dead including foreigners (Goldbaum, 2021).

ISIS-Khorasan Of special mention is another strand of IS, namely, ISIS-K, K standing for the Khorasan province, a historical region incorporating parts of modern-day Afghanistan and Pakistan. It is operative in Afghanistan since 2015 (Paybarah, 2021).[138] Listed as a Foreign Terrorist Organization (FTO) by the USA, it is a breakaway group from *Tehreek-E-Taliban Pakistan*, the Pakistani Taliban. The members of ISIS-K believe in the ISIS ideology and are opposed to the American and allied forces in Afghanistan as well as Taliban for its conciliatory approach to the USA and a lack of emphasis on Jihad as an objective. It has fought with both the allied forces and Taliban and survived. In August 2020, a prison complex in eastern Afghanistan was attacked, leaving 29 people dead, and this was claimed by ISIS-K.

It came to global limelight in August 2021 when a suicide bomber affiliated with ISIS-K carried out a deadly attack on Kabul airport killing thirteen US servicemen and nearly two hundred Afghani civilians who were trying to leave Afghanistan.

2.8.5 Al-Nusra, renamed Jabhat Fateh al Sham in 2016 and Tahrir al-Sham in 2017

Based in Syria and operating in Syria and Lebanon, this is a relatively unknown terror organization to the rest of the world at large. But experts consider it to be potentially no less dangerous than al-Qaeda or ISIS (Lister, 2016).

In 2011, a small group of Islamic State of Iraq (ISI) members led by Abu Mohammed al-Jolani crossed over to Syria to connect with Syrian jihadis. Together, they created in 2012 an Islamic extremist group, whose full name was Jabhat al-Nusra li-Ahl al-Sham min Mujahidi Al Sham fi Sahat Al Jihad, meaning "The Support Front to the People of the Levant by the Mujahideen of the Levant on the Fields of Jihad." Called Jabhat al-Nusra or simply al-Nusra, it considered itself allied with al-Qaeda and was also known as al-Qaeda in Syria or al-Qaeda in Levant.

Initially regarded as an outsider, it came to be recognized as a Syrian revolutionary opposition, fighting against Assad as a nationalist–Jihadist organization in the Syrian civil war.[139] But it was different from other terror organizations, particularly

[137] It came in the aftermath of a mosque shooting in Christchurch, New Zealand, in which fifty one people were killed and forty-nine were injured.

[138] Khorasan means the Land of the Sun.

[139] See *Supplement Break* 2.6 for a brief account of the Syrian civil war.

ISIS. Unlike ISIS, it did not engage in beheading prisoners or infidels. Nor did it try to enforce the Sharia law in very orthodox forms. The group wanted to be perceived as moderates. Unlike ISIS who alienated local groups, al-Nusra worked with other groups to oust Assad. It leveraged its victories against Assad's forces to create relationships with civil societies, population, and other Syrian opposition groups. And, by design, it did not want to be conspicuous or endeavor to occupy a terrain like ISIS. In brief, it was more collaborative, flexible, and consistently adhered itself to a "gradualist and localist approach" (Lister, 2016)—while its ultimate aim is the establishment of Sharia and Caliphate, no different from ISIS. Jabhat al-Nusra considers the USA and Israel to be the enemies of Islam.

Al-Nusra sought to make its position in Syria more acceptable and legitimate by creating the perception of leading through "people-oriented" policies, the "marrow" of which involved services and social welfare (Adraoui, 2017).

In 2012, al-Nusra grew in power and influence, largely owing to its success in attracting more foreign fighters, united by the desire to protect the Syrian majority. Al-Nusra's recruitment success in 2012 and 2013 was integral to its prestige and military success on the ground. There are differing estimates among experts regarding the extent of its expansion in recruitment, but the consensus is that the proportion of foreign fighters within al-Nusra increased over time.[140]

Supplement Break 2.6: Syrian Civil War

The origin of this civil war dates back to 2011 when Arab Spring uprising led to regime changes in Egypt and Tunisia, which, in turn, encouraged pro-democracy activists in Syria. The uprising began with a peaceful protest, which, unfortunately, led to torture and death of a teenager. President Bashar al-Assad responded by killing hundreds of protesters and incarcerating many more. Opposing this, a faction of the Syrian army formed a rebel group, the Free Syrian Army, against the Assad regime. The country plunged into a civil war. Initially, it was non-sectarian, but it became one soon after. The Shi'ite regimes in Iran and Iraq as well as Hezbollah in Lebanon supported Assad, while Saudi Arabia, Qatar, and Turkey sided with the opposition. Two terror groups, ISIS and al-Nusra, emerged in Syria both fighting against Assad's forces.

Russia entered the conflict in 2015 supporting the Assad regime in its fight against the rebel army group as well as the terror organizations. Turkey fought ISIS as well as the Kurdish forces, who, in turn, were supported by the US supported anti-Assad forces and also went after ISIS. Israel also got involved and particularly targeted Hezbollah, which is strongly anti-Israel.

[140] Adding to al-Nusra's strategic advantage was its ability to serve the interests of certain de facto sponsors. For instance, al-Nusra benefited from Qatar's intervention and funding, especially in terms of kidnapping negotiations, such as when Qatar facilitated discussions between the jihadi movement and foreign countries for the release of a group of Greek Orthodox nuns in March 2014. It is reported that at least until 2015, the Qataris were among the main fundraisers for al-Nusra. It has reportedly received support also from other nations like Saudi Arabia, UAE, Kuwait, and Turkey.

Apart from the USA and Russia, the main "players" in the civil war (see Chughtai, 2021) were: (i) Syrian government and forces under the Assad regime, (ii) Hezbollah, (iii) Free Syrian Army (a coalition of defectors from the Syrian army and civilians), (iv) SDF (militias led by Kurdish Women's Protection (Defense) Units or YPJ), (v) Syrian National Army (Turkey-backed rebels), (vi) ISIS, and (vii) Jabhat Fateh al-Sham.

Many groups, otherwise hostile of one another, fought against a common enemy, and some, otherwise allies, took sides to the dislike of one another. For instance, the USA and the Syrian government are strongly opposed to each other, but their forces fought against the ISIS. Turkey is a member of NATO, hence an ally of the USA, but the US worked with PKK, which was frown upon by Turkey. "An enemy of your enemy is always a friend" or "a friend of a friend is always friend" did not hold.

The casualty estimates of the civil war vary. According to United Nations (2021), an UN estimate, the death toll is at least 350,000. The Syrian Observatory of Human Rights, a war monitoring body in the USA, places confirmed fatalities at 387,111, and the number of people missing and thus presumed dead is estimated at 205,300 as of December 2020. About six million have been displaced internally and nearly 5.5 million live as refugees in neighboring countries. Regardless of the exact numbers, there is no doubt that the human cost of this long civil war has been huge.

The situation changed drastically when the USA pulled out from northern Syria in 2019. As of 2021, most of the regions are under the control of Assad regime. But it is weakened. Many groups that supported the regime now operate as local warlords. Furthermore, there are economic sanctions imposed upon the country.

In 2016 it severed its ties from al-Qaeda and renamed itself as Jabhat Fateh al Sham, meaning "the Levantine Conquest Front." The name change was intended for re-marketing itself as a central force among different groups within Syria in the war against the regime rather than as an organization like al-Qaeda whose aim is to change the global order toward Islamic extremism.[141] Although links with al-Qaeda existed, al-Nusra branded itself as a social movement, dedicated to Jihadist narratives.

In 2017, Jabhat Fateh al-Sham merged with four other groups. The new group is Hayat Tahrir al-Sham (also HTS or The Organization for the Liberation of the Levant). Its aim was to reinforce nationalization and challenge the regime more effectively. This notion was pushed to such an extent that a cleavage arose between al-Qaeda and al-Nusra in 2017. Over the period 2012–2017, al-Nusra mounted 276 attacks, killing 2977.[142] As of 2020, HTS was one of the strongest groups controlling parts of the northern province of Idlib (Ali, 2020).

2.8.6 Taliban

We all know that in August 2021, Taliban stormed to power in Afghanistan after the US administration's announcement of complete withdrawal of its armed forces from the country by the end of the month. Indeed, it caught the USA and the rest of world by surprise. Technically speaking, Taliban became a state actor; hence, no more a

[141] It was also reported that Turkey and Qatar would provide more funding to al-Nusra if it separated itself from al-Qaeda and thus become more acceptable in the region.

[142] More recent information on the group does not seem available.

terrorist organization according to how we have defined terrorism. How did Taliban originate and evolve over time?

2.8.6.1 Narrative

Taliban, meaning "the students" in Pashto, operates in Afghanistan. It came into existence in 1994, led by Mullah Mohammad Omar. It is important to differentiate this Afghan Taliban from Tehreek-e-Taliban (TTP), called Pakistani Taliban, to be described in Sect. 2.8.8. Although both Talibans share similar values like adherence to strict Islamic laws, their leaderships are different and aims are local. In what follows, just "Taliban" refers to the Afghan Taliban.

Taliban's origin lies in the Russian occupation of Afghanistan, during which some Afghan refugees were studying at religious schools in Pakistan funded by Pakistani and Arab philanthropists, whose purpose was to propagate an extreme but a non-violent interpretation of Islam. As the Russian occupation ended, Afghanistan plunged into a political turmoil. Warlords battled against one another, looted businesses and infrastructure (including telephone poles) and kidnapped and raped children. Banditry was ubiquitous. Disturbed by the suffering of the Afghani people, the leaders of the seminary students came to believe that this was due to a struggle among Afghan groups, who did not believe in the strict codes of Islam. Taliban was formed by Mullah Mohammad Omar to free Afghanistan from the influence of warlords and impose fundamentalist Islamic laws. Starting with less than one hundred students, it grew rapidly. The group received critical support from the ISI-Pakistan, which wanted to exercise some control over the politics of Afghanistan on behalf of Pakistan and obtain secure routes to open Pakistan's trade with the central Asian countries. Taliban started to arm itself and became well armed, thanks, in particular, to a tip that led to the discovery of a massive ammunition dump near the Pakistan border (Berman & Laitin, 2008).

Taliban's aim is to establish an Islamic theocracy in Afghanistan and impose a stringent version of the Sharia law. It is influenced by the Hanafi beliefs, while al-Qaeda and ISIS are led by the more radical Hanbali school of jurisprudence within the Sunni community (refer to Chap. 1). Also, it is important to know that:

Is That So? 2.16: Global Jihad is not an Objective of Taliban

Unlike al-Qaeda, ISIS or Boko Haram, global jihad is not an objective of Taliban.

Its enemies included the Afghan government, international coalition forces present in Afghanistan and other warlords.

In 1994 Pakistan tried to open the trade route through the southern city of Kandahar by bribing various warlords, some of whom would not trust Pakistan. A trial run was started when a convoy from Pakistan was stopped near Kandahar. But Taliban emerged from almost nowhere and freed it. Soon after, Taliban fought and won 12 out of 31 provinces/states in Afghanistan, intimidated the warlords, forcing them to surrender, as well as collected arms and imposed its own laws. The group took over most of Afghanistan like wild fire. By 1998, 90% of Afghanistan came under its influence, and it obtained diplomatic recognition from Pakistan, Saudi Arabia, and UAE. Legal and illegal trade prospered under the Taliban's protection. Smuggling worked smoothly to the extent that Pakistan lost about half a billion dollar worth of customs duties between 1993 and 1997 (Rashid, 2010). From the mid-1990s to 2001, Afghanistan was ruled, so-to-speak, by Taliban.

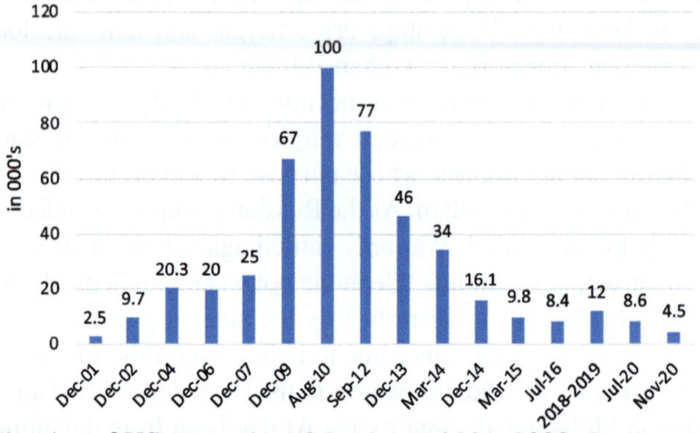

Fig. 2.24: The size of US troops in Afghanistan: 2001–2020. *Sources*: Al Jazeera (2019), Council of Foreign Relations (2020), Starr et al. (2020)

This came to a halt after the *9/11* attacks. As the American and allied troops descended on Afghanistan and Taliban were unwilling to hand over Bin Laden and other al-Qaeda operatives, it became the target of allied forces. Its leaders fled to Pakistan and Taliban remained dormant. A couple of years later, the US involvement in Iraq and its focus away from Afghanistan led to a resurgence of Taliban. It began to use suicide attacks against allied troops as well as the government of Afghanistan—which was essentially instituted by the Western powers. As Fig. 2.24 shows, the size of the US troops grew over years till 2011–2012 and since then has fallen drastically. However, all through this period, Taliban remained lethal.

Taliban is one of the four most dangerous terror organizations in the last two decades, certainly the most dangerous in 2018 and 2019; see Fig. 2.19. Figure 2.25 traces the number of attacks by Taliban and the number of deaths from the attacks over the period 2001–2019. Clearly, it was far more active and caused far more deaths in the 2010s than in 2000s.

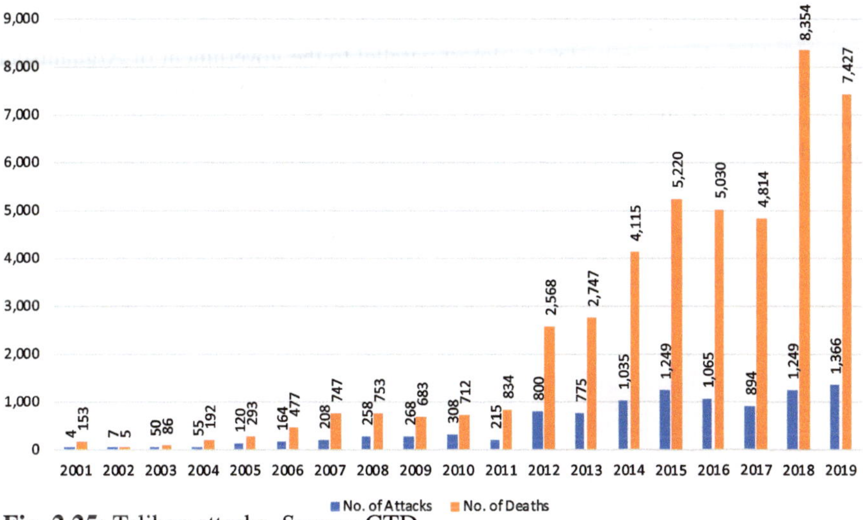

Fig. 2.25: Taliban attacks. *Source*: GTD

Like Hezbollah in Lebanon or Hamas in Gaza, Taliban participated in local governance. It is important to understand that it is a legitimate stakeholder in the Afghanistan political power structure, and we must understand that if it did not fight the allied forces, it would have faced strong resentment from within and considered as traitors. However, importantly and unlike al-Qaeda or ISIS, Taliban's aim is local. Indeed, Taliban is *not* considered as a direct enemy of the USA, nor is it even listed as an FTO by the USA[143]

2.8.6.2 Governance and Provision of Public Goods and Services

Concurrent with terror attacks, Taliban provided governance, law and order and safety of convoys and movement of ordinary people. Widespread corruption by the bureaucracy fueled Taliban's influence. Based on interviews with more than 160 Taliban fighters, civilians, and government officials, Jackson (2018) provides some insights into the nature of governance by Taliban. In the areas where the government and aid agencies supplied public goods and services, Taliban forces "coopt and control them." Taliban set the rules of operation by these agencies. It directed these agencies to move into areas hitherto neglected. In government schools, Taliban controlled the syllabi and supervised the administration. Utility and communication sectors were (partially) regulated by Taliban too. In many situations, governance preceded the capture of a territory (Jackson, 2018).

Figure 2.26 is a color-coded district-wise "control/influence" map of Afghanistan, showing control areas of Taliban starting from the pre-*9/11* era. The darker the region, the more is the degree of control by Taliban. It is easy to see progression. A large

143 It is listed as an armed insurgent group. Joe Biden, who was the Vice President of the USA in 2011, had said that "the Taliban per se is not our enemy."

fraction of districts were under some degree of Taliban's control even back in 2012. Thus, Taliban has a strong force, almost parallel to the government of Afghanistan for years even prior to 2021. Figure 2.26 underscores further that military victory by the USA and allied forces was not in sight despite their presence for nearly two decades.

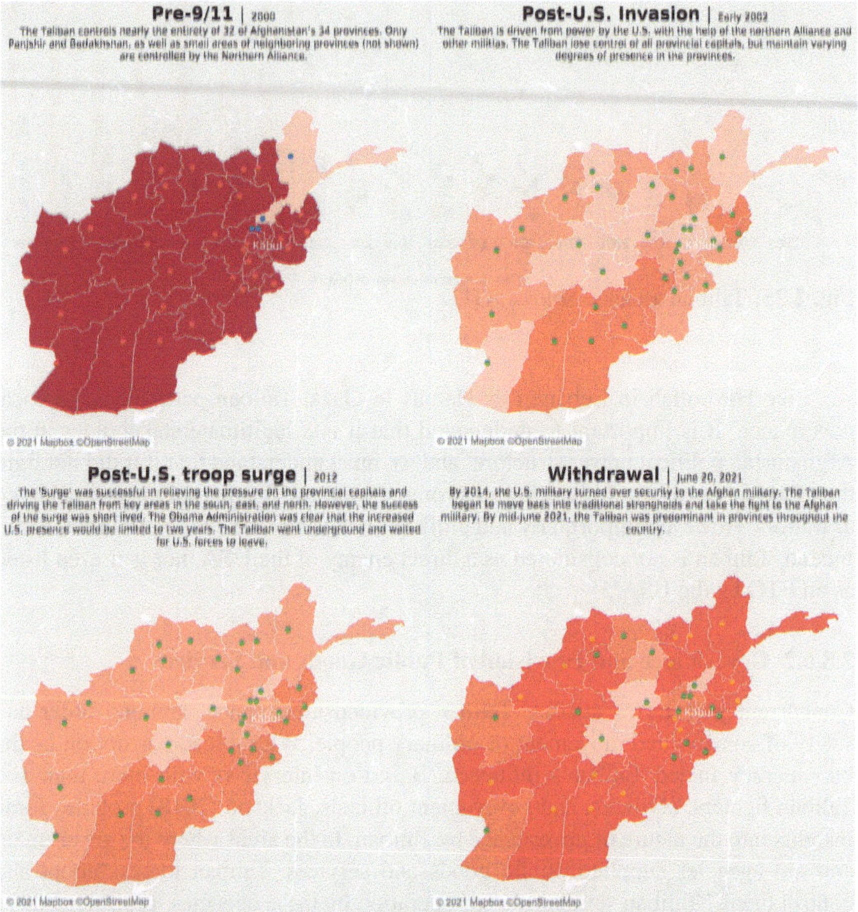

Fig. 2.26: District-wise control/influence map of Afghanistan. *Source:* FDD's long war journal; downloaded on November 19, 2021 from https://fdd-long-war-journal.github.io/2000-2020-Afghanistan/. The Foundation for Defense of Democracies (FDD) is a non-profit, non-partisan 501(c)3 policy institute focusing on foreign policy and national security. Founded in 2001, FDD combines policy research, democracy and counter-terrorism education, strategic communications, and investigative journalism in support of its mission to promote pluralism, defend democratic values, and fight the ideologies that drive terrorism

2.8.6.3 Funding

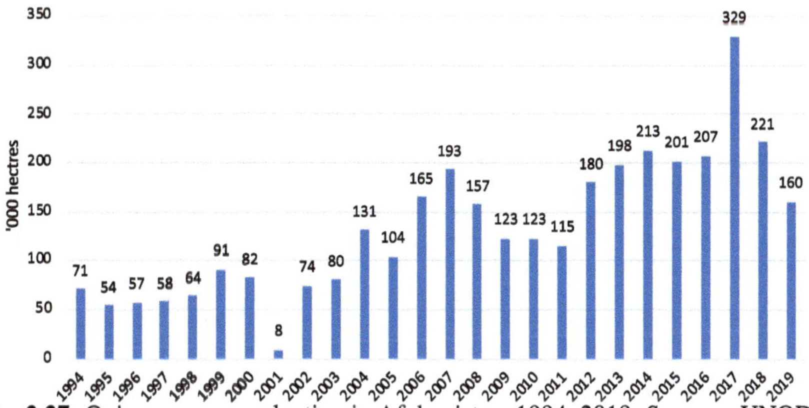

Fig. 2.27: Opium poppy production in Afghanistan, 1994–2019. *Sources*: UNODC, Afghan office survey, various years

The principal sources of funding for Taliban have been opium production and trade, external support and protection taxes.

Opium Production and Trade This was the largest source of revenues for Taliban. The morphine alkaloid content in opium is used to prepare heroin. As mentioned in Chap. 1, Taliban members did *not* directly produce opium leaves or engage in trafficking in opium poppies and heroin. Instead, they controlled and charged a protection tax from the farmers who grow opium poppies as an *usher* tax—up to 10% under Sharia law—paid in cash or in kind in terms of crops (which is stored in warehouses for future sale). In addition, as poppy crops are transported, Taliban charged up to 20% on consignment in return for safety of transit. Furthermore, it also levied protection fees for running heroin refineries located in Afghanistan (Peters, 2009).

Figure 2.27 depicts a time series plot of opium poppy production in Afghanistan over the period 1994–2019. According to the "2017 World Drug Report" of the UN Office on Drugs and Crime (UNODC), Afghanistan is the largest producer and exporter of opium in the world and responsible for the production of approximately 90% of the world's heroin. Zehorai (2018) states that the net value of opium exports alone constituted around 12% of the country's GDP. A report presented to the UN's Security Council states that roughly three out of eight million Afghani workforces were directly or indirectly employed by the drug industry.

Back in 2008 opium trade financed 40% of the Taliban's operations (Institute for Economics & Peace, 2014b). According to Tomas Olivier, a counter-terrorism expert, Taliban's revenue from opium production and trade reached somewhere between $100 million and $400 million per year in early 2010s (Dominguez, 2016).

It is interesting as well as important to understand how the opium production, the war in Afghanistan and Taliban, are intertwined over time. See *Supplement Break* 2.7.

Supplement Break 2.7: Opium Production and Taliban

The golden crescent consisting of Iran, Afghanistan, and Pakistan is known for opium poppy production. As the Soviet occupation in Afghanistan destroyed thousands of acres of farm land, poppy production—as a cash crop—rose steadily in Afghanistan. Between 1984 and 1986, it went up almost four times. Sale of opium poppy and heroin consistently financed the mujahideen commanders. Figure 2.7 charts the graph of opium production from 1994, the year Taliban came to power in Afghanistan. By 1999, Taliban had controlled most of the country and opium fields and Afghanistan produced about 75% of the total world produce of opium and 97% of it was grown in Taliban controlled areas. Taliban was already using it via extortion to finance itself and, in return, provided safety to public and commerce from regional warlords. By that time, Osama Bin Laden was the number one enemy of the USA, who was using Afghanistan as al-Qaeda's base. There was informal contacts between the USA and the Taliban through various channels. According to Teresita Schaffer, a former deputy assistant secretary of state for South Asia, the official position of the USA toward Taliban was that "we don't like you but we're willing to live with you if you give us al-Qaeda." In the meantime, the UN imposed sanction against the Afghan official airliner Ariana on the grounds that it was moving drugs, terrorists, and weapons. This hurt Taliban. At the same time, the UN continued to exert pressure on Taliban to clamp down on opium production, while Taliban needed international recognition. An agreement was reached, and Mullah Omar announced a total ban on the production of opium. Notice from Fig. 2.7 that, from 82,000 hectors in 1999, opium production in 2000 fell to 8000 hectors, most of it was being produced in areas not controlled by the Taliban. This was indeed confirmed by UN ground surveys and satellite photos.[a]

As Peters (2009) describes, it led to a humanitarian crisis as thousands of farmers became nearly income-less. The small farmers and share croppers "needed" opium production for their livelihood. Taliban too needed more resources for insurgency against the *9/11*-triggered occupation by the US and allied forces and the government of Afghanistan who supported the occupation. Both factors led to a rebound of opium production. By 2003, opium production nearly reached its level back in 2000 before Taliban had called for the ban of opium cultivation. Since then and till 2017, it has maintained a strong upward trajectory, reaching in 2017 a level that is nearly four times that in 2003. Since 2017, there is a decline in the cultivation of poppy. Whether it is transitory or a more sustained trend remains to be seen.

In any event, poppy production has remained a major source of funds for Taliban. It was not only a profitable business for farmers and Taliban but also (allegedly) supported by the country's administration that received its own share of bribery rent from the opium cultivation. As of early 2021, Taliban controlled all aspects of poppy production and processing and transport of heroin (SIGAR, 2021).
Sources: Peters (2009) and Clarke (2015).

---

[a] It is alleged that Taliban knowingly manipulated to reduce poppy production so as to gain from a price increase. It is estimated that Taliban's call for ban on poppy increased the price of poppy by 1000% (Clarke, 2015).

It is worth noting that while the USA had intelligence over the locations of the poppy fields, it did not target them militarily lest it should destroy the livelihood of farmers and thus turn the public opinion hostile toward the USA. In late 2017 the USA began to bomb, for the first time, the Taliban-controlled drug labs that processed the poppy seeds. Initially thought to be a game changer, it did not make any dent on drug processing. The bombing campaign, code-named *Iron Tempest*, was quietly abandoned in early 2019.

External Support and Donations This is believed as the second largest source of revenues for Taliban. According to Clarke (2015) and other sources, Taliban fighters received external support from ISI-Pakistan, although Pakistan has denied these claims. Further, it has also received support from Saudi Arabia in the form of weapons, ideological support, safe haven, *and funding*. Clarke (2015) reported that at one point of time 15% of Taliban's income came from donations from sympathizers in the Middle East. The network included businessmen from Karachi, goldsmiths in Peshawar, Pakistan military and intelligence services, and oil tycoons in Saudi Arabia and Kuwait. Some reports indicate the Taliban also solicited donations from local mosques and businessmen in dire times.

Extortion Taliban collected protection taxes and extortion money from sectors other than poppy production. For instance, in a secret meeting in December 2015, Taliban demanded a hefty new protection tax from Afghan telecom companies for not attacking towers and kidnapping employees (Dominguez, 2016). A significant source of Taliban's revenue came from the taxation of the general population in the areas of control, collected under the auspices of Islamic taxes. U.N. Security Council (2012) revealed that the Taliban collected *ushr* of 10% on harvest and *zakht* on personal and business wealth. It took payments for dispensing with justice and usage of water and electricity. Even supply trucks used by combat forces in Afghanistan paid protection taxes to Taliban (Dominguez, 2016).

KFR and Legal Businesses There is evidence that Taliban have engaged in KFR. For example, it captured an Italian journalist in 2006 and an Italian–Swiss journalist in 2007. The Italian government apparently paid (but it denied) $2.8 million and $2 million for these individuals, respectively. However, Taliban acknowledged that it was rewarded handsomely. More recently, Reuters (August 20, 2018) reported kidnapping of nearly 200 people traveling in bus for a holiday.

Legal businesses too have supported Taliban (Clarke, 2015). There were over 3500 export–import companies located near Chaman border between Afghanistan and Pakistan, having links with Taliban. UAE is a common destination for Afghan front companies, through which millions of dollars were reportedly laundered.[144]

[144] The art of front company is that a fictitious company is registered first. Next, an employment visa is procured for the director of the company, and then the director is paid handsomely as salaries, which are used to funds illegal activities.

Overall According to Zehorai (2014), in 2014 Taliban was the fifth richest terror organization in the world with an estimated revenue of $400 million per year.[145] By the end of 2017 it climbed to No. 2 position with $800 million (Zehorai, 2018). More recent reports suggest that Taliban is "mega-rich." According to Sufizada (2020) and other sources, Taliban's budget during April 2019 to March 2020 was $1.6 billion.[146]

2.8.6.4 Peace Efforts, The Leap Day Accord and Afterwards

In 2012 Taliban opened an office in Qatar to initiate talks with the USA regarding the political future of Afghanistan. However, the talks failed as the US administration could not complete a prisoner swap (New York Times, 2012). The first round of new talks between them began in 2015. While the talks were underway, Taliban announced the death of its leader Mullah Omar and the talks ended. Apparently, this was a result of a sharp division in opinion among Taliban members on the talks with one faction supporting the peace talks and others opposing on the grounds that Taliban was succeeding in the battlefield. Another initiative was undertaken by Afghanistan, the USA, China, and Pakistan in 2016. This failed too as the Taliban leader Mullah Mansoor was killed by a US drone strike. However, Taliban maintained a back-channel diplomacy and private talks with the USA and the Afghan government without much public information.

Shortly after a deadly early-2018 attacks by Taliban, the Afghan President Ghani offered peace talks, only to be rejected by Taliban, who said they would, instead, talk directly to the USA, the occupier.[147] A major publicly announced initiative was undertaken by the Trump administration in September 2018 when it appointed Zalmay Khalildad, an Afghan-origin American citizen and a former US ambassador to Afghanistan and Iraq, as the US Special Representative for Afghan Reconciliation. This was welcomed by Taliban. Several rounds of talks took place.[148] These negotiations were conspicuous by the absence of the Afghan government as Taliban remained opposed to it. Another major development occurred in early 2019 when Mullah Abdul Ghani Baradar, the co-founder of Taliban, joined the talks (after being

[145] Institute for Economics & Peace (2016b) also reported that during 2015, Taliban's estimated revenues were around $400 million, the principal source of which was smuggling opium and heroin.

[146] This was stated by Mullah Yaqoob, the son of Mullah Omar. Apparently, this information was obtained by NATO, which was passed on to Radio Free Europe/Radio Liberty, a US government financed news media.

[147] Around the same time, Kay Bailey Hutchison, the US Permanent Representative to NATO, confirmed that some initial contacts were made with Taliban. In mid-2018 President Ghani declared eight days of unilateral ceasefire. Taliban reciprocated it in three of the eight days that coincided with the holy Muslim festival of Eid ul-Fitr. Militants were seen mingling with civilians and taking selfies. Government security officers and Taliban fighters even smiled at one another.

[148] In 2018, Russia also involved itself in a political settlement in Afghanistan. Talks, not negotiations, were held in Moscow in November 2018. The Afghan government did not participate. Taliban was present along with Afghanistan's High Peace Council, a collective body in Afghanistan whose aim was to reach out to Taliban. There were eleven observer countries including the USA, China, and India. Taliban reiterated its position that foreign troops including the US forces must leave Afghanistan, and it wanted to engage in direct talks with the USA, not the Afghan government.

quietly released from a Pakistani prison in October 2018) as the new head of the Taliban team.

After at least a dozen rounds of talks punctuated by several interruptions and diplomatic efforts, a historic agreement was reached between the USA and the Taliban on the leap day of 2020 (when the world's preoccupation with corona virus had already begun but the virus was not yet seen as a major threat to the USA). I call this the ***Leap Day Accord***. Formally called the Agreement for Bringing Peace in Afghanistan, it was signed by Zalmay Khalilzad, and the Taliban leader Baradar in the presence of the Secretary of State Michael Pompeo, Qatar's Deputy Prime Minister Sheikh Mohammed bin Abdulrahman al-Thani, and many diplomatic dignitaries from around the world.[149] As a key facilitator for both the USA and the Taliban, Pakistan played a vital role in effecting the agreement.

The accord was a product of weariness of the USA (without any visible sign of victory), Taliban (which understood its inability to defeat the USA and the allied forces), and the Afghan people (tired of being subjected to foreign occupation of one kind or another since 1979).

The Leap Day Accord was not a final deal, but it exuded serious intent by both sides to end the longest war in the history of America. This is why it was historic. Apart from prisoner swaps, it stipulated a full withdrawal of American and allied forces within fourteen months, and in return, Taliban must deliver three things: (a) renunciation of violence, (b) talks with the Afghan government, and (c) a pledge "to prevent any group or individual, including al-Qaeda from using the Afghan soil to threaten the security of the United States and its allies."

By the end of 2020, the Taliban released 1000 Afghan security personnel and the Afghan government released 5000 Taliban prisoners, as stipulated in the Leap Day Accord. Negotiation between the Afghan government and the Taliban began in September 2020.[150] At the same time, Taliban continued to attack and kill personnel associated with Afghan government and military. But it did not target Americans or their facilities and equipment—which was a part of the deal. As Fig. 2.24 shows, the size of the US forces in Afghanistan as of mid-2020 stood at 8600.[151] In November 2020, the USA announced its intention of withdrawing troops from Afghanistan "by

[149] The signing ceremony took place at the Sheraton Hotel in Doha, Qatar in the afternoon of February 29, 2020. Before the deal was signed, Secretary Pompeo gave a speech with cautionary notes such as "This agreement will mean nothing and today's good feelings will not last if we don't take concrete action on commitments stated and promises made." He did not clap when the Taliban leader spoke briefly, nor did he shake hands with him whereas he was seen warmly mingling with others. After the signing ceremony, chants of "God is Great" and claims of victory in ending American "occupation" by the Taliban leaders were heard. It was the first time for a cabinet-rank official of the USA to meet-without-greet, or, at least, be in the civil company of, the leaders of a violent terror group that has killed over 2400 US service men. There are unconfirmed reports at the time that President Trump will meet Taliban leaders "soon."

[150] According to National Public Radio (2020), the talks quickly bogged down on issues like which type of Islamic law should apply to the disputes between the negotiators. But, commitment and progress in talks have been expressed by the Afghan government, Taliban, and the US special representative Khalildad.

[151] Since 2017, the US Department of Defense has stopped reporting personnel information on operations in Afghanistan, Iraq, and Syria.

thousands" in the very near future and, particularly, about 2000 of 4500 US troops to be recalled by January 2021. Renouncing Trump administration's condition-based withdrawal approach, the Biden administration announced a complete withdrawal of American troops (numbering around 2500) and allied troops from Afghanistan by the end of August 2021. This was consistent with the Trump administration's treaty with Taliban.

The turmoil in Afghanistan since August 2021 is well-known. To everyone's surprise, in almost "no time" and facing little resistance from the Afghan armed forces, Taliban captured most of Afghanistan including its major cities.[152] In September 2021, Taliban declared Afghanistan as an "Islamic Emirate." The political scene of Afghanistan may take several turns in the near future even before the book goes into print.

2.8.7 Haqqani Network (HN)

This is another experienced insurgent group in Afghanistan that fought against the Afghan government and the US-led forces. It is believed that the former Afghan President Burhanuddin Rabbani was killed by this group back in 2011. The USA declared it as a foreign terror organization in 2012. While the Haqqani Network works under the umbrella of Taliban, it maintains a distinct command and control. Originally formed back in 1970 (much earlier than Taliban) with Jalaluddin Haqqani as its leader (Stanford University, 2017b), the group enjoys a safe haven in north Waziristan, Pakistan, across Afghanistan's south-eastern border. The Pakistani Army has consistently refused to launch any military operation in North Waziristan despite the presence of al-Qaeda's senior leadership. It is because the elements within the Pakistani security establishment view the Haqqani Network as a useful ally and proxy force to represent Pakistan's interests in Afghanistan. To this end, Haqqani forces have repeatedly targeted Indian infrastructure and construction projects in Afghanistan (Weinbaum and Babbar, 2016). It has an elaborate system of funding of its own, relying on security payments from local, regional, and international businesses that operate in its zone of influence; see Peters (2012) and Clarke (2015).[153,154] In the interim government announced by Taliban in September 2021, the head of the Haqqani Network, Sirajuddin Haqqani, is the acting interior minister.

2.8.8 Pakistani Taliban: Tehreek-e-Taliban Pakistan (TTP)

As American forces marched into Afghanistan in 2001, many members of Taliban retreated to the Federally Administered Tribal Area (FATA) in the north-western part of Pakistan (see Fig. 2.28). They used this area to launch attacks on allied forces in Afghanistan and form a movement of Islamic fundamentalism in Pakistan similar to

[152] President Ghani went to hiding at the same time.

[153] Although an insurgent group, compared to Taliban, the Haqqani Network's indiscriminate violence and brutality makes it look more like a criminal gang than an insurgent group.

[154] The USA believes that more recently the Haqqani Network might have allied itself more to al-Qaeda (Farmer and Yousafzai, 2021).

Fig. 2.28: Federally administered tribal area (FATA) in Pakistan. *Source*: Google map

Taliban in Afghanistan. It was in ISI-Pakistan's good books insofar as it supported Taliban in Afghanistan and did not target Pakistan for its attacks. Other militant, fundamentalist groups with ideologies similar to those of Afghan Taliban started to grow within Pakistan where a significant fraction of the population were leaning toward fundamentalist Islam. They were facilitated by the sense of resentment within Pakistan against the US sponsored or supported drone strikes and Pakistani army attacks in FATA in its quest to destroy the elements of al-Qaeda.

The situation came to a head in 2007 when, under the US pressure, General Musharraf ordered the Pakistan army to storm into the Red ("Lal") Mosque in Islamabad, known as *Operation Silence* (White, 2017, Chapter 11). The mosque had housed militants of extreme groups as well as students and clerics who had openly expressed their support for Taliban and al-Qaeda, and had called for Musharraf's assassination. The seize and fighting continued for eight days, leaving at least 87 dead (Masood, 2007).

This was a watershed event that united militant groups including Taliban forces in FATA, and Pakistani Taliban—Tehreek-e-Taliban Pakistan (TTP)—was born. It aims to drive out Pakistani forces from FATA, establish Sharia law, expel the US forces from Pakistan, and wage a war against the state of Pakistan. In 2010, the USA designated it as an FTO. TTP carried out several terror campaigns against the Pakistani government and its forces. In 2012, it shot Malala Yousafzai in her head. As a young girl, she had campaigned for education of women. She survived the head injury and later became a Nobel peace prize winner. In 2014, TTP attacked a primary school for the children of Pakistani forces in Peshawar, killing 132 students.

TTP's leaders have been killed by US drone strikes, with Mullah Fazlullah being the latest victim in 2018. TTP's new leader is Mufti Noor Wali Mehsud (Ahmad and Mehsud, 2018). U.N. Security Council (2020) reports more than 100 cross-border attacks by TTP's and a consolidation of splinter groups overseen by TTP, all this attesting to an increase in the strength of TTP.

The takeover of Afghanistan by (Afghan) Taliban in 2021 has reportedly encouraged TTP toward its goals.

2.8.9 Boko Haram

2.8.9.1 Narrative

It is one of the deadliest terror organizations since 2010. Based in Nigeria and founded in 2002 under the leadership of Mohammad Yusuf, Boko Haram means "Western education is forbidden."[155] It was established with the aim of replacing the secular system of government by Sharia law under the Salafi beliefs. Yusuf set up a religious complex in the Maiduguri, which included a mosque and an Islamic school. It enrolled the children of poor Muslim families from Nigeria and neighboring countries. In 2004, it was shifted to Yusuf's home state of Yobe near the Niger Republic border. Boko Haram's first known attack occurred in 2003 near the Niger border that involved about 200 militants. Multiple police stations were attacked. It is unclear whether Yusuf played any direct role in it. He later denied it, saying the youths involved had simply studied the Quran with him. Overall, in its initial phase–between 2002 and 2009—Boko Haram, for the most part, was focused on "withdrawal from the society" (Cook, 2011), meaning organizing schools and preaching extreme versions of Islam, while opposing Western education. At the same time, the government was cracking down the organization.[156] Not much else is known about the group's activity between 2002–2003 and 2009.

Following the reports of the group becoming more radical and armed, in 2009 the Nigerian government launched an investigation into Boko Haram's activities. There were heavy reprisals by the army in 2009 through a task force named *Operation Flush II*. Yusuf angrily denounced the security forces and called on his followers to protest against them. This turned into a sudden uprising, during which Yusuf was killed. It was a turning point. From being an indigenous Salafist group, it became a violent Salafist Jihadi group. Creation of an Islamic state through jihad emerged as Boko Haram's political goal. His hard-line deputy Abubakar Shekau became the group's spiritual leader (who was thought to be dead by the authorities). In the same year, the group named itself as Jama'atu Ahlis Sunna Lidda'awati Wal-Jihad, meaning "People Committed to the Propagation of the Prophet's Teachings and Jihad." Following the uprising, Boko Haram went underground for more than a year and re-emerged in 2010 with assassinations and a spectacular prison raid. More than 700 inmates, many of whom were Boko Haram members, escaped. Under Shekau's brutal leadership and increased strength, Boko Haram turned into an extremely violent group. In 2010

[155] Yusuf was highly educated, lived a lavish life, and drove a Mercedes Benz (Adebayo, 2014).

[156] The group is referred to sometimes as the Nigerian Taliban.

it declared its jihad against the government of Nigeria and the USA (Refer back to Fig. 2.19 for the steep rise of deaths due to Boko Haram attacks, beginning in 2010.) Its operations included military as well as civilian targets such as schools, bus stations, mosques, and churches. It did not distinguish between Muslims and Christians (Schultz, 2014), and its modus operandi were suicide as well as armed attacks.

The year 2014 marked Boko Haram's territorial expansion. It seized several towns in the northeast part of the country, pushing the Nigerian army to the verge of defeat. In the state of Borno, Boko Haram took the town of Gwoza without any resistance. In the same year, it was the deadliest terror organization in terms of deaths from terror attacks, eclipsing ISIS (see Fig. 2.19).[157] In 2015 it launched terror attacks in Burkina Faso, Cameron, Chad, Niger, and Nigeria. Estimated deaths from its attacks numbered over 5000, a close second to ISIS (Institute for Economics & Peace, 2016b). In the same year it pledged its allegiance to ISIS and recognized al-Baghdadi, the leader of ISIS, as the Caliph of Muslims. ISIS named it Wilayat Gharb Afriqiyyah, meaning Islamic State in West Africa Province (ISWAP).

However, in 2016, Boko Haram began to implode and weaken (Onuoha, 2016). The Multinational Joint Task Force (MNJTF) inflicted defeats to Boko Haram forces in several areas.[158] Despite allegiance to ISIS, differences started to surface between the two organizations. ISIS named Abu Musab al-Barnawi as the new leader of ISWAP, who, shortly after his nomination, made a caustic rejection of Shekau's leadership, lambasting him for targeting ordinary Muslims and promising to target the Christians. Shekau however continued to claim as the leader of Boko Haram. The pressure from the MNJTF and disputes with ISIS led to a fragmentation of Boko Haram in 2016.[159] Internal division and intense pressure from security forces targeting the group led to much fewer attacks and deaths due to Boko Haram in 2016 than in 2015 (see Fig. 2.19).[160]

Boko Haram mainly targets civilians. Between 2009 and 2016, its attacks claimed at least 20,000 lives, displaced more than 2.6 million people, created over 75,000 orphans, and caused about $9 billion worth of damage (Onuoha and Oyewole,

---

[157] In 2014, Boko Haram also kidnapped about 200 schoolgirls vowing to hold them as "wives" for its fighters (Martin, 2018).

[158] Headquartered in N'Djamena, the capital city of Chad, MNJTF is a military task force formed by the governments of Benin, Cameroon, Chad, Niger, and Nigeria to end Boko Haram's insurgencies. It evolved from a Nigerian task force constituted back in 1994 to deal with banditry activities in the northern border areas of Nigeria.

[159] Three separate factions were visible: the Shekau faction (the most and indiscriminatingly violent), the al-Barnawi group aligned with ISIS, and a third faction led by Mamman Nur, a Cameroonian, affiliated with al-Qaeda.

[160] ISWAP is regarded as the largest splinter group. GTD treats terror attacks by Boko Haram and ISWAP as those by Boko Haram (Institute for Economics & Peace, 2020b). In 2016, it committed 61% fewer attacks and was responsible for 80% fewer deaths when compared to the previous year (Institute for Economics & Peace, 2017).

2018).[161] Internal division did not spell the end of Boko Haram. During 2016–2019, it attacks claimed between 1000 and 2000 lives in every year; see Fig. 2.19.

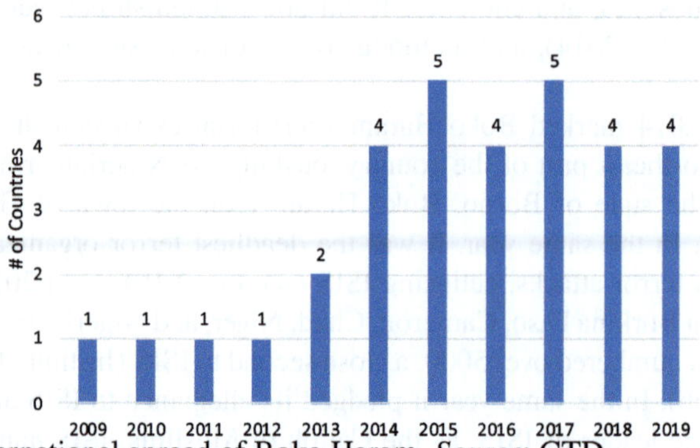

Fig. 2.29: International spread of Boko Haram. *Source*: GTD

2.8.9.2 International Spread of Boko Haram

Figure 2.29 shows the international spread of Boko Haram, and the country-wise number of attacks is shown in Table 2.4. We see that in the initial years, terror attacks by Boko Haram were confined to Nigeria. It activities started to spread across to neighboring countries in 2013. In 2015 and 2017, terror attacks by Boko Haram touched five countries.

2.8.9.3 Funding

Boko Haram has funded itself through illegal and legal means. The illegal channels include bank rubbery, KFR, trafficking, etc. As reported in Dingji Maza et al. (2020), bank robberies netted about $6 million between 2010 and 2013. Ransom demand for kidnapping ranged from $10,000 to $1 million. Boko Haram allegedly received €50 million for releasing 104 girls out of 106 in 2018. It engaged in narcotic trafficking from West Africa to Europe (Institute for Economics & Peace, 2014b). It is reported that it received $3 million from al-Qaeda as early as 2002, and in 2012, it received a much larger sum, $50 million from ISIS (Dingji Maza et al., 2020).

[161] GTD estimates of deaths from Boko Haram's attacks were in the 18,000s, less than the estimated reported by (Onuoha and Oyewole, 2018).

2009 Attacks		2010 Attacks		2011 Attacks		2012 Attacks		2013 Attacks		2014 Attacks	
Nigeria	10	*Nigeria*	18	*Nigeria*	127	*Nigeria*	424	*Nigeria*	232	*Nigeria*	436
								Cameroon	2	Cameroon	57
										Chad	1
										Niger	1

2015 Attacks		2016 Attacks		2017 Attacks		2018 Attacks		2019 Attacks	
Nigeria	404	*Nigeria*	169	*Nigeria*	275	*Nigeria*	207	*Nigeria*	269
Cameroon	71	Cameroon	53	Cameroon	55	Cameroon	18	Cameroon	34
Chad	27	Niger	17	Chad	1	Chad	7	Chad	14
Niger	39	Chad	4	Mali	1	Niger	10	Niger	28
Burkina Faso	1			Niger	6				

Table 2.4: Country-wise distribution of attacks by Boko Haram, 2007–2019. *Source*: GTD

Legal sources constituted a significant channel through which funds were raised by Boko Haram. It entered businesses-like phone centers and buying motor cycles and using it for commercial transportation in exchange for payments. It also controlled fishing business and agricultural production in the Lake Chad region. It received donation from shady charity organizations. The donors also included some well-known businessmen and politicians in Northern Nigeria.[162]

However, its financial structure of Boko Haram is not as sophisticated as that of ISIS. At the end of 2013, it ranked No. 10 among the top ten richest terror organizations (Zehorai, 2014). Its 2015 estimated revenues were $25 million (Institute for Economics & Peace, 2016b). Boko Haram's funding presumably shrank after 2016, although there are no estimates available.

2.8.10 Hamas

Hamas, meaning "Zeal" and an acronym for Harakat al-Muqawamah al-Islamiyya, or Islamic Resistance Movement, operates in the Gaza strip along the western flank of Israel and, to some extent, in the West Bank. These two regions are shown in Fig. 2.30. It has a base in Syria. There are evidences of Hamas operatives and sympathizers in Western Europe, the USA, and Latin America (Clarke, 2015).

2.8.10.1 Narrative

The Hamas movement originated in Gaza in 1987 by Imam Sheikh Ahmed Yassin and his aide Abdul Aziz al-Rantissi, shortly after the start of the First Intifada—the first Palestinian uprising against Israel's occupation of the Palestinian territories. Hamas is a Palestinian offshoot of Muslim Brotherhood (MB) in Egypt, which will be introduced shortly. The local organizers of MB urged its leader Yassin to endorse the Palestinian revolt and establish a militia, lest it would lose popular support to Fatah (already described in Sect. 2.7.5). After initial hesitations, Yassin agreed, and Hamas was born as a militant organization, calling for a violent opposition to Israeli occupation (see Encyclopedia Britannica and Berman and Laitin, 2008).

Muslim Brotherhood, initially a *non-violent* Islamic group, was established in Egypt in 1928 by Hasan Al-Banna. Its Arabic name is Ikhwan, and it aimed to (a) reinvigorate Islam through individual piety and self-improvement, i.e., *jihad* in its original and true meaning, (b) fight the insidious forces of assimilation into the "material" West, and (c) establish an Islamic state. It prohibited gambling, adultery, and usury and at the same time worked through a huge network of mosques and social service programs like schools of boys and girls, youth groups, clinics, hospitals, charities, and night school for workers. It earned widespread public support because of its social services. The MB also served as a forum for religious and political discourse and expression. However, in 1948 a splinter group within MB, called *Secret Apparatus*, killed the Egyptian Prime Minister Mahmoud al-Nuqrashi. As a result, MB fell out of favor from the Egyptian government. In 1950s an imprisoned

[162] One of them was Alhaji Buji Foi, the former Commissioner of Religious Affairs in Borno State (Dingji Maza et al., 2020).

Fig. 2.30: Gaza and West Bank. *Source*: Google map

member of Secret Apparatus, Sayyid Qutb, developed a theology of militant radical Islam. It was however rejected by Muslim Brotherhood on the grounds that Muslim theology is tolerant of other cultures, permitting warfare only as self-defense and rejecting violence in religious matters. A branch of MB appeared in Gaza and West Bank in the 1950s, which preached strict religious practices, dress codes, etc., and ran a huge network of social services. In 1971 Sheikh Ahmed Yassin founded an MB affiliate Congress, *Mujamah*, in Gaza. This branch of Muslim Brotherhood morphed into Hamas in 1987 (Berman & Laitin, 2008).

When Hamas came into being, it was welcomed by Israel thinking that it would serve as a counterbalance to Arafāt's PLO. Some argue that it is Israel's policy that helped to create Hamas (Tharoor, 2014a). On the contrary, Hamas called for the conquest of all Palestine territory that includes Israel and engaged in suicide attacks against Israel in the First Intifada (December 1987–September 1993).[163] The Intifada claimed many more Palestinian lives than Israeli ones, as the Israeli military responded to the protests by a heavy handed retaliation.

Later, Hamas opposed and attempted to rock the Oslo accord, signed in 1993 between Israel, Egypt, and PLO that recognized PLO as the main political authority of Palestinians. In a short time, Hamas became the singularly effective "rebel" organization vis-à-vis PLO: well trained, close-knit, well funded, and hard to penetrate. The Hamas members battled with Israeli soldiers and killed collaborators and Israeli

[163] The First Intifada began with non-violent actions like mass boycotts and Palestinians refusing to work jobs in Israel and attacks on Israelis by using rocks, Molotov cocktails, and occasionally firearms.

civilians. Its suicide bombing of buses in Israel in 1996 tilted Israeli election toward political right.

The Second Intifada began in 2000 with Ariel Sharon's visit of the Temple Mount in East Jerusalem. The visit seemed designed to display Israeli sovereignty over Muslim holy sites and was provocative. This prompted the birth of a new militant group, the al-Aqsa Martyrs Brigades, described earlier.[164] As soon as the entourage of Sharon began to enter the holy Temple Mount, fights broke out between the Palestinians and the security forces guarding Sharon. Seven Palestinians lost their lives, triggering the Second Intifada (Al Jazeera, 2003). While this was the immediate cause, the deeper cause was a sense of disappointment and discontent by Palestinians in the self-rule territories. They became increasingly resentful over their lack of economic development as promised by the Oslo peace accord. The Second Intifada lasted till 2005 and Hamas was at the center of it. Suicide terrorism was, again, the dominant tactic used (Matta & Rojas, 2016). The Second Intifada yielded a concrete outcome: Israeli forces withdrew completely from Gaza in 2005.

At the same time, Hamas became larger, entered politics and fought elections. As described earlier in Sect. 2.7.5, in 2006 Hamas won a slight majority of the seats in the Palestinian Authority legislative elections. This would have put Hamas in a commanding position in both the Gaza and West Bank, but there was a problem. Hamas refused to accept the previous deals that the PA had negotiated with Israel. That led Western powers to freeze out aid, which the PA depends on. Tensions between the PLO and Hamas escalated to a war between them, which, in 2007, ended up in Hamas governing Gaza independently from the West Bank-based PLO. The Gaza strip became Hamas's "homeland." At the same time, Israel imposed a blockade on the movement of goods between Israel and Gaza (except food and medical supplies) on the grounds that Hamas could use those goods to make weapons to use against Israel.

Since 2007, Hamas-in-Gaza and Israel have fought three "wars." Named after the Israeli military operations, these are (a) *Operation Cast Lead*, a three-week conflict in 2008–09 (known also as *Gaza War*, *Gaza Massacre* or *Battle of al-Furqan*), (b) *Operation Pillar of Defense* in 2012, and (c) *Operation Protective Edge*, alternatively *Operation Strong Cliff* or 2014 Gaza War.[165] The 2014 Gaza war lasted 51 days and left the Gaza devastated. More than 2000, mostly civilians and including 500 children were killed and another 100,000 displaced. Many secret tunnels beneath the ground that were built to overcome the land blockade were blown up. However, Hamas celebrated the war as "victory" because Gaza and Hamas survived. These wars were quite asymmetric in terms of the use of technology: high-tech Air Force bombing by Israel versus rockets and mortars and incendiary kites and balloons by Hamas.[166]

Because of the 2014 Gaza war, blockades imposed by Israel, pressures from PA and Egypt (see "Financing" below), the coffers of Hamas as well as the economy of Gaza began to suffer badly. Hamas eschewed its aggressive stance and reached

[164] Named after this group, the Second Intifada is also called al-Aqsa Intifada.

[165] In January 2008 Israel also led *Operation Hot Winter*.

[166] Flaming kites caused numerous wildfires and spread anxiety for Israeli population living close to Gaza.

a treaty with the Fatah/PA in 2017, which essentially forced Hamas to concede an upper hand to the PA in the administration of Gaza. Furthermore, in 2017 Hamas issued a political document effectively claiming to have broken ties with MB, its parent organization, a move apparently aimed at improving ties with Gulf Arab states and Egypt.[167] It has apparently accepted the notion of a Palestinian state in the West Bank and Gaza Strip only on the basis of 1967 border, although Hamas still refuses to recognize the legitimacy of the Israeli state and calls for the return of Palestinian refugees to Israel.[168]

By 2018, the economy of Gaza reached a dire state. With Hamas' encouragement, thousands of Gazans descended on the barrier separating Gaza from Israel in a series of peaceful protests, called *Great Return March*—aimed at drawing attention to the poor living conditions in Gaza, pressurizing Israel to open blockade, and showing a symbolic gesture toward reclaiming the lands in Israel that belonged to their grandparents. Israel fired back, leading to a bloodshed. Many feel that this was an overreaction on the part of Israel but Israel's contention was that two million people trying to cross the border cannot simply be deterred peacefully. Hamas threatened Intifada if the USA would recognize Jerusalem as Israel's capital. In mid-2018 the USA moved its Israeli embassy to Jerusalem, which effectively endorsed the US recognition of Jerusalem as Israel's capital. But no Intifada is in sight till date of writing this chapter.

Apparently, an informal "understanding" was reached between Israel and Hamas sometime in 2019 and to paraphrase Estrin (2020), "Strawberries and snacks from Gaza may now be sold abroad. Gazan fishermen can venture farther into the Mediterranean for a better catch. Thousands of unemployed Palestinians are suddenly allowed to leave the territory to work in Israel after more than a decade."

Hamas maintains its confrontational stance against Israel. During Covid-19 pandemic in 2020, it served a warning to Israel that if respirators and other medical aid are not supplied to Gaza to fight the virus, then Hamas would take extreme actions against Israeli citizens (Al Jazeera, 2021).

2.8.10.2 Public Service

Hamas has provided social services to Palestinians for a long time. They particularly expanded during the 1990s as Hamas began to grow in the West Bank and particularly in Gaza. By 2006, it was providing educational services, running summer camps, and providing food to the poor through affiliated charity organizations (Szekely, 2015). These activities were at least partly responsible for its (narrow) political victory in Gaza over Fatah in 2006. After it took over the political control of Gaza in 2007, it began to offer a wider and an efficient network of administrative, cultural, and social

[167] In a policy document presented in Doha by its leader Khaled Meshaal, Hamas said it would end its "umbilical chord" with the MB.

[168] This move has stirred fears among its loyalists that Hamas was giving up on the Palestinian cause. In response, Hamas has added the following clause: "Hamas rejects any alternative to the full and complete liberation of Palestine, from the river to the sea but considers the establishment of a sovereign Palestinian state on 1967 borders to be a formula of national consensus."

services to the population of Gaza—mostly refugee families from the Israel–Arab wars back in 1948—as an alternative to the deeply corrupt PA institutions.[169]

2.8.10.3 Funding

State Support Between 1987 and 2006, Hamas's chief patron for funding was Saudi Arabia, whose share was more than 50% of the Hamas's operating budget of $10 million per year (van Natta Jr. and O'Brien, 2003). After *9/11*, the Saudi portion of Hamas funding grew larger as donations from the USA, Europe, and other Persian Gulf countries dried up. However, starting in 2004, Riyadh reduced this funding, in part because, in the wake of *9/11* attacks in which most of perpetrators were Saudis, the Western countries began to closely scrutinize Saudi Arabia's financing of terrorist groups.[170]

However, when Hamas was elected to head the PA in 2006, Saudi Arabia publicly defied the US request to cut off funding to the group. In 2007, Riyadh helped negotiate what would be a short-lived coalition government between Fatah and Hamas. Even afterward when Fatah and Hamas fell out, Saudi Arabia maintained its financial support to Hamas, while emphasizing the importance of cooperation between the two rival groups.

It was at this point that Iran increased its support of Hamas, pledging $50 million aid per month (CNBC, 2017).[171] It was a strange relationship on paper: a Sunni Arab militant group receiving support from a Shi'ite Islamic Republic. But Iran was eager to exert any influence it could in Palestine in its quest to connect a crescent of Iranian satellites from Tehran to the Mediterranean. Iran provided both financial and military assistance to Hamas, and its influence over Hamas grew, much to Saudi Arabia's chagrin. This continued till 2012 when Hamas broke with the Assad regime in Syria partly because of the violent crackdowns Assad inflicted upon Sunni Muslims in Syria, which included displacement of the key members of Hamas's leadership stationed in Damascus and originally invited by Assad. This angered Iran and support from Iran started to ebb. Reportedly, Hamas managed to survive by support from Qatar and Turkey. The Iranian help to Hamas did not however dry up completely. During the 2014 Gaza War, Iran increased its funding to Hamas.

In the meanwhile, Saudi Arabia viewed Hamas with intense suspicion because Hamas was both an ally of Iran and an offshoot of the Muslim Brotherhood, a movement Riyadh has often viewed as a threat.[172]

---

[169] For instance, it revamped the police and security forces (Byman, 2010 and Roy, 2011).

[170] This is different from Saudi's official contribution to the Palestinian cause. The Saudi government claims that its support for Palestinian causes goes solely to the PA. For instance, it pledged $100 million to PA in 2013 (Reuters, 2013).

[171] During his trip to Iran in 2006, Ismail Haniyeh, the-then Prime Minister of Hamas, was believed to have received $36 million from Tehran (Frisch, 2009).

[172] Even more than Saudi Arabia or any other Arab government, the Egyptian regime sees Hamas as an enemy and a rival, in part because of its linkage to the Muslim Brotherhood, which poses a major threat to the regime in Egypt.

In 2017 Hamas and Iran relationship seemed to warm up. Iran apparently waived an earlier demand for Hamas to declare its support for Tehran in its struggle against Saudi Arabia. Further, Hamas's confrontation with Israel (e.g., three wars) is consistent with Iran's overall objective. At this point of writing, Iran, the Assad regime in Syria and Hezbollah appear to be aligned with Hamas.

In short, Saudi Arabia was a major financier of Hamas in earlier years, while more recently its biggest helping hand is Iran. There are allegations that Qatar also funds Hamas, which Qatar denies.[173] However, after the 2014 Gaza war, Qatar donated about $1 billion to Gaza for building new homes and fixing roads, and in 2018 it pledged $9 million to Hamas in order to avert a shutdown of emergency hospital generators in Gaza. According to ABC NEWS (2021), Qatar has provided $20 million per month, and for the year 2021, it has pledged $360 million to Hamas.

Palestinian Diaspora and Charities Hamas ran a sophisticated network to raise funds from the Palestinian diaspora in the Middle East, the Gulf, the USA, Canada, Western Europe, and parts of South America (the tri-border area).[174] Charities connected with Hamas have been identified in the USA, the UK, Germany, Denmark, Belgium, Netherlands, France, and some countries in Africa and Asia. For instance, an Islamic Charity named Holy Land Foundation for Relief and Development (HLFRD), based in Texas, was found contributing about $900,000 in 1999 and $2.4 million in 2000 to Hamas related accounts (Clarke, 2015). Increased scrutiny following *9/11* attacks led to the detection of HLFRD link to terrorism. In 2002 a jury in Chicago found HLFRD and the Quranic Literacy Institute, a non-profit organization based outside of Chicago, Illinois, tied to the death of David Boim who was shot by Hamas militants while waiting for a bus in Jerusalem in 1996 (Clarke, 2015).

Fraud At various points of time, the members and sympathizers of Hamas were involved in credit card, bank, cigarette, and food stamp frauds. For example, in 2005, two men from Michigan, USA, alleged to have links with Hamas, were convicted of mortgage fraud (Clarke, 2015).

Legal Businesses and Money Laundering Hamas was linked with many front companies alleged to have engaged in illicit revenue generation. A well-known front company was Sunuqrut Global Group, owned by Mazen Sunuqrut, a Hamas activist. An Internet company Infocom was indicted by a federal jury in 2002 for conspiring to conceal financial transactions with Mousa Abu Marzook, a well-known Hamas commander (Clarke, 2015). According to Zehorai (2014), Hamas directly ran a number of businesses in Gaza—namely, real estate, insurance, banking, hotels and tourism, fish farms, banquet halls, and so on.

[173] In a testimony in June 2018, Nikki Hailey, the US ambassador to the USA, stated that Qatar was "funding Hamas." But a few months later, she changed to say that "Qatar government does not fund Hamas" (Rogin, 2017).

[174] As a specific example, in 2003 an alleged Hamas conspirator, Jamal Akal, was arrested for planning to launch a terror attack in North America, relying upon funds by the Palestinian diaspora in Canada Clarke (2015).

Smuggling It has engaged in smuggling of drugs, arms, tobacco products, and counterfeit goods. Hamas allegedly uses its network of tunnels in Gaza for smuggling weapons (Clarke, 2015).[175]

Taxes and Fees There is no evidence of Hamas engaging in extortion and protection. Since it was politically ruling Gaza, it would obtain revenues from various legal taxes and fees, part of which would fund its violent activities. By 2014, 15% of Gaza's economy ended up in its pocket through taxes and levies including those on consumer goods entering the Gaza Strip, such as cigarettes and gasoline, and licensing fees for cars, motorcycles, and even carts (Zehorai, 2014).

Overall Financial State in Recent Times Zehorai (2014) listed Hamas as the second richest terror organization in the world presumably by the end of 2013, with an estimated turnover of $1 billion, about half of which came from taxes, fees, and duties, and from the businesses, it ran directly and indirectly. However, the tide of Hamas's fortune began to turn for the worse in 2014 as the 2014 Gaza war left Gaza and its economy devastated. Hamas was further squeezed from three fronts. First, the continuing Israeli blockades started to choke the already weakened Gazan economy.[176] Further, the power supply from the Israel was curtailed.[177] Second, the PA also cut back the salaries of its employees in Gaza by 20% in 2017 and slashed the PA staff numbers in Gaza from 60,000 by ordering early retirement for nearly a third of employees (Al Mughrabi, 2017). Both measures were designed to apply further financial pressure on the already financially weakened Hamas in order to force it to relinquish its control of Gaza. Third, Egypt too played a role. In 2013–2014, its military destroyed most of the 1200 smuggling tunnels connecting Gaza and Sinai, which were used to smuggle food, weapons, and other goods into Gaza and raised funds for Hamas in the form of *zakht.* In 2013 Egypt also had closed the Rafah border crossing, Gaza's main gateway to the outside world and the legal road passage to Egypt. This hurt Gaza's legal trade with Egypt, the effect of which was more painful to the already weakened economy of Gaza.[178]

A UN report of 2017 depicted an abysmal state of Gaza's economy and the lives of its population, with the poverty level approaching 40%. In 2018 the Gazan

[175] Hamas did engage in kidnapping but not for ransom. The motive was to secure the release of its members jailed earlier by authorities in different countries.

[176] Gaza typically exports strawberries and furniture to Israel through the Kerem Shalom crossing, which is the only commercial crossing between Israel and Gaza. Israel closed it on July 2018 on security grounds. It was reopened it a month later after the situation calmed down.

[177] Gaza's two million residents receive power from an electricity grid station, which is partly dependent on Israeli supplies. The bills of Israeli Electric Corporation (IEC) are paid by PA, not Hamas. But in 2017, the PA did not fully pay the bills on the ground that it was not reimbursed by Hamas. The Israeli government then directed the IEC to cut back on its supply of power to the grid in Gaza; see Al Mughrabi and Heller (2017). The power supply was restored back in early 2018.

[178] As noted earlier, Egypt's hostility toward Hamas stems from Hamas's link with the Muslim Brotherhood. Egypt also claimed that Hamas aided jihadists in Sinai.

economy shrunk by 3.1%, and it witnessed a marginally higher than zero growth rate in 2019 (World Bank, 2020).

The state of Gaza's economy is a major but not the only determinant of Hamas's finance. Zehorai (2018) estimated that Hamas's turnover in 2017 was about $700 million, made up from its business in Gaza, private donations, and the generous support from Iran. However, the continuing deterioration of Gaza's economy and economic sanctions on Iran are likely to further dry up funds for Hamas.[179]

2.8.11 Hezbollah[180]

2.8.11.1 Narrative

Hezbollah ("Party of God") operates mainly in Lebanon and Syria, while also active in Iraq and Yemen. The group's primary goals are: armed conflict against Israel, establishment of an Islamic-Shi'ite state in Lebanon, and implementation of the Iranian "Shi'ite Crescent" program (land bridge that connects Iran through Iraq to Syria, Lebanon, up to the Israeli border at Golan Heights). Unlike most Islamic terror groups that are Sunni, Hezbollah is a Shi'ite group.

It originated in 1982 from southern Lebanon and surprised and shocked Western forces with its capabilities. Right from start, it engaged in a deadly series of attacks including the 1983 suicide attack on a US Marine barrack that killed 241 service men. Its original members were some of the former seminary students who studied in Shi'ite holy cities of Najaf and Qom in Iran and who were expelled by Shah of Iran and Saddam Hussain. They came to Baalbek in Lebanon and later moved to the poor neighborhoods of Beirut inhabited by Shi'ites.[181] Like *Hamas*, it began as a non-violent religious group and, at some point, turned violent.

When Israel invaded Lebanon in 1982 to flush out Palestinian militants, it united the disenfranchised local Shi'ite population in southern Lebanon and facilitated Iran's Revolutionary Guard and Syria's Shi'ite regime to step in. Both countries needed a proxy to fight rather than to engage in a direct confrontation with Israel, lest they should be attacked by the USA or Israel. Hezbollah was formed as a response to the Israeli invasion—with the support of Iran's Revolutionary Guard and Syrian Baathists who are Shi'ites and who wanted to forge a relationship with Iran. While the Assad dynasty in Syria are the leaders of the Baathist party, which is secular, Hezbollah is not. It was inspired by two radical religious scholars: Ayatollah Khomeini of Iran and Mohammad Baqir al-Sadr of Iraq. In its initial phase it was led by Sheikh Mohammad Hassan Fadlallah, Abbas Musawi, and Hassan Nasrallah. Fadlallah was the spiritual leader, and Musawi facilitated the link with Iran, while Nasrallah was a military person who developed Hezbollah as a regional force. Starting out with a few hundred recruits, it expanded over time.

---

[179] A World Bank report updated on October 7, 2021 projected a mild contraction of the Gazan economy in 2021 because of the armed conflict with Israel in May 2021 that damaged infrastructure in Gaza.

[180] White (2017) contains a rich discussion of the history and organization of Hezbollah.

[181] Baalbek, a tourist attraction erstwhile, turned into a radicalized city over a few years.

After its pioneering 1983 suicide bombing, it kidnapped William Buckley, CIA station chief in Beirut in 1984, who died later in captivity. During the same year, a car explosion at the US embassy annexed in Beirut, attributed to Hezbollah, and claimed 24 lives. By the end of the Lebanese civil war in 1990, Hezbollah had become an important political player in Lebanon. But its violence continued. In mid-1990s, it executed a large number of high-profile attacks on Israelis and Jews. Hezbollah's popularity peaked in the late 1990s when its armed resistance against Israel's occupation of south Lebanon earned it immense admiration and sympathy. The Israeli occupation of southern Lebanon that started in 1982 ended in 2000, primarily due to Hezbollah's military strength.

The relatively quiet period and rapid growth in Lebanon beginning in 2000 ended in 2005 when President Hariri, a Sunni Muslim, was killed. An outrage over the killing, widely blamed on Syria, led to Syrian military's withdrawal and staged a confrontation between two groups to wrestle control of Lebanon. On one side was Hezbollah and its allies, backed by Syria and Iran; on the other, it was a coalition allied to Saudi Arabia and the West, led by Hariri's son and heir, Saad Hariri. A series of rocket attacks by Hezbollah in 2006 killed 12 Israeli army reservists and three civilians. An ambush ended in killing Israeli soldiers and taking two soldiers as hostages. Hezbollah demanded the release of its fighters imprisoned by Israel, to which Israel refused. A 34-day "Israeli-Hezbollah war" ensued, leaving more than a thousand dead, mostly Lebanese, and, displacing one and half million people including 300,000 to half a million Israelis. While the truce that concluded the Israeli–Hezbollah war called for restrictions on Hezbollah's military activities in southern Lebanon, it was not a defeated force by any means. Its survival against Israel's onslaught actually handed political dividends to Hezbollah. Following the war, a national unity government was formed in 2008, in which Hezbollah was accorded veto power in major political decisions and at the same time allowed to carry arms in order to "liberate and recover occupied lands."

Compared to Hamas, Hezbollah has a greater presence outside the Middle East. There is a tri-border region in Latin America overlapping Brazil, Argentina, and Paraguay, which is recognized as of one of the most ungoverned and lawless space in the world and where terror groups trained, plotted, and even raised money. It is also called the Triple Frontier. Interestingly, Hezbollah had a presence in Triple Frontier. Its attacks in these regions were financed by the local Lebanese diaspora. Hezbollah has also carried out attacks in Europe.

Hezbollah is a model example of a modern multi-tasking terror organization. It has four wings: military, political, social, and financial. The military wing, called Jihad Council, plans and carries out terror attacks. In the initial years bombing was its main tactics of terror: both suicide bombing and radio-controlled bombing for ambushes. Later, Hezbollah began to use rockets against the Israeli army.

While Israel is its prime enemy, it has also targeted Christians and other groups that are not supportive of its agenda. After the rise of ISIS in Syria, Hezbollah emerged as a stronger force in Lebanon. Hezbollah's international section or wing aids Iran to expand its political clout in the Middle East and elsewhere and at the same time serves as a buffer between Israel and Iran.

2.8.11.2 Governance and Social Services

Hezbollah's political wing, named Loyalty to the Resistance Bloc, represents Shi'ite Muslims in Lebanon. In 2018 elections, Hezbollah and its political allies secured at least 43 seats out of 128 in the Lebanese legislature, which allowed them veto power for passage of laws. This was hailed as a major victory by Hezbollah.[182]

Hezbollah runs a wide network of social services that includes managing nursing institutes, operating schools and hospital, and providing relief, welfare, and livelihood to large segments of the Shi'ite population in need. It is also involved in developing infrastructure in Lebanon. Through Hezbollah, Iran spends hundreds of millions of dollars on mosques, hospitals, schools, etc.

2.8.11.3 Funding

States and Diaspora Iran is Hezbollah's main benefactor. Levitt (2005) estimated that Hezbollah received between $200 and $350 million annually from Iran in the early 2000s. The level of support continued to remain the same in the earlier half of 2010s (Levitt, 2017). However, as of 2021, Iran's economy appears to suffer due to sanctions imposed by the USA. Hence, it is quite likely that Iran has curtailed its financial support to Hezbollah.

Apart from Iran, Hezbollah has received enormous financial support from Lebanese diasporas in different parts of the world (Clarke, 2015). Lebanese diaspora in Latin America helped in establishing a Hezbollah group in the Triple Frontier area overlapping Brazil, Argentina, and Paraguay, which attacked Israeli and Jewish population in Latin America in the mid-1990s. The Lebanese diaspora in Africa has also contributed funds to Hezbollah in Lebanon.[183] Israel claims that Hezbollah also collects huge amounts from the Lebanese expatriates living in the Senegal-South Africa belt in particular. In 2021, the USA imposed sanctions against Lebanon for its support to Hezbollah.

Charity Most notably, a charity organization called Bonyad-e Shahid, translating to "Martyrs Foundation", provided a substantial amount of financial and operational support to Hezbollah. It operated under different names in different countries. In Germany, it was known as the al-Shahid Social Relief Institution. Its satellite in the USA was the Goodwill Charitable Organization, based in Dearborn, Michigan (Clarke, 2015).

The Martyrs Foundation was involved in Hezbollah's conflict with Israel in July–August 2006 as well as financing for terror cells in Gaza related to both Hezbollah and Palestinian Islamic Jihad (PIJ). Money from the tri-border, South America has been traced directly to Martyrs foundation. According to Levitt (2005), the

---

[182] This politically weakened Saad Hariri, the prime minister, and seemed to consolidate Iran's influence on Lebanese political affairs.

[183] This became evident in 2003 when a Beirut bound *Union Transport Africaines* flight crashed shortly after takeoff in Benin, West Africa, killing, among others, a Hezbollah foreign relations officer along with two aides. These officials were reportedly carrying cash of nearly $2 million dollars from donations in West Africa.

Martyrs Foundation openly conceded to supplying charitable funds to the families of Hezbollah suicide bombers.

Fraud Hezbollah operatives and sympathizers outside Lebanon have engaged in various types of frauds to raise funds. For instance, some members of the Lebanese-origin population in the greater Detroit area have been implicated in mortgage and credit fraud (Clarke, 2015).

Legal Business Hezbollah maintains a portfolio of businesses, spanning over the globe, which is used to launder money, disguise criminal activities, and evade authorities and law enforcement officials (Clarke, 2015). Front companies with links to Hezbollah include Tajco Company, LLC, a property developer in Lebanon and Arosfram, a food import company in Angola. Both companies were managed by Ali Tajideen and Husayn Tajideen, designated as Hezbollah fundraisers by the US Department of Treasury.

Money Laundering The Lebanese Canadian Bank (LCB) was accused of helping Hezbollah to launder its profits from cocaine trafficking by mixing drug proceeds with money earned through the sale of used cars purchased in the USA and resold in Africa. A Drug Enforcement Administration (DEA) investigation found that the LCB also did business with a Belgian diamond trader named Ibrahim Ahmad, whose clan (according to a UN report) had ties to Hezbollah and was involved in counterfeiting, money laundering, and diamond smuggling (Clarke, 2015).

Smuggling and Counterfeiting[184] In February 2003 alone, it is alleged that Hezbollah raised nearly $2 million through the illegal diamond trade. Many of these diamonds were mined in Sierra Leone and then transported through Liberia and Guinea before reaching the world market—cities including Antwerp, Dubai, London, Tel Aviv, New York City, and Mumbai. Antwerp is the center of the global diamond trade, and authorities there estimated that less than a third of $600 million worth of diamonds exported annually from Congo through illegal channels. According to a Belgian intelligence report dating back to 2000, individual Lebanese merchants and entire companies were linked to Hezbollah. Hezbollah was particularly active in the war-torn Democratic Republic of Congo over the years, where its members exploited the country's vast natural resources, which include not just diamonds but also gold, uranium, and tanzanite. Perhaps even more troubling, al-Qaeda reportedly used the same model and contacted as Hezbollah when operating throughout West Africa.

Hezbollah has been known to be associated with a wide range of counterfeit goods including fake Nike sneakers, unlicensed T-shirts, knockoff sports jerseys, DVDs, and so on. Considering all of Hezbollah's counterfeiting, smuggling, and trafficking operations, among the most lucrative scams, the group executed was a cigarette smuggling ring based in Charlotte, North Carolina. Cartons of cigarettes purchased in North Carolina for $14 could be sold in Michigan for twice as much. In

[184] Almost entirely based on Clarke (2015).

all, it is believed that Hezbollah earned tens of thousands of dollars by transporting and selling untaxed cigarettes throughout the United States.[185]

Revenues in Recent Years As noted in Chap. 1, Hezbollah's annual turnover in 2014 was around $400 million, and it reached $1.1 billion in 2017 (Zehorai, 2014, 2018). However, in 2018 the Trump administration levied a series of sanctions against Iran as well as individuals and businesses linked with Hezbollah. According to Sly and Haidamous (2019) there are indicators supporting that sanctions have hard-hit Iran as well as Hezbollah beginning in Fall 2019. For instance, many Hezbollah fighters have been furloughed or kept as reserves. Al-Manar, the TV station financed by Hezbollah, has cut many programs. The group's economic assistance to the poor Shii'te population in Lebanon has been curtailed.

Notwithstanding the recent financial sanctions by the US government on Iran that has hit Hezbollah, it has progressed with various social and health-related programs. It has established a new grocery chain called, Al-Nour Markets. For its members and employees, it has devised a new social security plan through promoting the use of the Al-Sajed card. It has also created a parallel financial system (Ghaddar, 2020).

2.8.12 Kata'ib Hezbollah

Kata'ib Hezbollah (also KH, Hezbollah Brigades, or Brigades of the Party of God) is an Iranian-backed, Iraqi Shi'ite paramilitary founded by Abu Mahdi al-Muhandis in 2007 (Stanford University, 2016a). Relatively unknown, in its initial years it targeted the USA and coalition forces in Iraq and carried out some of the most lethal attacks against them. Later, the Iraqi government joined its list of targets, since it supported the coalition forces. As the Syrian civil war broke out, it was one of the first groups that fought alongside the Assad regime. According to Zehorai (2018), it has about 400 fighters; its goals are similar to those of Hezbollah, but it does not have a political wing. Funded by Iran and illegal means like KFR, it figured as the seventh richest terror organization by the end of 2017, according to Zehorai (2018).

2.8.13 Palestinian Islamic Jihad (PIJ)

2.8.13.1 Narrative[186]

Inspired by the Iranian Revolution, PIJ, whose native name is Harakat al Jihad al Islam fi Filistin, branched out of Muslim Brotherhood in 1979. Its founders, Fathi Shaqaqi, Bashir Moussa, and Abd al-Aziz Awda, were students in Egypt and members of the Egyptian Muslim Brotherhood until the late 1970s when they decided that the brotherhood was becoming too moderate and insufficiently committed to the Palestinian cause (BBC News, 2003). PIJ was opposed to any two-state solution

[185] Hezbollah also engaged in kidnapping. But, according to Clarke (2015), kidnapping by Hezbollah was less about collecting a ransom and more about terrorizing Israelis living abroad and acquiring persons that can be traded in future swaps for imprisoned terrorists.

[186] Based on BBC News (2003), The Mackenzie Institute (2016b) and Levin (2018).

of the Palestine–Israel issue. It sought to destroy Israel militarily and reestablish a sovereign Palestinian state with the geographic borders of the pre-1948 Palestine.

In 1981 it was implicated in the killing of the Egyptian President Anwar Sadaat and was expelled from Egypt. It moved to Gaza and remained there until 1987, when, due to ideological difference with Hamas, it moved from Gaza to Lebanon.[187] Since then, there have been occasional conflicts between Hamas and PIJ, but, for the most part, they have coordinated their attacks on Israel. It does not seek political representation within the PA. In 1989 PIJ moved its headquarters to Damascus, while still maintaining its presence in Lebanon.

While in Lebanon, the PIJ leadership cultivated a relationship with Hezbollah and received training from the Iranian Revolutionary Guards. The PIJ was accused of attempting to hinder the efforts of the 1993 Oslo Accords by launching several terrorist attacks on Israeli targets. The continued presence in southern Lebanon allowed the PIJ and Hezbollah to launch joint attacks on Israeli targets in the 1990s. At the same time, PIJ coordinated with Hamas too.

Since the 1990s, PIJ's military wing, the al-Quds brigades, has been responsible for dozens of suicide bombings against Israeli targets. In 1995, it carried out a series of attacks against Israeli service men (Levin, 2018). During the same year, PIJ's leader Shaqaqi was assassinated in Malta, reportedly by Mossad. He was replaced by one of his deputies, Ramadan Shallah. In 1997, the USA designated PIJ as an FTO. Hamas and PIJ coordinated their attacks during the Second Intifada too.

In 2012, PIJ reportedly relocated its headquarters from Damascus to Tehran because of the civil war in Syria. During the brief conflict between Israel and Gaza-based militants in 2012, Iran reportedly supplied PIJ with Fajr-5 rockets, having a range of up to fifty miles (Levin, 2018). As of 2013, the organization had less than 1000 members (The Mackenzie Institute, 2016b).

In contrast to Hamas, PIJ does not typically offer social services, although it provided food and other provisions in 2013 when Iran cut off funding to Hamas and pressed PIJ to compensate. PIJ distributed boxes of food with the PIJ logo and the Iranian flag (Levin, 2018).

2.8.13.2 Funding

Iran is the chief source of funds for PIJ (see Zehorai (2018) and Levin (2018)). But in 2015, Iran reportedly cut off funding to PIJ, because it refused to accept Tehran's involvement in Yemen in support of Shi'ite Houthis. However, after a declaration of loyalty to Iran, in 2016 Iran resumed its support for PIJ (Zehorai, 2018). Reportedly, Iran started to allocate $70 million annually. The decision followed a visit by a PIJ delegation to Tehran. According to Lieutenant General Gadi Eizenkot, chief of staff of Israel's armed forces, Iran increased funding to groups in the Gaza Strip starting

[187] Unlike Hamas, PIJ did not believe in the political process. PIJ identified with the Iranian concept of *waliyat al faqih*, which entrusts governance to clerics led by a supreme jurisprudence. Hamas rejected this notion.

in late 2017.[188] By the end of 2017, according to Zehorai (2018), PIJ ranked No. 8 among the richest terror organizations.

2.8.13.3 More Recent Status

In 2017, PIJ formed a joint command with Hamas to coordinate activities in Gaza, and it launched rockets into Israel in May 2018 (Levin, 2018). Its activities in more recent years remain unknown.

2.8.14 The Egyptian Islamic Group (IG)

This group with the native name of al-Gamaat al-Islamyya began as a radical umbrella for militant student groups in Egypt and was officially formed in early 1970s as a reaction to the Muslim Brotherhood's renunciation violence in 1970 (Stanford University, 2012). Instead of a centralized hierarchy it worked with a loosely connected network in several Egyptian cities. The group aimed to overthrow the Egyptian government and replace it with an Islamic state. It was indirectly involved in the assassination of the Egyptian President Anwar Saddat in 1981.[189]

From 1992 to 1998 the IG fought an insurgency against the Egyptian government, during which nearly 800 were killed, counting Egyptian policemen and soldiers, fighters of IG, and civilians including dozens of tourists.[190] A ceasefire negotiated with the government led to a split of the group in 1997. Those who denounced the peace treaty launched a deadly attack in 1997: *the massacre at Luxor*. Dressed as police, its members shot 58 foreign tourists, mostly of Swiss origin, and four Egyptian tourists visiting the Pyramids. They further attacked those wounded with knifes and mutilated the bodies of the dead. According to a BBC report, Luxor attack costs Egypt an estimated 50% of its average $3.7 billion tourism revenue in 1998. It took two years for the Egyptian tourism to rebound to the pre-Luxor attack numbers. The ghastly nature of this massacre and its major blow to the tourism industry dried out the sympathy for this group. It entered a ceasefire with the Egyptian government in 1999. By 2003, most members had renounced violence (The Economist, 1997 and Ashour, 2011).

In 2011 the organization reappeared in the media, forming its own political party known as the Building and Development Party. It was successful enough to gain seats in the lower house of the Egyptian Parliament in the 2011–2012 elections (Said Aly & Elkady, 2013). Recent whereabouts of this group are not known.

---

[188] In the words of Eizenkot, "In recent months, investment in the Palestinian arena has also been growing out of a desire to influence it—with an increase in the (annual) funding in the Gaza Strip for Hamas and Islamic Jihad to $100 million."

[189] It was directly executed by the members of Egyptian Islamic Jihad (see below).

[190] The 1993 bombing in the basement of the World Trade Center was linked, along with al-Qaeda, to IG's members or sympathizers in the USA

2.8.15 Egyptian Islamic Jihad[191]

Egyptian Islamic Jihad (EIJ), also known as *al-Jihad* or the ***Jihad Group***, was founded in Egypt in 1979 by Muhammad 'Abd al-Salam Farraj. Farraj was originally a member of the Muslim Brotherhood but split from the organization to form the EIJ, because of the Muslim Brotherhood's non-violent approach. Ayman al-Zawahiri, an eye surgeon by profession, who was later instrumental in forming al-Qaeda, was an influential member of EIJ. It gained international recognition in 1981 when its members together with members of IG killed Egypt's President Anwar Sadat in a spectacular fashion.

After serving a three-year jail sentence, Sharif, another future EIJ leader, and al-Zawahiri, along with many other EIJ members, moved in 1986 to Peshawar, Pakistan, and then to Afghanistan, where they set up new headquarters for the EIJ (BBC News, 2015b). While in Afghanistan, EIJ members actively fought alongside mujahideens against the Soviet Union. This helped the group to hone its fighting skills and strategic planning capabilities.

After returning from Afghanistan, Zawahiri became the leader of EIJ and its base moved to Sudan where Bin Laden's al-Qaeda was already based. EIJ focused on government targets. However, in 1993 its attempt to kill the Egyptian Prime Minister and the interior minister failed. But it was able to pull off a bombing attack on the Egyptian embassy in Islamabad, Pakistan in 1995.

This led to a massive crackdown by the government. Zawahiri and many members of EIJ left for Afghanistan in 1996. EIJ and al-Qaeda announced a formal alliance in 1998, and the two groups merged fully in 2001. Al-Zawahiri became Osama bin Laden's deputy and was affiliated with the attacks on the World Trade Center and the Pentagon on September 11, 2001.

In mid-2007, as part of a "deradicalization" program, Egypt released more than 130 jailed members of EIJ in exchange for their renouncing violence. That year also saw a series of publications by Sayyid Imam al-Sharif renouncing terrorism as un-Islamic. Sharif's writings drew a lengthy rebuttal from Zawahiri (see Encyclopedia Britannica).

2.8.16 Lashkar-e-Taiba (LeT) and Jamaat-ud-Dawa (JuD)

2.8.16.1 Narrative

Lashkar-e-Taiba (LeT), also known as the Army of the Pure or Army of the Righteous, is a Pakistan-based Islamic militant organization. It was founded in the early 1990s by Hafiz Mohammed Saeed as the military wing of Pakistani islamist organization Markaz-ad-Dawa-wal-Irshad (MDI), which practiced the Ahl-e-Hadith (AeH) interpretation of Islam.[192]

[191] Based on Encyclopedia Britannica and BBC News (2015b).

[192] AeH is a conservative interpretation of Islam, somewhat similar to but different from Wahhabism among Sunni Muslims. See Roy (2018).

LeT was initially active in the fight against the Soviet presence in Afghanistan but changed its focus to the disputed region of Jammu & Kashmir (J&K) when the state rebelled against Indian control in the early 1990s. LeT sees the fight against Indian control over Jammu & Kashmir as part of a global struggle against the oppression of Muslims and has opposed any Pakistani reconciliation with India in resolving the Kashmir issue. Its narrower objective is to unite Indian administered Kashmir with Pakistan under a radical interpretation of Islamic law, while it ultimately seeks to establish an Islamic caliphate in the Indian subcontinent.

Most of its members are Pakistani and Afghan. Its size is unknown but according to the Australian government's web page titled "Australian National Security," accessed on August 25, 2018, LeT's strength in the mid-2010s was in several thousands. It has reportedly been supported by ISI-Pakistan since its inception.

Fig. 2.31: Map of Kashmir. *Source*: Google map

The first known LeT operation in India was an ambush of a small group of Indian Air Force personnel in 1990. The group proved its mettle in 1993 in a successful attack on a heavily guarded Indian army base in Poonch. Until the end of 1990s, LeT almost exclusively focused on J&K.[193]

Despite LeT's operational focus on J&K, eliminating Indian power in the entire region has always been its broader goal. Its first strike inside India but outside of J&K was the Red Fort attack in New Delhi, India, in 2000. This attack established the group as a major threat to India.

[193] In 1996, the group gained notoriety for the first of many massacres targeting minorities in Kashmir, killing 16 Hindus in Barshalla, Doda. The most notable massacre, known as the Chattisinghpora attack, occurred in 2000, when LeT terrorists killed 35 Sikhs in Anantnag in J&K on the eve of President Bill Clinton's official state visit to India. Figure 2.31 presents a map of Kashmir.

The attack on the Indian parliament in 2001 was also attributed to LeT, although LeT denied the responsibility. It sparked a renewed confrontation between India and Pakistan and led to the US listing LeT as an FTO. Pakistan officially banned the group in 2002. In response, Hafez Saeed announced a split between LeT and MDI, and that he was no longer affiliated with LeT. MDI changed its name to Jamaat-ud-Dawa (JuD) (Stanford University, 2016b). The split and rebranding were superficial, however. JuD and LeT have continued to operate together, even retaining most of their joint offices, after the announced split.

In 2006, it was implicated in a considerably more deadly attack against civilians in Mumbai (Bombay), India's most populous city.[194] Two years later, LeT was linked to the most significant and innovative terror attack in Mumbai, which started on November 26, 2008 and goes by the acronym *26/11*.[195,196] The Mumbai attacks elevated LeT's status from being terror group targeting India exclusively to a global Islamic jihad group targeting its "enemies" like the "Crusader West," "Zionist Israel," and "Hindu India." At the same time, because of its increased visibility, it became a target of scrutiny and vigilance by advanced countries. Shortly after *26/11*, several people trained in LeT's camps were arrested.

The group actively holds rallies to protest on political issues such as US military cooperation with Pakistan, Indian water policies, and NATO agreements. In 2011, LeT founded Difa-e-Pakistan Council, a coalition of Islamist groups opposed to these efforts. LeT was designated as a terror organization by the USA, the UN, UK, Canada, and Australia. In 2012, the USA announced a $10 million bounty on the arrest of Hafeez Saeed. Saeed has been detained and subsequently released by Pakistani authorities on several occasions and continues to operate freely in Pakistan. He regularly appears on Pakistani TV and routinely addresses large anti-American rallies organized with the help of the ISI-Pakistan. LeT has continued terror activities in Kashmir and other states in India.[197]

---

[194] On "7/11" of that year, multiple bombs tore through Mumbai's commuter train system during the evening rush hour, killing more than 180 people and injuring more than 800. The bombs were all placed in first-class train compartments in an apparent effort to target India's professional class. Following the attack, which India linked to LeT, Pakistan detained Hafiz Mohammad Saeed and then released him, claiming that India's investigation was biased.

[195] Coming from Karachi, Pakistan by boat, the terrorists took over two luxury hotels and a Jewish outreach center. The seize lasted three days (over the Thanksgiving weekend) claiming 170 lives including six Americans and nine of the attackers. One terrorist was captured and later executed in 2012.

[196] Pakistan has continued to resist Indian pressure to prosecute LeT members including Hafeez Saeed. (The US government also held Saeed responsible for *26/11*.) Most of the individuals of LeT who planned the *26/11* attacks still remain free in Pakistan.

[197] As examples, in 2014, six militants wearing army uniforms attacked an Indian Army base in Uri, Kashmir. This was the first incident in a series of coordinated attacks undertaken that day that resulted in the death of eleven security force personnel, eight militants, and two civilians—as well as multiple people injured. Media reporting indicated LeT claiming responsibility for the attack against the army base. In 2017, LeT militants attacked Indian military personnel in Kulgam District, South Kashmir; one Indian soldier was killed. The suicide bombing attack on the Indian forces in the Pulwama district of Kashmir in 2019 was attributed to LeT by the Indian government. This led to a counter (surgical) strike on terrorist camps in the Pakistani occupied territory in Kashmir.

At a rally in 2017, Hafiz Saeed called for violent Jihad against the USA and Israel in response to President Trump's decision to move the US Embassy from Tel Aviv to Jerusalem. Saeed opined that "Pakistan's atomic bomb is the asset of Islam which should be used to free Jerusalem" (Financial Express, 2018). LeT supports proxy Islamist groups inside India with training, weapons, and funding. The Indian Mujahideen (IM), founded by Mohammed Sadiq Israr Sheikh, is LeT's primary ally in the country.[198]

It is noteworthy that in order to avoid US sanctions, LeT has repeatedly changed its name over the years. For instance, in 2017, LeT began operating under the name Tehreek-e-Azaadi Jammu and Kashmir (TAJK). In 2018, the USA amended the designation of LeT to include the aliases Milli Muslim League (MML) and TAJK.

2.8.16.2 Political Activities

JuD/ LeT has attempted but failed to make any headway in the political arena of Pakistan thus far. In 2017, soon after Saeed was released from detention, JuD/ LeT set up a political party, the Milli Muslim League, MML (which, as noted above, was declared as an FTO by the USA). The party was denied registration to contest in the Pakistan national elections. JuD fielded its candidates under the name of another party, Allaha-u-Akbar Tehreek, which failed to win any seat.

2.8.16.3 Social Services

Like Hezbollah, Hamas, and other terror organizations, LeT renders social services (through JuD). For instance, it runs schools, hospitals, and ambulance services across the country (see Roul, 2015 for more specifics). Besides its militancy and social services, it is dedicated to proselytize Pakistani society into a "pure" Islamic state by non-violent means. Despite its push for an extreme version of an Islamic state, many Pakistanis see JuD as a robust social welfare organization, not an alias for a lethal terrorist group. The Pakistani government still differentiates between LeT, which is banned, and JuD, which is not, even though the two wings remain as the two sides of a single organization, led by the same individuals.

This is one of the two reasons as to why LeT/JuD finds itself rooted in Pakistan. The other important reason is the support it receives from the military and the intelligence services, as it remains their most reliable terrorist ally against India.

[198] Analysts disagree on the degree of linkage between LeT and IM, with some arguing the latter is an independent organization, and others suggesting it is a direct product of LeT and ISI-Pakistan cooperation. LeT has kept "significant ties to global militant Islamist organizations" (Stanford University, 2016b).

2.8.16.4 Funding

It has "diverse and systematic" means of raising funds (Stanford University, 2016b). It collects donations from sympathizers in Pakistan. JuD donation boxes are present at several places and public gatherings (Kambera et al., 2011). Apart from ISI-Pakistan that presumably provides logistic and material support to carry out attacks, the Pakistani government itself provides funds through schools and hospitals sponsored by JuD/ LeT (Stanford University, 2016b). Its international benefactors include sympathetic Pakistani expatriates in other countries. A fund-raising method unique to LeT is collecting animal skins from religious sacrifices and selling them to tanneries. In 2010, JuD reportedly collected $1.2 million by selling these skins (Stanford University, 2016b).

2.8.16.5 More Recent Status

Despite the lack of direct political recognition, JuD/ LeT remains active because of its loyalty to Pakistan as well as the internal support from some section of the public, the Pakistani government as well as ISI-Pakistan, notwithstanding the international pressure on the Pakistan government to severe ties with JuD/LeT.

It is known to maintain and foster links with a variety of Islamist extremist groups including the Afghan Taliban, al-Qaeda, Harkat ul-Jihad al-Islami, and Jaish-e-Mohammad. Apart from partnering with militant groups in Kashmir, LeT receives support from and provides support to domestic based groups and networks in India, most notably the Indian Mujahideen and the Students Islamic Movement of India (SIMI).

In the midst of international pressure on Pakistan to act against LeT, in early 2020, Hafiz Saeed was convicted by anti-terrorism court of charges related to the 2008 Mumbai attacks and sentenced a prison term of five and half years. In late 2020, he was convicted of two charges of terrorist financing. These verdicts were overturned by a higher court in late 2021.

2.8.17 Al-Shabaab

It is an Islamic insurgent group in Somalia (see its map in Fig. 2.32). Al-Shabaab means "the youngsters" or "the youth." Its objective is to overthrow the Somalian government and establish a nation based on the Saudi-inspired Wahhabi version of Islam and Sharia law, while most Somalis are Sufis (BBC News, 2017b).

In early 2000s, the southern Somalia and the capital city, Mogadishu, were controlled by Islamic Courts Union (ICU), an alliance of Sharia Courts. Al-Shabaab emerged from within ICU in 2006 as a younger and more radical group. Both ICU and al-Shabaab opposed the officially recognized Transitional Federal Government of Somalia (Stanford University (2016c)).

Fig. 2.32: Map of Somalia. *Source*: Google map

Fearful of the spread of Islamic extremism, Ethiopia, a Christian-majority nation, invaded Somalia in 2006 with the help of the USA and ousted the ICU from Mogadishu with little resistance. The intervention came at the request of Somalia's transitional government, and this, according to analysts, radicalized al-Shabaab. After much of the ICU fled to neighboring countries, al-Shabaab retreated to the south, where it began organizing guerrilla assaults, including bombings and assassinations, on Ethiopian forces. Over time, the group morphed into a full-fledged insurgency, gaining control over a large territory in central and southern Somalia.

Following its declaration of allegiance to al-Qaeda in 2012, al-Shabaab began executing a series of violent attacks in Somalia's neighboring countries, including the 2013 Westgate Mall attacks in Nairobi, Kenya, which left 68 people dead and 175 wounded. The group was also responsible for the 2015 Garissa University attacks, wherein five al-Shabaab fighters stormed the Kenyan University, killing nearly 150 people. Since then, the group has continued to attempt terrorist attacks outside of its stronghold in Somalia.[199] Al-Shabaab reportedly killed more than 4200 people in 2016, making it the deadliest Islamic terror group in Africa. In 2017, al-Shabaab carried out the worst terror attack in Somalia to date: a truck bomb that killed over

[199] In its first attack on Western targets, an assailant detonated a concealed laptop bomb on a Daallo Airlines flight leaving Mogadishu for Djibouti City in 2016. However, the explosion killed only the attacker and was not strong enough to down the plane.

587 and injured 316 people in Mogadishu. It has been battling against the UN, and the Ethiopia backed regime in Somalia (Shay, 2018).

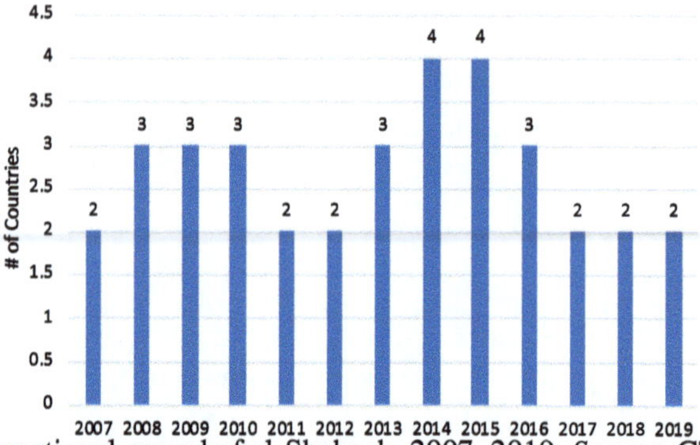

Fig. 2.33: International spread of al-Shabaab, 2007–2019. *Source*: GTD

2007 Attacks		2008 Attacks		2009 Attacks		2010 Attacks		2011 Attacks	
Ethiopia	1	Ethiopia	1	Kenya	1	Kenya	8	Kenya	33
Somalia	19	Kenya	1	*Somalia*	62	*Somalia*	62	*Somalia*	131
		Somalia	26	Uganda	1	Uganda	2		
2012 Attacks		**2013 Attacks**		**2014 Attacks**		**2015 Attacks**			
Kenya	54	Ethiopia	3	Djibouti	1	Kenya	57		
Somalia	182	Kenya	38	Ethiopia	1	*Somalia*	340		
		Somalia	284	Kenya	82	Tanzania	1		
				Somalia	787	Uganda	1		
2016 Attacks		**2017 Attacks**		**2018 Attacks**		**2019 Attacks**			
Kenya	57	Kenya	76	Kenya	46	Kenya	42		
Somalia	506	*Somalia*	497	*Somalia*	436	*Somalia*	286		
Uganda	1								

Table 2.5: Country-wise distribution of attacks by al-Shabaab, 2007–2019. *Source:* GTD

International proliferation of activities of al-Shabaab in the African continent around Somalia is illustrated in Fig. 2.33 and Table 2.5.In early 2017, the USA approved a Pentagon plan to escalate operations against al-Shabaab. It stationed more than 500 troops in Somalia and conducted 31 airstrikes in 2017, as opposed to 32 airstrikes over the period 2007–2016. The number increased to at least 45 over 2018.In November 2020 the Trump Administration ordered the departure of all US troops (around 700) from Somalia to be moved to bases in Kenya and Djibouti (Youssef & Phillips, 2020). Although the military operations have weakened al-Shabaab, the group engages in suicide attacks and exercises control of some areas in southern and central Somalia (Harper, 2020). As of 2020, it has extended its control in some parts of Mogadishu. Harper (2020) reports that, by means of violence and intimidation, al-Shabaab raises more revenues than does the government of Somalia. Businesses pay extortion fees to both al-Shabaab and the government.

2.8.18 Jemaah Islamiyah (JI)

Fig. 2.34: Map of Indonesia, Malaysia, Singapore, and Philippines. *Source*: Google map

Meaning "Islamic Congregation," it is a transnational Southeast Asian organization with cells in Indonesia, Singapore, Malaysia, and the Philippines. Figure 2.34 is the map of the region. It seeks a pan-Islamic state with strict Islamic laws.

JI's most notorious attack took place in 2002 when three bombs were detonated on the Indonesian island of Bali, a beach front city and international tourist destination. The most recent attack, believed to have been carried out by JI operatives, came in 2005, when a series of suicide bombings killed twenty people and wounded 129 in Bali. By the mid-2000s, national security efforts had begun to seriously degrade JI's operational capabilities. Since 2002, the governments of Southeast Asia have arrested more than 400 suspected terrorists linked to the group, including JI's operational chief in 2003 and two senior leaders in 2007. Many of its leaders were killed as well, including the group's senior bomb-maker in 2005, the operational leader Mohammed Noordin Top in 2009, and the senior leader Sanusi in November 2012.

There are some reports that the group may rebound after a decade of dormancy. As of 2015, its membership stood at 2000, nearly what it was before its crackdown (Stanford University, 2015e). However, there are no major terror attacks linked to this group since the mid-2000s.[200]

[200] In 2019 the Indonesian counter-terrorism unit was able to arrest a leader of JI, Para Wijayanto. In 2020 he was handed a seven-year jail sentence by an Indonesian court.

2.8.19 Islamic Revolutionary Guard Corps (IRGC)

In Iran, the IRGC came into existence in 1979 following the Iranian Revolution.[201] While the armed forces of Iran are entrusted with protecting the country's borders and internal security, IRGC's intended role is to safeguard the political system of the Islamic Republic, upholding the ideals of the Iranian revolution. It is a paramilitary force under the Iranian armed forces. Equipped with more than 150,000 troops, it has an army, air force, and navy (Qiblawi, 2019).[202] IRGC does not exactly fall within our definition of terrorism. First, it is not a non-state actor. Its duties are national and official, as per the Iranian Constitution. Second, it does not directly engage in standard terror tactics likes in bombing, assassinations, etc., that can potentially arouse public fear and a sense of insecurity, which separates terrorism as a distinct form of violence. However, according to the US Treasury Department, Quds Force, a unit of the IRGC, is a supporter of terrorism and Iran's "primary arm for executing its policy of supporting terrorist and insurgent groups."

Since 2018, it has been declared as a terror organization by Saudi Arabia and Bahrain. In 2019 the USA designated the IRGC of Iran as an FTO. It was speculated that other countries would also classify it as terror group.

2.8.20 The Lord's Resistance Army (LRA)

While all the fundamentalist terror groups described above are Islamic, The Lord's Resistance Army (LRA), which came into existence in 1988 in central Africa, is Christian. Figure 2.35 depicts the countries afflicted by this group. It emerged from the remnants of the Holy Spirit Movement army founded by Alice Auma Lakwena, a priestess, and distant relative of Joseph Kony, the LRA leader (Al Jazeera, 2014). The group first operated as the United Holy Salvation Army before it was named the Uganda Christian Army/Movement and eventually the LRA in early 1990s. Extremely brutal, it waged an armed rebellion to remove the government of Uganda and rule the country on the Biblical ten commandments. Many of its fighters were forcibly recruited, and most of those who resisted were either killed or maimed.

With the US help, it took the Ugandan government nearly two decades to contain the group. According to Cakaj and Ronan (2016), women and children numbering more than 200 escaped from LRA's captivity between 2012 and 2014. The strength of LRA fighters fell from around 400 in 2010 to 250 by 2013. By now it is no more a threat (Faber (2017)), although it is still in the Terrorist Exclusion List of the USA and its leader Kony is at large as of 2021.

Is That So? 2.17: The Lord's Resistance Army

In the post-World War II modern history of terrorism, the Lord's Resistance Army in Africa is the only Christian fundamentalist terror organization, which aimed to enforce Biblical ten commanders as the rule and practice of law.

[201] Its name in Persian is Sepâh-e Pâsdârân-e Enghelâb-e Eslâmi, briefly Sepâh, meaning "Army of Guardians of the Islamic Revolution."

[202] Its naval force maintains operational control of the Persian Gulf.

Fig. 2.35: Countries affected by LRA. *Source*: Own Mapping Software

2.8.21 Similarities and Dissimilarities among Islamic Terror Organizations

It is sometimes easy to be misguided that terror groups in the religious wave are clones of one another. But, there are major differences among them, which are implicit in our depiction of various terror organizations. In what follows, the similarities and dissimilarities among some of them are brought to the fore. From a policy perspective, this is important since specific information about the groups' beliefs and objectives would help us to better understand them and devise ways to deal with them effectively.

2.8.21.1 Al-Qaeda, ISIS, Boko Haram on One Hand and Taliban on the Other

These are extreme Islamic groups. They kill people and preach and try to enforce strict rituals including various prohibitions for women. Taliban has provided sanctuary to the members of al-Qaeda. However, there is a huge difference between al-Qaeda, ISIS and Boko Haram on one hand and Taliban on the other.

That is, the first group of three has a global ideological agenda, whereas Taliban does not. Barring a reported strand of Taliban in Pakistan, it does not have a global network or an aim to engage in terror activities outside of Afghanistan. Most Taliban members are Afghan, whereas al-Qaeda's and ISIS's members originate from Saudi Arabia, Egypt, and other middle eastern countries and elsewhere. Remember that of the nineteen hijackers who participated in the *9/11* attacks, fifteen were from Saudi Arabia, two from the UAE, one from Egypt, and one from Lebanon. Taliban's objective is local. Apart from preaching and enforcing fundamentalist, extremist, Islamic culture, it aims to establish a theocracy in Afghanistan and oust foreign occupation from Afghanistan.

Another difference is that while Taliban is influenced by Hanafi beliefs, al-Qaeda embraces the more radical Hanbali school.

2.8.21.2 Al-Qaeda versus ISIS versus Al-Nusra

These organizations share the same radical objective: to establish an Islamic caliphate along with extreme versions of Islam. The only but important difference between them lies in their tactics. As noted earlier, the crackdown by the USA and other nations following *9/11* attacks led to a less visible al-Qaeda central leadership and birth of al-Qaeda-like regional groups, e.g., ISIS, AQIM, AQAP, and al-Nusra, which vowed their allegiance to the spiritual leadership of al-Qaeda at some intervals of their evolution.

While both ISIS and al-Nusra are offshoots of al-Qaeda, ISIS differed from al-Qaeda and al-Nusra in three respects: (a) its brutal methods of killing those who are believed to be the infidels, (b) little attempt to build relations with other militant organizations with similar objectives or local population, and (c) aggressive territorial expansion. These are of course the factors that led to its own downfall.

Compared to ISIS, al-Nusra lies on the other side of the spectrum. It strives for reconciliation with other groups and building strong goodwill with local population and intellectuals. At the same time, it avoids visibility and refrains from occupying territories. It seeks to transform the society insidiously toward Islamic radicalism and caliphate.

In short, relative to al-Qaeda, ISIS is more brutal, whereas al-Nusra is less lethal and confrontational, while their ultimate goals are the same.

2.8.21.3 Fatah versus Hamas

Both groups share the common goal toward a Palestinian state on the territories based on 1967 borders (defined in Sect. 2.7.5). But there are some stark differences. Fatah has recognized Israel since 1993 or earlier but Hamas has not. Hamas is still intent on engaging in violence against Israel to achieve the Palestinian objective, whereas Fatah has taken the path of negotiations. Fatah is secular, while Hamas is not.

However, there are indications as of 2021 that Hamas has publicly accepted the existence of Israel as a separate state.

2.8.21.4 Hamas versus Hezbollah

While both have received funds in recent times from Iran, Hamas is a Sunni organization, whereas Hezbollah is Shi'ite and it was created by Iran. Both have fought for an independent Palestinian state and are sworn enemies of Israel. However, Hamas projects itself as an "independent" organization, whereas Hezbollah operates in the shadow of Iran.

2.9 Terror Groups in Russia, Central Asia, China, South and South-East Asia, and the USA

In this section, we outline terrorism problems in other regions that have not been covered or not adequately covered thus far. Our discussion leaves out the Australian continent the reason being that, while the threat of terrorism has not spared this continent, it has not witnessed any "major" event as yet—thanks to the Australian counter-terror measures in place.

2.9.1 Russia: The North Caucasus Region

Russia has faced terrorism problems in the era of the Religious Wave, stemming from its south-western border provinces, notably but not confined to Chechnya (see Fig. 2.36 for a map of this region). The terror/insurgent groups are Muslim. Many have sought autonomy, while others have harbored ideological goals.

This can be understood through Chechnya's struggle for independence from Russia. It is one of several semi-autonomous republics within Russia.[203] Following the Soviet collapse in the early 1990s, the separatists in the newly formed Russian Federation Republic of Chechnya started an independence movement called the Chechen All-National Congress. Russia was opposed, arguing that Chechnya was an integral part of Russia. From 1994 to 1996, Russia fought Chechen guerrillas in a conflict that became known as the ***First Chechen War***. While thousands of civilians died, Russia failed to win control of Chechnya's mountainous terrain, giving Chechnya de facto independence. In 1996, Russia signed a ceasefire with the separatists, and they agreed on a peace treaty the following year.

But violence returned in 1999 when Chechen militants invaded the neighboring Russian republic of Dagestan to support a local separatist movement. Five bombs exploded over a ten-day period—the largest coordinated attacks in the history of Russia, killing almost three hundred civilians. Moscow blamed the Chechen for these attacks and launched the ***Second Chechen War***, also known as the ***War in the North Caucasus***. In 2000, Russia recaptured the Chechen capital of Grozny, destroying a good part of the city center in the process and reasserting direct control over Chechnya. By this time, thousands of Chechens and Russians were killed or wounded, and hundreds of thousands of civilians were displaced.

[203] It means that Chechnya, unlike other constituent regions of Russia, can choose its own official language and may have its own constitution to better guarantee its unique ethnic, religious, or linguistic rights. But it cannot have its own armed forces as a sovereign nation, nor can it represent itself independently in the international fora.

Fig. 2.36: Map of North Caucasus Region, Russia. *Source*: Google map

Despite the direct control by Russia, Chechen insurgency continued. In 2002, a bomb blast killed at least forty-one people including seventeen children during a military parade in the south-western town of Kaspiysk. Russia blamed the attack on Chechnya rebels. In October of the same year, Moscow's Dubrovka Theater, where approximately seven hundred people were attending a performance, was seized by terrorists belonging to three Chechen-affiliated groups. Russian Special Forces launched a rescue mission that used the opium-derived gas to disable the hostage-takers. The operation resulted in the death of more than 120 hostages and as well as many of the terrorists. Shamil Salmanovich Basayev, a Chechen militant Islamist, assumed the responsibility for this attack. In 2003, the USA designated two Chechnya-based groups as FTOs: Special Purpose Islamic Regiment (SPIR) and the Riyadus-Salikhin Reconnaissance and Sabotage Battalion of Chechen Martyrs (RSRSBCM).

In 2006 Basayev was killed in an explosion, believed to have been orchestrated by Russia. Shortly after, the Russian security forces killed Abu Hafs al-Urdani, a Jordanian-born commander of foreign fighters in Chechnya. These two events severely cramped the Chechen insurgency for some time. But violence started to rise in 2008 and continued to increase till 2009.[204]

---

[204] Experts believe that there were ties between the al-Qaeda network and Chechen groups (Bhattacharji, 2010). Zacarias Moussaoui, who was convicted for his involvement in the September 11 attacks, was reported by the Wall Street Journal to be formerly "a recruiter for al-Qaeda-backed rebels in Chechnya." Chechen militants reportedly fought alongside al-Qaeda and Taliban forces against

Ramzan Kadyrov, a staunch supporter of Putin, became the President of Chechnya in 2007. In 2009, Russia officially ended the Second War of Chechnya.[205] Kadyrov took strong measures to squelch Chechnya's Islamist insurrection. Over the years however, he came under the criticism of international organizations for a wide array of human rights abuses in his watch.[206] The USA has imposed financial sanctions on Kadyrov, accusing him of a systematic campaign of repression.

In 2017, Kadyrov imposed the Sharia law on his population with an apparent eye on a global, Islamic stage. This seemed to defy Russia's foreign policy. While Kadyrov emphasizes that his republic is an integral part of Russia, he is "Putin's foot soldier" and that these measures are a part of bridging between Russia and the Muslims in Chechnya, it has raised concerns for Moscow (Halbach, 2018). However, as of 2021, Kadyrov has remained a strong supporter of Putin, and Chechnya is under firm control by Russia through Kadyrov.[207] In 2021 Kadyrov was reelected as the head of Chechnya.

2.9.1.1 Caucasus Emirate[208]

This is one of the relatively major terror groups operating in the Northern Caucasus region since 2007. The Caucasus Emirate is a Sufi nationalist organization created in 2007 by Doku Umarov, after he resigned from his position as president of the Republic of Ichkeria (the self-proclaimed secessionist government of Chechnya). The group aims to establish an independent Caucasus Emirate ruled under Sharia law within the territories of Russia, Georgia, Armenia, and Azerbaijan. It openly declared allegiance to the global jihadi movement in 2009 at a meeting of the group's top leaders in Chechnya. At this meeting, the Riyadus-Salikhin faction, which was active during the Chechen Wars and known for targeting civilians by suicide bombing, reformed and reconciled with the Caucasus Emirate.[209] Caucasus Emirate also served as an umbrella organization for other terrorist groups in the

the US-backed Northern Alliance in Afghanistan in late 2001. The Taliban regime in Afghanistan was one of the very few governments to recognize Chechen independence (Bhattacharji, 2010).

[205] Ramzan Kadyrov is the son of former Chechen President Akhmad Kadyrov, who was assassinated in May 2004. In February 2007, Kadyrov replaced Alu Alkhanov as President, shortly after he had turned 30, which is the minimum age for the post.

[206] He has also been criticized in Western press for his advocacy for restricted public lives for women and a campaign of mass detention for those who are suspected to have engaged in homosexual behavior.

[207] Kadyrov has supported Russian rebels in Ukraine and annexation of Crimea to the Russian Federation.

[208] The following write-up is based on Stanford University (2014) and The Mackenzie Institute (2015b).

[209] It consists of six vilayets (provinces) that report to their respective emirs who, in turn, report to Ali Abu Muhammad, the Emir of the Caucasus Emirate. These vilayets are located in the North Caucasus: Chechnya, Ingushetia, and North Ossetia, Nogay Steppe (Northern Krasnodar Krai and Stavropol Krai), Cherkess and Southern Krasnodar Krai, Dagestan, and Kabardino-Balkaria and Karachay.

North Caucasus, including the Yarmuk Jamaat (Kabardino-Balkaria), Shariat Jamaat (Dagestan), later known as Vilayat Dagestan, and Ingush Jamaat.

An attack in 2009 on the high-speed Nevsky Express train that runs between Moscow and Saint Petersburg and is used by members of the business and political elite killed twenty-seven people. In the following year, two female suicide bombers detonated bombs in a Moscow metro station, killing thirty-nine people. Both attacks were claimed by Doku Umarov.[210] He also claimed ownership of the 2011 bombing of Moscow's Domodedovo Airport that killed 36 people. Soon after during the same year, Caucasus Emirate was designated as an FTO by the USA.

In 2012, Umarov suspended attacks against civilian targets in response to protests against Russian President Vladimir Putin but left Russian military personnel as targets. He rescinded this order in 2013 and encouraged the members of the Emirate to strike the Winter Olympics in Sochi, scheduled in February. In late 2013, the members of Vilayat Dagestan carried out two suicide bombings in Volgograd as a future warning for the upcoming Winter Olympics. Umarov was killed by Russian security forces in 2014. He was succeeded by Aliaskhab Kebekov, also known as Ali Abu Muhammad. Kebekov was killed in 2015 by the Russian special forces. Following Kebekov's death, Magomed Suleimanov was appointed as the new leader of the Caucasus Emirate. In the same year, Suleimanov was killed in a Russian special operations raid in the Russian republic of Dagestan. More recent whereabouts of the Caucus Emirate are not known.

2.9.2 Central Asia[211]

Central Asia stretches from the Caspian sea in west to China in east and from Afghanistan in south to Russia in north. It consists of five countries: Kazakhstan, Kyrgyzstan, Tajikistan, Turkmenistan, and Uzbekistan (see Fig. 2.37).

As *Perestroika* got under way in the former Soviet Union in the mid-1980s, religious activities surged in central Asia and the Caucasus region. Because Central Asia shares a border of nearly 1500 miles with Afghanistan where terror groups like Taliban and al-Qaeda operated, this region is of strategic importance. As one would expect, along with moderate and traditional form of Islam, radical and militant Islamic trends appeared in Central Asia. However, compared to other regions, the terror incidents in Central Asia are rather infrequent: during the period 1992–2011, there were a total of 238 terror attacks in this region, compared to 383 in East Asia, 4628 in South East Asia, 15,683 in South Asia, and 15,567 in the Middle East.

[210] Two days after the metro station bombing in March 2010, two bombs exploded in the town of Kizlyar, in Russia's North Caucasus, killing at least twelve people. Russia believes that the two attacks in March 2010 are related.

[211] Based on Omelicheva (2013).

Fig. 2.37: Map of Central Asia. *Source*: Google map

Adolat or the "Justice Movement Group" is an early radical movement in Central Asia. It started in 1991 in the Uzbek part of the Fergana Valley that spreads itself across Uzbekistan, Tajikistan, and Kyrgyzstan. The leaders called for an Islamic State of Uzbekistan and engaged in terror activities against secular authorities. That invited reprisals from the Uzbek government.

In 1992, President Islam Karimov outlawed Adolat, forcing Yuldashev and Namangani, its leaders, to flee to the neighboring Tajikistan where they continued to launch cross-border terrorist and insurgent attacks against Uzbekistan. In 1998, Yuldashev and Namangani met with Taliban leaders in Kabul, Afghanistan. Together, they officially renamed Adolat to the ***Islamic Movement of Uzbekistan (IMU)***.

In 1999, Tashkent, the capital of Uzbekistan, witnessed a series of bombings ascribed to IMU. By early 2001, IMU had bases in Afghanistan, Tajikistan, and Kyrgyzstan, from which they could launch and support guerrilla campaigns. However, IMU's campaign against the Uzbek government ended in late 2001 after the US invasion of Afghanistan and overthrow of the Taliban. IMU, which had an estimated 2000 members before the war, diminished to a size of less than 1000 members. Namangani died in battle during November 2001. IMU carried out a series of bombings in the Kyrgyz cities of Bishkek and Osh in 2002–2004.

After the overthrow of Taliban in Afghanistan, IMU forces got scattered over the neighboring countries, became ethnically more diverse, and lost its focus on Uzbekistan. Even after finding various safe havens when fleeing from Afghanistan, IMU cadres faced continued counter-insurgent efforts by Pakistani, Afghani, and American forces. In 2009, Yuldashev was killed by CIA drone attacks in Pakistan. In spite of these setbacks, IMU continues to operate alongside Taliban and possibly ISIS and has claimed suicide bombings in Afghanistan, Pakistan, and Tajikistan.

In addition to IMU, there are two other major groups in Central Asia: East Turkestan Islamic Movement (ETIM) and Jund al-Khilafah (also known as JaK or the Soldiers of the Caliphate). These groups are reportedly associated with al-Qaeda and Taliban. The ETIM is an ethnic Uighur separatist organization that targets China, and its goal is to establish an Islamic State in the Xinjiang province of China, which is populated with Uighurs. JaK is a group by Kazakhstan radicals who made headline in 2011 when they organized a series of attacks in Kazakhstan, unaffected, hitherto, by terrorism.[212]

According to Omelicheva (2013), as of early 2010s the threat of radical Islam existed in central Asia, but it was overstated. The demise of the communist ideology rekindled people's interest in their spiritual and religious heritage. Most Muslims in this region follow the Hanafi school of jurisdiction, which is relatively moderate; see Chap. 1, Sect. 1.11. The rise of radicalism, according to Omelicheva (2013), was rather the result of policies that attempted to suppress religious and political freedom in the fear that it may lead to violent conflicts. By controlling Islam, the Central Asian governments have bred resentment and inadvertently contributed to forces that encourage violence and terrorism. The same conclusion of radical Islamism not being a serious threat in central Asia is also reached more recently by Bleuer (2020).

2.9.3 China

Somewhat similar to Chechnya, there were uprisings in the Xinjiang province of China starting 1990s (map in Fig. 2.38). The Uighars, who are ethnic Turkmen and sufi Muslims, are the traditional inhabitants of this region. As noted in Chap. 1, sufi Muslims are generally apolitical. Uighars have inhabited the Xinjiang province for two hundred years and governed it at some periods of time. China annexed this region in 1759. However, considering Xinjiang as their homeland, Uighars have demanded independence over centuries. The first revolt was witnessed in 1865 that lasted over a decade. In 1949, China suppressed Uighars' movement and took firm control of the region.

Buoyed by independence of central Asian countries from the Soviet domination, Uighars' national movement revived in the 1990s. In 1990 there was a major Islamic-inspired insurrection in Baren county, which proved to be a turning point (Welshans, 2007). Casualty reports of this revolt vary considerably. Between twenty and one hundred people were believed to have been killed.

Until this revolt, Xinjiang had remained a distant indigenous periphery of China. But the revolt led China to assert a tighter control over the Uighur society and launch a massive long-term strategy to accelerate the integration of Xinjiang with China by stepping up ethnic Chinese migration to Xinjiang. In 1949, Uighars constituted about 90% of the population, but their share as of 2018 declined to less than 50% (Lovelle, 2018). At the same time, China has undertaken a massive program of economic growth in the region, through exploiting Xinjiang's natural resources, notably oil and gas. These measures coincided with impressive economic growth in China, which made it possible to commit the capital and labor needed to carry them out. The Xinjiang province was transformed with new roads, industries, and cities, while new large-scale migration followed.

---

[212] Other groups operating in Central Asia include Hizb ut-Tahrir, Tablighi Jamaat, and others.

Fig. 2.38: Map of Xinjiang Province, China. *Source*: Google map

Concurrently, nationalist movements and violence proceeded side by side with peaceful demonstrations. A bus bombing in 1992 in Urumqi, the capital of the Xinjiang Uyghur Autonomous Region, resulted in three deaths, and this was attributed to the Shock Brigade of the Islamic Reformist Party. In Beijing's Xidan district, a bus bomb killed two people in 1997, and Uighur separatists claimed the responsibility for the attack.

China's official statement on "East Turkestan terrorists" published in January 2002 listed several groups allegedly responsible for violence in the province, including the , the East Turkestan Liberation Organization (ETLO), the Islamic Reformist Party Shock Brigade, the East Turkestan Islamic Party, the East Turkestan Opposition Party, the East Turkestan Islamic Party, the Uighur Liberation Organization, the Islamic Holy Warriors, and the East Turkestan International Committee. An ethnic riot in 2009 claimed about 100 lives in Urumqi (Lipscomb, 2016). In 2014, eleven members of an organization were killed by Kyrgyz security. They were identified as Uighars by their appearance, and their personal effects indicated that they were separatists (Reuters, 2014).

While China continues to face problems of violence and terrorism in the Xinjiang province, it is not as intense as in some other parts of the world. As soon as the USA launched a global war on terrorism in the aftermath of *9/11* attacks, it provided grounds for China to justify its own repressive measures against Uighars, branding them as jihadists like al-Qaeda and other Islamic extreme groups. However, experts generally categorize Uighars as moderate Muslims, and there is a general agreement that radical Islamic extremism is not a big threat in China. There are reports however that China is engaged in aggressive indoctrination programs for Uighur Muslims to adopt the Chinese system, culture and political norms, and remove their devotion to Islam. As Buckley (2018) narrates, indoctrination programs are conducted in some isolated part of western China where Uighar Muslims are forced to listening to lectures, singing hymns, praising the Chinese communist party, and writing self-criticism essays.

In 2021, the USA, the UK, and the European Union have imposed sanctions against some Chinese officials for their role in the abuse of human rights against Uighar Muslims.

2.9.4 South and South-East Asia

We have already discussed Naxalites in India, Khmer Rouge in Cambodia, The New People's Army in Philippines, and Jemaah Islamiyah that operated in Indonesia, Singapore, Malaysia, and the Philippines. In what follows, we briefly discuss the terror organizations in general in three countries: Indonesia, India, and Bangladesh.

2.9.4.1 Indonesia

When Suharto, Indonesia's dictator for over three decades, was forced to resign in 1998 amidst economic crisis, deadly riots, and political protests, the country's transition to democracy was threatened. Violence erupted between Christians and Muslims, and separatist insurgencies began to prosper. Lashkar Jihad (meaning Warriors of Jihad), an anti-Christian–Islamic group, came into being in 2000, and it fought with the Christians in the east (White, 2017, Chapter 11).[213] Jemaah Islamiyah, described earlier, came into existence to bring Indonesia and surrounding areas under strict Islamic laws. Both groups had links with al-Qaeda. The Bali bombings in 2002 served as a wakeup call for Indonesia and other the South East Asian countries to the threat of modern terrorism. Because of these groups' link with al-Qaeda,, the USA turned its attention to this region as well (Mckay and Webb, 2015). The Indonesian government accepted assistance from the USA and the international community to combat terrorism. As a result, terror incidences became less frequent over the years. Remarkably, Indonesia, with its largest population of Muslims among all countries, is a success story in countering terror (Caruso, 2018). Counter-terror operations are led by an elite police squad, Densus 88.

In 2018 Indonesia witnessed ISIS -inspired attacks (Jones, 2018). Notably, children were used to initiate some of these attacks, and this has been widely condemned. In response, Indonesia's parliament passed a tougher anti-terrorism law that allows more active participation of the military in counter-terror actions and longer detention period on the suspicion of involvement in terror activities.

[213] The group has remained dormant for years and is believed to have disbanded.

2.9.4.2 India

India's experience with terrorism predates the birth of Naxalites in 1967, described in Sect. 2.6.13. Recall that insurgency is a form of terrorism according to our definition of terrorism as long as civilians get killed generating public fear in the process of influencing a political, social, or ideological outcome. Insurgencies have afflicted the North-East region of India since its independence from the British in 1947 and till today.[214] There are numerous groups with their local political and/or social demands. None of these groups are national or have committed major terror attacks. The most prominent among them is the United Liberation Front of Assam (ULFA) that originated in 1979.[215] Later, it came to be known as United Liberation Front of Assam—Independent or ULFA-I. It is still an active group. Collectively however, their low-intensity attacks have caused major damage in terms of injuries and fatalities. According to the South Asia Terrorism Portal (SATP), https://www.satp.org accessed on August 21, 2020, the region witnessed 21,618 fatalities from terror attacks during the period 1992–2018. For the period 2010–2018, the count is 2205.[216] There has been an overall decline in the insurgency activities in the region from mid-2010s onward. However, in late 2021 a terrorist attack claimed lives of seven army personnel and family of a colonel in Manipur. This was claimed by MNPF and PLAM.

From the late 1960s onward, India has been facing the Naxalite movement, outlined in Sect. 2.6.13, which started from the state of West Bengal and spread to hilly areas in the South-Eastern part of the country.

The state of Punjab witnessed an insurgency situation during 1978–1993, called the Khalistan movement. It is embraced by Sikh extremists demanding a separate homeland (country) for the Sikhs.[217] While the demand for a sovereign Sikh nation has existed since India's independence in 1947—and continues—the movement became violent especially in the 1980s.[218] According to Singh (2015), about 33,000 people died in the hands of Khalistan extremists during the 1980s.[219]

---

[214] It started with the separatist Naga movement in the 1950s, represented by Naga National Council (NNC).

[215] It was banned by the Government of India in 1990.

[216] Active terror groups include, among many others, People's Democratic Council of Karbi Longri (PDCK) and Kamtapur Liberation Organization (KLO) in Assam, Tripura based PDCK, and National Liberation Front of Twipra (NLFT) in Tripura, Kanglei Yawol Kanna Lup (KYKL) and Kangleipak Communist Party (KCP)), People's Liberation Army of Manipur (PLAM) and Manipur Naga People's Front (MNPF) in Manipur and Hynniewtrep National Council (HNLC) in Meghalaya.

[217] This grew out of Sikh nationalism as well as political-economic grievances, unmet by both the Indian government and the government of Punjab.

[218] It was led by Sant Jarnail Singh Bhindranwale, who was initially supported covertly by the Congress party of India against a local political party in Punjab called Akali Dal (see Singh (2018) among many others). The power struggle between the two parties led to a lack of strong action by both the state of Punjab and the central government headed by the Congress party. In turn, the movement became extremely violent.

[219] Other estimates show both higher and lower numbers.

Fig. 2.39: Map of the Indian Subcontinent. *Source*: Google map

They received funds from the Sikh diaspora living in different parts of the world including the USA, Canada, and Europe, who supported the notion of a separate homeland for the Sikhs. The movement was aided by Pakistan. Bhindranwale and other extremists who had seized the Golden Temple in Amritsar were killed when the government forces attacked the Temple in 1984 to flush them out.[220] Strong military action in the late 1980s and early 1990s (Operation Black Thunder) led to the death or arrest of a large number of Khalistani extremists, and the insurgency was quelled.

The so-called Islamic terrorism in India grew out of insurgency in the Kashmir region of the state of Jammu and Kashmir in the 1990s. There were two types of groups: one demanding a separate homeland for Kashmiris, e.g., Jammu & Kashmir Liberation Front (JKLF) and the other leaning toward Pakistan. Both groups resented the state of India and its military presence in Kashmir and both rallied and attempted to thrive by invoking Islamism. The two objectives got mixed, and the insurgencies were "hijacked by cross-border terrorist groups based in Pakistan like LeT, Jaish-e-Mohammad (JeM), and Harkut-ul-Mujahideen" (Singh, 2018). Such cross-border terrorism has continued.[221]

[220] Then was named the Operation Blue Star.

[221] It is noteworthy that in 2019, by amending the constitution, the government of India removed the special political status and autonomy in administration that was accorded to the state of Jammu & Kashmir, and the state was divided into two "union territories" or quasi-states, "Jammu & Kashmir" (without the region of Ladakh) and Ladakh. The elected legislature of the previous J&K is now null and void, and the two regions are under the direct rule of the Indian government, which is called the "governor's rule." There are two schools of thought on the impact of this political integration of J&K into the Union of India on terrorism. The government of India as well as many other political parties and a large section of the Indian public think that this will reduce terrorism, while some fraction of the population believes that this will harden the attitude of local Kashmiris, who are predominantly Muslim and worsen the terrorism problem.

It is of interest to know more about the evolution of JKLF in the context of the Kashmir problem in the Indian subcontinent. This is outlined in the *Supplement Break* 2.8.

Supplement Break 2.8: Evolution of Jammu & Kashmir Liberation Front (JKLF)

Interestedly, JKLF was formed in Birmingham, UK, in 1977 by Amanullah Khan and Maqbool Bhat. Its aim was to establish self-determination of the people of Kashmir both in the Pakistan and Indian parts of Kashmir (respectively, *Azad Kashmir* and *Kashmir Valley*), which amounted to a separate country. It established several branches in the UK and was present in Europe, Middle East, and the USA. A militant outfit and supported by Pakistan, JKLF opened a branch in Azad Kashmir in 1982 and one in Kashmir Valley in 1987.[a] However, Pakistan began to withdraw its active support to it and leaned toward groups that wanted the accession of the whole of Kashmir to Pakistan. As a result, it became "sandwiched between Indian security forces and pro-Pakistan militants" (BBC News, 2012). It reportedly renounced violence in the mid-1990s. Since then, the Kashmir Valley "branch" of JKLF is headed by Yasin Malik. Initially, the JKLF of Azad Kashmir did not agree with Yasin Malik and separated itself. However, in 2005, they merged. Yasin Malik was arrested by the National Investigation Agency of India on several charges of murder and kidnapping. He remains incarcerated at the time of writing. The JKLF was banned by the Indian government in 2019 under its anti-terror law.

[a] See the report "Jammu and Kashmir Liberation Front (JKLF)" by Globalsecurity.org, an independent and a non-profit think-tank in the USA.

Apart from cross-border terrorism, India has also faced home-grown Islamic terrorism, especially since 1992 when a historic mosque was demolished by a Hindu religious group. The groups include Indian Mujahideen (IM), Students Islamic Movement of India (SIMI), and Tanzim Islahul Muslimeen (TIM). TIM was formed back in the mid-1980s after a communal riot in the state of Maharashtra. It, reportedly, has strong links with LeT in Pakistan. In 2014, the al-Qaeda leader Zawahiri announced the formation of al-Qaeda in the Indian Subcontinent (AQIS) with the objectives of global jihadism and a Caliphate inclusive of the Indian subcontinent (see Reed, 2015 and Singh, 2018). The Islamic State appears to have some presence in India too. However, no major attacks are ascribed to these groups.

As of 2018, India Ministry of Home Affairs (2018) deems 39 terror groups and their front organizations as banned under the Unlawful Activities (Prevention) Act 1967. These are the officially recognized terror organizations in India by the government of India.[222] The list does not contain any Naxalite groups because of the social-political reasons. The length of the list does not mean that all are super active. Currently, most terror activities take place in state of J&K. While the Indian government accuses that most attacks in J&K have the hand prints of the Pakistan-based organization, LeT, Pakistan denies it.

[222] Figure 2.39 depicts the map of the Indian subcontinent.

Besides LeT, the US government lists the IM as an FTO. According to United States Department of State (2018), IM has been active since 2005 and has links with LeT and other Muslim terror organizations. IM has expanded over to Nepal, now the biggest hub for IM operatives. A low-intensity blast in Bengaluru in 2015 that killed one and injured three has been attributed to IM. The arrest revealed that the group was planning attacks on the Republic Day of India (January 26) and had provided explosives for attacks at other places. In 2017, Indian law enforcement uncovered the plans of an IM militant (in custody) for various attacks, including killings and bombing a temple in Gaya in the state of Bihar. The US State Department's "Country Report on Terrorism 2018" states that the IM uses Nepal as its hub to organize its attacks in India by using the porous border between India and Nepal.

2.9.4.3 Bangladesh[223]

Militant groups in Bangladesh seek to establish an Islamist regime in the country. They include Harkat-ul-Jihad-al Islami Bangladesh (HuJI-B) and Jamaat-ul-Mujahideen Bangladesh (JMB). Newer groups are Ansarullah Bangla Team (ABT) and Ansar al Islam Bangladesh, which have been responsible for killing several secular bloggers and have strong links to al-Qaeda in the Indian Subcontinent (AQIS)).

It is suspected that a splinter group from JMB, referred to as neo-JMB, has allied itself to the ideology of ISIS. The neo-JMB claimed responsibility for an attack in mid-2020 on a police station in Dhaka, injuring five people, four among which were police personnel.

2.9.4.4 The United States

While the most spectacular terror attack was committed in the USA by al-Qaeda, a foreign terrorist organization, there are domestic groups too that have carried out attacks on the US soil.

The USA experienced 1500 terror attacks in the 1970s by groups and individuals together. Groups such as Fuerzas Armadas de Liberacion Nacional (FALN) and Armed Revolutionary Independence Movement (MIRA), who sought independence of Puerto Rico, were active during the 1970s and 1980s. There were left-oriented groups such as New World Liberation Front (NWLF) and the Weather Underground. Founded in 1968 in Brooklyn, the Jewish Defense League (JDL) perpetrated terror attacks in the New York area in the 1970s. An exhaustive list of groups that were/are active in the USA for at least ten years over 1970–2013 is given in Miller (2014). The list includes, among others, Ku Klux Klan, Neo-Nazi Group, White Extremists, Anti-Abortion Activists, Cuban Exiles, Jewish Extremists, Black Liberation Army, Army of God, and The Justice Department (*not* the US Department of Justice). Thanks to the robust security system and law enforcement, fatalities and damages from terror attacks in the USA are rather low compared to rest of the world.

---

[223] Based on Faber and Powell (2017).

2.10 "Quasi Terror" Groups

There are violent organizations around the world, which do *not* plan mass killings, have an explicit political agenda or sweeping ideological objectives similar to establishing a Caliphate. They are more aptly described as extreme hate groups like Ku Klux Klan in the USA and National Social Underground (NSU) in Germany. They may called quasi-terror groups.

2.10.1 Ku Klux Klan (KKK)

KKK has an ideological objective that is racial, but its ultimate target is not any government or authority. Unlike Hamas, Hezbollah, and Taliban, KKK does not nurture any political ambition of its own, although it has impacted American politics. Neither has it even planned or participated in any large-scale killing. Hence, it cannot be branded as a typical terror organization.

KKK has a long history dating back to 1866, formed by a group of Confederate veterans in the heels of the American Civil War. "Ku Klax" is believed to be derived from the Greek word *kyklos*, meaning circle, to which Klan was added. Supposed to be brainchild of General Nathan Bedford Forrest of the Confederate Army, the organization's original objective, according to White (2017), was to be anti-unionist and preserve the Southern tradition and culture. Instead, the KKK engaged itself in intimidating and using violence against the African–Americans to submission.[224] It had nearly vanished by the end of the nineteenth century, because its main cause of white dominance over the black in the South was more or less accomplished.

The late 1910s and the 1920s witnessed its resurgence, fueled by a surge in immigration, and emergence of organized labor and left-oriented thinking, inspired by the Bolshevik Revolution in Russia. Its hate campaign extended to Catholics, Jews, and organized labor. KKK adopted its burning-cross symbol and held rallies, parades, and marches around the country. At its peak in the 1920s, the Klan's membership exceeded 4 million nationwide. Ideologically, KKK blended into a xenophobic entity that championed racial prejudice and white supremacy within the broad purview of moral conservatism. Its membership however declined in the 1930s due to the Great Depression. In fact, the decline of its second generation was almost as fast as its rise. Internal corruption charges, and a criminal scandal led to its near collapse.

The third generation of KKK in 1960s coincided with the Civil Rights movement in the 1960s. In 1965, President Lyndon Johnson delivered a speech publicly condemning the Klan and announcing the arrest of four Klansmen in connection with the murder of a white female civil rights worker in Alabama. Over the next decades, it became fragmented and decentralized. Vigilante lynching is typical of the KKK's method of execution. Most recently, it was in news in 2017 when it attacked an African–American church in Charleston, S.C., and marched in Charlottesville, Virginia, with slogans against other races and ethnic groups.

[224] Forrest was later disillusioned and attempted to disband it; but it was too late.

2.10.2 National Social Underground

An extreme-right group, National Social Underground in Germany, consisted of a "terror trio" that killed ten people between 2000 and 2007, eight of whom were of Turkish origin. It also carried out two bombings and fifteen bank robberies (Koëhler, 2014). Two of the members, Uwe Böhnhardt and Uwe Mundlos, took their own lives in 2011 when police discovered the gang by chance. In 2018, the third member, Beate Zschäpe, was sentenced to life in prison. Koëhler (2014) describes how this group networked with a wide variety of extreme-right activists in and outside Germany.

2.11 End of the Fourth Wave and Beyond

Following Rapoport (2004), this chapter has organized the history of terrorism in terms of four waves—with the Religious Wave being the latest. We now touch upon theories about when the fourth wave is likely to end and what may be the nature of the next wave of terrorism.

To predict the timing of the end of the fourth wave is, of course, a difficult task.[225] Because the first three waves lasted for one to two generations, Rapoport submits that the fourth wave should end by 2025. Subsequent to Rapoport (2004), fifth-wave theories and predictions have indeed surfaced. We briefly review two of them.

Kaplan (2008) argued that the fifth wave might be dominated by a ***new tribalism***. He has identified a number of characteristics of such groups, including a breaking away from the established terrorist wave, physical withdrawal into the wilderness, an attempt to establish a new calendar, a radical quest for purity, and a focus on "localistic and particularistic concerns." Kaplan (2008) cited the Khmer Rouge of Cambodia and the Lord's Resistance Army (LRA) in Uganda as progenitors of this wave. Note that ISIS and to a large extent Boko Haram fit this description, but these groups were not in existence or active when Kaplan formulated his theory. Celso (2015) argues ISIS, and Boko Haram should be included into Kaplan's fifth-wave theory.

Simon (2011) speculates that the fifth wave will not be driven by a single ideology. Rather it will be largely dictated by technology, which he calls the ***technology wave***. Terrorism may be related to religion, narcotics, cessation from a state, etc., and, instead of large groups, there would be a large number of lone-wolf terrorists and leaderless jihads.

---

225 As Yogi Bera, an iconic baseball player, once said: prediction is a tricky business, especially about the future.

2.12 Take-Aways

- David Rapoport has classified modern terrorism since late nineteenth century into four waves: anarchism (1870s–1910s), anti-colonial (1920s–1960s), new left (1960s–1980s), and religious (1979–2020s).
- Modern terrorism began in Russia in the late nineteenth century with a group named Narodnaya Volya.
- The Irish Republican Army (IRA) of Ireland is a unique organization that spanned not one but three waves: second, third, and fourth.
- There are three major Jewish paramilitary groups working toward the independence of Israel as well as fighting with Arabs: Haganah, Irgun Zvai Leumi (an offshoot of Haganah), and Lehi (a splinter group of Irgun). After Israel's independence, Haganah and Irgun merged into Israel army and polity, whereas Lehi simply disbanded.
- FARC (*Fuerzas Armadas Revolucionarias de Colombia*), a left-wing terror organization in Colombia, is the oldest and largest terror groups in Latin America. It started in the 1960s and dissolved in 2016–2017 through a peace accord.
- Shining Path is one of the most dangerous terror organizations ever. It is a radical Maoist group that originated in Peru in 1970. During 1970s and 1980s, it killed about 70,000 people.
- Although not exactly a terror organization according to our definition (since it committed its atrocities while in "official" power), Khmer Rouge is the most ruthless group in Asia. It killed between one to two million people. Sculls of (some) Khmer Rouge victims are on display for tourists in Cambodia.
- The 1970s and 1980s mark the deadliest period in the history of IRA. It is called the period of "Troubles." The group's activities have abated substantially since the Good Friday Agreement (also known as Belfast Agreement) in 1998.
- An Islamic group spread over Turkey, Iraq, Syria, and Armenia, PKK is secular, which aggressively promotes the rights of women and women leadership.
- Palestine Liberation Organization or PLO is a conglomerate, dominant group within which Fatah is the most dominant group. A Sunni Muslim group, it is a secular organization. In the initial years, the objective of PLO/Fatah was to secure the homeland of the Palestine people by attacking Israel. Since the mid-seventies, it reoriented itself and became accommodating toward Israel. By the 1990s, it was no longer considered as a violent or terrorist group, although it supported other groups using violence against Israel at times. In 1993, Israel and PLO signed the Oslo accord. In the accord, PLO/Fatah recognized Israel's right to existence and formally eschewed violence against it. In return, Israel accepted PLO as the

lawful representative of the Palestine people, and both sides agreed for the establishment of a Palestinian Authority (PA), a semi-autonomous government body that would assume the responsibility of governing Gaza strip and West Bank until a deal is reached with Israel for the settlement of the Palestinian people. However, no permanent deal regarding the displaced Palestinians and their posterity is yet to see the light.

- The plane hijacking in 1968 by PFLP (Popular Front for the Liberation of Palestine), the second largest faction behind Fatah, marks the birth of Post-World War II modern terrorism in terms of tactics.
- A few rebel and breakaway groups from or within PLO/Fatah emerged who did not agree with the conciliatory and relatively peaceful approach of PLO/Fatah toward Israel and were violent. Black September was one, which ambushed the Israeli team for the Munich Olympics in 1972. It led to eleven Israeli athletes being massacred. Abu Nidal Organization (ANO) was another.
- ANO is considered as the predecessor of al-Qaeda in many ways. Its demise in early 1990s synchronized with the rise of al-Qaeda.
- In the pre *9/11* era, LTTE of Sri Lanka was the leader of all terror organizations in terms of suicide attacks.
- Modern terror organizations in the Post World War II era are complex entities. They do not contemplate murder, bombing, etc., 24 × 7. Many of them multi-task. They provide useful social and public services to the local populations—which generate support for their cause and aid in their recruitment process. Some of them have had political wings and have fought elections and have won—within a legitimate political framework.
- Most terror organizations in recent decades are Muslim. There exceptions however, namely, LTTE in Sri Lanka (Hindu) and Lord's Resistance Army in Central Africa (Christian).
- Some Muslim terror organizations are secular: they are not fundamentalists or adhere to extreme versions of Islam.
- All fundamentalist Islamic terror organizations do not have ideological goals like Muslim caliphate or Jihad. Hamas and Hezbollah in the Middle East are examples.
- The religious (Fourth) wave of terror and jihadism was born with three events: the Iranian Revolution, the attack on the Grand Mosque of Mecca in 1979, and the Russian occupation of Afghanistan, 1979–1989.
- Following the departure of Russian forces from Afghanistan, al-Qaeda was formed in the 1989 in Pakistan among the Afghan mujahideens under the leadership of Abdullah Yusuf Azzam and Osama Bin Laden. Azzam was killed in a car bomb during the same year, and this left Bin Laden as the undisputed leader of al-Qaeda.
- After four major attacks between 1998 and 2001 culminating in the *9/11* attacks, al-Qaeda became the No. 1 enemy of the USA. The US occupation

of Afghanistan immediately following *9/11* attacks drove al-Qaeda operatives out of Afghanistan including Bin Laden. Since then, it has not been able to rebuild itself as a single major force or organization.

- However, following the occupation of Iraq, al-Qaeda-inspired and affiliates sprang up in different regions, such as al-Qaeda of Iraq (AQI), al-Qaeda in the Islamic Maghreb (AQIM), and al-Qaeda in the Arabian Peninsula (AQAP).
- Al-Qaeda of Iraq morphed into the Islamic State of Iraq that in turn became ISIS or ISIL. In 2014 its name was changed to Islamic State. In terms of atrocities and territorial gain, ISIS rose meteorically in 2014. Its fall in 2016 and 2017 was equally dramatic. Control of oil production and distribution was the main source of revenue for the ISIS. Although the main ISIS remains subdued and appears disintegrated, ISIS-inspired groups have sprung up elsewhere such as West Africa, Greater Sahara, Libya, Congo, Central Africa, Egypt, Mozambique, Yemen, Pakistan, Bangladesh, Sri Lanka, Malaysia, and Philippines.
- Al-Nusra, based in Syria, is a relatively unknown Islamic extremist group that is equally dangerous as al-Qaeda or ISIS. But its modus operandi is different. It promotes a path of gradual transformation toward the practice of radical Islamic rituals and Caliphate while maintaining low visibility and integration into the local populace.
- As of 2020, only about 55% of the districts in Afghanistan were either controlled or influenced by the government—meaning that the rest were either under Taliban's control or contested.
- Opium leaf production and processing is the main source of revenue for the Taliban in Afghanistan.
- In 2020, Taliban negotiated an agreement with the USA to the effect that the US and allied troops will leave Afghanistan and Taliban would not harbor any groups hostile to the US and other Western countries.
- In 2021, as the US and allied forces were in the process of leaving Afghanistan, Taliban took control of Afghanistan without much resistance from the country's armed forces swiftly and surprisingly. At the time of finishing this chapter in late 2021, the structure of power and polity in Afghanistan remains fluid.
- Haqqani Network is another experienced insurgent group in Afghanistan that fights against the Afghan government and the US-led forces. While it works under the umbrella of Taliban, the Haqqanis maintain distinct command and control. The US Treasury believes that the Haqqani Network might have recently allied itself more with al-Qaeda.
- There is a Pakistani Taliban, Tehreek-e-Taliban Pakistan, which is different from (Afghan) Taliban. It runs terror campaigns against the Pakistani government and its forces.

- An Islamic fundamentalist group, Boko Haram, is one of the deadliest terror organizations since 2010, operating mostly in Nigeria but active also in Burkina Faso, Cameron, Chad, and Niger.
- Hamas is a Palestine terror/political group that originated from Muslim Brotherhood and controls the Gaza strip. Since 2007, Hamas-in-Gaza and Israel have fought three "wars," "2014 Gaza War" being the last. It has been funded by Saudi Arabia and Iran in different time periods. After the last war, its finances have taken a nose dip due to blockades and sanctions imposed by Israel, Egypt, and the Palestinian Authority.
- A Shi'ite group and sponsored by Iran financially and strategically, Hezbollah came into existence in the early 1980s in Lebanon. It is credited with the first major suicide attack in history when it attacked a US marine barrack killing 241 service men. It is heavily trenched in southern Lebanon in terms of providing social services to the Shii'te population and participating the state polity.
- Different from Hezbollah, Kata'ib Hezbollah is also an Iran-funded terror organization operating in Lebanon but without any political wing.
- Lashkar-e-Taiba (LeT) is a major terrorist organization in Pakistan. It is focused on India including the Jammu and Kashmir region. The famous *26/11* attacks in Mumbai in 2008 were carried out by LeT operatives. It has a sister organization called Jamaat-ud-Dawa (JuD), which is engaged in social services and deeply rooted in the population.
- Al-Shabaab, whose central base is in Somalia, has operated in Ethiopia, Kenya, Djibouti, and Uganda.
- Unlike al-Qaeda, ISIS or Boko Haram, global jihad is not an objective of Taliban.
- Although the vast majority of population in the Central Asian countries is Muslim and there is an increase in the practice of religious rituals that were earlier suppressed under the former USSR, violent Islamic extremism is not a major threat in the region.
- Despite claims by China, there are no major threats of terrorism from Uighirs in the Xinjiang region of China.
- Indonesia, whose Muslim population is the largest in the world, has successfully implemented counter-terrorism measures since the attacks on Bali resorts in the early 2000s.
- Terrorism in the USA did not begin with the *9/11* attacks or the unsuccessful attack on the World Trade Center in the 1990s by foreign terrorists. Indigenous terror groups have been active in the USA at various points of time with varied objectives like independence of Puerto Rico, instituting leftist ideals and prohibiting abortion, among others.
- KKK in the USA and National Social Underground in Germany are quasi-terror groups in that they do not attempt mass killing in the pursuit of their objectives.

- It is speculated that the fourth, Religious Wave of terrorism will end sometime in the 2020s.

Questions

2.1 Why is Narodnaya Volya considered the first "modern" terrorist organization? What was its main aim?

2.2 How is the first generation of the Irish Republican Army different from its second generation?

2.3 How is the third generation of the Irish Republican Army different from its fourth generation?

2.4 Which are the main Jewish terror groups before the independence of Israel and how are they different from one another?

2.5 What are the historical reasons for the conflict between Greeks and the Turks in Cyrus?

2.6 How were the leftist terror organizations in Latin America different from such organizations in other parts of the world?

2.7 "Suicide attacks have been carried out by Islamic terror organizations only." Defend or refute.

2.8 Is PLO a terrorist organization? Why or why not?

2.9 Do your own research and make an assessment of terrorist problems and the success of (political) power sharing between nationalists (republicans) and unionists in Ireland since the Good Friday Agreement in the late 1990s.

2.10 "All fundamentalist Muslim terrorist organizations in the Religious Wave are not jihadist." Defend or refute.

2.11 "Al-Qaeda is a spent force by now." Defend or refute.

2.12 In terms of upholding and promoting women rights, which is the most progressive among the Muslim terror organizations and why?

2.13 As noted in the chapter, ISIS-K came to global notice in 2021. How is it related, yet different from Taliban, Haqqani network and the TTP?

2.14 Who are the prominent terror groups that are active in politics and public services? Briefly describe their non-terror activities.

2.15 Why do groups like KKK and National Social Underground not fit the description of a typical terrorist organization?

Chapter 3

Tracking Terror: Trends and Patterns

3.1 Introduction

This chapter provides a global view of the evolution and spread of terrorism in the modern post-World War II era through the lens of data. For instance, how many deaths have occurred due to terror attacks in different regions of the world over the decades. Is there an increasing trend in the number of terror attacks over the years? What percentage of terror attacks results in fatalities? What fraction of the total number of terror attacks is the suicide attacks? Are most of lone-wolf terror attacks principally motivated by religion? Data helps us to understand trends and patterns of terror incidents and separate out facts from fiction and thus essential for a meaningful discourse on how to deal with the problem.

Systematic research on terrorism began in early 1970s when skyjacking graduated from a nuisance to a menace. The current chapter is filled with data-based graphs illustrating various trends and patterns. We begin with a brief description of various data sources available in Sect. 3.2, which should be of interest to students and researchers. Trend and patterns of terrorism are depicted in Sect. 3.3. Those particularly for the Organization of Economic Cooperation and Development (OECD) countries and the USA are outlined in Sects. 3.4 and 3.5.

S. P. Das, *Economics of Terrorism and Counter-Terrorism Measures*,
https://doi.org/10.1007/978-3-030-96577-8_3

3.2 Data Sources

Various sources of data on terrorism have become available over time. Indeed, there is an explosion of data on terrorism after *9/11*. This section describes some of the principal data sources over various time periods.

Terrorism in Western Europe: Events Data (TWEED) This is the first recorded data source on terrorism, which spans the period 1950–2004. Based on one news source, Keesing's Record of World Events, it was collected by Jan Oskar Engene of University of Bergen and contains information on domestic terrorism, covering 9730 terrorist events perpetrated by 214 terror groups in eighteen Western European countries (Engene, 2007).[1] The purpose was to understand the pattern of domestic terrorism in Western Europe in the light of historical and socio-political conditions.

RAND Database of Worldwide Terrorism Incidents The RAND Corporation of the USA has been at the forefront of studies on terrorism for over four decades. It maintained a database, called the RAND Database of Worldwide Terrorism Incidents (RDWTI), which compiled data from 1968 through 2009, providing comprehensive information on international and domestic (within USA) terrorism. Over the years, many public and private sponsors have contributed to the maintenance of the RDWTI and its predecessors, the RAND Terrorism Chronology and the RAND-MIPT Terrorism Incident Database. Terrorism Knowledge Base (TKB) was an online portal active from 2004 to 2008 (now defunct) that combined the RAND Terrorism Chronology and the RAND-MIPT Terrorism Incident Database. It was sponsored by the National Memorial Institute for the Prevention of Terrorism (MIPT), a non-profit organization funded by the US Department of Homeland Security.

With over 40,000 incidents of terrorism coded and detailed, the quality and completeness of the RDWTI is remarkable. The RAND conducted extensive research on candidate terrorist attacks, drawing on staff with regional expertise, relevant language skills, and in-country field work experience. The RDWTI is a fully searchable and interactive database, with the intention of providing quality and comprehensive data to users.

The database is free and publicly accessible for research and analysis. However, the use of the data must be attributed to the RDWTI.[2]

International Terrorism Attributes of Terrorist Events (ITERATE) and Data on Terrorist Subjects (DOTS) It is downloadable but not open source. It tracks terrorist incidents and characteristics of transnational terror groups from 1968 to 2012. The data is generated by using various research and media sources and organizations

---

[1] The included countries are: Austria, Belgium, Denmark, Finland, France, Germany (previously West Germany and East Germany separately), Greece, Iceland, Republic of Ireland, Italy, Luxembourg, Netherlands, Norway, Portugal, Spain, Sweden, Switzerland, and United Kingdom.

[2] It was last accessed by the author on October 21, 2021 at the url https://www.rand.org/nsrd/projects/terrorism-incidents/download.html.

including Associated Press, Reuters, Washington Post, New York Times, Al-Jazeera, US Department of State and FBI, among many others. It has Common Files, a Fate file, a Hostage File, and a Skyjack File. Common Files are comprehensive, featuring several attributes of terror events, whereas other files are more specific. For instance, the Fate file pertains to what happened to the terrorists (e.g., death, escape, and extradition requests) and the Skyjack file focuses on various characteristics of skyjacking events. Flemming et al. (2008).

ITERATE dataset is supplemented by DOTS that provides short biographies of terrorists and other individuals whose names appear in the ITERATE dataset.

Jane's Terrorism and Insurgency Centre (JTIC) It is a database that tracks terrorist, insurgent, and counter-terror events in the world since 2009. It monitors more than 1000 non-state armed groups and covers more than 250,000 terrorist and insurgent events. It also provides country briefings that assess each country's security situation, and case studies of landmark terrorist operations. It prepares an annual "Jane's Terrorism and Insurgency Centre (JTIC) Global Attack Index." Called simply as Jane's, it is published by IHS Markit, a market data company headquartered in London.

Chicago Project on Security and Terrorism (CPOST) Located at the University of Chicago, it is an open source, downloadable, database on suicide attacks only. Considered as the most authentic database on suicide attacks and called DSAT (Database on Suicide Attacks), it contains data from 1974 to through 2019 (at the time of writing this chapter). It stands out in terms of verification of data sources and various characteristics of suicide attacks. The url, as accessed on May 7, 2021, was https://cpost.uchicago.edu/research/suicide_attacks/.

Aviation Safety Network This is the website of the Flight Safety Foundation, an independent non-profit international organization, which keeps track of hijackings as well as aviation incidents and accidents. It provides annual data on the number of airliner accidents and fatalities, corporate jet accidents, and fatalities as well as the number of hijacking and fatalities. It also contains country-wise data on aviation accidents with specific dates and description. The url, as accessed on October 22, 2021, was https://aviation-safety.net.

Global Terrorism Database (GTD) Till date this is the most comprehensive, open source, and downloadable database on terrorism. Data is collected and collated by the National Consortium for the Study of Terrorism and Responses to Terrorism (START), a research and education center at the University of Maryland. Since 2005, START is one of the "centers of excellence," supported by the Department of Homeland Security of the USA. It covers all forms of terrorism including suicide attacks, both domestic and transnational terror events, from 1970. For each incident, it provides, among many other characteristics, the date–month–year, the place, state/province and country of occurrence, the perpetrators, whether it is a domestic or transnational terror event, tactics used, number of people killed, the target, and its type (e.g., business, property, police, government, public, etc.) If the data on some characteristics are not available, that is also clearly specified.

Indeed, *many data-based graphs in this book are generated from GTD, particularly its version released in early 2021, which covers from 1970 to 2019, except 1993 for which consistent data is not available.* The url, last visited on October 22, 2021, is https://www.start.umd.edu/gtd/.

Other Databases Within START There are other related databases that are available upon request.

Worldwide Incidents Tracking System (WITS) It is a database of transnational and domestic terror events spanning 2004 to 2009, maintained by the US National Counterterrorism Center (US Government). It has merged with GTD.

Terrorism and Extreme Violence in the USA (TEVUS) This database and portal provide information on terrorism and extremist violence in the USA by integrating four open-source datasets: The American Terrorism Study (ATS) GTD, The US Extremist Crime Database (ECDB), and Profiles of Perpetrators of Terrorism in the USA (PPT-US).

Profiles of Incidents Involving CBRN and Non-state Actors (POICN) Organized by Mark K. Blinder and Gary A. Ackerman, this is a dataset on chemical, biological, radiological, and nuclear terrorism attempts, covering the period 1990 to 2017 (at the point of writing this chapter). This is not confined only to actual CBRN (Chemical, Biological, Radiological, and Nuclear) terror attacks. It also records events where CBRN use is being contemplated.[3]

Big, Allied, and Dangerous (BAAD) Funded by the Department of Homeland Security and maintained by the Project on Violent Conflict at the University at Albany's Rockefeller College of Public Affairs and Policy, it contains narratives of fifty most dangerous among more than one hundred terror organizations since 1998.

Profiles of Individual Radicalization in the USA (PIRUS) Interactive and user-friendly, this database pertains to radicalization of individuals in the USA. Individual-level information on background and radicalization process are stored. Covering over 1948 to 2017, it has records of over 2100 violent and non-violent people who have embraced extreme left, extreme right, or single-issue ideologies.

Nuclear Facilities Attack Database (NuFAD) Created by Gary A. Ackerman and James Halverson, it records "assaults, sabotages, and unarmed breaches of nuclear facilities" across the globe for eighty cases over the period 1961–2014. It contains

[3] Events are classified into nine types: (i) proto-plot (evidence of groundwork for planning an attack, but no actual plot), (ii) plot (where the perpetrators seriously considered acquiring and using CBRN materials as a weapon), (iii) attempted acquisition (evidence of attempts to acquire CBRN substance), (iv) possession of a non-weaponized agent (evidence of possession but no evidence of weaponization of the substance), (v) possession of a weapon, (vi) threat with possession (evidence where the perpetrators have threatened after the weapon is possessed), (vii) attempted use of agent (where there is a failed attempt to disseminate the agent to cause harm), (viii) use of agent (successful use of the agent to cause harm), and (ix) unknown (where not enough information is available to determine which of the earlier eight types the event is).

information on map and location, the nature of the action against a facility (e.g., theft and sabotage), whether the action or attack succeeded, and so on.

Our World in Data, https://ourworldindata.org This is a website at the University of Oxford, England. It is not confined by terrorism only. Founded by Max Roser and co-authored with Esteban Ortiz-Ospina, Hannah Ritchie, Joe Hasell, and Daniel Gavrilov, it offers interactive global data and charts on hundreds of topics including terrorism.

In what follows, trends and patterns of terrorism in the modern era are presented by using GTD mostly but not exclusively.

3.3 Terrorism around the World: 1970 Onward

3.3.1 Number of Incidents and Fatalities: All Types of Terror Attacks

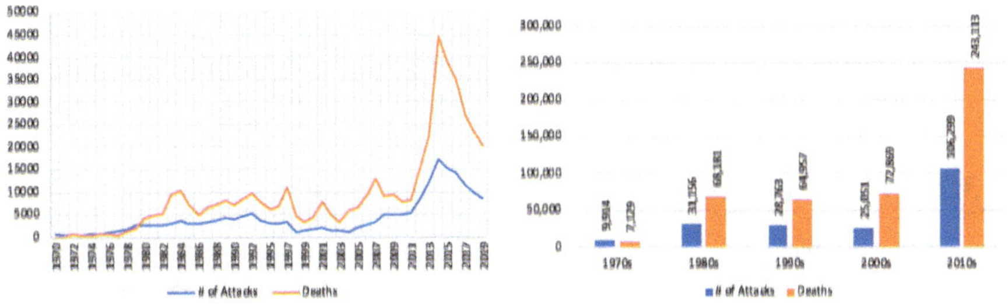

(a) (b)

Fig. 3.1: Number of terror attacks and deaths: globally, 1970–2019. (**a**) Annual. (**b**) Decadal. *Source:* GTD

GTD records over 201,000 terror incidents worldwide during the period 1970–2019 barring 1993 (for which consistent data is unavailable). Of these, whether or not there are fatalities, and, if yes, how many are reported for 189,233 (about 94%) of events. The total death count stands at 456,235. How does this number compare to another form of violence, namely, homicide?

Is That So? 3.1: Terrorism Versus Other Forms of Violence

According to UNODC (United Nations Office on Drugs and Crime), in 2017 alone, homicide, worldwide, claimed an estimated 464,000 deaths, which is higher than lives lost from terror attacks from 1970 to 2019.

This should not imply however that terrorism as a means of violence is overplayed—because, unlike homicide, terrorism creates a massive negative externality in terms of public fear and anxiety.

Figure 3.1a graphs the annual time series of the number of incidents and the number of deaths.[4] Clearly, the number of terror attacks as well as deaths resulting from terror attacks varies considerably over years and decades. Observe that

Is That So? 3.2: Terrorism since 1970

Terrorist activities increased globally from the 1970s to the mid-90s, after which it actually went down for some years. But, from 2000 until 2014, the world witnessed a surge in terror incidents and the number of deaths from it. Since then, there is a downward trend.

Whether this trend will continue is an open question, but terrorism exhibits a positive trend overall during 1970–2019. It is also interesting that

Is That So? 3.3: *9/11* Attacks relative to Global Incidence of Terror in 2001

While *9/11* was spectacular, the global incidence of terror in 2001 in terms of the number of incidents and deaths was actually less compared to the mid-1990s.

Figure 3.1b aggregates the data decade-wise and shows a positive trend of terrorism from 1970s to 2010s.

3.3.2 Success Rate

Are all terror attacks successful? For an event to be counted as a terror attack, GTD uses the criterion that the attackers must have been "out the door" on their way to execute it. An attack is counted as a success as long as it has some tangible effect. If, for instance, a bomb explodes while no one is hurt or there is no property damaged, it is still counted as a success, the rationale being that the act of violence has been committed. Otherwise, if the attackers have commenced their mission but the attack is aborted or foiled, it is termed as unsuccessful. Per this definition, if a bomb is neutralized before it detonates, the attack is not a success. Given this definition,

Is That So? 3.4: Success Rate of Terror Attacks

89% of terror attacks between 1970 and 2019 are successful.

3.3.3 How Deadly are Terror Attacks?

We may consider the average number of people killed per attack as a measure of lethality of terrorism on average. The lethality rate may also be called the kill ratio. Over 1970–2019, the lethality rate is $456{,}235 \div 189{,}233 = 2.41$. That is, on average, between 2 to 3 die from a single terror incidence. Figure 3.2 sheds some light on whether terrorism has become more lethal over time. While *9/11* terror attacks were

[4] As said earlier, the data on the number of deaths are available for 94% of all terror attacks.

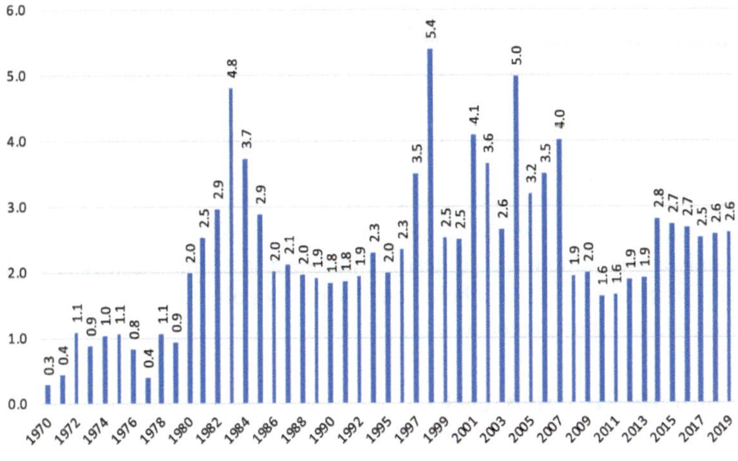

(a)

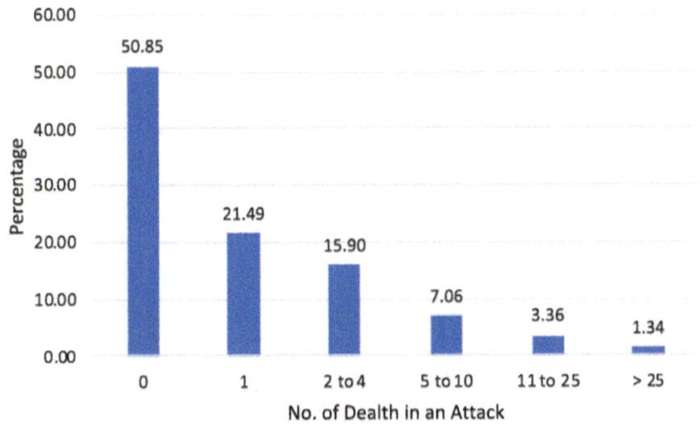

(b)

Fig. 3.2: Lethality or kill ratio and distribution of deaths: globally, 1970–2019. (**a**) Annual. (**b**) Distribution of deaths. *Source*: GTD

the most lethal and killed more than 3000 on September 11, 2001, on average, terrorism has *not* become more lethal. In 2010s, the number of attacks and the number of people killed have increased from the previous decade, but the kill ratio is actually smaller than the previous decade. Thus,

Is That So? 3.5: Lethality or Kill Ratio

The overall lethality or kill ratio (number of people killed on average in one terror attack) during 1970–2019 is 2.41. While the kill ratio increased from 1970s to the subsequent decades, from 1980s onward there is no increase in the kill ratio. It is less in 2010s compared to 1980s, 1990s, or 2000s. Hence, on average, terrorism has become less deadly.

How heterogeneous the terror attacks are in terms of causing death? In view of Fig. 3.2b,

Is That So? 3.6: Deaths from Terror Attacks

About half of all terror attacks do *not* lead to any death and less than 12% lead to more than four deaths.

This may be surprising to some. It is however worth emphasizing that even though only a small fraction of all terror attacks cause a large number of deaths, the major terrorism events create a heightened sense of public fear and anxiety. This is why terrorism is (rightly) seen as a big problem.

3.3.4 Suicide Terror Attacks

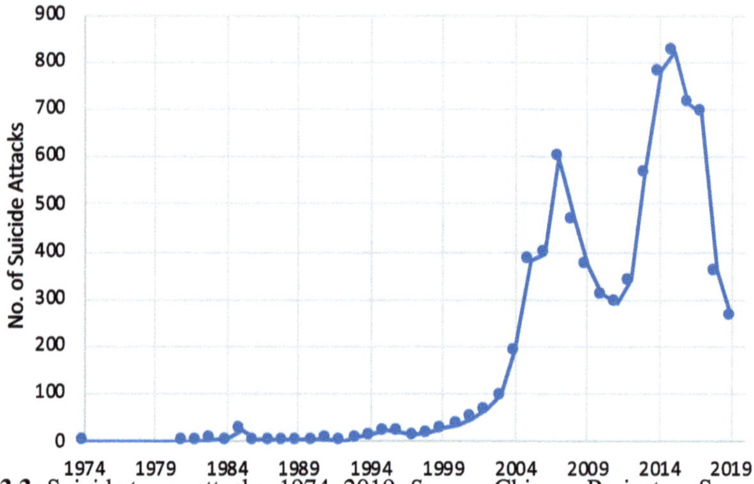

Fig. 3.3: Suicide terror attacks: 1974–2019. *Source*: Chicago Project on Security and Threats, CPOST (2020)

We can divide terror attacks into two broad types: those in which terrorists "plan" to end their lives, i.e., they do not have the intention of escaping and those in which they do not aim to be killed. The former defines the suicide attacks. The suicide attacks that are motivated by the ideology of Islam in the extreme version are commonly described as Jihad. Suicide attacks are special, because they symbolize the ultimate form of self-sacrifice and thus confront our notion of rationality. Note that

Is That So? 3.7: Advent of Suicide Attacks

In the history of terrorism, suicide attacks are relatively recent. The first confirmed suicide attack occurred in 1981.

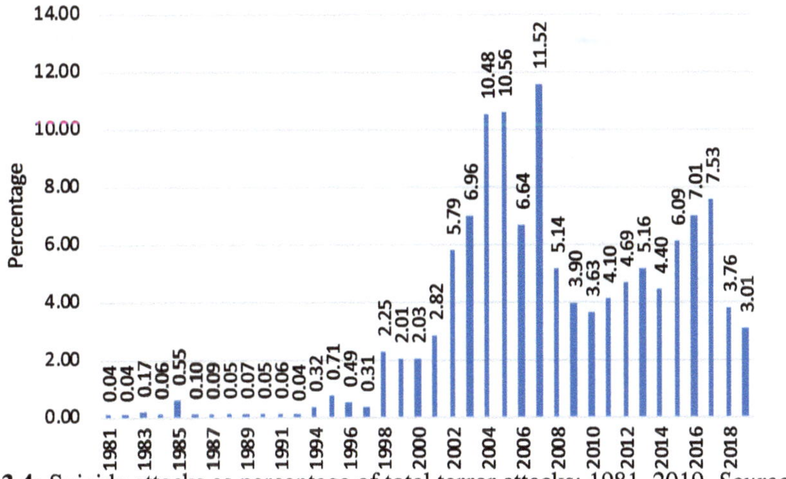

Fig. 3.4: Suicide attacks as percentage of total terror attacks: 1981–2019. *Source*: GTD

The 1981 suicide attack involved a sole attacker hitting the Iraqi embassy in Lebanon. It became a major modus operandi of terror attacks in 1983 when the US embassy in Beirut was hit by a truck killing 63, and, a military barrack housing American and French service members in Beirut was hit by bombs planted in car used by a suicide attacker in October of the same year killing 299. Both attacks were claimed by Hezbollah.

Figure 3.3 graphs the time series of suicide attacks, which includes those possible and confirmed according to Chicago Project on Security and Threats, CPOST (2020), while Fig. 3.4 graphs suicide attacks as percentage of total terror attacks recorded in GTD. We see that

Is That So? 3.8: Suicide Attacks

Suicide attacks are more prevalent in the post-*9/11* era than in the pre-*9/11* era. They constitute respectively 0.32% and 5.86% of all terror attacks during the 1970–2000 period and the 2000–2019 period.

Not only are suicide attacks far more frequent in the post-*9/11* era, their geographical pattern is markedly different, compared to the pre-*9/11* era. Figure 3.5 graphs the top five countries for the number of suicide attacks in these two era. The two sets of countries are completely different.

Is That So? 3.9: Countries Most Affected by Suicide Attacks: Before and After 2001

The top five countries in terms of the number of suicide terror attacks before 2001 are Sri Lanka, Lebanon, Israel, Turkey and West Bank and Gaza, whereas those after 2001 are Iraq, Afghanistan, Pakistan, Nigeria, and Syria.

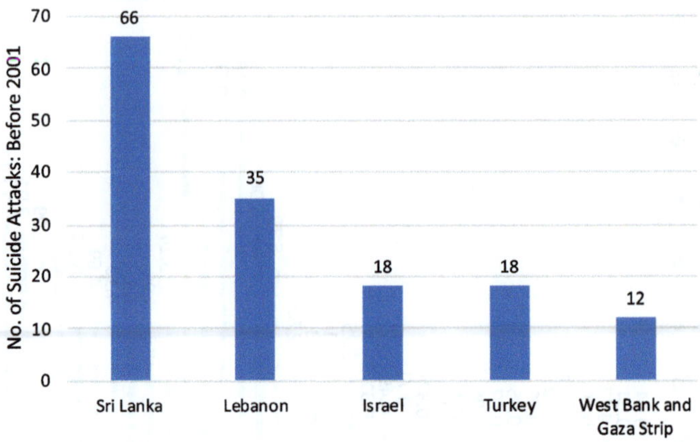

(a)

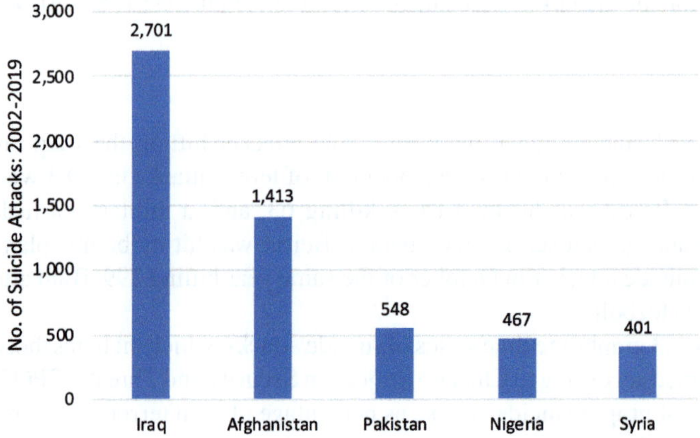

(b)

Fig. 3.5: Distribution of fatalities: suicide attacks before and after 2001. (**a**) Pre-*9/11* era. (**b**) Post-*9/11* era. *Source*: GTD

GTD reports 7269 suicide attacks from 1981 to 2019 (barring 1993) resulting in 73,067 deaths reported for 7146 incidents. This implies a kill ratio or lethality of 10.22. Interestingly, the success rate of a suicide attack is 84%, less than that of all types of attacks. According to Chicago Project on Security and Threats, CPOST (2020), 7982 suicide terror attacks, including possible but unconfirmed occurred during the period 1974–2016 causing 63,202 deaths, thus implying a killing ratio of 8.[5]

Comparing with the kill ratio for all forms of terrorist attacks, we can say that

[5] Chicago Project on Security and Threats, CPOST (2020) reports estimates of both a lower bound and an upper bound for the number of fatalities. In arriving at 63,202 deaths, we have used the annual averages of the two bounds.

Is That So? 3.10: Suicide Attacks as the "Lung Cancer of Terror Attacks"

The kill ratio associated with suicide attacks is in the range of 8–11, which far exceeds the kill ratio for all types of terror attacks (which is 2.41). Suicide terrorism is the most lethal form of terror attacks.

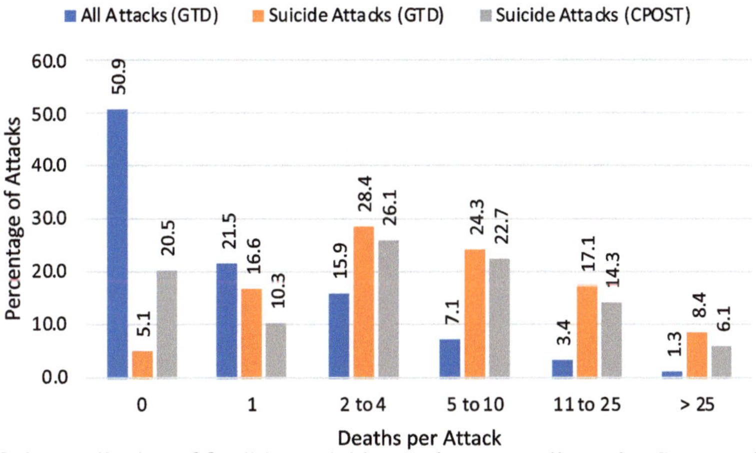

Fig. 3.6: Distribution of fatalities: suicide attacks versus all attacks. *Sources*: GTD (1970–2019); CPOST (1974–2019)

This is why Robert Pape, an expert on suicide terrorism, has described it as the lung cancer of terror acts. Overall, during 1970–2019, while these attacks constituted 3.6% of all terror attacks, they led to 16% of all deaths.

The distribution of fatalities associated with suicide attacks relative to all attacks is displayed in Fig. 3.6. It is an extension of Fig. 1.3 in Chap. 1 by including suicide terrorism data from GTD. Although we see some noticeable difference between GTD and CPOST datasets on suicide terrorism, the broad picture is similar: In contrast to around 50% of all attacks causing no death, nearly 50% of all suicide attacks kill 2 to 10 people.

3.3.5 Tactics and Weaponry

3.3.5.1 Bombing-Explosion and Armed Assault: The Main Tactics Used for Terror Attacks

Terrorists have used different tactics and weaponry like bombing, assassination, hostage-taking, armed assault, hijacking, etc. Figure 3.7 depicts the distribution of terror attacks according to the tactics and weaponry used. As we can see,

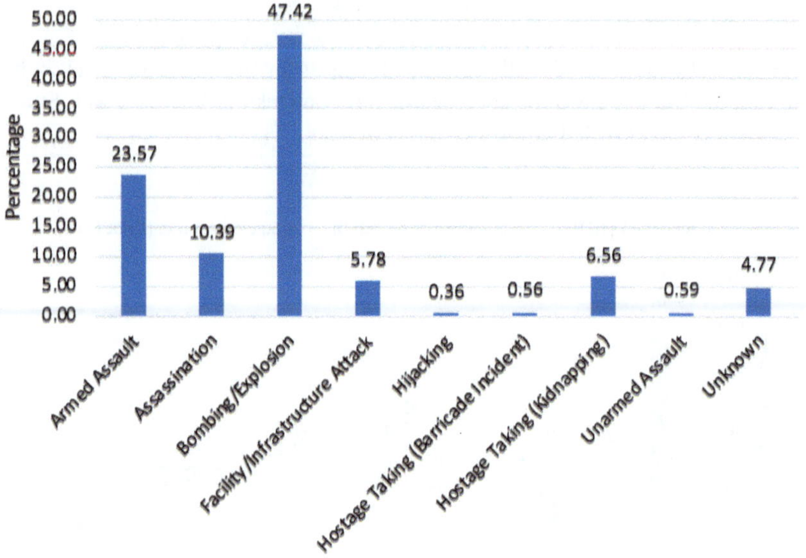

(a)

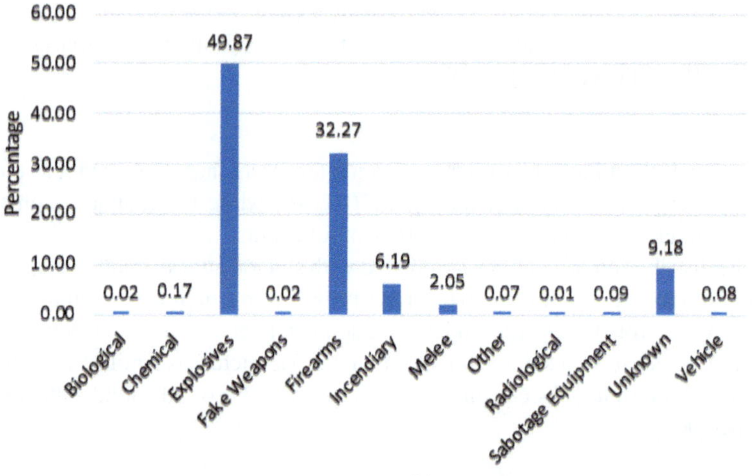

(b)

Fig. 3.7: Distribution of tactics and weaponry used in terror attacks, globally: 1970–2019. (**a**) Tactics or attack type. (**b**) Weaponry. *Source*: GTD

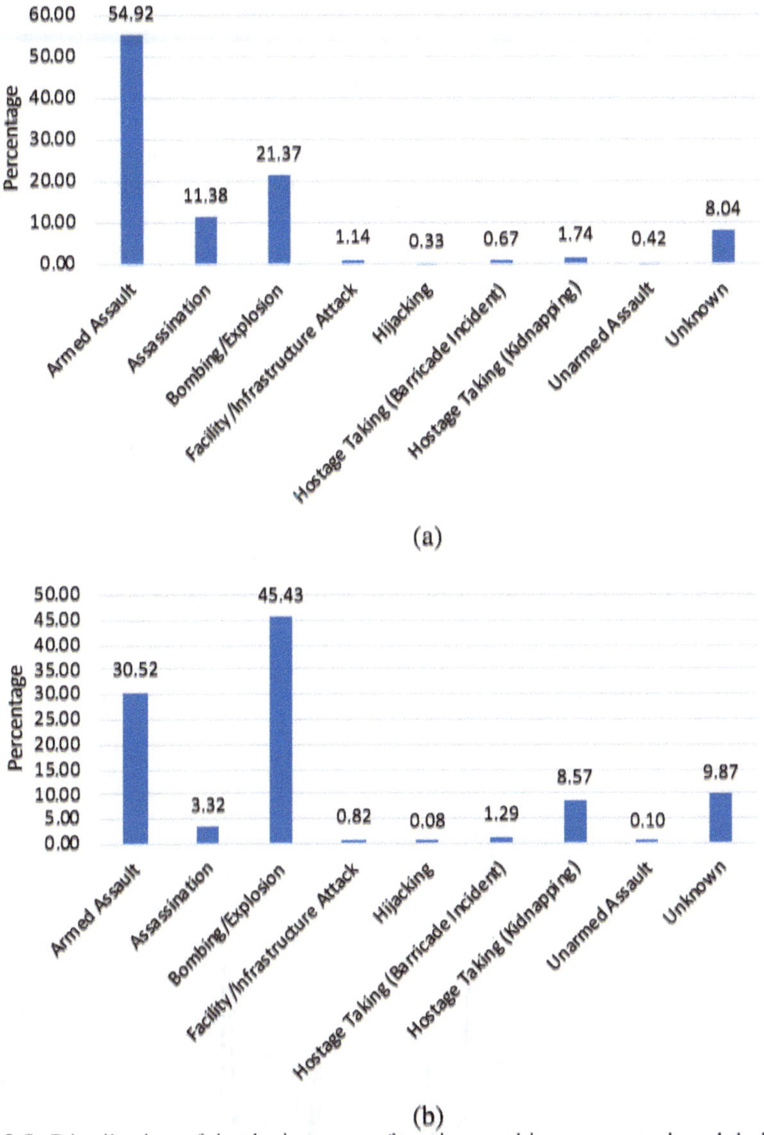

Fig. 3.8: Distribution of deaths in terms of tactics used in terror attacks, globally: 1970–2019. (**a**) Pre-*9/11* era. (**b**) Post-*9/11* era. *Source*: GTD

Is That So? 3.11: Common Tactics

Bombing-cum-explosion and armed assault are the most common tactics used in terrorist attacks.

It is because the logistics of these tactics to successfully execute an attack are the simplest among available options. In contrast, while plane hijacking could end up being spectacular, it is difficult to carry it out and hence used much less. Corresponding to bombing/explosion and armed assault, explosives and fire arms are the two most common weaponry used in terrorist attacks.

Figure 3.7 indicates that armed assault and bombing/explosion are likely to be the two principal tactics causing deaths from terror attacks. Figure 3.8 confirms this for both the pre-*9/11* and post-*9/11* era. Interesting however, the ranking between these two tactics are reversed between the two era. Together, these two tactics constitute more than 70% of terror attacks and cause more than 70% of deaths due to terror attacks.

Is That So? 3.12: Tactics Has Changed from Pre-*9/11* Era to Post-*9/11* Era

While armed assault ranks No. 1 in terms of causing death in the pre-*9/11* era, it is bombing and explosives that is No. 1 in causing death in the post-*9/11* era.

3.3.5.2 Plane Hijacking

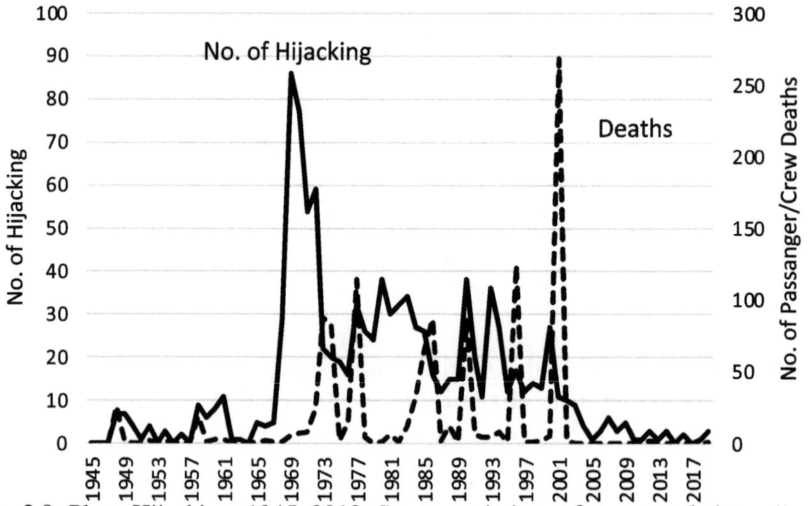

Fig. 3.9: Plane Hijacking: 1945–2019. *Source*: aviation safety network, https://aviation-safety.net; it is a private independent initiative, founded by Harro Ranter and Fabian I. Lujan; permission to use data is thankfully acknowledged

The first recorded skyjacking dates back to 1931 and it occurred in Peru. The first recorded skyjacking of a commercial airliner, a sea plane, took place in 1948. A Hong Kong based Cathay Pacific flight from Macau to Hong Kong was hijacked by four men, who killed the pilot after the take-off. The aim was to land the seaplane in a remote place and rob the passengers. The aircraft however crashed, killing twenty six, leaving only one survivor, a hijacker.

The first *successful* skyjacking took place in 1948 when a Greek T. A. E. airliner was hijacked by six pro-communist students who wanted passage to (the former) Yugoslavia. Many skyjackings involving US planes were undertaken in the late 1950s and the 1960s, most of which had Cuba as their destination. The first such event occurred in 1958. "Take This Plane to Cuba" was to become a common phrase later on. Toward late 1960s such hijacking was so common that FBI thought about setting up a fake Havana airport in southern Florida in order to trick hijackers to thinking they arrived in Cuba. The year 1968 witnessed 27 skyjackings. A surge occurred in 1969 with 82 skyjackings—higher than the sum total of all hijackings in earlier years. Overall, the 1961–1972 period was the golden age of skyjacking. However, it is on a decline ever since. The simple yet important reason for the downturn in skyjacking was the introduction of metal detectors for pre-board screening of passengers. During 2010 to 2018, the total number of plane hijacking was 12, a far cry from 82 during 1969 only.

A time-series graph of the number of plane hijacks and deaths of passengers and crew involved with these events is shown in Fig. 3.9.

3.3.5.3 Chemical, Biological, Radiological, and Nuclear (CBRN) Terrorism

One is always wary of weapons of mass destruction like chemical, biological, radiological, and nuclear arsenal falling into the hands of terrorists. This is CBRN terrorism. While the chances of such deadly weapons in the possession of non-state actors are rather small, the possibility remains and the cost of this happening is gargantuan, almost unthinkable. Billions of dollars have been spent to design and install protection against such terrorism (Binder and Ackerman, 2019).

The dynamics of CBRN terrorism is depicted in Fig. 3.10a. This is based upon POICN dataset, which records CBRN terrorism-related events since 1990. As described earlier, this dataset is not confined to CBRN terror attacks only and contains events where CBRN use is being contemplated. The upper line measures the total number of events, whereas the lower line graphs the number of attacks (both successful and unsuccessful), equal to the sum of "attempted use of agent" and "use of agent." The breakdown of events according to types is shown in Fig. 3.10b.[6] Most of the CBRN events use chemicals. None of the nuclear events actually led to any successful attack.

Out of 516 events recorded over 1990–2016, 240 have resulted in a CBRN attack and the death toll from CBRN terror attacks is 973. The most deadly CBRN attack is attributed to ISIS, which occurred in Iraq in 2016, killing or injuring around 1500. The chemical agents used were chlorine and mustard. The next worst attack dates

[6] The percentage points do not add up to 100, because many events use multiple agents.

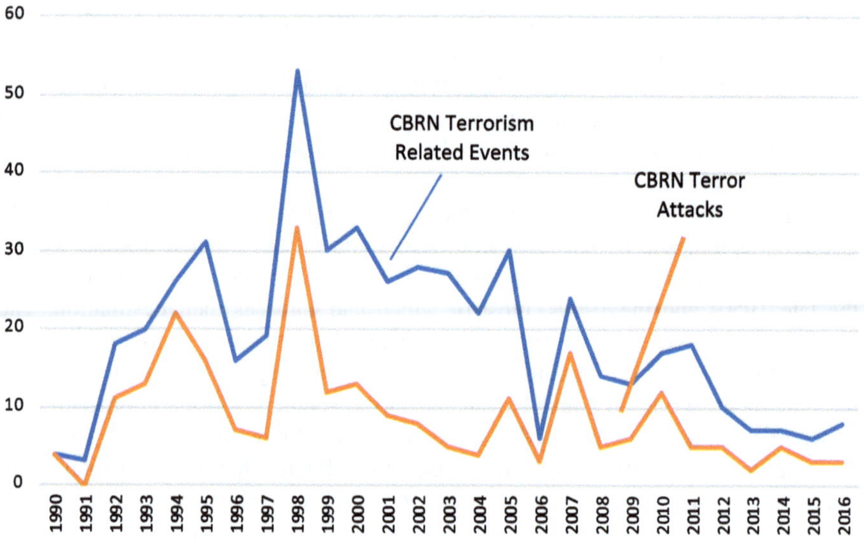

(a)

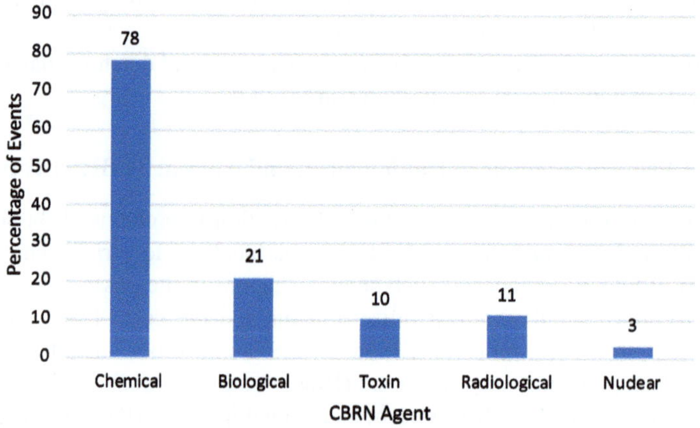

(b)

Fig. 3.10: CBRN Terrorism, 1990–2016. (**a**) CBRN related events and attacks. (**b**) CBRN events type. *Source*: POICN version 2.58

back to 1995 in Japan. The perpetrator was the Aum Shinrikyo group who used the chemical agent sarin. About 1038 people were killed or received injuries. These events and others that caused at least 100 death-plus-injuries are listed in Binder and Ackerman (2019).

3.3.6 Regional Distribution

The incidence of terrorism is greatly uneven across regions and countries. Figure 3.11a shows the percentage of all terror attacks and percentage of deaths from terror in different regions of the world. Various regions are defined in the chapter appendix 3.A. Figure 3.11b shows the same for suicide terrorism only. Clearly, the Middle East and South Asia have borne the brunt of terror attacks, followed by Africa. South America, Central America, and Caribbeans also figure among the relatively high-terror-incidence countries because of their experience in the pre-*9/11* era.

We can more precisely understand the incidence of terror in terms of individual countries afflicted by terrorism. Those most afflicted by terrorism in the pre-*9/11* era are shown in Fig. 3.12. It is no surprise that South and Central American countries feature prominently, given that left-leaning terror groups like FARC, Shining Path, Tupamaros were super-active in this region. Interestingly, Sri Lanka is the leading country by deaths caused by terror attacks, the perpetrator of which is LTTE. The United Kingdom, India, and Spain were victims of terrorism mostly due to IRA, Sikh extremists, and ETA, respectively.[7]

In comparison to Fig. 3.12 that shows the most affected countries in the pre-*9/11* era, Fig. 3.13 demonstrates an almost seismic shift in the landscape of terrorism in the post-*9/11* era. *There is no overlap of the worst-affected countries between the two era, except India.*

Is That So? 3.13: Top Countries Affected by Terrorism

In the Pre-*9/11* era (starting from 1970), the top five countries in descending order of fatalities from terrorist attacks are Sri Lanka, Peru, Colombia, El Salvador, and Nicaragua, whereas their counterparts post-*9/11* are Iraq, Afghanistan, Nigeria, Pakistan, Syria, Afghanistan, Nigeria, Iraq, and Pakistan (SANIP). There is a "continental shift" from South America in the pre-*9/11* era to Middle East and South Asia in the post-*9/11* era.

Iraq leads the post-*9/11* group in both the number of attacks and fatalities from the terror attacks, followed, in relatively recent years, by Afghanistan. Figure 3.14a and (b) illustrate how the number of terror attacks and associated deaths have evolved since *9/11* in each of the top five countries. Panel (c) depicts the share of deaths from terrorism in these countries together in the total number of deaths globally in the 2010s. In each year, more than 60% of deaths from terrorism have occurred in these

[7] There were other groups active in India and Spain, e.g., Naxalites and Catalan Liberation Front.

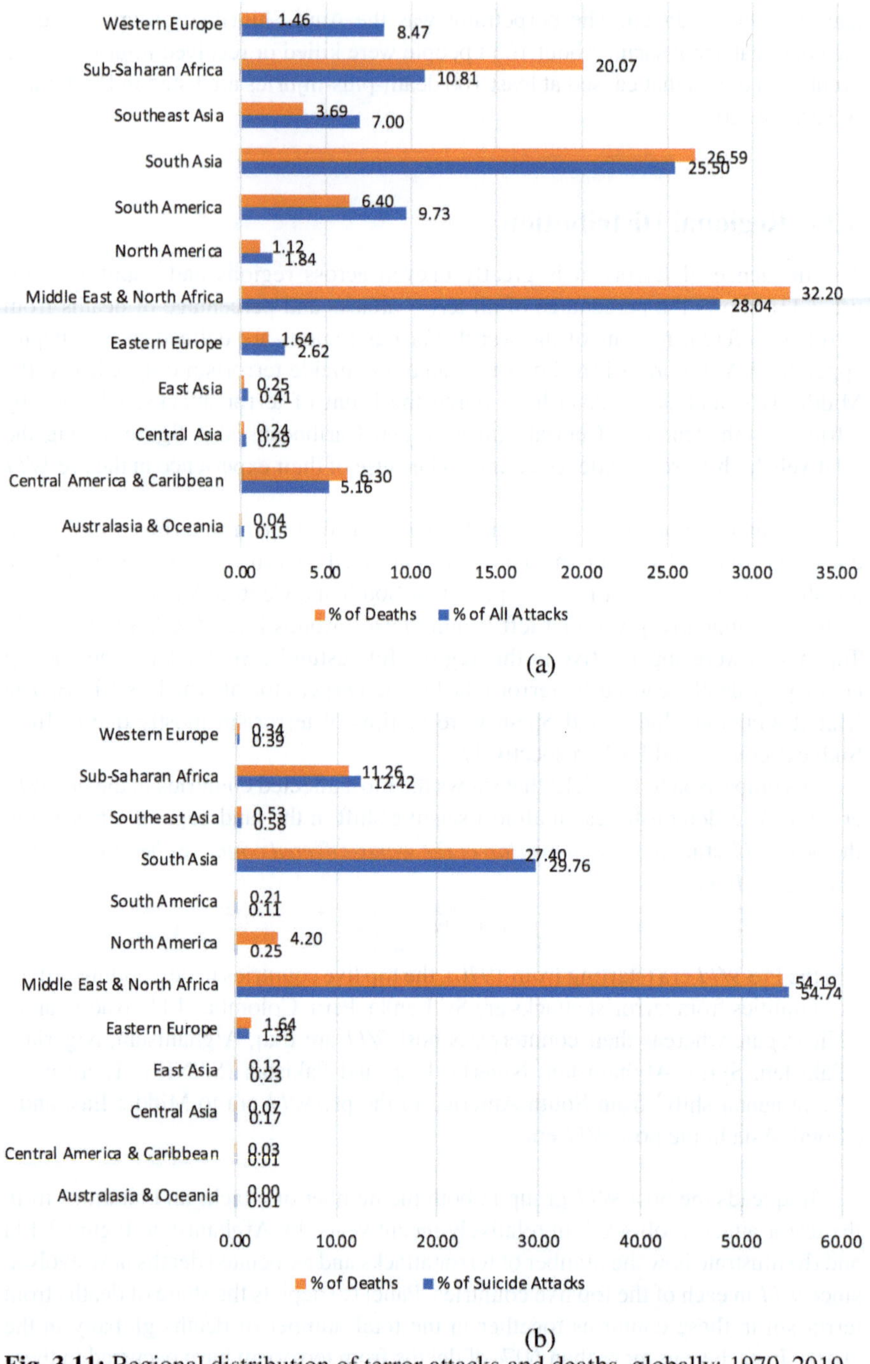

Fig. 3.11: Regional distribution of terror attacks and deaths, globally: 1970–2019, except 1993. (**a**) All forms of terror attacks and deaths. (**b**) Terror attacks and deaths: suicide Terrorism only. *Source*: GTD

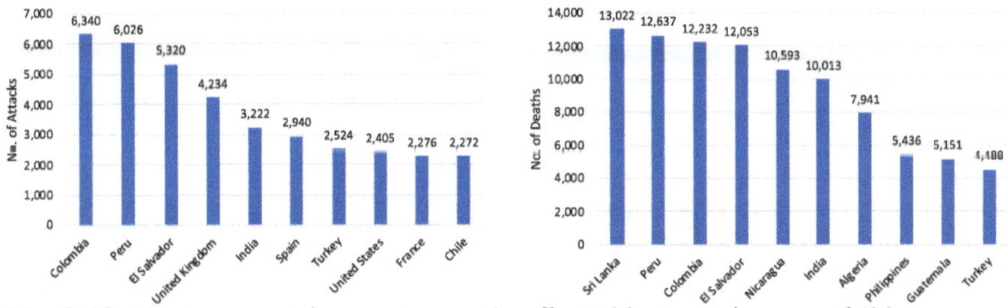

Fig. 3.12: Top ten countries most severely affected by terrorism: pre-*9/11* (1970–2000). *Source*: GTD

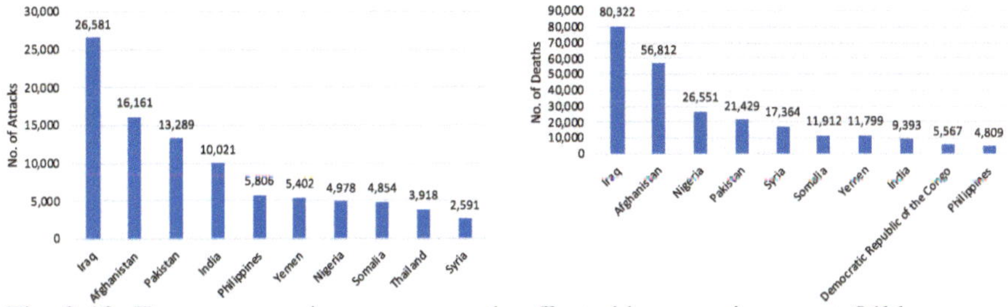

Fig. 3.13: Top ten countries most severely affected by terrorism: post-*9/11* (2002–2019). *Source*: GTD

five countries. *It is remarkable that there was no incidence of terrorism in SANIP countries prior to 2002.*

As noted in Chap. 1, beginning 2012, the annual Global Terrorism Index Report published by the Institute for Peace and Economics (IEP) ranks various countries in terms of the impact of the terrorism by a single number, called GTI that ranges from 0 to 10. It is constructed by taking into consideration four attributes of terror attacks in a country: the number of terror attacks, the number of deaths, the number of injuries as well as an index of physical property damaged during the current year as well as the past four years. The advantage of an index like GTI is that the scale of terrorism can be easily compared across countries and regions and over time. See the chapter Appendix 3.B for an illustration. Figure 1.1 in Chap. 1 presents color-coded world maps based on the magnitude of GTI scores for 2013, 2016, and 2019. The SANIP countries figure as the most severely impacted in terms of the GTI.

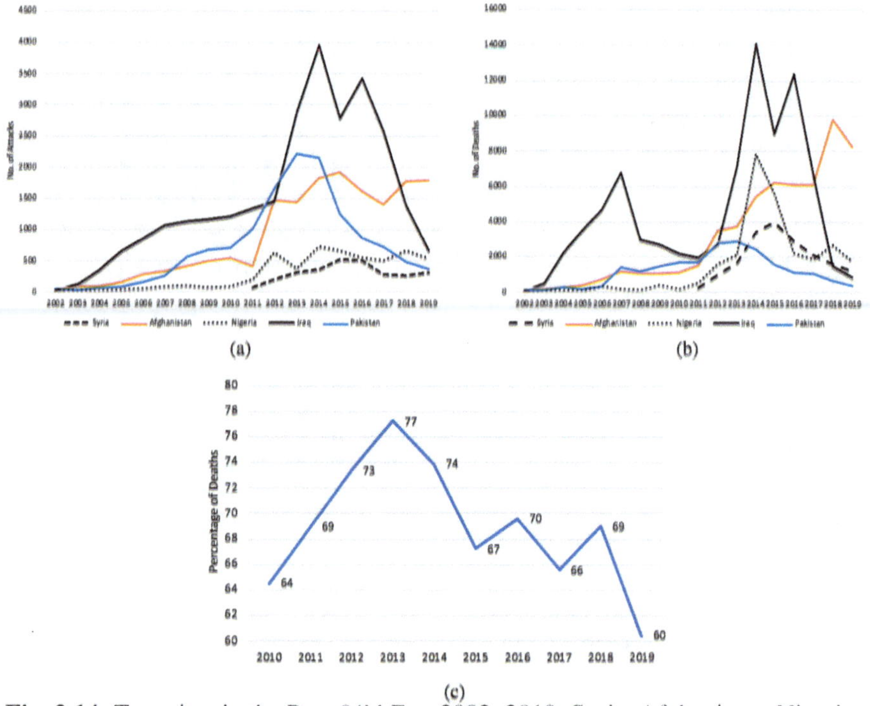

Fig. 3.14: Terrorism in the Post-*9/11* Era, 2002–2019: Syria, Afghanistan, Nigeria, Iraq, and Pakistan. (**a**) Number of attacks. (**b**) Number of deaths. (**c**) Share of SANIP countries in total number of deaths globally. *Source*: GTD

3.3.7 Domestic Versus Transnational Terrorism

In Chap. 1 we learned that domestic terrorism is much more prevalent than transnational terrorism. In GTD, given the information on all terror incidents, about half could be reasonably clearly identified as either domestic or transnational. Within this subset, the global distribution of domestic and transnational terrorism over the years is presented in Fig. 3.15. It may be surprising to note that

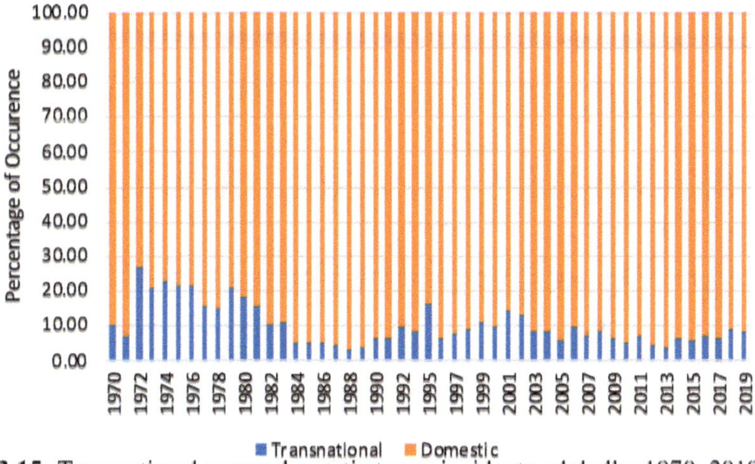

Fig. 3.15: Transnational versus domestic terror incidents, globally: 1970–2019. *Source*: GTD; Note: About half of all recorded incidents are neither identified as transnational nor as domestic. The graph pertains to those identified as transnational or domestic

Is That So? 3.14: Domestic Versus Transnational Terrorism

Compared to the 1970s or even 1990s, in the 2000s and 2010s transnational terrorism is relatively less incident than domestic terrorism.

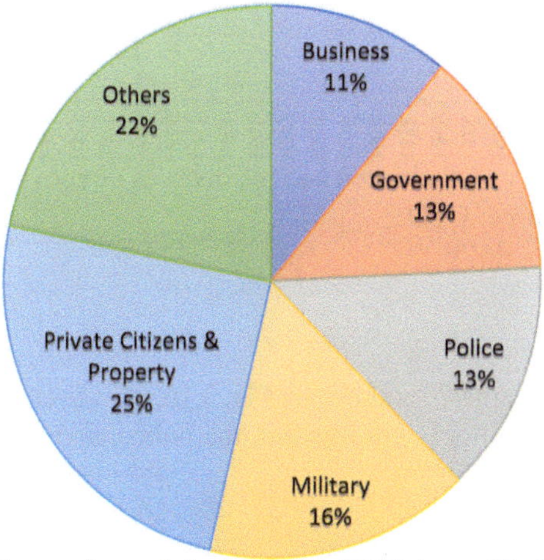

Fig. 3.16: Targets of terrorism, globally: 1970–2019 (overall). *Source*: GTD

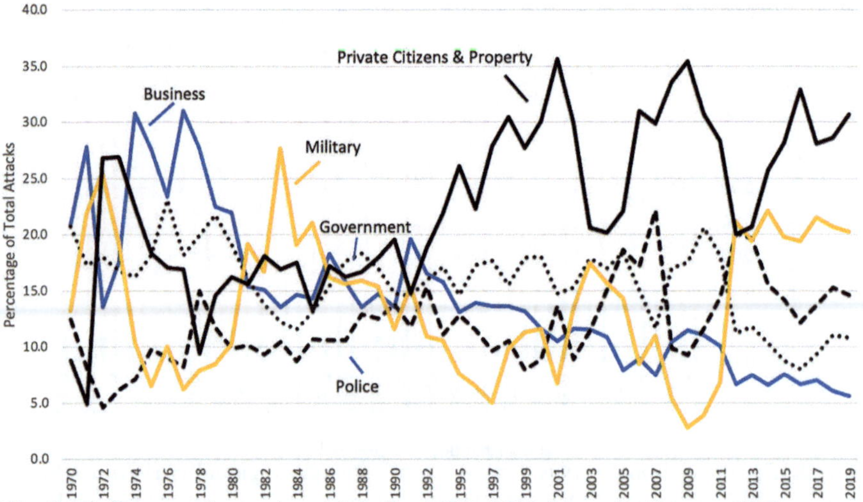

Fig. 3.17: Targets of terrorism, globally, 1970–2019 (annual). *Source*: GTD

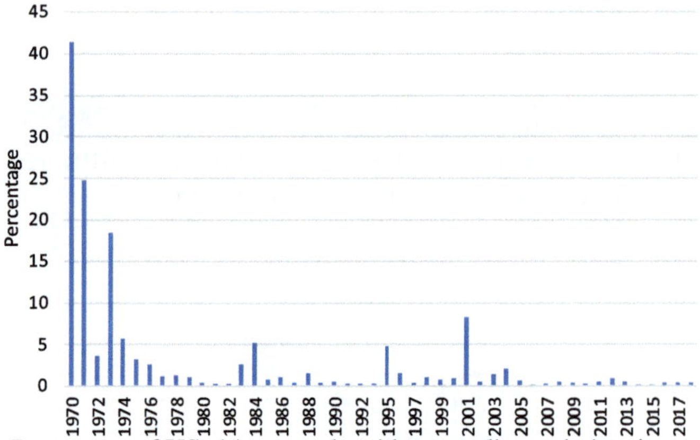

Fig. 3.18: Percentage of US citizens and residents as direct victims in terms of death and injury. *Source*: GTD

3.3.8 Targets

Who do the terrorists target? As shown in Fig. 3.16, private citizens and property top the list, followed my military, government, the police, and business. The evolution of the shares of these targets over time is depicted in Fig. 3.17. We may notice the share of businesses as a terrorist target has fallen over time, whereas, compared to the pre-*9/11* era, the share of private citizens and property is generally higher in the post-*9/11* years.

The USA being the most powerful and influential nation, for those who oppose Western values, education, and dominance, the USA becomes a target of dislike and hatred. It is therefore of interest to understand the dynamics of US interests being targets of terrorist attacks. As shown in Sandler (2015), the share of transnational attacks directed toward US interests has declined over time—numbering from 200+ in some years in the 1970s to less than 50 by 2012. Overall, about 35–40% of all transnational attacks during the same period were directed toward US interests. US "interests" include US citizens, residents, armed forces, businesses, and material properties belonging to US entities. Apart from *9/11* there are other prominent terrorist attacks against US interests, e.g., al-Qaeda attack on a US Navy destroyer in Yemen in 2000.

The GTD is not readily amenable to identify terror attacks against US interests. Hence, the precise numbers of attacks on US interests in more recent years are not readily available. But, as shown in Fig. 3.18, in terms of victims, killed, or injured in terror attacks, the percentage for the USA is well below 5% from 2002 to 2018.

Is That So? 3.15: Terror Attacks against US Interests and US Citizens and Residents as Victims

The number of transnational terror attacks against US interests has declined over time, very few of which occurs on US soil. Since 2002, the share of the USA in the number of victims of terror attacks is less than 5%.

3.3.9 Heterogeneity across Terror Organizations

Many terror groups were introduced in Chap. 2. These were the major groups whose count is certainly below one hundred. However, the *total* number of terror organizations, big and small, identified in the post-World War II era runs into thousands. A salient feature of the terror organizations and their activities is that there is considerable heterogeneity among them in terms of scale of activity or virulence and their lifespan. Indeed, only a small fraction of them have launched a large number of attacks, caused massive number of fatalities and remained active for a considerable length of time.

3.3.9.1 Heterogeneity in Terms of Number of Attacks and Fatalities

Which are the top terror organizations in terms of the number of attacks and causing deaths? Figure 3.19a depicts those, who have led more than 2000 attacks, whereas panel (b) lists those whose attacks have caused more than 5000 deaths. Taliban and ISIS are the leaders. Apart from the Islamic groups, The Shining Path of Peru and LTTE of Sri Lanka are credited with most terror attacks and/or deaths.

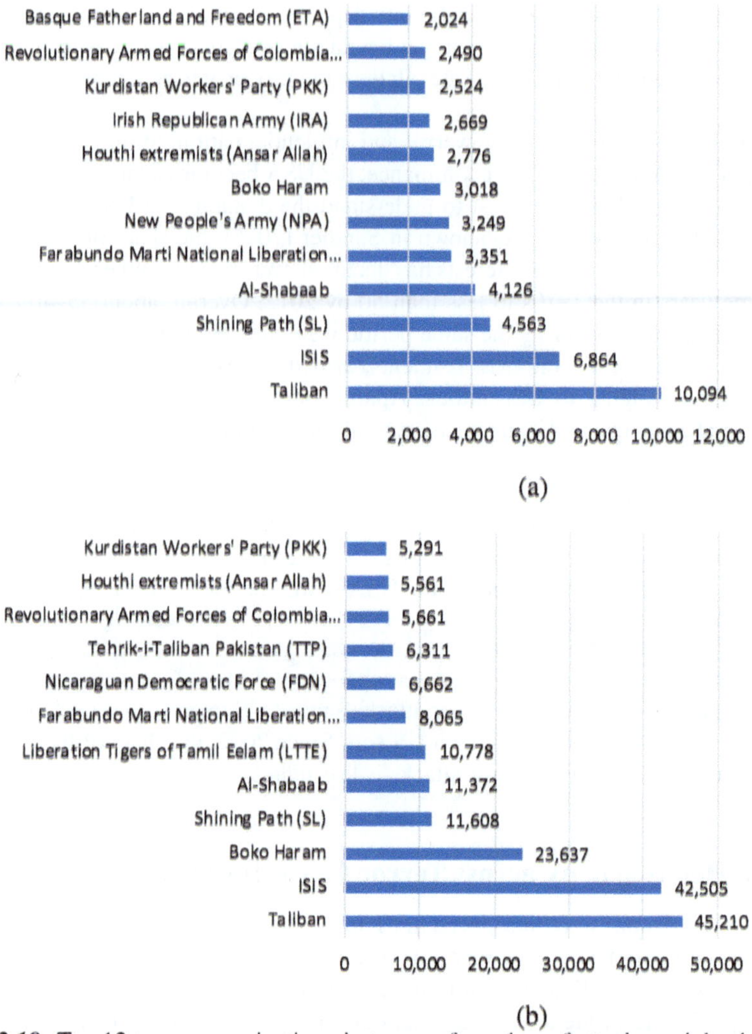

Fig. 3.19: Top 12 terror organizations in terms of number of attacks and deaths inflicted, globally: 1970–2019. (**a**) Number of attacks. (**b**) Deaths. *Source*: GTD

While a large number of terror groups have operated in different regions of the world over different time periods in the latter half of the twentieth century, the data reveals something interesting about the fraction of them who remain active over time and are lethal.

Is That So? 3.16: Lethality of Terror Organizations

Nearly half of the terror organizations mount one attack only and a little over half have caused no deaths in their terror attacks.

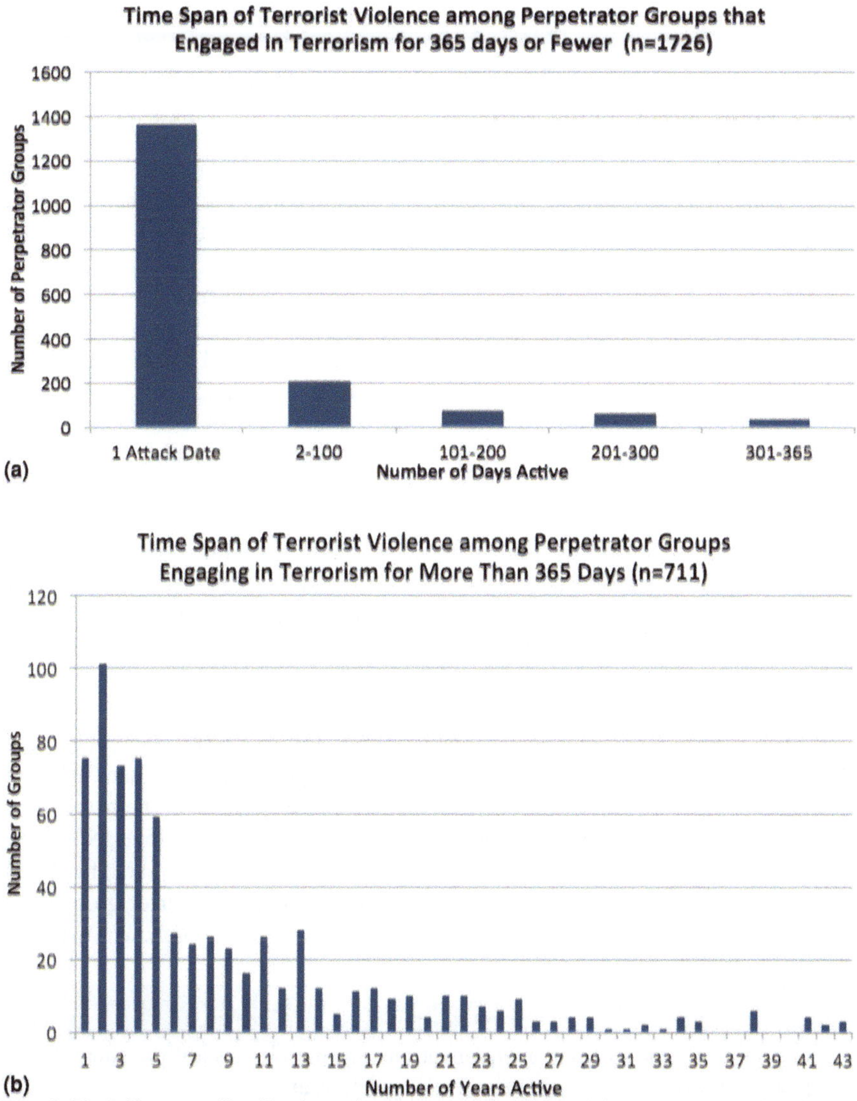

Fig. 3.20: Life-span distribution of terror organizations. (**a**) Among organizations that lasted no more than one year. (**b**) Among organizations that lasted over one year. *Source*: Miller (2016); permission to reproduce from the author is thankfully acknowledged

In other words, a large fraction of terrorist groups have caused minor damages only.

3.3.9.2 Heterogeneity in Longevity

What is the lifespan of terror groups? The conventional wisdom based on Rapoport (1992) is that as high as about 90% of terror organizations last less than one year, and, about 50% of those who survive beyond one year do not last more than ten years.

Miller (2016) has analyzed the lifespan of terror organizations by using GTD covering the period 1970–2013. She found 3120 unique entries for the perpetrator's name in the dataset, out of which 683 entries were discarded because no formal organizations could be associated with them. Of the remaining (2437), she found that 79% were active for a single day only. Furthermore, 71% of terror organizations (1726 in number) "lived" no more than a year. The distribution of these organizations according to their time span of violence is exhibited in part (a) of Fig. 3.20. The remaining 711 organizations (29% of non-generic perpetrators) were actively engaged in terrorist attacks for more than one year. The distribution of their longevity is graphed in part (b). It is heavily skewed to the right, as more than half of the organizations (55%) carried out attacks for no more than five years. Ranging from one year (75 organizations) to 43 years (three organizations), on average, these organizations engaged in terrorism for 8.7 years. Their terrorist activity comprises 94% of attacks and 95% of all fatalities perpetrated by non-generic organizations.

Other studies like Jones and Libicki (2008), Vittori (2009), Gaibulloev and Sandler (2013), and Phillips (2014), which are based on datasets other than GTD, find much less percentage of terror groups unable to survive a full year. The percentages of such short-lived terrorist groups in these studies are respectively 25%, 59%, 26%, and 28%.[8] However, the aforementioned studies did not cover the years after 2007. Phillips (2017) has calculated the average of the percentages of terror groups over eight studies relying on GTD and other datasets; it is equal to 52%. We may thus summarize that

Is That So? 3.17: Survival of Terror Organizations

A very large fraction of terror organizations are merely a one-time show. Less than 50% of terror organization survive over one year.

In Sect. 7.5 of Chap. 7, we will study the factors that explain the variations in longevity among terror organizations.

[8] In an early pre-*9/11* study, Crenshaw (1991) analyzed 77 terrorist groups from 1960s to 1980s and found that, among them, 11 (14%) lasted for 1–5 years, 19 (25%) for 5–10 years, and the remainder (61%) for 10 years or more. The "end" was defined as year in which a group openly declared its renunciation of violence. However, her study did not include one-hit wonders.

3.4 Terrorism in the Western and "Organization of Economic Cooperation and Development (OECD)" Countries

Born out of a coalition of European countries to run the US funded Marshall Plan, the OECD came into existence in 1961 in recognition of the interdependence and cooperation among the member countries. It is an intergovernmental organization. Beginning with twenty member countries, the membership has expanded to thirty six as of 2021.[9] Most of OECD nations are relatively affluent.

It is important to understand how these countries are directly affected by terrorism.

Is That So? 3.18: Israel and Turkey

Within the OECD countries, Israel and Turkey have been afflicted by terrorism the most.

Israel has been the target of Palestinian groups for obvious reasons, and most terror attacks in Turkey have been perpetrated by the Kurdish groups. The reasons of terror attacks by these groups are political, not ideological. Figure 3.21 shows the time-series plots of the number of terror attacks and fatalities for member countries except Israel and Turkey and those for Israel and Turkey combined. Observe that

Is That So? 3.19: Incidence of Terror Attacks in OECD Countries

Compared to the pre-*9/11* era, in the post-9/11 era the number of terror attacks in the OECD countries is smaller.

However, from 2005 onward there is a gradual increase in the number of terror attacks and fatalities till 2016. These numbers have declined since 2016. The kill ratios over the period 1970–2019 are respectively 0.54 and 1.38 for OECD countries barring Israel and Turkey, and, Israel–Turkey combined. Comparing with the kill ratio for all countries combined,

Is That So? 3.20: Kill Ratio in the OECD Countries

The kill ratio in OECD countries is much smaller than that for all countries combined.

This is because of the more efficient security measures in place in the OECD countries.

From now on, we will focus on OECD countries except Israel and Turkey. Figure 3.22 is the time-series graph of terror attacks and fatalities experienced by OECD countries as the percentage of the global totals. While during the 1970s,

[9] The original members were: Austria, Belgium, Canada, Denmark, France, Greece, Iceland, Ireland, Italy, Luxembourg, Netherlands, Norway, Portugal, Spain, Sweden, Switzerland, Turkey, USA, United Kingdom, and West Germany (now Germany). The additional sixteen countries are: Chile, Czech Republic, Estonia, Finland, Hungary, Israel, Italy, Japan, Korea, Latvia, Lithuania, Mexico, New Zealand, Poland, Slovak Republic, and Slovenia.

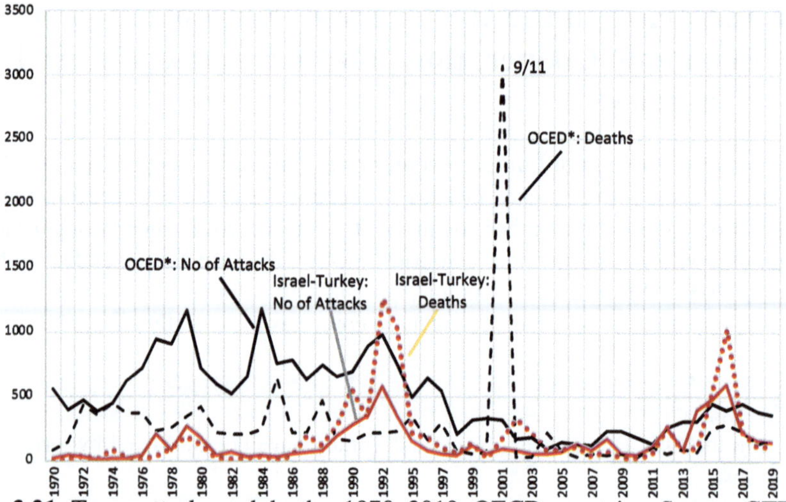

Fig. 3.21: Terror attacks and deaths, 1970–2019: OECD countries. *Source*: GTD; * denotes that Israel and Turkey are excluded

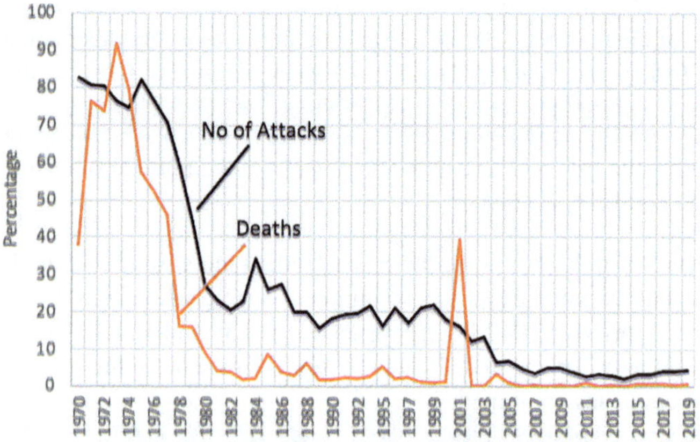

Fig. 3.22: Terror attacks and deaths, 1970–2019: OECD countries relative to the global totals. *Source*: GTD; Israel and Turkey are excluded

those in the OECD countries were somewhat high or significant compared to global totals, since then the relative incidence of terrorism in these countries has declined considerably. Overall, there is a sharp difference in the pattern between the pre-*9/11* period and the post-*9/11* years.

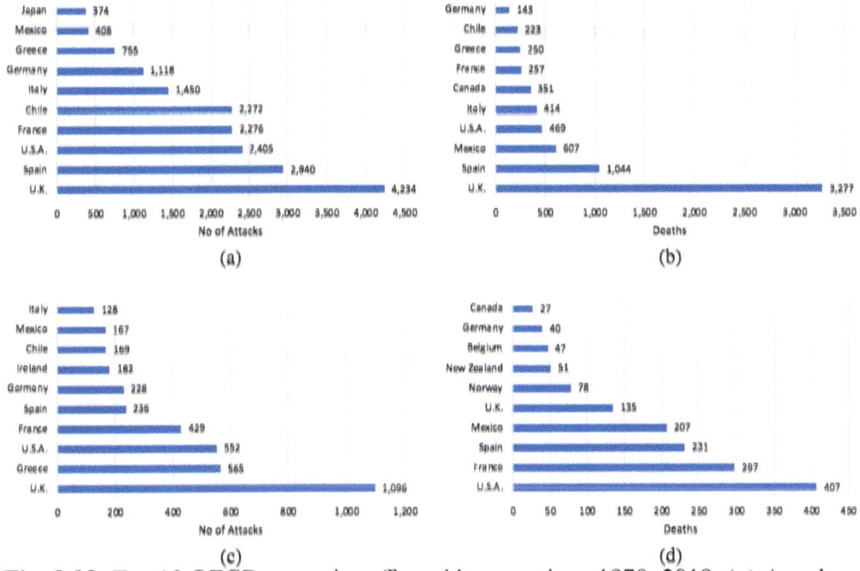

Fig. 3.23: Top 10 OECD countries affected by terrorism, 1970–2019. (**a**) Attacks: 1970–2000. (**b**) Deaths: 1970–2000. (**c**) Attacks: 2002–2019. (**d**) Deaths: 2002–2019. *Source*: GTD; Israel and Turkey are excluded

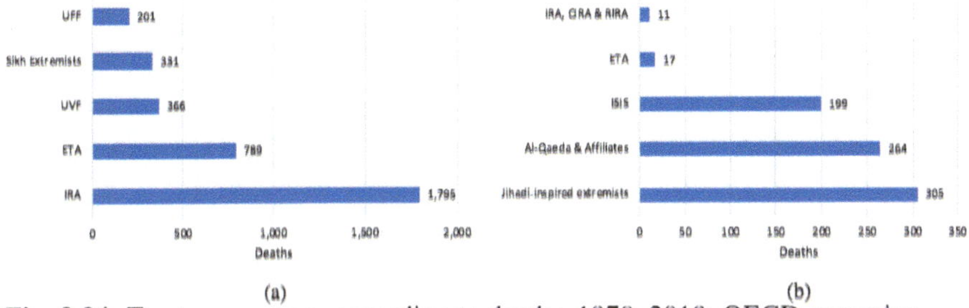

Fig. 3.24: Top terror groups according to deaths, 1970–2019: OECD countries (Israel and Turkey excluded). (**a**) 1970–2000. (**b**) 2002–2019. *Source*: GTD

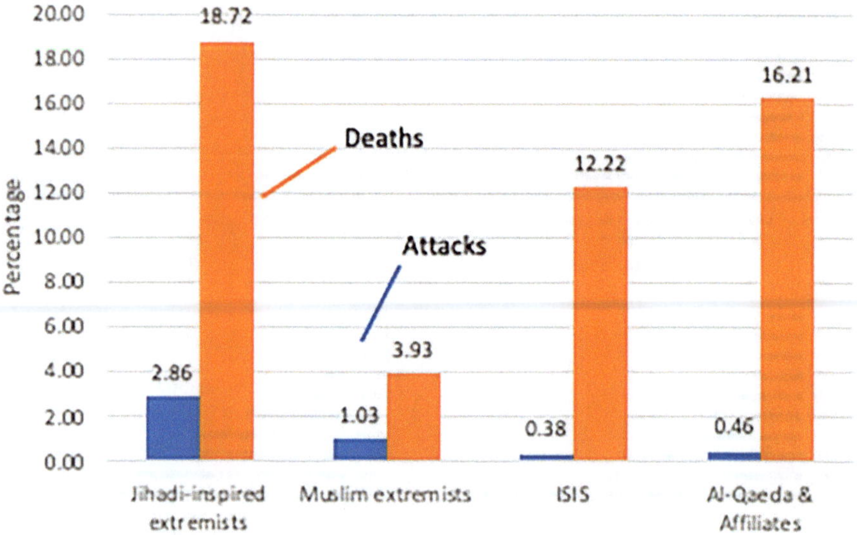

Fig. 3.25: Percentage of attacks by islamic fundamentalists in OECD countries, 2002 and onwards (Israel and Turkey excluded). *Source*: GTD

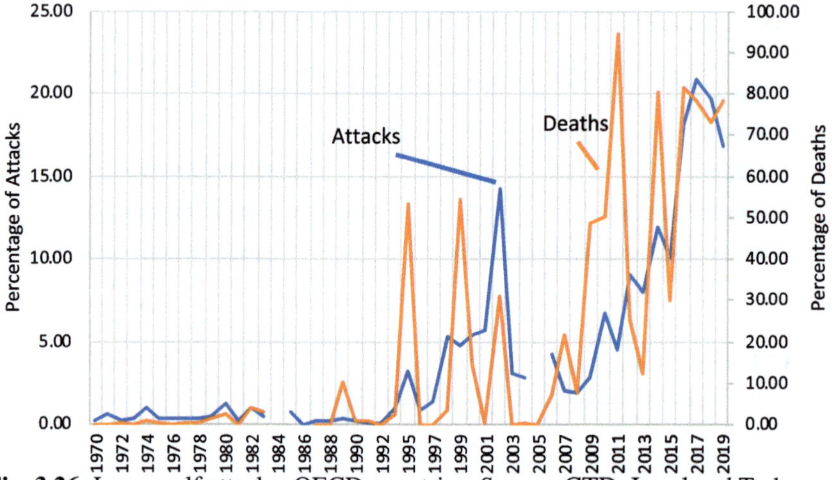

Fig. 3.26: Lone-wolf attacks: OECD countries. *Source*: GTD; Israel and Turkey are excluded

Is That So? 3.21: Share of OECD Countries in the Global Total of Terror Attacks and Deaths from Terror Attacks

Over 1970–2000, OECD countries except Israel and Turkey experienced 27% and 5% of global totals of attacks and deaths from terrorism, whereas over 2001–2019 (which includes *9/11* attacks)), the respective shares are 3.5% and 1.5%.

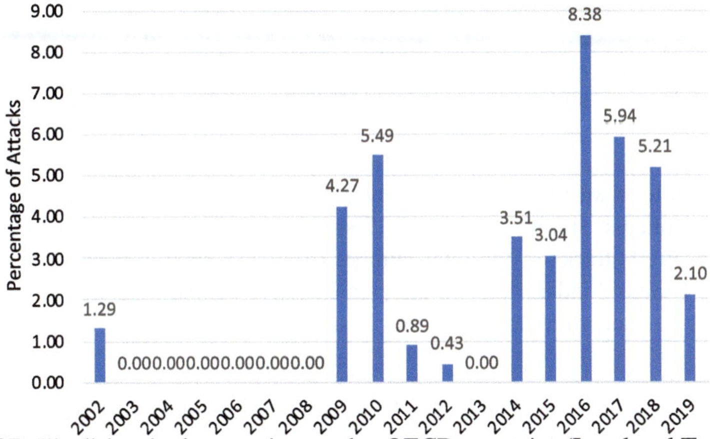

Fig. 3.27: Jihadi-inspired-extremist attacks: OECD countries (Israel and Turkey excluded). *Source*: GTD

Which are the OECD countries that are hit most by terrorism? Figure 3.23 shows the top ten OECD countries in terms of number of attacks and deaths. In the pre-*9/11* era, it is England and Spain who faced the burden of terrorism the most, attributed mainly to IRA and ETA, respectively. In the post-*9/11* period, it is the USA and France, which are most severely affected by terrorism in terms of death. In the following section, we will see which groups have been active in the USA. Fatalities from terror attacks in France in this period are mostly due to ISIS and jihadi-inspired extremists.

Which are the most active terror groups in the OECD countries? Figure 3.24 lists the top five in terms of fatalities they have inflicted in the pre-*9/11* and post-*9/11* periods. In the pre-*9/11* era, It is the IRA and other groups (in Ireland), followed by ETA (targeting Spain). Sikh extremists figure because of their planting of explosive devices in Air India flight en route from Toronto to London in 1985 that killed 329 passengers and crew. In the post-*9/11* period, it is the jihadi-inspired extremists and Islamic terror groups like ISIS and al-Qaeda that top the list in killing people. Figure 3.25 plots the number of attacks by four groups of Islamic fundamentalist groups and individuals and deaths caused by these attacks as percentage of total number of attacks and deaths by terrorism in the OECD countries (barring Israel and Turkey) during the 2002–2019 period. We see that the percentage of number of attacks compared to the OECD total is rather small, whereas the percentages of fatalities are high, consistent with Fig. 3.24b.

Lone-wolf (single-person and unaffiliated) attacks have become more common in the OECD countries. Notice from Fig. 3.26 that the percentage of lone-wolf attacks in total number of attacks and that of deaths from lone-wolf attacks in total number of deaths from all terror attacks in OECD countries are on the rise since 2005. Indeed,

Is That So? 3.22: Lone-Wolf Terror Attacks

In seven out of ten years in the 2010s, lone-wolf attacks have claimed at least 50% of deaths from all terror attacks in OECD countries not including Israel and Turkey.

Not all lone-wolf attacks or those by groups of individuals unaffiliated with any group are jihadis, although, as Fig. 3.27 shows, the number and the percentage of jihadi-inspired attacks in the total number of attacks show a positive trend since 2009. Is Islamic fundamentalism the prime motive behind lone-wolf attacks? The answer is no. According to Institute for Economics & Peace (2015),

Is That So? 3.23: Prime Motive behind Lone-Wolf Terror Attacks

Sixty-seven percent of deaths from lone-wolf attacks in the West over the period 2006–2014 resulted from those with a political motivation.

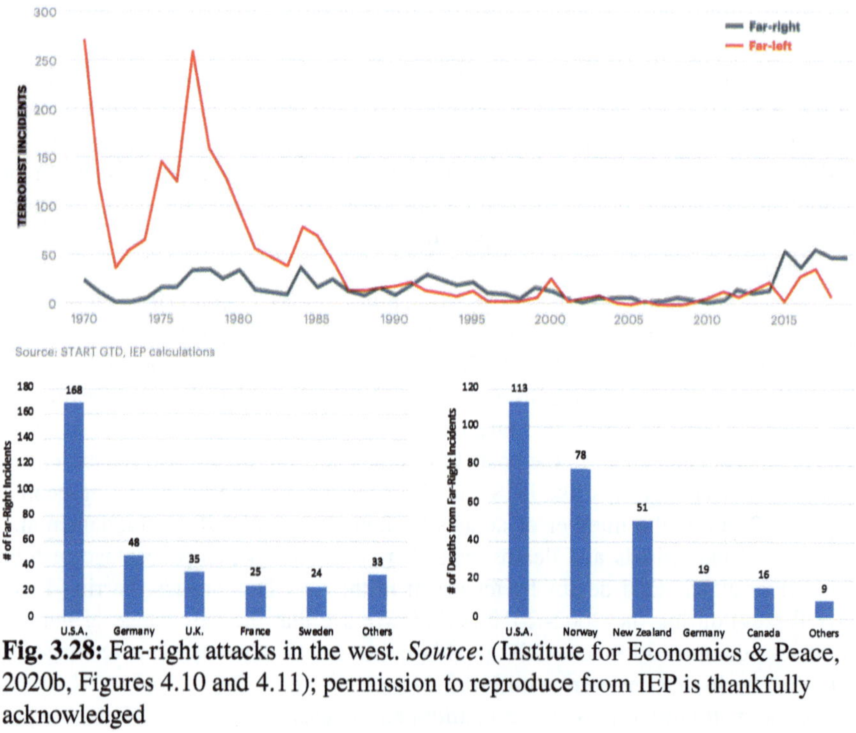

Fig. 3.28: Far-right attacks in the west. *Source*: (Institute for Economics & Peace, 2020b, Figures 4.10 and 4.11); permission to reproduce from IEP is thankfully acknowledged

Another noteworthy feature of terrorism in the West is the rise of far-right incidents in recent years. The top panel of Fig. 3.28 shows the graph of far-right and far-left terror incidents in the West. In the 1970s and 1980s, the far-left incidents dominated over the far-right incidents, whereas, in 2010s it is the opposite.[10] The bottom panel exhibits the country-wise distribution of such attacks and deaths from them, showing that these attacks are most incident and severe in the USA.

3.5 Terrorism in the USA: 1970 Onward

While the majority of terror attacks and deaths occur in a limited number of countries which are not affluent, advanced countries are not immune to terror attacks. The USA—arguably the most advanced country and certainly the most powerful—also has a history of terror attacks and groups. To begin with,

Is That So? 3.24: Terror Attacks in the USA

During 1970–2019 (excluding 1993) the USA witnessed 3004 terror attacks on its soil claiming 3890 lives.

The overall lethality rate is 1.33 (including *9/11* attacks), which is much less than the global average of 2.41.[11] Of 2794 attacks, 2340 (84%) were successful, and, 356, i.e., thirteen percent of attacks were lethal (killing at least one). It is worth noting that 77% of all deaths (3001) occurred on September 11, 2001, while the 1995 bombing of the Federal building in Oklahoma City, Oklahoma, resulted in 4% of all deaths (168 in number).

The annual time series of the number of terror attacks in the USA and deaths associated with them are depicted in Fig. 3.29a. We see that

Is That So? 3.25: Trend of Terror Attacks in the USA

Terror attacks drastically fell in number in the 1980s compared to the 1970s. Since then there has been a gradual decline followed by a modest upward trend in recent times.

Part (b) of Fig. 3.29 traces the time series of the percentage of lethal terror attacks, whereas part (c) presents the time series of the percentage of "successful" terror attacks. Clearly, terror attacks in the USA have not become more lethal or successful over the years. There is, however, a considerable variation in the share of lethal attacks and the success rate of terror attacks over the years.

Who are the perpetrators? Table 3.1 lists the top ten for each decade. In the 1970s the principal perpetrators were Puerto Rican nationalists as well as leftist radical groups emerging out of civil rights and anti-war movements of the 1960s. In the 1980s, attacks by left-wing extremists waned while those from anti-abortion extremists became more common. Their activities continued through the 1990s. Environmental extremists also became prominent, while attacks by left-wing extremists and Puerto Rican nationalists became a rarity. Compared to 1990s, attacks by anti-abortionists in 2000s were considerably smaller in number, but activities of animal protection and environment extremists continued. It is not surprising that

[10] It is interesting that the recent rise in far-right terror incidents coincides with the fall of ISIS.

[11] Data on fatalities are available for 2984 terror events. Hence lethality rate = 3890 ÷ 2984 = 1.33.

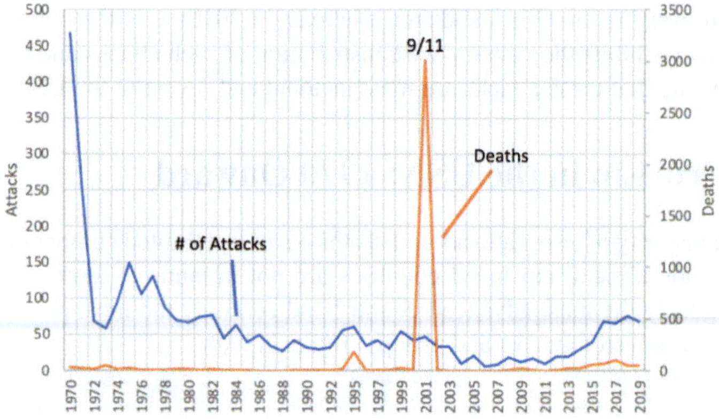

(a)

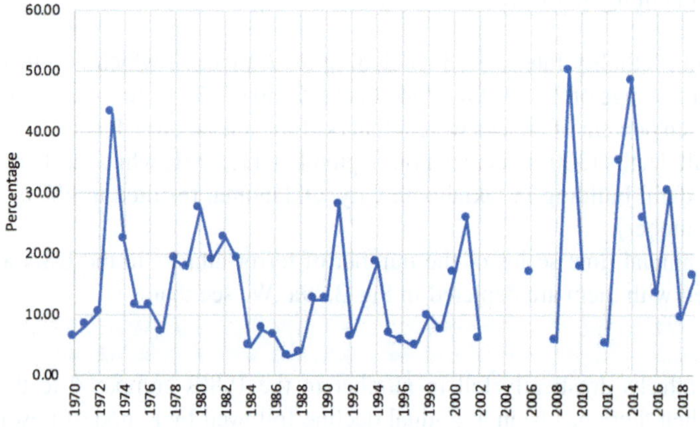

(b)

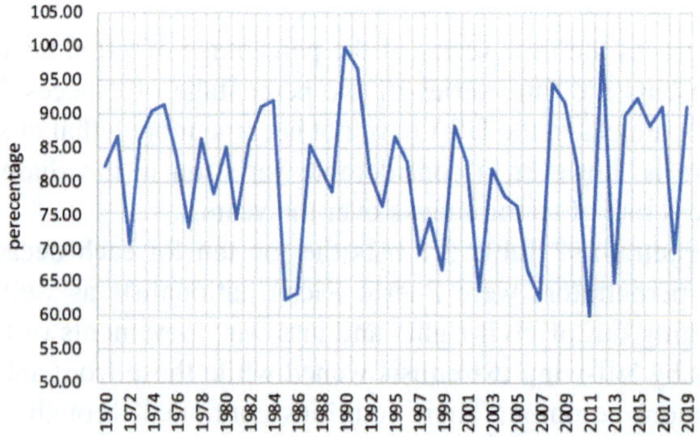

(c)

Fig. 3.29: Terror attacks, deaths, and share of lethal attacks: USA, 1970–2019. (**a**) Number of terror attacks and deaths. (**b**) Lethal attacks as percentage of total attacks. (**c**) Success rate. *Source*: GTD

Groups	# of attacks	Groups	# of attacks
1970s		**1980s**	
Left-Wing Militants	169	Anti-Abortion extremists	74
Fuerzas Armadas de Liberacion Nacional (FALN)	107	Macheteros	31
New World Liberation Front (NWLF)	86	Jewish Defense League (JDL)	30
Black Nationalists	82	Omega-7	25
Student Radicals	71	United Freedom Front (UFF)	19
White extremists	52	Army of God	15
Weather Underground, Weathermen	45	Organization of Volunteers for the Puerto Rican Revolution	15
Jewish Defense League (JDL)	44	May 19 Communist Order	14
Black Liberation Army	34	Fuerzas Armadas de Liberacion Nacional (FALN)	13
Chicano Liberation Front	31	Cuban Exiles	11
1990s		**2000s**	
Anti-Abortion extremists	114	Earth Liberation Front (ELF)	58
Animal Liberation Front (ALF)	33	(ALF)	31
Aryan Republican Army	16	Anti-Abortion extremists	20
The Justice Department	13	Anti-Government extremists	18
Earth Liberation Front (ELF)	8	White-supremacists/nationalists	11
Army of God	8	Coalition to Save the Preserves (CSP)	8
World Church of the Creator	8	Jihadi-inspired extremists	5
White extremists	6	Anti-white extremists	4
Anti-Government Group	5	Al-Qaeda	4
Anti-Semitic extremists	5	Anti-immigrant extremists	3
2010s			
Anti-Muslim extremists	43		
White extremists/nationalists	40		
Jihadi-inspired extremists	33		
Anti-Government extremists	19		
Anti-Semitic extremists	18		
Pro-Trump extremists	16		
Anti-Abortion extremists	13		
Anti-White extremists	12		
Anti-Police extremists	10		
Muslim extremists	9		

Table 3.1: Top ten groups in terms of number of attacks over the decades, US. *Source:* GTD

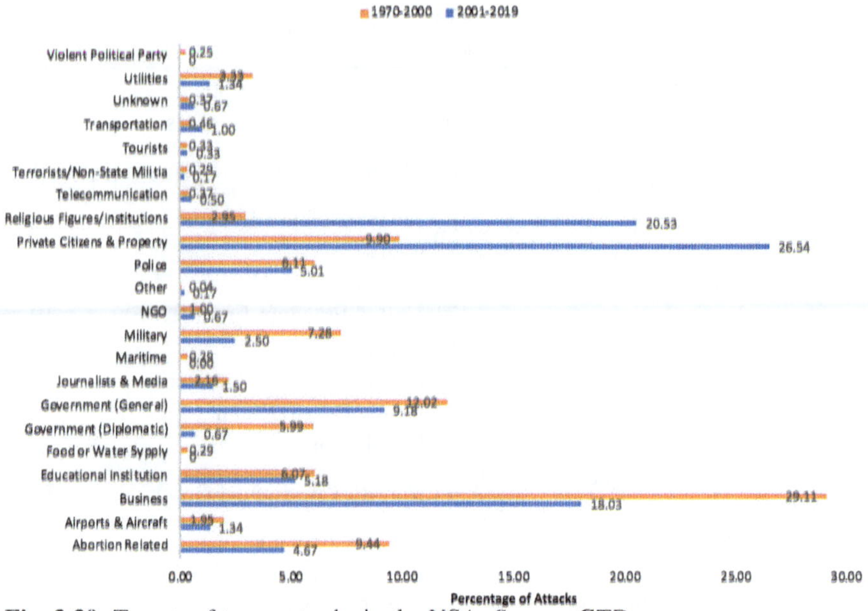

Fig. 3.30: Targets of terror attacks in the USA. *Source*: GTD

anti-Muslim extremists, white extremists/nationalists, and jihadi-inspired extremists top the list during 2010s.

The pattern of targets of terror attacks in the USA is exhibited in Fig. 3.30, showing a clear difference between the pre-*9/11* and post-9/11 era:

Is That So? 3.26: Types of Terror Attack Targets in the USA

In the pre-*9/11* era, businesses were targeted the most compared to private citizens, properties, educational institutions, etc., while in the post-*9/11* period, private citizens and properties, religious figures, and institutions became the prime targets.

In terms of spatial distribution of attacks, all fifty states plus District of Columbia and Puerto Rico have experienced terror attacks. Figure 3.31 exhibits the top five states in terms of number of terror attacks in each decade. It is evident that California and New York have been hit the most and most consistently.

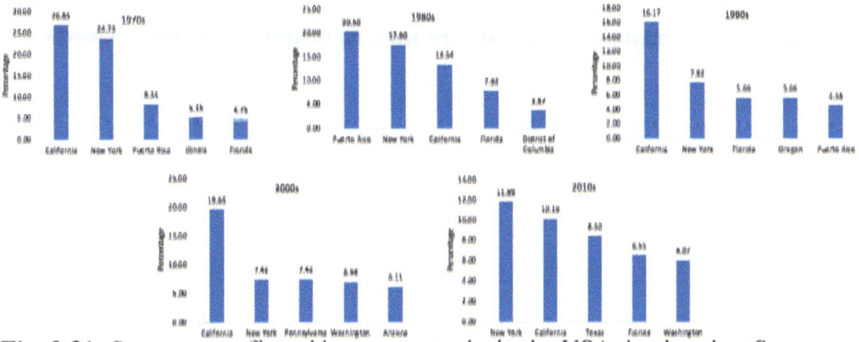

Fig. 3.31: States most affected by terror attacks in the USA: by decades. *Source*: GTD

3.6 Take-Aways

- According to UNODC (United Nations Office on Drugs and Crime), in 2017 alone, homicide, worldwide, claimed an estimated 464,000 deaths, which is higher than lives lost from terror attacks from 1970 to 2017.
- Terrorism increased globally from the 1970s to the mid-90s, after which it actually went down for some years. But, from the year 2000 until 2014, the world witnessed a surge in terror incidents and the number of deaths from it. Since 2014, there is a downward trend.
- While *9/11* was spectacular, the total global incidence of terror in terms of the number of incidents and deaths in 2001 was actually less compared to the mid 1990s.
- Following the definition of success by GTD, 89% of terror attacks between 1970 and 2019 are successful.
- The overall lethality or kill ratio (number of people killed on average in one terror attack) during 1970–2019 is 2.41. While the kill ratio increased from 1970s to the later decades, from 1980s onward there is no increase in the kill ratio. It is less in 2010s compared to 1980s, 1990s, or 2000s. That is, on average, terrorism has become less deadly.
- About half of all terror attacks do *not* lead to any death. Less than 12% of all terror attacks lead to more than four deaths.
- In the history of terrorism, suicide attacks are a very recent phenomena, beginning in 1981. The kill ratio associated with suicide attacks is between 8 and 11 (per attack).
- Suicide attacks are more prevalent in the post-*9/11* era, compared to the pre-*9/11* era. These attacks constitute 0.32% and 5.86% of all terror attacks in during the 1970–2000 period and the 2000–2019 period, respectively.
- The top five countries in terms of the number of suicide terror attacks before 2001 are Sri Lanka, Lebanon, Israel, Turkey and West Bank and

Gaza, whereas those after 2001 are Iraq, Afghanistan, Pakistan, Nigeria, and Syria.

- Bombing-cum-explosion and armed assault are the most common tactics used for terrorist attacks.
- While armed assault ranks No. 1 in terms of causing death in the pre-*9/11* era, it is bombing and explosives that is No. 1 in causing death in the post-9/11 era.
- Plane hijacking was in its peak in the early 1970s. Since then its incidents have fallen consistently, approaching almost zero in recent years.
- Chemical, biological, radiological, and nuclear(CBRN) attacks have been very limited in number (the definitions of CBRN events and attacks are different from conventional forms of terror attacks).
- The kill ratio associated with suicide attacks is over 10, which far exceeds the kill ratio for all types of terror attacks (which is 2.41). Suicide terrorism is the most lethal kind of terror attacks.
- In the Pre-*9/11* era (starting from 1970), the top five countries in descending order affected most by terrorism (in terms of fatalities) are Sri Lanka, Peru, Colombia, El Salvador, and Nicaragua, whereas after *9/11*, the top five countries in the descending order are Iraq, Afghanistan, Nigeria, Pakistan, and Syria (SANIP). There is a "continental shift" from South America to Middle East and South Asia.
- The Institute for Economics and Peace constructs a single index of terrorism, which varies from 0 and 10. It is called the Global Terrorism Index (GTI), which is available annually beginning in 2012 for different countries, by taking into consideration four attributes of terror attacks in a country: the number of terror attacks, the number of deaths, the number of injuries as well as an index of physical property damaged during the current year as well as the past four years.
- Compared to the 1970s or even 1990s, in the 2000s and 2010s transnational terrorism relative to domestic terrorism is less incident.
- The number of transnational terror attacks against US interests has declined over time, very few of which occurs on US soil.
- Nearly half of the terror organizations mount one attack only and a little over half have caused no deaths in their terror attacks.
- A very large fraction of terror organizations are merely a one-time show. Less than 50% of terror organization survive over one year.
- Compared to the pre-*9/11* era, in the post-*9/11* era the number of terror attacks is less in OCED countries.
- Within the OECD countries, Israel and Turkey have been afflicted by terrorism the most.
- Over 1970–2000, OECD countries except Israel and Turkey experienced 27% and 5% of global totals of attacks and deaths from terrorism, whereas over 2002–2019, the respective shares are 3.5% and 1.5%.

- Compared to the 2000s, terror attacks by Islamic fundamentalist groups and individuals are much greater in number in 2010s, although since 2016, their activities have declined.
- In seven out ten years in the 2010s, lone-wolf attacks have claimed at least 50% of deaths from all terror attacks in OECD countries not including Israel and Turkey.
- Sixty-seven percent of deaths from lone-wolf attacks in the West over the period 2006–2014 resulted from those with a political motivation.
- During 1970–2019 (excluding 1993) the USA witnessed 3004 terror attacks on its soil claiming 3890 lives.
- Since the 1970s, there have been a very limited number of terror attacks in the USA compared to the rest of the world.
- There are various terror and extreme groups that have been active in the USA in different time periods. In 2010s, the top three groups in terms of number of attacks are Anti-Muslim extremists, White extremists/nationalists, and Jihadi-inspired extremists.
- In the pre-*9/11* period, businesses were targeted the most compared to private citizens, properties, educational institutions, etc., while in the post-*9/11* period, private citizens and properties and religious figures and institutions became the prime targets.
- Among the states in the USA, California and New York have been hit by terrorism the most.

Appendix to Chapter 3

3.A Regions Defined in GTD

Table 3.2: Regions defined in GTD

Region	*Countries*
North America	Canada, Mexico, USA
Central America and Caribbean	Antigua and Barbuda, Bahamas, Barbados, Belize, Cayman Islands, Costa Rica, Cuba, Dominica, Dominican Republic, El Salvador, Grenada, Guadeloupe, Guatemala, Haiti, Honduras, Jamaica, Martinique, Nicaragua, Panama, St. Kitts and Nevis, St. Lucia, Trinidad, and Tobago
South America	Argentina, Bolivia, Brazil, Chile, Colombia, Ecuador, Falkland Islands, French Guiana, Guyana, Paraguay, Peru, Suriname, Uruguay, Venezuela
East Asia	China, Hong Kong, Japan, Macau, North Korea, South Korea, Taiwan
South East Asia	Brunei, Cambodia, East Timor, Indonesia, Laos, Malaysia, Myanmar, Philippines, Singapore, South Vietnam, Thailand, Vietnam
South Asia	Afghanistan, Bangladesh, Bhutan, India, Maldives, Mauritius, Nepal, Pakistan, Sri Lanka
Central Asia	Armenia, Azerbaijan, Georgia, Kazakhstan, Kyrgyzstan, Tajikistan, Turkmenistan, Uzbekistan
Western Europe	Andorra, Austria, Belgium, Cyprus, Denmark, Finland, France, Germany, Gibraltar,Andorra, Austria, Belgium, Cyprus, Denmark, Finland, France, Germany, Gibraltar, Greece, Iceland, Ireland, Italy, Luxembourg, Malta, Netherlands, Norway, Portugal, Spain, Sweden, Switzerland, United Kingdom, Vatican City, West Germany (FRG) Greece, Iceland, Ireland, Italy, Luxembourg, Malta, Netherlands, Norway, Portugal, Spain, Sweden, Switzerland, United Kingdom, Vatican City, West Germany (FRG)
Eastern Europe	Albania, Belarus, Bosnia-Herzegovina, Bulgaria, Croatia, Czech Republic, Czechoslovakia, East Germany (GDR), Estonia, Hungary, Kosovo, Latvia, Lithuania, Macedonia, Moldova, Montenegro, Poland, Romania, Russia, Serbia, Serbia- Montenegro, Slovak Republic, Slovenia, Soviet Union, Ukraine, Yugoslavia
Middle East and North Africa	Algeria, Bahrain, Egypt, Iran, Iraq, Israel, Jordan, Kuwait, Lebanon, Libya, Morocco, North Yemen, Qatar, Saudi Arabia, South Yemen, Syria, Tunisia, Turkey, United Arab Emirates, West Bank and Gaza Strip, Western Sahara, Yemen

Sub-Saharan Africa	Angola, Benin, Botswana, Burkina Faso, Burundi, Cameroon, Central African Republic, Chad, Comoros, Democratic Republic of the Congo, Djibouti, Equatorial Guinea, Eritrea, Ethiopia, Gabon, Gambia, Ghana, Guinea, Guinea-Bissau, Ivory Coast, Kenya, Lesotho, Liberia, Madagascar, Malawi, Mali, Mauritania, Mozambique, Namibia, Niger, Nigeria, People's Republic of the Congo, Republic of the Congo, Rhodesia, Rwanda, Senegal, Seychelles, Sierra Leone, Somalia, South Africa, South Sudan, Sudan, Swaziland, Tanzania, Togo, Uganda, Zaire, Zambia, Zimbabwe
Australia and Oceania	Australia, Fiji, French Polynesia, New Caledonia, New Hebrides, New Zealand, Papua New Guinea, Solomon Islands, Vanuatu, Wallis, and Futuna

3.B An Illustration of the GTI Calculation

The following exposition is based on Institute for Economics & Peace (2015, Annex C). Let us denote the number of attacks, the number of deaths, the number of injuries, and the index of physical damage by x_1, x_2, x_3, and x_4, respectively. There are three steps in IEP's construction of GTI. In step 1, an index of immediate (current-year) impact of terrorism is constructed by taking a weighted average of x_1, x_2, x_3, and x_4 with respective weights equal to 1, 3, 0.5, and 2. Note that x_1, x_2, and x_3 are natural numbers, whereas property damages are valued in monetary units. For each terror incident within a year, the associated property damage is assigned a pure number between 0 and 3: 0 if the value of the property damage is unknown, 1 if the estimated damage is less than $1 million (minor), 2 if it is between $1 million and $1 billion (major), and 3 if it exceeds $1 billion (catastrophic). These 0 to 3 scores are summed over all terror incidents during the current year and the sum is attached with the weight 2. As a hypothetical example, if suppose country A experiences 35 terror attacks that killed 100 people and 200 injured and the sum total of property damages indicators over all 35 attacks is 40, then the annual impact number is $1 \times 35 + 3 \times 100 + 0.5 \times 200 + 2 \times 40 = 35 + 300 + 100 + 80 = 515$. Step 2 accounts for the after effects of terror attack into later years (in terms of the trauma the terror attacks cause). The GTI is based on the annual impact numbers for the preceding four years, in this case, for 2014 back to 2011. Suppose these are 400, 450, 300, 556 respectively. Step 2 calculates a weighted average of the current-year impacts for five years, the weights being equal to 16 for the current year, 8 for the preceding year, 4 for the second preceding year, 2 for the third preceding year, and 1 for the fourth preceding year. In this example, annual impact numbers for 2015 back to 2011 are assigned the weights 16, 8, 4, 3, 2, and 1. The five-year weighted average is then equal to $16 \times 515 + 8 \times 400 + 4 \times 450 + 2 \times 300 + 1 \times 556 = 8240 + 3200 + 1800 + 600 + 556 = 14{,}393$. These five-year weighted averages are computed for all countries. In the third and final step, the five-year-weighted averages are mapped on a range between 0 and 10 by using a logarithmic banding formula.

Questions

3.1 "Because of various counter-terrorism measures in place, global incidence of terrorism has a declining trend since 2002." Defend or refute.

3.2 How and why has the geographical concentration of terrorist incidents shifted from the pre-*9/11* era to the post-*9/11*?

3.3 "In terms of fatalities per attack, terrorism has become less lethal over time." Defend or refute.

3.4 Do majority of terror attacks claim more than ten lives? Justify your answer.

3.5 "Terrorism has become more transnational over the last four decades." Defend or refute.

3.6 What is CBRN terrorism? Is it growing over time?

3.7 What are the top ten countries in the twenty-first century thus far in terms of the number of suicide attacks? (You would have to download the GTD to answer this question.)

Part II
Financing, Costs and Consequences of Terrorism

Chapter 4

Cost of Organizing, and, Financing of Terror

There are two things a brother must always have for jihad, the self and money.
— An al-Qaeda operative, according to 9/11 Commission Report (2004)

4.1 Introduction

PLANNING and executing terror attacks cost money. Terrorists and their families need to be compensated and paid pension in case of death of a terrorist. The Washington Post, November 18, 2015, reported that ISIS paid its fighters about $400 per month. In addition, guns, bombs, and other materials have to be procured. Terrorists and material may have to be moved from one place or country to another. Transport is costly. There are recruitment, training, and maintenance costs too. The list goes on.

As we have seen in Chap. 2, many terror organizations engage in public service, which also involves resource costs. Some terror groups are a part of bigger organizations that have political wings: They take part in elections and govern. These are costly activities. Like businesses, the funds are necessary to turn the wheels of terror so-to-speak and finance social and political programs of terror groups.

In Sect. 4.2, we look at the estimated costs of selected terror attacks and jihadi cells, while we discuss the financing of terror organizations in general in Sect. 4.3.

4.2 Estimated Cost of Terror Attacks

4.2.1 Individual Terror Attacks

Beginning with *9/11* attacks, according to the 9/11 Commission report, the cost estimates of these attacks range from $400,000 to $500,000. Not much is known about the original sources of the funds except that most of it was financed by al-Qaeda. Prior to the attacks, nearly $300,000 was deposited into the hijackers' bank

S. P. Das, *Economics of Terrorism and Counter-Terrorism Measures*,
https://doi.org/10.1007/978-3-030-96577-8_4

accounts in the USA. There is however not much information on how they spent this money. But, interestingly,

Is That So? 4.1: Planning of *9/11* Attacks

The planning of *9/11* attacks apparently went so well prior to September 11, 2001 that the hijackers returned $26,000 to al-Qaeda.

Table 4.1 summarizes the cost of organizing prominent terror attacks by al-Qaeda since 1998.

Incidence	*Location and date*	*Estimated fatalities*	*Estimated cost ($)*
US Embassy bombings	Kenya and Tanzania, 1998	223	50,000
USS Cole	Yemen, 2000	17	10,000
9/11	USA, 2001	2977	400,000–500,000
Bali Night Club Bombing	Indonesia, 2002	202	50,000
Jakarta Marriott hotel bombing	Indonesia, 2002	12	30,000
Madrid train bombings	Spain, 2004	191	10,000–70,000
London transport bombings	UK, 2005	52	15,000
Failed London Car Bomb Attacks	UK, 2007		14,000
Attacks in Paris	France, 2015	130	≤10,000

Table 4.1: Cost of attacks by Al-Qaeda.
Sources: Prober (2005), Reuters (2007), Wittig (2011, page 63), Windrem (2015), Institute for Economics & Peace (2017)

4.2.2 Financing of Jihadi Terror Cells Targeting Western Europe

A revealing case study by Emilie Oftedal of the Norwegian Defence Research Establishment, namely, Oftedal (2014), records 123 jihadi plots in Europe during 1994–2013 that were perpetrated by 110 jihadi cells. Of these, Oftadel gathered financing details of forty jihadi cells from court documents and media. Here are some of the highlights.

(1) There was a downward trend over time in the proportion of cells that received support from organized terrorist groups and their support networks, and a corresponding increase in cells that were—somewhat surprisingly—self-financed through legal activities.

(2) The fund-generating activities were ordinary: 90% of cells in the sample were funded by income-generating activities, and half of them were entirely self-financed by own salaries and savings.
(3) Only five per cent relied entirely on external support from international groups like al-Qaida or ISIS, while 43% of cells in the study combined self-financing with external support. As we shall see in Sect. 4.3, in other regions of the world, Islamic charities have been extensively used to fund Islamic terror groups, and, money moves between locations through an informal transfer system called *hawala*. However, very few jihadi terrorist plots in Europe involved money traced to such charities or hawala transactions.
(4) Perhaps the most striking, the jihadi terror attacks in Western Europe were relatively inexpensive. Only 8% of attacks cost more than $20,000, 12% cost between $10,000 and $20,000, while nearly 50% of all attacks involved funds ranging from $1000 to $10,000 (Oftedal, 2014, Table 3.1). The average cost per attack was less than $10,000 (see *Is That So?* No. 4.2). Money was used to finance activities like travel, communication, storage, acquiring of weapons and bomb-making material.[1]

Is That So? 4.2: Cost of Organizing Terror Attacks by Jihadi Cells in Europe

In three quarters of the forty terror plots in Western Europe studied over 1994–2013 by Oftedal (2014), the estimated average cost of an attack was less than $10,000.

4.3 Financing of Terror Organizations

We now discuss the various ways the terrorist organizations finance themselves. The extent of their activities depends on their operational and organizational capabilities. Funds help them to maintain and enhance their capabilities. Since they are not legal entities, they rely on illegal sources like KFR and extortion. This is called a ***dark economy***, which is unaccounted. Terror groups also use "legal" sources. Even if a source is non-criminal and legal in and of itself, as long as it is channeled to finance illegal activities like terrorism it cannot be totally legal. These sources are labeled as the ***gray economy***. Figure 4.1 lists various dark- and gray-economy sources of funds for terror, which are described in Sects. 4.3.1 and 4.3.2.[2]

In organizing large-scale terror attacks, moving funds between different locations is almost as important as generating funds. Different channels through which terror organizations transfer funds are outlined in Sect. 4.3.3. Financial rankings of top terror organizations in recent years are presented in Sect. 4.3.4.

[1] In recent years, using motor vehicles as weapons has become more common.

[2] Note that "External State Support" appears in the gray-economy category, but it can argued that it is illegal and thus should be included in the dark-economy category.

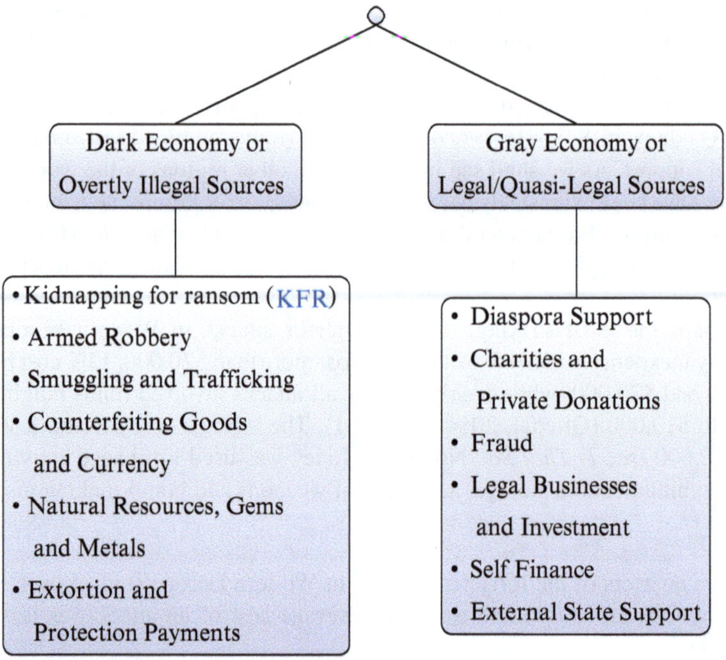

Fig. 4.1: Sources of funds for terrorism

However, note that, unlike data for GDP, employment, inflation, population, etc., the data on terror financing are not readily or systematically available. Some of them are not surely recorded, and, even if available, are proprietary information. Estimates are obtained from various intelligence reports, interviews, etc. and are prone to high variance. We outline the general sources of terrorism finance along with some examples and numbers. This contrasts with Chap. 2 where we discussed the financing of specific terror organizations in more detail.[3]

It is interesting that large terror organizations manage their money flows professionally. For instance, according to FATF (2015a), the financial records seized by the US military reveal that AQI's (al-Qaeda in Iraq) administrative emirs made "extensive use of tracking spreadsheets, expense reports, and standardized financial accounting reports."

4.3.1 Dark Economy: Illegal Sources

Kidnapping for Ransom (KFR) This is a common practice, since it is a relatively low-risk venture with a high reward. Videotaped beheadings frequently used by ISIS are a chilling reminder of what could happen if ransom demands are not met.

[3] There are several specialized books, e.g., Adams (1986), Wittig (2011), Vittori (2011) and Clarke (2015) that provide much more insightful and interesting accounts of terror financing. Also see White (2017, Chapter 3).

Most terror organizations use it for profit but some like FARC and Hezbollah have used it as a bargaining chip for future exchange of prisoners. According to FATF (2015c), the US government estimated that groups including al-Qaeda, ISIL, and their affiliates and allies raised at least $222 million from KFR between 2008 and 2014. In a statement in 2012, David S. Cohen, the then US Undersecretary for Terrorism and Financial Intelligence said that al-Qaeda affiliates in North Africa, Somalia, and Yemen collected nearly $122 million over the period 2002–2012 from KFR. Malik (2017) reports that, in 2016 alone, ISIS raised from $10 to $30 million from KFR. There are several instances of very large ransom payments made to terror organizations. We list three of them here (Clarke, 2015).

- In 2006, the Italian government reportedly paid the Taliban about $5 million for releasing two Italian citizens.
- In 2007 a busload of missionaries from South Korea were held hostage by Taliban. They were released after a ransom payment around $5 million.
- In 2013, Boko Haram was paid $3 million in ransom to release a French family of seven.

Extortion Extortion of businesses is a common method of raising funds used by terrorist groups. In the 1970s, PLO charged some airlines five to six million dollars per year (Freeman, 2011). LTTE extorted members of the Tamil diaspora who resisted making donations. The average extortion rate charged by LTTE for targeted individuals and families in Canada ranged from CAN$2500 to CAN$5000; it was often higher for business owners (Human Rights Watch, 2006).

Drugs and Protection Taxes Large parts of the funding of two Colombian terror organizations, FARC and ELN, were based on the production of coca leaves that produce cocaine. The production of opium leaves (used to prepare heroin) was (is?) the financial backbone of Taliban in Afghanistan. One should carefully note that

Is That So? 4.3: Taliban, FARC and Drug Money

Taliban and FARC have not produced or traded in drugs. Instead, they "protect" the production and transport of the drug leaves and collect "protection taxes."

Taliban collected 10% *ushr* tax from opium farmers, shop keepers, and small business owners. FARC vehemently denies any involvement in the illicit drug trafficking business or being any part of the so-called drug mafia.

However, unlike Colombian terror organizations and Taliban, the PKK, based in Turkey and also present in northern Iraq, eastern Syria, western Iran, and southern Armenia, reportedly took part in the smuggling of heroin originating from Afghanistan, Iran, and Pakistan. According to Freeman (2011), 80% of drugs in Europe had some link with PKK.

Oil In its heydays, ISIS raised millions of dollar per day by trading oil when it occupied the oil fields in Iraq. Institute for Economics & Peace (2016b) reported that about half of estimated $2 billion revenues raised by ISIS in 2014 and 2015

came from oil smuggling.[4] ISIS being an illegal entity, no individual, organization, or country could legally buy oil from ISIS directly. Instead, it sold the crude oil extracted from the captured oil fields to a mafia of middle men in a black-market network, which presumably existed from the days of Saddam Hussain when Iraq tried to circumvent sanctions imposed on it by the U.N. In turn, the middle men sold crude oil to refineries in Iraq, Syria, and Iran.

Smuggling and Trafficking of Commodities and Humans Terror groups smuggle commodities like diamond, cigarette, ivory, and charcoal. According to Washington Post, November 2, 2001, al-Qaeda earned millions over three years around the year 2000 from illicit trade in diamonds mined by the rebels of Sierra Leon. It also reported that the al-Shabaab group in Somalia raised funds from illicit trade in charcoal (van der Merwe, 2017).[5]

According to Levitt (2014), excavating and selling artifacts from archaeological sites in Iraq was the second-largest source of revenue for ISIS, next to oil.

ISIS and Boko Haram reportedly engaged in human trafficking—sale and resale of human bodies—to raise funds. According to Freeman (2011), PKK would smuggle people from Middle East and other parts of Asia to Europe. Interpol estimated that PKK would charge up to €2000 or €3000 per person. IRA raised $1 million in one year from smuggling pigs between Northern Ireland and Irish Republic border.

Counterfeiting Goods Alastair Gray presents a fascinating TED talk on how organized crime—and terrorism—are funded by counterfeit goods like fake leather bags, brand-name shoes, etc., where profit margins could be as high as 2000% with much less risk, compared to 200–300% in selling drugs.[6]

In 2002 an al-Qaeda manual recommended counterfeit selling as a good way to fund terror cells. Saïd Kouachi and Chérif Kouachi (two brothers), who carried out terror attacks in Paris in 2015 when they barged into the office of the weekly magazine *Charlie Hebdo* and shot twelve people to death, were previously engaged in the selling of fake Nike trainer shoes (Wash and Smith, 2017).

Armed Robbery Two groups in particular, PIRA and LTTE have extensively used armed robbery to finance themselves (Clarke, 2015).

4.3.2 Legal/Quasi-Legal Sources: The Gray Economy

Diaspora Support Diasporas refer to immigrant communities outside of the country of their origin. All major terror and insurgent groups, except those in Latin America, have received finance from their sympathizing diasporas, e.g., Irish community in the

[4] Other estimates such as by Heißner et al. (2017) place the oil revenues to be significantly less than ISIS's funds raised from looting, confiscations, and fines.

[5] There are controversial claims that al-Shabaab also raised funds from trade in ivory.

[6] Overall, counterfeiting businesses constitute about $2.3 trillion underground economy. According to Alastair Gray there is (or was) a store in Turkey called "I love genuine fakes."

USA supporting IRA, Tamils outside Sri Lanka helping Tamil Tigers during 1990s and 2000s, and Sikhs outside India contributing to Khalistan separatist movement in Punjab, India in early 1980s.

Charities and Private Donations Money flows into terror activities via non-profit organizations (NPOs) and charity organizations, which are legal entities with socio-economic-environmental objectives like poverty reduction, environmental consciousness, fighting infectious diseases, etc. These organizations are funded by donations from private individuals and grants from autonomous, semi-government, and government bodies. This is *not* to say that majority of NPOs or charity organizations funnel funds to terror; only some have. There is evidence that PLO and IRA received funds through charities in the 1970s (Clarke, 2015, Page 6).

Legal sources of finance for terror organizations include private donations. According to FATF (2015b), ISIS received funding from wealthy private donors in its occupied regions.

According to Washington Post, November 18, 2015, some estimates suggest that the Islamic State received up to $40 million in 2013–2014 from businessmen, wealthy families, and other donors in Saudi Arabia, Qatar, Kuwait, and the U. A. E. Many of these elite donors chose to fund the Islamic State because of fear for and animosity toward Iran and the Syrian President Bashar al-Assad.

In an innovative empirical study using terror attacks (nearly 12,000 in number) in Pakistan between 1992 and 2015, Limodio (2019) estimates the impact of terror financing through donations on the number of terror attacks. The impact is statistically significant and positive with an elasticity of 0.25.

Fraud Fraud is typically committed at the grass-root level, where small cells of sympathizers not directly connected to a group raise funds in different ways. Fraud tends to be a crime with low barriers to entry, which is one of the reasons it is favored by terrorist fund-raisers.

It has many dimensions including identity theft, illegal credit card use, cyber crimes, etc. As a concrete example, the Australian Transaction Report and Analysis Centre (2014) reported an official investigation in Australia of a Melbourne-based group that was allegedly planning a terror attack in Australia and funding its activities through small cash contributions by the members that amounted to 19,000 Australian dollars (roughly equal to $14,000) at the time of its members' arrests. The suspects systematically bribed taxi cab drivers and obtained from them credit card numbers of unsuspecting passengers.

Self-Finance This is an important legal source of funding terror. We have noted it earlier in this chapter for jihadi cells in Western Europe between 1994 and 2013 (Oftedal, 2014). According to a video posted online by the al-Qaeda leader Ayman al-Zawahri one year after Osama Bin Laden was killed in 2011, Osama Bin Laden led a frugal life and financed al-Qaeda from (legal) investments of his own personal wealth.[7]

[7] This is unsubstantiated however and probably false (Roth et al., 2004).

Legitimate Business and Investment Terrorists and insurgent groups run front companies and through them channel profits to their activities. The type of businesses does not matter much. But those involving more cash transactions are more convenient for channeling funds for terror and other criminal activities. For instance, between 1992 and 1996 Bin Laden and al-Qaeda operated many legal business in Sudan like farming peanut butter and honey, furniture making company, tannery, and bakery (Burke, 2004). According to a testimony by an FBI official, prior to *9/11*, an al-Qaeda cell in Europe operated a construction and plumbing company and some other cell members ran a business in buying, fixing, and reselling used cars (Levitt, 2002).

External State Support Terror organizations receive financial support from states who back their causes. In the 1980s Libya provided financial support to many groups such as Abu Nidal, the Red Brigade, and IRA (Freeman, 2011). Iran provides material as well as financial support to Hezbollah and has funded Hamas.[8] It is believed that Qatar supports the Muslim Brotherhood in Egypt (from which Hamas originated), Ahrar al-Sham in Syria, and other groups (Block, 2017). Qatar denies this however. Pakistan is reported to have provided support to Afghan Taliban and those in Pakistan-controlled Kashmir like Lashkar-e-Taiba, Harakat-u-Mujahideen, and the Hizbul Mujahideen (Freeman, 2011).[9]

It is worth noting that while terror organizations welcome financial help from nation states, there may be strings attached: The benefactor may ask the organization to wage crime against entities that may not be the top priority of the organization. Hence terror groups have sought other means of finance.

4.3.3 Moving Funds

Along with raising funds, it is important to move funds between individuals and locations. Terrorists use several ways to do so.

Cash Couriers and Use of Money Service Businesses (MSBs) Western Union, money orders, and currency dealers are examples of MSB. These institutions are subject to regulations like those the banks face, but are not rigorous.[10] In 2013, a federal jury in San Diego convicted four Somali immigrants of conspiring to fund

[8] As will be noted in Sect. 4.3.4, Iran has contributed $700 million per year to Hezbollah in recent years. Katzman (2018, page 38) reports that Iran's assistance to Hamas in cash and weapon may have reached at times $300 million per year.

[9] Some scholars find that terror organizations with external state support tend to be more lethal than those that do not enjoy state support (Clarke, 2015, page 14).

[10] For instance, banks must follow the "know your customer" (KYC) procedures, but MSBs do not have to.

al-Shabaab.[11] *Supplemental Break* No. 4.1 describes how *9/11* hijackers obtained funds through MSBs.

Supplement Break 4.1: Money Transfer to the *9/11* Hijackers

Fig. 4.2 depicts funds flow to *9/11* terrorists, as noted by the 9/11 Commission Report. Khalid Sheik Mohammed, a Pakistani, and, believed to be the mastermind behind the *9/11* attacks, delivered cash to 13 terrorists in Pakistan before they left Pakistan. He also gave cash in Dubai to Ali Abdul Aziz Ali, also a Pakistani, who transferred funds to the hijackers via MSBs. Ali Abdul Aziz Ali is believed to have been directly involved in the planning and execution of the *9/11* attacks and reportedly taken into custody by US authorities in 2003. Mustafa al-Hawsawi, a Saudi, and, considered to be financial facilitator behind the *9/11* attacks, transferred funds to the hijackers directly as well as through Ramzi al-Shibh, a Yemeni, later arrested in 2002. The hijackers brought with them cash and travelers' checks as they entered the USA and deposited the funds in Bank of America and other smaller banks. Among the hijackers, Zacarious Moussaoui brought most cash, $35,000, which was declared with the US Customs.

Notice that both formal and informal financial intermediaries were used across multiple locations.

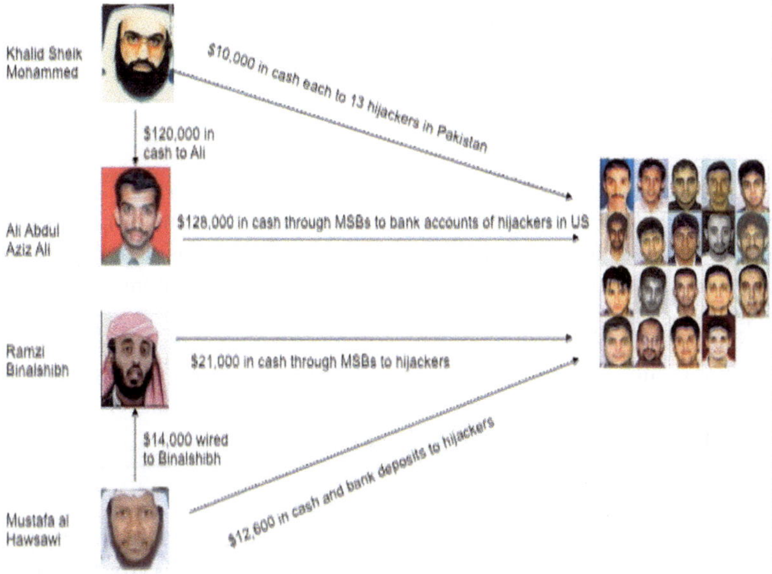

Fig. 4.2: Money transfer before *9/11*.
Source: Freeman and Ruehsen (2013), based on 9/11 Commission Report; permission to reproduce from the authors is thankfully acknowledged

[11] While all four men were involved in raising funds, one of them, Issa Doreh, worked at the Shidaal Express, a registered MSB from which he sent funds directly to one of al-Shabaab leaders, Aden Hashi Ayrow, who was in regular telephone contact with one of the other defendants.

Informal Transfer Systems These include Hawala/Hundi in South Asia, Fei Ch'len in China, and Phoe Khan in Thailand. Hawala is an ancient form of money dealing and funds transfer that competes with state-governed finance in developing countries across the globe, especially Middle East and South Asia. It is mostly secure, relatively anonymous, and convenient for those who do not wish to deal with the scrutiny or due diligence procedure of banks.[12] A typical hawala transaction looks as follows.

An Illustration of a Hawala Transaction

Shekhar, a worker in Kuwait wants to send $5000 to his father, Ramesh, in India. One option for Shekhar will be to use his bank account in Kuwait and pay a transaction fee, say 2%, which amounts to $100. The bank in India that Ramesh uses may very well charge him a transaction fee too and the whole process may take four, five business days before the equivalent money in Indian rupees, net of various fees, is deposited to Ramesh's account. An alternative for Shekhar is to use Hawala, whose transaction fees are much less and money is delivered much faster. Shekhar meets a Hawaladar (an agent) in Kuwait in a coffee shop and delivers him $5000. In turn, the Hawaladar gives Shekhar a code number and the name of a Hawaladar in or near the town where Ramesh lives. Over phone or SMS, Shekhar passes on the code number to Ramesh, who, the very next day can meet the Hawaladar in his town and collect money at a significantly more favorable exchange rate, by revealing the code number.

The Hawala network is huge and exists in many countries. The transactions are unaccounted for and illegal, yet they work efficiently. Such networks exist because of lack of access to adequate banking system, and banking regulations. Most customers use them for legitimate purposes. However, terror organizations use them also.[13]

Is That So? 4.4: Hawala

Terror groups have extensively used the Hawala system for transferring funds. It is a huge network of an informal international money transfer system, used by common people and terrorist organizations.

Money Laundering through Regular Banks Some regular banks and their employees have facilitated money laundering that have reached nefarious groups including terror groups. Money laundering involves three sequential processes: (1) placement, (2) layering, and (3) integration (Livescu, 2017).

The placement stage involves the physical introduction of a bulk amount of illegal cash into the financial system, typically through cash deposits and purchase

[12] See Jost and Sandhu (2000) for a lucid account of how the Hawala system works.

[13] Moore (2015) writes that "Known as hawala, the system is being used as a conduit for the financing of fighters aligned to terror groups such as ISIS and the al-Qaeda-affiliated al-Nusra Front through a network of 250 to 300 shops—such as butchers, supermarkets, and phone call centers—run by mostly Pakistani brokers across Spain."

monetary instruments. In the layering stage, these funds transit through a complex layer of transactions using checks, money orders, wire transfers, etc. It typically involves more than one financial institution for obscuring an audit trail. At this phase, for the sake of privacy, protection from lawsuits, and regulatory advantages, the launderer may choose an offshore financial center, a large regional business center, a world banking center, or any location that provides an adequate financial or business infrastructure. In the final stage, that is integration, laundered proceeds reenter the financial system appearing as legitimate funds. During this phase, legitimate explanations are furnished for the money launderer's wealth. In general, this is accomplished through schemes like real estate purchases, shell companies (companies that do not maintain a physical presence in any country), investments in securities, and other investments. The funds thus become "white."

Terrorists and terror organization have used banks that do not ask too many questions. Al-Madina bank of Lebanon is an example. Before it closed in 2003, it allegedly helped to launder funds by Saddam Hussain's sanctions regime, Russian mafia group as well as an arms dealer for Hezbollah (Prothero, 2005).

Corrupt bank employees have facilitated laundering and movement of funds for illegal purposes. This was the case with the Lebanese Canadian bank. The bank was implicated in Hezbollah financing as well as other groups in South America and West Africa (Becker, 2011).

False trade invoicing This is accomplished through inflating invoice without raising suspicion. If a US-based terrorist purchases some American honey, exports that to Yemen, he could overprice shipment by $100,000 without attracting much attention. When the Yemeni importer pays for the overpriced honey, some of that money will go toward paying off the US honey producer, but much of the additional $100,000 can fill the pockets of the terrorists in the USA. According to one government source, this is believed to have happened in the months leading up to *9/11*.

4.3.4 Richest Terrorist Organizations

2014		2017	
1. ISIS	2000	1. Hezbollah	1100
2. Hamas	1000	2. Taliban	800
3. FARC	600	3. Hamas	700
4. Hezbollah	500	4. al-Qaeda	300
5. Taliban	400	5. ISIS	200
6. al-Qaeda	150	6. PKK	180
7. Lashkar-e-Taiba	100	7. Kata'ib Hezbollah	150
8. al-Shabaab	70	8. Palestinian Islamic Jihad	100
9. Real IRA	50	9. Lashkar-e-Taiba	75
10. Boko Haram	25	10. Real IRA	50

Table 4.2: Estimated revenues of top ten richest organizations (in million $).
Sources: Zehorai (2014, 2018)

The overall estimated budgets or revenues have varied greatly across terror organizations and time. Table 4.2, based on Zehorai (2014, 2018), reports the estimated 2014 and 2017 revenues of the ten richest organizations. Here are some relevant notes.

[a] There are three names here, which are not included in the list of terror organizations stated in Chap. 1, Table 1.1, namely Real IRA, Kata'ib Hezbollah, and Palestinian Islamic Jihad. As already discussed in Chap. 2, Real IRA is a splinter group of the Provisional IRA, which has remained opposed to the Good Friday Agreement of 1998 and continues to use violence. Kata'ib Hezbollah is a relatively recent Shi'ite group based in Iraq, which started in 2007, whereas Palestinian Islamic Jihad is an old organization since the 1970s. The last two groups are recipients of financial support from Iran.

[b] In 2014, ISIS gained a vast amount of territory including oil fields (and was the most prominent and the most brutal terror organization). It is thus unsurprising that it was the richest among all terror groups in 2014. But, by 2017, ISIS practically lost all its territory and its financial fortune dwindled.[14]

[c] FARC, the most deadly organization in Colombia, was dissolved in 2017—thanks to a U.N. sponsored peace treaty between the group and the Colombian government. Hence, it does not appear in the list of 2017.

[d] Speaking at the Foundation for Defence of Democracies in Washington on June 5, 2018, Ms. Sigal Mandelker, the US Treasury under-secretary for terrorism and financial intelligence, stated that Iran's support of Hezbollah increased considerably after the US–Iran nuclear deal. She said: "Iran provides upwards of $700 million a year to Hezbollah." This explains why Hezbollah topped the list in 2017.

[e] We have noted earlier that al-Qaeda is like a holding company or conglomerate with virtually independent affiliates. The al-Qaeda listed for 2017 includes al-Shabaab but that for 2014 does not.

[f] Opium production in Afghanistan has witnessed a massive growth in 2010s and that had led to a major rise in the fortune of Taliban. *The New York Times*, October 29, 2017 reports how Taliban was awash in heroin cash.[15]

It is significant that

Is That So? 4.5: Terror Organizations getting Financially Weaker Over Time

Overall, all terror organizations, except Hezbollah and Taliban, became financially weaker in the latter half of 2010s.

[14] According to NBC News, June 30, 2017, the estimated second quarter revenue of ISIS was $16 million. This translates into an annual turnover of $64 million, which is considerably less than its reported income of $200 million by Zehorai (2018).

[15] In 2015, estimated revenues of al-Qaeda and Boko Haram stood at $150 million and $25 million, respectively (Institute for Economics & Peace, 2016b).

At the time of writing this chapter, there is no public information available on comparative financial strengths of major terror groups for later years.

4.3.5 Terror Financing as a Value Chain

Wittig (2011, Chapter 4) portrays terror financing as "epistemologically similar to a commercial value chain." This is useful from the standpoint of economic analysis, because a terror organization can be viewed as a firm or a business organization. What does it produce? Terror attacks. What are the inputs? Volunteers, labor, and equipment like guns, bombs, and computers. What is the equivalent of revenues or benefits to a terror enterprise? This is a bit more subtle. We may hypothesize that in the short run the revenue equivalent is the value of damage inflicted upon the targets, which depends on the quantity and quality of terror attacks. However, if we consider the ultimate socio-political objective of a terror organization, then the revenue or benefit equivalent is the value attached to a terrorist organization's long-run objective, e.g., the utility from more political rights or being a separate country, whereas the damage from terror is an intermediate value added in this value chain.[16]

Considering terror financing as a value chain does *not* mean that all those involved in the value chain are (direct) supporters, sympathizers, or perpetrators of terror. As Wittig (2011, Chapter 2) argues rightly, a big public company like General Electric (GE) has a vast network of businesses and individuals. A small glass factory may be supplying certain kind of glass to GE for manufacturing bulbs. Computer maintenance may be outsourced to a company whose employees attend server issues. But this does not mean that the glass company is a part of GE or the computer engineers are in the payrolls of GE. Similarly, a terror organization's sympathizer may have a legitimate account in a bank, from which the account holder withdraws funds and simply gifts these funds to the terror organization. Unless the bank is aware of such activities, it cannot be held as a party abetting terror. As another example, at least some of us buy fake goods and the proceeds may very well be used to organize a terror attacks. Are we then directly responsible for the terror attacks or should we be arrested for abetting terror if we buy counterfeit products? The answer is no, although in a very general way we all are collectively responsible for terrorism as a problem.

4.4 Take-Aways

- The estimated cost of *9/11* attacks is about \$400,000–\$500,000.
- Most of the Jihadi cells in Western Europe were self-financed from ordinary sources of income like salaries. The average cost of organizing and executing a terror attack in Western Europe was no more than \$10,000.

---

[16] The theme of a terrorist organization as a firm will be developed in detail in Chap. 7.

- Big terror organization manage their funds professionally.
- Terror organizations raise funds from various sources: both illegal and quasi-legal. Illegal sources include kidnapping, armed robbery, natural resources (like illegal control and sale of oil by ISIS), extortion and protection payments (like FARC in Colombia collecting protection taxes from cocoa growers), and Taliban collecting *ushr* (tax on agricultural product) from opium poppies in Afghanistan. Quasi-legal sources cover diaspora support (like US residents supporting IRA, Tamils outside Sri Lanka financing LTTE), money funneling through charity organizations, businesses and investments and external state support (e.g., Iran financing Hezbollah).
- For transferring funds, terror groups have extensively used the Hawala system, a huge network of an informal international money transfer system, used by common people as well as terror organizations.
- In a 2017 financial ranking of terror organizations, Hezbollah topped the list following by Taliban.
- Terror financing can be thought of as a value chain, just as financing of a private firm.

Questions

4.1 Download the paper, Oftedal (2014), from the internet and list the other relevant details of costs of executing terror attacks that are not covered or emphasized in the text.

4.2 In the terminology of economics, a terrorist organization "produces" terror. In the light of this, give three (hypothetical) examples of variable costs and three (hypothetical) examples of fixed costs that a terrorist organization ("firm") would typically face?

4.3 Trace the history of the hawala system as best as you can and assess its prevalence by citing specific examples.

4.4 Researching from the internet, write a short essay on how and where ISIS was able to sell oil for money.

4.5 Researching from the internet, describe two specific examples of KFR by prominent terrorist organizations that are not covered in the text.

Chapter 5

Economic Costs of Terrorism and Costs of Counter-Terrorism Measures

5.1 Introduction

TARGET countries incur two types of costs associated with terrorism: (1) The cost of the adverse consequences of terror attacks—which will be called the ***economic cost of terrorism***. (2) The cost of counter-terror measures.

It is natural to ask, how much damage do the terror attacks cause to an economy and a society in a monetary unit? What is the socio-economic cost of terrorism? The questions look simple, but the answers are not. There are inherent difficulties. First, *what are the cost items to be included?* Obviously, one should include the cost of properties damaged and the values of lives lost and injuries. But there are indirect costs like the adverse impact of terror attacks on the local or national economy. One may also want to include the cost of increased security apparatus a government deploys in the aftermath of terror attacks. Second, *how much value to ascribe to or what would be the price tag on items to be included* like injuries, death, health services offered, and business losses? Third, there are impacts of terrorism that are hard to measure and thus hard to evaluate—the loss of civil liberty due to security restrictions, mental suffering of families of the deceased, and public fear and anxiety caused from terror attacks.

In principle, we can distinguish three types economic costs of terrorism in terms of time horizon: short term, medium term, and long term. In each type, we can think of direct and indirect costs. Buesa et al. (2007) explain this nicely.

Short-Term Costs Short-term *direct costs* are associated with the immediate consequence of terror attacks. It includes the costs of loss of lives, loss of private property and public infrastructure, delays and interruptions, attending to injuries, removing debris, etc. Short-term *indirect costs* address the disruptions caused to an economy. An example will be the losses by the tourism-affected industries like hotel and restaurant businesses.

S. P. Das, *Economics of Terrorism and Counter-Terrorism Measures*,
https://doi.org/10.1007/978-3-030-96577-8_5

Medium and Long-Term Costs Rehabilitation of the affected areas is a cost of this type. For instance, the destruction of the World Trade Center buildings in *9/11* attacks led to a newly designed ground-zero structure. Another example is disability pensions for severely injured survivors. These are direct costs. But the bulk of medium- and long-term costs of terrorism are indirect. Examples would include new permanent security systems against the conventional as well as non-conventional attacks with the help of biological and possibly nuclear weapons, resource cost of counter-terrorism units, reduction in an economy's growth rate and foreign direct investment, and so on. Needless to say, valuing medium and long-term costs are fraught with measurement issues.[1]

The preceding discussion has two implications. First, *the cost estimates are bound to have high variance.* Studies trying to assess the cost of the September 11 attack provide estimates ranging from \$35 billion to \$109 trillion. This is *not* to say that the estimates are inconsistent *per se*, because different items are included or excluded in different studies and their valuations may somewhat differ. Even if we limit ourselves to direct short-run costs, the variability can be considerable. For instance, a bio-terrorist attack could be delivered using a poison, virus, or bacteria, each of which would have varying degrees of damage. According to Institute for Economics & Peace (2014b), the estimated economic cost of such an attack could range from \$477.7 million to \$26.2 billion for every 100,000 persons exposed. Second, *estimating indirect costs associated with the loss of civil liberty, mental suffering of the families of the deceased and public fear and anxiety that terror attacks cause are very difficult to quantify.* Terrorism also leads to change of behavior that can have costs too. For instance, *9/11* attacks led to an increased fear of flying as well as loss of time due to more intense security checks at airports, which, in turn, led to more travel by road, causing more accidents (Blalock et al., 2009). Most estimates of terrorism costs simply ignore these. Hence, *the estimates presented in this chapter are to be regarded as lower bounds of the true cost of damage from terror.*

Section 5.2 lists costs of some specific, high-profile terror attacks. There are estimates available for all terror attacks combined for various countries and the world as a whole for different years. These are discussed in Sect. 5.3. In order to deter terrorist attacks, potential target countries incur costs of security, intelligence, regulations, assistance to foreign countries as well as cost of attacking terrorists, their leaders, terror camps, etc. An account of the *direct* costs of counter-terror measures is included in Sect. 5.4.

[1] Sometimes it is not easy to draw a line between direct and indirect costs of terrorism. For instance, should we consider increased security costs as direct or indirect?

5.2 Costs of Specific Attacks

5.2.1 *9/11* Attacks

Various estimates of costs associated with *9/11* attacks are available. A little over a month after the attacks, Gary Becker and Kevin Murphy wrote a piece in the Wall Street Journal (Becker & Murphy, 2001), which stated that capital equipment (including the value of planes lost) and property damages from the attacks amounted to $13 to $14 billion, equal to about 0.05% of the value of total physical assets in the USA. If we include the productivity of the individuals killed, the loss was between $25 to $60 billion, whereas the upper limit is 0.06% of the total productive assets of the US economy at the time. The authors viewed that, generally, advanced countries rebound from natural disasters rather quickly. Thus, "prosperities will rise out of the ashes" [from the *9/11* losses].

Navaro and Spencer (2001) provided an early yet detailed estimates of losses from *9/11* attacks. They valued property damages between $10 and $13 billion (close to Becker and Murphy's).[2] Apart from physical damages, $6.67 million was taken as the average value of a human life lost in the *9/11* attacks. The box below outlines a simple back-of-the-envelop method of calculating the value of human life.

Calculating the Value of Human Life

Suppose an individual decides to cross a busy road in order to save two minutes. If he/she earns $120 an hour, then two minutes of his time are worth $120/30 = $4. If the chance of getting killed while crossing the street is say 1 in 1 million, then choice of the crossing the road amounts to preferring $4 over the value of life divided by one million. Hence the value of life cannot exceed $4 × 1 million = $4 million. We can thus consider $4 million as the value of human life.

The amount $6.67 million was reached on the basis of similar calculations, accounting for the fact that people who lost their lives in New York were more highly educated and had higher income than the national average. Hence 3000 fatalities translate into $6.67 × 30,000 = $20 billion.[3,4] Adding this to the earlier total of $10 and $13 billion, the value of physical and human capital loss then ranges from $30 and $33 billion.[5]

Compared to Navaro and Spencer (2001), others have included additional sources of loss and arrived at higher estimates. Kunreuther et al. (2003)'s estimates of losses due to *9/11* attacks equal $80 billion—which takes into account workers' compensation lost, values of commercial properties destroyed, business

[2] Between 50–60% of this figure is attributed to the loss of World Trade Center buildings ($3 to $4.5 billion) and office equipment and software ($3.2 billion). See the authors' Table 2.

[3] See (Enders & Sandler, 2012, Chapter 10).

[4] At the time of their writing, Navaro and Spencer (2001) did not have a precise estimate of fatalities. They assumed that it was $6000, and hence the total value of lives lost was placed at $40 billion.

[5] This is less than the estimate obtained by Becker and Murphy (2001).

interruptions, aircraft hull, health, and disability effects, etc. According to Rose et al. (2009), the attacks on the World Trade Center directly entailed business disruption costs amounting to $19.8 billion and relocation costs of $5.3 billion. Indirect costs of these attacks in terms of air travel and other related travel were $35.3 billion and $55.9 billion, respectively. All these estimates are in 2006 dollars.

Institute for Economics & Peace (2014b) notes that fatalities and infrastructure damage from the *9/11* attack on the World Trade Center cost $55 billion in New York alone, while secondary effects such as increased security and decreased economic activity cost respectively $589 billion and $123 billion. Insurance premiums on large structures increased considerably. For instance, the annual insurance premiums on Chicago's O'Hare airport surged from $125,000 to $6.9 million while its insurance coverage for terrorism declined from $750 million to $150 million per year.[6,7]

Although estimates vary widely, the overall impact of the *9/11* attacks on the GDP of the USA is rather small, less than one percent.

However, in their web-interactive piece, Carter and Cox (2011) arrive at a much higher number: The total estimated costs of the *9/11* attacks are nearly $3.3 trillion. These are in 2011 dollars, translating into roughly 3 trillion 2006 dollars.[8] This figure includes long-term indirect costs like expenditures on homeland security and intelligence, subsequent wars in Iraq and Afghanistan, etc. Out of this total, the costs of lives lost, injuries, and property damages and economic impacts like business disruption, reduced air travel, and event cancelations were estimated at 178 billion in 2011 dollars (thus 159 billion 2006 dollars).[9]

5.2.2 Madrid Commuter Train Bombing in 2004

Direct costs of train bombings on March 11, 2004 in Madrid have been estimated by Buesa et al. (2007). They amount to €211 million, roughly 0.03% of Spain's GDP at the time.

The authors clearly state their methodology and items included in estimating various components. Costs are based on the number of people killed and injured, number of people mobilized to help the victims, resources used as well as damage to property and railways infrastructure. Quantities are estimated from official and

---

[6] The insurance-value losses of World Trade Center and Pentagon buildings were $22.7 billion. See Enders and Sandler (2012, Chapter 10).

[7] Following the *9/11* attacks, reduction in coverage for damage due to terror attacks was feared to cause lending problems. As a result, the USA passed the Terrorism Insurance Act in 2002, which created a temporary federal program. The Act provided a risk-sharing mechanism between the Federal government and to the insurance industry to share losses in the event of major terror attacks on business infrastructures. It has been periodically extended ever since. The latest is the Terrorism Risk Insurance Program Reauthorization Act of 2015, which places the end of 2020 as the expiration date of this insurance program.

[8] This conversion is based on consumer price index being 11.58% higher in 2011 than in 2006, according to the Bureau of Labor Statistics.

[9] Another estimate due to Riedel (2011) places the cost of property damage in New York and Washington alone at about 100 billion and cumulative economic cost to the global economy at 2 trillion, both in 2011 dollars.

journalistic sources. The evaluation of damages and compensations accords with scales stipulated by the Ministry of Interior. As an example of the comprehensiveness of their coverage of direct costs, there was a massive demonstration by 2.3 million people in Madrid (against these attacks) a day after the attacks (March 12, 2004). The authors estimated that among 2.3 million present, about one million were employed. At the rate of €60 per one employed person, the total opportunity cost of these individuals was valued at €57.36 million. A summary of various types of direct costs is given in Table 5.1.

It is clear from our discussion on *9/11* and Madrid terror attacks that

Is That So? 5.1: Economic Cost of Large-Scale Terror Attacks

As percentage of GDP, large-scale individual terror attacks have caused small direct losses.

Cost item	Cost in million €
Rescue and initial care of the victims cost, based on detailed accounts of various resources used and their costs like police, firemen, vehicles, administrators, health professionals, etc.	2.18
Health care of the injured	5.15
Cost of compensation to the victims	134.12
Loss of wages of the injured in the attacks	2.37
Damages in infrastructure and houses	5.27
Performing autopsies and identification of victims cost	0.18
Psychological support for the victims	4.9
Opportunity cost of employed people who took part in the demonstration	57.36
Total	211

Table 5.1: Components of direct cost of March 11, 2004 Madrid train bombings. *Source:* Buesa et al. (2007, Table 11); permission to reproduce by the Taylor & Francis Group is thankfully acknowledged.

5.3 Country-Wise and Global Cost of Terrorism

Considering all recorded terror events within a country during a year, the Institute of Economics and Peace (IEP) publishes the annual costs of terrorism for selected countries as well as for some regions and the entire world. This is useful for comparing economic burden of terrorism across countries as well as the burden for the same country over time.

5.3.1 IEP's Methodology

It uses the number of deaths and injuries and valuation of properties destroyed associated with all recorded terror attacks within a year. In addition, if the number of deaths from all attacks within a year exceeds 1000, then a macro economic cost is included. The information on death, injury, and property damage is obtained from GTD. The unit costs of death and injury due to terrorism are proxied by those of homicides and aggravated assault, which are sourced from McCollister et al. (2010).[10] To account for the income differences across countries, the unit costs are scaled on the basis of the country's Purchasing Power Parity (PPP) GDP per capita, relative to the source of the unit costs (see Institute for Economics & Peace, 2014a, 2016b).[11] For instance, a country with a PPP GDP per capita equal to 26% of the US per capita GDP would have a homicide unit cost equal to 26% of the US homicide unit cost. If the costs are to be expressed in prices of a year different from 2008, the corresponding rate of inflation in the USA for that year relative to 2008 is factored in.

Evaluating property damages is more involved.[12] Global estimates are obtained by aggregating the costs across countries. IEP's calculations include direct costs that are quantifiable and leave out the indirect costs of terrorism, except for significant GDP costs. Hence the estimates are conservative and should be regarded as lower bounds of true costs associated with terrorism. The advantage of IEP's methodology is that the estimates are comparable across countries and time.

---

[10] The cost of one death is $8,888,692 and that of one injury is $120,622, both at 2008 dollars for the USA. These are a bit different from the numbers in McCollister et al. (2010), as they are adjusted for terrorism-related death and injury, as opposed to other forms of violence.

[11] PPP per-capita GDP is based on PPP-adjusted exchange rate. Purchasing power parity compares the cost of a common representative basket of goods across a pair of countries. If, say, in the USA it is $100 and in Japan it costs ¥8000, then the PPP-adjusted exchange is $1 = ¥80. (The costs of the representative basket of goods may be imputed from the respective consumer price index.) This is the different from the nominal exchange rate between two currencies that is based on daily trade in the world currency market and thus can vary daily. There are some common factors affecting the two exchange rates, but there are different factors as well.

[12] GTD categorizes terror events into four types: minor, major, catastrophic, and unknown. For the unknown category, property damages are assumed to be zero. For events with available reported costs of property damage, the figures are converted to the US dollars. Those associated property damage costs less than $1 million, between $1 million and $1 billion and higher than $1 billion are defined as minor, major, and catastrophic, respectively. The GTD dataset also contains information on the tactics used in terror events like bombing/explosion, armed assault, hijacking etc., and, the cost of property damage from some, not all, terror events during a year. From this information, IEP calculates, for each country, the average cost of property damage for each tactic and for each of the three aforementioned categories (minor, major, and catastrophic). These averages are applied for all terror events in terms of tactic whether or not property damage estimates associated with them are available, and, then summed over all events. Next, they are scaled on the basis of the income type of the country: high-income OECD, high-income non-OECD, upper middle income, and lower income country groups (Institute for Economics & Peace, 2016b).

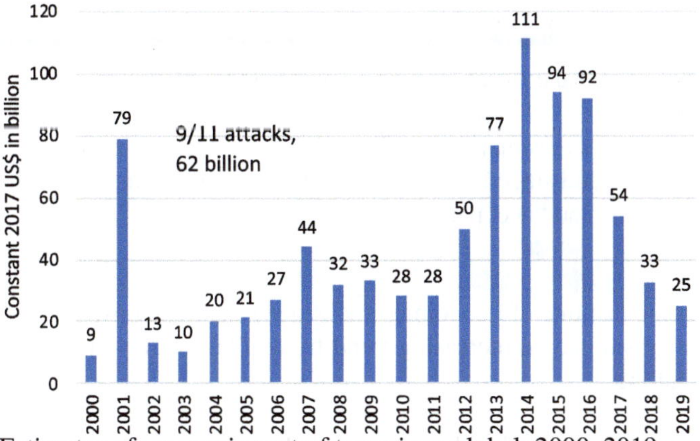

Fig. 5.1: Estimates of economic cost of terrorism: global, 2000–2019.
Sources: Institute for Economics & Peace (2019, Figure 1.6), Institute for Economics & Peace (2020b, Table 2.1); permission to reproduce from IEP is thankfully acknowledged

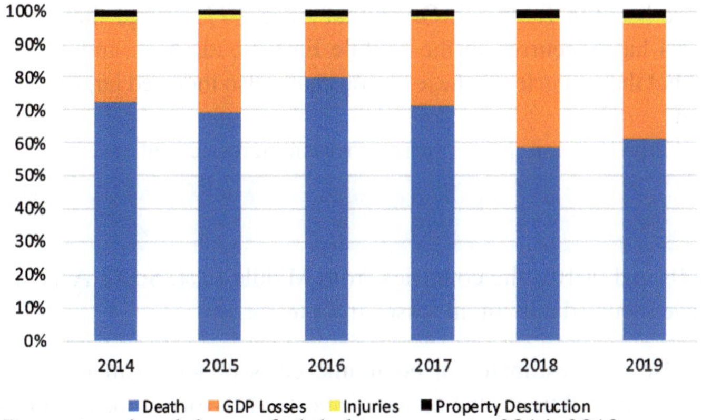

Fig. 5.2: Percentage breakdown of global terror costs: 2014–2019.
Source: Institute for Economics & Peace (2020b, Table 2.2); permission to reproduce from IEP is thankfully acknowledged

5.3.2 Patterns and Trends

A time-series of global costs of terrorism during 2000–2019 is presented in Fig. 5.1. (Needless to say, the *9/11* attacks explain the spike for the year 2001.) Observe that there is an overall increasing trend in the global cost of terrorism from 2000 to 2014 and a downward trend since 2014, whereas the year 2014 coincides with the zenith of ISIS's atrocities and "occupation."

Is That So? 5.2: Global (Direct) Costs of Terrorism

Following the Institute of Economics and Peace's methodology, the global direct cost of terrorism had an increasing trend from 2000 to 2014, and, since then it has been falling.

Figure 5.2 presents the breakdown of global terrorism costs over the years 2014–2109 according to the sources. As we can see, among the four categories of the impact of terrorism, deaths constitute the major share, followed by GDP loss.

There are however considerable differences of terror costs across countries. Top ten countries in terms of incurring the cost of terrorism for years 2015–2017 and 2019 are listed in Table 5.2. Given that since *9/11*, a large share of worldwide terror attacks have occurred in the Middle East, South Asia, and Africa, it is not surprising that the countries in these regions have also incurred large economic costs of terrorism.

Comparing economic losses from terrorism across countries,

Is That So? 5.3: Economic Costs of Terrorism: Middle East, South Asia, and North Africa

Over 2000s and 2010s, the countries from Middle East, South Asia, and North Africa have incurred maximum losses from terrorism.

There also exist estimates of economic costs of terrorism for the developed economies. Figure 5.3 tracks the economic costs of terrorism for Europe from 2007 to 2019. Note that these costs are less than $1 billion in 2014 PPP$ in every year during 2007–2014, while 2015 was a really bad year. It is because Belgium, France, and Turkey witnessed a dramatic increase in the number of terror attacks during this year. The economic costs of terrorism crossed $4 billion in 2015. In more recent years the economic cost for Europe from terrorism is around $600 million.

Detailed estimates of economic cost of terrorism incurred by individual countries in the European Union over the period 2004–2016 and over 2013–2016 as a whole are given in (van Ballegooij & Bakowski, 2018, Tables 2 and 3). Figure 5.4 shows the total figures for the entire region. It may be noted that while the IEP's methodology is used in this study in estimating costs of fatalities, injuries, and property damage, the GDP costs are based on econometric estimation of the impact of terrorism on

	2015		2016		2017		2019	
Rank	Country	% of GDP	Country	% of GDP	Country	% of GDP	Country	% of GDP
1.	Iraq	17.3	Iraq	24	Afghanistan	12.8	Afghanistan	16.7
2.	Afghanistan	16.8	Afghanistan	13	Iraq	10.8	Syria	3.4
3.	Syria	8.3	South Sudan	9	Syria	5.8	Nigeria	2.4
4.	Yemen	7.3	Syria	6	Somalia	5.0	Burkina Faso	1.9
5.	Libya	5.7	Libya	3	South Sudan	3.9	Mali	1.9
6.	South Sudan	4.8	Nigeria	3	Central African Republic	2.6	Somalia	1.2
7.	Nigeria	4.5	Yemen	2	Nigeria	2.6	Iraq	1.1
8.	Pakistan	2.8	Central African Republic	2	Libya	1.8	Yemen	1.0
9.	Niger	2.1	Burundi	1	Egypt	0.8	Sri Lanka	1.0
10.	Central African Republic	2.1	Turkey	1	Yemen	0.7	Central African Republic	0.9

Table 5.2: Top 10 Countries in terms of economic costs of terrorism in 2015–2017, 2019.
Sources: Institute for Economics & Peace (2016b, 2017, 2018, 2020b); permission to reproduce from IEP is thankfully acknowledged

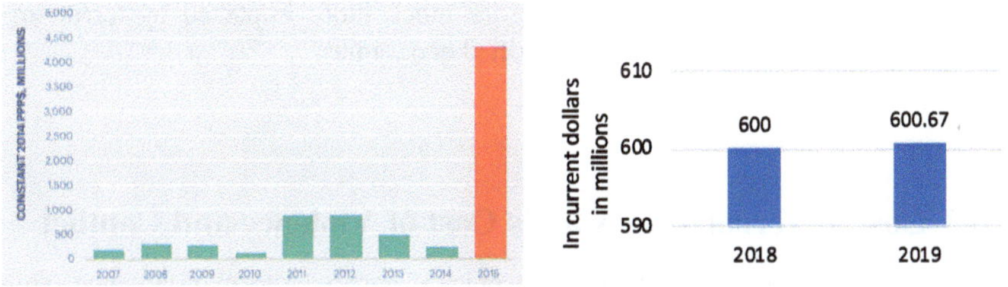

(a) (b)

Fig. 5.3: Estimates of Economic Cost of Terrorism: Europe. (**a**) Economic Costs of Deaths and Injuries from Terrorism for Europe, 2007–2015. (**b**) Total economic costs for Europe, 2018–2019.
Sources: (**a**) Institute for Economics & Peace (2016a, Figure 14), (**b**) (Institute for Economics & Peace, 2019, Table 1.4), (Institute for Economics & Peace, 2020b, Table 2.5); permission to reproduce from IEP is thankfully acknowledged

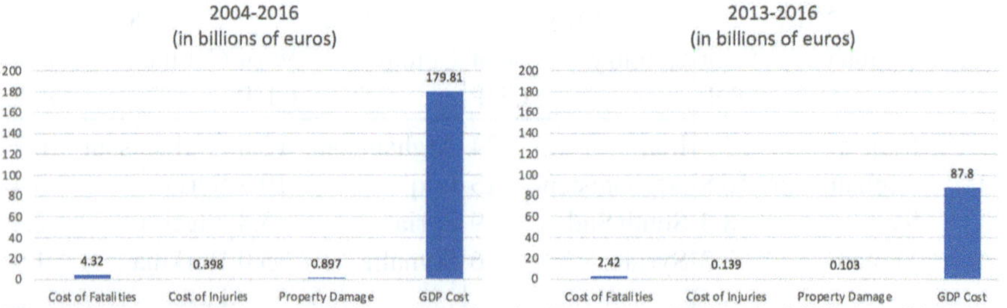

Fig. 5.4: Economic costs of terrorism for the European Union in billions of 2016 €: 2004–2016 and 2013–2016.
Source: van Ballegooij and Bakowski (2018, Tables 2 and 3)

growth. As a consequence, well over 90% of total cost of terrorism is attributed to GDP losses. Also notice that the total cost over the period 2013–2016 is nearly half of the total cost over the period 2004–2016, which is consistent with our earlier observation that terrorism problems in Europe are more severe in relatively recent years than in the first decade of this century.

The annual GDP of the European Union runs in trillions of euros. Obviously, the total cost of terrorism, indicated in Fig. 5.4, is much less than one percent of the total GDP. In contrast, referring back to Table 5.2, we see that for countries like Iraq, Afghanistan, Syria, and Somalia among others, the costs of terrorism bear a much higher proportion to the respective GDPs. Thus,

Is That So? 5.4: Economic Costs of Terrorism: Small Versus Advanced Economies

Small and less diversified economies are much more impacted by terrorism compared to advanced and more diversified economies.

5.3.3 Cost of Terrorism vis-à-vis Cost of Violence and Conflict

It is important to keep in mind that terrorism is "a" particular form of violence, while violence manifests also in other forms like homicide, civil war, external war, etc. As it turns out, the economic costs of terrorism are a small fraction of the economic costs of overall violence and conflict.

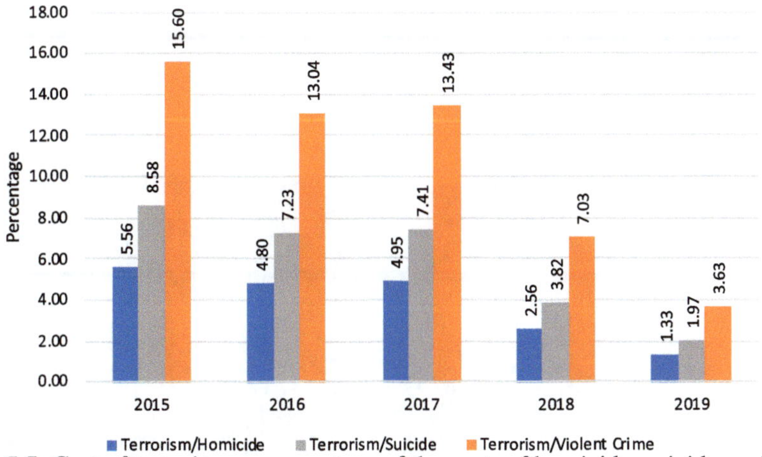

Fig. 5.5: Cost of terrorism as percentage of the costs of homicide, suicide, and violent crime: global, 2015–2019.
Source: Institute for Economics & Peace (2020a, Table 3.2); permission to reproduce from IEP is thankfully acknowledged

Globally, in 2014, interpersonal violence—which includes homicide, violent and sexual assault, fear of crime, and terrorism—cost 32 times higher than terrorism and claimed 13 times the lives lost in terror attacks (Institute for Economics & Peace, 2015). Figure 5.5 shows that the economic cost of terrorism is a small fraction of that of homicide, suicide, or violent crime.

Comparing the economic costs of terrorism with another category of violence, namely, conflict also shows how small the cost of terrorism is relative to that of conflict. Figure 5.6 presents a comparative time-series of the economic impact of terrorism and conflict from 2007 to 2015. In 2015, the economic costs of terrorism were 14.2% of that of conflicts (Institute for Economics & Peace, 2016b). Conflict is a "driver of terrorism." In 2019, 96% of global deaths from terrorism occurred in countries that experienced conflict (Institute for Economics & Peace, 2019).

Is that So? No. 5.5 is a notable observation.

Is That So? 5.5: Economic Costs of Terrorism and Conflict

Estimates of economic cost of terrorism are a small percentage of homicide, suicide, violent crime, or conflict. Further, the economic cost of terrorism is positively and strongly correlated with that of conflict.

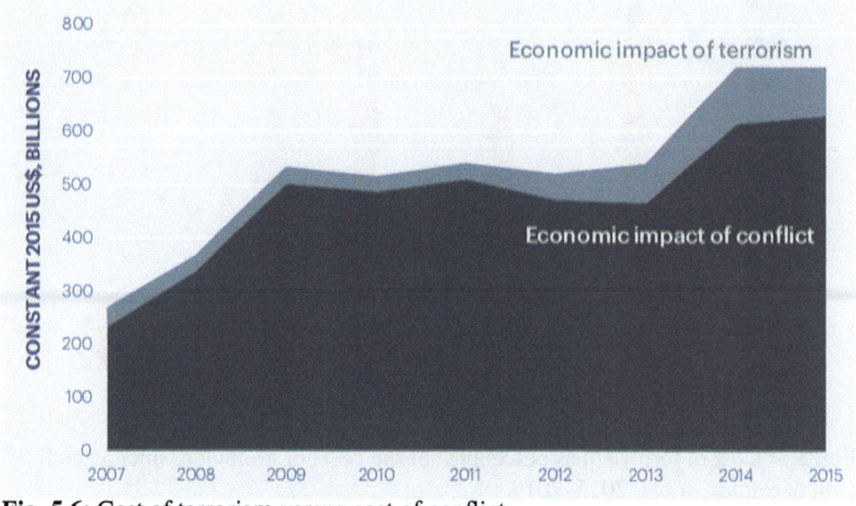

Fig. 5.6: Cost of terrorism versus cost of conflict.
Source: Institute for Economics & Peace (2016b, Figure 4.3); permission to reproduce from IEP is thankfully acknowledged

The costs of terrorism in comparison to cost of overall violence is even much smaller than in comparison to interpersonal violence or conflicts. In 2015, the global economic cost, using Purchasing Power Parity, of overall violence—inclusive of interpersonal violence, communal and ethnic conflicts, internal, and external military conflicts—was \$13.6 trillion, whereas that of terrorism was \$89.6 billion, which is 0.65% of the total cost of violence. The corresponding numbers for 2017 and 2019 were (\$14.76 trillion and \$52 billion) and (\$14.5 trillion and \$26.4 billion).[13]

Is That So? 5.6: Economic Costs of Terrorism vis-à-vis Economic Costs of Violence

The economic cost of terrorism is less than one percent of the economic cost of violence.

However, what sets terrorism apart is the unexpectedness of collective injury, death, and devastation and thus the aggregate sense of fear and anxiety it creates. Monetary equivalent of these adverse effects is not easy to measure and typically not included in the estimation of the cost of terrorism. If they are quantified, the measured cost of terrorism would be surely higher.

[13] See Institute for Economics & Peace (2016b, 2018, 2020b). The cost of violence does not include domestic or self-directed violence.

5.4 Direct Cost of Counter-Terrorism (CT) Measures

Many countries do not divulge much information on the cost of their CT measures. However, *some* worldwide estimates as well as accounts of expenditure on CT measures by the USA are publicly available, albeit a bit dated.

In principle we can divide these costs into three categories: ① security including intelligence, ② preemptive attacks against terrorists and their bases, and ③ foreign aid or assistance to other countries to act toward containing terrorism in their countries.

5.4.1 Security Costs

Needless to say, worldwide security measures increased dramatically in the aftermath of the *9/11* attacks. It is however difficult to separate out these costs for terrorism only, because spending on immigration, border protection, domestic law enforcement, etc. is only partly used for containing terrorism. According to Institute for Economics & Peace (2015),

Is That So? 5.7: USA is the Leader in terms of Spending on National Security Agencies

Global security costs totaled $117 billion in 2014 and the US accounts for 70% of the total global spending on national security agencies.

In the USA, 41% of expenditure on domestic security agencies is devoted to terrorism, while in the UK, 81% of budget for M15 is targeted toward terrorism. Over 2005–2014, USA spent $650 billion on intelligence (including terrorism and other concerns). For G20 countries combined, the spending on national security and intelligence that target terrorism and other concerns reached $117 billion in 2014.

European Parliament (2016) reported that European Union's spending on CT security measures increased from €5.7 billion in 2002 to €93.5 billion in 2009, a 16-fold increase. Following the 2015 January attacks, France increased its CT spending by €3.8 billion for the next four years. EU's budget for "Security and Citizenship" increased from €2.52 million in 2015 to €4.05 million in 2016. Founded in 1992, *Europol* is the law enforcement agency of the European Union. Counter-terrorism was not included in its mandate till 1999. Between 2002 and 2009, *Europol*'s budget increased from €53 million to €68 million. In 2016, its budget exceeded €100 million.[14] During 2007–2013, the European Commission made €1.4 billion available

[14] In the same year, the European Counter-Terrorism Centre was created within *Europol*.

for security research. Under the 2014–2020 Multiannual Financial Framework of the European Union, a fund named Internal Security Fund (ISF) was created to support security-enhancing initiative in the EU. The fund has a budget of €3.8 billion, which is divided between borders, visa, and police issues. The portion allocated for police is used for CT measures.

According to the UK Home Office, in 2017 an estimated amount of £824 million was spent by the Office of Security and Counter-Terrorism. Of £8.5 billion allotted to Crime, Police, and Fire group, £731 million was slated for counter-terrorism policing (van Ballegooij & Bakowski, 2018).

The facts and figures on security measures indicate considerable variation across countries and regions.

5.4.2 Cost of Preemptive Strikes

These costs refer to launching offensives against terrorists and terror organizations. During the height of "The Troubles" in the 1970s when PIRA was very active, the British government spent about $6 million per day to counter PIRA (Clarke, 2015, page 30).

Data are available for *Operation Inherent Resolve* (OIR), the operational name for the military campaign against ISIS in Iraq and Syria by the USA in concert with the coalition forces. The data contains # of air strikes by allied forces as well as ***weekly data*** on the costs of operations of OIR by the USA (not other members of the coalition): visit https://www.defense.gov/OIR/. Figure 5.7 graphs the breakdown—by category, expense, and service—of total cost of US air campaign against ISIS in Iraq and Syria over a two-year and ten-month period: from August 6, 2014 to June 30, 2017. By category, military "operational tempo" (OPTEMPO in brief), which refers to the rate of military actions or missions, tops the list. Because these are costs of air strikes, air force constituted the lion's share of total expenditures toward army, navy, air force, and SOCOM combined.[15]

Figure 5.8 tracks the average daily cost of OIR, which increased from $9.1 million in May 2015 to $13.6 million per day in June 2017.

Is That So? 5.8: Cost of US Air Campaign against ISIS

By June of 2017, the US spending on air campaign against ISIS in Iraq and Syria reached $13.6 million per day.

[15] SOCOM stands for Special Operations Command.

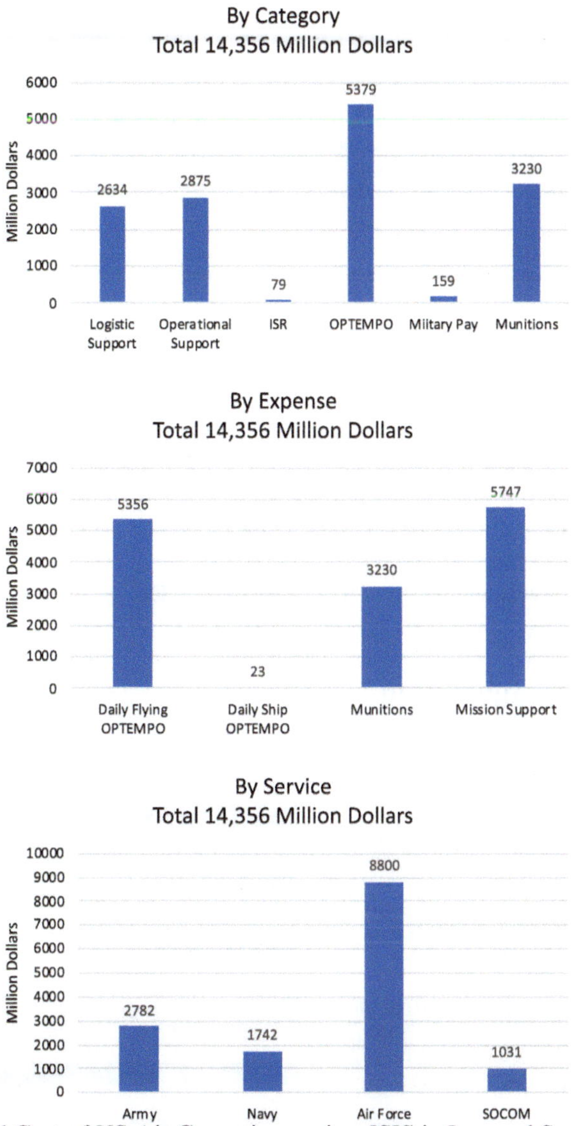

Fig. 5.7: Total Cost of US Air Campaign against ISIS in Iraq and Syria: August 8, 2014 to June 30, 2017.
Source: https://www.defense.gov/OIR/, Accessed on Dec 4, 2019

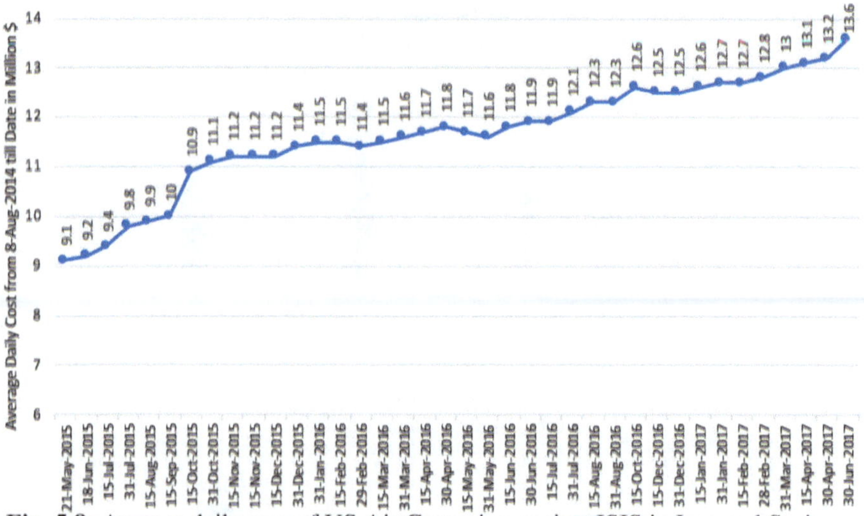

Fig. 5.8: Average daily cost of US Air Campaign against ISIS in Iraq and Syria: August 8, 2014 to June 30, 2017.
Source: https://www.defense.gov/OIR/, Accessed on Dec 4, 2019

5.4.3 War in Afghanistan

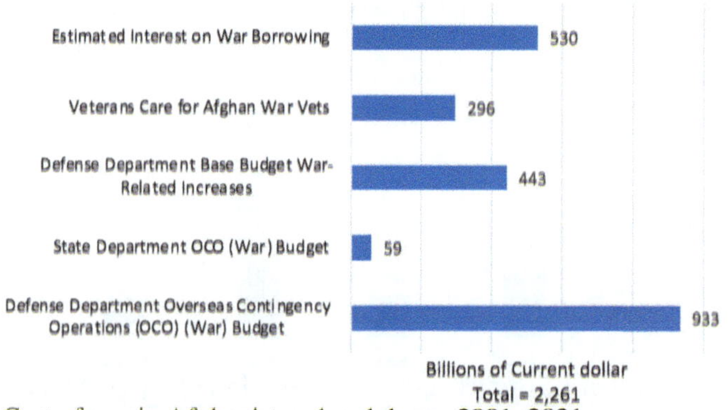

Fig. 5.9: Cost of war in Afghanistan, breakdown, 2001–2021.
Source: Crawford and Lutz (2021); permission to reproduce by the authors is thankfully acknowledged

The US war in Afghanistan is covered by two mission names: *Operation Enduring Freedom* (2001–2014) and *Operation Freedom's Sentinel* (since 2015). In a broad sense, most of the expenses in Afghanistan can be interpreted as the cost of

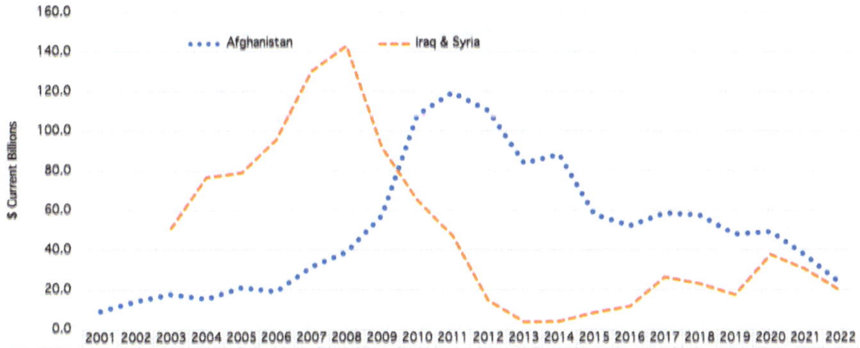

	2001	2002	2003	2004	2005	2006	2007	2008	2009	2010	2011	2012	2013	2014	2015	2016	2017	2018	2019	2020	2021	2022
Afghanistan	9.0	14.0	17.6	15.2	20.9	18.8	31.4	38.8	57.2	107.	119.	110.	83.7	88.1	57.8	52.1	58.6	57.5	47.8	49.0	37.1	22.9
Iraq & Syria			51.0	76.6	79.1	95.6	130.	143.	91.8	65.3	47.1	14.7	3.7	4.1	8.4	11.6	26.3	23.0	17.4	37.6	30.3	19.4

Fig. 5.10: Cost of War in Afghanistan–Pakistan and Iraq–Syria under Defense and State Department Appropriations.
Source: Reproduced from (Crawford, 2021, Figure 4); permission to reproduce by the author is thankfully acknowledged

counter-terror measures, because, in the first place, the USA moved into Afghanistan in order to counter-terrorist threat, both direct and indirect, emerging from Afghanistan.

Is That So? 5.9: Cumulative Cost of Afghan War to the USA

According to Crawford and Lutz (2021) as well as other sources, the estimated total cost, both direct and indirect, of the Afghan war (including operations in Afghanistan and Pakistan) from fiscal year 2001 to the fiscal year 2021 is over 2 trillion in current dollars.

The breakdown of costs, constructed according to the departments or agencies that are budgeted, is shown in Fig. 5.9. The spending under the heading of Defense and State Department Appropriations approximates the direct cost of involvement in Afghanistan (including Pakistan). The evolution of spending under this heading is exhibited in Fig. 5.10.[16] The total is 1.16 trillion in current dollars.

[16] The number for the fiscal year 2022 is amount requested by the Biden administration.

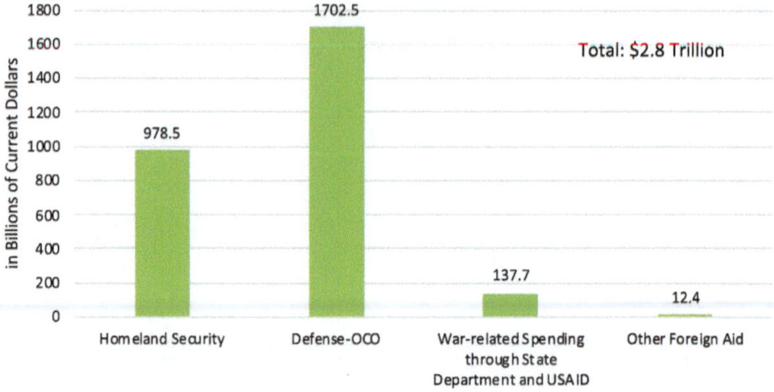

(a)

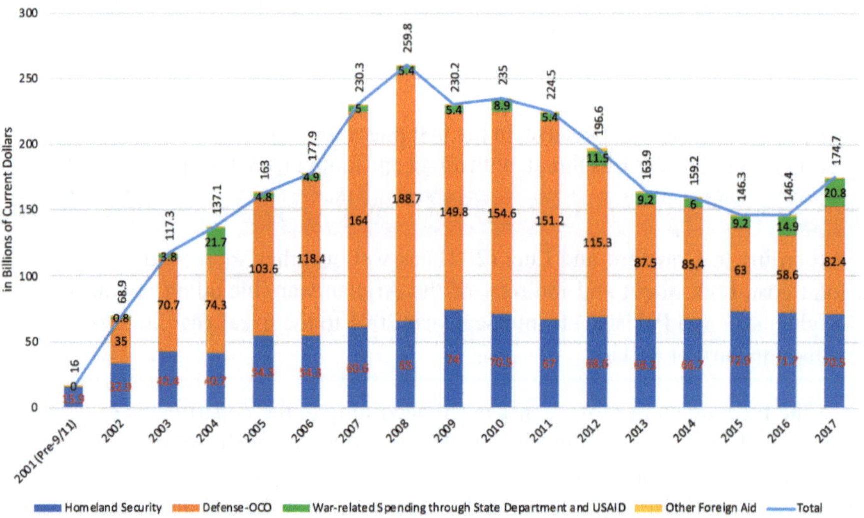

(b)

Fig. 5.11: US Spending on CT Measures: 2001–2017. (**a**) Overall CT spending during 2002–2017. (**b**) Time-Series of Spending on CT Measures.
Source: Stimson Study Group (2018, Figure 3); permission to reproduce from the Stimson Center is thankfully acknowledged

5.4.4 Aggregate Counter-Terrorism Spending by the USA since *9/11*

In contrast to most of the available information on the cost of CT measures being fragmented, Stimson Study Group (2018) documents a systematic account of these costs for the USA from *9/11* to the year 2017. They are organized into four broad categories depending on where the expenses are itemized in the federal budget, namely,

Homeland Security It includes government-wide homeland security spending, distributed over the Department of Homeland Security *and* other agencies.
Defense-OCO It refers to the Department of Defense (DOD) spending designated as emergency and overseas contingency operations (OCO). This includes a major part of war-related expenses in Afghanistan, Iraq, and Syria.
War-Related Spending at the State Department and USAID Some of the overseas spending on security, related CT measures as well as foreign aid are financed through budget to the State Department and US Agency for International Development USAID.
Other Foreign Aid It covers foreign aid through various US initiatives specifically created for counter-terrorism. Foreign aid to countries with significant presence of al-Qaeda, its affiliates, ISIS and Iraq falls in this category.[17]

As Fig. 5.11a shows, the total federal CT spending in the post *9/11* years till 2017 totaled 2.83 trillion in current dollars, 35%, 60%, and 5% of which are spent respectively for homeland security, defense-OCO, and war-related spending at the State Department and USAID. Other foreign aid is only a tiny fraction (less than 0.5%) of the CT spending. Year-wise CT spending is shown in Fig. 5.11b.[18] We see that CT spending by the USA surged after *9/11* and peaked in 2008, representing 16-fold increase over the pre-9/11 total. Since 2008, total CT spending has declined, and this is due to reduced spending on war. As of 2017 the total CT spending was still pretty high—11-fold higher—compared to 2001 before *9/11*. The cost of preemptive measures against terrorism falls mostly under defense-OCO. Recall that between August of 2014 and June of 2017, the US air campaign in Iraq and Syria cost 14.36 billion, which is about 7% of CT spending spending on defense-OCO during 2015–2017.

Note that the spending on homeland security more than doubled in 2002 compared to pre-*9/11* 2001 and steadily climbed till 2009, when it reached $74 billion. It remained relatively stable afterwards varying between $66.3 and $72.9 billion. Stimson Study Group (2018) divides homeland security spending under the headings: border and transport security, defense against catastrophic threats, domestic counter-terrorism, emergency preparedness and response, intelligence and warning

[17] Stimson's estimate of CT-related US spending from 2002–2017 does not include foreign contributions to counter-terrorism; state and local investments in counter-terrorism; some dual-use programs and spending, such as drones; economic losses and secondary effects associated with the long-term cost of counter-terrorism operations and homeland security; and classified CT spending.

[18] No numbers are shown for other foreign aid as these are too small compared to the other three categories.

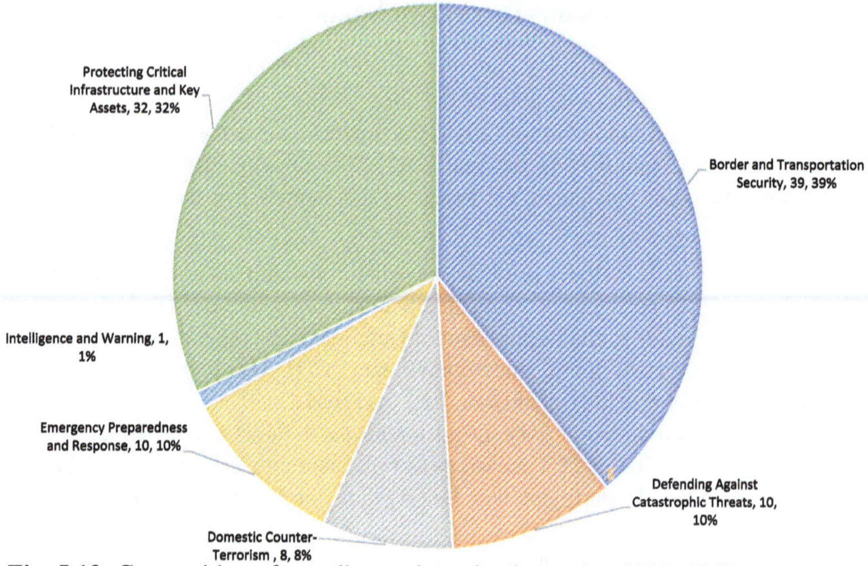

Fig. 5.12: Composition of spending on homeland security: 2002–2017. *Source*: Stimson Study Group (2018, Figure 8); permission to reproduce from the Stimson Center is thankfully acknowledged

and protecting critical infrastructure and key assets. As shown in Fig. 5.12, the major shares of spending on homeland security are held by border and transport security (39%) and protecting critical infrastructure and key assets (32%).

Before *9/11*, the CT spending was less than 2% of the total discretionary spending of the federal government that spans a wide range of areas, including defense, education, and medical research. At its peak in 2008, CT spending amounted to 22% of total discretionary spending. By 2017, CT spending had fallen to 14% of the total. During 2002–2017, the overall CT spending was 15% of the total discretionary spending.[19] Despite this drop, the study group found no indication for CT spending to decline further.

[19] Discretionary spending is spending that is subject to the appropriations process, whereby Congress sets a new funding level each fiscal year (which begins October 1st) for programs covered in an appropriations bill. As opposed to discretionary spending, there is mandatory spending, which does not take place through appropriations legislations. It includes entitlement programs, such as Social Security, Medicare, and required interest spending on the federal debt. Mandatory spending accounts for about two-thirds of all federal spending. In most cases, but not all, mandatory spending is ongoing; it occurs each year absent a change in an underlying law that provides the funding.

Is That So? 5.10: Counter-Terrorism Spending in the USA

According to Stimson Study Group (2018), the counter-terrorism spending by the USA in 2017 was nearly $175 billion and this is not likely to decline in the subsequent years.

While both discretionary and CT spending rose rapidly since *9/11*, CT spending increased more sharply. At the 2008 peak, CT spending had increased 277%—primarily because of the wars—while overall discretionary spending had grown by 116% since 2002. By 2017, CT spending increased by 154% from 2002, whereas overall discretionary spending increased by 102%.

5.4.5 Indirect Cost of Counter-Terrorism Measures

There are indirect costs of CT measures as well, which are quite important but have not been measured. For instance, various security measures including collection of intelligence infringe upon our civil liberty and privacy, which are an integral part of liberal democracy that we all cherish. Preemptive strikes cause collateral damage in terms of civilian lives. This may be unacceptable to us on humanitarian grounds, lead to lack of local support undermining our military efforts and very well breed resentment and encourage more participation in terrorism.

5.5 Are Such Large Spending on Security and Counter-Terrorism Rational?

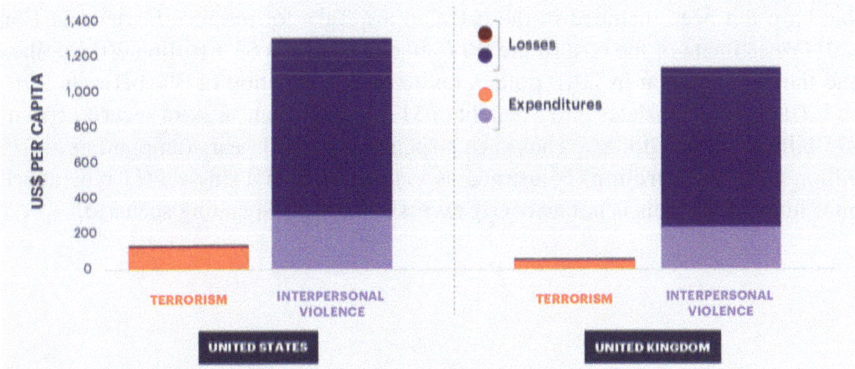

Fig. 5.13: Security expenditure vis-à-vis economic losses.
Source: Institute for Economics & Peace (2015, Figure 36); permission to reproduce from IEP is thankfully acknowledged

Of course, large spending on security and other CT measures has made us safer than otherwise: Just imagine how much suffering would result in the modern age from terror attacks without enhanced CT measures. However, a natural economic question is whether the size of expenditure on CT measures justifies the magnitude of the benefits from them. Keeping aside the expenditure on preemptive measures, as Fig. 5.13 (adapted from Institute for Economics & Peace, 2015) shows, the direct security expenditure on containing terrorism is much larger than the economic loss from terrorism for the USA and the UK[20] For instance, in 2014 the USA spent $115 per capita on national security agencies, whereas the per-capita economic losses from terrorism were only 61 cents.

Mueller and Stewart (2011, 2014) provide an interesting back-of-the-envelope cost–benefit calculation, showing that the cost of security measures far outweigh the estimated benefits from security measures. They first estimate that before *9/11* the security costs per year for the USA were around 25 billion in 2010 dollars. After *9/11*, these costs increased by 75 billion 2010 dollars per year on average till 2011.[21] They also estimated that a $75 billion increase in security is likely to reduce the chance of a successful terror attack on the US soil by 50%. Suppose the estimated economic cost of a *9/11* type attack is $200 billion. Then $75 billion extra security spending would save us an expected cost of a *9/11*-type attack, equal to $100 billion. Hence a four-year security spending of $75 billion per year, that is, a total spending of $300 billion over four years would breakeven with the benefit if there were three *9/11* type attacks over four years (which would yield a benefit of $3 × 100 = $300 billion). Over ten years (2.5 × 4 years), $75 billion per year spending would then break even with benefits if there were 3 × 2.5 = 7.5 September 11-type attacks. This obviously has not happened. Therefore the security costs are much higher than their expected benefits.

However, let us be reminded that there are many indirect costs of terror attacks that have not been included in the calculations. Take for instance Carter and Cox (2011)'s estimate of the cost of the *9/11* attacks, which is $3.3 trillion 2011 dollars and thus $3.2 trillion in 2010 dollars (assuming an inflation of 3% between 2010 and 2011). This translates into a benefit of $1.6 trillion from an extra security cost of $75 billion in 2010 dollars. Thus such a spending over 21 years (amounting to $75 billion ×21 =1.57 trillion) is justified as long as there is a single *9/11*-type attack once in 21 years. This is not an overly excessive security spending scenario.

[20] In contrast, for interpersonal violence in general, the expenditure is considerably less than the economic losses.

[21] This includes security spending by the Department of the Homeland Security, the Department of Defense, the Department of Justice, the Department of Energy, the Department of Health and Human Services and 26 other federal agencies, while it does not include the cost of war in Afghanistan and Iraq or CT-related assistance to foreign governments. Additionally, it includes indirect opportunity costs.

Is That So? 5.11: Economic Costs of Terrorism vis-à-vis Costs of Counter-Terrorism Measures

Cost–benefit analysis of counter-terror measures suggests much less benefits than costs when the benefits only account for direct losses from terror attacks. If the values of indirect losses from terrorism are included, it is likely to yield a more balanced outcome.

5.6 Sum-Up and Take-Aways

- Costs of terrorism can be grouped into short-term direct and indirect costs and medium- and long-term direct and indirect costs. Indirect costs are hard to identify and measure.
- The estimates of *9/11* attacks vary widely, starting from $60 billion to $8.3 trillion depending on what are included and what their estimated cost is.
- According to Buesa et al. (2007), the direct cost of Madrid attacks in March 2004 was around €211 million.
- Based on a methodology developed by the Institute for Economics and Peace, the global direct cost of terrorism increased from 2002 to 2014 and has declined thereafter.
- In more recent years, the countries from Middle East, South Asia, and North Africa have incurred maximum losses from terrorism.
- In general, small and less diversified economies are impacted more by terrorism compared to the advanced economies that are more diversified.
- The economic cost of terrorism is less than one percentage of the economic cost of violence, which includes terrorism, homicide, etc. However, the cost of terrorism does not typically incorporate the public fear and anxiety factor that is the hallmark of terrorism.
- The USA accounts for well over 50% of the total global spending on national security agencies.
- By June of 2017, the US spending on air campaign against the ISIS in Iraq and Syria reached $13.6 million per day.
- The estimated overall cumulative cost of Afghan war for the USA during the period 2001–2020 is over two trillion in current dollars.
- According to Stimson Study Group (2018), the counter-terrorism spending by the USA in the Afghan war was nearly $175 billion in 2017.
- Total US spending on CT measures over 2001–2017 was $2.8 trillion. Defense-OCO and homeland security constitute respectively the first and the second highest categories of expenditure out of the four broad categories of CT spending by the USA.

- Cost–benefit analysis of counter-terror measures suggests much less benefits than costs of the benefits that include only the values of direct losses from terror attacks. If the values of indirect losses from terrorism are included, it is likely to yield a more balanced outcome.

Questions

5.1 "Major terror attacks have exerted heavy losses to national economies." Defend or refute.

5.2 The Afghan war has cost the USA in trillions of dollars. Can you articulate some of the benefits (in concrete terms) from this long war on terror? (You would have to do your own research to develop a good answer.)

5.3 Do you agree with Mueller–Stewart analysis and conclusion that the costs of CT measures far exceed the benefit from them? Justify your answer.

5.4 Develop a back-of-envelope calculation of the expected damage in terms of dollars from a nuclear warhead falling into the hands of a jihadist terrorist group.

Chapter 6

Economic and Health Effects of Terrorism

6.1 Introduction

In Chap. 5, we discussed the direct and indirect economic costs of terrorism, which were estimated by using various accounting methods. In contrast, the current chapter studies the impact of terrorism on real income, growth of an economy, physical and mental health of people, etc., measured by statistical/econometric estimation. The focus is on understanding of the cause–effect relation between terrorism and these outcomes, rather than how these outcomes translate into a dollar value. Not only will the quantitative estimates be presented as information, but emphasis will also be placed on the underlying methodologies as learning tools.

The current chapter has several sections. Sections 6.2 through 6.9, respectively, review the impacts of terrorism on per-capita income and growth, international trade, foreign direct investment, labor market, financial markets, tourism, psychological well-being, and physical well-being. Section 6.10 outlines the role of media coverage of terror events on mental health and Sect. 6.11 discusses available evidence of terrorist attacks leading to adaptive changes in behavior in order to "live" or cope with terror attacks.

Given the enormous volume of the literature on various ramifications of terrorism, our review will be selective and in varying details. As said earlier, different methodologies are introduced—without placing much technical burden on the reader—for learning purposes. For further reference, many individual studies are outlined in the chapter appendix.[1]

6.2 Real Per-Capita Income and Real GNP

It is natural to ask how terrorism has affected the overall economic performance of an economy or a group of economies in terms of the real per-capita income (a *level effect*) and the growth of real per-capita income (a *growth effect*). An increase in

[1] Summary information in tabular form on the methodology, variables used, data source, time period, etc. presented in individual studies are available from the author on request.

S. P. Das, *Economics of Terrorism and Counter-Terrorism Measures*,
https://doi.org/10.1007/978-3-030-96577-8_6

Fig. 6.1: Real per-capita GDP of the US: 1995–2015. *Source*: World Bank

terrorism is likely to heighten uncertainty about the future and decrease returns from business, investment and commerce as well as exert a negative impact on the labor markets. These factors would tend to reduce the level and the growth rate of real income.

To begin with, as noted in Chap. 5, there is no significant effect of single terror attacks, major or minor, on the overall macro indices of developed nations. Consider, for instance, the time-series of the US real per-capita GDP from 1990 to 2015, exhibited in Fig. 6.1. It rose steadily in the 1990s and through 2000, during which there were terror attacks on the US soil and US interests abroad, e.g., on the World Trade Center in 1993, Alfred P. Murrah Federal Building Oklahoma City in 1995 and the Navy destroyer USS Cole in 2000 in Yemen. Except from the year 2000 to 2001, the per-capita real GDP again rose steadily in the 2000s up until 2008, before the advent of the Great Recession. The flat segment between 2000 and 2001 covers the *9/11* attacks of course, but the `dot.com` bust in the IT sector also happened during 2000–2001. Thus, the impact of terror attacks—including *9/11* attacks—on the overall performance of the US economy is rather modest, at best. The reason is that the developed economies are well-diversified and resilient, thus able to absorb the "shocks" of terror attacks without much difficulty.

However, this is not true for less developed countries or regions since these economies are typically less diversified and hence less resilient. If plagued by persistent problems of terrorism over some interval of time, they are significantly affected.

In what follows, we review the impact of terrorism on the level and growth of per-capita real income of selected countries and regions as well as on the world economy.[2]

6.2.1 Per-Capita Real Income of Individual Countries

There are studies on Spain, Israel, and Turkey.

6.2.1.1 Basque Country (Spain)

In Sect. 2.7.3 of Chap. 2, we studied the ETA, a terror organization in the Spanish Basque Country. Its objective was to gain independence or at least greater autonomy for the region. ETA's atrocities began around 1970, although its origin dates much earlier. Prime Minister Blanco who was close to General Franco was killed by its attack in 1973. ETA's violence escalated through the 1970s and the early 1980s, after which it began to abate. Various intermittent ceasefires came to exist since late 1990s. ETA was active in the 2000s. A multilateral settlement was brokered in 2011. In 2017 ETA self-declared to be totally disarmed. During the entire conflict period, ETA's terror attacks claimed more than 800 lives and around 2600 injuries.

In an innovative study, Abadie and Gardeazabal (2003) measured the impact of terrorism by ETA on the real per-capita income of the Basque Country in Spain. Their main result is that

Is That So? 6.1: Per-Capital Income Loss of the Basque Country, Spain

During 1980s and 1990s when ETA's violence was prominent in the Spanish Basque region, the region's real per-capita GDP was 10% lower on average annually than what it would have been in the absence of ETA's terrorism.

The authors deduced this by using a novel methodology. That is, they created a counterfactual of what would have been the time path of the per-capita real GDP of the Basque Country in the absence of terrorism, which was then compared with the actual. The innovation lies in constructing the counterfactual, or, what the authors called a *synthetic Basque economy without terrorism.* They first computed several "growth characteristics" like per-capita GDP, population density, investment to GDP ratio, etc. of the region in the 1960s, which was the period before the ETA's violence began. This served as the reference period. Next, they constructed a weighted average of the same characteristics of the other (sixteen) regions of Spain, such that the resulting hypothetical economy closely resembles the observed characteristics of the Basque Country. This was the synthetic Basque Country without terrorism.

[2] The combined impact of conflicts and terrorism on the growth of real per-capita income for low- and middle-income countries is studied in Gupta et al. (2004).

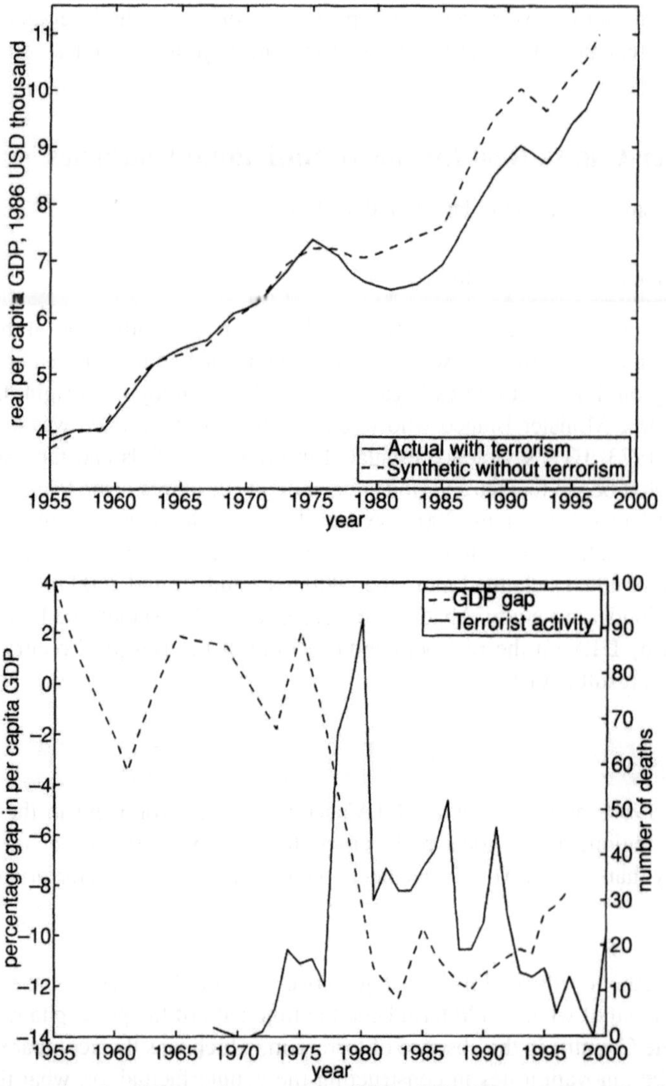

Fig. 6.2: Terrorism by ETA and per-capita GDP of The Basque Country. *Source*: Abadie and Gardeazabal (2003, Figures 1 and 2); permission to reproduce by the authors and the American Economic Association is thankfully acknowledged

With the regional weights in hand it is straightforward to construct the time path of each growth characteristic of the synthetic Basque. In particular, the dotted line of the top panel of Fig. 6.2 is the time path of the real per-capita GDP of the synthetic Basque, whereas the solid line represent the actual real per-capita GDP of the Basque region. Check that the counterfactual and the actual per-capita income (real per-capita GDP) paths run very close to each other from 1955 till 1975. But, thereafter—and coincident with a rise in ETA's atrocities—they diverge: the actual falls behind the counterfactual. The annual percentage difference between the two is graphed as the dotted line in the bottom panel of Fig. 6.2. This panel also graphs the magnitude of terrorism by ETA in terms of the number of deaths. We see that the per-capita income gap and terrorism are positively correlated. Based on data exhibited in the top panel of Fig. 6.2, the number given in our *Is that So* Box 6.1 is obtained.

6.2.1.2 Israel

Ever since its independence in 1948, Israel has faced numerous conflicts and terrorist attacks. Eckstein and Tsiddon (2004) provided evidence that terrorism did adversely affect the real per-capita income and other macro variables of Israel over the period 1980–2003, which witnessed two waves of *Intifada* (Palestinian uprising) against Israel. Recall from Chap. 2 that the First Intifada began around 1987–1988 and lasted well into 1993. It ended with the loss of civilian Israeli occupation and control of the West Bank and Gaza territories. However, the individual security of Israeli citizens was not affected significantly.

The Second Intifada, also known the al-Aqsa Intifada, that began in the fourth quarter of 2000 and lasted till 2004–2005, was bloodier and more severely impacted Israel. Palestinian attack tactics included suicide bombing, rocket launch, and sniper fire. There were about 151 suicide attacks (Benmelech and Berrebi, 2007). Nearly 4000 Palestinians and more than 1000 Israelis were killed (Becker and Rubinstein, 2011).

Eckstein and Tsiddon (2004) used the time-series VAR analysis (see General Appendix B, Sect. B.13.4) to assess the impact of terrorism on Israel's per-capita income as well as investment, exports, and non-durable consumption over two sample periods 1980Q1–2000Q3 and 1980Q1–2003Q3, where "Q" denotes a quarter of a year. Note that the end of 2000Q3 marks the beginning of the Second Intifada. whereas 2003Q3 falls in the middle of it. A novelty of Eckstein and Tsiddon (2004) is their construction of an index of terrorism, which has been subsequently used by other researchers:

$$\begin{array}{l}\textit{Eckstein-}\\\textit{Tsiddon (ET)}\\\textit{Terrorism}\\\textit{Index}\end{array} \equiv \ln\left(e + \frac{\#\text{ of attacks} + \#\text{ of deaths} + \#\text{ of injuries}}{3}\right), \tag{6.1}$$

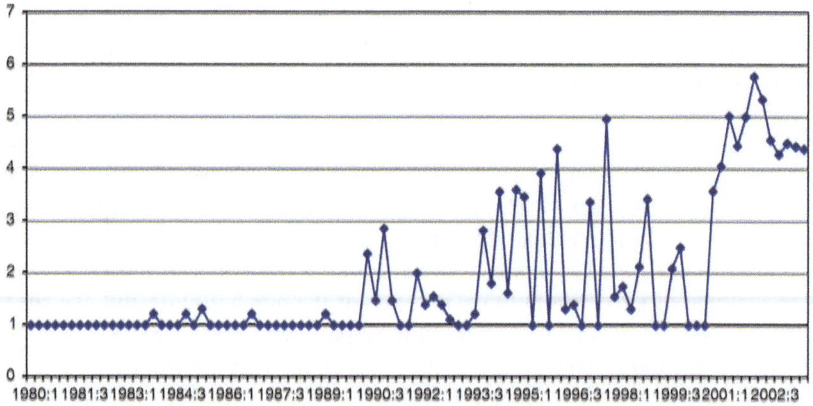

Fig. 6.3: Terror index for Israel from 1980:1 to 2003:3. *Source*: Eckstein and Tsiddon (2004, Figure 5); permission to reproduce by the authors and Elsevier is thankfully acknowledged

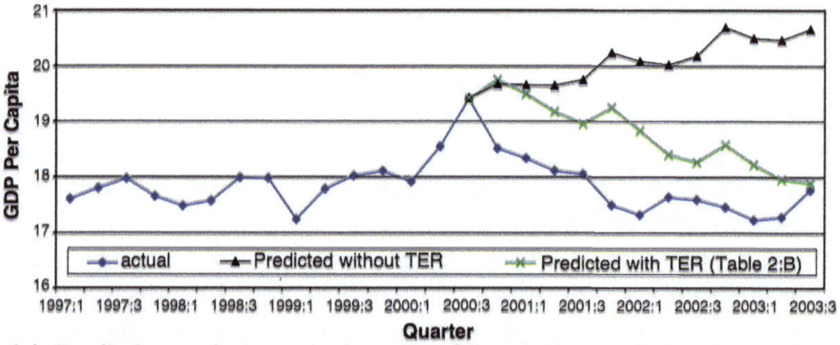

Fig. 6.4: Predicting real per-capita income of Israel. *Source*: Eckstein and Tsiddon (2004, Figure 6(a)); permission to reproduce by the authors and Elsevier is thankfully acknowledged. *Note:* Quarterly GDP per capita is measured in 000s of chained 2000 NIS

where e is the exponential constant $\simeq 2.718$. This formula is such that if there are no terror attacks, i.e., if # of attacks + # of deaths + # of injuries = 0, then the ET terrorism index = 1. Figure 6.3 graphs the time-series of the terror index for Israel over the sample period. We see that Israel began to be hit by terrorism in a relatively large scale in 1988, which coincides with the beginning of the First Intifada.

The estimated time-series equations yield negative and statistically significant coefficients on terror (the ET terrorism index). The main result of Eckstein and Tsiddon (2004) is shown in Fig. 6.4. Comparing the actual to the predicted counterfactual by forcing ET = 0 in the estimated equation on terrorism, i.e., comparing the bottom branch to the top branch (ignore the middle branch),

Is That So? 6.2: Per-Capital Income Loss of Israel

If terrorism did not occur during 2000Q4–2003Q3, the Israeli per-capita income in 2003Q3 would have been 10% higher than the actual.

Note the similarity with the magnitude of the effect of terrorism on per-capita income of the Basque Country studied earlier.[3]

6.2.1.3 Turkey

Araz-Takay et al. (2009) studied the impact of terrorism in Turkey on its real gross national product over 1987–2005. During this period most of terrorist attacks in Turkey were perpetrated by PKK (see Chap. 2). Using the time-series method of Granger causality tests (General Appendix B, Sect. B.13.3) and the ET terrorism index, the authors found that *terrorism had severe adverse effects on the economy when it was in an expansionary phase, and, overall, a one-standard-deviation increase in the terrorism index led to a 0.05% fall in the real GNP, and it was statistically significant.*[4]

6.2.2 Per-Capita Real Income Growth: Different Regions

The studies on the impact of terrorism on the overall economic performance of different regions (as opposed to individual countries) of the world economy and the world economy as a whole have typically focused on the *growth rate* of real per-capita income. The units of observation are a collection (sample) of countries. There are cross-sectional as well as panel-data analyses.[5]

6.2.2.1 Western Europe

Gaibulloev and Sandler (2008) studied eighteen Western European countries over the period 1971–2004, differentiating between domestic terrorism and transnational terrorism. Their panel regression equation is of the form:

$$\text{Growth}_{it} = a + b_1 \cdot \text{Terror}_{it} + b_2 \cdot \left(\frac{I}{\text{GDP}}\right)_{it} + \boldsymbol{\beta} \mathbf{Z} + u_{it}, \tag{6.2}$$

where i stands for a country, t is time, and "Growth" is the annual growth rate of real per-capita GDP. For each year, the variable "Terror" was measured in three alternative ways: the number of domestic-terror attacks, the number of transnational terrorism or the sum of the two, each divided by population in million. In other words, terrorism is measured relative to the size of a country. The estimated coefficient of

[3] Eckstein and Tsiddon (2004) also estimated "out-of-sample" counterfactual prediction for the period 2003Q4–2005Q3.

[4] One-standard-deviation change is explained in the General Appendix B, Sect. B.7.

[5] The cross-sectional and panel data are explained in General Appendix B, Sect. B.3.1.

b_1 is of central importance. The equation also includes current investment (I) to GDP ratio, an important determinant of a country's growth rate. The vector $\mathbf{Z}$ denotes other control variables that include last period's real per-capita GDP and a measure of a country's international-trade openness (these are also standard and important determinants of growth) as well as unobserved country-specific effects and unobserved time-specific effects.[6]

The main findings were as follows. *Transnational terrorism had a greater negative marginal influence on real per-capita income growth than did domestic terrorism. Each additional transnational terrorist incident per million persons reduced economic growth by about 0.4%. When both types of terrorist attacks are aggregated into a single measure, the resulting marginal impact was less yet statistically significant.*[7]

6.2.2.2 Asia

Using a similar econometric framework while allowing for more controls like external and internal conflicts and degree of democracy, Gaibulloev and Sandler (2009b) quantify the impact of terrorism and conflicts on the real per-capita income growth for Asia during 1970–2004. Similar to Gaibulloev and Sandler (2008), panel regression using data on 42 Asian countries yields that transnational terrorist attacks have a significant growth-limiting effect: *an additional transnational terrorist incident per million persons reduces gross domestic product per-capita growth by about 1.5%. Growth reductions occur through the twin channels of reduced private investment, coupled with increased government expenditures.*[8]

Note that the negative impact of terrorism on growth is stronger in Asia than in western Europe. It attests to the hypothesis that poorer countries are less resilient to terrorism compared to richer nations.

---

[6] As discussed in General Appendix B, Sect. B.14, the inclusion of unit (countries, here) and time-specific effects that are unobserved is common in panel estimation. For instance, the geographical location or landscape of a country, or its political system may have some effect on its growth rate. Country-specific effects capture these effects collectively. Similarly, common happenings in a particular calendar year may have some impact on growth rate of countries. These are reflected by time-specific effects.

[7] Two other equations are estimated so as to understand the mechanism of how terror events impact on growth: one for the investment to GDP ratio and the other for government spending to GDP ratio. These are the dependent variables, whereas the regressors are the log of last period's per-capita real GDP, trade openness in the current year, current measure of terror as well as unobserved country- and time-specific effects. The impact of terror on the investment to GDP ratio is negative, signifying that *terrorism reduces growth via affecting the investment/GDP ratio.*

[8] Note that *the impact of terror on growth is greater for Asiatic countries than for the Western European countries.* The same authors, namely Gaibulloev and Sandler (2011) analyze the adverse effects of domestic and transnational terrorism on the real per-capita income growth for 51 African countries during the period 1970–2007, while accounting for cross-sectional (spatial) dependence and conflict (i.e. internal conflicts and external wars). Their results suggest that transnational terrorism has a significant but modest marginal impact on the real per-capita income growth, while domestic terrorist events have no significant effect on the growth of real per-capita income.

6.2.3 Per-Capita Real Income Growth: World Economy

There are studies estimating the impact of terrorism on growth by utilizing large samples of countries over time. Generally speaking, the results show that *on average, a minor, albeit statistically significant, effect of terrorism on growth.*

For example, using data covering 177 countries from 1968 to 2000, Blomberg et al. (2004a) performed cross-country regression, panel-data regression as well as VAR (see General Appendix B, Sect. B.13.4) to estimate the impact of transnational terrorism—vis-à-vis that of external and internal conflicts—on the growth rate of per-capita real income.[9] On average, terrorism exerts a significantly negative effect on growth, whose magnitude is considerably smaller and less persistent than that associated with either external wars or internal conflict.[10]

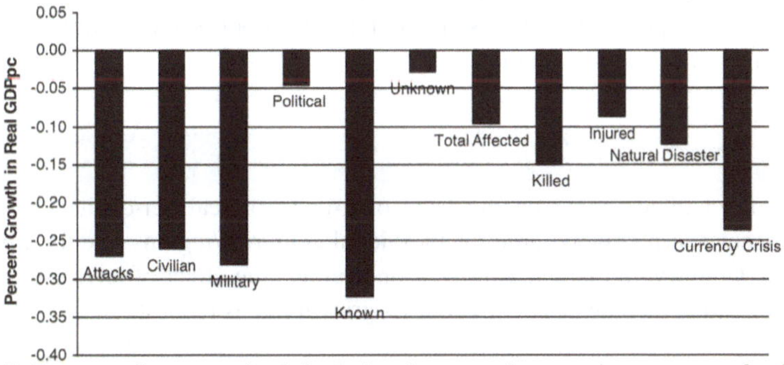

Fig. 6.5: Impact of one standard deviation increase in terrorism on growth of per-capita real GDP across countries. *Source*: (Tavares, 2004, Figure 1); permission to reproduce by the author and Elsevier is thankfully acknowledged

In his cross-country analysis of the impact of terrorism on real per-capita GDP growth over 1987–2001, Tavares (2004) controls for political rights, currency crisis and natural disasters including earthquakes, floods, hurricanes, and other events. Figure 6.5 displays the results, where each bar indicates the impact of a one-standard-deviation change in each regressor on the growth of real per-capita GDP. The first four columns refer to the total number of attacks, number of attacks on civilian areas,

[9] Two measures of terrorism are used. One is a dummy variable: equal to 1 if a country experienced terrorist attacks in a year and 0 otherwise. The other is the number of incidents per capita in a given year.

[10] According to one estimate, a one-standard-deviation increase in the incidence of terrorist activity (e.g. raising the number of incidents from 0.2 to 1.2 incidents per million of population per year) is associated with a decline in real per-capita GDP growth of about one-quarter of a percentage point (see their Table 5).

that on military and that on political targets.[11] We see that the attacks on civilian and military targets impose the greatest potential damage: a 0.25% decrease in the real per-capita GDP growth. These cost estimates are small yet comparable to the estimated cost of a currency crisis and much larger than the impact of a natural disaster.

Using the time-series test of *Granger causality* (see General Appendix B, Sect. B.13.3) on panel data over a sample of 160 countries and over the period 1970–2007, Meierrieks and Gries (2012) differentiate between the Cold War era and the post-Cold War era. The main findings are that during the Cold War era, terrorism had the highest impact on the real per-capita income growth of the Latin American countries, which were, generally speaking politically unstable yet at intermediate levels of development, whereas in the post-Cold War era terrorism has had its most detrimental effect on African and Islamic countries which are generally characterized by "low level of political openness and high levels of political instability."

We may thus summarize that

Is That So? 6.3: Terrorism and Per-Capital Income Loss, Overall

The impact of terrorism on the level or growth of real per-capita income is significant and relatively large for individual countries/regions like the Spanish Basque Country and Israel. However, on average, the effect of terrorism on the real per-capita income of countries or its growth rate is modest.

It does not imply however that terrorism is not a serious issue. Firstly, terrorism has forced nations to allocate valuable resources to set up and continuously fund counter-terrorism measures without which business, trade, and commerce cannot conceivably grow at the rate they do. Secondly, the economic well-being is not same as psychological or mental well-being. In Sect. 6.8 we will review various studies that have analyzed how terrorism has impacted on mental well-being of population in different localities, regions, and countries.

6.3 International Trade

International trade is an important factor of growth and development in an integrated world economy. Terrorism can adversely affect international trade, both indirectly and directly. For instance, if the GDP or its growth rate falls due to terrorism, it would affect export supply of and import demand for products. Terrorism may divert government expenditure from more productive public investment to less directly

[11] In Fig. 6.5, "Known" and "Unknown" refer to known and unknown terror organizations; "Killed" and "Injured" stand for the number of people killed and injured in terror attacks and "Total Affected" is the sum of "Killed" and "Injured." The last two bars indicate the impact of natural disasters and currency crises.

productive security measures, which would tend to reduce economic growth, export production, and import demand. These are indirect effects.

More directly, terrorism increases the cost of producing export-oriented goods in terror-prone areas. If terror attacks target industries, their capacity to produce and export competitively would fall. Terrorism also creates uncertainty in the transport of goods to their destinations, which increases the cost of insurance and property damage in exporting and importing. Various security and inspection requirements as counter-terrorism measures at borders and ports tend to cause delays and increase the cost of international transport. If an increase in terrorism in country A increases the cost of doing business with country B that imports products from A, B will purchase goods or services either domestically or from other, more peaceful countries. There is a substitution effect.

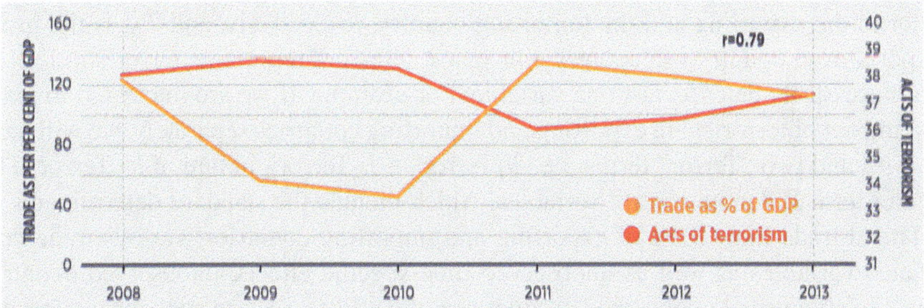

Fig. 6.6: Terrorism and international trade: Colombia. *Source:* (Institute for Economics & Peace, 2014b, Figure 23); permission from IEP is thankfully acknowledged

Institute for Economics & Peace (2014b) presents a specific example, Fig. 6.6, showing how trade to GDP ratio (sum of gross exports and imports divided by GDP) is negatively correlated with terrorist events in Colombia from 2008 to 2013. While the large drop in trade in 2008 can attributed to the global recession, there is a significant correlation between trade and terrorism over the six-year period (the correlation coefficient is −0.79).

Formal econometric models have assessed the impact of terrorism on international trade by extending the so-called ***gravity model of international trade***. As explained in the General Appendix B, Sect. B.23, the original gravity model (developed in early 1960s) estimated how, on average, bilateral trade between countries—measured by *gross exports*, *gross imports* or the sum of gross exports and imports between two countries—is explained by the size of the exporting country's and importing-country's economies and physical distance between them.[12]

[12] In any product category in which international trade takes place (say in cars), there is gross international trade and there is net international trade. For example, during any given time period, say, a year, if the US exports cars to Japan valued at $10 billion and Japan exports cars to the USA valued at $14 billion, then the gross exports of cars by the USA to Japan is $10 billion and that by

Modern gravity models include many more explanatory variables like per-capita income of exporting and importing countries, trade-cost related variables other than distance—like whether the exporting and importing countries are geographically contiguous, whether they share a common language as well as a host of other variables depending on the specific objectives and scope of the study at hand and data availability.[13]

Indeed, all research papers reviewed below use some variant of the gravity model applied on panel data in order to estimate the impact of terrorism on international trade. The estimated equations have the following form:

$$\text{Trade}_{ijt} = a + b \cdot \text{Terror} + \boldsymbol{\beta Z} + u_{ijt}, \tag{6.3}$$

with some variations, except Egger and Gassebner (2015). The subscripts i and j refer to the exporting and the importing country, respectively, and T_{ijt} is the gross exports from country i to country j in year t. "Terror" represents terrorism. It does not necessarily enter as just one variable. For example, if we are interested to learn the impact of terrorism in exporting and importing countries separately, we will have two b's and two "Terror" terms, i.e., $b_1\text{Terror}_{it} + b_2\text{Terror}_{jt}$ in lieu of $b \cdot \text{Terror}$. The vector term $\mathbf{Z}$ denote control variables, which include the standard determinants of bilateral trade like GDPs of exporting and importing countries, various trade-cost related variables as well as unobserved time-specific effects, unobserved country-specific effects and unobserved product-specific effects. (These concepts are briefly explained in General Appendix B, Sect. B.14.)

Specifics of individual studies are outlined in the chapter Appendix 6.A.1.[14] In sum, the general finding from estimated equations like (6.3) is that

Is That So? 6.4: Terrorism and International Trade

Both domestic and transnational terrorism have significantly negative and delayed effects on international trade among countries. Exports from a country are not only affected by terrorism in the exporting country but also terrorism in its neighboring countries.

6.4 Foreign Direct Investment (FDI)

Like international trade, international movement of capital, i.e., *foreign direct investment* (*FDI*) is critical for growth, especially for smaller or developing countries.

Japan to the USA is $14 billion, whereas net exports of cars by the USA to Japan is $−4 billion and net exports by Japan to the USA is $4 billion.

[13] The gravity model is also used to study the flow of capital between countries, that is, foreign direct investment or FDI.

[14] The list includes Nitsch and Schumacher (2004), Blomberg and Hess (2006), Baier and Bergstrand (2009), Mirza and Verdier (2014), de Sousa et al. (2009), Egger and Gassebner (2015), de Sousa et al. (2018) and Bandopadhyay et al. (2018).

This is important for developed countries too as investors seek better returns for their capital in order to enhance their income and wealth.

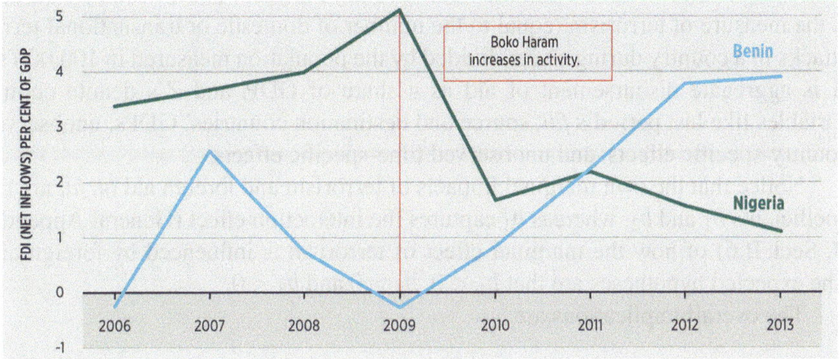

Fig. 6.7: Terrorism and foreign direct investment in Colombia, Nigeria, and Benin. *Source:* (Institute for Economics & Peace, 2014b, Figure 22); permission from IEP is thankfully acknowledged

Terrorism in a country is a potential deterrent of FDI inflow, as it poses an additional risk for foreign investors in terms of loss of plant and equipment, threat and injury to its executives (as happened in South America), anticipation of weak markets, etc. Foreign investors would tend to move their capital away to other safer destinations.[15]

As an example, Fig. 6.7 depicts the time-series of FDI/GDP ratio of Nigeria and its neighboring country Benin. As Boko Haram turned violent from 2009, FDI in Nigeria began sliding, while that in Benin climbed up sharply as investing in Benin became relatively more attractive. Between 2009 and 2010 The FDI flows in Nigeria dipped dramatically by $6.1 billion, representing a decline of almost 30% from the previous fiscal year (Adebayo, 2014).

Different individual studies that estimate the impact of terrorism on FDI are summarized in the chapter Appendix 6.A.2.[16] Here we elaborate upon one particular study, namely Bandopadhyay et al. (2014), which estimates the impact of foreign aid on FDI inflow directly and on the marginal effect of terrorism on FDI inflow. The authors posit and estimate an empirical equation which is similar to Eq. (6.3). The hypothesis is that higher foreign aid received by a country should lower the impact of terrorism in that country on the FDI inflow, since foreign aid may be tied to counter-terrorism efforts by the host country and foreign aid may lead to increase in the standard of living, thereby tending to reduce general grievances and proclivity for using violence. The regression equation is

---

[15] By the same token, terrorism and violence in a country can lead domestic capital to flow out of the country; this is FDI outflow.

[16] These are, namely Enders and Sandler (1996), Blomberg and Mody (2005), Enders et al. (2006), Abadie and Gardeazabal (2008) and Bandopadhyay et al. (2014).

$$fdi_{it} = a + b_1 \cdot T_{it} + b_2 \cdot A_{it} + b_3 \cdot (T \times A)_{it} + \beta \mathbf{Z}_{it} + u_{it}, \quad (6.4)$$

where fdi_{it} is the ratio of NFDI inflow into country i in year t to the country's GDP, T is the measure of terrorism (equal to the number of domestic or transnational terror attacks in a country during a year divided by the population measured in 100,000's), A is aggregate disbursement of aid as a share of GDP, and $\mathbf{Z}$'s denote control variables like last period's *fdi*, source and destination countries' GDPs, unobserved country-specific effects, and unobserved time-specific effects.

Notice that the own marginal impacts of terrorism and foreign aid on *fdi* are the coefficients b_1 and b_2, whereas b_3 captures the interaction effect (General Appendix B, Sect. B.6) of how the marginal effect of terrorism is influenced by foreign aid. The expected hypotheses are that $b_1 < 0$, $b_2 > 0$ and $b_3 < 0$.

The overall implications are:

Is That So? 6.5: Terrorism and Foreign Direct Investment

Like international trade, foreign direct investment is adversely affected by terrorism. The magnitude of the impact widely varies across countries. Foreign aid mitigates the negative impact of terrorism on and thus is conductive to foreign direct investment into developing countries afflicted by terrorism.

6.5 Labor Markets

Terrorists may target business and specific industries in an area, creating fear-driven future uncertainty about the prospects of conducting business and discouraging investment and buyer's confidence. This would impinge on the local and regional labor markets.

Regions from where terrorists originate can also face negative labor market consequences as terror attacks may spur security and retaliatory measures that can hamper regular work by local residents. Successful attacks may lead to radicalization of the local population, which would affect the size of the labor force for work.

We review two research works, one investigating local labor market of target regions and the other analyzing that of the source regions.

6.5.1 Target Economies

Supporting evidence of negative effects of terrorism on the labor markets of local target economies is provided by Brodeur (2018) for the USA over the period 1970–2013. Using panel regressions, the author estimates the impact of "successful" terror attacks (relative to failed once) on employment and total earnings at the county level.[17] Comparing between successful and failed terror attacks does not require controlling for employment shocks or characteristics of local economies, since these factors are unlikely to affect the effectiveness of terror attacks.[18]

A major finding is that successful attacks, compared to failed attacks, reduce the number of jobs and total earnings in targeted counties by approximately 2% and 2.5% in the years following an attack. These are "huge," given that most terror attacks in the USA during this period are not catastrophic. The effects for neighboring counties are smaller and less precisely estimated suggesting that the employment and earnings effects are, by and large, quite local.

Analyzing the channels of causation, the author finds that successful attacks affect specific industries like housing. In comparison to failed attacks they reduce housing prices by 1.3–1.7%. Another plausible channel is the increased (perceived) uncertainty due to fear, which is captured by media coverage. The estimates suggest that the number of news stories and minutes of coverage for successful attacks are about 15% higher than for failed attacks.[19]

Is That So? 6.6: Terrorism and Labor Market in Target Economies

Brodeur (2018) provides county-level evidence that successful terror attacks in the USA during the period 1970–2013 had relatively large impact on the local labor markets, reducing employment and wages by 2% and 2.5%, respectively.

6.5.2 Source Economies

In an interesting study, Benmelech and Berrebi (2007) analyzed how Palestinian violence and terrorist acts originating from West Bank and Gaza strip during the Second Intifada affected the labor market in these regions.

What are the mechanisms of this cause–effect relationship? Terror attacks would prompt security measures that prevent local residents from continuing to work regularly. If attacks are successful, they may encourage the radicalization of the local population, leading to self-deprivation and de-prioritization of personal economic achievement, translating into less active labor market participation.

Using data on Palestinian suicide attacks during the Second Intifada and combining that with economic and demographic characteristics and Israeli security measures undertaken at the district level in the two regions, the authors quantified the impact of successful attacks on the three labor market outcomes: unemployment rate, average wage and the percentage of the district's population working in Israel.

---

[17] The definition of a successful/failed attack depends on the type of attack. For instance, an assassination is considered successful if the target is killed, while an explosion is considered successful if the explosive device detonates.

[18] Brodeur's analysis includes controls such as year, month, county, attack types, and weaponry fixed effects.

[19] The study also finds that successful attacks affect consumer sentiment.

The regression equations explain the *change* in the labor market outcomes by the success of attacks, changes in demographic variables and changes in security measures, i.e., they are of the form:

$$\begin{aligned}\Delta(\text{Labor market outcome})_{it} = {} & b_1 \cdot (\text{Outcome of attack})_{it-1} \\ & + b_2 \cdot \Delta(\text{Security measures})_{it} \\ & + c \cdot \Delta(\text{Demographic variables})_{it} + u_{it},\end{aligned}$$

where Δ denotes "change in," equal to the respective value in the quarter following an attack minus the respective value in the quarter prior to the attack.

To measure persistence, another set of regressions defines Δ(Labor market outcome), equal to the difference between the respective value in the *second quarter* following an attack and that in the quarter prior to the attack. If a coefficient is significant, it means the effect is present for at least half a year.

Ordinary least squares (OLS) regressions yield strong results. A successful attack (a) causes an increase in unemployment by 5.3%,(b) increases the likelihood that the district's average wages fall in the quarter following an attack by more than 20%, and (c) reduces the number of Palestinians working in Israel by 6.7% relative to its mean. Importantly, these effects are persistent and last for at least six months after the attack.

Is That So? 6.7: The Impact of Terror Attacks during Second Intifada on the Labor Market in Gaza and West Bank

Estimates by Benmelech and Berrebi (2007) imply that Palestinian terror attacks during the Second Intifada led to worse outcomes in the labor markets in Gaza and West Bank, suggesting that "terrorism may not pay."

6.5.3 Discrimination in the Labor Market of Target and Potential Target Economies

Major terrorist attacks may engender adverse perceptions of the ethnicity of the perpetrators in people's mind. This can lead to hate crimes and discrimination against those ethnicities in the labor market. In view of the *9/11* and other prominent terror attacks by Islamic groups, we may expect that Muslims would be discriminated in the labor markets of host nations following such attacks.

6.5.3.1 *9/11* Attacks and Discrimination in the US Labor Market

In one of the earliest studies, Dávila and Mora (2005) addressed the issue of discrimination toward Arabs and Muslim workers in the USA following the *9/11* attacks. Using data covering 2002–2004, which is obtained from the American Community Survey, they analyzed the wage earnings of Middle Eastern Arab men and Afghan, Iranian, and Pakistani men relative to non-Hispanic whites. Their finding was that Middle Eastern Arab men experienced a large increase in the wage gap (more than

20%), whereas Afghan, Iranian, and Pakistani men experienced insignificant changes in relative wages.[20]

By analyzing employment data over 1998 to 2004 from Current Population Surveys, Kaushal et al. (2007) found less evidence of discrimination following *9/11*. Employment and hours of work of Arab and Muslim men were not significantly affected, but there was a 9–11% decline in their real wage and weekly earnings, with some evidence that this decline was temporary. These authors used Difference-in-Differences or DiD regression (see Appendix B, Sect. B.17.)

Rabby and Rodgers III (2011) who used DiD regressions as did Kaushal et al. (2007), analyzed the ratio of employment to population and hours worked for individuals in the age group of 16–25 whose nativity profiles were similar to the perpetrators of *9/11* attacks. Their main finding was that employment to population ratio as well as hours worked declined for Muslim men shortly after the *9/11* attacks. However, by 2004, most losses had begun to dissipate.[21]

6.5.3.2 2005 London Attacks

Using data from the Labor Force Survey, Braakmann (2010) argued that wages, hours worked and employment probabilities of Arab men in the UK were unaffected by the 2005 London attacks. However, Rabby and Rodgers III (2010) estimated a 10% decrease in the employment of very young Muslim men (between 16 and 25 years of age) relative to non-Muslim immigrants. Hence, the impact of 2005 London attacks on labor market discrimination in the UK seems inconclusive.

6.5.3.3 Terror Attacks in Norway in 2011

In 2011, Anders Behring Breivik, a Norwegian far-right terrorist, detonated a car bomb at the government quarters in Oslo, killing 8 people and maiming over 200. He then drove to the summer camp of the Workers' Youth League (Arbeidernes Ungdomsfylking) in the island of Utøya, where he shot and killed 69 people, most of whom were teenagers. These are by far the worst terrorist attacks in modern Norwegian history. What was the impact of Breivik's anti-Muslim, anti-migrant attacks on the Norwegian society? Survey evidence offers the impression that Norwegians became more positive about immigrants after these attacks. However, in an interesting study, Birkelund et al. (2018) provides evidence showing that the incident did *not* change the existing discrimination against immigrants. People of Pakistani origin are the largest immigrant community in Norway. An experiment was conducted after the

[20] Surprisingly, the wage gap for African Arab men narrowed significantly by 24%.

[21] Fear and perceptions travel fast and wide. It is conceivable that *9/11* attacks may have contributed to discrimination in the labor market of other Western countries. However, Åslund and Rooth (2005), who analyzed whether *9/11* led to more discrimination toward minorities in Sweden, find no significant difference in the unemployment-to-employment exit rates of ethnic groups, hence no sign of increased discrimination. Similar conclusion was reached for the German labor market (Braakmann, 2009) and the labor market in England (Braakmann, 2010): *9/11* did not cause a significant or major decline in job prospects in Germany and England for individuals from predominantly Muslim countries.

attacks in which 556 fictitious CVs and cover letters were sent out in response to 278 job postings. It turned out that applicants with typical Pakistani names were significantly less likely to get a job interview compared to those with a typical Norwegian name. This suggests that Pakistanis in Norway still experienced the same degree of discrimination as earlier, despite the claims that Norwegians become more tolerant about migrants after the far-right, anti-migrant terrorist attacks of 2011.

Is That So? 6.8: Terror Attacks and Discrimination in the Labor Market

There is mixed evidence to the effect that *9/11* attacks and London attacks in 2005 led to discrimination against Muslim men in terms of employment and wages. Contrary to the common perception, the large-scale home-grown terror attack by Anders Behring Breivik in 2011, a Norwegian far-right terrorist, did not lead to a more favorable attitude toward Pakistani-origin individuals—who constitute the largest immigrant community in Norway.

6.6 Financial Markets

Terror attacks hamper businesses, trade and the economy. More intangibly yet importantly, they create anxiety and uncertainty. This can affect financial markets, particularly the stock market. There are tens of studies on how terrorism impacts the stock markets around the world. How big are the effects on stock prices and stock returns? How persistent are these effects? Do terror attacks in advanced nations have a contagion effects on financial markets in other countries? How do terror attacks affect stock-market volatility? Various studies on these issues/questions can be grouped into two categories: one measuring the impacts of major terror attacks individually and the other on the implications of terror attacks within a time interval and confined to a country or region.

6.6.1 Single-Attack Studies

They include *9/11* attacks and other attacks like Madrid attacks in March 2004, London attacks in July 2005 and Boston Marathon bombings in April 2013.

A common approach in studying how individual terror attacks affect stock prices or returns is the *event-study method* (see General Appendix B, Sect. B.16), which measures the "excess" or "'abnormal" returns on securities by comparing the actual returns on the day of the event (e.g. *9/11*) and after some days of the event with a counterfactual of what the returns would have been if the event had not occurred.

6.6.1.1 *9/11* Attacks

Scholars have studied the effect of these infamous attacks on the US stock market, airline industries and air-freight carriers and their contagion effects on global markets. Individual studies (i.e. Carter and Simkins, 2004; Chen and Siems, 2004; Drakos, 2004; Hon et al., 2004; Richman et al., 2005 and Nikkinen et al., 2008) are briefly reviewed in chapter ppeandix 6.A.3. The grand summary from these studies is:

Is That So? 6.9: Stock Market Reactions to *9/11* Terror Attacks

9/11 attacks had strong negative impacts on stock-market returns across the world over the days following September 11, 2001. Airlines stocks were one of the worst sufferers. However, almost all markets recovered to their pre-*9/11* levels in a few weeks following the attacks. The global impacts varied across regions depending on how integrated they were into the global economy. Financial markets in the Middle East and North Africa were affected the least.

6.6.1.2 Madrid and London Train Bombings, and Boston Marathon Bombing

These events are studied by Kollias et al. (2011) and Baumert et al. (2013), brief descriptions of which are relegated to chapter appendix 6.A.4. Overall,

Is That So? 6.10: Stock Market Reactions to Madrid, London and Boston Terror Attacks

These attacks also affected stock markets but in a much smaller scale compared to the *9/11* attacks.

6.6.1.3 Group of Selected Terror Attacks

Brounrn and Derwall (2010) consider price dynamics of international stock markets—both immediately on the event day and thereafter—in response to thirty-one major terror attacks across the world between 1990 and 2005, and (for comparison) fifty-nine earthquakes with Richter scale between 4.0 and 9.2 during the same time period.

Price declines in major stock markets were mild, except for the *9/11* attacks, and they were more pronounced for terror attacks than for natural disasters like earthquakes. However, in case of terror attacks and natural disasters both, prices rebounded within the first week of the aftermath. Moreover, terror attacks had impacts on both the domestic stock market and stock markets outside the country, while the reactions were stronger in the domestic market and for industries that were directly affected by terror attacks.

Karolyi and Martell (2010) examined the long-run stock price impact of 75 different terrorist attacks that took place between 1995 and 2002 on publicly-traded domestic and international companies. In their sample, McDonald's suffered the most number of attacks (10), followed by Royal Dutch Shell with nine attacks. On average, stock prices declined by 0.83%, translating into a huge loss in a firm's capitalization on average. Attacks that involved human capital losses from terrorism in the form of kidnapping of company executives had a greater impact on stock prices, compared to those that mostly involved loss of physical assets like buildings and facilities (by bombing).

Daily stock-market returns for a sample of top 22 countries in terms of the share of worldwide terrorist attacks during the period 1994–2004 were studied by Drakos (2010). Terrorist activities led to significantly lower returns on the day an attack occurred, averaging −0.6%. In particular, distinguishing between attacks on the basis of their severity as classified in the GTD dataset, the negative stock-market impacts of terrorist activity were found to be substantially amplified when terrorist incidents caused higher psycho-social impact.

Chesney et al. (2011) estimated the impact of terrorism on stock, bond, and commodity markets from seventy seven relatively major individual terror attacks over twenty five countries during 1994–2005.[22] Approximately two-thirds of the terrorist attacks in the sample led to a significant negative impact on at least one stock market. In terms of the numbers of attacks affecting a particular stock market, the Swiss stock market was at the top, while the American stock market was at the bottom, underscoring the resilience of the latter. Insurance and airline sectors exhibited the highest vulnerability to terrorism, while the banking industry was the least sensitive.

The pattern of spillover from terrorist attacks through trading partners in international stock markets was studied by Kumar and Liu (2013). The authors focused on terror attacks globally between 1990–2010 that targeted business interests. They documented that when a bigger economy is targeted, the spillover is quite prominent for economically smaller trading partners. Furthermore, democratic countries appeared to be more vulnerable to this effect.[23]

Is That So? 6.11: Stock Market Reactions to Terror Attacks in General

In general, terror attacks have exerted greater impact on financial markets compared to natural disasters like earthquakes. Stock-market effects are stronger in the country where terror incident takes place than in other countries. More severe attacks and those involving loss of human capital as opposed to physical capital losses are associated with more pronounced impacts on stock markets. Adverse impacts are temporary, however, lasting over a few weeks only. Attacks targeted toward bigger economies have greater spillover effects to other financial markets.

Markoulis and Katasikides (2018) analyze the relationship between eleven major terrorist attacks that occurred in the twenty-first century and the stock indices.[24]

---

[22] The countries included were: Argentina, Austria, Chile, Colombia, Egypt, France, Germany, Greece, India, Indonesia, Ireland, Israel, Japan, Malaysia, Mexico, Morocco, Pakistan, Peru, Philippines, Russia, Spain, Thailand, Turkey, the UK and the USA.

[23] Volodin and Mikhalev (2017) analyze the stock-market effects of 117 terrorist attacks committed in different countries within the 1988–2016 period. The stock-market dynamics was shown to depend on factors like the number of victims, level of country's economic development, day of terrorist attack, etc. Overall, many terror attacks significantly affected the dynamics of stock-market indices, while, for some, the impact was insignificant and transitory.

[24] These are, namely *9/11* attacks, Istanbul Bombings on November 20, 2003, Madrid Train bombing on March 11, 2004, bombings in London on July 7, 2005, Domodedovo (Russia) airport attack, Boston Marathon Bombing dated April15, 2013, Paris Attacks on November 13, 2015, Nice

Results suggest that earlier events appear to result in higher negative abnormal returns when compared to more recent ones, suggesting that "investors have learned to better assess terror events and react more calmly to them." The negative abnormal returns seem to persist beyond the date of the event, but tend to disappear rather quickly. Some of these events exhibit a "spill-over" effect on international stock markets.

In summary,

Is That So? 6.12: Stock Market Reactions to Major Terror Events

Among major terror attacks in the twenty-first century thus far, relatively recent events do not seem to affect local or international markets.

There are country-specific studies other than the USA. For example, Christofis et al. (2013) investigate the impact of three major terrorist incidents in Istanbul in 1999, 2003, and 2008 on the Istanbul Stock Exchange and its sub-sector indices. Their results indicate that the effects were only short-lived and the tourism sector index was affected the most. Aksoy (2014) tracks the effect of thirteen terror attacks in Turkey between 1996 and 2007 on the Turkish stock market and finds that the stock market continued to fall in the days following most terror incidents.

6.6.2 Attacks in a Region/Country over an Interval of Time

Instead of single or a group of single events, we now review studies that consider the financial-markets implications of terror events in general over a span of time.

Cease-Fire with ETA and Stocks of Firms doing Major Businesses in the Basque Country In September 1998, ETA declared and began a cease-fire that lasted till November 1999. Comparing between fourteen Basque and fifty-nine non-Basque stocks, Abadie and Gardeazabal (2003) showed that Basque stocks performed better in terms of cumulative abnormal returns than did the non-Basque stocks as the cease-fire took hold and just the opposite happened toward the end of the truce period. This is illustrated in Fig. 6.8. Such stock price dynamics accords with the ***efficient market hypothesis*** which tells us that if the financial markets are efficient, asset prices reflect all available information, and they would react only to new information.

Israel Eldor and Melnick (2004) showed evidence to the effect that during 1990–2003 the Israeli stock and foreign exchange markets were significantly affected by terrorism. In this period 639 terror attacks were recorded, in which 1212 people in Israel were killed and 5726 were maimed or injured. The number of suicide attacks and the number of victims from terror attacks had long-term effects on both the stock and foreign exchange markets.

Turkey Using monthly data from December 1987 to December 2003, Eruygur and Omay (2014) analyzed the effects of terrorist activities on the Istanbul stock market

(France) Attack dated July 14, 2016, Brussels bombings on March 22, 2016, Berlin market Attack on December 19, 2016 and Westerminister (U. K.) attack dated March 22, 2017.

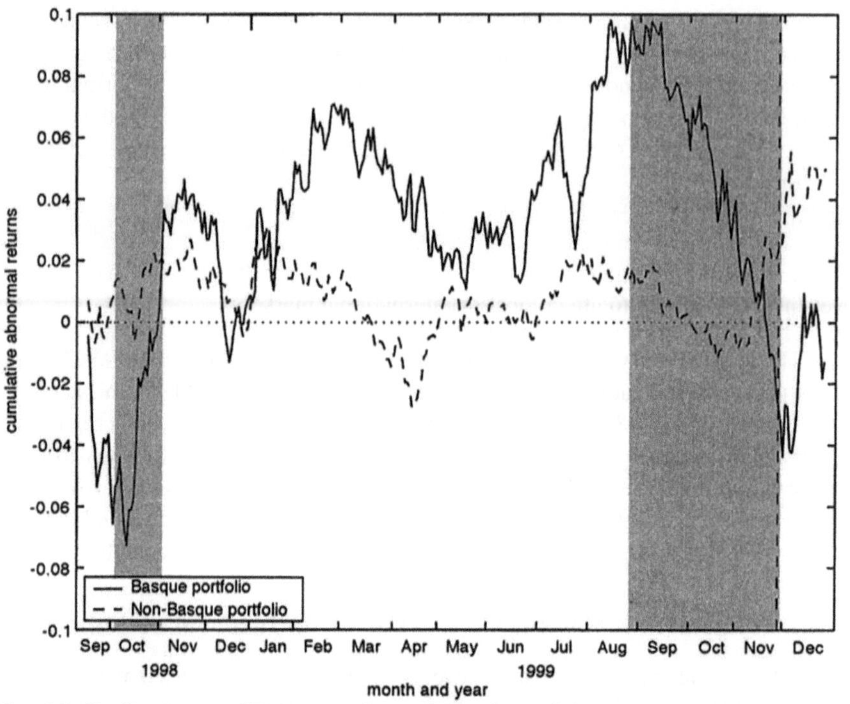

Fig. 6.8: Performance of Basque and non-Basque portfolio. *Source*: Abadie and Gardeazabal (2003); permission to reproduce by the authors and the American Economic Association is thankfully acknowledged

(BIST100). They found a negative and non-linear relationship between terrorism and BIST100. Aksoy and Demiralay (2019) explore how the Turkish stock market, foreign exchange market, and foreign investors in the stock market reacted to the terror attacks in Turkey as well as attacks in the USA, the UK, Italy, and Spain. Their analysis, which used the ET terrorism index (see the expression (6.1)) showed that stock returns, abnormal returns, and cumulative abnormal returns as well as the foreign exchange market were *not* affected by the terror attacks, but, the portfolio value of foreign investors in the stock market were.

Pakistan Aslam and Kang (2015) found that terrorist events in Pakistan adversely affected the Pakistani stock market. They analyzed daily observations on the Karachi stock index (KSE-100 index) over the years 2000–2011, during which 300 major terrorist attacks were reported, causing 10,743 deaths and 22,451 injuries. The stock-market effect was short-lived: the market bounced back from terror attack shocks in one day. The impact of attack depended on the locations and types of attack. The more severe the attack (i.e., the larger the number of fatalities), the more negative was the return on the KSE-100. Interestingly, different tactics of terrorists had varied effects on stock returns.

Asia Aslam et al. (2018) examined the impact of 410 terrorist attacks on the performance of five Asian stock markets (Bangladesh, India, Indonesia, Philippine, and Sri Lanka) between 1997 and 2011. The findings indicate that terrorism had a significant impact on the stock markets, although the magnitude of the effects varied across countries, attack type, target type and the severity of the attacks. In target type, terrorist attacks on business sector and security forces were particularly harmful for the stock markets. Among the attack types, suicide attacks and bomb blasts specifically generated a significant downward movement in the stock markets. Also, more severe attacks had larger negative impact on market returns.

6.6.3 Terrorism and Market Volatility

Terrorism has not only influenced the financial-market returns but also the *volatility* of returns. Arin et al. (2008) tested whether there is a causality effect running from terrorist activity to stock-market returns and volatility. Analyzing daily data in six different countries, namely Indonesia, Israel, Spain, Thailand, Turkey, and the UK, over the years 2000–2006, terrorism, as measured by the daily ET terrorism index, was found to have significant impacts on both the stock-market returns and the stock-market volatility: a negative impact on the stock returns and a positive effect on volatility. European stock markets (Spain and the UK) were generally less effected in terms of both mean and in variance, compared to other countries with emerging markets. For Turkey, Aksoy (2014) (who studied thirteen major terror attacks between 1996 and 2007) found that terror incidents increased the volatility of the BIST100 index. The same conclusion for daily returns over a larger sample period, 1988–2015, was reached by Aksoy and Demiralay (2019).

Is That So? 6.13: Terrorism and Financial-Market Volatility

Terrorism increases volatility of stock prices and returns in the short run.

6.7 Tourism

In 2018, travel and tourism contributed 10.4% of world GDP (World Travel & Tourism Council, 2019). This sector is quite sensitive to terrorism as tourists are soft targets. Since 2000, Yemen, India, Algeria, Colombia, and Pakistan have witnessed the largest numbers of terrorist attacks directed against tourists (Institute for Economics & Peace, 2016b). Tourists tend to avoid countries and regions where the fear of terrorism is strong and particularly where the terrorists have targeted tourists. If the flow of tourists dwindles, tourism-related service industries like aviation, transport, and hotel businesses suffer. It is thus important to understand the magnitude of the effect of terrorism on the tourism industry.

As described in Chap. 2, in one of the most gruesome attacks on tourists, known as the *Luxor massacre* that occurred in Egypt in 1997, some members of an Egyptian Islamic group, namely *al-Gamaat al-Islamyya*, dressing as police, killed 62 tourists in Luxor who were visiting the temple of Queen Hatshepsut. A BBC report estimated a loss of tourism revenue for Egypt amounting to nearly $1.8 billion, attributed to the Luxor massacre.

Bali, a popular tourist destination in Indonesia, suffered two major attacks in the early 2000s. The first that occurred in October 2002 claimed nearly 200 lives, mostly of tourists. It seriously disrupted Bali's tourism industry. While still in the process of recuperation, the second attack was perpetrated in October 2005, after which the number of foreign tourists fell by 31% (APEC, 2017).

In 2015, a Russian airliner (Metrojet), carrying tourists mostly, went down over the Sinai peninsula of Egypt. It was believed to be shot down by terrorists with links to the Islamic State. Grave concerns were raised about the impact of this incident on tourism in Egypt (Glusac, 2015).

Figure 6.9 graphs change in tourism revenues in two developed and two developing countries: (France, Italy) and (Tunisia, Morocco). In 2015 France and Tunisia were hit hard by terrorism, while in Italy and Morocco there were no deaths from terrorism. Look at the tourist revenue losses and gains. While France and Tunisia lost $1.27 billion and $1.2 billion, respectively, Italy and Morocco, respectively, gained $.9 billion and $400 million.

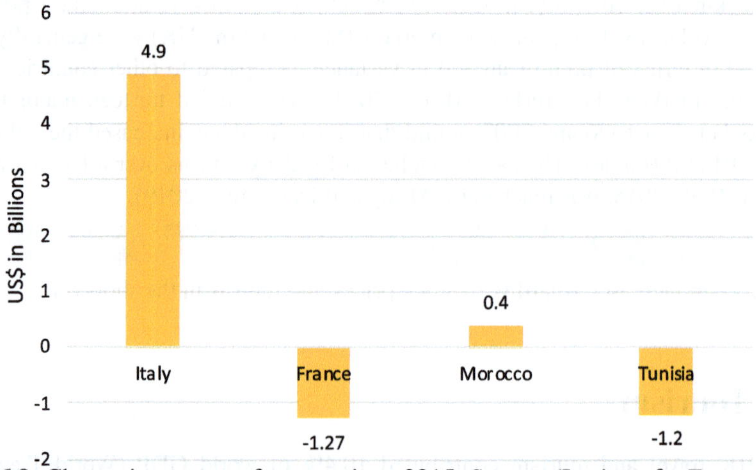

Fig. 6.9: Change in revenues from tourism: 2015. *Source*: (Institute for Economics & Peace, 2016b, Figure 4.5); permission to reproduced from IEP is thankfully acknowledged

Beginning with Enders and Sandler (1991), there are several econometric studies on the impact of terrorism on the tourism industry, e.g., Enders et al. (1992), Fleischer and Buccola (2002), Pizam and Fleischer (2002), Drakos and Kutan (2003), Yaya (2009), and van Ballegooij and Bakowski (2018). These are described in chapter Appendix 6.A.5. The overall finding is that the number of tourists as well as revenues from tourism decline strongly with terrorist attacks.

Perhaps the most comprehensive and interesting work till date on how much terrorism affects tourist arrivals is Neumayer and Plümper (2016). The estimated equation is outlined below along with details on which variables are present. Covering the period 1995–2013, the authors explore the effect of terror attacks in "Islamic countries" on tourists in those countries who hail from "western countries."[25] Tourism is an important source of revenue for many predominantly Islamic countries. For instance, Jordan, Lebanon, Morocco, Tunisia, and Bahrain generate more than 5% of their GDPs from tourism, and the Maldives substantially more than that. Based on the country of origin of the attack-victims from the "West" and in which Islamic country the attack took place, the authors posit the following panel-data model (see General Appendix B, Sect. B.14):

$$\begin{aligned} y_{ijt} &= a + b_1 \cdot terr_{ijt} + b_2 \cdot terr_{ijt-1} + b_3 \cdot \sum_{m \neq j} terr_{imt} + b_4 \cdot \sum_{m \neq j} terr_{imt-1} \\ &+ b_5 \cdot \sum_{k \neq i} terr_{kjt} + b_6 \cdot \sum_{k \neq i} terr_{kjt-1} + b_7 \cdot \sum_{m \neq j} \sum_{k \neq i} terr_{kmt} \\ &+ b_8 \cdot \sum_{m \neq j} \sum_{k \neq i} terr_{kmt-1} + \beta \mathbf{Z} + u_{ijt}.^{26} \end{aligned} \tag{6.5}$$

Here i is the western source country, j is the Islamic destination country, t is year, and y_{ijt} is the annual number of tourists from the Western country i to the Islamic country j during the year t. The vector $\mathbf{Z}$ is the list of control variables, namely unobserved destination-country-specific effects, unobserved origin-country-specific effects, unobserved bilateral origin-destination-country specific effects and unobserved time-specific effects.[27]

There are eight terrorism-related variables with coefficients b_1 through b_8. The variable $terr_{ij}$ is either the number of fatal terror attacks or the fatalities in the Islamic country j that involved victims from the Western country i, and this can be called the *specific target effect*. The estimates of b_1 and b_2 measure the specific target effects, which are contemporaneous and one-period lag, respectively.

The estimates of b_3 through b_8 measure three contagion effects. The variable $terr_{im}$ is the index of terror in Islamic country m except j that involved victims of the Western country i, and thus coefficients b_3 and b_4 capture the *target contagion effect*. The variable $terr_{kj}$ is the index of terror in Islamic country j that involved victims of the Western country k except i. Hence the coefficients b_5 and b_6 reflect the *source contagion effect*). Next, $terr_{km}$ is the index of terror in the Islamic country m except j that involved victims of the Western country k except i. Accordingly, the coefficients b_7 and b_8 capture the *dyad contagion effect*.

In sum, the number of tourists from a western country i to an Islamic country j depends on how many tourists from country i and how many from other western

---

[25] Which countries are counted as "West" follows the work of Russett et al. (2000).

[26] The models were estimated by a regression called the "Pseudo-Poisson Maximum Likelihood."

[27] Unobserved "fixed" effects are explained briefly in General Appendix B, Sect. B.14.

countries are involved in terror attacks in the destination Islamic country j as well as other Islamic countries. The contagion effects are the *spatial spillover effects*, arising because the terror message is strategically addressed at western citizens in general rather than the tourists' countries of origin per se.[28]

Results strongly support specific target as well as all three contagion effects. Indeed, the negative effect of terrorism is large. For instance, in the estimation model (6.5), one fatal terror attack involving a victim from the source country reduces tourist inflow by 4.2% contemporaneously and 7.4% in the next year. Contagion effects are strong too. These results imply that tourists understand one aspect of transnational terrorism fairly well: that is, terrorist attacks in Islamic countries are executed by terror groups with transnational strategic objectives toward western countries as a whole.

In summary,

Is That So? 6.14: Terrorism and the Tourism Industry

By and large, terrorism has exerted large adverse impacts on the tourism industry in terms of number of tourists and tourism revenues. In addition, tourism in Islamic countries by residents of western countries is subject to contagion effects: it is sensitive to terror attacks against all western tourists in all Islamic countries.

6.8 Subjective Well-Being

Terrorism breeds fear, anxiety as well as grief and mourning especially among people living in areas directly affected by terror attacks. People outside of the areas where terrorists hit are indirectly exposed and affected too. Psychological impacts can be thought of as a public good which is involuntarily consumed. This public good is indeed a *public "bad"* that lowers people's mental or subjective well-being. Such effects have been studied and quantified by social scientists and medical professionals. Given the enormity of the volume of this literature, we will mostly review terror events or episodes from the year 2000 onward only, except one study on the UK and France in Sect. 6.8.4.

6.8.1 *9/11* Attacks

As one can imagine, there exist a large number of studies on the impact of *9/11* attacks on mental well-being of residents in the USA and outside of the USA. Because of the sheer volume, we organize them into three categories on the basis of the statistical/econometric techniques used. This is consistent with one of the objectives of this book: to encourage learning the methodologies of analysis.

One group of papers estimate the impact of *9/11* attacks on subjective well-being by analyzing post- *9/11* data only. Another group incorporates both pre-*9/11*

[28] The authors estimate another regression that includes all variables in Eq. (6.5) plus the one-period lagged dependent variable, y_{ijt-1} to account for own dynamics of tourist arrivals.

and post-*9/11* data during the year 2001 in order to obtain more reliable estimates of *9/11* as an event. In the process they use the Regression Discontinuity Design (RDD) approach. A third group of papers go even further to isolate the impact of *9/11* event by using pre- *9/11* and post-9/11 data in 2001 as well as data in some other year so as to control for changes from the pre- *9/11* period to the post- *9/11* period due to factors other than *9/11* that are not observable. That is, they make use of the Difference-in-Differences (DiD) approach.

Both RDD and DiD methods are discussed in the General Appendix B, Sect. B.17.

6.8.1.1 Impact on US Residents

Post-Event Data In varying degrees of detail, telephonic interview based studies show an association of post-traumatic stress disorder (PTSD) with direct and indirect exposure to the *9/11* attacks, e.g., Schuster et al. (2001), Galea et al. (2002), Silver et al. (2002), Schlenger et al. (2002) and Eidelson et al. (2003). Schlenger et al. (2002), however, report that the overall psychological distress levels in the USA were within normal ranges, whereas, interestingly, Eidelson et al. (2003) record more visits to psychologists in the vicinity of the World Trade Center in comparison to elsewhere. There are patient-based studies too. Neria et al. (2006) examined PTSD in 930 primary care patients seven to sixteen months after *9/11*, among whom 10.2% of them were found to exhibit PTSD symptoms.

By conducting a nationwide, large-sample, telephonic survey covering 75,000 households across the USA, Lerner et al. (2003) studied how fear and anger from learning about the massive tragedy and destruction from *9/11* attacks changed people's attitudes. While fear triggered pessimism, anger bred more optimistic beliefs on safety of air travels due to greater safety measures and a national resolve to undertake strong actions to contain or eliminate the problem of terrorism.

How did the *9/11* attacks impact on the survivors from the collapsed and damaged buildings in New York and those who lost their near and dear ones in the event? Based on interviews of the survivors, Brackbill et al. (2006) found severe physical and mental problems such as depression and anxiety even three years after *9/11*.[29] A telephone survey one and a half years after *9/11* found that of those who had been bereaved, 44% had *complicated grief*, a condition where grief is present together with adjustment disorders manifested by some combination of depression, disturbed emotions, anxiety, substance abuse, etc. This was related to the loss of a family member as opposed to an acquaintance (Shear et al., 2006). By using a web-based survey that took place 2.5 and 3.5 years after *9/11*, Neria et al. (2007) examined the levels of complicated grief among those bereaved as a result of *9/11*; 43% of them still experienced the same symptoms.

Pre- and Post-Event Data, RDD Approach The limitation of using post *9/11* data only is that the results could not be compared with the mental well-being outcomes

---

[29] The long-terms physical problems were due to exposure to dust and debris clouds during the event.

prior to *9/11*. Ford et al. (2003) is one of the earliest and comprehensive studies on how 9/11 affected the mental health of young-adult individuals by comparing the pre- and post- *9/11* observations. Using Wave III of the National Longitudinal Study of Adolescent Health that interviewed young adults between 18 and 26 years (2913 respondents within two months prior to *9/11* and 4182 respondents within two months after *9/11*), the authors found that the percentage of men expressing sadness increased from 33.6 before *9/11* to 39.0 after *9/11*, and the same percentage for women jumped from 43.8 to 53.3.[30]

Knudsen et al. (2005) analyzed the effect of *9/11* attacks on depressive symptoms and drinking, based on data from the National Employee Survey. Using random digit dialing in which American households were randomly selected for interviewing, the respondents were asked about depressive symptoms like the number of days during the last week when they felt sad, had trouble getting to sleep or staying asleep, felt everything was an effort, felt lonely, felt they just could not get going, etc. as well as the number of drinks they had in the past one month.

There were two regressions: one with the depressive symptoms in the past week as the dependent variable and the other with the number of drink during the past month. The principal independent variable of interest is temporal proximity of the date of the respondent's interview to September 11, 2001.[31]

The results indicated a significant jump in the number of depressive symptoms reported during the four weeks after the *9/11* attacks; but, in the subsequent weeks, the levels of depressive symptoms returned to pre- *9/11* levels. Contrary to expectations, there was some indication of a modest decrease in alcohol consumption after *9/11*. Thus, *9/11 attacks negatively affected mental well-being for a short period only.*

Pesko (2014) estimated the effect of *9/11* attacks (and Oklahoma City Bombing) on stress, smoking, and quit-smoking attempts by using the Behavioral Risk Factor Surveillance System (BRFSS) data from 1994 to 2003 for all US states and Washington, D.C. As Oklahoma City Bombing occurred on April 19, 1995, the data covers time periods before and after this terror attack as well as before and after *9/11*. More specifically, the periods 1994–1995 and 1999–2003 were used, respectively, to estimate the impact of Oklahoma City bombing and 9/11 attacks.[32]

The results suggest that in the fourth quarter of 2001 the stress level increased by nearly an extra half day per 30 days (11.9%). In the two years after 9/11, smoking prevalence increased by 1.1 percentage points (2.3%) among ever smoking adults, resulting in between 950,000 and 1,300,000 adult former smokers becoming smokers again because of terrorism.

Pre- and Post-Event Data with a Control Year, DiD Approach By using DiD, Tsi and Venkataramani (2015) investigated the impact of *9/11* attacks on mental health

[30] The question eliciting the level of sadness was "Were you sad during the past seven days?", the response to which was to be expressed on a 4-point scale. The interview also asked about other aspects of mental well-being such as their perception of general health and life expectancy.

[31] In addition, basic demographic measures were included as controls.

[32] Control variables included gender, race/ethnicity, household income, age, education attainment, marital status, employment status, etc.

working with a broader BRFSS (survey) dataset compared to Ford et al. (2003) and Knudsen et al. (2005).[33] The subjective well-being question in the survey asked the number of days in the last month when the respondents considered themselves being in poor mental health.[34]

The findings indicate a significant overall mental health deterioration between September 11 and September 17, 2001 and more so between September 25 and October 1 of 2001. The impacts on the number of days during the past month when the respondents felt being sad, blue or depressed and worried, tense or anxious were also highly significant during the September 25-October 1, 2001 period.[35]

6.8.1.2 The Impact on Residents in the UK

Metcalfe et al. (2011) presented a causal evidence of international spillover of subjective well-being effect due to *9/11* attacks. Using a variety of estimation methods, all within the class of DiD models, they studied how *9/11* attacks impacted on the subjective well-being (SWB) of UK residents. The data was obtained from the British Household Panel Survey (BHPS). Administered annually, with a significant proportion of it takes place during September in a random manner, this permits comparing SWB levels of the UK population between the periods before and after 11th September in 2001, while controlling for the variation between the same time periods in the preceding year 2000. Their regression equation has the form:

$$\begin{aligned} D_{it} &= a + b_1 \cdot (\text{Post- } \mathit{9/11})_{it} + b_2 \cdot (\text{Year} = 2001)_{it} \\ &\quad + b_3 \cdot [\text{Post- } \mathit{9/11} \times (\text{Year} = 2001)]_t + \boldsymbol{\beta Z} + u_{it}, \end{aligned} \tag{6.6}$$

where D_{it} is index of mental distress and t takes values 2000 and 2001.[36] Mental distress—the dependent variable, indicated by General Health Questionnaire

[33] The control year is 2000 and the period covered is August 14 to October 8 of both 2000 and 2001.

[34] The specific question was, "Now thinking about your mental health, which includes stress, depression, and problems with emotions, for how many days during the past 30 days was your mental health not good?"

[35] Instead of measures of subjective well-being, there are tens of studies that analyze the impact of terrorist events like the 1994 Oklahoma City building and *9/11* on cigarette smoking, alcohol consumption, and substance abuse (DiMaggio et al., 2009). According to one particular study, Vlahov et al. (2002), that is based on a random digital telephone survey 5–8 weeks after *9/11* among the residents of Manhattan, New York City that covered 988 respondents, 28.8% reported an increase in use of any of these three substances, 9.7% reported an increase in smoking, 24.6% reported an increase in alcohol consumption, and 3.2% reported an increase in marijuana use. These numbers represent substantial increase in these habits.

DiMaggio et al. (2009) conducted a meta-analysis based on 31 research articles on smoking, alcohol, and substance consumption, finding 7.3% of the population showing an increase in alcohol consumption during the two years following a major terror attack. The prevalence of increased cigarette smoking and substance abuse were noticed with 6.8% and 16.3% of the population, respectively.

[36] Another set of regression uses a large-sample period, namely 1997–2004.

(GHQ)—is a composite measure of twelve subjective states.[37] Both (Post- *9/11*) and (Year = 2001) dummy variables, taking value 1 for the post- *9/11* period and for the year 2001, respectively, and 0 otherwise. The focus of interest is the estimated coefficient b_3 on the interaction term Post- *9/11* × (Year = 2001), which captures the filtered effect of the post *9/11* period. Several controls (**Z**) are used, e.g., interview month dummies, gender, age, household income, dummies for marital status, labor force status, education, etc. as well as unobserved individual specific effects.

The main finding is that the *9/11* terrorist attacks lowered the levels of SWB of those UK residents who answered the survey after *9/11*, and the effect was large. According to one set of estimates, the effect on the overall mental distress measured by GHQ is between 0.17–0.27, which is approximately 7% of the standard deviation of the GHQ responses. Out of the twelve components of GHQ, four, namely ability to concentrate, loss of sleep, ability to play useful role and ability to make decisions, drive the impact of *9/11* attacks on SWB. The adverse effects lasted till the end of November 2001 and petered out afterwards.

6.8.2 Madrid Bombings in 2004 and London Attacks in 2005

There are several studies on PTSD symptoms from these major terror attacks (Freedman, 2009). Using a large-sample telephone survey one and two months following the Madrid Train bombings on March 11, 2004, Miguel-Tobal et al. (2006) reported 2.3% of individuals with PTSD, and 8% with depression. Among the injured survivors, PTSD remained significant even after one year. A study on injured survivors by Conejo-Galindo et al. (2008) showed PTSD among 35.7% one month later, 34.1% six months later and 28.6% a year later.

A little over a week after the London attacks on July 7, 2005, a random-dial telephone survey over 1000 people (between 18th and 20th July) conducted by Rubin et al. (2005) found 31% of individuals had one or more substantial stress symptoms. According to a seven-month follow-up study by Rubin et al. (2007), the incidence had declined to 11%.

6.8.3 Boston Marathon Bombing in 2013

Perpetrated by two youths of Chechen background, it was the first major terror attack on the US soil after *9/11*. It was homegrown and attracted considerable domestic and international media coverage. Clark et al. (2017) analyzed the mental health effects of this incident. The authors used the repeated cross-sectional data from the Well-Being module of American Time Use Survey (ATUS) and applied the

[37] These are, namely losing sleep over worry; constantly feeling under strain; feeling that difficulties cannot be overcome; feeling unhappy and depressed; losing confidence; feeling like a worthless person; feeling of playing a useful part in things; feeling capable of making decisions; ability to enjoy day-to-day activities; ability to concentrate; ability to face up to problems; and feeling reasonably happy.

DiD methodology.[38,39] The indicators of experienced wellness (see footnote 39) are computed for 28 days before and 28 days after the day of attack in 2013 (that is April 15, 2013) as well as 28 days before and 28 days after April 15, 2012 as the controlling period.[40]

The estimations imply that the Boston marathon bombing significantly affected the well-being of individuals and more so for women than for men and for those living in the states closer to Boston than for those living further away. There was an overall decline in experienced well-being equal to one-third of the standard deviation.[41] This is a sharp decline, equivalent to an increase of about two percentage points in the annual unemployment rate. But, the impact of the attack appears to have dissipated by one week after the bombing—reflecting the resilience of people in terms of quickly bouncing back from the emotional effect of this attack.

In sum,

Is That So? 6.15: Terrorism and PTSD

Subjective well-being, as inversely measured by post-traumatic stress disorder, depression, etc., declines for people directly affected by and indirectly exposed to major terror events (via general information and news media). It includes residents outside the country where an event occurs. However, the effect is mostly temporary for a few weeks or a few months at most for those indirectly exposed, but people who are directly affected (like the injured survivors and those who lost their near and dear ones) remain mentally affected over a longer haul.

6.8.4 Terrorism in France and British Isle

Frey et al. (2009) present empirical estimates of the impact of terrorism on the perception of life satisfaction by people, covering France, Great Britain and the Republic of Ireland over the period 1973/1975–2002. In western Europe, France witnessed the highest number of international terror attacks from the 1970s till the end of 1990s, whereas during most of this period, the Great Britain and the Irish Republic experienced worst episodes of terror attacks by the IRA and rival

[38] "Repeated" cross-sectional data is defined in the General Appendix B, Sect. B.3.1.

[39] The survey, done daily for a representative sample of the American population, contains information on daily activities of an individual and solicits well-being status on six emotional experiences, namely happiness, meaningfulness, sadness, tiredness, pain, and stress. The first two are positive emotions and the rest are negative. Each emotion is scaled between 0 and 6. From these indices an overall indicator of "experienced wellness" being is constructed, equal to the difference between the average of the two positive emotions and that of the four negative emotions.

[40] Control variables include individual, family and demographic characteristics, dummies for holidays, whether the respondent lives in a metropolitan area, state of residence, year, month, and day.

[41] Measuring changes in terms of the standard deviation is explained in the General Appendix B, Sect. B.7. The magnitudes of the emotions and hence the experienced well-being change with the scale chosen (that is, if the scale was different from [0,6], the magnitude of changes would be different). To keep it unit-neutral, the changes in a variable are expressed as the multiple of its standard deviation in the data.

Protestant groups in Northern Ireland. Life satisfaction responses are a measure of psychological well-being but different from those measuring mental illness. One novelty of Frey et al. (2009) is that this effect is quantified by the scale in which life satisfaction is measured *and* in monetary units, so that the estimates can be compared across regions.

The authors used life satisfaction scores (scaled from 1 to 4) obtained by Euro-Barometer Survey Series, which enabled them to derive large samples over Great Britain, Northern Ireland, Republic of Ireland and France.[42] Terror incidents were classified into three regions in France—Paris, Provence-Al-pes-Côte d'Azure—and three regions in the British Isles—Great Britain, Northern Ireland and the Irish Republic.[43] The regression equation was:

$$LS_{irt} = a + b_1 \cdot T_{rt} + b_2 \cdot \ln(m_{irt}) + \boldsymbol{\beta Z} + u_{irt}, \tag{6.7}$$

where LS is the life satisfaction score, i is the individual, r stands for the region, t is time, T the indicator of terrorism (number of attacks or the number of fatalities in the region), and m is the reported individual income. The vector $\mathbf{Z}$ includes control variables like individual characteristics such sex, age, marital status, employed or not, retired or not, etc., and unobserved region-specific and time-specific effects. Equation (6.7) was estimated for France and the British Isles separately.

The primary focus was on the estimated coefficient on terrorism, $\hat{b}_1$. The coefficient on income, $\hat{b}_2$, also assumed importance since it was necessary to derive the monetary equivalent of the impact of terrorism on life satisfaction. The values of $\hat{b}_1$ across the regressions (negative and highly significant) imply that a one-standard-deviation increase in the fatalities—translating into 14.42 fatalities in British Isles and 1.78 fatalities in France—lowered life satisfaction by 0.009 points in both countries, whereas an increase of one-standard-deviation in the number of recorded incidents, i.e., an increase of 154.03 incidents in the British Isles and an increase of 5.59 incidents in France, lowered life satisfaction by 0.012 and 0.013 points, respectively, on the four-point scale. These magnitudes are large, evidencing strong negative impacts of terrorism on life satisfaction.

The estimates $\hat{b}_1$ and $\hat{b}_2$ enable one to calculate the monetary equivalent of the estimated loss of life satisfaction due to terrorism, by appealing to the concept of *compensating surplus*, explained in Sect. A.1 of the General Appendix A. The idea is the following. Start with some given level of monetary income say m_{i0} for individual i and a given level of terror T_{r0} in the region r together with given levels of other explanatory variables. In view of Eq. (6.7) let the corresponding life satisfaction index be LS_{i0}. Now suppose terror increases from T_{r0} to T_{r1} while all

[42] The dataset constitutes 30,244 observations for Great Britain, 7891 for Northern Ireland, 24,185 for the Republic of Ireland, and 38,062 for France over the period 1972/1975–2002. The survey asks a random cross-section selection of people the following question: On the whole, are you very satisfied (4), fairly satisfied (3), not very satisfied (2) or not all satisfied (1), with the life you lead? It also records the respondents' income and other characteristics.

[43] The data on terrorism was obtained from the RAND dataset (for France and Great Britain excluding Northern Ireland) and TWEED dataset (for the Republic of Ireland and Northern Ireland).

other determinants including individual income are unchanged. Since $\hat{b}_2 < 0$, the life satisfaction indicator will decrease from LS_{i0}. Now ask yourself the hypothetical question: how much extra income the individual i in region r would need so that her life satisfaction would remain unchanged at LS_{i0} rather than fall from this level? The answer to this question defines and measures the compensating surplus (CS), measuring the monetary equivalent of the loss of life satisfaction from an increase in terror from T_{i0} to T_{i1}.

Based on the resulting expression of compensating surplus, that is, Eq. (6.8) derived in the chapter Appendix 6.B, the authors calculated that

Is That So? 6.16: Monetary Cost of Terrorism in France and British Isles

During the period 1973/1975–2002, compared to the least terror-prone regions, the monetary equivalent of the losses of the perception of life-time satisfaction in the most terror affected regions of France and British Isles amounted, respectively, to 4% and 26% of annual household income.

Note that the life-time-satisfaction cost of terrorism was particularly severe for the residents in the British Isles.

6.8.5 Second Intifada: Israel

We have noted earlier that the worst phase of terrorism experienced by Israel was during the Second Intifada from October 2000 to February 2005. There is a large number of studies on stress effects in Israel from terror attacks during this period, which are cataloged by Freedman (2009). We review a few of them.

Using data from a survey conducted from June to August of 2001, Shalev et al. (2006) compared the incidence of PTSD among the residents of two suburbs of Jerusalem, namely Efrat and Bét Shemesh, the former being more directly affected by terrorism than the latter. While the residents of the more exposed community reported more severe PTSD symptoms, the difference was not large. Bleich et al. (2003) estimated the nationwide impact on PTSD resulting from terror attacks during the early stage of the Second Intifada. Based on a nationwide telephone survey conducted in April and May of 2002 (at the height of the Second Intifada), the authors concluded that the psychological impact seemed to be moderate. Although the survey participants showed distress and lowered sense of safety, they did not develop high levels of psychiatric distress. This may be related to a habituation process and coping mechanisms. In a follow-up work, Bleich et al. (2006) analyzed the long-term impact of terrorism during the Second Intifada. The authors conducted a survey in May 2004, a relatively calm period, the results from which were similar to the previous study.

In contrast to the earlier authors who used surveys covering less than 1000 individuals, Romanov et al. (2012) used the comprehensive Social Surveys conducted in Israel in 2002–2004 covering more than 20,000 observations and estimated the effect of terrorism on the self-reported happiness. Happiness was measured on an ordinal scale from four possible answers to the question, "Overall, are you satisfied with your life?" The choices are: "very satisfied," "fairly satisfied," "not very satisfied," and "not at all satisfied."[44]

In order to estimate the impact of terrorism measured by the fatalities from terror attacks on happiness, other determinants like gender, age, education and health status as well as income and employment status were controlled. Terrorism can impact on happiness directly as well as indirectly via its effect on income and employment. Thus, controlling for these two variables in particular brings out the direct effect of terrorism from the coefficient on the fatalities from terror attacks.

The main finding is rather striking.

Is That So? 6.17: Second Intifada and Happiness

According to Romanov et al. (2012), during the Second Intifada, the number of country-wide terrorism fatalities in Israel had no direct effect on the life satisfaction of Jewish Israelis. In contrast, the Arab citizens of Israel (Arab-Israelis) displayed a robust negative reaction to terrorism fatalities.

What can be a reason? The authors hypothesized that the negative reaction of Arabs may be related to increasing concerns of discrimination against them because of terror attacks rather than the fear of terror itself.

6.9 Physical Health Effects

Major terror attacks have been associated with fear and anxiety related physical health problems like heart conditions and birth outcomes.

6.9.1 *9/11* Attacks and Cardiovascular Health

In an innovative study, Steinberg et al. (2004) showed that *9/11* attacks contributed to an increase in the heartbeat of heart patients who had ICDs (implantable cardioverter-defibrillators) implanted into their bodies. A small battery-powered device placed in the chest to monitor heart rhythm and detect irregular heartbeats, an ICD can store all serious arrhythmias for months.[45]

---

[44] The data contains the date, the time and the location in which each of the survey interviews was conducted, and this is linked to the daily data on terrorism, covering the same period as do the Social Surveys. The sources of data on terrorism are B'Tselem (the Israeli Information Centre for Human Rights in the Occupied Territories), the Israeli Ministry of Foreign Affairs, the Israeli Ministry of Defense and the Israeli National Insurance Institute. Each terror attack is assigned a date and time. The data on terrorism cover all politically motivated and fatal attacks inside Israel and in the Occupied Territories (Judea, Samaria, and the Gaza Strip). They include attacks against both civilians and security forces. In each case we have information about the number of fatalities, location, and other relevant variables.

Logit and ordered logit regressions were used (see Sect. B.4.2 of the General Appendix B).

[45] An ICD is similar to a pacemaker but has more functionality. For instance, if the heart fails, a pacemaker acts when the heart functions slowly but it cannot revive it if it fails. But a defibrillator can jump start the heart.

The authors conducted an observational study on two hundred consecutive ICD patients who presented themselves for regularly scheduled follow-ups to six affiliated clinics in Manhattan, Staten Island, the Bronx, northern New Jersey and upstate New York. The electrograms stored in the ICDs for the three months before *9/11* and 13 months thereafter were scrutinized for all ventricular tachyarrhythmias (faster heartbeat) triggering ICD therapy.

The major findings were that the frequency of tachyarrhythmias increased significantly for the 30 days post- *9/11* (with*p* value equal to 0.004) relative to all other months between May 2001 and October 2002. In the 30 days post- *9/11*, sixteen patients (8%) demonstrated tachyarrhythmias, compared with only seven (3.5%) in the preceding 30 days, the difference being significant at a 3%. Similar qualitative results were reported by Shedd et al. (2004) on heart patients in Florida.

The effect of *9/11* attacks on cardiovascular ailments based on a nationwide survey was studied by Holman et al. (2008). It was a Web-based sampling, carried on over three years after *9/11* and covering more than 2500 adults. The main finding was that there was a 53% increased incidence of cardiovascular ailments over the three subsequent years, after adjusting for pre- *9/11* cardiovascular and mental health status, degree of exposure to the attacks, cardiovascular risk factors, demographics, etc.[46]

The general conclusion is that

Is That So? 6.18: *9/11* Attacks and Cardiovascular Health

9/11 terror attacks were associated with poorer cardiovascular health.

6.9.2 Stress-Induced Birth Outcomes

There is evidence that terror attacks have impacted on birth outcomes.

6.9.2.1 USA: *9/11* Attacks

Bruckner et al. (2010) examined the fetal-death sex ratio in the USA resulting from *9/11* attacks. Using fetal death and birth data from 1996 to 2002 over the entire USA obtained from the National Vital Statistics System and applying the time-series intervention analysis or the interrupted time-series analysis (see Sect. B.13.2 of the General Appendix B), the results support the hypothesis that the fetal-death sex ratio, i.e., the odds of a male fetal death, increased above its expected value in September 2001—which can be attributed to increased stress resulting from the *9/11* attacks. It holds for fetal deaths over the USA except California.

[46] The study used a Generalized Estimating Equation (GEE) approach, a statistical approach to fit a marginal model for longitudinal/clustered data analysis, which has been popularly applied into clinical trials and biomedical studies. It is a semi-parametric regression technique and a special case of generalized method of moments approach.

6.9.2.2 Colombia

In an interesting study, Camacho (2008) uncovered that in Colombia terror attacks impacted on the weight of newborn babies, due to fear and shock experienced by expectant mothers. Fear and shock were proxied by landmine explosions in the area, which were loud and shocking and which were presumably planted by terror organizations.[47] The author used 4.3 million birth certificates filed in hospitals in 1120 municipalities in Colombia from 1998 to 2003.[48] Birth weights of newborns were regressed against indicators of landmine explosions in the area during four time periods separately: the three trimesters and the trimester just before the first trimester of pregnancies.[49,50] Two sets of regressions were run. In one, landmine explosion is incorporated as a dummy: whether or not there was any such explosion in the respective trimester. In the other, the number of explosions is a regressor.

The main result is that exposure to landmine explosion in the *first* trimester of pregnancy had the strongest negative impact (-11.6 grams, i.e., 0.4 ounce) on birth weight of newborns. According to one of the estimates the marginal impact of landmine explosion experienced in the first trimester reduced the baby weight by 11.6 grams (0.4 ounces), while the combined effects of that in three trimesters prior to the birth trimester, compared to no explosions, reduced the baby weight by 27.76 grams, which is 0.8% of the average weight of a newborn in Colombia for the period of study.[51]

Is That So? 6.19: Terrorism and Fetal-Death Sex Ratio and Birth Weight of Newborn Babies

In the USA, *9/11* attacks led to an increase in the fetal-death sex ratio in September of 2001. During 1998–2003, landmine blasts (a result of planting of landmines by terror groups) in Colombia were associated with a 0.8% decline of birth weight relative to the average weight of newborns.

[47] Landmine explosions capture the shocks of violence rather than persistent levels of violence. Data on them was obtained from National Planning Department of Colombia.

[48] This is obtained from the Vital Statistics Records, collected by the Administrative Department of Statics of the Government of Colombia. Among these records, the empirical analysis of the paper uses a sample of 781,000 birth records, in which mothers appeared more than once, i.e., the sample contains mothers with two or more pregnancies.

[49] The regressions also included control variables like age, education, marital status of mothers, sex of the newborn as well as dummies for years, months, areas of residence (*departmento* or municipality), etc.

[50] Colombia is a unitary, not federal, republic, consisting of thirty-two *departmentos* (which are like districts or administrative units) and a capital district. Each *departmento* is formed by grouping municipalities.

[51] The average weight was 3.15 kilograms or 6.94 pounds.

6.10 Role of Media

One can imagine that seeing news coverage of major disasters continuously can add to anxiety and affect mental health. Indeed, there are studies which quantify and confirm this hypothesis.

Based on random-digit-dial telephone survey conducted between October 16 and November 15, 2001 and covering more than 1000 respondents, Ahern et al. (2002) sought their television exposure to *9/11* attacks as well as demographic characteristics including age, race/ethnicity, sex, income, and education. Respondents were asked whether or not they saw these images on television, and if they did, how many times over seven days following September 11. The images included "an airplane hitting the WTC," "buildings collapsing," "people running away from a cloud of smoke," and "people falling or jumping from the towers of the WTC." Among these, the last image—"people falling or jumping from the towers of the WTC"—was most consistently found to be associated with both PTSD and depression. Respondents who saw this image repeatedly had higher prevalence of PTSD (17.4%) and depression (14.7%) than those who did not (6.2% and 5.3%, respectively).

There is evidence that watching the first anniversary of *9/11* had adverse mental effects too. With the help of random-digit-dial longitudinal telephone surveys conducted six months and twelve months after *9/11* Bernstein et al. (2007) found that watching 12 or more hours of *9/11* attacks anniversary news coverage was associated with a 3.4-fold increased risk of new-onset probable PTSD (with p value equal to 0.004).[52]

Silver et al. (2013) analyzed the TV coverage of *9/11* attacks as well as the Iraq War. Their findings strongly suggests that widespread media coverage of terrorism and war can have negative mental- *and* physical health consequences like asthma and hypertension over time.

Holman et al. (2014) studied the impact of media coverage on the Boston Marathon bombing. They compared the impact of media versus that of direct exposure, on acute stress response to collective trauma. An internet-based survey was undertaken following the Boston Marathon bombings between April 29 and May 13, 2013, with representative samples of residents from Boston, New York City and the remainder of the United States. Acute stress symptom scores were comparable between Boston and New York but lower nationwide when compared with Boston. Adjusting for pre-bombing mental health, demographics, and prior collective stress exposure, six or more daily hours of bombing-related media exposure in the week after the bombings were associated with higher acute stress than direct exposure to the bombings.

---

[52] See General Appendix B, Sect. B.2 for a description what p-value is. The lower the p-value, the higher is the degree of significance for a coefficient or a number to be different from zero.

Is That So? 6.20: Media Coverage of Terrorism

Media coverage of terror attacks has contributed to PTSD and depression. In case of *9/11* attacks, the scene of people falling or jumping out WTC buildings was particularly harmful. Even the media coverage of the first anniversary of *9/11* was linked to PTSD.

6.11 Behavioral Impact

Fear and anxiety from the prospect of terror attacks can trigger changes in individual behavior. This is reflected, for example, in the stress-related habits like smoking and alcohol and substance abuse. Apart from such effects that have been already discussed in the preceding sections, people's risk perceptions change when there is a major terror attack or a series of successful terror attacks. In turn, this leads to behavioral changes. For instance, *9/11* attacks increased people's fear of flying and that combined with expected delays at airports due to security checks led to a substitution of flying toward driving.

If subjected to repeated terror attacks, people may become more resilient as they consciously try to overcome fear. In what follows, we briefly discuss evidence for such behavioral changes.

6.11.1 Substituting Flying for Driving

It was noticed by scholars and press reports that road traffic deaths in the USA increased in the aftermath of *9/11*. This was attributed to the fear of flying instigated by the fatal *9/11* attacks, which led to more travel by road.[53,54] In addition, the inconvenience of unprecedented security procedures may have contributed to the substitution of air travel by car travel. More road travel meant more road accidents and deaths.

Blalock et al. (2009) presented a careful econometric analysis of these causal factors for road accidents while controlling for other reasons. Changes in relative prices would affect substitution of air travel for road travel. Weather, traffic conditions, state regulations, highway maintenance, etc. can also affect fatality rates on roads. In assessing the impact of *9/11* attacks, the authors considered driving fatalities in the USA, focusing on the deaths of non-commercial drivers. Commercial driving fatalities were used as controls, because while these fatalities are likely to be affected by other factors such as road or weather conditions, they are much less likely influenced by the fear and security inconvenience stemming from *9/11*.

One series of regressions have a post- *9/11* dummy which takes values 1 for October 2001 to December of 2001, 0 for all other months of 2001 as well as for all

[53] See Gigerenzer (2004), Sivak and Flannagan (2004), Begley (2004) and Science News (2004).

[54] Statistically, the probability of dying from road accidents is higher than that from flying. However, the substitution effect is driven by the individual *perception* of risk rather than what the statistics shows.

other years.[55] This represents the short-run impact of *9/11*. Another set of regressions use a time-trend after September 2001 in order to capture the long-run effects of *9/11*.[56]

The main dependent variable is the number of non-commercial vehicle fatalities per each month over the years 1994–2003.[57] The central findings are the following. Non-commercial driving fatalities increased substantially after *9/11*; but there was no increase in commercial driving fatalities. An additional 327 driving fatalities per month can be ascribed to *9/11* attacks for the period from October to December of 2001. These effects mostly dissipated by October 2003, a little over two years following September 2001. Cumulatively, 2300 lives may have been lost because of the reaction to the attacks. Moreover, there was much larger increase in driving deaths in the Northeast corridor than elsewhere in the USA.

Is That So? 6.21: Substitution of Air Travel for Road Travel following September 11, 2001

Following the *9/11* attacks, there was a substitution of air travel for road travel. Fatalities from non-commercial driving increased substantially. The Blalock et al. (2009) study estimates that between October and December of 2001, approximately 2300 road accident deaths can be attributed to this substitution effect.

6.11.2 Overcoming Fear

Becker and Rubinstein (2011) have studied the fear-overcoming behavioral changes of Israeli residents as a response to terror events during the Second Intifada. They examined the demand for two services, namely bus travel and going to cafés, both targeted by suicide terror attacks during those years. The key idea is to differentiate between the behavioral patterns of individuals who are frequent users and who are occasional users of these services. If the response of the frequent users to terror attacks is less than that of the occasional users, then it is consistent with the hypothesis that people do control their emotions in order to overcome terrorism-triggered fear. Such behavior is attributable to economic considerations—since these services are economically more important for the frequent users than for occasional or infrequent users.

The Israeli bus companies offer three major types of tickets: standard single-ride tickets, multiple-ride tickets and monthly passes. Last two categories are naturally associated with frequent users. Consumption of café visits vary by age, income, and especially marital status. Most social and dating activities take place in such

[55] September of 2001 is excluded as an outlier.

[56] There are many control variables used like gasoline price, air fare, rail freight, unemployment, personal income, year and month dummies, and many interaction terms. Unemployment and personal income are included as control variables in order to reflect that general economic conditions may also have an effect of fatalities from auto accidents.

[57] Some regressions use deaths associated with accidents of commercial vehicles and the total number of deaths from accidents of non-commercial and commercial vehicles. There are also regressions where the dependent variable is the natural log of the number of fatalities.

"public locations." The authors disaggregated the young-adult population into two types: singles and married couples without children. It is presumed that singles are the frequent visitors, while young married couples without children are occasional users.

The main results are that (a) while a bus-related attacks reduced the number of single-ride tickets purchased during the following week by approximately 9%, the multiple-ride tickets or monthly passes issued remained on average unchanged, and (b) suicide attacks on cafés reduced the number of visits of married couples by about 15% during the first week, whereas they had no impact on the number of visits or spending habits of singles.

Clearly, terrorism exerted differential impacts on different types of users. Regular users were affected less compared to occasional users. It is, however, possible that this may be due to less price elasticity of demand for services by the frequent users. The authors, however, noted that demand for services by regular users is more price-elastic than that by occasional users. Therefore, the results are reflective of behavioral changes toward overcoming fear, not price-elasticity differences in demand.

Is That So? 6.22: Developing Resilience toward Terror Attacks in Israel during the Second Intifada

In their study of demand for bus rides and café visits in Israel during the Second Intifada period, Becker and Rubinstein (2011) showed that, as Israel witnessed several terror attacks, the Israelis developed an inner resilience to overcome terror-triggered fear, because of economic motives.

6.12 Take-Aways

- Single terror events including *9/11* attacks have had negligible impact on the real per-capita income, GDP or growth of any economy.
- According to Abadie and Gardeazabal (2003), during 1975–1997 when ETA's violence was prominent in the Spanish Basque region, the region's real per-capita GDP declined by 10% on average annually from what it would have been in the absence of ETA's terrorism. There is evidence that terrorism during the First and the Second Intifadas lowered the real per-capita income of Israel.
- On average over many countries, the effect of terrorism on the real per-capita income or its growth rate is modest at best.
- Both domestic and transnational terrorism have had a significant negative effect on the size of international trade among countries. Exports from a country are not only affected by terrorism in the exporting country but also terrorism in its neighboring countries. There is evidence to suggest that there is a delayed effect of terrorism on the size of international trade.
- Like international trade, FDI is adversely affected by terrorism. The magnitude of the impact varies considerably across countries. Foreign aid

mitigates the negative impact of terrorism on FDI and thus is conductive to FDI inflow into developing countries afflicted by terrorism.
- Brodeur (2018) provides county-level evidence that successful terror attacks in the USA during the period 1970–2013 exerted a relatively large impact on the local labor markets, reducing employment and wages by 2% and 2.5%, respectively.
- Estimates obtained by Benmelech and Berrebi (2007) imply that Palestinian terror attacks during the Second Intifada led to worse outcomes in the labor market in Gaza and West Bank, suggesting that "terrorism may not pay."
- There is mixed evidence to the effect that *9/11* attacks and London attacks in 2005 led to discrimination against Muslim men in terms of employment and wages. Contrary to the common perception, the large-scale homegrown terror attack in 2011 by Anders Behring Breivik, a Norwegian far-right terrorist, did not lead to a more favorable attitude toward Pakistani origin individuals—who constitute the largest immigrant community in Norway—in the Norwegian labor market.
- *9/11* attacks had strong negative impacts on stock-market returns across the world over the days following September 11, 2001. Airlines stocks were hit the hardest. However, almost all markets recovered to their pre- *9/11* levels in a few weeks following the attacks. The global financial-market impacts of 9/11 attacks varied across regions depending on how much integrated they were into the global economy. Those in the Middle East and North Africa were affected the least.
- Madrid, London, and Boston marathon terror attacks have affected the stock markets but in a much smaller scale compared to *9/11* attacks.
- Financial markets have been affected more by terrorist attacks than by natural disasters like earthquakes. More severe attacks and those involving loss of human capital as opposed to physical capital losses are associated with greater impacts on stock markets. Adverse impacts are, however, temporary: they remain for a few weeks only. Attacks targeted toward bigger economies have greater spillover effects on other financial markets.
- Among major terror attacks in the twenty-first century thus far, relatively recent events do not seem to affect local or international markets.
- Terrorism also increases volatility of stock prices and returns in the short run.
- By and large, terrorism has had large adverse impact on the tourism industry in terms of number of tourists and tourism revenues. In addition, tourism in Islamic countries by residents of Western countries is subject to contagion effects: it is sensitive to terror attacks against all Western tourists and in all Islamic countries.
- Subjective well-being, as inversely measured by post-traumatic stress disorder, depression, etc., declines for both people directly affected by and

those indirectly exposed to major terror events (via general information and news media). It includes residents outside the country where an event occurs. However, the effects stay over a few weeks or a few months at most for those who are indirectly exposed. But people who are directly affected—like the injured survivors and those who lost their near and dear ones—remain mentally affected over a longer haul.

- According to Frey et al. (2009), during the period 1973/1975–2002, compared to the least terror-prone regions, the monetary equivalent of the losses of the perception of life-time satisfaction in the most terror affected regions of France and British Isles amount, respectively, to 4% and 26% of annual household income.
- According to Romanov et al. (2012), during the Second Intifada, the number of country-wide terrorism fatalities in Israel had no direct same-day effect on the life satisfaction of Jewish Israelis. The evidence of delayed reaction was minor. In contrast, the Arab citizens of Israel (Arab-Israelis) displayed a robust negative reaction to terrorism fatalities.
- *9/11* terror attacks were associated with poorer cardiovascular health.
- In the USA, *9/11* attacks led to an increase in the fetal-death sex ratio in September of 2001. In Colombia, landmine blasts (a result of planting of landmines by terror groups) during the period 1998–2003 were associated with a 0.8% decline of birth weight relative to the average weight of newborns.
- Media coverage of terror attacks affects PTSD and depression. In case of *9/11* attacks, the scene of people falling or jumping out WTC buildings was particularly harmful. Even media coverage of the first anniversary of *9/11* contributed to PTSD.
- Following the *9/11* attacks there was a substitution of air travel for road travel. Fatalities from non-commercial driving increased substantially. The Blalock et al. (2009) study estimated that between October and December of 2001, approximately 2300 road accident deaths can be attributed to this substitution effect.
- In their study of demand for bus rides and café visits in Israel during the Second Intifada period, Becker and Rubinstein (2011) showed that, as Israel witnessed several terror attacks during this period, the Israelis developed an inner resilience to overcome terror-triggered fear, because of economic motives.

Appendix to Chapter 6

6.A Individual Studies

6.A.1 Terrorism and International Trade

Using data for over 200 countries and the period 1968–1979, Nitsch and Schumacher (2004) estimate the impact of terrorism on trade as the sum of gross exports and imports. Terrorism is measured in three ways: (i) the sum of terror incidents in a pair of exporting and importing countries within a year, (ii) sum of two dummy variables, one for the exporting country and the other for the importing country (that takes value 1 if there is at least one terror attack in a year and zero otherwise), and (iii) total terror events in the exporting country and importing-country pair over the entire sample period.[58,59] According to one estimated regression equation, if terror is measured as (i) above, a doubling of terror attacks in a pair of countries reduces total bilateral trade by 4% on average.

Blomberg and Hess (2006) use data on 177 countries from 1968 to 1999 and treat *real* bilateral trade as the dependent variable.[60] Control variables include other forms of organized violence, namely internal revolutions, internal ethnic fighting and external wars.[61] The authors also construct a composite or synthetic measure of organized violence by applying the Principal Components Analysis, a technique to compress the data by reducing the dimensionality of a dataset.[62] Panel gravity regression yield that, on average, bilateral trade falls by 5.8% if a pair experiences at least one terror incident, which, under reasonable assumptions, is equivalent to a tariff equivalent of 0.65–1.46%.[63]

---

[58] In case of (i) and (iii) the regressors appear as the natural log of 1+ the sum, in order to accommodate Terror = 0 for some years.

[59] Control variables include standard gravity-model variables, indices of internal and external conflicts, defense expenditure as share of GDP and size of military.

[60] It is measured in two ways: sum of gross exports and imports in real terms, and the ratio of this sum to the product of the exporting and the importing countries' GDPs.

[61] Terrorism and other types of organized violence appear as dummy variables, taking value 1 if at least one event occurs in the exporting country, or the importing country or in both.

[62] The estimated synthetic measure is:

$$TERIF_{ijt} = 0.41873 \cdot N(T_{ijt}) + 0.04526 \cdot N(E_{ijt}) + 0.58256 \cdot R(T_{ijt}) + 0.50414 \cdot N(IF_{ijt}),$$

where N denote the standard normal value of the variable, equal to (the value a variable takes − the mean of the variable) ÷ (standard deviation of the variable in the dataset), and T, E, R, and IF, respectively, denote terrorism, external conflict, internal revolutions, and internal ethnic conflicts. Here, four different forms of violence are compressed into one composite or synthetic measure.

[63] Moreover, for a given country in a given year, on average, the presence of terrorism together with internal and external conflict—organized violence as a whole—is equivalent to as much as a 30% tariff on trade. This is indeed larger than estimated tariff-equivalent costs of border and language barriers and tariff-equivalent reduction through generalized systems of preference and WTO participation.

Mirza and Verdier (2014) explore how terrorism abroad impacts on US imports from countries that are exposed to terrorism—via how terrorism may prompt security measures undertaken by the USA and hence increased the cost of trading with the USA. To elaborate, if country X is a potential exporter of some products to the USA and faces terrorism problems, the USA would, as a response, undertake more terrorism-related security measures in that country. This would tend to increase cost of trading and hence adversely affect country X's exports to the USA. Hence, exports to the U.S. are expected to be negatively affected by terrorism in the exporting countries, reflective of the impact of security measures on international trade.

In order to proxy US counter-terror measures on which direct data is not available, the authors use the ratio of terror attacks in the exporting country i against US interests relative to total number of terror attacks worldwide during the same year, the ratio of total terror attacks worldwide against US interests relative to total number of terror attacks worldwide during the same year and other such measures as explanatory variables. The dependent variable is US bilateral imports of products in different sectors from various countries during the period 1968–2000.

To further understand the mechanism of how terrorism affects US imports, another set of regression use the share of business visas issued to individual exporting countries in the total number of visas issued to that country as the dependent variable over the years 1997–2002 for which data on business visas is available. The rationale is that business visas facilitate bilateral trade.[64]

The estimates show that a one-percent increase in the frequency of terrorism acts originating from a high terrorism origin country, say, Colombia, reduces U. S. imports from Colombia by 3%. This effect reaches as high as 10% when terrorism attacks are major in terms of claiming large number of victims (death and injuries). This high figure is an exception, however. For most cases, the elasticity of US imports is much lower. Furthermore, terrorism does have a negative impact on the share of business visas used, indicating that terrorism abroad, by prompting counter-terror measures, tends to reduce bilateral trade of the USA.

Following the Mirza-Verdier study, de Sousa et al. (2009) and de Sousa et al. (2018) pursue the idea that terrorism in individual exporting countries may not just lead to an increase security measures in those countries but in neighboring countries as well since terrorists are internationally mobile. This would tend to reduce exports from the neighboring countries too. If the neighboring countries share common language and/or religion, there is a greater likelihood of terrorism spreading to these countries and hence a greater reduction in their ability as exporters.

Empirically, this translates to the following scenario. Consider a given country j, say the USA, and its gross imports, X_{ij}, from country i. The preceding discussion implies that X_{ij} is expected to be negatively related to the extent of terrorism not only in country i but also in the countries neighboring country i (because terrorism in the neighboring countries induces more security measures in country j too). The closer the neighboring countries are in terms of common language and religion, the more severe will be this effect.

de Sousa et al. (2009) analyze US imports from different countries. The regressions include terrorism in those exporting countries as well as in the countries that share border with the exporting country, while de Sousa et al. (2018) include (bilateral) imports of many countries including the USA from other countries. For any given country as an exporter (say country i), they consider neighboring countries of three different types: those which share common border with country i (say B_i-countries), those which share common border and language (say BL_i-countries) and those which share common border, common language and common religion ((say BLR_i-countries). The focus is on how terrorism in the B_i-, BL_i-, and BLR_i-countries affect the exports from country i to other countries (j) as importers. Both de Sousa et al. (2009) and de Sousa et al. (2018) use panel estimation and find evidence supporting the negative "neighborhood effect" of terrorism on exports. For instance, de Sousa et al. (2009) find that each terror attack is estimated to reduce trade by about 1% when happening in the exporting country and by about 0.5% when happening in the exporter's neighboring (B-) countries.[65]

---

64 A variety of controls are used including standard explanatory variables in the gravity equations for bilateral trade as well as indicators of military disputes and internal security.

65 Mores specifically, the estimated equation by de Sousa et al. (2009) is:

Using monthly data on the exports of 31 OECD countries to 181 OECD and non-OECD countries over the period from January 1970 to December 2008, Egger and Gassebner (2015) estimate the impact of contemporaneous as well as lagged effects of terrorism in the exporting and importing countries on bilateral trade.[66] The main result is that international terrorism displays effects on bilateral and multilateral trade only in the medium run (more than one and a half years after an attack-/incident). The short-run impact of international terror on trade appears very small, if not negligible.

In the latest of the research papers reviewed here, Bandopadhyay et al. (2018) depart from the earlier literature by allowing domestic and transnational terrorism separately and distinguishing between trade in manufactured goods and trade in primary products. Three measures of trade are considered: gross exports, gross imports and total trade (which is the sum of the two). Further it uses a joint indicator of terrorism in an export-country-importing-country pair, one for domestic terrorism and another for transnational terrorism. The authors' sample period is 1995–2012 which corresponds to dominance of religiously fundamental terror groups.

Terrorism does not affect trade of primary products but does affect that of manufactured goods. Both domestic and transnational terrorism have a detrimental effect on manufactured imports. On average, a 1% increase in domestic (respectively, transnational) terrorist incidents either in the exporting country or importing country reduces total trade of manufacturing by 0.025% (respectively, 0.013%).

6.A.2 Terrorism and Foreign Direct Investment

Enders and Sandler (1996) is probably the first econometric study on the impact of terrorism on FDI. They estimated how much the real net FDIs (NFDIs) into Spain and Greece were impacted by terrorist attacks in the respective countries.[67] Their sample period was from mid-1970s to 1991 and time-series VAR was the estimation method. Terror incidents led a decline in NFDI into Spain and Greece by about half a billion US dollars amounting to 13.5% of NFDI for Spain and 11.9% for Greece—equivalent to 7.6% and 34.8% of annual gross fixed capital formation for Spain and Greece, respectively.

Abadie and Gardeazabal (2008) analyze the impact of terrorism on NFDI positions of countries in a global context. Instead of the number of fatalities or injuries from terror incidents, terrorism is represented by a terrorist risk index for different countries, along with other controls like indices of country risk, indices of capital flows and foreign investment restrictions and regional dummies. The ratio of NFDI to GDP in the year 2003 is regressed against the terrorism index and the controls. On average, a one-standard-deviation increase in the terrorist risk (equivalent to an increase in terrorism risk from the level of Italy to the level of the USA) is associated with a fall in the NFDI of about 5% of GDP. Further, terrorism reduces the expected return to foreign investment and increases the uncertainty of returns to foreign investment.

Instead of NFDI of individual countries, Blomberg and Mody (2005) attempt to explain *bilateral* FDI flows that can be attributed to terrorism and violence in general. An index of violence

---

$$
\begin{aligned}
m^s_{it} &= a + \text{unobserved country-specific effects} + \text{unobserved time-specific effects} \\
&\quad + \boldsymbol{a} \cdot \text{gravity variables} + b_1 \cdot incid_{it} + b_2 \cdot neighbor - incid_{it} + \epsilon_{ist},
\end{aligned}
$$

where i denotes the country that exports to the USA, s is the sector or the product and "incid" denotes the number of terror incidents. The parameters of importance are b_1 and b_2, both expected to be negative and significant. The numbers 1% and 0.5% refer to the estimates of b_1 and b_2, respectively.

The studies by de Sousa et al. (2009) and de Sousa et al. (2018), respectively, cover the period 1993–2002 and 1997–2007. The gravity variables include dummies for regional trade arrangements and currency union.

[66] They use general equilibrium estimation of the gravity model *a la* Baier and Bergstrand (2009), which differs substantially from Eq. (6.3).

[67] NFDI equals gross inflow during a period, typically a year, minus receipts from the repatriation of capital and repayment of loans and plus reinvested earnings, etc.

is constructed as a weighted average of terror incidents and incidences of internal conflict and external wars. The regressions included terrorism and violence in both exporting and importing countries. Estimating a gravity-type model yields that all three forms of violence—terrorism, external conflicts and external wars—are harmful to global investment. As one would expect, violence in the source country has a positive impact on investment outflow, while that in the host country reduces the inflow of investment (as well as international trade).

The USA is the largest investor in the world in terms of FDI outflow, and, at the same time, the US interests have been some of the major targets of terrorism in many parts of the world. Enders et al. (2006) study how the US FDI abroad was affected by attacks on US interest abroad during1989–1999 as well as *9/11* attacks. Using the time-series intervention analysis (General Appendix B, Sect. B.13.2), the authors found that *9/11* generally had little lasting influence on US FDI outflow. Only a few countries that experienced subsequent terrorist attacks displayed a post-*9/11* drop in the US FDI flows into those countries.[68]

Furthermore, the results of estimation of the effect of transnational terrorism against US interest on the stock of US FDI during 1989–1999 indicate minor or no significant effects.[69] In the regressions, terror is measured in three ways: number of events, casualties, and deaths.

As mentioned earlier, FDI is a major source of total investment and growth for developing countries. Bandopadhyay et al. (2014) studied how terrorism in developing countries affect FDI flows.[70] As mentioned in the text, a novelty in their analysis lies in considering the role of foreign aid in the causal link between terrorism and FDI. Eq. (6.4) is their main equation of estimation. Both domestic and transnational terrorism significantly affect FDI in developing countries. A one-standard-deviation increase in domestic terror incidents per 100,000 people reduces NFDI between $324 million and $513 million for the average sample GDP country, while a one-standard-deviation increase in transnational terror incidents per 100,000 people reduces NFDI between $296 million and $736 million.[71] In particular, the negative effects on NFDI are less severe in the presence of foreign aid. For example, the aforementioned lower estimate of NFDI loss from domestic terrorism of $324 million is reduced to about $113 million for the average aid-receiving nation, while the lower estimate of loss due to transnational terrorism is reduced to about $45 million from $296 million.

6.A.3 *9/11* Attacks and Financial Markets

As one of the earliest studies, Carter and Simkins (2004) investigated the returns on the stocks of airlines (American, Delta, Northwest, United, etc.) and air-freight carriers (Airborne Express, FedEx, UPS, etc.) in the first day of trading after *9/11*, that is, September 17, 2001. They found negative excess returns for the airline stocks and even negative returns for air-freight firms. However, Drakos (2004) estimated that the airline stocks recovered their full value in less than a year after *9/11* (see their Table 3).

Chen and Siems (2004), who studied the short-term global stock-market reactions to several cataclysmic events during the period 1915–2001, found statistically significant and negative impacts of *9/11* attacks on the US stock-market returns up to six working days after September 11, but the

---

[68] In term of FDI inflow, in Spain it actually increased by $6 billion in 2005 following the 2004 Madrid train bombings and by another $11 billion in 2006 (Institute for Economics & Peace, 2014b). It means that single events do not affect FDI inflow, while it does not mean that terrorism encourages FDI inflow.

[69] Terror attacks against US interests abroad lowered US FDI by 1% in the OECD countries, but had no statistically significant effect in non-OECD nations. Only Greece and Turkey (OECD members) suffered relatively large damages, amounting to US FDI reductions of 5.7% and 6.5%, respectively.

[70] Their sample contains data on 78 developing countries over the period 1984–2008.

[71] The loss of FDI, however, was much smaller when calculated at the median value of GDP in the sample.

abnormal negative returns became statistically insignificant by eleven days after the event. Global capital markets also reacted to *9/11* attacks in a similar fashion: strong immediate effects, but statistically insignificant in most global markets after eleven days. The world stock indices recovered their lost value within 30–40 days.

Using stock-market indices from thirty three industrial and emerging economies, Richman et al. (2005) obtained statistically significant negative short-run reaction to *9/11* attacks in twenty eight stock markets in the sample.

Hon et al. (2004) analyzed stock prices in twenty five countries with the objective of finding contagion effects of *9/11* attacks across global markets. Following the crisis, international stock markets, particularly those in Europe, responded closely to United States stock-market shocks.

Nikkinen et al. (2008) considered stock markets of fifty-three countries, including developed economies, emerging markets as well as the MENA (Middle East and North Africa) that is typically ignored in financial-market-impact studies of terrorism. Using daily stock indices and covering the period from March 10, 2001 to March 12 2002, the authors compared the behavior of stock markets in six different regions before and after the September 11 attacks. The results indicated short-run negative effects and increased volatility across the markets. Moreover, the impact of attacks varied across geographic regions, depending on the degree of their integration into the global economy. Less integrated regions such as the MENA seemed to be less exposed.

6.A.4 Stock-Market Effects of Madrid and London Bombings and Boston Marathon Bombing

Kollias et al. (2011) estimated the impacts of Madrid train Bombing in 2004 and London train bombing in 2005 on the Spanish and London stock markets, respectively. The two attacks shared the common characteristics that the bombings targeted the transport system of the respective capitals. The study used daily prices of the three major stock exchanges in Spain (Madrid, Valencia, and Barcelona) and the London Stock Exchange, and investigated the impact of these events on the general and sector indices.[72] The main findings were that the terrorist events significantly and negatively impacted on the abnormal returns of stocks across most sectors in the Spanish markets but not so in the London stock market; furthermore, the market rebounded more quickly in London than in Spain and the impacts were transitory in general.

Baumert et al. (2013) is the only study, or one of the few that has analyzed the stock-market impact of Boston bombings in 2013. It measured the impact of this event on a number of international financial markets (Frankfurt, London, Madrid, Paris, Milan, New York, and Tokyo) and compared with the impact of the *9/11* attacks, 2004 bombings in Madrid and 2005 bombings in London. The central finding was that the market indices exhibited statistically significant negative abnormal returns on the day of the Boston marathon bombing event, but the losses were smaller than those following the previous three prominent terror attacks.

6.A.5 Terrorism and Tourism

Enders and Sandler (1991) was the first to estimate econometrically the impact of transnational terrorism in Spain on tourists visiting Spain during the period 1970–1988. Using monthly data, their main finding was that one additional transnational attack would, over years, reduce the number of tourists to Spain by more than 140,000. This implies that 18 international terrorist events that occurred in Spain in 1988 would have scared away 2.5 million tourists.[73]

---

[72] The sample period for the Madrid event was April 2003 to March 2005 (500 trading days) and that for the London event was June 2004 to June 2006 (500 trading days).

[73] One can argue that there may be a reverse causality: disorganized and insecure tourist facilities can encourage terrorist attacks. The authors showed that terrorism impacts on the inflow of tourists, not the vice versa.

Enders et al. (1992) estimated the impact of terrorism on the loss of tourism revenue for Western European countries, especially, Greece, Italy, and Austria, for years 1974–1988. The estimated revenue losses were large, collectively amounting to 572 million to 3.372 billion Special Drawing Rights (SDRs) for the three countries combined.[74] For the whole of Western Europe, there was an estimated revenue loss of over $16 billion. A similar time-series analysis was undertaken by Sloboda (2003) for tourism in the USA and terrorism within the USA over the period 1998–2001. His results indicate that the effect of terrorism on the tourist receipts dissipated quickly over time.

An econometric demand-supply model for the Israeli hotel industry over the years 1987–1999 was formulated by Fleischer and Buccola (2002). One finding is that the foreign demand for Israeli hotels was moderately sensitive to terrorist events. Pizam and Fleischer (2002) studied the impact of terrorism on tourism demand (the number of tourists) in Israel during the period May 1991–May 2001. Between the two indices of terrorism considered, namely the severity and the frequency of terror attacks, the frequency of attacks exerted a larger decline in international tourist arrivals.[75]

Drakos and Kutan (2003) examined the impact of terrorism on the share of tourists in three Mediterranean countries—Greece, Israel, and Turkey—for the period 1991–2000 during which all three countries were severely troubled by terrorist attacks.[76] The study emphasized the spillover or contagion effects, e.g., how terrorist attacks in Turkey may affect tourism in Greece and Israel. By the substitution effect, tourism revenues in Israel would tend to increase if there are more terror attacks in, say, Turkey. However, risk-aversion would imply that tourism revenues would tend to decline in both Turkey and Israel as tourists may want to stay away from the entire region. The findings constituted the evidence of both substitution and risk-aversion spillover effects—thus significant own and spillover effects of terrorist activity—on the tourism market shares of these three countries.

Yaya (2009) studied the effect of terrorism on the number of tourists visiting Turkey from January 1997 to December 2006.[77] Using time-series methods, the results indicate a negative but small impact of terrorism. During 1997–2006, terrorist attacks in Turkey accounted for a decline of six million foreign tourists.

In a relatively recent study, van Ballegooij and Bakowski (2018) analyze the impact of terrorism in the E.U. on the tourists arriving in the E.U. over the period 1990–2016. It uses terrorism index of countries constructed by the Institute of Economics and Peace (IEP). One unit increase in the IEP terrorism index for a month is associated with 1.6% reduction in tourist arrivals and 2.3% decrease in the nights stayed.[78]

---

[74] One SDR was roughly equal to $1.38 US dollars. SDRs are monetary units used by the International Monetary Fund (IMF) during that period.

[75] Frequency was measured by the number of terror attacks, while severity was represented by an index based on the number of deaths and injuries from the attacks.

[76] Italy was included as a bench-mark, such that the respective shares are defined in reference to the total number of tourists in the four countries combined.

[77] Turkey began to be significantly affected by terrorism in the early 1980s. Between 1985 and 2006, three types of terrorist groups were active in Turkey: Kurdish terror groups, radical Islamic groups and leftist terror groups.

[78] The empirical model is:

$$\ln y_{it} = a + b_1 \cdot T_{it} + b_2 \cdot T_{it-1} + b_3 \cdot T_{it-2} + b_4 \cdot T_{it-3} + \boldsymbol{\beta Z} + \epsilon_{it},$$

where y_{it} is the monthly number of arrivals or nights spent in tourist accommodations for non-residents in country i and year t, T_{it} is the IEP terrorism index and the vector $\boldsymbol{Z}$ denotes the control variables. The model estimates include $\hat{b}_1 = -0.0162$ for ln (arrivals) and -0.0228 for ln (nights), which, respectively, correspond to the percentage figures cited.

6.B Compensating Surplus to Measure the Monetary Equivalence of the Effect of Terrorism on Life Satisfaction in Model of Frey et al. (2009)

By definition,

$$LS_{ir}(m_{i0}, T_{r0}) = LS_{ir}(m_{i0} + CS, T_{r1}) \quad \text{or } LS_{ir}(m_{i0}, T_{r0}) - LS_{ir}(m_{i0} + CS, T_{r1}) = 0,$$

where the notation $LS_{ir}(m_{i0}, T_{r0})$ denotes the life satisfaction indicator associate with income m_{i0} and terror level T_{i0}, CS stands for compensation surplus and $LS_{ir}(m_{i0} + CS, T_{r1})$ denotes the life satisfaction indicator with income $m_{i0} + CS$ and terror level T_{i1}. Referring to Eq. (6.7), the above equation is written as

$$\hat{b}_1 \cdot T_{r0} + \hat{b}_2 \cdot \ln m_{i0} - \hat{b}_1 \cdot T_{r1} + \hat{b}_2 \cdot \ln(m_{i0} + CS) = 0,$$

which simplifies to

$$\frac{m_{i0}}{m_{i0} + \text{CS}} = \exp\left(\frac{\hat{b}_1 \cdot \Delta T}{\hat{b}_2}\right), \text{ where } \Delta T \equiv T_{r1} - T_{r0} \equiv \text{Increase in Terror.}$$

In turn,

$$\text{CS} = m_{i0}\left[\exp\left(-\frac{\hat{b}_1 \cdot \Delta T}{\hat{b}_2}\right) - 1\right], \tag{6.8}$$

the solution expression for the compensating surplus.

Questions

6.1 Briefly describe the construction of a "synthetic economy" without terrorism *a la* Abadie and Gardeazabal (2003). Why is it useful in estimating the impact of terrorism?

6.2 What is the Eckstein-Tsiddon terrorism index? What are its limitations in your opinion?

6.3 During a year, a hypothetical economy experiences 100 terror attacks causing 300 deaths and 500 injuries. Computer the Eckstein-Tsiddon terrorism index for the economy for that year.

6.4 Briefly explains different channels through which terrorism may adversely affect international trade in goods and direct foreign investment.

6.5 "Financial markets remain depressed for a long time after a terror attack." Defend or refute.

6.6 By using examples, explain how media coverage of terrorist events contribute to mental well-being of people.

Part III

Behavior, Organization and Survival of Terror Groups

Chapter 7

Behavior, Internal Organization, and Survival of Terror Groups

7.1 Introduction

How do we "model" or think of a terror organization in the lens of economic analysis? This chapter builds an answer:

a terrorist organization is similar to a firm.

Similarity is not the same as total equivalence. There are dissimilarities. A coffee shop in your neighborhood, a financial firm on the Wall Street, Microsoft Corporation or Amazon is not exactly like IRA or al-Qaeda. An obvious difference, among others, is that a terrorist organization is a non-state illegal entity. Apprehension of the leadership and rank and file for being caught is a constant worry. This is not a typical headache for legitimate business or firm in operation. However, similar to a business or a firm, a terrorist group employs resources like labor services (terrorist operatives), equipment (capital), raw materials (bombs, chemicals, etc.), and so on. It has a leader like CEO of a company. It raises funds in various ways. What does a terrorist group "produce"?

Terrorist attacks.

In turn,

terror attacks produce damage, both physical (injuries, death and property damage) and psychological (fear and anxiety).

We know from Chap. 1 that generating public fear is a hallmark of terrorism as a distinct form of violent activity.

Moreover, terrorist groups are not isolated from one another. Like firms in a business sector that compete and sometimes cooperate with each other, different terror organizations compete for dominance and prominence and strive to build and

S. P. Das, *Economics of Terrorism and Counter-Terrorism Measures*,
https://doi.org/10.1007/978-3-030-96577-8_7

expand their support base—and at times, they coordinate certain activities together. We begin our study on terror groups by noting examples of *rivalry and cooperation* among them in Sect. 7.2.

We often depict the inside of a business corporation as a network of individuals. Some are "connected" with a small number of people in terms of active interaction and reporting, while others are linked with a large number of people. There are delegations of tasks, which are, on the one hand, necessary, but, on the other hand, raise motivational and incentive issues. For instance, a salesperson may have been asked to visit 100 homes in a week, but he may have visited only 80 homes. A rental manager is hired to attend repair jobs in an apartment complex as quickly as possible, but he may be doing it in a leisurely fashion. The same holds for terror organizations.

Large terror groups are very often described as (terrorist) networks. In Sect. 7.3, we first learn the basic concepts of network theory, a branch of mathematics. We then analyze a few real-world terrorist networks in the light of these concepts. In Sect. 7.4, we view a terrorist organization as hierarchical, in which there is delegation of tasks from individuals higher up in ranks to those in lower ranks. Delegation entails problems. For example, a group of terrorist operatives may have been advised to minimize injury to public while killing policemen in duty in a busy street, but some of the operatives may not use restraint. Similar to workflow inside firms, delegation issues pose organizational challenges for terror groups.

An important policy implication is that counter-terrorism measures must interpret the behavioral response of terror organizations in the light of organizational difficulties and use tools that can make these challenges more difficult for terror groups.

Just as there are small, mid-size, and large firms, there are small and large terror groups. In a market economy, there is typically a high turnover of small firms. Only a small fraction of firms are able to grow to become big. The same holds for terror groups. As noted in Chap. 3, Sect. 3.3.9.2, a large percentage of terror organizations are *one-hit wonders* (associated with one attack only) and less than 50% of terror organizations "live" beyond one year. In the media, we hear and read about those "few" who survive for longer periods. Section 7.5 reviews empirical evidence on the types of ending of terrorist organizations and the determinants of their longevity.

7.2 Rivalry and Cooperation Among Terror Groups

In a market economy, firms compete with each other. In the global smart phone market, Apple, Samsung, Huawei, and many other compete with one another. In the auto market, General Motors, Tesla, Honda, Toyota, BMW, and many other well-known companies are rivals of one another. FedEx, DHL, UPS, and various national postal services compete in the express delivery market.

At the same time, competing firms exhibit cooperative behavior as well. In the pharmaceutical industry, there are numerous instances of R&D collaboration in national and international markets. As specific examples (see Banerjee & Siebert, 2015), in early 2000s, three companies, Tanox, Novartis, and Genentech, jointly worked to select and develop anti-Immunoglobulin E antibodies; in 2011, the pharmaceutical companies Takeda Ltd. and XOMA Ltd. signed an R&D cooperation at the early stage of drug development process for developing a monoclonal antibody in the oncology market.

Industry magazines and websites provide useful information and analysis that benefit all firms in the industry (as well as interested public). In the oil sector, magazines include Oil & Gas Monthly, Oil & Gas Journal, and many others. Auto-sector magazines and websites include Automotive Industries and Automotive News (https://www.autonews.com). These are cooperative projects.

Sometimes, firms collude illegally by engaging price fixing, bid rigging, etc. Court convictions abound. For instance, in 2007, British Airways was fined £121.5 million by the Office of Fair Trading in England for colluding with Virgin Atlantic. Later, British Airways was fined $300 million by the US Department of Justice. As reported by Geis (1967), back in 1961, in an anti-trust case, a federal district court imposed a fine totaling $1,924,500 on twenty-nine electrical manufacturing companies and forty-five individuals for fixing prices and rigging bids on heavy electrical equipment.

In a similar vein, rivalry as well as cooperation exist between terror groups. Some examples of rivalry and cooperation are in order.

7.2.1 Armed Rivalry

There are terror groups whose objectives are almost opposite of each other. Rivalry between them falls into the category of *inter-field rivalry*, e.g., between left-wing and right-wing groups. Those with similar objectives also fight with one another in order to gain supremacy and public support from the same group of sympathizers. This is *intra-field rivalry*, e.g., Hamas versus Fatah and Shining Path versus the Túpac Amaru Revolutionary Movement.[1]

7.2.1.1 Examples of Inter-Field Rivalry

As FARC started to control coca production in Colombia and imposed taxes, ranchers, drug traffickers, and some self-defense groups started to fight with leftist groups. Many left-leaning politicians, union leaders, and common people were killed. FARC intensified its attack on the self-defense, right-wing, paramilitary groups in the late 1980s. The rivalry and attacks-and-counter-attacks continued into the 1990s. Several groups combined their resources and manpower to form The United Self-Defense Forces of Colombia (AUC) in 1997 to counter leftist groups. AUC was prominent and engaged in armed conflict with FARC. The rivalry between them spilled over to the 2000s. In the year 2000, AUC foiled the peace talks between the Colombian

[1] The terms "inter-field" and "intra-field" are borrowed from Phillips (2015).

government and leftist groups. It also fought with the National Liberation Army (ELN), the second largest leftist terror group in Colombia.[2]

From Chap. 2, recall that the Provisional Irish Republican Army (PIRA) became a separate entity in 1969. Since then it fought with the Ulster Volunteer Force (UVF) (formed in the mid-1960s) and the Ulster Defence Association (UDA) that came into existence in 1971. Both UVF and UDA are Loyalist groups that supported Northern Ireland to be a part of the UK. Along with killing unaffiliated civilians, PIRA on the one hand and UDA/UVF on the other engaged in attacks and counter-attacks against each other. Rivalries continued well into the 1990s.

In Spain, ETA, which demanded autonomy for the Basque Country in Spain, fought with Anti-Terrorist Liberation Groups (GAL), a paramilitary group; see Chap. 2.

During the Syrian civil war, not only did the USA and allied forces counter ISIS (and the Syrian government), at least five terrorists groups were battling with ISIS. They include PKK, Hezbollah, Kata'ib Hezbollah, al-Qaeda and al-Nusra. ISIS's fights with the first three belong to the category of inter-field rivals.[3]

7.2.1.2 Example of Intra-Field Rivalry

The FARC and the ELN, both leftist groups and, respectively, the first and the second largest terror group in Colombia, periodically fought with each other. There are no detailed accounts of this intra-field rivalry, but they are briefly cited by various authors at various points of time, e.g., the mention of bloody confrontations between the two groups in the early 2000s (InSight Crime, 2020) and in the oil-rich region of Arauca in 2009 (Hennigan, 2009). Fights between ELN and the dissident faction of FARC that was opposed to the 2016 peace treaty between the FARC and the Colombian government took place in the Magui Payan city of Nariño in 2017 (Daily Sabah, 2017).

In the early 1970s, late 1990s, and 2000s, the Loyalist groups, UDA and the UVF, in Northern Ireland also fought with each other (see Coogan, 1995 and van Um, 2016). On the Republican side, the PIRA fought with the Original IRA in the 1970s, and, later, it had fights with splinter groups like the Irish National Liberation Army (INLA) and the Irish People's Liberation Organization (IPLO), who were opposed to negotiations with the British. INLA also fought with IPLO (van Um, 2016, Chapter 3).

Returning to ISIS, it faced hostility from al-Qaeda and al-Nusra, who had similar objectives like a fundamentalist, pan-Islamic state (Caliphate), and global jihadism. This is a prime example of intra-field rivalry in recent times. It arose because al-Qaeda and al-Nusra resented ISIS's indiscriminate brutal killings and an over-driven territorial ambition. Such an extreme approach, they believed, would undermine their

[2] An agreement between the Colombian government and AUC was reached in 2005. The group effectively disbanded 2006. Since 2006, small groups perpetrated attacks claiming to be the AUC.

[3] PKK stood against ISIS, partly because ISIS tortured thousands of Yazidis (mostly women), who are an ethic minority within the Kurdish population. Hezbollah and Kata'ib Hezbollah are Shi'ite groups who support the Assad regime and thus are opposed to ISIS; see Tharoor (2014b).

cause as it would invite hostility from the global community including Muslims. This happened indeed. The meteoric rise of ISIS was followed by a precipitous fall in a span of two to three years.

7.2.2 Cooperation Among Terror Groups

In August 2001, three men were arrested at the Bogota international airport. They had spent about a month in the rebels-dominated regions of Colombia. Tests on clothes they were wearing indicated traces of explosives and cocaine. They were identified as James Monaghan, Martin McCauley, and Niall Connolly, all from Ireland. Colombian authorities charged that they were traveling with false passports, and, while in Colombia had trained FARC guerillas on bomb making. The three denied the charges, saying that they were ecotourists and observers of the peace process between the Colombian government and FARC.

According to Jordan (2002) and other sources, the first two had links with IRA. James Monaghan was the inventor of the first homemade mortar known as Jim "Mortar" Monaghan. According to police reports in Ireland, he was the head of the engineering with PIRA and McCauley was his deputy. Niall Connolly was affiliated in Sinn Féin but based in Cuba.

In 2003, a trial court in Colombia gave its verdict that all were traveling under false passports, while they were found "not guilty" on charges of helping FARC. Sentences up to 44 months in jail and fines were meted out. They were not jailed but asked to stay in Colombia, while the prosecution challenged the verdict in the appeals court. In December 2004, the appeals court overturned the trial court's decision and sentenced them a seventeen-year prisoner term. The three later became known as *Colombia Three.* As in crime thrillers, the day after the conviction, the Attorney General of Colombia reported that three had escaped from Colombia. The legal case persisted, while the Colombia Three stayed free in Ireland as Ireland and Colombia do not have an extradition treaty. Finally, in 2020, a Colombian special court granted them amnesty, citing no evidence that "the three had been part of a terrorist group." Moreover, it was noted that none of the crimes for which they were convicted at the time had any victims. For this reason, a full amnesty would be issued. This was a controversial decision. Strong suspicions over the trio's involvement with FARC continue to remain. A US Congress Report back in 2002 ("The Nexus among Terrorists, Nacrotics, Traffickers, Weapons Proliferators, and Organized Crime Networks in Western Europe" by Glen E. Curtis and Tara Karacan) said that, according to the British intelligence reports, the FARC paid IRA operatives about "US$2 million for training in arms, explosives, and techniques of urban warfare, using offshore bank accounts." If true, it is an example of cooperation between terror groups.

There are other examples of cooperation among terrorist groups. Several instances of terror group alliance and cooperation are listed by Karmon (2005). In 1970, seven or eight members of the West German Red Army Faction (RAF) went to Jordan and Lebanon to receive training in Fatah camps. There was cooperation between Revolutionäre Zellen (RZ), also a left-leaning terror group in West Germany and the Palestinian groups in the 1970s. The Italian Red Brigades partnered with PLO in the 1970s. Its members were trained and fugitives were assured shelter by PLO. In return, the Red Brigades would store weapons for PLO in Italy and participate in attacks against Israelis in Italy (Karmon, 2005, Chapter 4).[4] The Japanese Red Army leader Fusako Shigenobu fought with the PFLP in the 1970s. Her association with Palestinian groups lasted over two to three decades.

In 2001, the allied forces in Afghanistan found al-Qaeda blueprint documents on a planned attack in Singapore by Jemaah Islamiyah, a proof of alliance between the two groups (Horowitz and Potter, 2014). Tankel (2009) describes cooperation between Lashkar-e-Taiba (LeT), based in Pakistan, with other groups. For instance, it aided al-Qaeda operatives to escape from Afghanistan after the US occupation of Afghanistan in 2001 and, allegedly, helped AQI in its recruitment drive. In course of its campaign against India, its main target, and Kashmir in particular, LeT took help of local terrorists rather than used its own personnel and resources. According to the Indian government, many terrorists apprehended or killed in Kashmir were either trained by LeT or secured ammunition from it.[5] Ties between LeT and Hizbul Mujahideen, a separatist group in Jammu & Kashmir, are well-known.

It is important to know that coordination between terror groups leads to learning of tactics. As noted by Horowitz (2010), Bin Laden sent his men to Hezbollah, a Shi'ite Muslim group, in Lebanon to learn the art of suicide attacks, although "his" al-Qaeda was a Sunni group.

In sum,

Is That So? 7.1: Rivalry and Cooperation among Terror Groups

Similar to firms within an industry or across industries, there are rivalries among terrorist groups with similar objectives and among those with opposite objectives, except that the rivalries are violent. At the same time, like firms and industries, terrorist groups exhibit cooperative behavior too.

7.3 Terrorist Networks

We commonly describe *large* terror groups in terms of cells and networks, meaning how the terrorists *within* a group are "connected" with one another. Networks exist *across* terror groups too. This is again similar to the business world where networks exist within and across firms in any given industry—and even across industries. Two (hypothetical) examples of within-firm networks are illustrated in Fig. 7.1. Panel (a) is a top-down, hierarchical network, whereas panel (b) is a "hub-spoke" network. There are other kinds of networks too. Internet is itself a huge global network.

[4] Karmon (2005) also analyzes cooperation among the European leftist groups.

[5] In December 2007, Riyazuddin Nasir, alias Mohammed Ghouse, a native of Hyderabad, India, was arrested while planning a series of blasts on the crowded beaches of Goa, a famous beach town along the west coast of India. He was apparently targeting American and Israeli tourists (Tankel, 2009, Page 22).

Computers and other communication devices within a home are also a network. The list goes on.

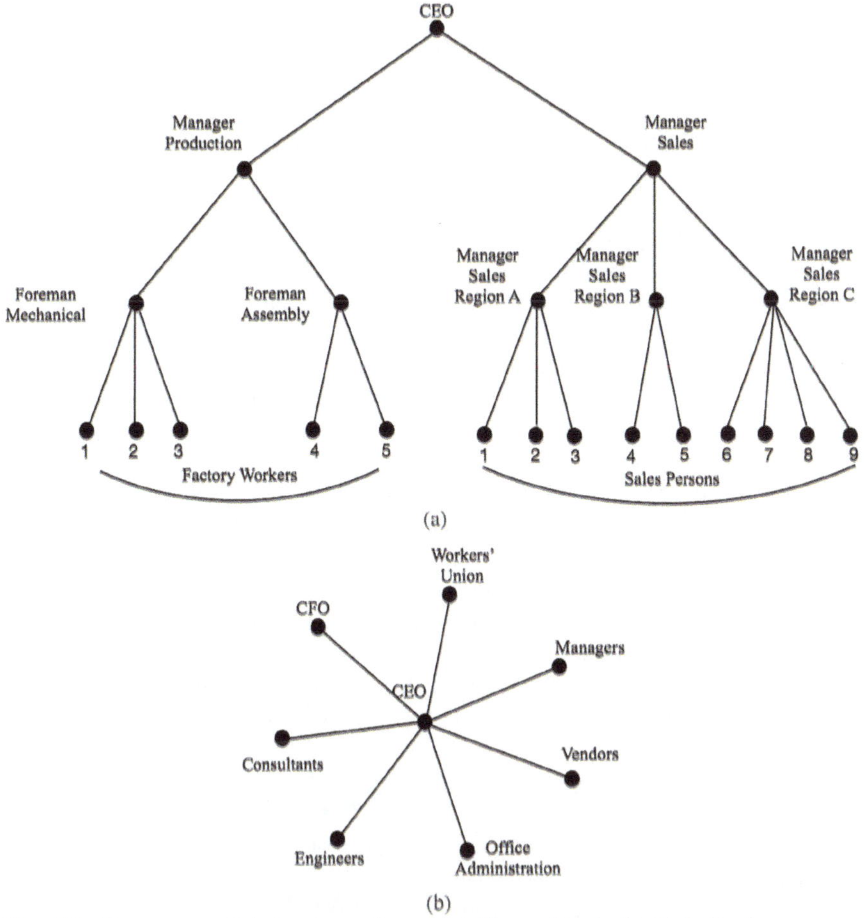

Fig. 7.1: Networks within business firms. (**a**) Hierarchical. (**b**) Hub-Spoke

There is a branch of mathematics called the ***network theory***. We will first review some preliminary concepts associated with it and then look at two terrorist networks in the light of these concepts.

7.3.1 Basic Concepts of Network Theory

Network theory captures relationships and connections between two individuals or units in a multi-individual or unit setting and borrows concepts from what is called the ***graph theory***. There is not really any difference between the network theory and the graph theory except that the latter is abstract and deals with graphical structures in general, whereas the former is invoked in a particular context. The most elementary concept in network theory is a ***a node*** ("vertex" in graph theory), which represents an individual or unit. A network is a collection of nodes (individuals) that are "connected" to some other nodes. A terrorist cell can be interpreted as a node in a terrorist network.

In Fig. 7.1a, there are altogether twenty-two nodes: the CEO, the two managers, the two foremen, the four sales managers, the five factor workers, and the nine salespersons. The connection is hierarchical. The CEO is connected with two managers, whereas the managers have their subordinates and the subordinates have their own subordinates. In Fig. 7.1b depicts a less hierarchical network of eight nodes with the CEO at the center, who is directly connected with all other nodes. The latter report to or communicate with the CEO only, while they are not connected among themselves. It has a hub-spokes look.

Our next concept is a ***link*** ("edge" in graph theory). Two nodes are said to be linked if they "communicate" or are linked with each other either directly or through other nodes. If it is direct, then it is ***direct link***. In Fig. 7.1a, the CEO is directly linked to the production manager and the sales manager, while she/he is *not* directly linked to factory workers or salespersons. But she/he is indirectly linked to them via managers, foremen, and sales managers.

Direct links are bilateral. This implies that the maximum number of direct links that is possible must equal "N combination 2," where N is the total number of nodes in a network.[6] That is,

Result 7.1

In a network with N nodes, the maximum possible number of direct links is equal to

$$^{N}C_2 = \frac{N!}{2!(N-2)!} = \frac{N(N-1)}{2}.$$

An ***indirect link*** is defined as follows: if node A is directly linked to node B and node B is directly linked to node C, but nodes A and C are not directly linked, then nodes A and C are indirectly linked. In Fig. 7.1b, the CEO is directly linked with each of the seven nodes (and vice versa). Nodes other than the CEO are only indirectly linked to one another (through the CEO).

We may denote a direct link or an indirect link between two nodes by •–• and ∘–∘, capturing "direct communication" and "indirect communication." For instance, in Fig. 7.1a, Mechanical foreman •–• Factory workers 1, 2, or 3, and CEO ∘–∘

[6] This is equivalent to the total number of possible pairs among N objects.

Mechanical foreman. In Fig. 7.1b, CEO ●–● Workers' Union, CEO ●–● CFO, and so on, while Worker's Union ○–○ CFO, Vendors ○–○ CFO, Engineers ○–○ Consultants, etc. Depending on how nodes in a network are connected or not connected, networks are named differently.

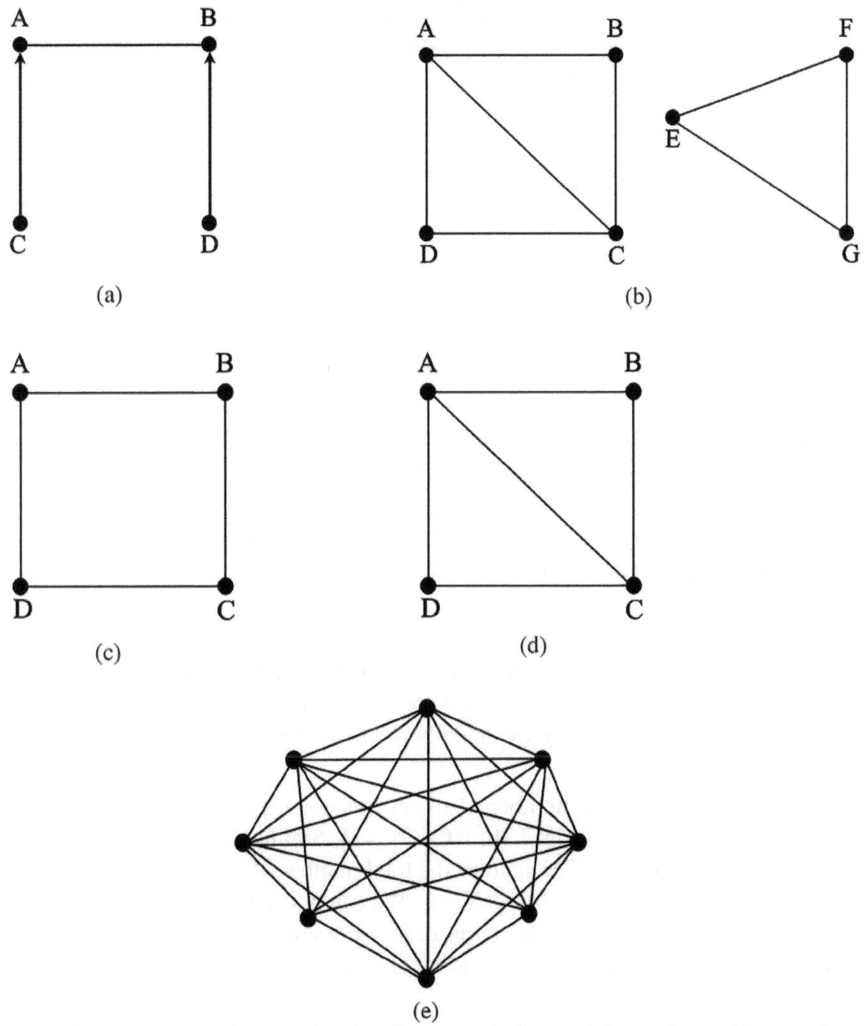

Fig. 7.2: Categories of networks. (**a**) Connected, directed, irregular and incomplete. (**b**) Disconnected, undirected, irregular and incomplete. (**c**) Connected, undirected, regular and incomplete. (**d**) Connected, undirected, irregular and incomplete. (**e**) Connected, undirected, regular and complete

Connected Versus Disconnected Networks A network is connected if any two nodes have a direct or an indirect link between them; otherwise, it is a disconnected network. All graphs in Fig. 7.2 are connected, except panel (b). By definition, nodes A through G constitute a single network in Fig. 7.2b.

Directed Versus Undirected Network A network is directed if there are at least two nodes among which the relationship is asymmetric. For example, if we are interested to understand an extended family network or family history and know who is a child of whom, we can capture the link between parent A and child B by line between the two nodes with an arrow pointing toward B. This is an example of a directed network.[7] All panels in Fig. 7.2 except panel (a) are undirected. *From now on, we will not be concerned with directed networks. By a network, we will mean an undirected network.*

Regular Versus Irregular Network A network is regular if the number of direct links is the same for all nodes; otherwise, it is irregular. In Fig. 7.2, panels (c) and (e) are regular networks, and the rest are irregular.

Complete Versus Incomplete Networks A network is complete if any two nodes are directly linked. Otherwise, it is an incomplete network. Figure 7.2e is an example of a complete network, and others are not.

We now discuss notions that capture the degree of connectedness of individual nodes and the network as a whole.

Neighborhood of a Node It is the set of nodes that are *directly* linked to the node in question. For instance, in Fig. 7.1b, the neighborhood of CEO is the set {CFO, Workers' Union, Managers, Vendors, Office Administration, Engineers and Consultants}. In Fig. 7.2a and d, respectively, the neighborhood of A is {B, C} and {B, C, D}.

Degree of a Node It is the number of direct links or neighbors associated with a node. Denoting it by r, in Fig. 7.1b, $r(\text{CEO}) = 7$. Similarly, $r(\text{A})$ in Fig. 7.2a is 2 and $r(\text{A})$ in Fig. 7.2d is 3. If N denotes the total number of nodes in a network, it is obvious that for any node v, $r(v) \leq N - 1$. We can normalize the degree of a node by dividing it by $N - 1$, the maximum degree possible for any node. That is, the normalized degree of node v is equal to $r^n(v) \equiv r(v)/(N - 1)$.

Cluster Coefficient of a Node This is a measure of clusterness around a node. As before, let $r(v)$ denote the number of neighbors or degree of node v. Among the neighbors only, ${}^{r(v)}C_2 = r(v)(r(v) - 1)/2$ is the maximum possible number of direct links. Additionally, let $k(v)$ denote the actual number of direct links among the $r(v)$ neighbors of a node. The cluster coefficient of node v, say $c(v)$, is equal to the actual

[7] Another example will be the network of animals in a forest in terms of predators and preys.

number of direct links divided by the maximum possible number of direct links among the neighbors; that is,

$$\boxed{c(v) \equiv \frac{2k(v)}{r(v)(r(v)-1)}}. \tag{7.1}$$

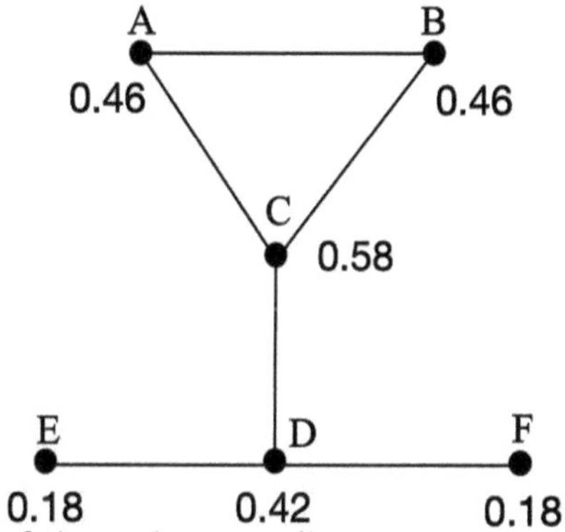

Fig. 7.3: An example of eigenvalue centrality

Eigenvector Centrality of a Node Highly technical-sounding, it is an indicator of how important or influential a person or a node is in a network. It is measured not just by how many neighbors the node in question has but also by how the neighbors are linked to rest of the nodes in a network. Intuitively, compared to node A, node B will be more important—and will have a higher eigenvector centrality score—in a network even if B has fewer neighbors than does A (i.e., B has a lower degree than A) provided that B's neighborrs are sufficiently highly connected with others in the network. Put differently, a node or an individual is central if connected with other individuals who are central. The concept takes into account both direct and indirect links of a node and its neighbors.

An illustrative example is given in Fig. 7.3. There are six nodes, A to F. Note that A or B has degree = 2, whereas D has degree = 3. But A or B's eigenvector centrality score (0.46) is higher than that of D (0.42). We do not get into calculating the scores, which involves matrix algebra. However, we can see intuitively that although D has three neighbors, two of them, namely, E and F, are not connected directly with other nodes in the network, whereas A and B are connected with each other and C, which is connected with D. This is why A and B have a higher eigenvalue centrality score than D, i.e., they are more central in the network compared to D.[8]

[8] Because C is most centrally located in the network, its score is the highest, whereas E and F are weakly connected with the network and thus have the lowest eigenvalue centrality score.

Length of a Path between Two Nodes Two nodes in a network may be linked directly, indirectly, or both directly and indirectly. Consider Fig. 7.2. In part (a), the nodes A and C are directly linked with each other, where A and D are indirectly linked. However, in part (d), A and C are both directly and indirectly linked. One can easily imagine that there may be multiple indirect links between two nodes.

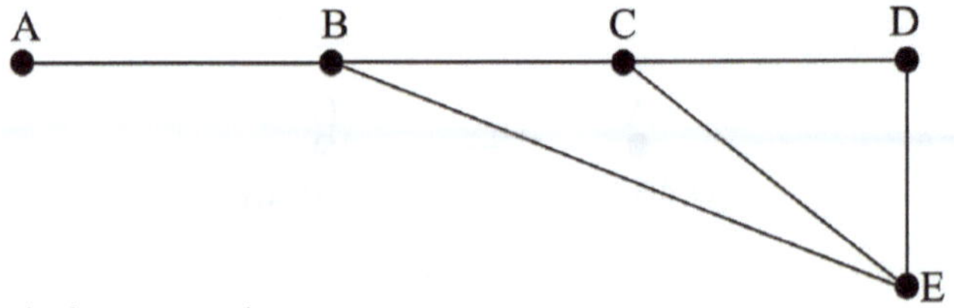

Fig. 7.4: Paths in a network

The length of a path between two nodes equals the number of vertices in the path including the two nodes *minus* one, which is equal to the number of steps. Consider two paths between A and C in part (d) of Fig. 7.2. The path $A \to B \to C$ has the length $3 - 1 = 2$, whereas the direct path $A \to C$ has length equal to $2 - 1 = 1$.

Now consider Fig. 7.4. There are three paths from A to E or, which is the same, from E to A. The order does not matter. Their lengths are

Path	Length
$A \to B \to C \to D \to E$	$= 5 - 1 = 4$
$A \to B \to C \to E$	$= 4 - 1 = 3$
$A \to B \to E$	$= 3 - 1 = 2.$

Distance Between Two Nodes It is simply the length of the shortest path between them, also called the ***geodesic distance.*** The shortest path itself is called the ***geodesic path***. There can be one or more than one geodesic path between two nodes. If we denote the distance between two nodes, say u and v, by $d(u,v)$, then in Fig. 7.4, $d(B,C) = 1$, $d(A,C) = 2$, $d(A,D) = 3$, $d(A,E) = 2$, and so on.

Between-Centrality of a Node It captures the extent to which a node lies on the shortest (geodesic) paths between all other nodes and measures the node's importance in terms of how much of information or communications between other nodes "pass through" the node in question.

Consider node C in a network with six nodes, A to F as in Fig. 7.5. If we exclude C, there are ten pairs of nodes. For each such pair, consider the number of geodesic paths and among these geodesic paths how many include the node C. This is compiled in Table 7.1.

We are thus led to the following (general) formula for the normalized between-centrality for node v:

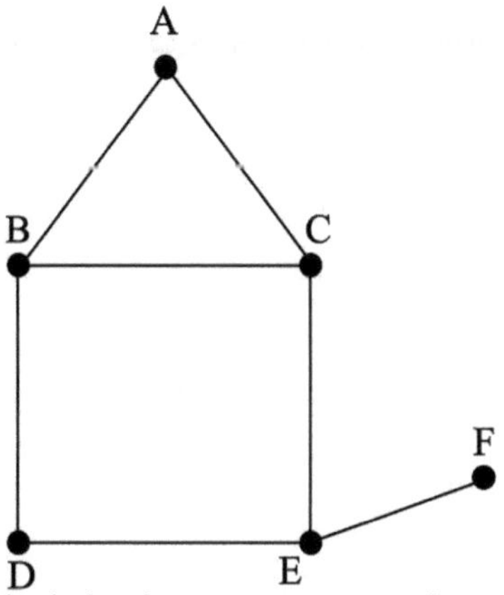

Fig. 7.5: Example for calculating betweenness centrality

	Pairs of nodes not containing C									
	AB	AD	AE	AF	BD	BE	BF	DE	DF	EF
# of geodestic paths (Π_C)	1	1	1	1	1	2	2	1	1	1
# of geodestic paths passing through C (π_C)	0	0	1	1	0	1	1	0	0	0
$\pi_C/\Pi_C =$	0	0	1	1	0	0.5	0.5	0	0	0

Between-centrality of C ≡ $b(C) = 1 + 1 + 0.5 + 0.5 = 3$

Between-centrality of other nodes: $b(A) = 0$, $b(B) = 1.5$, $b(D) = 1$, $b(E) = 4$ and $b(F) = 0$

Normalized between-centrality: this is equal to between-centrality divided through the total number of pairs among $N - 1$ nodes = $(N - 1)(N - 2)/2 = 10$ (in this case).

Thus normalized between-centralities are:
$\beta(A) = 0$, $\beta(B) = 0.15$, $\beta(C) = 0.3$, $\beta(D) = 0.1$, $\beta(E) = 0.4$ and $\beta(F) = 0$

Table 7.1: Calculation of between-centrality in the network in Fig. 7.5

$$\boxed{\beta(v) \equiv \frac{\sum_{j \neq k} g_{jk}(v)/g_{jk}}{(N-1)(N-2)/2},} \tag{7.2}$$

where $g_{jk}(v)$ is the number of shortest paths connecting nodes j and k passing through v and g_{jk} is the total number of shortest paths connecting j and k that includes those passing through v and those not passing through v.

Closeness-Centrality For any node, say v, take the sum of distances from it to every other node. This is equal to $\sum_{i \neq v} d(v, i)$. This is a measure of farness or peripherality of node v. The closeness-centrality of node v is the inverse of this: $\frac{1}{\sum_{i \neq v} d(v,i)}$.

We may normalize farness by dividing it by $N - 1$, i.e., normalized farness is equal to $\sum_{i \neq v} d(v, i)/(N - 1)$. The normalized closeness-centrality of node v is then

$$\gamma(v) \equiv \frac{N-1}{\sum_{i \neq v} d(v,i)}.^{9} \tag{7.3}$$

Density or Link Density of a Network If n is the # of direct links in a network, then its density, same as link density, say ρ, is equal to the ratio of n to the maximum possible number of direct links, $N(N - 1)/2$, i.e.,

$$\rho \equiv \frac{2n}{N(N-1)} \in [0, 1].$$

Realize that if a network is connected, the minimum number of direct links must be $N - 1$, and thus minimum density is $\rho = 2(N - 1)/[N(N - 1)] = 2/N$. Hence if we already know that a network is connected, ρ falls in the interval $[2/N, 1]$.

Density quantifies the degree of communication in a network. Notice that if we think of the neighbor of a node as a network by itself (which does *not* include the node itself), the density of this subnetwork is the cluster coefficient of the node.

Average Cluster Coefficient of a Network We have already discussed the cluster coefficient of a node. That of the (entire) network is simply the average of the cluster coefficients of all nodes, i.e.,

$$C \equiv \frac{\sum_{v=1}^{N} c(v)}{N}.$$

Average Path Length of a Network It is a measure of the efficiency of information in a network, defined as the average number of steps along the shortest (geodesic) paths for all possible pairs of network nodes:

$$\bar{D} \equiv \frac{\sum_{i,j,i \neq j} d(i,j)}{N(N-1)}. \tag{7.4}$$

The summation $\sum_{i,j,i \neq j}$ means that in a network with three nodes 1, 2, and 3, for example, we refer to the sum $d(1, 2) + d(2, 1) + d(1, 3) + d(3, 1) + d(2, 3) + d(3, 2)$. Realize that each pair of nodes is counted twice in this summation. Hence there

[9] There are other measures of centrality, e.g., Katz centrality, PageRank centrality, and Bonacich centrality, which we shall skip.

are $\sum_{i,j,i\neq j} d(i,j)/2$ pairs of distances among $N(N-1)/2$ pairs. Thus, the average is $\frac{\sum_{i,j,i\neq j} d(i,j)/2}{N(N-1)/2}$, which is the same as (7.4).

7.3.2 Random, Small-World, and Centralized or Scale-Free Networks

Typically, three types of networks are associated with terrorist and other "dark" organizations, namely, random, small-world, and scale-free (also called centralized) (Xu and Chen, 2008). Gone are the days of Red Brigades of Italy, which was very hierarchical. Because of the hierarchy, the capture of its top leaders led to that of hundreds of its rank and file, and the group was virtually destroyed in the late 1980s. In the 2000s and 2010s, terror groups have operated in more interactive and more loosely connected networks.[10] The three-way classification is a good way to judge the resilience of a terrorist network against *random attacks* and *targeted attacks* on the nodes.

The distinction is based on the distribution of the degrees (i.e., the number of neighbors) among all nodes of a network, the average path length, and the cluster coefficient. *Random network* is a very loosely connected network, having a small average path length and a small average clustering coefficient.[11] *Small-world networks* are characterized by relatively small average path length but a significantly larger cluster coefficient than random networks. *Centralized networks* have a large share of nodes with just a few direct links, i.e., a small degree of connectivity and a small percentage of nodes having a large number of direct links, i.e., a large degree of connectivity. A hub-spokes model is an example. A more prominent example is the Internet network, where sites like Google or Yahoo have many links, while "countless" other nodes have a relatively small number of neighbors.[12]

Random networks are resilient against random failures, captures, or infiltration. However, the drawback is that, because of smallness of the clusters, there are likely to be coordination problems in planning and executing a mission. Small-world networks are similar to random networks except that there is more clustering. Both random and small-world groups respond to random and targeted attacks in a similar way. On the other hand, scale-free networks are reasonably protected from random attacks but susceptible to targeted attacks.

7.3.3 Examples of Terrorist Networks: *9/11* and Bali Attacks

We now look at some actual terrorist networks. For obvious reasons, the network of terrorists associated with the *9/11* attacks has been studied in detail. Soon after the

[10] Although a vertical hierarchy is one kind of networks, the study of networks focuses on non-hierarchical organizations.

[11] Formally, the degree has a bell-shaped Poisson distribution.

[12] Mathematically, a centralized network has a degree distribution following the power law. That is, the fraction $P(k)$ of nodes in the network having k connections to other nodes approximates $k^{-\gamma}$, where γ is typically between 2 and 3. So the proportion of nodes with a higher number of degrees of connectivity falls exponentially.

9/11 attacks, using information from various sources including newspaper articles, Krebs (2002) was able to construct the network of terrorists who took part in these attacks and their associates. The nineteen hijackers consisted of subsets of individuals who knew each other for a long time and some were buddies from their school days. But it is *not* that each hijacker knew all or most others. It was the opposite. One group of people did not know another group. Figure 7.6a exhibits the network between them based on history of their prior contacts. Part (b) adds six "short-cuts" (indicated by red edges) meaning that they actually met before the attacks took place in order to coordinate. See how the last-stage short-cuts altered the network of hijackers. The density of the network of hijackers with short-cuts was 19% compared to 16% without. The average path length with short-cuts was 40% lower than that without short-cuts. These network theory concepts measure and illustrate the importance of the "last-minute" coordination meetings.

Part (c) of Fig. 7.6 depicts the degree of each hijacker without and with short-cuts. Among the nineteen hijackers, four stand out for high (nodal) degrees: Nawaz al-Hazmi, Hamza al-Ghamdi, Marwan al-Shehhi, and Hani Hanjour.

One may recall however that Mohamed Atta (of Egyptian origin) was the leader among the *9/11* hijackers. But his "degree" was only 3 and 5 without and with short-cuts. This may appear odd given that he was the leader. Interestingly, his importance in the network is revealed when we include not just the hijackers who directly participated in the attacks but also others who were connected in planning the *9/11* attacks. Figure 7.7 depicts a bigger network of 37 terrorists, which include the infamous "Hamberg cell" that provided major support to the *9/11* attacks. Figure 7.8 tabulates the top five terrorists in terms of degree, between-centrality, and closeness-centrality. Here we see the importance of Mohamed Atta.

Lindelauf et al. (2013) have studied the network of terrorists involved in the Bali attacks. Figure 7.9 is their constructed network. The rankings of terrorists in terms of the degree, between- and closeness-centralities are shown in Table 7.2.[13]

In order to weaken or break a terrorist network (as a counter-terror measure), intelligence and infiltration first enable a construction of the network structure of a terrorist organization: who is connected with who else and how. Next, the computation of centrality measures can tell which nodes are relatively important and, in particular, who the high-value targets are. This is useful in designing counter-terrorism measures in terms of targeting individuals for attack or infiltration.

7.4 Internal Organization and Agency Problems

Within a firm, a variety of tasks are delegated and they eventually lead to outputs of goods or services. Shareholders—the ultimate owners of a public firm—delegate the task of managing to the CEO, who, in turn, delegates various duties to mangers in different areas of operation. There is a hierarchy. Similarly, there are hierarchies within terror groups and those in upper strata in the hierarchy delegate functions

[13] The actual numbers for these measures can be easily computed from Fig. 7.9 by using the formulas developed in Sect. 7.3.1.

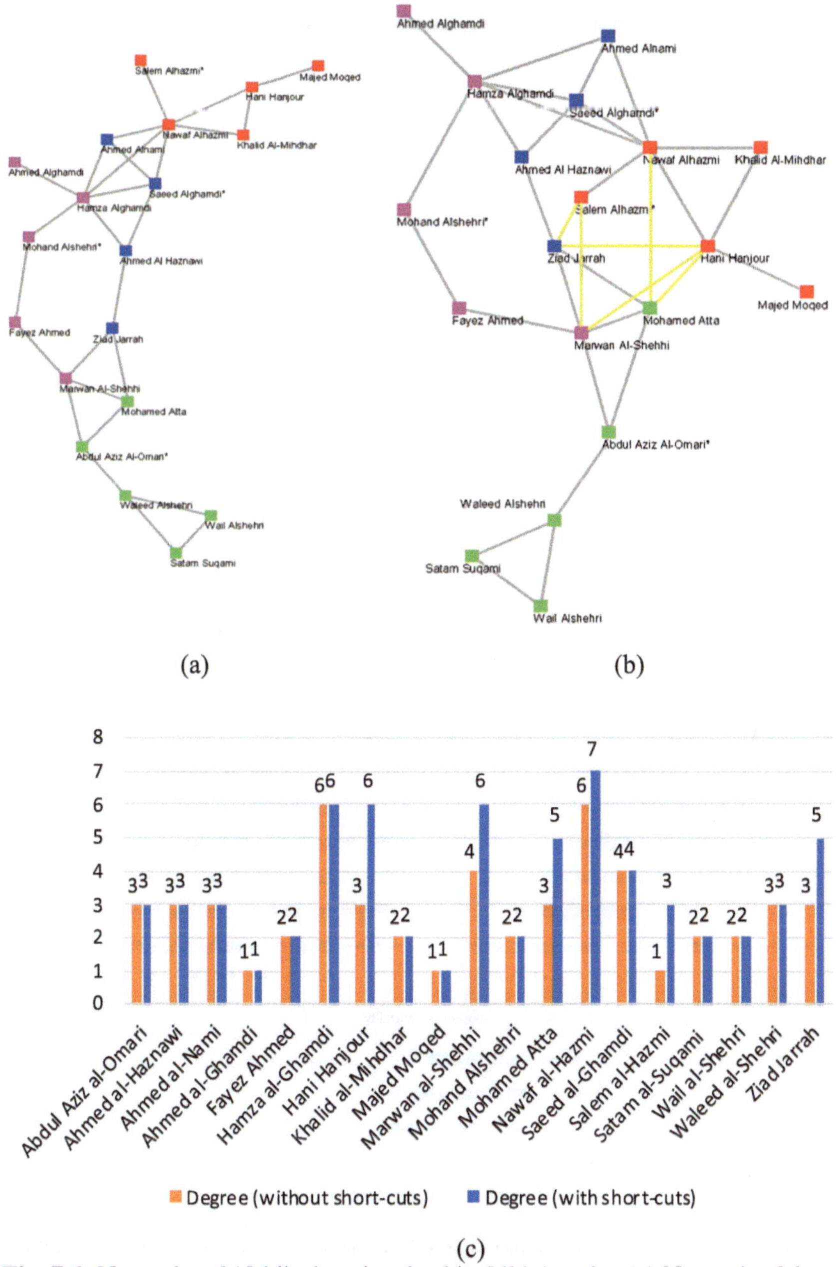

Fig. 7.6: Networks of 19 hijackers involved in *9/11* Attacks. (**a**) Network of the *9/11* Hijackers without short-cuts. (**b**) Network of the *9/11* hijackers with short-cuts. (**a**) and (**b**) *Source:* Krebs (2002); permission to reproduce from the author is thankfully acknowledged. (**c**) Inferred from (**a**) and (**b**) above

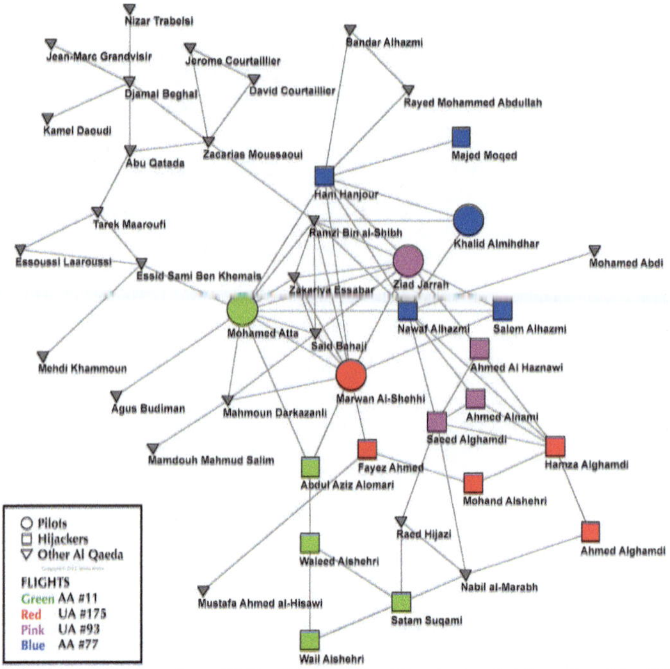

Fig. 7.7: Extended networks of hijackers and other terrorist involved in *9/11* Attacks (37 of them). Obtained from Valdis Krebs with many thanks

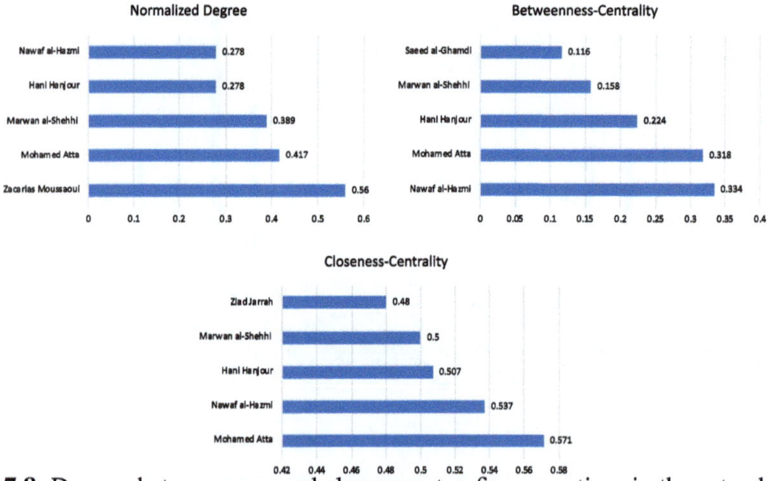

Fig. 7.8: Degree, betweenness, and closeness: top five operatives in the extended networks of hijackers and other terrorist involved in *9/11* attacks computed from (Krebs, 2002, Table 3)

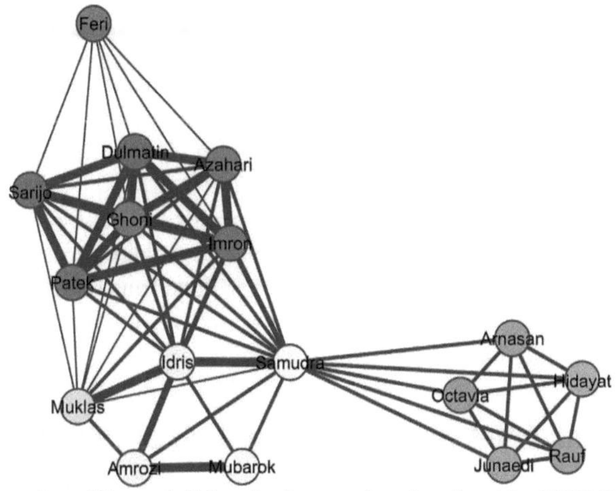

Fig. 7.9: Networks of Jemaah Islamiyah terrorists involved in 2002 Bali attacks. *Source:* (Lindelauf et al., 2013, Figure 4); permission to reproduce from Elsevier is thankfully acknowledged

Degree	Betweeness	Closeness
Samudra	Samudra	Samudra
Idris	Idris	Idris
Muklas	Muklas	Muklas
Ali Imron	Ali Imron	
Dulmatin	Dulmatin	Dulmatin
Azahari	Azahari	Azahari
Patek	Patek	Patek
Ghoni	Ghoni	Ghoni
Sarijo	Sarijo	Sarijo
Feri	Amrozi	Arnasan
Arnasan	Feri	Junaedi
Junaedi	Arnasan	Abdul Rauf
Abdul Rauf	Junaedi	Octavia
Octavia	Abdul Rauf	Hidayat
Hidayat	Octavia	Amrozi
Amrozi	Hidayat	Mubarak
Mubarak	Mubarak	Feri

Table 7.2: Ranking of terrorists on centrality measures: Bali attack. *Source:* Own calculations

to those in the lower ranks. In the network approach, a terror organization consists of various nodes or individuals, whose importance is judged by the nature of links with other individuals in the network. However, it does not capture the notions of subordination and delegation of task. The problems associated with delegation and how counter-terrorism measures may be designed in view of these problems are the subject matter here.

For the sake of understanding the internal organization issues, we view a terror group being constituted by leadership, on the one hand, and terrorist operatives and others managing finance- and non-finance-related functions on the other. The leadership delegates the task of attacks to terrorist operatives and financial management to people who are essentially middlemen.

7.4.1 The Principal-Agent Problem of Delegation and Agency Costs

Economists analyze delegation of tasks in terms of what is known as the *principal-agent problem*. The principal wants certain tasks to be done. But she/he does not have the expertise, time, information, or aptitude to undertake the tasks. They are delegated to agents or an agent. The tasks generate revenues or, more generally, utility for the principal. In return, the agent is compensated. The principal's net payoff equals the utility that the agent delivers minus his compensation. There could be multiple agents and multiple principals, but typically the analysis is focused on a scenario with one principal and one or many agents. In a public firm, the shareholders and the CEO are the principal and the agent, respectively. In selling a product or service, the sales manager and the salesperson are the principal and the agent, respectively. Likewise, for a terrorist organization, the leader is the principal and the terror operatives and financial managers are the agents.

The core problem is that the principal and the agents being different individuals, their preferences may not be aligned. Think of a sales manager (the agent), who must report to the CEO (the principal). It is quite possible that the former may have other interests than just working for the CEO. He might be just lazy for example, that is, he is someone with a preference for leisure. He may have a side project of his own, which the principal may be unaware of and which does not permit sufficient time or effort toward the principal's job. This is called a *moral hazard problem*, which almost always accompanies the task of delegation. Obviously, preference divergence and the resulting moral hazard problem do not serve the interest of the principal.

The question is how can a principal motivate or incentivize an agent to work in his interest? One solution may be a threat of punishment: if the agent does not work hard, he/she would face the prospect of being fired. This may work well if effort can be observed or verified. But this is not always feasible. The agent may be working far away from the principal and there may not be live video cameras. We may think that although the principal may not be able to observe the effort by the agent, he can observe the output and from that infer the effort by the agent. This may not be that straightforward however, because typically an output or an outcome of an enterprise would partly depend on random factors. A bad output may be a result of an adverse random occurrence, not lack of effort by the agent. Hence, an output or outcome may be a noisy signal of an agent's efforts or preferences.

One may think that if the principal pays the agent a high-enough wage or other compensations, he/she would work sincerely in the principal's interest. This may not work as long as there is a scope for blaming a bad outcome on luck or random factors, which is not verifiable by the principal. Suppose that I am a college professor and do not have time to manage my own finances. I hire a financial advisor. If, in a given year, I get bad returns on my investments, it could be that there were indeed random factors due to which returns are lower, or it could be that the financial advisor did not exercise sufficient due diligence in identifying good securities and trading them in time.

A standard solution in such moral hazard situations is to make the agent a "shareholder" in that his remuneration is a fraction of the profit she generates. That is, it is not a fixed-fee or fixed-salary contract: it is a contract contingent upon the outcome. The examples are stock options for employees, salespeople, or lawyers being paid commission on the volume of sales or outcome, discretionary bonus and vacation plans, law firms offering a partnership, etc. The idea is that in a profit-sharing contract, the higher the profits, the greater is the compensation of the agent. Hence it should motivate the agent to look after the project of the principal in the earnest.

There may be problems with this solution too. Since profits are influenced by random factors, a purely performance-based compensation may be too risky a proposition for the agent, who may not simply accept this contract. Also, profit- or output-based payments to employees may lead to "working too hard" and avoiding safety measures. If workers injure themselves, it may become a liability to a firm. Quality may suffer too. One may think of combining a lump-sum fee with a profit- or performance-based compensation, but finding the right mix so that the agent accepts the job and is fully motivated to work in the interest of the principal is difficult.

Furthermore, in some cases, the principal's return or utility cannot be measured in monetary units or the agent's performance cannot be measured well. For instance, I hire a nurse to take care of my ailing parent or hire a babysitter to watch my child, while I am away at work. It is hard to devise a performance-based wage structure for these functions. In these situations, it is not feasible to write a precise contract based on profit, outcome, or output.

Another way to motivate an agent will be that the principal combines a reward scheme to the agent with monitoring or control of the agent. But that comes with a price: increased time and effort exerted by the principal for this purpose, which can be potentially used for other uses that the principal is good at.

To summarize, if an agent's preferences are fully aligned with the principal, there is no issue with delegating tasks. But, if not, there are ***agency problems***, i.e., ***agency costs*** associated with delegation. The lack of preference alignment presents two types of agency costs.

(a) As efforts of the agent do not fully match with the goal or interest, there is a lower output or less desired outcome. This is a cost to the principal.

(b) Control by means of monitoring and supervision is (personally) costly to the principal in terms of time, effort, and resources.

Preference divergence, moral hazard, and agency costs are common with almost any business firm. They cannot be eliminated but can be "managed." A rational principal would strive to minimize agency costs.

7.4.2 Delegation and Agency Costs of Facing a Terror Organization[14]

As said earlier, like business firms, the leaders of terrorist "firms" delegate tasks in executing attacks, raising and using funds and recruiting, etc. to low ground-level operatives and middlemen, who act as the leader's or the principal's agents.

These tasks are partly dependent on random factors. In particular, terror attacks are highly susceptible to random sources of failure. Shapiro (2013) narrates how Ahmed Ressam, an al-Qaeda man, was planning to attack the Los Angeles airport in the year 2000, but chance factors led to suspicion on him, while he was entering the USA and he was apprehended.[15] Not just chance factors, other factors including financial constraints can contribute to the failure of attack missions.[16]

If all agents are perfectly committed to the cause and synced with the leaders in terms of objectives, tactics, and information, then agency problems from delegation are a non-issue. But preferences and beliefs may not be aligned. The objective of terrorist operatives may partly differ from that of the leadership. Monitoring and control of the operatives demand time, resources, and effort costs for the leaders. As described earlier, random elements play a role, and, this makes accountability a difficult proposition.

Hence, like business firms, terrorist "firms" face preference divergence leading to moral hazard issues and agency costs. In addition and importantly, compared to business firms, the covert nature of a terrorist organization exacerbates the moral hazard problem: operatives (agents) in the lower cadre can take advantage of secrecy as they prefer rather than what their principals would have wanted.

There is a massive evidence of serious dissensions and differences among the members of terror groups reflective of preference non-alignment and the allied agency costs. Shapiro's study covers from Narodnaya Volya in Russia in the late nineteenth century to modern day terror organizations like al-Qaeda and its affiliates. Umpteen examples of dissensions and differences within terrorist and militant groups

---

[14] The material of this and following subsections closely follows Shapiro (2013).

[15] At the time of entry, he was sweating and fumbling that led to further scrutiny and apprehension. Apparently, his physical condition was not due to nervousness from what he was planning to do. It was a result of malaria he had caught during his stay in Afghanistan. It was simply bad luck for al-Qaeda.

[16] In the 1993 World Trade Center attack, nearly 1500 pounds of homemade explosives were detonated inside the parking garage. The explosion killed six and injured more than 1000. However, it could have been much worse as the rented van had a cargo capacity of more than 4000 pounds. The leader of the attack, Ramzi Yousef, testified later that he did not have enough funds to purchase more explosive to build a larger bomb and the attack was rushed as funds go exhausted.

are provided, derived from a wide variety of historical accounts, terrorists' own public writings (108 memoirs), and seized documents. Captured documents from al-Qaeda and other groups are contained in the US Department of Defense's Harmony Database. It has more than one million documents secured during operations in Afghanistan, Iraq, and elsewhere. Roughly, a quarter of the documents have been translated and a large number have been released.

In particular, a lot of micro-level information on the operational and financial management of al-Qaeda in Iraq (AQI) was obtained from 109 internal documents seized by the allied forces in 2007 near Sinjar in Iraq (located near the Syrian border). These are called *Sinjar records*.

Here are some examples of internal disagreements and concerns.

Jemaah Islamiyah (JI) After the first Bali attack, Norodin Mohammed Top, the leader of a breakaway faction, asked a mid-level JI leader, Sarwo Edi Nughraho, for funds, explosives, and operatives for "... fighting America, and its interests, assets, citizens, and allies, wherever they may be." Nughraho refused the request saying that JI's vision, mission, and selection targets were different from his. This is an example of preference divergence on the choice of violence.

Original al-Qaeda Saif al-Adel, a member of al-Qaeda, criticized Osama bin Laden's leadership in a letter dated 2002. He argued that the group needed to take a time-out in order to regroup after some setbacks in East Asia, America, Europe, and elsewhere. This is another example of disagreement over the use of violence.

Internal disagreements happen not only over the use of violence but also on financial management. Shapiro narrates an account of L'Hussein Kherchtou, a member of al-Qaeda's operational cell in Nairobi during the 1998 US Embassy bombings. In the subsequent bombing trial for the prosecution, he testified that he disagreed with the spending priorities of the senior members of his team and personally resented the leadership for this and other reasons.

In 1999, al-Zawahiri, the al-Qaeda's second-in-command, wrote a letter to a Yemeni cell about financial irregularities in a business-as-usual tone (Shapiro, 2013, Chapter 5). Zawahiri chastised his subordinates through seven bullet points.

Lehi and Irgun Zavai Leumi In her book, Guela Cohen of Lehi or the Stern Gang talked about disagreements within the Lehi about the course of action after World War II. After the war, the Lehi group joined hands with Irgun Zavai Leumi and Haganah (a relatively moderate group) to wage insurgency against the British. This was seen by some Lehi members as a weakening of the group.

Hezbollah After Israel withdrew from Lebanon in 2000, Hezbollah decimated the South Lebanon Army (SLA), a proxy of Israel. Shapiro narrates how, by issuing warnings and threat of punishment, the leadership of Hezbollah successfully dissuaded its fighters from taking revenge on SLA members. This is an example of internal dissension with respect to targets and objectives.

Al-Qaeda in Iraq Sinjar records reveal many accounts of disagreements within AQI on both tactics and spending. In a 2007 instance, the AQI's leadership did not want to fight the Islamic Army of Iraq (IAI), an indigenous Sunni militant organization, who criticized AQI for killing Sunnis without sufficient evidence, lest it should lead to a bad publicity. Interestingly, the AQI leaders addressed its members through a pamphlet ordering them to stay home. This an example of disagreement between the leadership and the rank and file over tactics (Shapiro, 2013, Chapter 1).

7.4.3 Two Sets of Problems

Shapiro summarizes that preference divergence leads to two sets of problems:
(1) Uncontrolled and indiscriminate use of violence[17]
(2) Inefficient use of resources, especially the management of money.

A prominent example of failure due to delegation and agency problems is Louis Beam, who, after serving the US army, became a white supremacist intellectual and a member of the Ku Klax Klan. He called for no coordination at all in order to minimize the risk of any compromise. As Shapiro puts it, this kept him out of jail but his armed resistance movement failed completely.

7.4.4 Control and Security Vulnerability

So, what does a terrorist leader do to deal with the problem of preference divergence on the choice of violence and inefficient use of internal resources? While most normal organizations solve such problems by writing contingent contracts on performance or profit, this is unrealistic and impractical for terror groups. The only choice left is monitoring, control, and reprimand, the instruments of which include, among other means, writing memos, auditing, organizing group activities so as to detect shirking, reprimand for deviations, and creating mechanisms to screen out potentially insincere candidates at the time of recruitment. For instance, recall the letter from al-Qaeda's al-Zawahiri to a Yemeni cell on financial mismanagement described earlier.

Sinjor records reveal AQI's increasing effort over time toward control, particularly with respect to financial management.[18] The leaders of ISI (not ISIS) noted that too much of violence or illegal fund raising through theft, robbery, kidnapping, etc. can damage the reputation of the group. They recognized the political benefits of control over subordinates, even though it was costly.

Not only do the tasks of monitoring and reprimand entail time, cost, and resources that can be more efficiently used for directly "productive" purposes by the

[17] The Real IRA bombing in Omagh, Northern Ireland, in August 1998 is a prime example. The attack led to a public outrage at the Real IRA and substantial weakening of the group. Shapiro identifies three sources of preference divergence between terrorists and their leader over the tactics to be used. First, operatives recruited on their specialty in violence would opt for excessive violence. Second, in an environment of secrecy, the leaders and the operatives may have different information and perception about the world. Third, the leaders and the terrorist operators may process the same information differently.

[18] There is a discussion of "expelling those who exploit" suggesting that the appearance of financial impropriety hurts AQI's politically.

leaders, there is *an additional problem of security* that is particular to covert and non-state entities. That is, too much interaction with subordinates and low-level operatives runs the risk of exposure, apprehension, and death. Even reprimand can create security problems. The leader can be physically attacked by subordinates or they can defect to the government and reveal logistic information about the leaders.[19]

7.4.5 Twin Tradeoffs

The additional problem of *security vulnerability* imposes two challenging tradeoffs that a terror group's leaders must contend with.

Security-Control Tradeoff To reduce the political risk from operatives executing indiscriminate violence, leaders adopt controlling actions. In turn, such actions create security issues for the leadership and entire group.[20]

Security-Efficiency Tradeoff In order to check financial mismanagement by middlemen and low-cadre operatives, the leaders institute managerial systems, which, in turn, entails security vulnerabilities.[21] Such security-efficiency tradeoff arises in recruiting too. In the business world, bad performance can easily trigger firing on the presumption that getting replacement is not very costly. But, for a terrorist organization, the pool of potential dedicated or high-ability individuals may be small. Hence, the leaders must be extra careful in selecting individuals to the group. The problem is that it is very difficult for leaders to perfectly judge a potential entrant's ability or aptitude. Relatively undedicated or unworthy individuals can slip through the recruitment process. In the economics of information, this is called the *adverse selection problem*. On the other hand, rigorous selection procedures to eliminate uncommitted/inefficient "applicants" create security leakages.

Combining the two, we can simply state that *too much control in order to minimize agency costs creates serious security issues.*

7.4.6 Evidence on Preference Divergence and Control

The tradeoffs between agency problems and control facing terror organizations imply the theoretical predictions that

(1) The greater the discrimination required by a group's political goals, the more control the leaders will exert.

(2) The greater the degree of preference divergence, the lesser is the scope for control.

---

[19] Shapiro described that groups like Ulster Volunteer Force (UVF) and Ulster Defense Association (UDA) in Ireland were very much afflicted by the first problem, as their operatives were prone to use mafia-style tactics.

[20] Shapiro lists the necessary conditions behind this tradeoff: operatives' indiscretion in choosing targets, the number of attacks and tactics of attacks due to preference divergence, and limitations to monitoring and reprimanding them.

[21] Agents' lack of commitment or preferences for allocation of funds and the inability to perfectly monitor or reprimand enough are the underlying factors behind this tradeoff.

We now briefly review the statistical evidence put forth by Shapiro that supports these hypotheses in the context of two areas of conflict and terrorism: Ireland and Palestine.

7.4.6.1 PIRA versus UVF versus UDA in Ireland

These three main terrorist groups that were involved in Ireland's conflict differed in the levels of discrimination in the use of violence warranted by their political goals but were otherwise comparable. Their members hailed from similar working-class populations. They all began during the violence in the late sixties, and their military wings were non-state entities. In the early years of the Troubles era, the PIRA and UVF faced higher security pressure from the British forces, compared to the UDA (as the UDA used a covered name Ulster Freedom Fighters (UFF) in perpetrating sectarian violence), but by the mid-1980s, all faced similar counter-terrorism pressure.

Compared to the UVF and UDA, PIRA's political goals demanded more careful selection in the application of violence. The PIRA had to apply balance between (a) putting sufficient pressure on the British military so as to force them to leave Northern Ireland and (b) avoiding indiscriminate and excessive violence risking its support from the moderate Catholics as well as making it politically very difficult for the British to leave Northern Ireland. The demand for discrimination in violence by PIRA grew over time as Sinn Féin gained an increasing prominence in the Republican strategy toward the independence for the entire island of Ireland.

Within the Loyalist side, UVF's goals required it to be more cautious about using violence than did UDA, since UVF became affiliated with the Progressive Unionist Party (PUP), a relatively successful political party in 1979, whereas the UDA did not form its political wing, the Ulster Democratic Party (UDP), until 1989. Furthermore, unlike PUP, UDP did not have much electoral success. The political edge for UVF's called for more discretion in terror attacks on its part.

	Target choice	Operational procedure	Personnel assignment	Resources management	Fund-raising	Recruiting
PIRA	No	Yes	Yes	Yes	Yes	No
UVF	No	Yes	No	No	No	Yes
UDA	No	No	No	No	No	No

Table 7.3: Control exercised by PIRA, UVF, and UDA|indexUDA, 1969–2001. *Source*: (Shapiro, 2013, Table 7.2); permission from the Princeton University Press is thankfully acknowledged

Greater discrimination in violence requires more control. Hence, the hypothesis is that *the PIRA exercised greater control than the UVF, which in turn exercised greater control than the UDA.* To measure control, Shapiro considered six dimensions of organizational activities: (1) target choices, (2) operational procedures, (3) personnel assignments, (4) resource allocation, (5) fund-raising methods, and (6) recruiting practices. Based on data, a binary yes–no indicator was created. As we see in Table 7.3, PIRA exercised control in four out of the six areas of operation, where it is two for UVF and none for UDA. These rankings are in conformity with the above hypothesis.

Among those killed in the attacks by Republican groups, civilians and combatants constituted 36 and 46%, respectively, compared to 86 and 14% for civilians and combatants who lost their lives from attacks by Loyalist groups Shapiro (2013, Table 7.1). The lower percentage of civilians killed by the Republican groups supports the hypothesis that these groups were more discriminate in their violence than the Loyalist groups.

7.4.6.2 Fatah Versus Hamas

How does religious extremism affect the organizational tradeoffs facing Islamic groups? Shapiro compares Fatah with Hamas. Both groups have similar objectives—homeland or autonomy for Palestinians. We noted in Chap. 2 that Fatah is secular, while Hamas is not. Religious ideology being a unifying factor, one would expect Hamas to be more effective in screening its operatives to reduce preference divergence.

Fatah established a paramilitary presence in the Occupied Territories during the First Intifada, but its military operations were managed by commanders based outside of the Occupied Territories. Their ideas about how to effectively resist Israeli rule were vastly different than those of their inside operatives and they did not want strong inside leaders. As a result, there was a divergence of preference between activists who grew up under the Israeli rule in the Occupied Territories and the militants in Fatah guerrilla forces abroad. When Fatah, as the dominant party in the PLO, began to work cooperatively with Israel in 1994 under the Oslo Accord, it faced a major challenge of mutually accommodating the two groups of operatives.

In contrast, Hamas did not have to face such issues. The group originated from Muslim Brotherhood and it recruited almost entirely within the territories, thus drawing upon a relatively homogeneous population. Thus preference divergence is expected to be a lesser problem for Hamas than for Fatah.

The relevant hypothesis is that *Hamas leaders exercised greater control than Fatah leaders during both Intifadas.* As in the case of Ireland, Shapiro evaluated the same six forms of organizational activity and deduced a yes–no indicator for each. Table 7.4 shows that Fatah exhibits control in three areas, compared to at least five out of six by Hamas. This supports the hypothesis than less preference divergence is associated with more control.

	Target choice	Operational procedure	Personnel assignment	Resources management	Fund-raising	Recruiting
Fatah	No	No	Yes	Yes	Yes	No
Hamas	Yes	Yes	May be	Yes	Yes	Yes

Table 7.4: Control exercised by Fatah and Hamas, 1987–2005. *Source*: (Shapiro, 2013, Table 8.1); permission from the Princeton University Press is thankfully acknowledged

The upshot is that it was *not* the Islamic commitment of members that made Hamas more efficient. Greater efficiency resulted from the ability to exercise more control since it faced an easier managerial challenge of reconciling conflicting sub-groups.

In a nutshell,

Is That So? 7.2: Internal-Organization Issues facing Terrorist Groups

Like business firms, terrorist organizations face internal-organization issues of preference divergence associated with delegation of tasks, which lead to moral hazard problems. However, unlike firms, in controlling these issues, terrorist groups face security issues and thus internal organization problems are more severe for them. All else the same, these problems are less among groups based on religious ideology than among secular groups.

7.4.7 Implications for Counter-Terrorism Actions

We have argued that agency problems are more acute for terrorist "firms" than for business firms. The larger the group, the more prevalent these problems are. In the face of these mounting internal challenges, Shapiro submits that while large groups may be capable of occasionally delivering spectacular attacks, by and large they are not able to pose an existential threat to target states. Terrorist organizations ". . . are nothing close to the threat that many in the policy community once claimed them to be" (Shapiro, 2013, Chapter 1).

9/11 attacks can be regarded as an exception. It was possible only because al-Qaeda had the propensity to organize and maintain a hierarchical system under which a large number of terrorists could be trained and monitored. The groups that eventually win political power or major concessions do *not* succeed on the strength of their violence. Their success results from political mobilization and participation in normal politics.

Since *9/11*, the American counter-terror efforts have largely focused on capturing or killing Islamic terrorists who are vehemently anti-American or anti-Western. This may have been the right strategy to deal with an organization like al-Qaeda in its heydays or ISIS. But there are other groups like al-Nusra, Hamas, Hezbollah, and Taliban, which have strong political and/or social wings. For these organizations, selection of violence is more critical than those driven mostly by ideology and global jihad. To contain these organizations, Shapiro argues a more efficient allocation of scarce counter-terrorism resources should entail less use of military and more of measures that can exacerbate the internal agency problems. Shapiro (2013, Chapter 9) suggests a number of counter-terror measures that are based on understanding of the agency problems within terrorist groups, some of which are outlined below.

7.4.7.1 Specific Suggestions

Interpret Behavior in the Light of Intra-Organizational Dynamics There are instances where aggressive counter-terror measures have or would have backfired. How so can be understood in the light of organizational response.

Consider Israel's policy of pressurizing Hamas in the 1990s, following the latter's suicide bombings in 1994. Israel did so for mistakenly interpreting those attacks as the choice of a unified leadership of Hamas. By cracking down Hamas in the Occupied Territories, Israel paradoxically made it harder for Hamas's leaders in controlling its operatives. It actually empowered a more militant faction that was largely immune from Israeli pressure because its managers were operating from Jordan and Syria: a few militants carried out a number of high-profile attacks on Israel.

Similarly, Israel's policy of targeted assassinations against senior Hamas leaders in 2004 helped create a situation in which the group's more moderate leaders in Gaza and the West Bank were unable to enforce ceasefire agreements. This made it impossible to break the cycle of violence that started with the Second Intifada.

Consider PIRA in Ireland in the 1990s, when its key leaders like Martin McGuinness and Gerry Adams were struggling to rein in their organization, as many operatives within PIRA consistently demanded more action against the British. In this situation, strong military actions by the British toward PIRA like arresting its leaders and close associates would have made it harder for the PIRA to operate and removed those who could ensure restraint at the negotiating table.

In both of these cases, an agency theory perspective is able to bring to the fore the costs of crackdowns that are not apparent if we treat terrorist groups as monolithic. The general lesson here is that *it is a mistake to presume that an aggressive, high-profile approach always succeeds*.

Refrain from Actions that Encourages Preference Alignment Recall the email by al-Zawahiri to the Yemeni cell leader in 1999. Measures to incriminate financial agents and propagate narratives that arouse suspicions of graft and corruption in the eyes of their leaders should weaken terrorist organizations.

Make Credible Punishment of Operatives by Their Leaders Harder This can be achieved by providing an exit option for members other than indefinite detention or death. This would make it harder for groups to enforce discipline and control on operatives through the use of force. A good example of this tactic is the defection of Ali Abd al-Rahman al-Faqasi al-Ghamdi from Saudi Arabia in June 2003. Al-Ghamdi was involved in the May 12, 2003 bombings in Riyadh and was known to have close ties with al-Qaeda. There are varied accounts of al-Ghamdi's reasons for giving himself up, but his own father told this to the reporters: "... security agencies have promised that if he gives in and is convicted of the alleged crimes, his punishment would be reduced to half."

Offering well-publicized amnesty or reduced sentences for voluntary defectors from terror groups can effectively reduce the demands a terrorist organization can make on its members and make it less lethal.

Provide Information That Makes the Political Impact of Actions Less Clear Dissensions within the group stem from debates over how the struggle is going politically. Hence information or misinformation may be fed strategically in order to purposefully confuse the group members.

Question the Motive of Financial Managers This can be achieved by publicizing how uncommitted some operatives are. The Indian government followed this tack in publicizing how the foot-soldiers of the Indian Mujahideen (IM), an Islamic group, had stolen from their superiors and how higher level managers had ripped off their foreign sponsors. As the story in a major Indian English-language daily newspaper put it, "Money meant to fund terror activities or recruit new operatives was on many occasions siphoned off and used for 'personal benefit'." In the article, an Indian counter-terror official described how an IM operative, Mirza Himayat Baig, used roughly 20% of the funds sent to him for a terror mission to pay off his debts, saying, "Most IM operatives use this modus operandi since there is no accountability where money is concerned in the outfit. The top functionaries are bothered only about operations. The money does not come out of their pockets and hence they do not care to keep tabs on it."[22]

Make the Screening Strategies Appear Risky Openly monitoring family relations of known terrorist operatives makes the job of a terrorist group's screening for recruitment harder.

Create an Environment in Which Terrorists Place a Premium on Discrimination in Selecting Attacks Governments can ramp up the value of discrimination by highlighting the human cost of terrorism among a group's supporting population.

Deny Terrorist Groups a Safe Haven A safe haven in the form of secured locations granted by any regime reduces a terror group's organizational challenges and makes it more effective. In case of Northern Ireland, the South Armagh unit of PIRA could exercise tighter control than other PIRA units, because it had a safe haven in the Republic of Ireland. Expulsion of Hamas in 1995 from Jordan, a safe haven, played a key role in pushing the group into a more peaceful stage.

[22] Another way would be to refrain from publicizing freezing of assets. In that case the financial managers have to take a lot of pains to explain to their superiors. This would tend to create a stress in their relationships.

We should however be clear that a safe haven does *not* mean administratively uncontrolled areas, because in such areas the terror groups have to fight with local bandits and other violence outfits. Also, they may be more prone to bombing by the target countries. The idea is not to allow a terror group a safe sanctuary in a relatively efficient administrative area.

Understand That Decentralization in Terror Groups May Be Sign of Weakness In devising counter-terror measures, we should be clear that the decentralization of al-Qaeda that occurred after allied forces occupied Afghanistan and Iraq is *not* a sign of moving into a more effective organizational structure or it has become more dangerous. Instead, it is a testimony to the weakening of al-Qaeda.

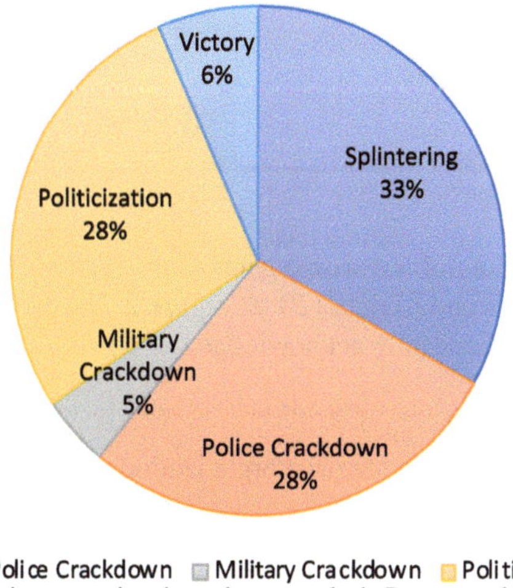

Fig. 7.10: How terrorist organizations have ended: Jones and Libicki (2008), total number of groups = 404. *Source*: It is an extension of (Jones and Libicki, 2008, Figure 2.1); permission from the RAND Corporation is thankfully acknowledged

7.5 Ending of Terrorist Organizations and the Determinants of Their Longevity

Business firms do not last forever. Like living beings, their "lives" end. In adverse market conditions, many small individual firms go out of business by simply closing "shops" or services or filing bankruptcy. Large firms file bankruptcy too. A firm also ceases to exist when it is bought by another or when a hostile takeover takes place. Trans World Airlines, a renowned American airliner, started in 1930 and filed its third and final bankruptcy in 2001 and was acquired by American Airlines. Radio Shack, a famous retailer in electronic goods which came to existence in 1921, went bankrupt in the mid-2010s. Likewise, terrorist groups have finite lifetime. In this

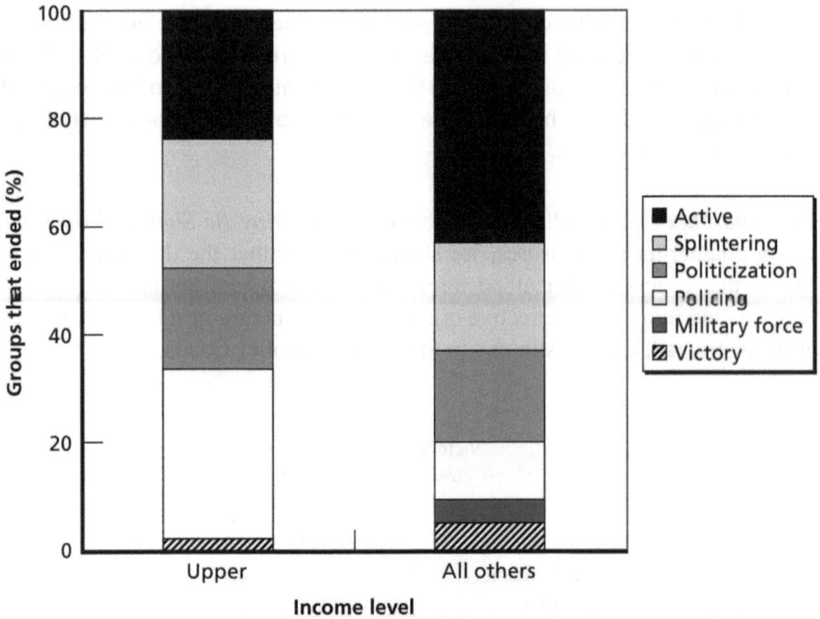

Fig. 7.11: How are ending of terrorist organizations related to per-capita income of countries. *Source*: Jones and Libicki (2008, Figure 2.7); permission from the RAND Corporation is thankfully acknowledged

section, we study the ending of terrorist organizations and the factors that influence their lifetime.

7.5.1 Types of Ending

The "ending" of a terror organization is of course different in nature from that of a business firm. Different authors have classified the ending of terror groups into five to seven categories. In an influencing study, Jones and Libicki (2008) analyzed 648 terror groups that were active between 1968 and 2006, including those started prior to 1968. Terror-group endings were divided into five categories: police crackdown, military crackdown, politicization, victory, and splintering. The last category simply means that the group became divided into separate entities. As examples, the end of LTTE was achieved by military force. Politicization refers to the situation where terrorism by a group ended following a negotiated settlement, e.g., ETA in 2011 and FARC in 2016. There are a few examples of victory or success, e.g., Irgun Zvai Leumi in Israel, EOKA in Cyprus, and FLN in Algeria.

The distribution of the types of ending in the Jones–Libicki dataset is exhibited in Fig. 7.10.[23] Notice that,

---

[23] In generating these percentages, of the total of 648 groups in the study, those still active by 2006 (244 of them) were excluded. Hence the total number of "dead" groups equals 648 – 244 = 404.

Is That So? 7.3: Ending of Terrorist Groups

Apart from splintering, among different modes or types of ending of terrorist groups, police crackdown and politicization constitute the two most frequent types.

Local police is likely to have a good knowledge of how a terror organization operates locally and be able to receive good intelligence. Using these, it can effectively bust terror groups. Interestingly, Jones and Libicki (2008) also correlates the mode of ending to per-capita income of countries, as shown in Fig. 7.11. Observe that the percentage of groups ending by police crackdown is higher in the upper-income countries.

Cronin (2006, 2009) identifies an additional type of termination, namely, loss of a group's public support or sympathy.[24] Examples include Shining Path of Peru and ETA in the Basque Country of Spain. Dugan et al. (2008) present a lucid account and statistical analysis of the decline of two groups in Armenia which fizzled out due to loss of popular support, namely, the Armenian Secret Army for the Liberation of Armenia (ASALA) and the Justice Commandos of the Armenian Genocide (JCAG).[25,26]

7.5.2 Measuring the Life Span of Terror Organizations

To study longevity or survival of a terror organization, we need to ascertain its beginning and end. The beginning date is typically associated with an organization's first recorded attack, rather than when the group was formed or announced its

Of these, how many ended which way are given in footnote 33 of Jones and Libicki (2008). This is the basis of Fig. 7.10.

[24] She analyzed terrorist groups identified in the MIPT event database.

[25] As Dugan et al. (2008) narrate, both groups emerged in the mid-1970s and were quite violent in the early 1980s. But by the late 1980s, they simply disintegrated. The former was a left-wing and the latter was a right-wing group, whose main objective was to attack Turkish people and leaders. There was a genocide in Turkey in 1915 that killed nearly one million Armenians, which shocked Armenians all over the world. Their main demands were the recognition of this genocide and apology by Turkey (which Turkey denies). The other demands were reparation and reclamation of the ancestral homeland.

The main differences between ASALA and JCAG were that the latter was selective, solely focusing on Turkish targets, whereas the former killed non-Turkish and Armenian people who were not supportive. Initially, native Armenians and the Armenian diaspora were supportive of both groups, financially and morally. The turning point came when ASALA attacked the Orly airport in 1983. An explosive device was denoted near the Turkish Airlines counter that killed eight (four French, two Turkish, one American, and one Swedish) and injured more than fifty. This was a watershed event that completely overturned the attitude of Armenian toward ASALA. By using data on attacks and fatalities from terror acts committed by both groups, Dugan et al. (2008)'s regression analysis found that the Orly attack had a strong negative impact on the activities of *both* groups, the point being that this attack by ASALA created a negative feeling toward not just ASALA but also JCAG.

[26] Cronin (2006) includes a seventh mode of ending: failure to transit to the next generation, i.e., no generational transition.

intentions. However, determining the end date for a terror organization is not easy. For instance, suppose we have a dataset of terrorism for a period, say 2017–2021, and an organization's last attack in the dataset is in October 2021. From this information only, we cannot say that October 2021 is the end date of the organization. Also, a terror organization may remain dormant for even a few years before surfacing again. A group can be divided into two or more groups with different identities too. Hence, it is not straightforward to put a date on the "death" or end of a terror organization. Jones and Libicki (2008) and Cronin (2009) actually traced the history of each terror organization in their studies and determined *when* and *how* they ended. Later studies like Blomberg et al. (2011) and Gaibulloev et al. (2013) confine to the same time period as do Jones and Libicki (2008) and use Jones–Libicki's estimates of terror organization duration to uncover what explains the variation in the duration of terror groups.

In other situations, when a dataset is available to a researcher that records the date of incidence of attacks and their various attributes including who the perpetrators are, nature of attack, etc., but case-by-case historical narratives of various organizations are either not considered or available, some assumptions on the pattern of occurrence of terror attacks by a group in the dataset are used to pin down a group's end date. For instance, Vittori (2009) treats the last date of attack as the end date of an organization, unless it is within the last three years of the dataset. His dataset covered from 1968 to 2007. If the last date of attack fell within the last three years, that is, 2005–2007, other information was taken into consideration to judge whether a group was active or not active. Young and Dugan (2014), who use terror attacks data from GTD from 1970 to 2010, simply take the last recorded attack date by an organization as its end date. A hybrid method is employed by Phillips (2014, 2015), who combines the information from Jones and Libicki (2008) with new sources as well as the Terrorist Organization Profiles dataset (TOPs).[27,28]

Obviously, "dataset-based-only" criteria for the end date are arbitrary to some extent. For instance, some terrorist groups—like ETA and Shining Path—suspended operations for three or more years but came back with attacks later.[29] Despite these limitations, different measures on the end date of a terror organization do have merits insofar as they are indicative of potential weakening of an organization, which, in many cases, essentially marks the end of it as a major force.

Once the beginning period is known and the end period of a terror organization is determined, the difference between the two is its life span or the duration of its survival.

---

[27] This is availed from the Memorial Institute for the Prevention of Terrorism (MIPT).

[28] In the absence of any of the above, the last attack date for an organization in the GTD is regarded as its end date.

[29] The Black September, the dissident faction of the Palestine Liberation Organization was responsible for the September 1972 attack on the Israeli team at the Munich Olympic Games (see Chap. 2). After this attack, the Israeli Mossad targeted this group. Many members were either captured or killed. The group was presumed to be decimated by the mid-1970s. However, nearly a decade later, the group announced that it was "resuming revolutionary activities" (Miller, 2016).

7.5.3 Determinants of the Longevity of Terror Organizations

We now study the factors that help explain the longevity or survival of terror groups. To begin with, Jones and Libicki (2008) not only characterized types of ending but also attempted to shed light on what may contribute to the life span of terror organizations. Five factors were considered: ideological motivation, economic conditions in the country, regime type in the country, the size of groups, and the breadth of terrorist goals. Ideological motivations were divided into four types: left-wing, right-wing, nationalist, and religious. In their dataset, among these four types, religious organizations tend to last the longest.[30] In terms of regression analysis, however, only one factor came out to be significant, namely the peak size of a group, defined as the maximum recorded size at some point of an organization's life. The greater the peak size, the longer was the life span of a terror organization, on average.

Econometric models have identified several explanatory factors (variables) that are statistically significant. They can be grouped into three categories:
(1) those that are specific (internal) to an organization,
(2) interaction among terror organizations, and
(3) external factors like politico-economic environment in which the organizations operate and the country's geographical characteristics.

In terms of estimation, all studies that are referred to below apply survival analysis methods except Carter (2012), who use multinomial logit.[31]

7.5.3.1 Group-Specific Factors

Several such factors have been uncovered.

Autonomy and Capability The higher the autonomy and capability of an organization, the longer should it survive. This is tested by Vittori (2009). How are these factors quantified? Vittori's measurement of autonomy depends on external donations as well as the amount and the variety of internal resourcing available to the group. Based on some formula that includes these variables, the autonomy of various organizations is grouped into three categories, 1, 2, and 3, low, medium, and high autonomy, respectively.[32] Capability is measured by an organization's quality and quantity of resources. Terror groups were grouped into four different capability categories: very low, low, medium, and high—assigned values 1–4.[33] Both autonomy and capability were found to have positively influenced the life span of terror organizations.

[30] Nearly 62% of all terrorist groups have ended since 1968, but only 32% of religious terrorist groups have ended.

[31] See General Appendix B, Sects. B.21 and B.4.2 on introduction survival analysis and multinomial logit. Individual studies along with the methodology, sample time period, and data sources are summarized in Table 7.5 in the chapter appendix 7.A.

[32] In his study, five groups out of 100 were assessed as having low autonomy, 18 had medium autonomy, and 77 had high autonomy.

[33] Of 100 groups in the dataset, 41 were assigned 1 (the lowest range), 44 were assigned 2 (the second lowest range), 7 were of medium-range capability (No. 3), and 8 were classified as having high-capability capacity (No. 4).

Age All else the same, how does age affect survival? Similar to conventional firms, Blomberg et al. (2010) show negative duration dependence for terrorist organizations: the chances of failing or dying decreases with time, i.e., the survival increases as a terror organization ages.

Lethality The same authors show that the more lethal an organization, the longer is it likely to last. This is more so in terms of the number of attacks than in terms of deaths the attacks cause.

Diversity of Attacks Those who deploy a greater variety of tactics, e.g., assassinations, armed assaults, and bombings, etc., tend to survive longer (Blomberg et al., 2011; Gaibulloev et al., 2013; Young & Dugan, 2014).

Size The size of an organization has been shown to be positively related to survival (Blomberg et al., 2011; Gaibulloev et al., 2013; Jones & Libicki, 2008; Phillips, 2014, 2015).[34]

Share of Domestic Terrorism Blomberg et al. (2011) and Gaibulloev et al. (2013) find that greater engagement in domestic terrorism is associated with a longer period of survival. Mounting domestic terrorist attacks, as Gaibulloev et al. (2013) argue, is less risky than transnational terrorist attacks. It is more difficult to "blend in on a foreign soil" than at home. Transnational attacks involve the additional risk of crossing the border. It is easier to main ties with the support base at home. Transnational terrorist incidents are more likely to invite retaliation by foreign target countries, whereas governments are generally less willing to take punitive actions against their own citizens. These are the reasons why a higher share of domestic terrorism contributes to the longevity of a terror group.

Religiosity The last two cited research works also find that religiosity tends to enhance a terror organization's survival, the reason being that religious groups tend to be more homogeneous and committed.[35] The authors classify terror organizations into four types based on their orientation: left-wing, right-wing, nationalist, and religious. These categories are introduced by dummy variables.

State Sponsorship A question of interest and vital importance is the role of state sponsorship in the longevity of a terror organization. As we discussed in Chap. 2, in the pre-*9/11* era, the Abu Nidal Organization was supported by Iraq, Libya, and Syria. Since the 1980s till date, Iran has remained as the benefactor of Hezbollah in

---

[34] (Blomberg et al., 2011 and Gaibulloev et al., 2013) consider "peak size," the largest recorded size of an organization over its lifetime. Phillips (2014, 2015) models size differently. His size variable, *Group size*, is coded 0 if the group has fewer than 100 members, 1 if the group has between 100 and 999, 2 if the group has 1000–9999, and 3 for the few groups with 10,000 or more members.

[35] We shall discuss the link between religious orthodoxy and terrorism in Chap. 14.

Lebanon. Some terror groups active in the Kashmir valley in India are supported by Pakistan.

A detailed empirical analysis of how state sponsorship affects the survival of terror organization *and* how they end is carried out by Carter (2012). Carter considers two types of ending: internal reasons or forceful elimination. (Other types of ending like victory and a negotiated settlement are not treated.) The conventional wisdom is that state sponsorship—in terms of financial help and possibly logistic support—should make terror organization more durable because of financial and possibly logistic support. However, Carter argues that it could be the opposite—as sponsors that provide safe haven to terror organization may have incentives to provide information to the target about the groups in order to avert military operations by target countries within their territory. If so, state sponsorship would increase the risk of being forcefully eliminated.[36] Carter's major finding is that groups that have a state sponsor which provides a safe haven face *less* chance of survival and are *more* likely to be eliminated and that by force.[37]

7.5.3.2 Interaction Among Terrorist Organizations

A business firm's life span depends on its interaction with other firms in terms of competition and cooperation. This is true for "terrorist firms" too.

Competition Young and Dugan (2014) articulate three hypotheses on how competition may affect the survival of terror groups. In the face of competition, they would want to distinguish themselves from one another. This leads to an *outbidding hypothesis*: terror groups that operate in a more competitive environment are more likely to fail. Also, larger groups with more resources can undermine and eliminate other groups in order to gain prominence and would tend to receive larger financial support from the sympathizers. This is a predatory behavior, leading to a *top dog hypothesis*: top dog terror organizations are less likely to fail than their competitors. As the number of groups increases, the power differential between the top dogs and other groups widens. This gives rise to the *interactive hypothesis:* as the number of terror groups increases, less likely are the top dogs to fail compared to other groups.

The question is: how are these concepts "operationalized" from data? The unit of Young–Dugan's analysis is group-year. For each organization, the authors determine the primary target country, defined as the country in which the organization carries

[36] To illustrate his point, Carter refers to the Jammu & Kashmir Liberation Front, JKLF, described in Chap. 2. The JKLF was a major group fighting in the Kashmir Valley, India, until the early 1990s, during which time it was generously financed and given a safe haven by Pakistan. But all this started to dry up and it was nearly decimated by the Indian security forces. Its leadership accused that Pakistan was providing information about it to Indian forces. Although this claim is not verified, it is consistent with the fact that Pakistan leaned more toward other groups that wanted Kashmir to belong to Pakistan, whereas JKLF's objective was an independent statehood of Kashmir.

[37] There are other group-specific factors that significantly affect longevity too. For instance, dealing with drugs is positively related to longevity, the reason being that it provides a good source of revenue (Phillips, 2015). The statistical significance of this effect is mild however (10%). Gaibulloev et al. (2013) show that multiplicity of bases also contributes to a group's longevity.

out attacks the most often.[38] If T_x is the main target country of the terror organization x in a given year, then the number of terrorist organizations that have mounted attacks in T_x is paired with x and interpreted as the relevant variable for the outbidding hypothesis.[39] Whether an organization is the "top dog" is captured by a dummy variable: if x has mounted the greatest number of attacks among all terrorist groups operating in T_x in a given year, then it is assigned 1 (indicating that is the top dog); otherwise, it is assigned value 0. Interactive hypothesis is modeled by creating an interactive variable, top dog dummy × the number of groups in T_x in a given year.

The dependent variable is a dummy coded 1 if the group stopped operating after the current year, and zero otherwise. The main result from Young and Dugan's analysis is that the coefficients on the number of groups, top dog, and the interaction term are all statistically significant at 5% or less and have the right signs. That is, all three hypotheses are empirically supported.

Violent Rivalry In Sect. 7.2.1, we discussed two types of rivalry: intra-field and inter-field. The former refers to rivalry among groups that have the same broad objectives, whereas the latter refers to that among groups who have taken opposite positions. How does such rivalry impact on the longevity of groups?[40] This is studied by Phillips (2015), who, contrary to common intuition, argues that violent rivalries can enhance the longevity of terrorist groups. The logic is that violent rivalry would draw more civilians to take sides, inspire innovation, and provide new incentives to group members. Because of violent rivalry, the leadership would try hard to instill a sense of purpose and solidarity.[41]

Phillips's dataset covers the period 1987–2005 and considers nearly 600 terrorist groups, about 15% of which had a violent rival at some point. He runs two types of regression, one that has, among many controls, the variable *Violent rival*, a dummy which is coded 1 if the group has a violent rival and 0 otherwise and the other that distinguishes between intra-field and inter-field rivalry (also captured by dummy variables, namely, *Violent rival—intra-field* and *Violent rival—inter-field*). The former tests when violent rivalry is a significant predictor of longevity and the latter tests which type of rivalry has a stronger impact. The dependent variable is *Group end*, coded 1 in the year that the terrorist group ended, if it ended during the sample, and 0 otherwise.[42]

---

[38] It is possible that a country could be the primary target of two or more terror groups. These organizations are then the country's primary groups.

[39] However, the number of groups as a proxy for competition is criticized by Miller (2016), who argues that the number of groups may capture not just competition but also cooperation.

[40] Young and Dugan did not directly consider armed conflicts among terror groups.

[41] As Miller (2016) observes, this is similar to assertion by Frederic Thrasher, a well-known sociologist in the 19920s who studied gangs, that gangs "develop through strife and thrive on warfare."

[42] Following Cronin (2009), terrorist group has "ended" when it has either ceased to exist as an organization or given up terrorism as a tactic even if it remains a political group.

The author hypothesizes that (a) violent rivalry per se has a positive effect on longevity and (b) the effect is stronger in case of inter-field rivalry than intra-field rivalry. The estimates support both hypotheses.

Cooperation We noted examples of cooperation among terrorist groups in Sect. 7.2.2. In a separate paper, Phillips (2014) has empirically examined how cooperation among terrorist groups affects their longevity. In order to survive, these groups need to "mobilize" resources, where mobilization refers to the process of maintaining resources like manpower and money. Terrorists groups often share resources. Cooperation can help groups meet the organizations' needs relating to personnel, training, weapons, and information, among other essentials. This helps them to endure and mount attacks more effectively, which, in turn, contributes to further recruitment and other ends. In short, cooperative relations, through mitigating mobilization challenges, help terrorist groups survive. When a terrorist group has difficulty mobilizing resources, it is more prone to ending. Hence the hypothesis is that cooperation would increase the survival rate of terror groups.

Of course, there is a counter-argument that cooperation may create dependence and that can prove to be harmful. As Halloran (1987) speculates, this is why Shining Path did not collaborate with other terror groups. In spite of this counter-argument, Phillips posits that cooperation increases a group's longevity (presuming that benefits outweigh the costs). He also posits a second hypothesis that cooperation has a greater impact on longevity in countries where it is more difficult to cooperate. Difficulties in cooperating are proxied by how capable the state is in gathering intelligence and undertaking direct counter-terrorism measures and how undemocratic the state is. A dictatorial regime will be more trigger-happy to deal with terrorists than a democratic regime.

As examples, it is a generally held view that organizations like FARC and ELN in Colombia survived for decades because of the weakness of the Colombian government in dealing with these groups firmly.[43] On the other hand, countries like the USA or the UK have relatively more efficient systems of intelligence and counter-terror measures to deal with terrorism (barring, of course, the occurrence of a spectacular event like *9/11*). Recall how an autocratic state like Russia heavy-handedly dealt with Moscow theater terror attack in 2002 and Beslan school bus attack in 2004.

One of the Phillips's independent variables is *Capacity*. It measures the state's capability to deal with terrorists by World Bank Government Effectiveness Estimate index, which, in turn, is based on various attributes like bureaucratic competence, degree of independence from political pressure, etc. Like many other research work, the degree of democracy is proxied by Freedom House's Polity index.

Measuring a group's cooperative interaction is the central innovation of Phillips (2014). A variable *Allies* for each terror organization in the dataset is constructed as equal to the number of its cooperative allies. A terrorist group is considered to be in

[43] As we discussed in Chap. 2, the Colombian government has recently signed a pact with FARC, whose members have surrendered their arms and eschewed violence.

a cooperative relationship with another terrorist group if a source indicates that the groups have logistically or operationally cooperated. In the data *Allies* ranges from 0 to 33 and the group with 33 ties is al-Qaeda, as one would expect; all other groups have 12 or fewer allies with the average of 1.2.

While *Allies* measures the degree of a group's *direct interaction* with other groups, a broader measure of interaction by a group is its position in a network and particularly how a group is connected with others, who, in turn, are connected with others. From Sect. 7.3, recall the notion of eigenvector centrality, which captures the notion of how importantly connected a person or unit is in a network. Suppose that unit *A* has a small number of direct links (direct friends) than does unit *B*. Unit *A* can still be more connected in a network if its (fewer number of) friends are sufficiently more connected with others than the direct friends of unit *B*. Eigenvector centrality is a measurement of such "potential" interaction by a unit. Phillips creates another variable for interaction for each terrorist group, namely, *Allies' ties* which is equal to the group's eigenvector centrality in the network.[44]

Two hypotheses are proposed: (I) survival increases with each additional ally and/or a higher eigenvalue centrality and (II) the survival-enhancing impact of co-operation will be higher in countries with higher *Capacity* and/or in more autocratic regimes. Here are Phillips's findings:

[a] The coefficient of *Allies* is negative and significant. But that on *Allies' ties* is not. Thus hypothesis (I) is supported in terms of the number, not the importance, of allies an organization has, signifying that *the number of relationships matters but to whom a group is connected is not significant.*[45]

The counter-terrorism implication is that the governments or authorities should be concerned about a terrorist group's number of connections and not just its link with a highly connected group such as al-Qaeda.

[b] Interaction terms of *Allies* with regime type and capability are both significant, and their signs are consistent with hypothesis (II).

Some of the factors explaining longevity of terror organizations are summarized here.

Is That So? 7.4: Longevity of Terrorist Organization

A terrorist group's lethality, diversity of attacks, autonomy, dominance over, and alliance with other groups contribute toward its longevity. Religious groups tend to live longer.

[44] The author provides two illustrative examples. The Islamic Movement of Uzbekistan has only two ties, which is near average for *Allies*. However, its *Allies' ties* score (0.111) is well above average, because its ties are to al-Qaeda and the Taliban. A group with a high value for *Allies* and a low value for *Allies' ties* is the Ulster Defence Association. Its allies were local groups with few or no other ties.

[45] To paraphrase Phillips (2014), "The lack of significance for *Allies' ties* could occur because more well-connected groups might be occupied cooperating with so many groups that they cannot devote much attention to every single ally, and therefore, there is less resource sharing. A partner with no other connections, however, is likely to focus substantial attention on its lone tie."

7.5.3.3 External Factors

The politico-economic characteristics, namely, population and per-capita real income and democratic institutions of target countries positively affect survival of terrorist groups (see Blomberg et al., 2010, 2011; Gaibulloev et al., 2013; Young & Dugan, 2014).

Regional factors and geography play a role too. Blomberg et al. (2011) and Gaibulloev et al. (2013) show that terrorist groups based in the Middle East and North Africa survive longer than groups based in other regions. The hypothesis is that a terrorist organization's ability to survive is higher in regions and regimes with more fragile counter-insurgency institutions. Groups based in a landlocked country are more likely to fail, while those in tropical countries are more likely to survive (Gaibulloev et al., 2013).

7.6 Take-Aways

- Like business firms, a terrorist organization faces competition. The critical difference is that competition among terror groups manifests in violent rivalries. There are inter-field and intra-field rivalries, referring, respectively, to groups with opposite and similar objectives.
- We studied some elementary concepts of network theory like a node, direct and indirect links, connected versus unconnected, regular versus irregular networks, degree, density, geodesic path, length between two nodes, between-centrality, and closeness-centrality, among others.
- In the light of some of these concepts, we studied the network of perpetrators involved in *9/11* and Bali attacks in early 2000s.
- Like business firms, terrorist "firms" face problems of delegation and control with the organization because of difference in preferences. Delegation of tasks by the leaders of group to middlemen and terror operatives entails moral hazard problems. However, to reduce these problem by control leads to serious security issues, and this is unique for clandestine and non-state groups including terror groups.
- This leads to two tradeoffs (Shapiro, 2013): the security-control tradeoff and the security-efficiency tradeoff. The author draws evidence of various internal organizational problems starting from Narodnaya Volya in Russia in the late nineteenth century to modern day Islamic terror groups.
- He argues that counter-terrorism measures should also include instruments that can potentially create or exacerbate these organizational issues and weaken the groups. A variety of specific recommendations are offered.
- Terrorist organizations end in different ways like police crackdown, military crackdown, political negotiations, victory, and splintering. Police crackdown is the most common type of ending for terrorist groups.

- Various factors tend to significantly explain the longevity of terror organizations. They can be summarized into three types: group-specific factors, interaction among terror groups, and external factors like politico-economic characteristics and geography of target countries.
- These factors and the direction of their impact on longevity include an organization's autonomy and capability (+), age (+), lethality (+), diversity of attacks (+), size (+), share of domestic terrorism (+), competition (−), being the top dog (+), the number of allies (+), population, per-capita income, and democratic institutions of target countries (+). In addition, religious groups tend to survive longer. Terror groups based in the Middle East and North Africa have higher lifetimes, on average, than groups in the other regions of the world. Interestingly and paradoxically, state sponsorship that includes providing a safe haven for a terrorist group tends to exert a negative effect on survival (Carter, 2012). A possible reason, it is argued, is that such states have an incentive provide damaging information about terror groups to the target countries in order to avert military reprisal from them.

Appendix to Chapter 7

7.A Individual Studies on Survival of Terrorist Organizations

Authors	Method of analysis	Time period	Dataset
Vittori (2009)	Survival analysis	1968–2007	TBK dataset
Blomberg et al. (2010)	Survival analysis	1970–2007	ITERATE
Blomberg et al. (2011)	Survival analysis	1970–2007	GTD
Carter (2012)	Multinomial logit	1968–2006	GTD and Jones and Libicki (2008)
Gaibulloev et al. (2013)	Survival analysis	1970–2007	RAND event data and Jones and Libicki (2008)
Young and Dugan (2014)	Discrete-time survival analysis (logit regression)	1970–2010	GTD
Phillips (2014, 2015)	Discrete-time survival analysis	1987–2005	GTD, TOPs, Asal and Rethemeyer (2008), Jones and Libicki (2008), Lexis-Nexis and targeted research and books

Table 7.5: Studies on duration of terrorist organizations. *Note:* ITERATE tracks transnational terrorism only

Questions

7.1 Figures 7.3 and 7.5 both have six nodes. Calculate which of the two networks has higher density.

7.2 In the post *9/11* years, al-Qaeda as a centralized organization does not exist. Different al-Qaeda groups in Asia and Africa are loosely connected at best. Is it a sign of al-Qaeda's strength or weakness?

7.3 Like businesses, terrorist organizations face risks. Which kinds of risks for a terrorist group are dissimilar to those facing a firm in an industry?

7.4 Empirical analysis shows that terror groups who have focused on domestic attacks and who are religious tend to survive longer. Give examples of terror groups to explain these findings.

Part IV

Fighting the War on Terror: How Direct Counter-Terrorism Measures Work

Chapter 8

Security

8.1 Introduction

In Chap. 1, we categorized different types of CT (counter-terror) measures. This chapter marks the beginning of the economic-theoretic analysis of these measures, starting with security, a defensive strategy. You may ask what do we mean by an *economic* analysis of security? Is not it obvious that a nation should increase security in the face of a greater threat of terrorism? Yes, of course. However, an economic analysis goes deeper into how security measures work from a cost–benefit perspective by unraveling the mechanisms implied by incentives facing the terrorists and the target states.

Our analysis illustrates two mechanisms at work, through which security measures tend to thwart terror incidents and limit damage from terror.

① Suppose, for a moment, that terrorists keep up their level of planned attacks on a country or region despite more security measures. Even then, greater security would lead to more planned attacks being foiled or the same number of attacks being less harmful. This is a ***direct effect***.

② The other channel is that, in anticipation of greater security and hence less success, the terrorists will be induced to reduce their attacks. This is a ***deterrence effect***.

S. P. Das, *Economics of Terrorism and Counter-Terrorism Measures*,
https://doi.org/10.1007/978-3-030-96577-8_8

Transnational terror groups often target more than one country. If one of the target countries steps up its security measures, it will have repercussions on the threat of terrorism facing another, as terrorists and terror groups would tend to shift their attacks from one to another depending upon the variations in security measures employed by different target countries. This creates an *interdependence* of security measures adopted by multiple target countries. The problem assumes special significance if the target countries happen to be neighbors like Belgium and France or Iraq and Syria, because it is less costly for the terrorists shift their operations. In this chapter, we learn the nature and the implications of such interdependence.

The current chapter also makes an important point that the effects of CT measures *can* be econometrically measured, given relevant and sufficient data. In fact, the first analytical cum economic model of terrorism—due to William M. Landes (Landes, 1978)—quantified the negative effect of the installation of metal detectors at airports in the early 1970s *and* legal measures to mete out punishment to captured hijackers on plane hijacking.

In Sect. 8.2, we begin with Landes's work and its extensions. We will clearly see how terrorism is framed as an economic problem, how behavioral predictions can be derived from economic theory, and how they can be empirically tested. In Sect. 8.3, we use game-theoretic models to analyze the direct and deterrence effects of security measures and, particularly, how far a targeted country would respond in terms of security measures to an increase in the threat of terror attacks. The nature of the strategic interdependence among multiple target countries is analyzed in Sect. 8.4.

8.2 Landes's Analysis of Plane Hijacking and Its Extensions

Since we are talking about plane hijacking, it will be useful to know a bit about its history. The first recorded skyjacking goes back to 1931 in Peru. The first recorded skyjacking of a commercial airliner took place in 1948, a failed attempt. A Hong Kong-based Cathay Pacific flight from Macau to Hong Kong was hijacked by four men, who killed the pilot after take-off. The aircraft crashed and twenty-six people died. Interestingly, one of the hijackers was the sole survivor. The first *successful* skyjacking also occurred during the same year: a Greek T.A.E. airliner was hijacked by six pro-communist students wanting a passage to Yugoslavia.

A US carrier was hijacked over the US airspace for the first time in 1961. A Puerto Rican born American citizen locked himself in a bathroom onboard in a National Airlines flight from Miami to Key West, Florida and passed a note saying that he had a bomb that could destroy the airplane. Complying with his demand, the plane was diverted to Havana, Cuba, where he deplaned without any incident and was granted asylum. The plane returned to Key West. No one was hurt.

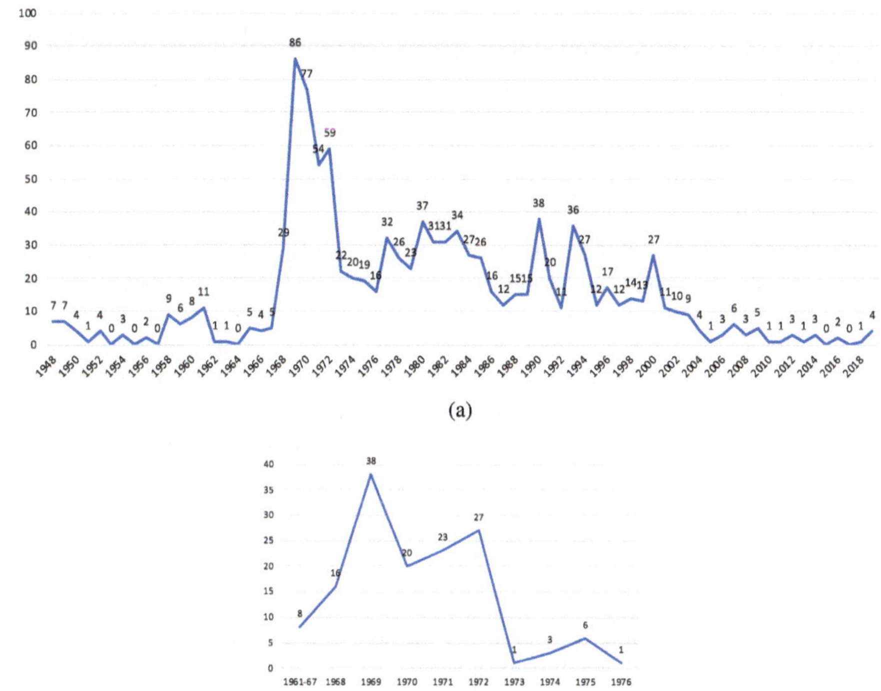

(a)

(b)

Fig. 8.1: Time-Series of Plane Hijacking. (**a**) No. of hijacking: global, 1948–2019. (**b**) No. of hijacking: US carriers, 1961–1976. *Sources*: (**a**) Aviation Safety Network, https://aviation-safety.net; it is a private independent initiative, founded by Harro Ranter and Fabian I. Lujan; pension obtained, with thanks and (**b**) Landes (1978)

Figure 8.1 graphs the number of global plane hijackings and that of US carriers in panels (a) and (b), respectively. During 1961–1967, the respective numbers were 27 and 8. In 1968 alone, these numbers jumped to 29 and 16, respectively. Remember the high profile 1968 hijacking by the Palestinian group, PFLP, described in Chap. 2, in which an Israeli El Al flight from Rome to Tel Aviv was redirected to Algiers and passenger lives were threatened in exchange for the hijackers' demand. Marking the beginning of modern terrorism tactics, this incident catalyzed a surge of plane hijacking around the world in the ensuing years.

The 1961–1972 period was the "golden era" of skyjacking, during which more than 50% of the events were "successful." In the majority of incidents involving US carriers, the planes were diverted from the USA to Cuba. Toward the late 1960s, hijacking attempts with destination Cuba became so common that the FBI reportedly contemplated setting up a fake Havana airport in southern Florida to trick hijackers to thinking they arrived in Cuba. There were incidences where the terrorists wanted to divert the plane elsewhere. For instance, in 1969, Raffaele Minichiello, an Italian-American marine, who had a pay dispute with the higher authorities, hijacked a plane from Los Angeles to his native country, Italy.[1] It was not a hostage situation. Outside the USA, some of the plane hijackings from 1968 to 1972 were motivated to secure the release of prisoners by using passengers and crew as hostages.

From the viewpoint of counter-terrorism measures, 1973 was a landmark year, when, for the first time, metal detectors were installed at the airports to screen passengers and their carry-on luggage. For our purpose, notice the precipitous fall in the number of plane hijackings beginning in 1973. Globally and in respect to the US carriers, there were 22 and one hijackings, respectively, compared to 59 and 27 in 1972. The installation of metal detectors as a security measure obviously dealt a severe blow to skyjacking attempts. The downward trend in plane hijacking has continued over the following decades despite notable spikes including the *9/11* attacks.

Two paradigm shifts have occurred in terms of motives behind plane hijacking and risk to passengers.

① In 1968, for the first time, the hijackers used the lives of passengers as a bargaining chip to achieve something beyond a safe passage to a destination of their choice. Killing passengers was not a priority, however.

② In 2001, the *9/11* hijackers' intention was to kill passengers and themselves toward achieving a long-term political/ideological goal.

8.2.1 Theory

As the first economic analysis of terrorism and counter-terror measures, Landes (1978) formulated a theoretical model of economic choice of participating in a plane hijacking in the celebrated tradition of Gary Becker's economic approach to the understanding crime and punishment. This was followed by econometric estimation.

Think of an individual (an economic agent) contemplating to carry out a plane hijacking. Let us ignore (for now) any moral considerations and assume that the individual is guided by economic benefits and costs only. Furthermore, suppose that the individual would want to hijack only for the purpose of going to and living in a foreign country. There is no intention of harming anyone.

Let i denote the country of current residence of the individual (say, the USA) and j his destination country (say, Cuba). Suppose the estimated monetary value of the individual's wealth and income, i.e., life in the current country of residence (if she/he stays in country i) is worth W_i. Likewise, let W_j be the (expected) monetary value of life in country j. An obvious yet sensible assumption is that

Assumption 8.1. *Life is worth more to the individual contemplating plane hijacking in the destination country than in the current country of residence, i.e.,* $W_j > W_i$.

[1] He was greeted in Italy as a hero for this "adventure." After serving a short jail sentence, he ended up with signing a contract to be a star in a Westerner movie.

Otherwise, there is no scope for plane hijacking from an economic perspective. We shall call $W_j - W_i$ the *wealth gap*. However, if the person decides to hijack, there is positive probability, π_a, that she/he will be apprehended. If apprehended, there is a positive probability π_c that she/he will be convicted. Hence, π_c is a conditional probability. Let L_a and L_c denote, respectively, the losses in monetary terms from being apprehended but not convicted and from being apprehended and convicted. Another natural assumption is that

ASSUMPTION 8.2. *Monetary loss associated with being apprehended and convicted is greater than that from being apprehended but not convicted, i.e., $L_c > L_a$.*

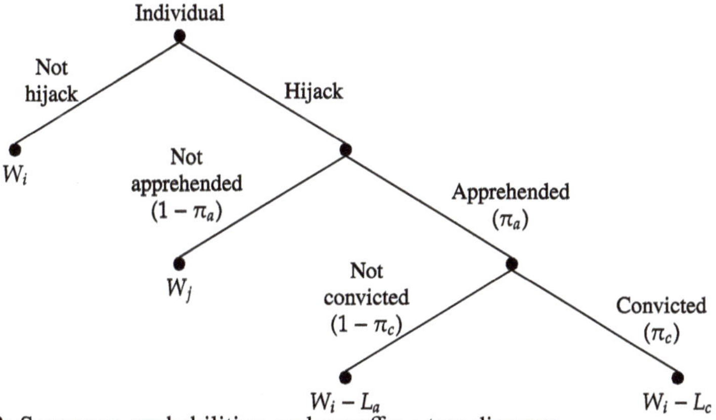

Fig. 8.2: Sequence, probabilities, and payoffs: a tree diagram

State	Probability	Payoff
(1) Not apprehended	$1 - \pi_a$	W_j
(2) Apprehended but not convicted	$\pi_a(1 - \pi_c)$	$W_i - L_a$
(3) Apprehended and convicted	$\pi_a\pi_c$	$W_i - L_c$

Table 8.1: Different states, probabilities, and payoffs (if the individual decides to hijack)

Of course, hijacking invites other risks for a hijacker like being injured and/or killed by passengers, crew, or police, crashing of the plane, etc. Let us ignore these risks for the sake of simplicity.

The question is whether the individual will decide to hijack a plane or not, a *binary choice* problem. The answer depends naturally upon his "payoff" in alternative states. For instance, if he decides not to participate in hijacking, his payoff is W_i. Of course, a person is interested ultimately in his utility or satisfaction that the payoff provides him. For simplicity, let us suppose that

Assumption 8.3. *A potential hijacker's utility or satisfaction is proportional to his payoff.*[2]

As long as this factor of proportion is constant, the magnitude of it is immaterial in the binary decision making. Therefore, for notational simplicity, we take this factor of proportion equal to unity. Hence, payoff and utility are, analytically, one and the same thing.[3]

8.2.1.1 Sequence of Events, Probabilities, and Payoffs

Consider Fig. 8.2, a *tree diagram*. There are two branches from the top, representing the binary choice problem: hijack or not hijack. If he does not hijack, he enjoys W_i (end of the story before it really begins).

If he hijacks, there are two possibilities: either he is apprehended or he is not. Accordingly, there are two branches. The respective probabilities are π_a and $1 - \pi_a$. In case of no apprehension, the mission is successful. The terrorist reaches his dreamland and enjoys the payoff W_j. But he is apprehended two possibilities open up, shown as two branches down from the branch "Apprehended." Either he is convicted or he is not, with probabilities π_c and $1 - \pi_c$. In the former scenario, his payoff is $W_i - L_c$, where L_c is cost of being apprehended and convicted. In the latter case, the payoff is $W_i - L_a$ with L_a being the cost of being apprehended but not convicted. Different states, their probabilities, and the associated payoffs are summarized in Table 8.1.

Notice that the states (2) and (3) in Table 8.1 are conditional upon the person being apprehended, and thus the respective probabilities, depending upon whether he is not convicted or not, appear in the multiplicative form. Check that the probabilities over all three rows add up to one—as it must.

Because the payoffs from hijacking are uncertain, we calculate the expected payoff, equal to the sum of the payoffs weighted by their respective probabilities.

$$\begin{aligned}\text{Expected Payoff}_{\text{hijacking}} &= (1 - \pi_a)W_j + \pi_a\left[(1 - \pi_c)(W_i - L_a) + \pi_c(W_i - L_c)\right]\\ &= (1 - \pi_a)W_j + \pi_a(1 - \pi_c)(W_i - L_a) + \pi_a\pi_c(W_i - L_c).\end{aligned}$$

The expression is consistent with the right-hand side nodes of the tree diagram and Table 8.1.

8.2.1.2 Binary Decision

Presuming that the individual is rational, it is natural to assume the following decision rule:

---

[2] In the theory of uncertainty and risk, it means that the individual is risk-neutral.

[3] Landes (1978) assumes a more general utility function $U = U(W)$, where the function $U(W)$ is nonlinear.

Do not hijack or hijack according to the payoff from not hijacking $\gtrless$ the expected payoff from hijacking.

This is equivalent to

$$W_i \gtrless (1 - \pi_a)W_j + \pi_a(1 - \pi_c)(W_i - L_a) + \pi_a\pi_c(W_i - L_c), \tag{8.1}$$

which simplifies to

$$W_i \gtrless \bar{W} \equiv W_j - \underbrace{\frac{\pi_a}{1 - \pi_a}\left[(1 - \pi_c)L_a + \pi_c L_c\right]}_{\text{risk cost associated with hijacking}}. \tag{8.2}$$

Here $\bar{W}$ simply defines the whole right-hand side of the above expression. We can interpret the second mathematical term inside $\bar{W}$ (with a negative sign in front) as the cost of risk associated with hijacking, i.e.,

$$\text{Risk Cost of Hijacking} = \frac{\pi_a}{1 - \pi_a}\left[(1 - \pi_c)L_a + \pi_c L_c\right], \tag{8.3}$$

so that $\bar{W}$ is the value of living in the destination country minus the risk cost of engaging in plane hijacking. As you would expect, the risk cost of hijacking increases with the probabilities π_a and π_c as well as the magnitudes of punishments L_a and L_c.

The inequality (8.2) is the implied choice rule, which is intuitive. It says that the person will decide not to hijack or hijack according as the payoff from not hijacking (W_i) exceeds or falls short of the expected payoff from hijacking.[4]

Within a given population in the original country of residence, who would be then motivated to hijack a plane? We first restrict to those who think they will be economically better off living in the destination country j than in the current country of residence i. Consider the distribution of wealth-cum-income (briefly wealth) W among individuals in this sub-population. In principle, those with wealth W less than $\bar{W}$ will be motivated to undertake hijacking. But, we recognize that all such individuals will not be influenced by economic considerations only. A host of non-economic considerations can come into play like physical ability and morality, to name a few. It seems reasonable to assume that only a fraction of those having wealth $(= W) < \bar{W}$ will be guided by economic factors solely and attempt hijacking.

Overall then, in view of the choice rule (8.2), the model predicts that

[4] The remaining razor-edge possibility is where the two sides of (8.2) are equal to each other. In this case, the person will be indifferent between the two choices.

Result 8.1

The number of plane hijacking increases with the wealth gap $(W_j - W_i)$ and decreases with (i) the probability of apprehension, (ii) probability of conviction, (iii) the length and complexity of the legal process, and (iv) severity of sentencing if convicted.

Note that (iii) and (iv) of Result 8.1 are reflected in the terms, L_a and L_c.

A few important remarks are in order.

[a] We began this section with a discussion of installation of metal detectors at airports as security measures. Where is the installation of the metal detectors in the model? The answer is that it is represented by the probability of apprehension π_a.

[b] The model illustrates that, besides the security measures, the legal system can also serve as a deterrence of terrorism.

[c] Here is a subtle point. In (8.2) or (8.3), mark that π_a appears in both the numerator and the denominator, reflecting that an increase in the probability of apprehension acts as a deterrence in two ways: by reducing the chance of a successful hijack $(1 - \pi_a)W_j$ and increasing the opportunity cost of attempting a hijack. In contrast, π_c and the loss terms are present in the numerator only, indicating that they only affect the opportunity cost of hijacking.

[d] As mentioned earlier, the model is in the tradition of Gary Becker's economic theory of crime and punishment in framing that hijacking a plane is similar to an act of any other crime (see also Ehrlich, 1973).

8.2.2 Empirical Analysis

To test the theoretical predictions, Landes worked with data from the US Federal Aviation Administration on US carrier plane hijacking as well as the number of flights over the US airspace from the third quarter of 1961 (1961Q3) to the fourth quarter of 1976 (1976Q4). Altogether, there were 143 incidences. Multiple regression was used.

In one set of regressions, Landes used the number of quarterly hijackings as the dependent variable.[5] Landes's focus was on security and legal measures as "deterrence variables," which included the probability of apprehension, the conditional probability of conviction, and the length of sentencing of a person following conviction. Realize however that the probabilities of apprehension or conviction are not observable. Landes employed another set of regressions to estimate these probabilities. (This is not explained here.) The independent variables included but were not limited to the deterrence variables, just described. The wealth gap, which is hard to measure, was proxied by two macro variables: quarterly data on the rate of unemployment in the US economy and per-capita consumption. These variables reflect the opportunity cost of attempting a plane hijack. The size of the population in the

[5] In addition, he used two alternative measures of the incidence of hijacking: (a) the number of days between two consecutive hijackings (the reciprocal of which will be the probability of hijacking on a given day) and (b) the number of flights between two successive hijackings.

USA was also used as another explanatory variable in order to capture the number of potential hijackers.

8.2.2.1 Landes's Findings

① Among the deterrence variables, the probability of apprehension and length of sentencing were highly significant (at less than 5%), whereas the probability of conviction or incarceration was marginally significant (at nearly 10%).
② The estimated regression equation implied that *an increase in the probability of apprehension from 0.75 to 0.95, which was close to the estimated increase in probability from 1972 to 1973–1976, the estimated number of plane hijackings decreased by 1.1–2.2 per quarter.* This is huge.
③ The regression equation was also used to generate important "counterfactuals," meaning thought experiments. If mandatory screening were not instituted and the probability of apprehension from 1973 to 1976 remained the same as in 1972, there would have been 41–67 additional hijackings during the 1973–1976 period (whereas the actual number of hijackings in this period was 11 only). This is also huge and measures the combined effect of metal screening and more effective apprehension in general.[6]

8.2.2.2 Intervention Analysis *a la* Enders et al. (1990a)

A subsequent study, namely, Enders et al. (1990a), empirically analyzed the effect of metal detector screening (not legal measures) on plane hijacking by using a different dataset and a different method: monthly data on plane hijacking from 1968 to 1988, including those over the USA and outside of the USA, and, a time-series intervention analysis, which essentially treats a regime change as a dummy variable. Sections B.13 and B.13.2 in the General Appendix B explain the time-series analysis and the intervention analysis.

The authors considered three categories of plane hijackings: US domestic (including hijacking inside the USA and from the USA to Cuba), transnational (those where the origin and the destination countries are different, except USA–Cuba), and other (domestic hijackings outside of the USA and those that are not politically motivated). The intervention analysis provides estimates of the impact effect—the short-run effect on hijacking at the time of introduction of metal detectors—as well

[6] It can be argued that the success of the famous 1968 hijacking generated a worldwide fad to attempt hijacking, and, as long as fads are considered as a temporary shift of preference, we should expect hijackings to decline after a few years. If this preference shift was true, then deterrence measures are less effective than what these regressions imply. Landes also tested this ***fad hypothesis***. He did it in two alternative ways: (i) include foreign hijacking as an additional explanatory variable and (i) use foreign hijacking as a dependent variable while keeping US deterrence measures as the regressors. The idea is that if the fad hypothesis is significant, then, in regression (i) the marginal impact of deterrence variables will be less significant and less in magnitude, and, in regression (ii) the coefficients on the deterrence variables will be close to those when domestic hijacking was treated as the dependent variable. However, the regression results found support for neither. Therefore, although foreign and US carrier hijackings were positively correlated, the US deterrence measures were indeed the major determinants of US carrier hijackings.

as the cumulative long-run effect. Their main result is that the installation of metal detectors had a dramatic effect on the US domestic hijackings compared to transnational hijackings. The impact and long-run effects on the former were −5.62 and −5.62, while those for transnational hijackings were −1.29 and −1.78, respectively. Notice that for the US domestic hijackings, there is no difference between impact and long-run effects, which means that the installation of metal detectors had exerted a permanent effect which played out right from the start. Lesser impact was seen outside of the USA, probably because metal detectors were not installed or less effectively installed in many airports in other countries.

8.2.2.3 General Significance

The general significance of Landes's analysis and the follow-up work by Enders et al. (1990a) is the demonstration that

Is That So? 8.1: Metal Detector Installation and Skyjacking and Quantification of the Deterrence Effect of Security

The installation of metal detectors at airports in the early 1970s had a major dampening effect on skyjacking incidents. More generally, Landes's analysis demonstrated that deterrence effects of security as a counter-terror measure can be quantified.

8.3 A Model of Attack-Defend: One Terror Organization and One Target (Defending) State

Landes modeled plane hijacking as an individual act, which was appropriate since in the 1960s and 1970s many hijackings were individual attempts. However, in more recent decades, majority of terror acts are perpetrated by members of terror groups.[7]

We now explore the theoretical models of counter-terror measures when the acts of terror are "produced" by a terrorist firm, as portrayed in Chap. 7. Our fundamental premise is that the terrorist firm, which we call the "Org," is a rational entity. Furthermore, for now, terror is assumed to be directed toward one target country or state (briefly, "the State"), which tries to defend itself from the terror attacks by instituting security measures. It is an elementary attack-defend game-theoretic model of terrorism, whose scenario is similar to a regular warfare between two countries, except that the defending state does not attempt to attack or undermine the terror organization by preemptive strikes and other aggressive measures.

Our objective is to understand (a) the production process of terror attacks, (b) the link between terror attacks, security, and damage from terror attacks as well as, (c) the two mechanisms through which security acts as a counter-terror measure: a direct effect and (as highlighted in Landes's model) a deterrence effect.

[7] Lone-wolf attackers are "inspired" by terror groups too.

8.3.1 General-Damage, Terror-Damage, and Damage-Control Functions

As in Chap. 7, the Org produces terror attacks, which, in turn, serve as an input to cause or produce damages like death, injury, loss of property—and public fear, the hall mark of terrorism as a distinct form of violence. There are, hence, two "production functions" or technologies here:

1. One that produces a terror input, which we will call an *aggregate terror input*
2. The transformation of the aggregate terror input into damage

To elaborate, just as a regular firm that produces a good or a service with the help of labor, capital, etc., an Org produces the aggregate terror input with the help of terrorists (labor), equipment and funds (capital), etc. There are "technologies" associated with this production, e.g., suicide attacks, bombing, suicide-bombing, etc. For analytical simplicity, we will presume the terror producing technology to be one and given. Hence, we can think of the aggregate terror input as planned or attempted attacks. More generally, the given technology can be thought of as a given mix of different technologies. Security measures force terror organizations to find new technologies of organizing terror. But these issues are not addressed here. Thus, the choice of technology of the terror attack is ignored (for simplicity).

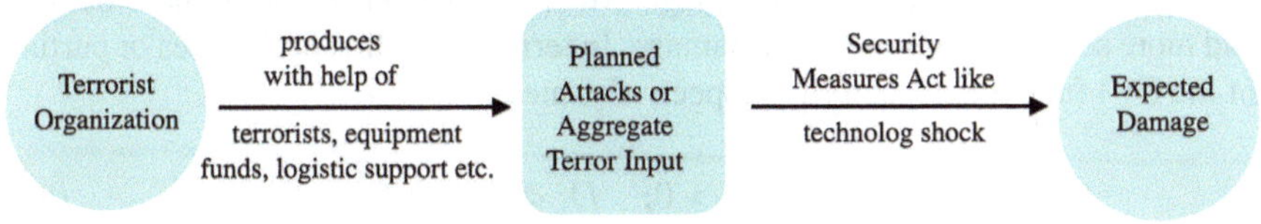

Fig. 8.3: Terrorist organization, attacks, and damage

To reiterate, the Org produces terror which acts as an input to produce damage. The sequence is illustrated in Fig. 8.3. As shown, realized damage is caused by the level of planned attacks, the magnitude of which is moderated by security measures. Hence, we can view security as a negative technology shock to the production of damage. For analytical purposes, let the planned attacks (X) and security (s) be measured by single indicators or numbers, both ranging from zero to infinity continuously. Let us measure damage—more precisely ***expected damage***—by a monetary unit and denote it by D. The damage process just described can be written compactly as

$$\boxed{D = D(X, s).} \tag{8.4}$$

We call the algebraic expression (8.4) a *a general-damage function.* For simplicity, *let us use "damage" for expected damage and "terror" to mean planned attacks.* When we keep security, s, fixed at some level and refer to the variation in damage due a change in terror, we call it a *terror-damage function.* It will be denoted by $D(X, \cdot)$, where the "$\cdot$" represents the suppressed argument or parameter s. Similarly, variations in damage due to changes in the security level at any given level of terror will be called a *damage-control function* and denoted by $D(\cdot, s)$. Obviously, the terror-damage and the damage-control functions are closely related to each other and both express damage as the outcome. But the distinction is important from an analytical perspective.

To make analytical progress, we need to impose some reasonable assumptions on *how* damage $D(\cdot)$ depends on terror (X) and security (s). This amounts to specifying restrictions on the terror-damage function $D(X, \cdot)$ and the damage-control function $D(\cdot, s)$.

ASSUMPTION 8.4. *(i) Given the level of security, an increase in terror implies more damage. (ii) Given the level of terror, an increase in security leads to less damage. (iii) Given the level of security, an increase in terror has a diminishing marginal effect of terror on damage. (iv) Given the level of terror, security has a diminishing marginal controlling effect on damage. (v) An increase in security reduces the marginal effect of terror on damage. (vi) Finally, an increase in terror increases the marginal damage-controlling effect of security.*

We must understand clearly what these assumptions mean or imply. They are explained below.

[a] (i) and (ii) refer to the direction of respective *marginal* or *incremental* effects of terror and security measures on damage. More terror tends to cause more damage and more security tends to reduce damage. In terms of the first derivatives or partials of the $D(\cdot)$ function, (i) and (ii), respectively, mean

$$\boxed{D_X > 0; \quad D_s < 0.} \tag{8.5}$$

Graphically, if we keep security level unchanged and plot X and D on the horizontal axis and the vertical axis, respectively, we will obtain a positively sloped line. This is the terror-damage function. Likewise, keeping the level of terror unchanged, varying s will generate a negatively sloped damage-control function in graph. These functions are illustrated in the top part of Fig. 8.4. The terror-damage function is drawn with security fixed at s_0. Similarly, the damage-control function assumes a given level of terror, X_0. Accordingly, we may rewrite the general-damage function a bit more informatively:

$$\boxed{D = D(\underset{+}{X}; \underset{-}{s}),} \tag{8.6}$$

where the symbols beneath the variables show the signs of the respective partials.

[b] (i) and (ii) also imply the shifts of damage-control and terror-damage functions, respectively. A variation in security changes damage at any given level of terror and thus shifts the terror-damage function. Part (ii) implies a downward shift of the terror-damage function as the level of security increases. This is shown in the bottom left part of Fig. 8.4 where a higher level of security s_1 is associated with the lower $D(X; \cdot)$ curve. (Ignore, for now, the points X_a and X_b and the slope lines.) Similarly, an increase in terror results in more damage at any given level of security and thus

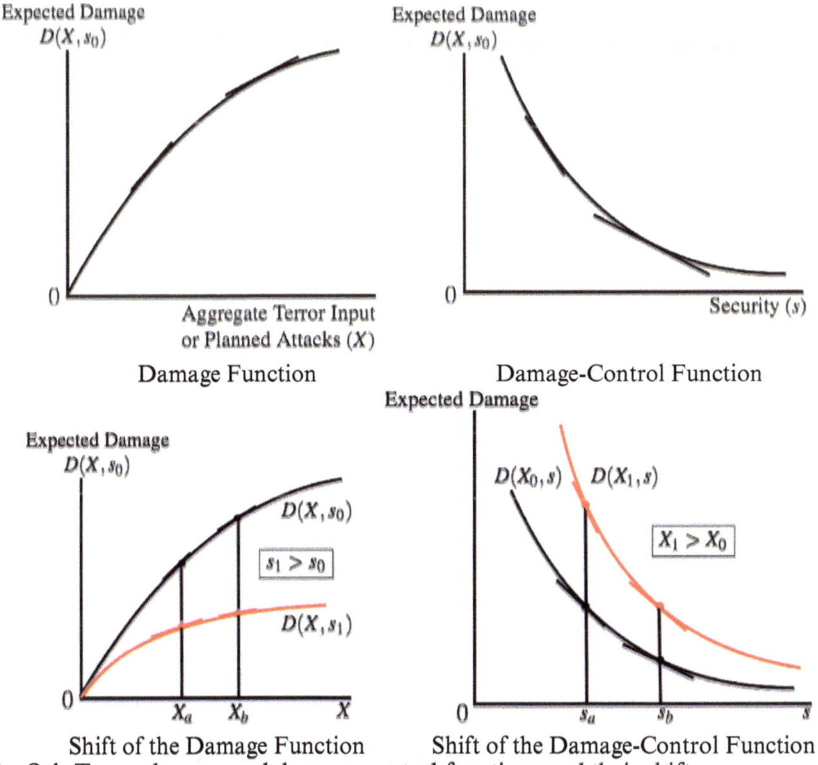

Fig. 8.4: Terror-damage and damage-control functions and their shifts

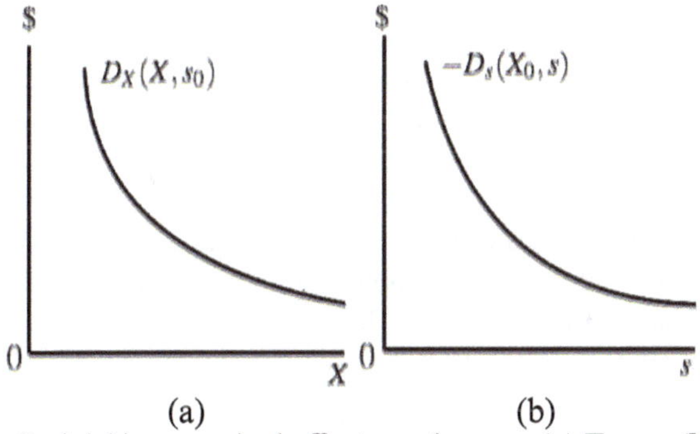

Fig. 8.5: Own diminishing marginal effects on damage. (**a**) Terror. (**b**) Security

shifts the damage-control function up, illustrated in the bottom right part, where $X_1 > X_0$. Ignore for the moment the points s_a and s_b and the slope lines.
[c] Parts (iii) through (vi) of Assumption 8.4 are a bit more subtle: they refer to how the *marginal* effects of terror and security on damage may vary. (iii) says that as terror increases, its marginal impact on damage diminishes. This is analogous to the principle of diminishing marginal utility or diminishing marginal returns in the microeconomic theory. Algebraically, it is equivalent to the second partial being negative, i.e.,

$$\boxed{D_{XX}(X, s) < 0.} \tag{8.7}$$

In Fig. 8.4, (iii) means that the (positive) slope of the terror-damage function becomes smaller for higher X. This is shown in the top left part of Fig. 8.4. Alternatively, we can see Fig. 8.5a, where the marginal effect of terror is plotted against the level of terror at security level fixed at s_0.

Is this reasonable? If damages were physical, one can put forth a reasonable argument that more attacks may not lead to proportional increase in the number of casualties or death. At any given level of security provided by the State, as terror strikes increase, people would become more watchful. But remember that damage from terror includes the value of the psychological impact in terms of public fear. If more attacks feed a fear psychosis, then diminishing returns may not hold since the marginal impact on damage will increase with terror. But if people develop a sense of resilience, it is reasonable to suppose that diminishing returns set in even if damages include the (negative) value of fear. Part (iii) of Assumption 8.4 presumes a scenario in which the problem of terrorism may be a major worry facing the populace, but it has not reached a stage of such high anxiety so as to create a sense of fear psychosis and near panic.

Assumption 8.4 part (iv) says that security is also subject to diminishing returns: more security implies less marginal effectiveness. The absolute value of the (negative) slope of the damage-control function falls with a higher level of s (see top right part of Fig. 8.4). Diminishing marginal effectiveness of security is also depicted in Fig. 8.5b.

Algebraically, the declining absolute value of a variable that is negative amounts to an increase in the value of the variable itself (you can imagine a variable taking values −5, −4.5, and −3 successively). Thus the second partial of the damage-control function is positive:

$$\boxed{D_{ss}(X, s) > 0.} \tag{8.8}$$

[d] Parts (v) and (vi) of Assumption 8.4 refer to the impact of one variable on the marginal effect of the other toward expected damage, i.e., how security affects the marginal effect of terror on damage and how terror affects the marginal damage-reducing effect of security.

Part (v) says that enhanced security makes terror less effective also *at the margin* in producing damage. This is captured in bottom left part of Fig. 8.4. See that, *at any given level of* X, e.g., X_a or X_b, the slope of the damage function or curve—

that measures the marginal impact of terror on damage—is smaller at security = s_1 than at security = s_0. That is, an increase in security shifts down the terror-damage function and makes it flatter.

Part (vi) states that an increase in security reduces damage more at a higher level of terror than at a lower level of terror. This is depicted in the bottom right part of Fig. 8.4. At $s = s_a$, the slope of the damage-control function is greater at $X = X_1$ than at $X = X_0$. The same is also true at $s = s_b$. Putting it differently, due to an increase in terror, the damage-control function not only shifts out but also becomes steeper.

Parts (v) and (vi) both imply that the cross partial of the general damage function is negative, i.e.,

$$\boxed{D_{Xs}(X, s) < 0.} \tag{8.9}$$

In fact, (v) and (vi) are the two sides of the same coin, i.e., the cross partials of damage with respect to terror and security are the same irrespective of the order of the partials.

Level of Terror X	Damage D at $s = 5$	Increase in damage at $s = 5$	Damage D at $s = 7$	Increase in damage at $s = 7$
(1)	(2)	(3)	(4)	(5)
0	0	–	0	–
1	100	100	95	95
2	190	90	180	85
3	275	85	260	80
4	345	70	326	66
5	408	63	386	60
6	458	50	431	45

Table 8.2: Restrictions on the terror-damage function: an illustrative numerical example

[e] Parts (i), (ii), (iii), and (v) of Assumption 8.4 pertain to the terror-damage function and can be further understood from the patterns of (hypothetical) numbers in Table 8.2. Column (1) lists different level of terror. Columns (2) and (3) are based on security level = 5, whereas columns (4) and (5) correspond to a higher level of security = 7. The total damages are given in columns (2) and (4) for $s = 5$ and $s = 7$, respectively, whereas the entries along the columns (3) and (5) are the respective incremental damages derived from columns (2) and (4), respectively. First, notice from columns (2) and (4) that total damage increases with terror, that is, part (i) of Assumption 8.4. Second, for each level of terror, compare column (4) with column (2): the entries are smaller along column (4), which is part (ii). Third, look at the pattern of increase in damage in columns (3) and (5) separately. They fall with X, confirming part (iii) of Assumption 8.4. Finally, compare columns (3) and (5) at each level of terror. Entries are smaller in column (5), i.e., incremental/marginal damage from terror is less at a higher security level, which is part (v).

Level of Security s	Damage D at $X = 10$	Decrease in damage at $X = 10$	Damage D at $X = 14$	Decrease in damage at $X = 14$
(1)	(2)	(3)	(4)	(5)
1	300	–	500	–
2	240	60	430	70
3	190	50	375	55
4	150	40	330	45
5	115	35	289	41
6	90	25	259	30
7	75	15	236	23

Table 8.3: Restrictions on the damage-control function: an illustrative numerical example

[f] Table 8.3 illustrates parts (i), (ii), (iv), and (vi) of Assumption 8.4 that relate to the damage-control function. The falling pattern of numbers along columns (2) and (4) represents part (ii) and the numbers in column (4) being higher than those along column (2) are consistent with part (i). Derived from columns (2) and (4), columns (3) and (5) exhibit a decreasing pattern, implying diminishing marginal effectiveness of security, part (iv). Now compare between columns (3) and (5): the *marginal* effectiveness of security is stronger when the terror level is higher, which is a part (vi) of Assumption 8.4.

8.3.2 Behavior of the Org

In Chap. 7, we studied a terror group as a network of individuals or as a collection of individuals with different objectives in a hierarchy with associated agency costs. In this chapter and Chap. 9, we abstract from the organizational aspects of a terror group. From the prospective of learning insights on how direct counter-terror measures work, except for intelligence and infiltration (to be studied in Chap. 11), it suffices to treat a terror group as unitary entity.

If so and given that the Org is rational, what is its objective function? In all chapters in Part IV including the current chapter, we abstract from the long-term objective of a terror organization and suppose that

ASSUMPTION 8.5. *The objective of a terror organization is to cause damage to a target country by unleashing terrorist attacks.*

Let us suppose that the total benefit or utility to the Org is proportional to the (expected) damage it inflicts upon the State. For simplicity, let this factor of proportionality be one, so that the damage from terror is equal to the Org's total benefit.

It then follows that the marginal benefit of the Org from producing the aggregate terror input is equal to the marginal damage from terror, D_X, measured by the slope of the terror-damage function. Figure 8.5a shows the MB curve facing the Org. This is replicated in Fig. 8.6a where the labeling is different only. Its downward slope

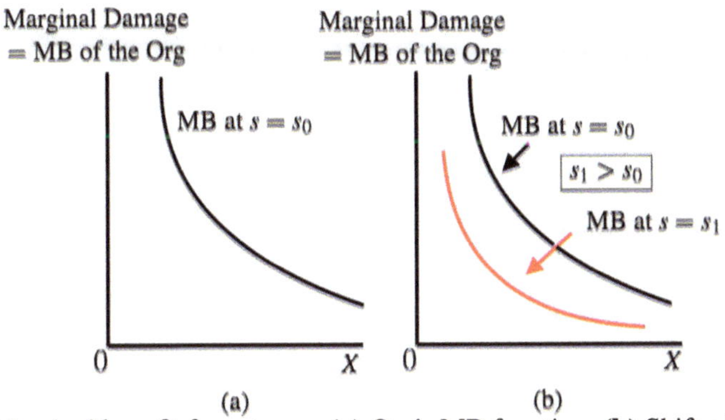

Fig. 8.6: Marginal benefit from terror. (**a**) Org's MB function. (**b**) Shift of Org's MB function

reflects part (iii) of Assumption 8.4. Furthermore, according to part (v), an increase in security shifts the Org's MB curve to the left (see panel (b) of Fig. 8.6).

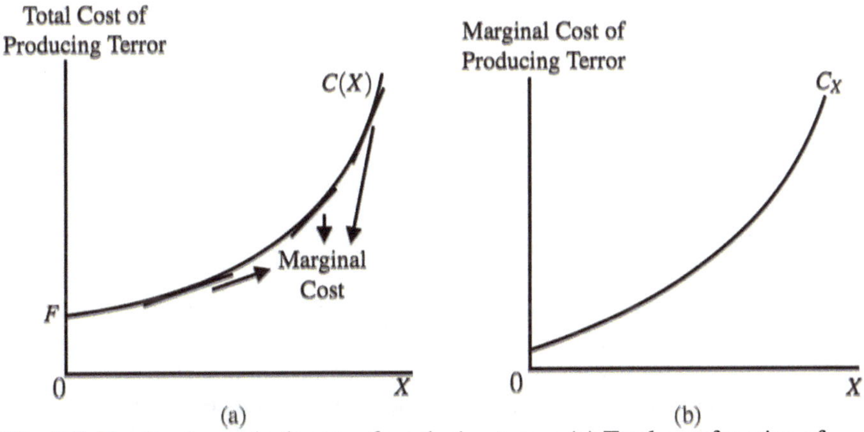

Fig. 8.7: Total and marginal costs of producing terror. (**a**) Total cost function of producing terror. (**b**) Marginal cost function of producing terror

Producing terror is, by no means, costless. The Org will have to compensate the families of terrorists, procure equipment, arrange transport, etc., which require funds. Let $C(X)$ denote the total cost function of producing terror. We assume that

Assumption 8.6. *The total and the marginal cost functions facing the Org in producing terror are increasing, i.e.,* $C_X > 0$ *and* $C_{XX} > 0$.

These functions are shown in Fig. 8.7.

Given its benefits and costs, we assume that

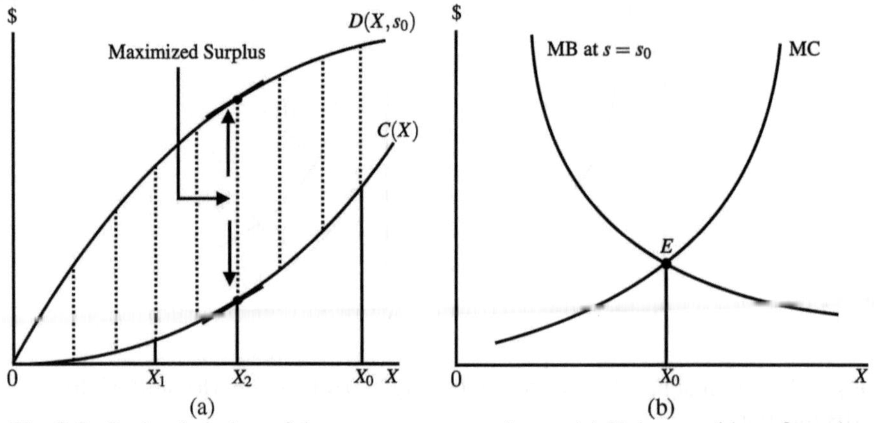

Fig. 8.8: Optimal choice of the aggregate terror input. (**a**) Using total benefit and total cost functions. (**b**) Using MB and MC functions

ASSUMPTION 8.7. *The Org, a rational entity, chooses the level of terror so as to maximize its surplus, equal to the difference between the total benefits and the total costs.*

Symbolically,

$$\begin{aligned}&\text{Org's Surplus}\\&\equiv \text{Damage (in \$)} - \text{Cost of Producing the Terror Input (in \$)}\\&= D(\underset{+}{X};\underset{-}{s}) - C(\underset{+}{X}).^{8}\end{aligned} \tag{8.10}$$

The signs underneath the argument X in the expression (8.10) illustrate the tradeoff facing the Org: as the Org increases terror, it tends to increase its benefits as well as costs. Just like a firm's profit maximization with respect to output that you learned in principles of microeconomics, the first-order marginal condition dictates the level of production of terror that maximizes the Org's surplus, that is, the MB from terror must equal the MC of terror. In symbols, the first-order condition (equation) is

$$\underbrace{D_X(X,s)}_{\text{MB}} = \underbrace{C_X(X)}_{\text{MC}}, \tag{8.11}$$

which solves the rational or optimal choice of the aggregate terror input.

Refer now to Fig. 8.8a. It depicts the total damage curve at $s = s_0$, the total cost curve of producing terror, and the surplus—-equal to the vertical difference between the total damage in \$ and the total cost at different levels of terror, X. Various levels

[8] The symbol "≡" means "equal to, by definition."

of surplus are indicated by the dashed lines. As we can see, *the surplus is maximized at the terror level* X_0*, which is identified as that X where the slope of the (expected) damage curve (= MB) is equal to slope of the cost curve (= MC).* This is the level of terror that a rational Org would choose. Panel (b) of Fig. 8.8 draws the MB and MC curves. The intersection point *E* marks where MB=MC. The corresponding optimal choice of terror is X_0, which must be the same X_0 in panel (a).

We are interested in the predictions of the model. In the present context, we ask how the Org's choice of terror (*X*) and the damage from terror (*D*) are impacted when the parameters of choice facing the Org change. A change in the predictions of variables in a model due to parametric changes is called *comparative statics* in economics.

We do two comparative statics:

1. The effects of an *exogenous increase* in terrorism or militancy
2. An increase in security measures

8.3.2.1 An Exogenous Increase in Terrorism or Militancy

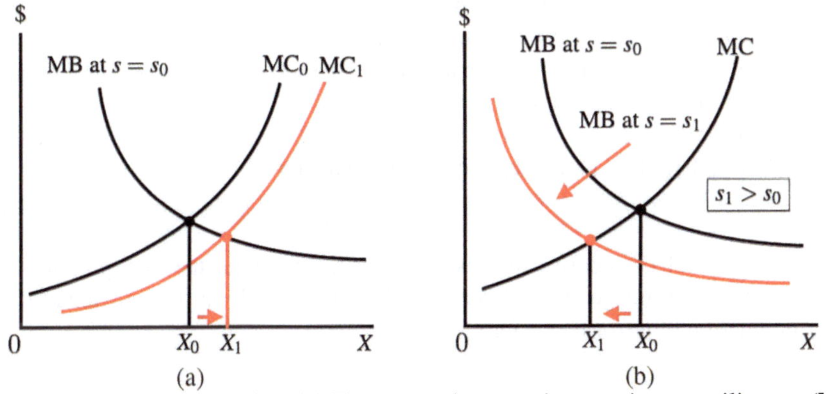

Fig. 8.9: Comparative statics. (**a**) Exogenous increase in terrorism or militancy. (**b**) Increase in security

We need to be first clear on what we mean by an increase in terrorism or militancy. It refers to more people willing to join terror organizations, more financial support for them, a higher propensity to launch attacks, etc. How does it translate into the terminology of economics? We interpret *an increase in terrorism or militancy as an exogenous decrease in the marginal cost of producing terror, which shifts the MC curve facing the Org downward.* Plainly put, *an increase in terrorism or militancy amounts to producing terror at lower total and marginal costs.* Given this interpretation, it is straightforward to deduce the implications of an increase in terrorism or militancy.

In Fig. 8.9a, the MC_1 curve, as opposed to the MC_0 curve, represents an exogenous fall in the marginal cost curve facing the Org. To understand its effect, let us keep the level of security measures unchanged (for now). Beginning with the MC_0 curve, we see that the equilibrium level of terror is X_0. If an exogenous increase in terrorism shifts the Org's marginal cost curve to MC_1, we observe that the new equilibrium terror level is X_1. That is, there is more production of terror. In turn, this leads to more damage.

Result 8.2

The level of security deployed by the target country remaining unchanged, an increase in militancy, or an exogenous increase in terrorism induces the Org to produce more terror in equilibrium. As a result, expected damage from terror attacks increases.

8.3.2.2 An Increase in Security Measures

Suppose the Org faces an increase in the security level employed by the State from say s_0 to s_1. How does it respond? In terms of Fig. 8.9b, this shifts the Org's MB curve inward or left, because an increase in security reduces the marginal effect of terror on damage (recall part (v) of Assumption 8.4). As we would expect, the new optimal choice of terror is X_1, which is less than X_0.

The next question is how does an increase in the security measures affect damage from terror? Refer to the damage function $D(X, s)$. As s increases and X decreases, D falls on *both* accounts. These are the *direct* and *deterrence effects* of security, respectively, discussed in the beginning of this chapter.

Result 8.3

As the level of security increases by the target State, the Org produces less terror. Damage from terror falls directly as well as through reduced production of terror by the Org.

This is one of the main take-away points from this chapter.

We now proceed to analyze the State's choice problem.

8.3.3 Behavior of the Defending State

The State suffers the damage from terror, which is the *cost of terrorism* to it. It attempts to reduce this cost by deploying security measures, which are costly too. Hence the State faces two types of costs:

1. The costs of terror
2. The security costs

Note that *incurring one type of cost (of security) tends to reduce the other (cost of terror).*

The cost of terror is simply the value of damage, $D(X, s)$, which we have already discussed. Moving on to security costs, we can categorize them into two types: direct resource costs and the loss of civil liberty. Direct security costs refer to the

State's expenditure to maintain its police and armed forces, secure borders, gather intelligence, etc. However, some of these measures infringe upon our civil liberty, and this is an important societal cost. A rational State that values personal liberty will be cognizant of this.

Let $T(s)$ denote total security costs. Analogous to Assumption 8.6,

Assumption 8.8. *The total and marginal security costs increase with security, i.e.,* $T_s > 0$ *and* $T_{ss} > 0$.

Obviously, the total security cost would increase with security. Increasing "marginal" cost of security is the second part of Assumption 8.8. Apart from other considerations, if more and more security makes us incrementally more averse toward our loss of civil liberty, that, by itself, would tend to imply increasing marginal cost of security.

Summing up the terror-damage and security costs, the total cost facing the State has the expression:

$$\Gamma \equiv D(\underset{+}{X}, \underset{-}{s}) + T(\underset{+}{s}). \tag{8.12}$$

We suppose that

Assumption 8.9. *The rational State's objective is to minimize the total cost by choosing the level of security measures.*

The signs under s in the expression (8.12) reveal the tradeoff: an increase in security entails higher resource costs of security but reduces the damage from terror (a benefit). The damage-control function $D(\cdot, s)$ inversely reflects the benefit from security.

8.3.3.1 Marginal (First-Order) Conditions

Realize that the total benefit from security is read along the damage-control function, already shown in the right panels of Fig. 8.4, *at some given level of terror* X_0. This is also drawn in the positive (top) quadrant of Fig. 8.10a. Given our assumptions, the total security cost function $T(s)$ will have a shape similar to the cost function facing the Org. The function $T(s)$ is drawn (unconventionally) in the negative (bottom) quadrant of panel (a) where it is measured downward from the origin. We can see that its slope is positive and increasing.

Although unconventional, the rationale for drawing the $T(s)$ function this way is following: at any level of security, the total cost of terror is the upward distance from the horizontal axis up to the corresponding point on the damage-control function, while the total security cost is equal to the downward distance from the horizontal axis to the total security cost line, and therefore, *the (grand) total cost facing the State is the sum of the two vertical lines.* For instance, at security = s_1, terror cost = s_1A_1, security cost is = s_1B_1, and thus the total cost is the dashed vertical line A_1B_1. Similarly, at security levels s_0, s_2, and s_3, the total costs facing the State are A_0B_0, A_2B_2, and A_3B_3, respectively. What is the security level at which the total cost facing the State minimized? The answer is that level of security where the slopes

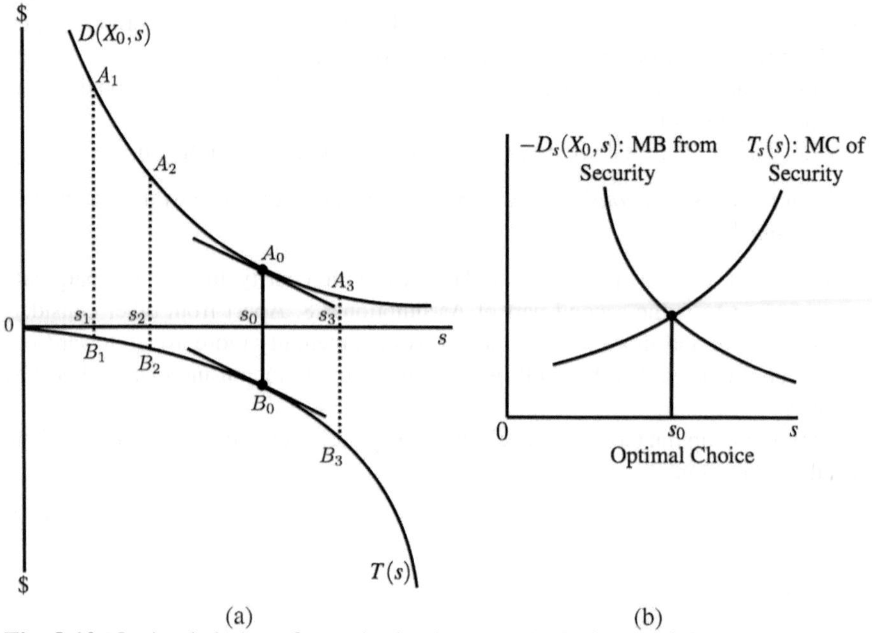

Fig. 8.10: Optimal choice of security by the state. (**a**) Using total damage and total security cost curves. (**b**) Using MB and MC functions of security

of the total terror cost function and the total security cost functions are equal. In Fig. 8.10a, that cost-minimizing level of security is s_0. This is the optimal choice of security by the rational State.

Going back to the State's total cost expression (8.12), the marginal principle of minimizing the total cost with respect to security measures s, i.e., the first-order MB = MC condition, is

$$\boxed{D_s(X,s) + T_s(s) = 0 \Leftrightarrow \underbrace{-D_s(X,s)}_{\text{MB}} = \underbrace{T_s(s)}_{\text{MC}}\ .} \tag{8.13}$$

Recall that the subscripts denote the respective partials. Since, at any given X, damage falls with more security measures, we have $D_s < 0$. So, the MB to the State equals to the absolute value of the decline in damage, $-D_s$.

Figure 8.10b illustrates the first-order condition (8.13), *assuming a fixed level of terror*, e.g., X_0. It plots the MB and the MC curves facing the State. Their intersection point defines s_0, where the condition MB = MC holds. Obviously, the two panels of Fig. 8.10 must be consistent with each other. The point s_0 should match between the two panels, defining the optimal or rational choice of security at the terror level X_0.

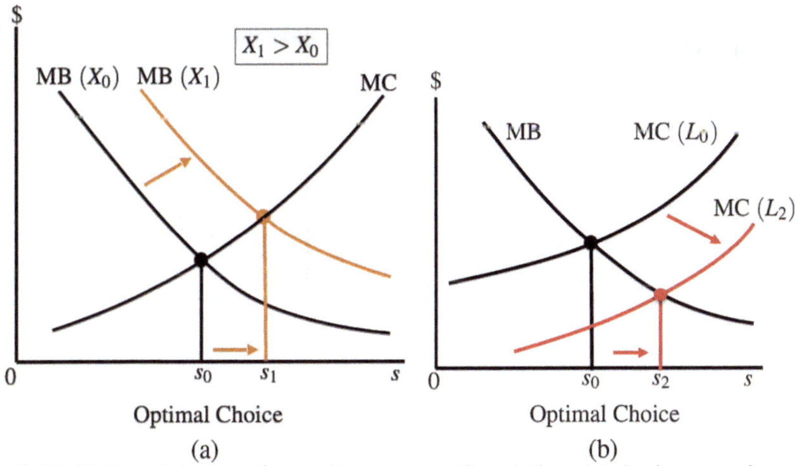

Fig. 8.11: Rational choice of security: comparative statics. (**a**) An increase in terror. (**b**) Security technology improvement

8.3.3.2 Comparative Statics

We will consider two comparative statics:

① How the State would respond to an increase in terror attacks X by the Org

② A technology improvement in security.

If the Org steps up terror attacks, the State's MB from security increases, i.e., one extra dollar spent on security has a larger damage-reducing effect. This is part (vi) of Assumption 8.4. Now refer to Fig. 8.11a. Starting with an original level of terror X_0 and the equilibrium level of security s_0, if the level of terror increases to X_1, the MB curve shifts to the right. The new equilibrium point is where the MC curve and new MB curve intersect. We see that the security level is higher at s_1: as one would expect, the State responds to more terror attacks by enhancing its security measures.

The technology of security measures improves over time. As examples, a new type of instrument may better detect contents in a vehicle; a new computer program can better decipher suspicious chats over the Internet, and so on. These technology improvements tend to reduce the marginal cost of security. In part (b) of Fig. 8.11, L_2 denotes a more effective technology than L_0. We see that the State employs a higher scale of security: s_2, compared to s_0. In general, security is not just measured by the number of security personnel but also by more and better equipment that leads to better and more effective inspection, information, etc.

Both comparative statics results are intuitive and thus lend support to the plausibility of our economic model as a vehicle to analyze a target or defending country's behavior facing terrorist attacks.

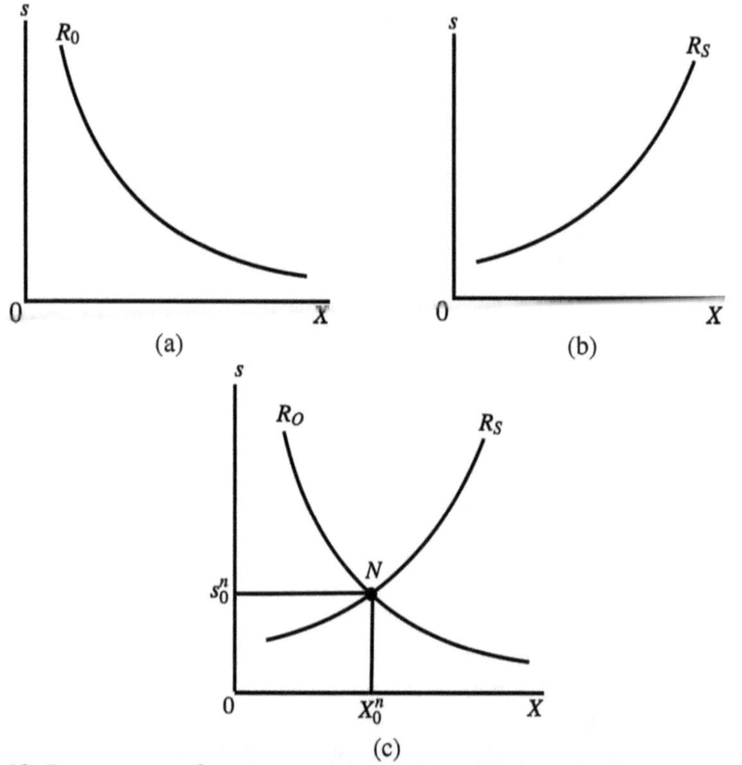

Fig. 8.12: Best response functions and the Nash equilibrium. (**a**) Best response function of the Org. (**b**) Best response function of the state. (**c**) Nash equilibrium

8.3.4 Nash Equilibrium

We have analyzed the behavior of the Org and that of the State separately. The rational choice of terror by the Org was determined, assuming a given level of security chosen by the State. Similarly, the optimal choice of security by the State was contingent upon a fixed level of terror produced by the Org. But this is like saying "if you tell me the value of a variable x, I can determine y, and, if I know the value of y, then I can derive the value of x," a sort of circular reasoning or Catch-22. We do not yet have a *joint* analytical solution of the level of terror X and the level of security s.

Simultaneous solutions are obtained by posing the scenario as a simultaneous move "game."[9] At this point, we may brush up some basic elements game theory (see General Appendix A), which will be used here and later in the chapter and in some of the subsequent chapters. In general, a game is defined by a number of players, two or more, their possible strategies, and their payoffs or utilities at different combinations of strategies across the players. All these elements are present in our model. We have two players, the Org and the State. Their respective strategies are

[9] The theoretical model here is similar to Das and Lahiri (2006).

$X \in (0, \infty)$ and $s \in (0, \infty)$. The payoffs are defined by the values of their objective functions, namely, (8.10) and (8.12).

The joint solution of X and s is ensured by invoking the concept of Nash equilibrium. Simply put, the Nash equilibrium strategies by players in a game are such that no player has any unilateral incentive to deviate from his/her respective strategy, given the strategies chosen by other players. Assuming that the Org and the State simultaneously choose the level of terror production and the level of security, respectively, a particular strategy combination, say (X_0^n, s_0^n), will constitute the ***Nash equilibrium*** or be the ***Nash equilibrium strategies*** if two conditions are met (one for each player), that is,

(1) The Org would not prefer to choose or "play" any strategy other than X_0^n as long as the State chooses $s = s_0^n$.

(2) Likewise, the State would not wish to "play" any other level of security than s_0^n when the Org plays X_0^n.[10]

Nash equilibrium reflects individualistic, non-cooperative decision making in a strategic environment.

No incentive to deviate amounts to a rational choice. Given s_0^n, X_0^n must be the optimal or best strategy for the Org, and given X_0^n, s_0^n should be the optimal or best strategy for the State. Now go back to the choice behavior of the Org and the State described in Sects. 8.3.2 and 8.3.3. The optimal choice of terror X by the Org was conditional upon a given s and the choice of s by the State was conditional upon a given X.

This leads to a method of finding the Nash equilibrium: find different optimal levels of X, from the Org's standpoint, at different levels of s, and similarly find different optimal levels of s by the State at different levels of X. We will have two different *schedules* of X and s, one based on rational behavior of the Org and the other based on that of the State. Nash equilibrium is that combination of (X, s) which is common to, i.e., falls on both schedules. That is, Nash equilibrium is the point of intersection between the two schedules. More precisely, we proceed as follows.

Refer to Result 8.3. Higher security induces the Org to produce less terror. We can present this cause–effect relation by a downward sloping curve in Fig. 8.12a relating to X to s. In a two-player game, such a curve relating the optimal choice of strategy by one player corresponding to a strategy by the other is called the *best response function*. The curve R_O in Fig. 8.12a is the best response function of the Org.

Turning to the State's choice, we have seen that an increase in terror induces the State to deploy more security. This cause–effect relationship translates into an upward sloping best response function for the State, shown as the curve R_S in Fig. 8.12b. Note that the best response functions are derived from and hence represent the respective the first-order conditions.

Panel (c) of Fig. 8.12 jointly depicts the two best response functions. Realize that the intersection point N lies on both best response functions and hence must be the Nash equilibrium that we are looking for. Being on R_O, it means that given $s = s_0^n$,

---

[10] See General Appendix A, Sect. (A.2).

$X = X_0^n$ is the best choice of the Org, so that the Org does not have any incentive to deviate from X_0^n. Similarly, being on the curve R_S, the point (s_0^n, X_0^n) implies that given $X = X_0^n$, the State's best choice is $s = s_0^n$, and hence the State does not have any incentive to move away from s_0^n. The strategies s_0^n and X_0^n reinforce each other in a way and constitute the Nash equilibrium joint solution.

8.3.5 Increase in Terrorism and Response: A Comparative Statics

We now put our model to work by considering a change in the environment and determining its impact on the equilibrium levels of terror (X) and security (s). A central question of interest is how would an increase in terrorism or militancy affect a target country's counter-terror measures? We have already addressed this question earlier, but only partially in the sense that the Org's choice of terror was given. The big difference in the simultaneous game model here is that both X and s vary as endogenous variables.

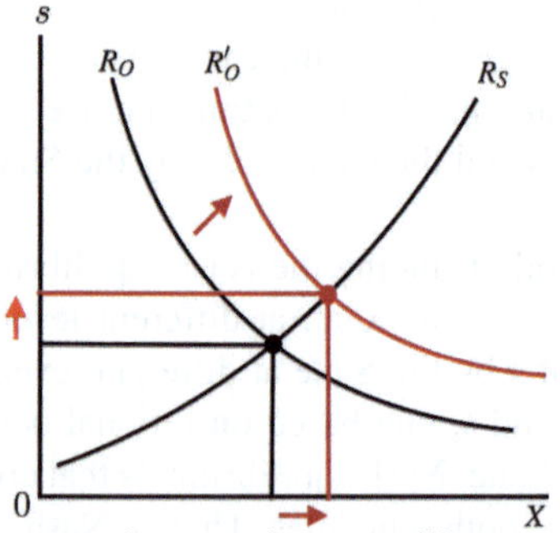

Fig. 8.13: Effects of an increase in terrorism or militancy

As before, we view an exogenous increase in terrorism or militancy as a downward shift of the Org's marginal cost function. We already know (see Result 8.2) that, at any given level of security, the Org would choose a higher level of terror. This implies a rightward shift of the Org's best response function in Fig. 8.12a (not shown). The shift is shown in Fig. 8.13: the best response function of the Org shifts out from R_O to R'_O. We see that the Nash equilibrium shifts from N to N'. Comparing the two points,

Result 8.4

As a result of an increase in terrorism or militancy, there are more terror attacks as well as a higher level of security deployed by the State.

While it is obvious that the State would undertake more security measures in the face of an increase in militancy, it is less obvious and interesting to see that *the Org would engage in more terror attacks despite higher security.*

What happens to damage from terror? Recall the damage function $D(\underset{+}{X}, \underset{-}{s})$. As X increases, it tends to increase the damage from terror, while an increase in security tends to reduce the damage from terror. The overall effect is thus ambiguous. This suggests that security measures alone may not be enough to offset the damage stemming from an increase in terrorism. Indeed, imagine a situation where a growing resentment of population leads to more and more militancy. In response, as the target state increases security more and more, it is bound to more severely curtail civil liberty which we all cherish. This may very well limit the State's ability to increase security measures sufficiently so as to fully offset the increase in terrorism or militancy.

The upshot is that, while security is an essential counter-terror measure, we need to do more in order to contain or reduce the problem of terrorism.

8.4 Many Target Countries

Among others, some terror organizations like al-Qaeda, Hezbollah, and ISIS target more than one country. This creates an interdependence and problems of coordination between target countries. Suppose two countries, say, France and Germany, are targeted by a terror group. All else the same, if Germany bolsters its security against terror, the terror organization would deflect its activities toward France. It is a *terror diversion* effect, which leads to more expected damage from terror for France. Thus, more security measures by one target country is, in and of itself, can be a bad news for another target country. This is *a negative externality*, introduced already in Chap. 1.[11] That is,

> **Is That So? 8.2: Security Measures Have a Negative Externality Effect**
>
> In the context of many target countries, an increase in the security by one target country creates terror diversion and acts as a negative externality effect on other target countries.

We can view the example of France and Germany as two players in a game with respective security measures as strategies, where the strategy of one player affects the payoff or welfare of the other—because of the common enemy, the terror organization, or a group of terror organizations, whose aim is to harm both countries.

We develop below a game model (similar to the dormitory game elucidated in General Appendix A, Sect. A.4, and, similar to the model of terrorism in Sandler and Siqueira (2006)) with two target countries as two players, where the two countries rationally choose the level of their security measures *and while the terror organization remains in the background and is not modeled explicitly.*

[11] It is like passenger A sitting beside passenger B in a vehicle enjoying loud music without an earphone and thereby disturbing B, or, passenger A's smoking causing passenger B a headache or health risk.

We first characterize the Nash equilibrium in terms of the two target countries' choice of security measures.

8.4.1 The Scenario and the Damage Functions

Two countries, a and b, face terror threat from one or more foreign organizations. They use security levels, s^a and s^b, respectively, as the only counter-terror measure. The expected damage from terror received by either country depends on security measures deployed by both countries. Let

$$\boxed{D^a(\underset{-}{s^a},\underset{+}{s^b}); \qquad D^b(\underset{+}{s^a},\underset{-}{s^b})} \tag{8.14}$$

denote the respective damage-control functions. As earlier, the expected damage facing a country decreases with own security measures, i.e., $D^a(\cdot)$ and $D^b(\cdot)$, respectively, decrease with s^a and s^b. Terror diversion is the additional element here:

Assumption 8.10. *If country a (respectively, country b) increases security, then country b (respectively, country a) faces more terror attacks X^b (respectively, X^a).*

Thus s^b (respectively, s^a) tends to increase the expected damage from terror in country a (respectively, country b). These are negative externalities. The partials of the $D^a(\cdot)$ and $D^a(\cdot)$ functions have the signs accordingly.

Furthermore,

Assumption 8.11. *(i) Given s^b (respectively, s^a), an increase in s^a (s^b) reduces its own marginal damage-reducing effect on damage received by the own country. (ii) Given s^a (respectively, s^b), an increase in s^b (s^a) increases the marginal damage-reducing effect of s^a (respectively, s^b) on damage received by country a (respectively, country b).*

Part (i) is analogous to part (iv) of Assumption 8.4 and says that own security measures are subject to diminishing returns. Part (ii) says that if one country enhances its security, the marginal damage-reducing effect of own security by another target country gets stronger. This should be intuitive too: if, say, country b steps up security, terror is diverted to country a, and, in the face of a higher terror threat, one extra dollar spent by country a on security will contain a greater amount of damage.

Figure 8.14 illustrates how the damage from terror attacks in one country is influenced by security measures undertaken by both countries. Panel (a) shows that damage to country a falls with the own security level, given the security level by country b. Panel (b) illustrates that, at any given level of s^a, a higher s^b implies more damage to country a (Assumption 8.10). Thus an increase in s^b (respectively, s^a) shifts out the damage function facing country a (respectively, country b), reflective of terror diversion, and the negative externality.

Part (i) of Assumption 8.11, that is, diminishing returns from own security, is shown in panel (c). The label of the vertical axis reflects that marginal damage-reducing effect of own security is the marginal benefit from it. Part (ii), which states

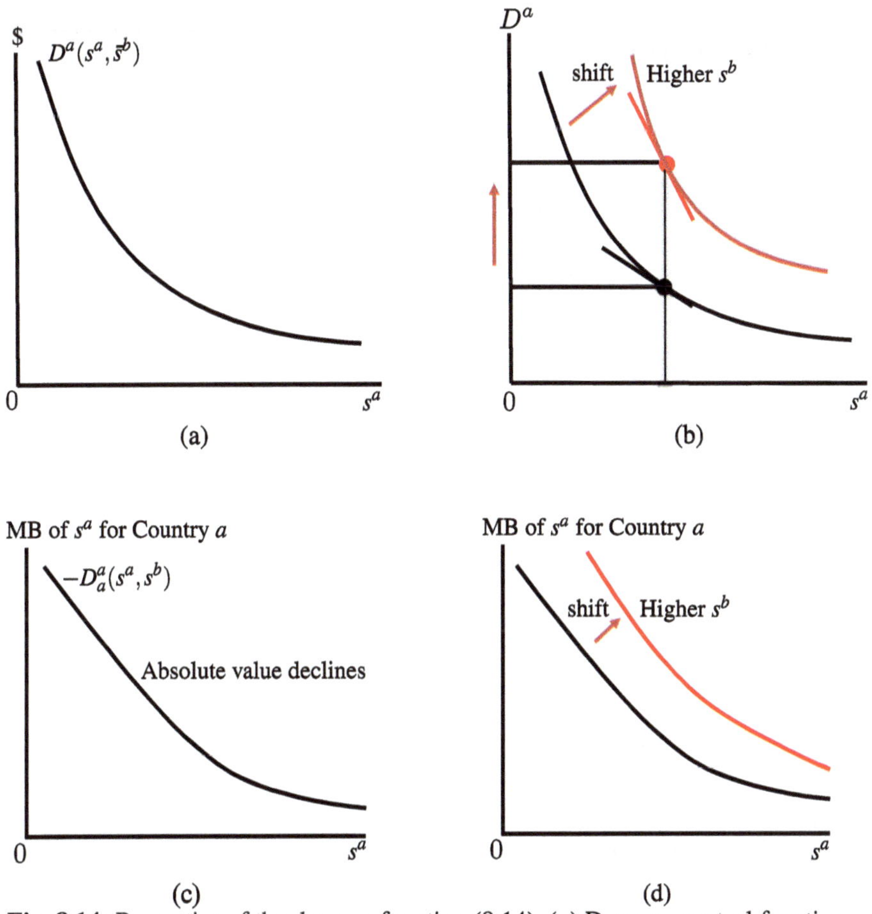

Fig. 8.14: Properties of the damage function (8.14). (**a**) Damage-control function. (**b**) Shift of the damage-control function: the negative externality effect. (**c**) Diminishing marginal effect of security. (**d**) Shift of the marginal damage-reducing effect

that an increase in security by another target country makes own security measures marginally more effective and thus is equivalent to saying that the MB curve for own security shifts out as the other country increases security, is shown in panel (d) of Fig. 8.14.[12]

8.4.2 Rational Choice of Security

The damage-control functions inversely reflect the total benefit from security. Let $T^a(s^a)$ and $T^b(s^b)$ denote the respective security cost functions with the same prop-

[12] This is also shown in panel (b) too, where the slope of the damage function is higher for a higher level of security by the other country.

erties as in Sect. 8.3.3, i.e., the total and the marginal costs increase with security. A rational target country aims to minimize the sum of its terror costs and security costs *at a given level of security chosen by other target country;* that is,

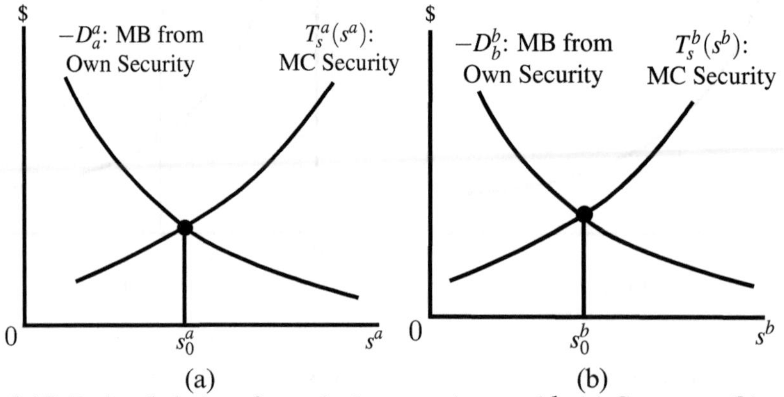

Fig. 8.15: Rational choice of security by countries *a* and *b*. (**a**) Country a. (**b**) Country *b*

$$\text{State } a \text{ minimizes } D^a(\underset{-}{s^a}, \underset{+}{\bar{s}^b}) + T^a(\underset{+}{s^a}) \text{ with respect to } s^a;$$

$$\text{State } b \text{ minimizes } D^b(\underset{+}{\bar{s}^a}, \underset{-}{s^b}) + T^b(\underset{+}{s^b}) \text{ with respect to } s^b.$$

These objective functions lead to the following total cost minimizing marginal principles or first-order conditions:

$$\text{State } a\text{: } D^a_a(s^a, \bar{s}^b) + T^a_s(s^a) = 0 \Leftrightarrow \underbrace{-D^a_a(s^a, \bar{s}^b)}_{\text{MB to State } a} = \underbrace{T^a_s(s^a)}_{\text{MC of State } a} \tag{8.15}$$

$$\text{State } b\text{: } D^b_b(\bar{s}^a, s^b) + T^b_s(s^b) = 0 \Leftrightarrow \underbrace{-D^b_b(\bar{s}^a, s^b)}_{\text{MB to State } b} = \underbrace{T^b_s(s^b)}_{\text{MC of State } b}, \tag{8.16}$$

where D^a_a and D^b_b are, respectively, the partials of D^a and D^b functions with respect to own security, and T^a_s and T^b_s are first derivatives of the respective total security cost functions, i.e., the marginal security cost functions. The tradeoffs are clear and similar to what we have seen in Sect. 8.3.3: more security reduces damage from terror but imposes higher costs of its own. The marginal principles are illustrated in Fig. 8.15. The respective solutions, i.e., s^a_0 and s^b_0, are conditional on some given level of s^b and s^a, respectively.

As comparative statics, let us ask how country *a* and country *b* would react to an increase in security undertaken by country *b* and *a*, respectively. For example, if country *b* deploys more security measures, it encourages more attacks on country *a*

(Assumption 8.10) and thus makes the *marginal* damage-reducing effect of security measures taken by country a stronger (Assumption 8.11 (ii)). Therefore, as seen in Fig. 8.16a, the marginal benefit curve facing country a shifts out. The implication is clear and intuitive: as a response to more security measures by country b, country a anticipates more terror attacks and hence institutes more security measures as well. Likewise, if country a uses more security measures, the MB curve for country b shifts to the right and it chooses a higher level of security. Hence

Result 8.5

If one country enhances its security, it induces the other country to step up its security.

Both Fig. 8.16 and Result 8.5 are based on the first-order conditions for the optimal choice of security by the two countries individually. Negative externality effect of security measures by one country on the other's welfare is the key behind the direction of the response of one country's security to a change in the other target country's security measures.

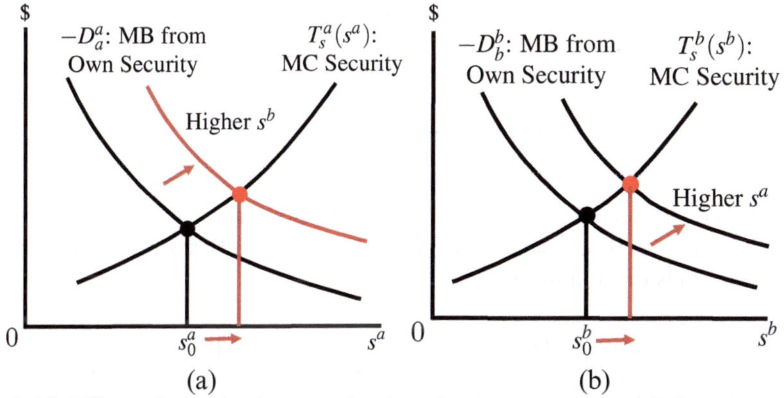

Fig. 8.16: Effect of security increase by the other target country. (**a**) Country a. (**b**) Country b

8.4.3 Best Response Functions, Nash Equilibrium, and a Comparative Statics

The individually rational behavior of countries a and b with respect to security, marked by the respective first-order conditions, was based on some given level of security chosen by the other country—b and a, respectively. The simultaneous equilibrium solutions of both s^a and s^b are obtained by invoking the concept of the Nash equilibrium.

First, we obtain the best response functions: locus of the optimal value of s^a for different values of s^b and similarly for country b. These are positively sloped since one country raises its security level if the other does the same, a restatement

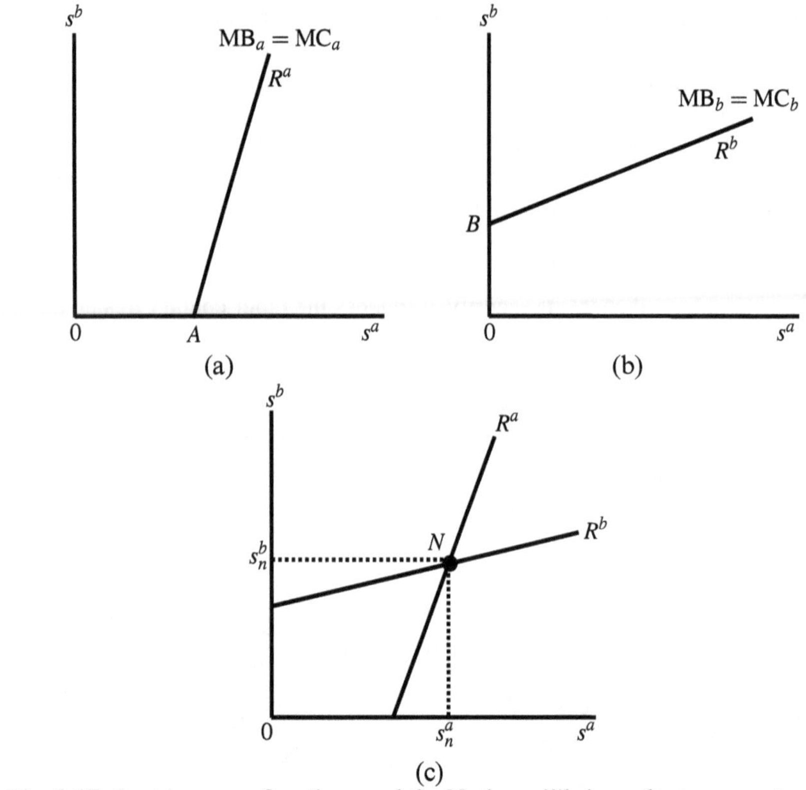

Fig. 8.17: Best response functions and the Nash equilibrium: the two-country security game. (**a**) Best response function: country a. (**b**) Best response function: country b. (**c**) Nash equilibrium

of Result 8.5. These are depicted in panels (a) and (b) of Fig. 8.17 and labeled as R^a and R^b, respectively. *For simplicity, the lines drawn are straight, but they need not be.*[13] Consider the intersection point N of R^a and R^b in panel (c). Since the associated levels of security, s_n^a and s_n^b, lie on the best response functions of both players, the point N marks the Nash equilibrium point and the associated strategies are the non-cooperative Nash equilibrium strategies.

Let us initiate a comparative statics to see if the model yields sensible predictions. Suppose country a perceives a greater threat from the terror organization possibly because of some political or military actions which are outside the scope of this model or simply because there was a successful attack in the recent past which has worsened the target country's sense of fear. We can incorporate this by slightly modifying the damage-control function facing country a: $\alpha D^a(s^a, s^b)$, where $\alpha > 0$. Let an increase in α capture a higher level of terror threat, meaning a higher expected damage at given levels of security.

---

[13] Notice that the intercept points A and B have natural interpretations: they are the level of security that will be chosen by the respective countries when the other country selects zero security.

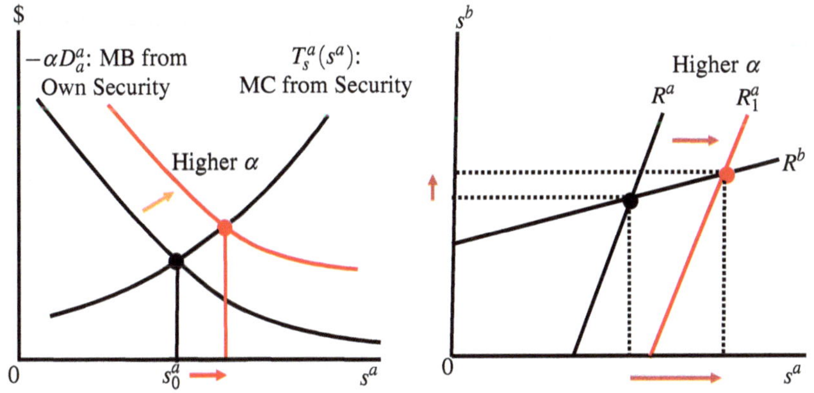

(a) (b)

Fig. 8.18: An increase in the threat perception of one target country. (**a**) Country a's decision. (**b**) Shift of Nash equilibrium

Realize that an increase in α not only increases the expected damage from terror at given levels of security, but it increases the marginal damage-reducing impact of own security (that is, $-\alpha D_a^a$) as well. Hence the MB curve facing country a would shift to the right, implying a higher level of s^a at any given level of s^b. This is shown in Fig. 8.18a. In turn, this leads to a rightward shift of country a's best response function (see panel (b) of Fig. 8.18). The new Nash equilibrium point (of intersection) compared to the original tells us that both countries will adopt more security measures. Country a enhances its security due to the higher threat perception, and, country b steps up its security because of terror diversion and the negative externality effect.

Result 8.6

A higher threat perception by either country leads to more security measures by both countries.

8.4.4 Cooperative Solution

When there is a common issue facing a group—whether at the local, regional, national, or international level—we often advocate a coordinated, cooperative strategy as the preferred approach. The members of a community form a coalition. As examples, when burglary and theft increase in a residential colony, residents jointly decide and pay for more security personnel and cameras. When ISIS was causing havoc in Syria and Iraq in the mid-2010s, it was a problem for many countries and groups. The USA was partnering with PKK (which irked Turkey) to defeat ISIS. In the present context, there is a group of target countries facing the same set of terror organizations. They have an incentive to cooperate.

To begin with, let us first understand how exactly there is a gain from a cooperative solution. Remember a central result in economics about the functioning of markets. That is, if a market is perfectly competitive, then it is "efficient": it serves the society—producers and consumers—the best. In our context, if all target countries choose their levels of security by maximizing respective surplus (or minimizing cost) and their actions did *not* directly affect the welfare of other target countries—similar to perfectly competitive firms being unable to influence the market on their own—then there would be no need for cooperation or coordination in setting security measures. But that is not the case. One country's security measures do affect the expected damage inflicted upon another target country. This negative externality effect implies that the uncoordinated or non-cooperative choice of security levels *cannot* maximizes joint welfare of target countries—because *the individually rational decisions do not internalize the (negative) cross effect*. Keep in mind that the cross effect (externality) is external to the individual countries but internal to the group. However, a group decision will internalize the externality and can, thereby, potentially make all countries better off. To understand this clearly, we now characterize cooperation—or joint decision making—and how it differs from the Nash equilibrium, which is founded on individual decision making.

In order to do so, we have to first define the group's or coalition's objective function.

ASSUMPTION 8.12. *As a group, the target countries aim to minimize the unweighted sum of total costs facing all members.*

In effect, this objective assigns equal weight to all target countries. In reality, however, a coalition may have a different objective function. For instance, if country a is affluent and country b is relatively poor, a more egalitarian objective function would put a higher weight on security cost borne by the poorer country b. We abstract from such distributive considerations and treat all target countries equally, since this is sufficient from the standpoint of understanding the tradeoffs under a cooperative solution and how they differ from the non-cooperative Nash equilibrium.

In our scenario, the two-country coalition's objective is to

$$\boxed{\underset{\text{by choosing } s^a \text{ and } s^a}{\text{Minimize}} \quad D^a(\underset{-}{s^a}, \underset{+}{s^b}) + T^a(\underset{+}{s^a}) + D^b(\underset{+}{s^a}, \underset{-}{s^b}) + T^b(\underset{+}{s^b}),} \tag{8.17}$$

where the plus/minus signs are the signs of respective partials or first derivatives. The "minus" and the "plus" indicate the respective marginal benefits and the marginal costs. Note that, for the group as a whole, there are, with respect to say s^a,

(1) One source of benefit, that is, reduction of terror cost in the own country

(2) Two sources of costs, namely, own security cost and the negative externality cost

An important point to understand is that the cooperative choice of s^a would factor in its negative externality effect on country b, and likewise that of s^b would account for its negative externality effect on country a.

We may imagine that the two countries have constituted a joint body or committee which has estimates of the damage and cost functions facing both countries and which selects s^a and s^b that minimizes the objective function (8.17). The first-order conditions with respect to s^a and s^b are

$$\begin{aligned} & D^a_a(s^a,s^b) + T^u_s(s^a) + D^b_a(s^a,s^b) = 0 \\ \Leftrightarrow\ & \underbrace{-D^a_a(s^a,s^b)}_{\text{MB}_a} = \underbrace{T^a_s(s^a) + \underbrace{D^b_a(s^a,s^b)}_{-\text{ve externality}}}_{\text{SMC of } s^a} \end{aligned} \tag{8.18}$$

$$\begin{aligned} & D^a_b(s^a,s^b) + D^b_b(s^a,s^b) + T^b_s(s^b) = 0 \\ \Leftrightarrow\ & \underbrace{-D^b_b(s^a,s^b)}_{\text{MB}_b} = \underbrace{T^b_s(s^b) + \underbrace{D^a_b(s^a,s^b)}_{-\text{ve externality}}}_{\text{SMC of } s^b}\ . \end{aligned} \tag{8.19}$$

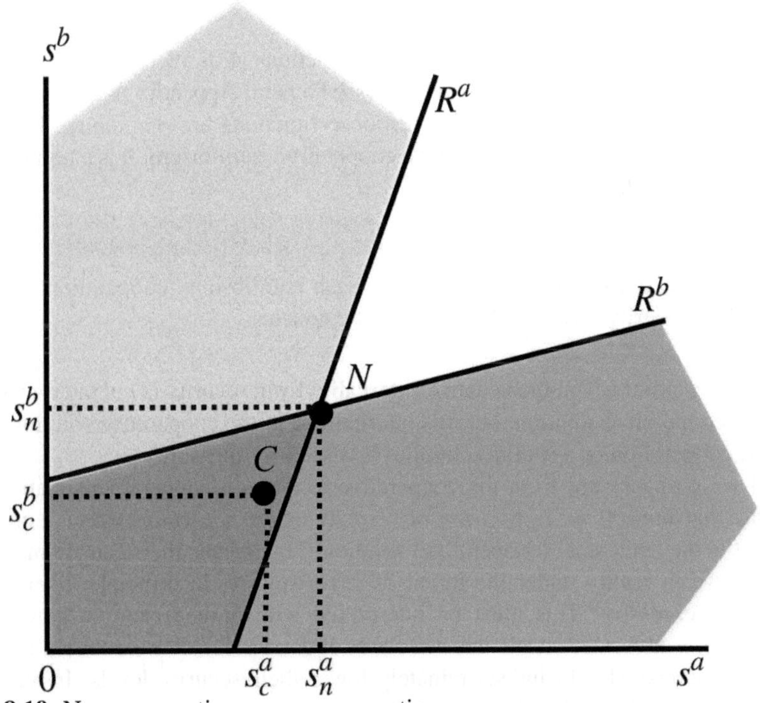

Fig. 8.19: Non-cooperation versus cooperation

Notice that, compared to the first-order conditions in the non-cooperative equilibrium, that is, Eqs. (8.15)–(8.16), here the source of marginal benefit is the same, but the marginal cost to group—which we will call the *social* marginal cost (SMC)—

is different from the country-specific, "private," marginal cost, $T_s^a(s^a)$ and $T_s^b(s^b)$. The right-hand sides of Eqs. (8.18) and (8.19) are the expressions of the SMCs of country a's and country b's security levels. In general,

$$\underset{\text{of security}}{\text{Social marginal cost}} = \underset{\text{of security}}{\text{Private Resource cost}} + \underset{\text{of security}}{\text{Negative Externality}}.$$

What does this imply for the cooperative solutions of s^a and s^b? Because of the additional marginal cost, comparing (8.18) to (8.15) yields that, at any given s^b, the cooperative solution of s^a would be smaller than that under non-cooperation. The same holds for s^b: at any given s^a, the solution of s^b will be lower in cooperative than in the non-cooperative equilibrium.

Refer now to Fig. 8.19, where R^a and R^b are the best response functions of countries a and b, respectively, and their intersection point N marks the non-cooperative Nash equilibrium as in Fig. 8.17c. Since the best response function R^a plots the non-cooperative solutions, the cooperative solution, s_c^a of s^a, must lie to the left of R^a. By the same logic, s_c^b, the cooperative solution of s^b must lie below or to the right of the R^b line. Thus, the cooperative solution point, say C, must fall in the darker region in Fig. 8.19.

Parallel to the standard best response functions, Eqs. (8.18)–(8.19) spell the respective cooperative response functions (see General Appendix A, Sect. A.4). For simplicity, however, the cooperative response functions are *not shown*. However, their intersection point would define the cooperative equilibrium. It is a point like C. Comparing it with point N,

Result 8.7

In comparison to the non-cooperative Nash equilibrium, cooperation calls for less security measures by both target countries.

The key point is that the negative externality from security is *not* internalized in the non-cooperative solution, but it is internalized in the cooperative solution. This is why, cooperation or a coalition implies less security measures.

If we go backward from the cooperative to the non-cooperative situation, we can say that *there is over-provision of security under non-cooperation*, compared to what is the "efficient" (cooperative) solution. This means that security measures we observe in reality under the threat of terrorism are, in principle, likely to be somewhat excessive. This must be interpreted with utmost caution, however. It is being *not* advocated at all that (in view of Result 8.7) the countries afflicted by terror attacks should indiscriminately lower their security levels. Instead, the target countries should jointly select at least some security measure savings to avoid duplication but without increasing the risk of terror, e.g., sharing of information on profiles of suspected individuals and groups, freer movement of security personnel between countries for investigative matters, coordinated border patrol, etc.

8.5 Takeaways

- Effects of counter-terrorism measures can be statistically or econometrically measured.
- Landes (1978), which deals with plane hijacking, is the first theoretical and empirical analysis of terrorism and counter-terrorism measures. The estimated quantitative negative impact, by standard regression techniques, of metal detector installation at the airports in the early 1970s on plane hijacking was large. Similar conclusions were obtained by Enders et al. (1990a) who used intervention analysis.
- Terrorism and the damages from terrorism can be viewed in terms of two production processes: (a) one is the production of planned attacks in the form of an aggregate terror input (toward causing damage) by means of labor, capital, and raw materials (i.e., terrorists, equipment, and other materials) and (b) the other is the production of damage—including both physical and psychological in terms of fear—from the aggregate terror input.
- Security measures affect the latter process, similar to a (negative) technology shock to production of a good or a service: they tend to reduce terror at any given level of terror attacks.
- As the level of security increases by the target State, the terrorist organization produces less terror. Security measures tend to reduce the damage from terror in two ways, directly and acting as a deterrent to a terrorist organization.
- An exogenous increase in terrorism or militancy leads to more terror attacks as well as a higher level of security deployed by the State.
- In the context of many target countries, an increase in the security by one target country leads to terror diversion and thus as a negative externality effect on other target countries. As a result, if one country increases its security, it induces other countries to step up their securities. In this scenario, a higher threat perception by one target country leads to more security measures by all target countries.
- In comparison to the non-cooperative Nash equilibrium, cooperation calls for less security measures by all target countries. Inversely, compared to cooperation, there is over-provision of security at the non-cooperative Nash equilibrium.
- It does not mean that countries should indiscriminately lower their security measures. Instead, the target countries should avoid duplication of security tasks without increasing the risk of terror.

Questions

8.1 In the Landes model, recall the expression of the risk cost of hijacking, equal to

$$R \equiv \frac{\pi_a}{1-\pi_a} \cdot [(1-\pi_c)L_a + [\pi_c L_c],$$

where π_a is the probability of apprehension, π_c is the probability of conviction if apprehended, and so on. Introducing the counter-terror technology of pre-boarding metal detection amounts to an increase in π_a. Consider a 1% increase in the probability of apprehension, e.g., from 0.27 to 0.28, where all other terms remain unchanged. Prove that the risk cost of terror increases by no less than 4%. [Hint: The answer does not depend on the particular initial value of π_a.]

8.2 Consider the game model between the State and the Org. The Org chooses X, the aggregate terror input, which, in turn, produces damage, and, the State chooses security s. We learned that a security-enhancing technology improvement leads to a decrease in X and an increase in s. The expected damage to the State $D(X, s)$ falls on both accounts, which are interpreted, respectively, as a direct effect and a deterrence effect. In this question, you are asked to decompose, in percentage terms, the fall in expected damage into the direct effect and the deterrence effect.

Let expected damage function be $D(X, s) = 27X/s$. The total cost function facing the Org is $C(X) = X^2/2$ and the total security cost function facing the State is $T(s) = 27s$ (so that the marginal security cost is constant and equal to 27).

(a) Derive the Nash solutions of X and s. Denote them X_0^n and s_0^n. Also compute the expected damage level and denote it as D_0.

(b) Suppose the State is able to devise new security-enhancing technologies so that the new total security cost function is $T(s) = 9s$. There is no change in the cost function facing the Org. Derive the new Nash solutions and denote them as X_1^n and s_1^n. Compute the new level of expected damage, say D_1. Note that $D_1 = 27X_1^n/s_1^n$.

(c) Comparing your answers to parts (a) and (b), briefly argue whether they make sense.

(d) What is the percentage change in the expected damage from terror due to the security technology improvements?

(e) Consider the counterfactual when the equilibrium security is at the new level s_1^n, while the terror level is the old level X_0^n. Let D_2 be associated level of expected damage, i.e., $D_2 = 27X_0^n/s_1^n$. It captures what will be the new expected damage after technology improvement if the State adjusted its security level, but the Org did not change X. Compute the percentage difference between D_0 and D_1, which is the *direct effect*.

(f) The difference between your answers to parts (d) and (e) is the *deterrence effect*. What is it equal to?

8.3 In the multiple-target country model, consider the following expected damage functions for target country a in the security-deterrence model. (For (ii) and (iii), we assume that the values of s_a and s_b are such that D^a is always positive.)
(i) $D^a(s_a, s_b) = \frac{10 + 500s_a}{s_a} s_b$
(ii) $D^a(s_a, s_b) = 2000 - 100\sqrt{s_a} + 50s_b$
(iii) $D^a(s_a, s_b) = 2000 - s_a^2/s_b$.
For each of the three functions, determine which parts of the Assumptions 8.10 and 8.11 are satisfied and which are not.

8.4 Suppose the damage function for country i, $i = a, b$, in the security-deterrence game is

$$D^i = \frac{1 + s_j}{s_i},$$

while the total cost functions of security-deterrence are, respectively, $T^a(s_a) = 20s_a$ and $T^b(s_b) = 30s_b$. Notice that marginal costs are constant and, respectively, equal to 20 and 30.
(a) What are the equations for the best response functions, i.e., the relationships between s_a and s_b implied by the first-order conditions?
(b) Assuming that the countries choose their security-deterrence measures non-cooperatively, what will be the Nash solutions, s_a^n and s_b^n? State the solutions up to the ninth decimal. Which country uses security-deterrence measures more and why? [Hint: Nash solutions are solutions to the two first-order conditions. These are nonlinear equations in s_a and s_b however and need to be solved numerically. You can solve them by using Excel's equation solver.[14]]
(c) Suppose the two countries collectively decide their security-deterrence measures by minimizing the sum of their total security costs. What are the cooperative solutions, say s_a^c and s_b^c? How do these solutions compare with the non-cooperative solutions (s_a^n, s_a^n)? What is the economic rationale behind the differences between cooperative and non-cooperative solutions?

[14] In the Excel 2016, choose say cells C10 and C11, where you enter "guesses" for s_a^n and s_b^n, respectively, e.g., $s_a^n = 0.25$ and $s_b^n = 0.24$. In D10, enter the expression (formula in Excel starting with "=") of −MB + MC for country a where s_a^n = C10 and s_b^n = C11. Although -MB + MC = 0, do not put "0" or "= 0." Do the same in D11 for country 2. Next, in D12, enter the formula "= $D10$^2 + $D11$^2." Now go to Equation Solver in Data. Choose "set objective" to D12; choose "value of" = 0; under 'by changing variable cells', type 'C10, C11.' Then hit "Solve" at the bottom. You will see that Excel Solver changes your initial entries in C10 and C11. The new entries in these two cells are the respective solutions.

Chapter 9

Preemptive Strikes, Can We Win the War on Terror?

9.1 Introduction

Although an absolutely essential counter-terror (CT) measure, security does not catch our imagination of war on terror, WoT, since it is defensive, hence inward. On the other hand, offensive measures like military crackdown to degrade the capability of terror groups by taking the war to the door of the enemy so to speak capture the spirit of WoT. In this chapter, we study how offensive CT measures work from an economic standpoint. Apart from military operations, financial controls that curb the flow of funds to terror organizations tend to weaken them too. Hence both military interventions and financial regulations are preemptive in that they tend to forestall terror groups from mounting attacks. In this and other chapters, we use the terms preemptive measures and preemption interchangeably.

In Chap. 8, we learned that security reduces the damage from terror in two ways. Even if terror organizations keep up terror attacks, enhanced security would reduce the damage from terror; this is a direct effect. Additionally, increased security discourages terrorists or terror groups from attacking: this is a deterrence effect, which is indirect in a sense. There is however no presumption that a direct effect is always stronger than an indirect effect. Realize that preemption exerts a deterrence effect only. It does *not* however imply that because preemption exerts only an indirect effect, its effectiveness is somewhat limited. In fact, preemptive measures constitute a frontal attack in the WoT and can deliver major blows to the production and propagation of terror.

How far a target country would step up its preemption in response to an increase in militancy or terrorism is a central question of interest in this chapter. Our analysis lends itself to formulate—and answer—the question of whether or under what conditions preemptive measures can help win the WoT. For simplicity, to focus on preemptive measures work, *we hold security measures fixed throughout this chapter.*

Section 9.2 conceptualizes preemption in a cost–benefit framework. In Sect. 9.3, we learn, in a one-organization and one-defending-state scenario, the terrorist organization's choice of the level of its production of terror and reaction to the state's

S. P. Das, *Economics of Terrorism and Counter-Terrorism Measures*,
https://doi.org/10.1007/978-3-030-96577-8_9

preemptive measures. Taking into account the response of the terror organization, the state chooses the level of its preemptive measure; this is analyzed in Sect. 9.4.

Having characterized the choice behavior of the terrorist group and the state, the model will be able to frame the central question of whether preemptive measures can help win the WoT. Of course, this presupposes what we mean by winning the WoT. In Sect. 9.5, we define "winning or losing WoT" and then analyze whether or under what conditions, preemptive measures can or cannot deliver a win.

Like in Chap. 8, we also examine the interdependence among multiple target countries in regard to their choice of preemptive measures and compare the non-cooperative solutions with the cooperative solutions. This is explored in Sect. 9.6. An adverse side effect, so to speak, of using preemptive strikes is that it may lead to a backlash due to the collateral damage caused from such strikes. The ramifications of this are discussed in Sect. 9.7.

9.2 Preemptive Measures in an Economic Model

In an economic decision making setting, we can think of preemption in two ways: one is *static* where time does not play any role and the other *dynamic*. As in Chap. 8, we call a terror organization an Org and a target country a State.

9.2.1 Shift of the Marginal Cost Function of Producing Terror

This is a *static* view. Recall the terror cost function introduced in Chap. 8, which is a schedule of total costs associated with different levels of terror production. A decrease of a terror organization's capacity to produce terror can be viewed as an increase in the total and marginal costs of producing terror. Military strikes and financial controls tend to decrease the capability of terror groups in organizing attacks and thus affect both variable and fixed costs of producing terror. For our purpose, *we will regard preemptive measures as interventions that shift up a terror organization's marginal cost function, thus increasing the variable cost of producing terror.*

Let us divide the marginal cost (MC) of producing terror into two parts: one that is independent of the terror output and thus fixed from the perspective of the terror organization, and the other that varies with terror output, i.e.,

$$\text{MC of producing terror} = \underbrace{z + m}_{\text{fixed}} + \underbrace{v \cdot X}_{\text{variable}},\ z + m > 0;\ v \geq 0. \tag{9.1}$$

In the above expression, X is the level of terror production, m denotes the level of preemptive measures, and thus an increase in preemption shifts up the marginal cost of producing terror, whereas z denotes that part of the marginal cost of producing terror which includes, among other components, the cost of equipment, hiring and training terrorists, and volunteering to join terror group. The "z" in the marginal cost function does not vary with the production of terror. Turning to the variable component, if $v > 0$, the marginal cost increases with terror output.

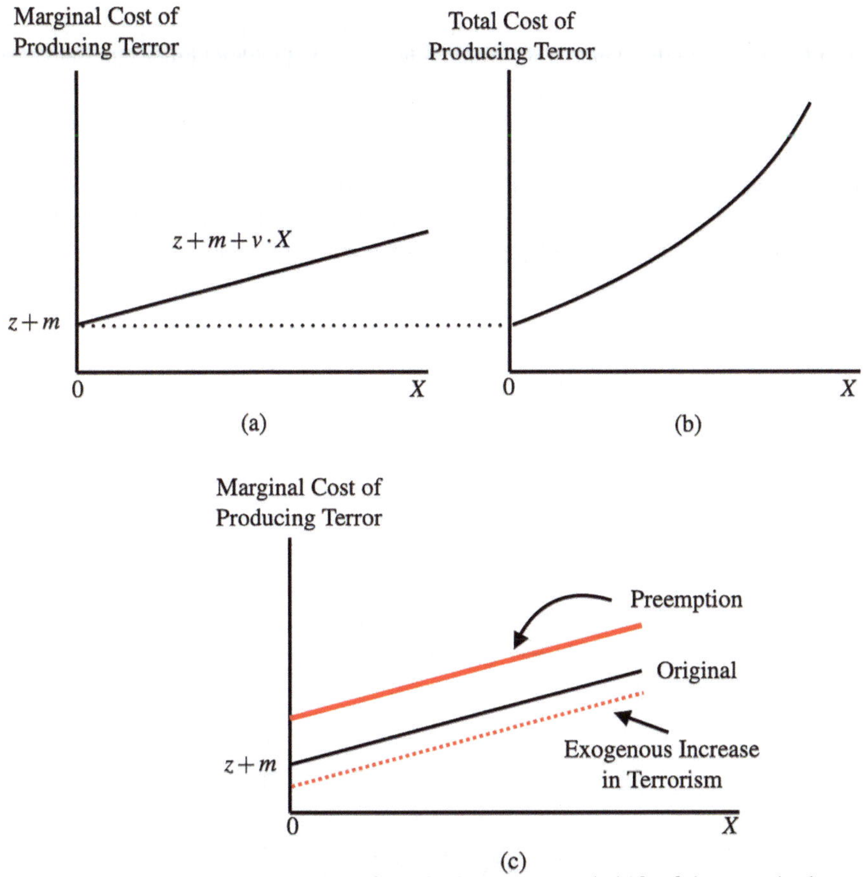

Fig. 9.1: Marginal and total costs of producing terror and shift of the marginal cost function . (**a**) Marginal cost function. (**b**) Targinal cost function. (**c**) Shift and marginal cost function

The total cost function, which gives rise to the marginal cost function in (9.1), is

$$\boxed{C(X) = (z + m)X + \frac{1}{2}vX^2.} \tag{9.2}$$

Check that $C_X(X) = \partial C/\partial X = z + m + vX$, which is the same as the expression (9.1).

Figure 9.1a illustrates the marginal cost function (9.1), whereas panel (b) exhibits the total cost function (9.2).[1] An increase in preemptive measures, via an increase in

[1] These are indeed the same terror cost functions shown in Fig. 8.7 in Chap. 8, except that these are more structured and thus less general so as to illustrate how preemption affects the cost function of a terror organization.

m, is illustrated in panel (c). Starting with middle line, which is the original marginal cost function, a higher level of preemption is associated with a higher marginal cost function such as the heavier line.

At any given level of preemption, an exogenous increase in terrorism or militancy is captured by a decrease in the exogenous component z and hence a downward shift of the marginal cost function, exhibited by the dotted line in panel (c).

Thus, z acts (inversely) as the parameter of the level of militancy. We shall refer to the sum, $z + m$, as the "level" of an Org's marginal cost function.

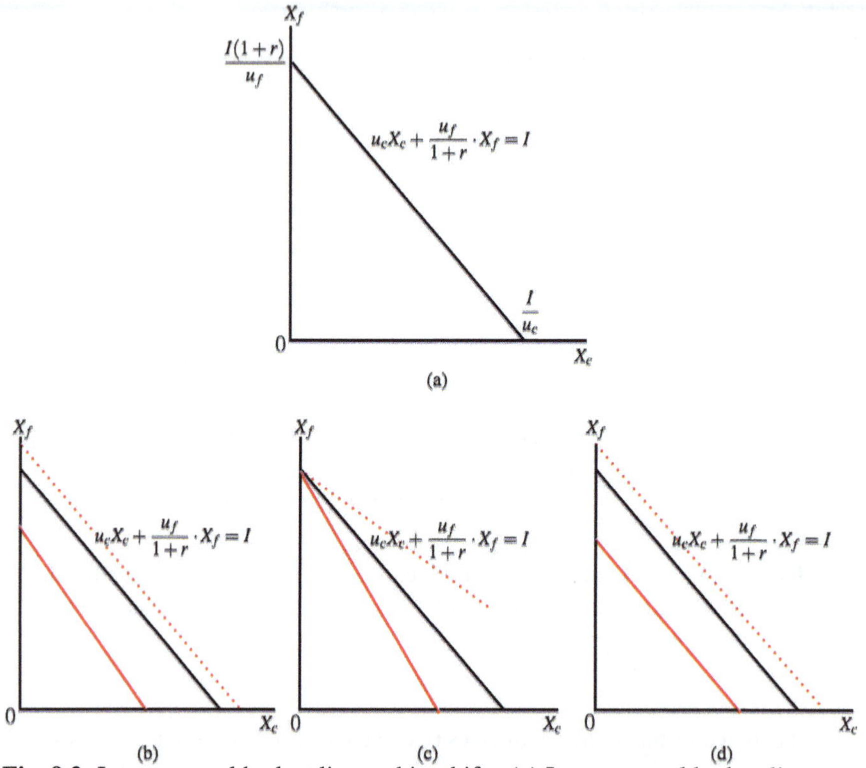

Fig. 9.2: Intertemporal budget line and its shifts. (**a**) Intertemporal budget line. (**b**) Preemptive strikes having a permanent effect. (**c**) Preemptive strikes having a temporary effect. (**d**) Financial controls

9.2.2 Shift of the Intertemporal Budget Line

This refers to a *dynamic* framework having an element of time, in which military strikes and financial controls can be discerned. Over time, money flows into the hands of terror groups, which organize attacks for the current as well as future periods. We can imagine a terrorist organization planning its attacks over time subject to a budget constraint. For simplicity, suppose only two periods, say, present or current (c) and future (f). Let X_c and X_f denote an Org's production of the aggregate terror input in the present and in the future period, respectively. Assuming that an Org can borrow or lend at a given interest rate r, we can write its budget constraint as

$$\boxed{u_c X_c + \frac{u_f}{1+r} \cdot X_f = I_c + \frac{1}{1+r} \cdot I_f \equiv I,} \tag{9.3}$$

where u_c is the current period unit cost of producing X_c, I_c is the flow of funds to the Org in the same period, u_f is the *expected* unit costs of producing X_f and similarly I_f is the *expected* flow of funds in the future, and I is the discounted value of the flow of funds available to the Org in the current period.

We presume that the Org has access to loan/credit markets in which it can freely borrow or lend, i.e., transfer funds between the two periods. This leads to a single budget constraint rather than one for each period. Equation (9.3) states that the discounted value of the costs of terror attacks equals the discounted value of the flow of funds to the Org. Of course, borrowing or lending is not an easy task for a non-state entity like a terrorist organization. We however abstract from the loan market problems facing a terrorist groups in order to highlight that they do have "some" access to the loan or credit market.

Notice that unit costs depend on technology as well as prices of various inputs like salaries of terrorists and personnel, cost of transport, training and equipment, etc. that enter the production of the aggregate terror input.

In sum, Eq. (9.3) is a simple intertemporal or "over time" budget constraint, which is illustrative of the tradeoff between current and future production of terror, given technology, input prices, flow of funds, and the interest rate. This is depicted in Fig. 9.2a. The shifts of this intertemporal budget line are exhibited in panels (b) to (d). Military interventions raise the unit costs through the destruction of facilities, personnel, etc. and thus shift the budget line inward. If they diminish both present and future capabilities, the inward shift occurs on both axes, as in panel (b). If they reduce only the current capabilities of a terror organization to produce terror, the budget line pivots on the horizontal axis that measures X_c—shown in panel (c). For example, damage caused by bombing certain roads that a terror organization uses can be rebuilt after some time.

The effect of financial controls is depicted in panel (d). These controls affect the current or the future flow of funds and will have similar qualitative effects as do military strikes: they lead to a parallel shift of the budget line. Notice that, in terms of consumer choice theory in microeconomics, preemptive strikes work like a price effect or an income effect, while financial controls are analogous to an income effect.

Comparing panel (b) to panel (d), we can see the similarity of shifts due to preemptive strikes that exert a permanent effect and financial controls. The implication is that

Result 9.1

Preemptive strikes that permanently reduce the capability of producing terror and controls on the flow of funds to terror organizations have similar implications toward the production of terror.

Result 9.1 underscores the importance of financial control as a means to combat terrorism.

An exogenous increase in terrorism can manifest in more participation and thus lower unit cost of producing terror or more funds supporting a terror organization. This is shown by the dotted lines in panels (b) to (d). Those in panels (b) and (d) illustrate more participation and/or more financial support, while the dotted line in panel (c) reflects more participation in the current period only. As in the static model, preemption and an exogenous increase in terrorism work in opposite directions.

It is important to note that the static and the dynamic versions of representing preemptive measures are *not* unrelated: the total cost of producing terror in the static model can be interpreted as money at disposal in the current period after the borrowing or lending is done. As an example, if the total cost of producing terror in the static model turns out to be 100 units (say in thousands of dollars), whereas the Org has 90 (respectively, 115) units, it then borrows 10 units (respectively, lends 15 units).

9.3 The Org's Choice of the Terror Input and the Impact of Preemption

9.3.1 The Static Model

In a timeless or one-period framework, the rational choice of terror production by the Org is guided by the principle that the marginal cost of terror production equals its marginal benefit in terms of damage caused to the target country. Assuming one target country, the State, recall the damage function for the State introduced in Chap. 8, namely $D(X, s)$, where X is the amount of terror produced and s stands for the security measures. If security is unchanged, we can ignore s and write (expected) damage as $D(X)$, the terror damage function. As in Chap. 8, let us assume positive but diminishing marginal effect of terror on damage inflicted upon the target country. Hence the Org's marginal benefit (MB) curve from terror is downward sloping.

A rational Org is assumed to maximize its surplus $D(X) - C(X)$, where $C(X)$ is the total cost of producing terror. The expression of the marginal cost $C_X(X)$ is

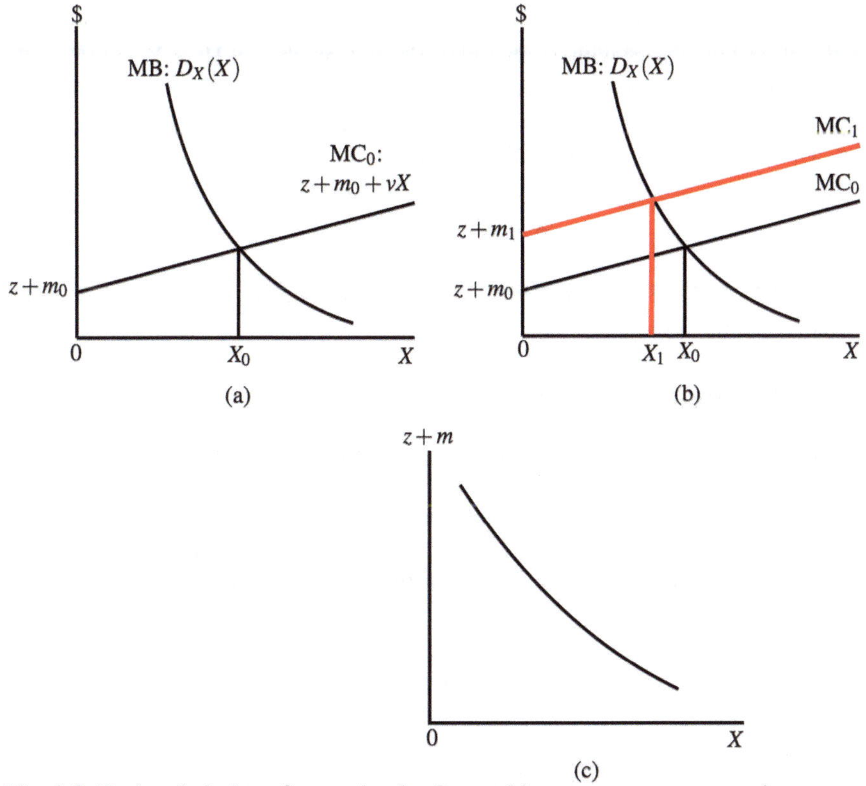

Fig. 9.3: Rational choice of terror by the Org and its response to preemptive measures in the static model. (**a**) Choice of production of terror. (**b**) Org's response to preemptive measures. (**c**) Best response function of the Org

given in (9.1). The first-order condition for the optimal choice of terror is thus

$$\boxed{\underbrace{D_X(X)}_{\text{MB}} = \underbrace{C_X(X) = z + m + vX}_{\text{MC}}.} \tag{9.4}$$

Figure 9.3a depicts the Org's marginal benefit function (the same as in Chap. 8) and, at a given level of preemptive measures, $m = m_0$, the marginal cost function. The intersection point is where the condition (9.4) is met. The corresponding X, that is X_0, is the optimal/rational choice of terror by the Org at the preemptive measures level m_0.

We can now see the Org's response to an increase in preemptive measures. Turning to panel (b), a higher level of preemption (m_1) implies a higher MC function for the Org and hence a lower equilibrium level of terror X_1. An increase in preemptive measures leads to a decline in the production of terror, as one would expect.

Recall the definition of the best response function, which states how one player's rational strategy varies with another player's strategy choice. Here X and m are the strategies of the Org and the State, respectively. From Fig. 9.3b, it follows that the best response function of the Org is downward sloping, as shown in Fig. 9.3c. It will be helpful to write this down algebraically:

$$\boxed{X = X(z + m),\ X' < 0.} \tag{9.5}$$

Figure 9.3c and the above equation summarize the impact of preemption on the behavior of the Org.

9.3.2 The Dynamic Model

We now consider the dynamic model of preemption, which differentiates between preemptive strikes and financial controls. Since there are two periods, present (c) and future (f), we can postulate two damage functions facing the State, $D^c(X_c)$ and $D^f(X_f)$, the functional forms of which may be the same or different. Let us now define a utility function of the Org from the terror-damage functions in the two periods:

$$\boxed{U = \bar{U}(D^c(X_c), D^f(X_f)) = U(\underset{+}{X_c}, \underset{+}{X_f}),} \tag{9.6}$$

which measures the overall benefit to the Org. In the static model, the damage $D(X)$ to the State spells the utility or benefit of the Org. In the same vein, the utility, $\bar{U}(D^c(X_c), D^f(X_f))$, to the Org here can be seen as an aggregate function of damage over the two periods caused to the State.

In this setup, it is natural to assume that the rational Org would choose X_c and X_f, the current and the future aggregate terror inputs, so as to maximize its total benefit $U(X_c, X_f)$, subject to the intertemporal budget constraint (9.3). A reader can immediately recognize that this is analogous to the household utility maximization problem studied in microeconomic theory. We can define an *iso-benefit curve* (IBC) or an *iso-damage curve* (IDC) as the locus of current and future terror production that generate the same level of total benefit to the Org or the same level of aggregate damage to the State. Henceforth, we will refer to this as an iso-damage curve or IDC.

Given the utility function $U(\cdot)$, IDC is downward sloping. Let us further assume that like a standard indifference curve it is convex to the origin. Figure 9.4a shows the Org's rational choice of current and future production of terror, defined by the point of tangency E_0 along with X_{0c} and X_{0f} as the optimal solutions. In general, the optimal choice of terror production for the present and the future depends on the position and slope of the budget line and the shape of IDCs that depend on the per-period terror damage functions and the aggregate damage function $\bar{U}(\cdot)$.

We are ready now to analyze the implications of preemptive measures. A higher level of preemptive measures shifts the budget line in (see panels (b)–(d) of Fig. 9.2),

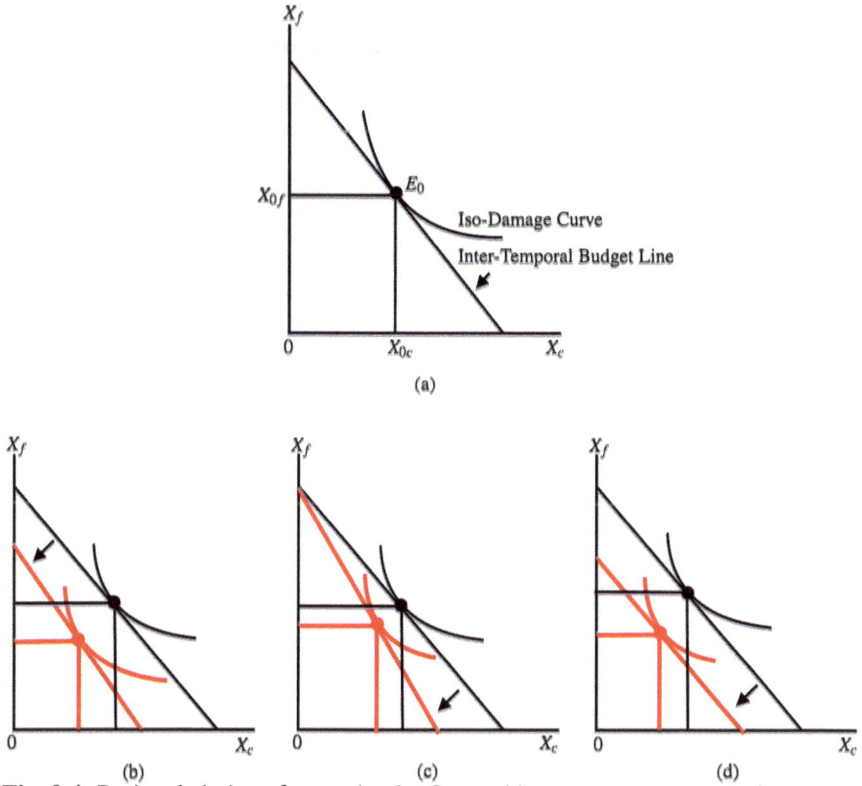

Fig. 9.4: Rational choice of terror by the Org and its response to preemptive measures: The dynamic model. (**a**) Choice of terror for present and future. (**b**) Preemptive strikes having a permanent effect. (**c**) Preemptive strikes having a temporary effect. (**d**) Financial controls

whereas the nature of the shift depends on the type of the preemptive measure, already discussed in Sect. 9.2. The impacts on X_c and X_f individually are ambiguous, however. But, an inward shift of the budget line implies that the terror production for at least one of the two periods would decline; that is,

Result 9.2

Preemptive measures in terms of either military strikes or financial controls lead to a decline in aggregate damage associated with a decrease in the current or/and future production of terror.

Specifically, if the current and future damage functions are similar and preemptive strikes that damage present *and* future capability of the terror organization in similar magnitudes, we can deduce the following from Fig. 9.4:

Result 9.3

(i) Preemptive measures that have permanent effects tend to reduce both present and future productions of the aggregate terror input.
(ii) In response to preemptive measures that reduce only the current capability, the current production of terror falls, while the future production of terror may increase or decrease.
(iii) Present *or* future financial controls tend to reduce present *and* future production of the aggregate terror input.

Part (i) of Result 9.3 follows from the implications shown in panel (b) of Fig. 9.4. Part (ii) is derived from panel (c). Whether funds are available in the present period or will be generated in the future, as long as borrowing and lending allow fund transfer between present and future, part (iii) of Result 9.3 follows in view of panel (d) of Fig. 9.4. An upshot is that

Is That So? 9.1: Equivalence between Military Strikes and Financial Controls

Financial controls are as potent as military measures to contain or degrade the capability of terror organizations.

The dynamic model is richer than, yet consistent with, the earlier static approach. Both approaches lead to the same broad conclusion that *preemptive measures directly discourage the production of terror.*

9.4 The State's Choice of Preemptive Measures: A Sequential Game

For now on, we shall suppress security-deterrence measures and focus on the choice of preemptive measures by the State. Furthermore, for simplicity of exposition, we will use *the static model of the Org's behavior*, because it delivers, in a simple way, the prediction that an increase in preemptive measures induces the Org to reduce the production of terror.

Recall that in Chap. 8, we employed the concept of one-shot, simultaneous-move Nash equilibrium to study security measures. But we cannot do the same here, because, unlike security measures, there is no (direct) effect of preemption on damage from terror (if the Org keeps the level of its terror production unchanged). Put differently, if the terror output is unaffected, there is no benefit to the State from preemptive actions and thus a simultaneous-move Nash equilibrium where a player optimizes over his actions given the strategy of other players would imply zero preemptive measures (i.e., $m = 0$). This does not make sense.

Instead, because preemption (the State's strategy) works *only* through its impact on terror production (the Org's strategy), we must use a *sequential game* (see General Appendix A, Sect. A.6) to study the choice of preemption. In a two-player sequential game, one player moves first and chooses an action, and the other player moves next and chooses his action after observing the action of the first player. In other words, the second player has a prior knowledge of the strategy of the first player but not vice versa. The game is "solved" by backward induction. We first characterize the second player's choice of action conditional upon the first player's action. Factoring in this behavior of the second player, we then solve the behavior of the first player in stage 1. There is a refined concept of Nash equilibrium used here called the *sub-game perfect equilibrium*, requiring that the strategies be such that a Nash equilibrium holds *at each stage of the game.*[2]

In our context, it is natural to assume a two-stage sequential game in which the State moves first and chooses the level of preemption in stage 1, and, in stage 2, the Org chooses the level of production of terror after observing the level of preemption selected by the State.

We are ready to "solve" the game, beginning with stage 2 and working backward. In stage 2, it is the Org's turn. Realize that we have already characterized the Org's choice of terror, given the level of preemptive measures chosen by the State. In other words, we already have the solution of the game in stage 2: it is the best response function of the Org defined in Eq. (9.5) and illustrated in Fig. 9.3c. We proceed to characterize the State's choice of preemption in stage 1 of the game.

It should be clear now why this sequential game—where the State chooses its action (preemption) first and the Org chooses its action (production of terror) next—is the appropriate game model. The level of preemption in stage 1 fixes the marginal cost function facing the Org. Having observed this function, the Org chooses its level of terror in stage 2—which determines the expected damage facing the State. This is the mechanism of benefit to the State from the preemptive measures. To be more specific, an increase in preemption leads to less production of terror, which, in turn, implies less damage from terror. Connecting the chain effects,

$$\boxed{D(X) = D(X(z+m)) = \bar{D}(z \underset{-}{+} m).} \tag{9.7}$$

We call this the *damage-deterrence function*, as it capsules that preemption delivers benefits to the State by deterring the Org from attacking the State.

The negative (beneficial) impact of preemptive measures on damage means $\bar{D}_m(z+m) \equiv \partial\bar{D}/\partial(z+m) < 0$, the magnitude of which is $-\bar{D}_m(z+m)$. We assume that the marginal benefit diminishes with m, i.e., $-\bar{D}_{mm}(z+m) < 0$, that is,

$$\boxed{\bar{D}_{mm}(z+m) > 0.} \tag{9.8}$$

[2] Since in a sequential game only one player "moves" at any given stage of the game, at the sub-game perfect equilibrium, each player chooses its optimal strategy whenever her/his turn comes.

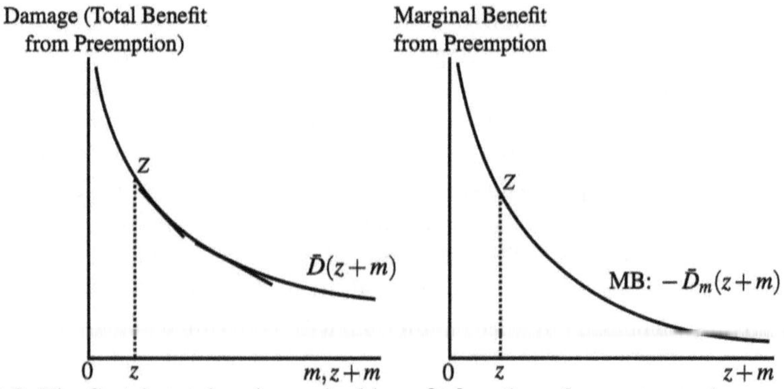

Fig. 9.5: The State's total and marginal benefit functions from preemption

The total and marginal benefits to the State from preemption are illustrated in Fig. 9.5 at some given level of z. The absolute value of the slope of the $\bar{D}(z+m)$ curve (equal to MB) decreases in conformity with condition (9.8). In both panels, m is measured along the horizontal axis from z to the right and the total and marginal benefits on the vertical axis from Z to the right.

Turning now to the costs associated with preemptive actions, there are direct costs of military engagement. Injury and death of soldiers entail their opportunity costs as well as the cost of pain and suffering of relatives and the nation at large. Furthermore, there are collateral damages. If terrorists and facilities are located in populous areas, there would be civilian casualties and loss of property. These are direct costs to the population where the terrorists reside but at the same time impose implicit costs to the State in terms of increased hostility and loss of goodwill. Let $H(m)$, with $H_m > 0$, denote the total cost function of preemptive measures. In view of the preceding discussion, it is compelling to assume *increasing* marginal cost of preemptive measures: $H_{mm}(m) > 0$.[3] However, for the sake of understanding the implications of increasing marginal cost of preemption, we need to consider constant marginal cost of preemption as a benchmark. Thus, for analytical purposes, we shall assume constant or increasing marginal cost of preemption, that is,

$$\boxed{H_m(m) \geq 0.}$$

Figure 9.6 depicts the graphs of the preemption cost functions.

Having understood the benefits and costs associated with preemption, we move on to the State's rational choice of preemption. Assume that the State chooses preemptive measures m in order to minimize the sum of total terror-damage cost and the total cost of preemption, i.e., its objective is to

$$\boxed{\text{Minimize} \quad \bar{D}(z \underset{-}{+} m) + H(\underset{+}{m}) \text{ with respect to } m.} \tag{9.9}$$

[3] See Bueno De Mesquita (2005), who also assumes increasing marginal cost of preemption.

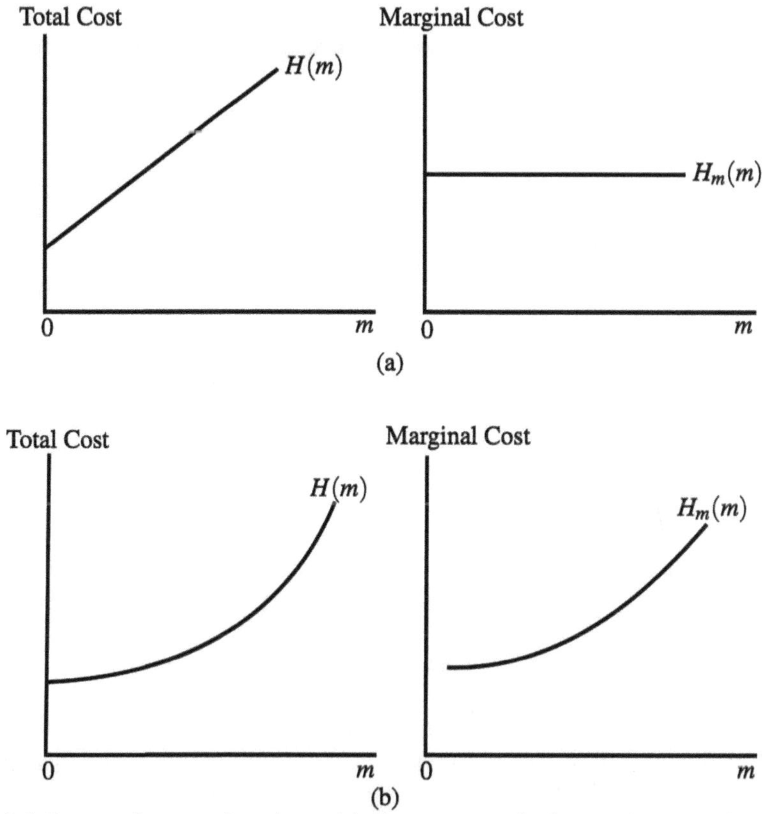

Fig. 9.6: Preemption cost functions. (**a**) Constant marginal cost of preemption. (**b**) Increasing marginal cost of preemption

The tradeoffs are clear from the signs underneath. The first-order condition for the rational choice of m is

$$\boxed{\bar{D}_m(z+m) + H_m(m) = 0 \Leftrightarrow \underbrace{-\bar{D}_m(z+m)}_{\text{State's MB}} = \underbrace{H_m(m)}_{\text{State's MC}} .} \tag{9.10}$$

Figure 9.7 illustrates this, where the exogenous level of militancy is given at z_0.

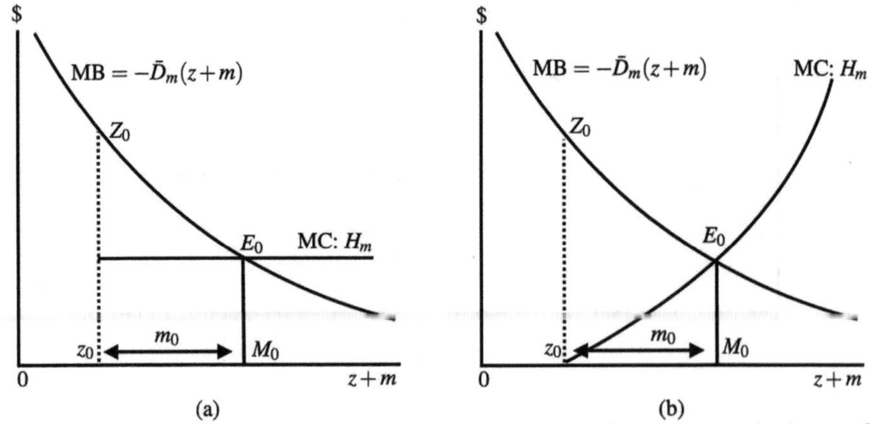

Fig. 9.7: Rational choice of preemption by the State . (**a**) Constant marginal cost of preemption. (**b**) Increasing marginal cost of preemption

Notice that the State's MB depends on the level of the marginal cost function facing the Org, $z+m$, which is measured on the horizontal axis. If $z = z_0$, we read MB from the point Z_0 on the curve. The MC of preemption depends on m only, and thus the MC function is drawn from z_0. Panels (a) and (b) depict the constant-preemption-marginal-cost and increasing-preemption-marginal-cost situations, respectively. The intersection point between the MB and the MC curves (E_0) locates where the first-order condition (9.10) is met. The optimal solution of $z_0 + m$ is M_0 and the optimal level of preemption is m_0. Of course, since the two panels graph different MC functions of preemption, E_0, M_0, and m_0 in the two panels represent different points and magnitudes.

Given the solution of m, the optimal production of terror is determined from Fig. 9.3c. The "solution" of the model is complete.

9.5 Can the State Win the War on Terror?

We are in a position now to pose and answer some fundamental questions. First, how would the Org and the State respond to an increase in militancy? Technically, it boils down to a comparative statics with respect to a decrease in the militancy parameter z. Interestingly, this leads to an answer for another fundamental question: can we win the WoT?

We first define winning or losing WoT. Start with an initial level of militancy say z_0. Given z_0, the State chooses a level of preemption, say m_0. Given z_0 and m_0, the level of the Org's marginal cost function is $z_0 + m_0$. In turn, in Stage 2, let the corresponding level of Org's rational production of terror be X_0. From this initial situation, consider an increase in militancy, i.e., a decline in z from z_0 to, say, z_1. We expect that the State would respond with more preemptive measures, say $m_1 (> m_0)$. Now, if m_1 is high enough such that the Org produces a level of terror, say X_1, which is less than how much terror it produced before (that is X_0), we say that the State has successfully overcome the problem of terrorism by preemptive measures, i.e., the State has won WoT. If $X_1 = X_0$, we would say that the State has weakly won WoT. But if $X_1 > X_0$, the State is losing WoT: its response in terms of preemptive measures is not strong enough to turn the rising tide of terror attacks. Hence, we have the following definition:

Definition of Winning or Losing the WoT

The State loses WoT if, following an exogenous increase in militancy or terrorism and the State's response in terms of CT measures, the Org still produces more terror than earlier. Otherwise, the State wins.

We next argue that winning or losing WoT depends on the nature of the State's marginal cost of preemptive measures. Refer to Fig. 9.8, which has two panels: one for constant marginal cost of preemption and the other for increasing marginal cost of preemption. Each panel has two quadrants. The upper one depicts the marginal benefit and marginal cost functions for the State. The lower quadrant graphs the best response function of the Org, which is the same as in Fig. 9.3c but drawn upside down.

In both panels, z_0 and z_1, respectively, denote the original and the new level of militancy. We first analyze the case of constant marginal cost of preemptive measures.

9.5.1 Constant Marginal Cost of Preemption

In panel (a), at the original level of militancy z_0, the MB curve of preemptive measures for the State starts from Z_0 in the top quadrant. The MC curve of preemptive measures is the flat line "MC: H_m." The original equilibrium point for the State is E_0 where the State chooses the level of preemption equal to m_0. The level of the Org's marginal cost function is $z_0 + m_0$, which marks the point M_0. In the bottom quadrant, we read the equilibrium production of terror corresponding to M_0. It is X_0.[4]

Now suppose there is an increase in militancy such that z falls from z_0 to z_1. How do the Org and the State respond? The MB curve for the State begins from Z_1. However, notice that its intersection with the MC curve occurs at E_0 as before, and thus the equilibrium $z + m$ is at M_0. This means that the State responds to the increase in militancy by increasing preemption from m_0 to m_1. The point is that, despite the increase in militancy, this response by the State leaves the level of Org's marginal cost function unchanged. As a result, the equilibrium production terror remains unchanged at X_0. The increase in militancy is neutralized by the State's preemptive actions. Per our definition, the State has won WoT, albeit in the weak sense! Since the marginal cost of preemptive measures is constant, the economically rational response for the State is to increase preemption that exactly offsets the

[4] Note that the best response function of the Org in the bottom quadrant is implicit in the MB curve in the top quadrant. They are drawn separately to show the equilibrium responses.

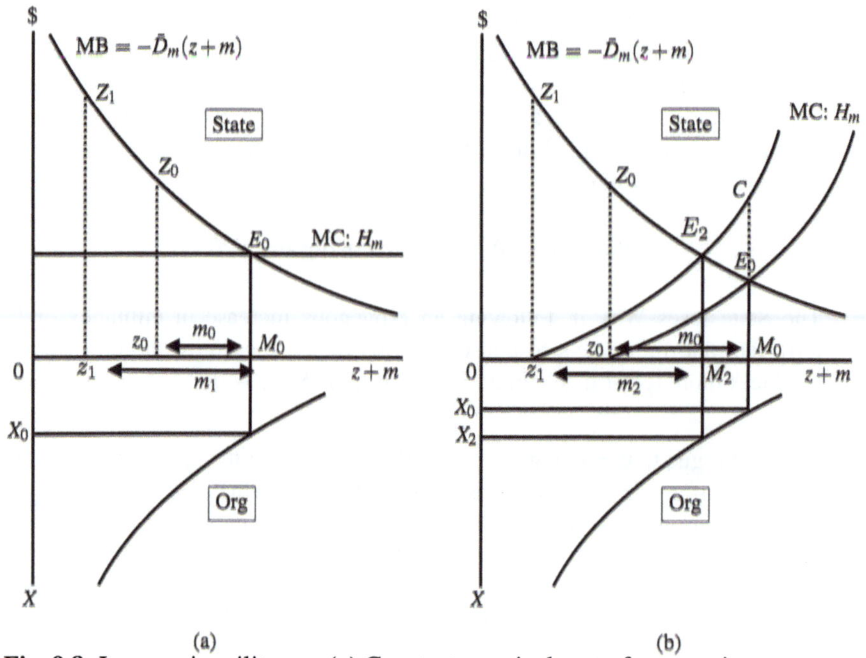

Fig. 9.8: Increase in militancy. (**a**) Constant marginal cost of preemption. (**b**) Increasing marginal cost of preemption

decrease in z due to the increase in militancy. Consequently, increased militancy does not translate into an increase in the capability of the Org. There is no increase in terror production, and the State wins.

9.5.2 Increasing Marginal Cost of Preemption

This is shown by the upward sloping MC function facing State in panel (b) of Fig. 9.8. We will now see that the implications are vastly different if the marginal cost of preemption to the State is increasing—which, as we have argued, is more realistic.

Consider the initial level of militancy z_0. The upward sloping curve starting from z_0 is the marginal cost function and reflects increasing marginal cost of preemption. The MB and the MC curves intersect at E_0. The initial optimal level of preemption is m_0 and the initial level of terror production is X_0.

Starting from z_0, m_0, and X_0, if the level of militancy increases so that $z = z_1$, the MB curve starts from Z_1, while the (same) MC curve starts from z_1 instead of z_0. The two curves intersect at E_2, implying the new level of preemption m_2. Although it is not evident from the diagram, one can show that $m_2 > m_0$. That is, the State responds to an increase in militancy by increasing the preemptive actions. However, the key point is that the increase in preemption from m_0 to m_2 does *not* fully offset the decrease in z. *The new level of marginal cost facing the Org is M_2, which is less than M_1 even after the State's response.* In the bottom quadrant, the associated new level of terror production is X_2, which is *higher* than X_0. The State loses the WoT.

The underlying reason is that if the marginal cost of preemption is increasing, it is too costly for the State to enhance preemption to fully neutralize the increase in militancy. Notice that if the State did so (such that the marginal cost to the Org remains unchanged at M_0), its MC would be at the point C in panel (b), which exceeds its MB. The State would not maximize its surplus. This is why the State does *not* fully offset the exogenous increase in militancy or terrorism and thus (rationally) loses the WoT. The State willingly accepts a higher level of terror.

This may appear odd at first but not at all unrealistic. Just think about why the USA did not engage in a full-scale military operation to defeat Taliban, although, undoubtedly, it has the military capability to obliterate Taliban soldiers and their strongholds. It is the prospect of huge collateral damage that withheld the USA from engaging in a full-scale attack on Taliban, which is the equivalence of increasing marginal cost of preemption. It explains why the USA could not win over Taliban.

Here is our model's prediction.

Is That So? 9.2: Winning/Losing WoT

Preemptive actions can help the State to win WoT if the marginal cost of preemption is constant but cannot win WoT if the marginal cost of preemption is increasing.

One would think that if preemptive measures are not enough, it can be combined with more security measures and win. Well, it is possible but not for sure—because a rational state would substitute between security and preemptive measures: if the State enhances security, its response with respect to preemption may be less than otherwise from a cost–benefit standpoint. Hence it is unclear that the State would win WoT: *winning is highly unlikely if the marginal costs of both preemption and security are increasing.* The same logic applies.

It is worth noting that if the State were not a liberal democracy and did not care about the cost of preemption and security measures, it can simply "go after" terrorists and terror organizations and suppress the problem effectively. But as long as the State is a liberal democracy—as most of the developed western nations, Japan, Australia, India, and some others are—it would care about the loss of civil liberty and collateral damage. This would constrain the State from unleashing enough preemptive actions required to win the WoT as long as the marginal costs of preemption are increasing.

Our analysis thus suggests that military intervention alone may not be sufficient to mitigate the problem of terrorism. In Chap. 13, we examine how it may be combined with other measures to tame terrorism.

9.6 Interdependence Among Target Countries

We now relax the assumption of one target country and consider a scenario where multiple target countries face the threat of terrorism from the same terror organizations. In Chap. 8, we analyzed the interdependence of security measures by target countries, whereas here we examine preemption. Our objective is to understand the nature and implications of interdependence of preemptive measures by the target countries that arises because of a *common-enemy situation*. For simplicity, assume two target countries, a and b (the results are generalized to many target countries). Security measures are kept unchanged so as to focus on preemptive measures. As in Chap. 8, in order to understand the interaction between the target countries, we keep the behavior of a terror organization implicit: it is not treated as a separate entity. Thus, we have a two-player game with State a and State b.

Remember that an increase in security by one target country exerts a terror diversion effect and a negative externality on other target countries. In contrast, *preemptive measures entail a positive the externality effect*. If country a (say the USA) steps up its attack on the facilities of terror organizations that plan attacks on the USA as well as country b (say Britain) and raises their marginal cost, it is good news for country b, Britain. Hence,

Is That So? 9.3: Preemptive Measures Have a Positive Externality Effect

In the context of multiple target countries, an increase in the preemption by one target country acts as a positive externality for other target countries.

The implication is that if target countries choose their preemptive measures individually, i.e., non-cooperatively, they do not factor in the positive externality effect. Hence they *under-provide* preemptive measures compared to what may be the best for them jointly. Another way to look at it is that one target country tends to free-ride on another's preemptive measures and thus undertakes less preemptive measures compared to a cooperative arrangement. For instance, if France bombs ISIS, there is less incentive for the USA to do so and vice versa.

The model below is based on Sandler and Siqueira (2006).

9.6.1 The Model

9.6.1.1 Damage-Deterrence and Cost Functions

Let m^i denote country i's measure of preemption, where $i = a, b$.

Assumption 9.1. *Preemptive actions m^a or m^b shift up the terror organizations' marginal cost function, reducing their terror producing capabilities. As a result, they unleash less terror attacks on both countries.*

It essentially says that *preemptive actions by either country reduce terror damage received by both countries.* Accordingly, let us define more general terror-deterrence functions $D^a(m^a, m^b)$ and $D^b(m^a, m^b)$:

$$\boxed{D^a = D^a(\underset{-}{m^a}, \underset{-}{m^b}); \quad D^b = D^b(\underset{-}{m^a}, \underset{-}{m^b}).} \tag{9.11}$$

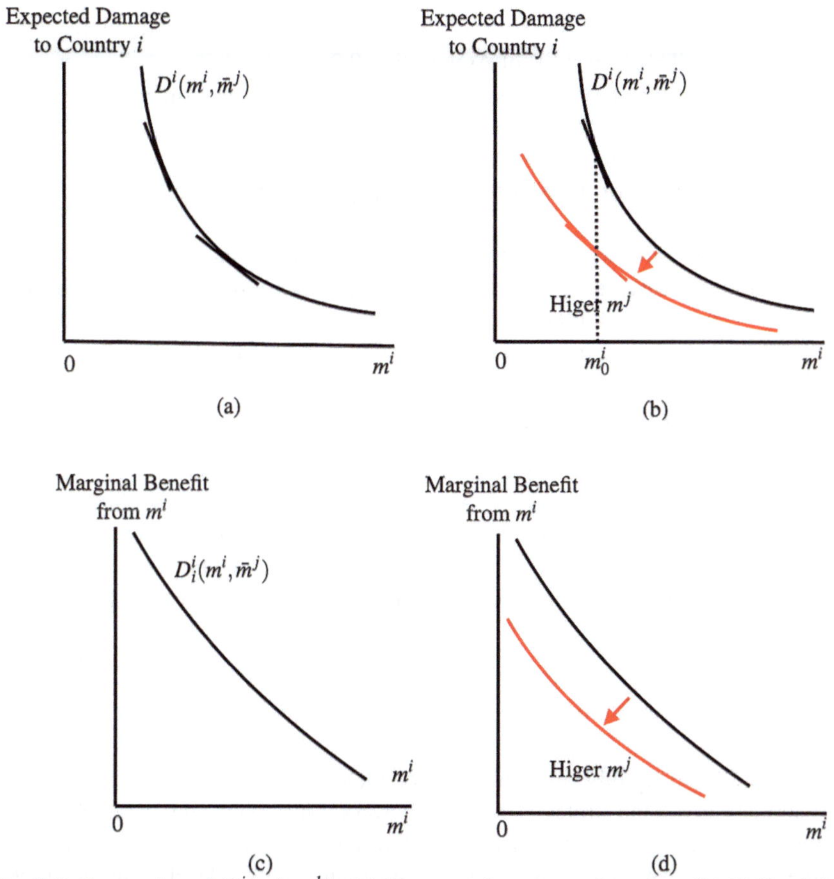

Fig. 9.9: Properties of $D^i(m^a, m^b)$. (**a**) Damage deterrence function. (**b**) Shift of the damage deterrence function. (**c**) Marginal benefit function. (**d**) Shift of the marginal benefit function

We impose the following conditions:

ASSUMPTION 9.2. *(i) The marginal damage-reducing effect of own preemptive measures is subject to diminishing returns. (ii) The marginal damage-reducing effect of own preemptive measures falls as other country steps up its preemptive actions.*

The positive externality effect is reflected by the negative marginal effect of m^b on D^a and m^a on D^b in the damage-deterrence functions as well as part (ii) of Assumption 9.2. Assumptions 9.1 and 9.2 are illustrated in Fig. 9.9. The convex curvature of the damage-deterrence functions implies that the absolute value of its slope falls with own preemption. This is reflective of diminishing returns ((i) of Assumption 9.2). Given m_0^i, an increase in m^j by country j implies less damage for country i and hence leftward shift of the damage-deterrence function. In panel (b), note that, at any given m_0^i, the slope of the damage-deterrence function falls with an increase in m^j. This is part (ii) of Assumption 9.2.

Damage-deterrence functions describe the States' benefits from preemptive measures. The marginal benefit from own preemptive measures falls with own or the country's preemptive measures (Assumption 9.2). These are shown, respectively, by the downward slope of the MB function in panel (c) and the leftward shift of the same in panel (d).

In the cost side, we continue to assume constant or increasing marginal cost of preemptive measures. However, there is no qualitative difference in implications here between the constant and increasing marginal cost situations. To fix ideas, we will suppose increasing marginal cost of preemption, as shown in Fig. 9.6b.

9.6.1.2 Rational Choice of Preemptive Measures and Nash Equilibrium

Since in the present context, preemptive measures by any country have their own direct impact on terror damage when the levels of preemptive measures by other target countries remain unchanged, we can work with a simultaneous-move Nash game, where countries a and b simultaneously choose m^a and m^b, respectively. Each country's objective is to minimize the sum of terror damage costs and the costs of preemption, i.e.,

$$\boxed{\text{Minimize} \quad C^i = D^i(m^a, m^b) + H^i(m^i), i = a, b.}$$

Recall that Nash equilibrium is where each player has no incentive to deviate from his strategy given the strategies of other players. Thus, each country minimizes its total cost with respect to its own preemptive measures, i.e., C^i is minimized with respect to m^i, given m^j. That is, each country chooses the level of its preemptive measures optimally on its own. The first-order conditions are

$$m^a : D_a^a(m^a, m^b) + H_m^a(m^a) = 0 \Leftrightarrow \underbrace{-D_a^a(m^a, m^b)}_{\text{MB}_a} = \underbrace{H_m^a(m^a)}_{\text{MC}_a} \tag{9.12}$$

$$m^b : D_b^b(m^a, m^b) + H_m^b(m^b) = 0 \Leftrightarrow \underbrace{-D_b^b(m^a, m^b)}_{\text{MB}_b} = \underbrace{H_m^b(m^b)}_{\text{MC}_b}. \tag{9.13}$$

In Fig. 9.10a, the intersection of the respective marginal benefit and marginal cost curves defines the respective optimal choice of preemptive actions.

How does the choice of preemption by one country affect that of the other? It is shown in panel (b). Assumption 9.2(ii) implies that a higher m^j by country j leads to a lower level of the MB curve from preemption for country i. The equilibrium or optimal level of m^i is thus lower. This implies, in turn, that the best response functions are downward sloping, shown in panel (c). The positive externality effect is the underlying reason: if one country steps up preemption, the other country

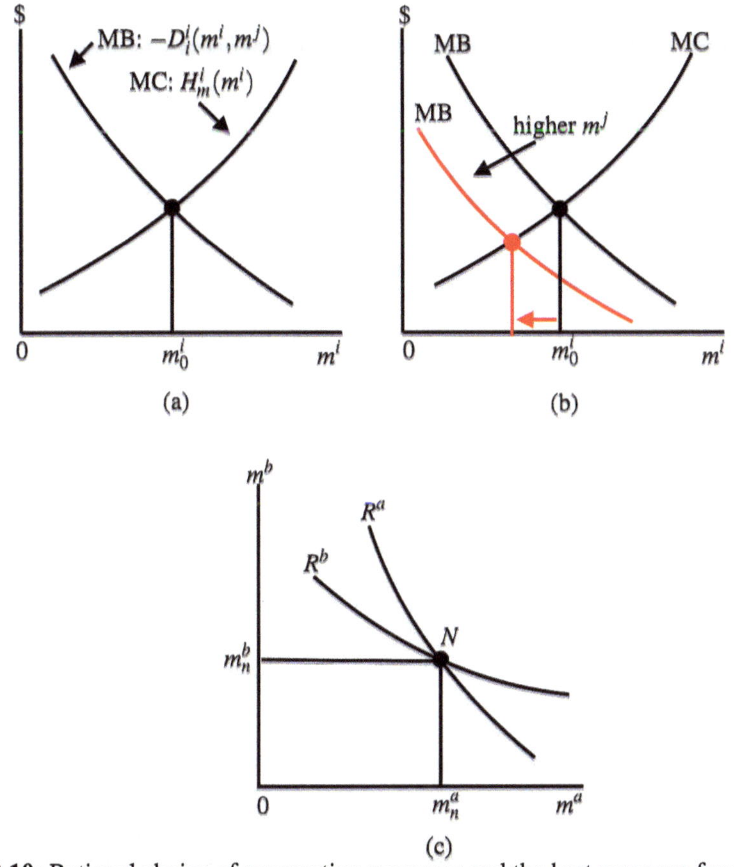

Fig. 9.10: Rational choice of preemptive measures and the best response functions. (**a**) Choice of m^i, given m^j. (**b**) Effect of an increase in m^j on m^i. (**c**) Best response functions and the Nash equilibrium

benefits and hence has an incentive to free ride and reduce its preemptive actions. The intersection point N of the best response functions locates the Nash equilibrium choice of preemption strategies (m_n^a and m_n^b).[5]

9.6.1.3 Comparative Statics

In economic terms, preemptive measures work like a common fund for a common purpose, to which every member contributes. Here, the common purpose is to defeat the common enemies that target them, and contributions to the fund are akin to preemptive measures. Which target country will "contribute" more and which will

[5] Using some other assumptions, it can be established that the R^a curve is steeper than the R^b curve.

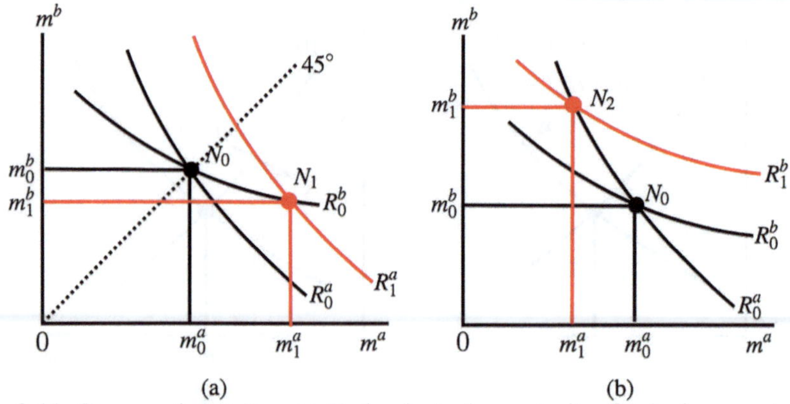

Fig. 9.11: Comparative statics. (**a**) Technological superiority. (**b**) An increase in the valuation of damage from terrorism

"contribute" less? Difference in technological capabilities is one of the factors. Suppose country a is technologically superior to country b in delivering preemptive measures. All else the same, we should expect country a to use more preemptive measures. Our model predicts this indeed.

Let us start with a situation where the damage and cost functions are the same for the two countries. Their best response functions will be mirror reflections of each other and the Nash equilibrium will lie on the 45° line like the point N_0 in Fig. 9.11a. The equilibrium preemptive measures are m_0^a and m_0^b, where $m_0^a = m_0^b$. Now, suppose country a develops a superior technology of attack. One could think of more powerful aircrafts or drones, more rigorously trained armed forces, etc. This amounts to a lower marginal cost of preemptive measures for country a. It will tend to deploy more preemptive measures, which will shift its best response function out to the right. There is no shift of country b's best response function. The new Nash equilibrium will be at a point like N_1 in panel (a). We have $m_1^a > m_0^a = m_0^b > m_1^b$. More preemptive actions are undertaken by the technologically superior country. Particularly notable is the outcome that as country a employs more preemptive measures, country b free-rides on it and scales down its preemptive measures—thanks to the positive externality effect of country a's initiative. This explains, for instance, why the USA is the natural leader in the war against terror.

Turning to our next comparative statics, whenever there is a successful terror attack causing fatalities and injuries to several people it is a big news, heightening public fear. Imagine that country a, but not country b, has experienced such a terror attack in the recent past. All else equal, another terror attack would cause greater fear among the people in country a. In other words, the damage valuation of country a is now greater. In Chap. 8, we modeled this via an increase in a multiplicative parameter α in the terror-damage function. Following the same approach, let us modify country a's damage-deterrence function as $\alpha D^a(m^a, m^b)$, where an increase in α represents a proportional increase in the valuation of damage from terror. The comparative statics question is how does an increase in the valuation of damage from terror by country a (i.e., an increase in α) affect the choice of preemption by both countries?

Note that an increase in α shifts up not just the total damage-deterrence function but also the marginal benefit function of country a's preemptive measures. At any given m^b, country a will choose a higher m^a. As shown in Fig. 9.11b, starting with an initial Nash equilibrium at N_0, the best response function of country a will shift out. The new equilibrium will be at point like N_2. Country a chooses a higher level of preemptive measures. Country b scales down. The positive externality effect is the key again, because of which country b tends to free ride on preemptive strikes by country a and chooses a lower level of preemption.

9.6.1.4 Cooperation

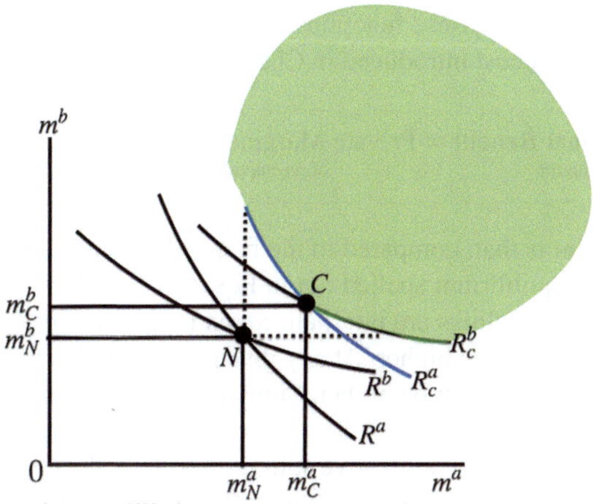

Fig. 9.12: Cooperative equilibrium

Because the positive externalities associated with preemption are not internalized at the Nash equilibrium, there is a scope for a better outcome through a joint cooperative decision making by target countries in attacking terror groups militarily and financially. It amounts to forming a coalition on terror. The question is how does the cooperative solution compare with the non-cooperative Nash solution?

Assuming that the objective of the coalition is to minimize the unweighted sum of total costs facing all target countries, in our two-target country model, countries a and b jointly decide m^a and m^b so as to minimize

$$\boxed{D^a(\underset{-}{m^a},\underset{-}{m^b}) + H^a(\underset{+}{m^a}) + D^b(\underset{-}{m^a},\underset{-}{m^b}) + H^b(\underset{+}{m^b}).}$$

The trade-offs are clear. An increase in m^i tends to reduce expected terror damage to and hence enhance the benefit of both countries, while it imposes an increase in costs for country i only. The first-order conditions are

$$m^a: \underbrace{-D_a^a(m^a, m^b) \underbrace{-D_a^b(m^a, m^b)}_{\text{+ve externality}}}_{\text{SMB of } m^a} = \underbrace{H_m^a(m^a)}_{\text{MC of } m^a} \tag{9.14}$$

$$m^b: \underbrace{-D_b^b(m^a, m^b) \underbrace{-D_b^a(m^a, m^b)}_{\text{+ve externality}}}_{\text{SMB of } m^b} = \underbrace{H_m^b(m^b)}_{\text{MC of } m^b}, \tag{9.15}$$

where SMB stands for social or collective marginal benefit, which includes own marginal benefit as well as the positive externality effect. These equations spell the respective cooperative response functions, shown as R_c^a and R_c^b in Fig. 9.12. Parallel to the social marginal cost introduced in Chap. 8, here

$$\underset{\text{of preemption}}{\text{Social Marginal Benefit}} = \underset{\text{of preemption}}{\text{Private Marginal Benefit}} + \underset{\text{of preemption}}{\text{Positive Externality.}}$$

The main point is that, compared to the first-order conditions defining the non-cooperative Nash equilibrium spelled out in Eqs. (9.12) and (9.13), under cooperation, the positive externalities are internalized, and thus the social marginal benefits of preemptive measures are higher. At any given m^b, the collectively optimal or the cooperative choice of m^a will be higher. Similarly, at any given m^a, the cooperative choice of m^b will be greater.

Figure 9.12 depicts the cooperative solution vis-à-vis the non-cooperative Nash solution. The cooperative response functions R_c^a and R_c^b must lie to the right of R^a and R^b, respectively, since the positive externalities are internalized and the social marginal benefit of m^a and m^b are higher than the individual or private benefit. The cooperative equilibrium point must lie in the shaded area (and beyond), which is to the right or both R^a and R^b lines.

Looking at the shaded area, the most likely cooperative equilibrium point will be like the point C where the solutions, m_C^a and m_C^b, are higher than the respective solutions at the Nash equilibrium point N. That is, compared to no cooperation, every target country is expected to undertake more preemptive measures. But it need not be the case. The intersection point of R_c^a and R_c^b may not lie to the north east of point N, if the two countries differ greatly in terms of cost or damage functions. The reason behind why all countries may not necessarily be called upon to engage in more preemptive strikes under cooperation is that preemptive measures by target countries are substitutes of one another. Thus

Result 9.4

Compared to non-cooperation, under cooperation at least one country chooses a higher level preemptive actions. If both countries are not too dissimilar, both would have to choose higher levels of preemptive actions.

We can generally say that the aggregate preemptive actions by the two countries together will be greater, and hence the terror organizations will be under more pressure if the target countries act collectively. Reversing the sequence,

Result 9.5

Compared to what is collectively or cooperatively the best for a group of target countries, there will be an ***under-provision of preemptive measures*** when they (non-cooperatively) choose preemption on their own (at the Nash equilibrium).

9.7 Side Effects

There are side effects of preemptive strikes that tend to encourage terrorists and terror production. One is a backlash effect arising out of resentment and anger, and the other is a negative economic externality that preemptive strikes create when economic assets of affected areas are damaged. This does not however apply to financial controls as preemptive actions.

9.7.1 Backlash

Collateral damages generate anger, vengeance, and thus more hostility toward the attackers. Such concerns have been voiced by many leaders and experts, who do not support heavy-handed military intervention as a general strategy to address the problem of terrorism. How do we think of the backlash effects in our model? There are two (generic) ways: anger and vengeance

① Lead to more support for terror organizations in terms of finance and willingness to join terror organizations

② Translate into more satisfaction to a terror organization from the same level of damage it causes to the target country that has carried out the preemptive strikes.

The first is physical and tangible, while the second is psychological. Both lead to a change in the behavior.

9.7.1.1 Greater Support for Terrorism

Sympathy and anger from crackdown and collateral damage can motivate more support to terror organizations in the form of more financial support and/or more recruitment opportunities for terror groups. We view this as a decrease in the marginal cost of producing terror *induced by preemption*. Algebraically, we can write the Org's marginal cost function as

$$\text{MC of producing terror} = z + m - \gamma m + v \cdot X,\ \gamma > 0, \tag{9.16}$$

which is a generalization of (9.1) and where $\gamma > 0$ represents the backlash coefficient. Note that the backlash effect depends on preemptive actions (m); notice that it is 0 when $m = 0$. If $\gamma \geq 1$, then preemptive measures have no benefit to the State and thus totally ineffective as CT measures. This is highly unrealistic. It is reasonable to suppose $0 < \gamma < 1$. Hence, without the backlash effect, a unit increase in m leads to a unit increase in the MC facing the Org, whereas with a backlash effect, the marginal impact is less than unity ($= 1 - \gamma$). Two conclusions follow immediately.

Result 9.6

(i) Collateral damage-induced backlash effects tend to reduce the impact of preemption on the Org's marginal cost function and therefore reduce the effectiveness of preemption as a CT measures. (ii) However, this does not imply that preemptive measures are ineffective. WoT can still be weakly won if the marginal cost of preemption is constant. Of course, compared to the case of no backlash, a higher level of preemption will be necessary for the purpose. But, if, more realistically, the marginal cost of preemption is increasing, the backlash effect further diminishes the role of preemptive measures in limiting the problem of terrorism.

9.7.1.2 Preference Shift

Backlash may breed of a sense of intense hatred, such that the same amount of damage caused to the State engenders more satisfaction to the terrorists. We can modify the utility function of the Org as $U_D = \beta(m)D(X)$, where β increases with m and captures the backlash-induced shift in preferences of the Org. The Org maximizes the surplus $\beta(m)D(X) - C(X)$, the first-order condition of which is

$$\beta(m)D_X(X) = z + m + vX. \tag{9.17}$$

Notice that an increase in preemption increases the MC of as well as the MB from producing terror. While the former tends to reduce the production of terror, the latter tends to encourage the production of terror and captures the backlash effect. In symbols,

$$X = \bar{X}(\underset{-}{z + m}, \underset{+}{m}). \tag{9.18}$$

Similar to the increasing-support argument effect, the preference shift effect also implies a diminished effectiveness of preemptive measures.

9.7.1.3 Targeted Backlash Effect: A Third Aspect

Another kind of backlash effect arises in the context of multiple target countries. It can be argued that if, for example, country a takes more preemptive actions, it would incur the wrath of the terror organization more so compared to other target countries. As a result, in terms of carrying out terror attacks, the preference of the Org would shift away from country b to country a.

We can capture this by augmenting the damage-deterrence functions. For countries a and b, we can define them as

$$\boxed{D^a(\underset{-}{m_a}, \underset{-}{m_b}) + L^a(\underset{+}{m_a}, \underset{-}{m_b}); \quad D^b(\underset{-}{m_a}, \underset{-}{m_b}) + L^b(\underset{-}{m_a}, \underset{+}{m_b}).,} \tag{9.19}$$

where $D^a(m_a, m_b)$ and $D^b(m_a, m_b)$ are the earlier damage-deterrence functions, and, $L^a(m_a, m_b)$ and $L^b(m_a, m_b)$ are the respective targeted backlash effects. The backlash effect is such that, all else the same, preemption actions by one country tend to invite more damage to that country and less to other target countries. There are two implications.

Result 9.7

In the presence of targeted backlash effect, (a) the preemptive actions chosen by the partner country remaining unchanged, a given target country will use less preemptive actions—because the terror organization becomes more focused on this country, and (b) there is an additional positive externality effect of one country's use of preemption on another target country's welfare or payoff: that is, as a country steps up its preemptive actions, the Org shifts its attention away from other target countries.

Result 9.7b implies that in Nash equilibrium, preemption will be under-provided because of two positive externality effects, and hence, cooperation would improve the joint welfare of all target countries more strongly than otherwise.[6]

9.7.1.4 Evidence on Backlash Effects

Estimating backlash effects is not an easy task. Scholars like Walsh (2013) and Gill (2015) have attempted to correlate the number of drone attacks or the civilian causalities from drone attacks in Afghanistan and Pakistan between mid-2000s and early 2010s one hand and insurgent violence in terms of terror attacks within the same or succeeding periods. They find no systematic relationship, i.e., drone strikes did not appear to have any significant deterrence effect. It means, albeit indirectly, that backlash effects cancel out *short-term* deterrence effects of drone strikes, a rather strong backlash effect. However, it does *not* say anything about the long-run deterrence effects.

---

[6] For a detailed analysis of this point, see Siqueira and Sandler (2007).

In terms of regression analysis, strong evidence of backlash effects is reported by Santifort-Jordan and Sandler (2014). They analyzed panel data on suicide terrorism at the global level from 1998 to 2010, covering 48 countries. Controlling for country-specific variables that may explain suicide attacks (e.g., per-capita income, unemployment, whether a country has a democratic system of government, etc.) and attack-specific variables like whether attackers belong to a secular or religious fundamentalist group, whether targets are business, official, or military, the authors use a time dummy variable, assuming value 0 for 1998 to 2001 and 1 for 2002 to 2010, to represent WoT that began in late 2001.

With other plausible determinants of suicide terrorism accounted for, the authors interpret the coefficient of WoT as the backlash effect.[7] Among other results, the authors find that, at the margin, WoT resulted in an *increase* of the number of transnational suicide attacks by 70%. The effect was particularly strong for suicide-attack-prone countries like Afghanistan and Iraq. Overall, "...this war created a deadlier world by enhancing grievances and expanding the use of suicide attacks by terrorists against hardened targets."

9.7.2 Negative Economic Externality

Bueno De Mesquita (2005) has argued that military crackdown on terrorists and terror facilities that produce collateral damages of economic assets like factories, infrastructure, and so on can reduce economic opportunities in the marketplace and force young people to join terror organizations. This side effect results from purely economic consideration rather than through an elevated psychological sense of anger, resentment, or ideology. This point can be understood more precisely in a simplified version of Bueno de Mesquita's self-selection model of choice in which an individual decides between working in an economy and volunteering for a terror group.

Assume an eligible workforce in a geographic area prone to preemptive strikes by a State. Individuals in the workforce differ in their ability to earn based on innate and/or education-enhanced skill. Let a denote a unidimensional index of ability that varies across individuals over an interval say from $\underline{a}$ to $\bar{a}$. Let the earning potential of an a-level-ability person be $W(a)$, where W increases with a.

Crackdown or preemption reduces economic opportunities when economic assets providing employment are damaged or destroyed. Thus, actual earnings, say w, will depend also on the level of preemption. Define $w = (1 - \mu m)W(a)$, where μ is a fraction such that $\mu m < 1$. Thus an increase in preemption reduces the earnings of all individuals irrespective of their abilities. Figure 9.13 graphs w against ability a at two levels of preemption, m_0 and m_1, where $m_1 > m_0$. The earnings lines are upward sloping, drawn as a straight lines for simplicity, and the higher the level of preemption, the flatter is the earnings line.

Suppose that all individuals are sympathizer of the cause of terror organizations. If some of them decide to volunteer for a terror organization, they receive some utility,

[7] Suicide terrorism is measured by the number of suicide missions, casualties from and the likelihood of these attacks, and the authors differentiate between domestic and transnational suicide terror attacks.

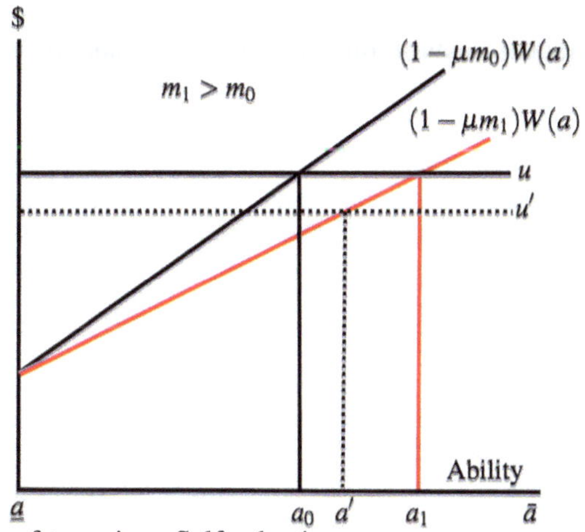

Fig. 9.13: Choice of terrorism: Self-selection

say, $u > 0$. It can be argued that u decreases with preemption, because degrading a terror organizations' capabilities reduces the chance of success and fulfillment as a terrorist. On the other hand, higher preemption can also increase u by increasing resentment—which we have already discussed. A person's ideological sentiments would also affect the magnitude of u. But, in order to isolate the effect of economic options, suppose that the net effect of preemption on u is zero. In Fig. 9.13, this is depicted as the flat line labeled u.

An individual in the labor force faces a binary choice: either work or join a terror group. Thus he/she weighs $w = (1 - \mu m)W(a)$ against u. He works or volunteers for terror organizations according to $(1 - \mu m)W(a) \gtrless u$. This comparison can be seen in Fig. 9.13. At the preemption level m_0, individuals with ability in the range $(\underline{a}, a_0)$ join terror organizations and those with ability higher than a_0 prefer to work in the economy. It is a self-selection mechanism that yields an expected outcome: those who have relatively higher ability work in the economy and those with relatively lesser ability and lesser earnings potential choose to join a terrorist group.

Beginning with the preemption level of m_0, if the State escalates it to m_1, the earnings line shifts down: all potential workers face the prospect of lower earnings because of the negative economic externality effect of preemptive strikes. At the margin, this affects the composition of individuals who opt to work and who opt to become or remain as a terrorist. We see that the new cut-off point is a_1, which implies a greater number of terrorists: those with ability in the range $(\underline{a}, a_1)$. Individuals in the ability range (a_0, a_1) become fresh entrants to terror groups. This is the main point: that is, the negative economic externality effect associated with preemptive strikes creates more terrorists.

It is not an unqualified outcome, however. By damaging the ability of terror organizations to carry out attacks, preemptive strikes may very well lower the utility from being a terrorist. If $u'(< u)$ is the new utility level from terrorism associated with $m = m_1$, the cut-off point is a'. A smaller number of people freshly join terror organization. It is, of course, possible that if the capability of the terror organizations is sufficiently degraded so that utility from terrorism falls by a sufficiently large magnitude, some may leave terror organizations and hence participation in terrorism falls. Hence the outcome depicted in Fig. 9.13 assumes that the negative economic externality effect outweighs the capability-damaging effect of preemption. However, even then the point remains that, all else the same, reduced economic opportunity, i.e., the negative economic externality (shown by the downward shift of the earnings line) is, in and of itself, a push factor toward greater participation in terrorism.

Returning to our assumption that the negative economic externality effect is dominant, there is another important and interesting implication. Observe that the new entrants to terror organizations, whose abilities range from a_0 to a_1 in Fig. 9.13, are more skilled than the existing members. This would tend to increase the *quality* of terrorism as well. Thus

Result 9.8

If preemptive strikes reduce economic infrastructure of areas that are affected by these strikes, they would tend to reduce job opportunities in those areas and encourage participation in terror organization, especially by relatively more skilled workers, thereby increasing the *quantity and quality of terrorism.*

9.8 Take-Aways

- Preemptive measures can be viewed as shift parameters of the marginal cost function of a terror organization that produces terror.
- Preemptive strikes that permanently reduce the capability of producing terror and control of funds flow to a terror organization have similar implications toward the production of terror. That is, preemptive strikes and financial controls are equivalent to some extent.
- In a game-theory setup, preemption can be studied as a sequential game where the State first chooses the level of preemptive actions, followed by the Org's choice of the level of terror production.
- Losing or winning WoT is defined such that the State loses WoT, if after an exogenous increase in militancy or terrorism and the State's response in terms of CT measures, the Org is induced to produce more terror; otherwise, the State wins.
- Preemptive measures can help the State to win WoT if the marginal cost of preemption is constant but cannot win WoT if the marginal cost of preemption is increasing.
- In the context of many target countries, an increase in the preemptive measures by one target country exerts a positive externality effect on other target countries.

- When there are two or more target countries, compared to non-cooperation among them, under cooperation at least one country must choose higher level preemptive measures, and the equilibrium level of terror is lower. If target countries are highly dissimilar among one other in terms of the cost-efficiency of counter-terror measures, relatively inefficient target countries may be called upon to scale down their preemptive actions under cooperation than under no cooperation.
- Compared to what is collectively or cooperatively the best for a group of target countries, there will be an ***under-provision of preemptive measures*** when they (non-cooperatively) choose preemption on their own (at the Nash equilibrium).
- Collateral damage induced backlash effects tend to reduce the impact of preemption on the Org's marginal cost function and therefore weaken the effectiveness of preemption as CT measures. However, this does not imply that preemptive measures are ineffective. WoT can still be weakly won if the marginal cost of preemptive measures is constant. Of course, compared to the case of no backlash, a higher level of preemption will be necessary for the purpose. But, if the marginal cost of preemption is increasing—which is more realistic—the backlash argument further diminishes the potency of preemptive measures, on their own, to contain the problem of terrorism.
- In a multiple target country scenario and targeted backlash effects, (a) the preemptive measures chosen by the partner country remaining unchanged, a given target country will use less preemptive actions—because the terror organization becomes more focused on this country, and (b) there is an additional positive externality effect of one country's use of preemption on another target country's welfare or payoff; that is, as a country steps up its preemptive actions, the Org shifts its focus away from other target countries.
- If preemptive strikes reduce infrastructure of areas that are affected by these strikes, it would tend to reduce job opportunities in those areas and encourage participation in terror organization, especially by relatively more skilled workers, thereby improving the quantity and quality of terrorism.

Questions

9.1 How would you differentiate between an exogenous and an endogenous change in terrorism or militancy?

9.2 Which of the following preemption cost functions, $H(m)$, satisfy the assumption of increasing marginal cost and why?

(i) $10 + \sqrt{m}$
(ii) $10 + m^2$
(iii) $10 - 2m + 5m^2$?

9.3 Consider the two-period model in which a terrorist group chooses the level of terror attacks in the current period and the future period. The present value of its resources in the two periods is \$340,000. Assuming that all attacks are of the same magnitude in either period, the unit costs of organizing terror attacks (cost per one attack) in the present and future periods are \$20,000 and \$33,000. The interest rate is 10%. If the Org chooses 5 terror attacks in the current period, how many terror attacks can it plan for the future period?

9.4 Describe in words why preemptive measures may fail to ensure a win in the war on terror if the marginal cost of such measures is increasing.

9.5 In multiple target country preemption game, the damage function for country i ($i = a, b$) is given by

$$D^i = 10 - \ln(m_a + m_b).$$

You may check that this function satisfies the relevant assumptions. Let the preemption cost function be $H^a(m_a) = m_a/100$ for country a and $H^b(m_b) = m_2^b/4000$ for country b.
(a) Derive the Nash solutions, m_a^n and m_b^n, and compare the two.
(b) Set up the cooperative or coalition problem and find the cooperative solutions, m_a^c and m_b^c.
(c) Compare m_a^c with m_a^n, m_b^c with m_b^n, and $m_a^c + m_b^c$ with $m_a^n + m_b^n$, and interpret.

9.6 "Backlash against preemptive actions causing collateral damage may fully neutralize the effect of such measures in degrading terrorist organizations." Defend or refute.

Chapter 10

Combating Financing of Terror

10.1 Introduction

Unlike other chapters in Part IV, this is a descriptive chapter. Terrorist resources are costly. Hence, combating the flow of funds toward supporting terrorist activities is similar to preemptive strikes on terrorists and their bases or hideouts in that it weakens the capacity of terrorists and terror organizations to produce terror attacks by raising costs. Therefore, the measures to curb the financing of terror are preemptive in nature.

Financial activities of terrorists and terrorist organizations fall into two categories (Clunan, 2006). One involves funds to carry out particular terrorist operations, which include expenses for lodging, food, transportation, purchase of audio-visual equipment, etc. These transactions are, however, legal until they are linked to terror acts, hence quite difficult to track before an event takes place.

The second category of terrorism-related financial activities are like general overhead expenses of terror organizations, training, propaganda, etc. Funds for these activities come from individual contributions, money laundering, charity organizations, control of drug production and trade, etc. These financial transactions are also hard to detect. For instance, funds are transported through the informal *hawala* markets already described in Chaps. 1 and 4. Yet they are relatively more tractable than the first category. Curbing terror financing mainly addresses the second category of financial activities.

Section 10.2 outlines efforts to check terror financing in the pre-*9/11* era. The *9/11* attacks triggered unprecedented financial restrictions all around the world so as to deter flows of funds to terrorists and terror groups. The scope of the intergovernmental agency, namely Financial Action Task Force (FATF) (to be described),

S. P. Das, *Economics of Terrorism and Counter-Terrorism Measures*,
https://doi.org/10.1007/978-3-030-96577-8_10

a watchdog of money laundering in its initial years, was broadened to include measures to fight terror financing. World bodies like the U.N., IMF, and World Bank have developed their own initiatives. In their individual capacities, the USA and the European Union have undertaken several important measures. These, along with other collective and country-specific efforts and measures, are outlined in Sect. 10.3.

10.2 Pre-*9/11* Efforts to Check Terror Financing

Before *9/11*, the primary focus was on state sponsoring of terrorism by countries like Libya, Iran, Syria, and Sudan as well as money laundering and finance by organized crime (mafia groups) and drug traffickers. Explicit reference to terror organizations, which are non-state entities, as targets for limiting the flow of funds began to surface in the late 1990s only.

State sponsorship of terrorism began to decline with the demise of the cold war. This led terror organizations to rely more on other sources of finance, both legal and illegal. The attention on terror finance began to mount after the terror attacks on the US embassies in Tanzania and Kenya in 1998. Before these events, the U.N. Security Council resolutions and treaties authorized economic sanctions and unilateral military strikes by the USA as the punitive instrument for the state sponsors of terror. These attacks compelled the USA and the Western Europe to recognize and emphasize the non-state actors, i.e., terror organization like al-Qaeda and others, as equally "complicit in supporting terrorism as states" (Clunan, 2006).

Also, several U.N. Security Council Resolutions recognized the seriousness of the financing of terror organizations and called for actions: Resolution 1214 in 1998 asked Taliban to stop trade in opium and heroin and Resolution 1267 in 1999 urged the member states to freeze Taliban's assets as long as it sheltered al-Qaeda. Resolution 1269 in 1999 used the word "terror financing" for the first time. Resolution 1333 in 2000 recognized that drug production and trade enabled Taliban to harbor terrorists and called for a freeze on financial assets of Bin Laden and his associates. These resolutions signaled a serious beginning of efforts to curb terror financing.

In 1999 France led the U.N. to host an *International Convention for the Suppression of Terrorist Financing*. The member states were urged to coordinate among themselves as well as work with private financial institutions to tackle the problem. This landmark convention specifically required member states to issue domestic legislations to criminalize terrorist financing, regulate the financial sectors, and implement checks that can ebb the flow of funds toward terrorist activities.

10.3 Post-*9/11* Efforts and Regulations

Financial regulations to choke the flow of funds to terrorists and terror organizations proliferated in the post- *9/11* era. Several multilateral, regional and national measures and regulations were instituted.

10.3.1 FATF

One of the major steps undertaken soon after *9/11* attacks was to enhance the scope of the Financial Action Task Force (FATF). Located at the OECD headquarters in Paris, FATF, an inter-governmental body, is the leading watchdog and international standard setter to tackle money laundering and terror financing.

It came into existence from the G-7 Summit held in Paris in 1989. The original sponsors were the G-7 countries (the USA, the UK, Canada, France, Germany, Italy, and Japan), the European Commission—the executive branch of the European Union, which initiates legislations and implements them once passed, manage day-to-day business, etc.—and eight other nations. FATF membership reached twenty eight in 1991–1992 and thirty one by 2000. As of 2020 the membership number stood at thirty nine. In addition, Indonesia is an observer country, and FATF has several associate members that are regional groups aiming to regulate money laundering and terror financing in the respective regions, e.g., Asia Pacific Group on money laundering (APG), Financial Action Task Force of Latin America (GAFILAT) among others. It also has observer organizations consisting of banks and financial institutions like IMF, World Bank, African Development Bank among many others as well as international bodies like OECD and the U.N.[1]

In its initial years, FATF was assigned tasks of analyzing money laundering trends and techniques, reviewing the actions already been taken at a national or an international level, and proposing new measures to counter money laundering. In 1990, it issued a report containing a set of Forty Recommendations, which were intended to provide a comprehensive plan of action against money laundering.

After the *9/11* attacks, terror financing was incorporated in its mission. Measures recommended or set by FATF have the acronym AML/CFT, meaning "anti-money laundering and combating financing of terrorism". To specifically deal with terror financing, in 2001 the FATF prescribed the eight *Special Recommendations*. Its AML/CFT recommendations have evolved and expanded over the years. They were revised in 2003, and it issued the ninth Special Recommendation in 2004. The scope of FATF's activity was further broadened after the 2008–2009 global financial crisis, lest a weakened financial system will be more prone to illegal activities. In 2012 its standards were thoroughly reviewed and financing weapons of mass destruction was added to its purview. As of 2021, it has forty recommendations that have consolidated the previous 40 + 9 recommendations.

FATF's tasks can be grouped in to six categories (Jackson, 2017).

Recommendations We have already mentioned 40 + 9 recommendations, as of 2004. Since 2012 FAFT has had a combined and revised list of 40 recommendations. The subject areas of these recommendations are enlisted in the chapter appendix.

High-Risk and Non-cooperative Jurisdictions In evaluating the compliance its recommendations, FATF designates some countries/jurisdictions as high-risk and non-

[1] FATF'S original mandate was temporary and that was renewed from time to time. Since 2020, it has an open mandate.

cooperative. For example, the FATF October 2015 statement listed three counties—Iran, North Korea, and Myanmar—as non-cooperative jurisdictions and high-risk countries with strategic deficiencies. These are *black-listed countries.* It is highly likely that black-listed countries are subject to economic sanctions and other prohibitive measures by FATF member states and other international bodies.

There are also countries classified under the *grey list*, typically referred to as "jurisdictions under increased monitoring." The FATF grey list, as of October 2021, included twenty-three countries: Albania, Barbados, Burkina Faso, Cambodia, Cayman Islands, Haiti, Jamaica, Jordan, Mali, Malta, Morocco, Myanmar, Nicaragua, Pakistan, Panama, Philippines, Senegal, South Sudan, Syria, Turkey, Uganda, Yemen, and Zimbabwe.

Curbing Financing of WMD Proliferation This is targeted toward proliferation of weapons of mass destruction (WMD), i.e., transport and export of nuclear, chemical and biological weapons, and related material. For example, the Public Statement, dated October 18, 2019, FATF notes serious concerns about North Korea's illicit activities related to the proliferation and financing of WMD.

Mutual Evaluations The FATF undertakes detailed analyses and evaluates, by peer review, each member's implementation of its recommendations in the context of the member's financial system. It also reviews countries or jurisdictions that are not its members but are members of regional watchdog organizations. For instance, Pakistan is not a member of FATF but it has membership in the Asia Pacific Group.

It is noteworthy, albeit unsurprising, that the USA consistently scores high marks for its effort to combat money laundering and terror financing. Yet, the FATF notes some deficiencies, such as no uniformity in the approach to money laundering by the individual states within the USA. While casinos and dealers in precious stones and metals are subject to close AML/CFT scrutiny, only minimal measures apply to certain non-financial businesses and professions. While the financial intelligence system in the USA is strong and robust, there are technical gaps that hinder relevant information being passed timely to competent authorities (Jackson, 2017).

Financial Intelligent Units (FIUs) are national bodies that collect information on unusual financial transactions that may be used for money laundering or terror financing. These are analytical units, not law enforcement agencies. If sufficient evidence is found, a FIU reports a transaction to the public prosecutors and law enforcement agencies. The Financial Crimes Enforcement Network (FinCEN) is the FIU of the USA.

Methods and Trends FATF continuously monitors and updates various methods used to launder money and support terrorist activities in order to effectively counter new methods of money laundering and terror financing.

Countering Corruption FATF recognizes the link between corruption and money laundering. More specifically, corruption thrives when public-sector and state officials use their positions for personal gain. Also, private sector institutions like banks, insurance companies, security firms, casinos, real estate agents, dealers in precious metals and stones are the venues and professions that are typically prone to laundering the proceeds of corruption. For example, in order to deter such activities, FATF recommends that persons in management or holding a significant controlling interest in a designated private sector institution must be vetted.

Another instrument of checking corruption and money laundering refers to *politically exposed persons* (PEPs) and their close relatives and associates. Financial institutions must incorporate systems to engage in financial dealings of such persons. The aim is not to stigmatize these individuals but to ensure that monetary transactions are legal, above the board and transparent.

10.3.2 FATF-Like Regional Groups

There are FATF-like regional groups such as

- Asia Pacific Group (APG)
- Caribbean Financial Action Task Force (CFATF)
- Eastern and Southern Africa Anti-Money Laundering Group (ESAAMLG)
- Euro Asian Group (EAG)
- Financial Action Task Force of Latin America (GAFILAT)[2]
- Inter-Governmental Action Group Against Money Laundering in West Africa (GIABA)

These organizations are committed to implement internationally accepted standards on money laundering and terror financing. APG has 41 members, different organizations as well as outside observers; CFATF has 25 member countries and so on.

10.3.3 The United Nations

The U.N. has played an active role in countering terrorism and terror financing. The 40 + 9 Recommendations of FATF indeed complied with the *International Convention for the Suppression of the Financing of Terrorism* hosted by the U.N. in 1999.

10.3.3.1 Various Resolutions and Institutions within the U.N.

The Security Council Resolution 1617 (2005) recognized FATF's 40 + 9 Recommendations. In 2006 the *Plan of Action* annexed to General Assembly Resolution 60/288 (2006) became an important tool in combating global terrorism. It marked the first time that all member states agreed to a common strategic approach to fight terrorism, defining four "pillars" upon which measures were to be undertaken. These are to

[2] Its former name was Financial Action Task Force on Money Laundering in South America (GAFISUD).

(I) address the conditions conducive to the spread of terrorism;
(II) prevent and combat terrorism;[3]
(III) build the states' capacity to prevent and combat terrorism and to strengthen the role of the U.N. system in this regard; and
(IV) ensure respect for human rights and the rule of law while fighting terrorism.

A Counter-Terrorism Implementation Task Force (CTITF) was established by the Secretary-General in 2005 and endorsed by the General Assembly resolution in 2006. Working with limited staff and capabilities CTITF was assigned the task of fighting terrorism keeping in view the four aforementioned pillars. It coordinated with at least 24 entities inside the U.N. system and some outside institutions as well, totaling more than thirty. Eight CTITF working groups were established, each headed or co-chaired by CTITF members. They are based on the following tasks:

(1) preventing and resolving conflicts;
(2) supporting and highlighting victims of terrorism;
(3) countering the use of internet for terrorist purposes;
(4) preventing and responding to WMD terror attacks;
(5) tackling the financing of terrorism;
(6) strengthening the protection of vulnerable targets;
(7) protecting human rights while countering terrorism;
(8) border management related to counter-terrorism.

As examples of bodies or institutions affiliated with CTITF, Al-Qaida Analytical Support and Sanctions Monitoring Team was established in 2004 and it had membership in CTITF working groups numbered (3), (5), (7), and (8). The Department of Peace Keeping Operations (DPKO) belonged to the working groups (1), (3), (6), and (8).

However, coordinating a large number of institutions is hardly efficient. A more focused approach of counter-terrorism efforts and dealing with financing of terror was adopted in 2011, when the U.N. Counter-Terrorism Center (UNCTC) was created within CTITF with the help of a $10 million grant from Saudi Arabia. UNCTC organizes capacity-building workshops for interested member states to counter terrorism including financing of terrorism and assists them on asset freezing requirements. In 2018 and 2019, UNCTC efforts led to the adoption and implementation of a decree in Tunisia that allowed the country to designate individuals and entities connected to terrorism. It also helped develop the Counter-Financing of Terrorism Regional Operational Plan for the ESAAMLG and helped the regional organization meet the key FATF requirements.

The U.N. Security Council has addressed countering the financing of terrorism in relatively recent years too. The measures include, among others, Resolution 2133 (2014) on kidnapping and hostage-taking by terrorists, Resolution 2178 (2014) on suppressing the flow of Foreign Terrorist Fighters (FTFs), financing and other supports to terrorist groups in Iraq and Syria, Resolution 2195 (2014) on prevent-

[3] This includes various agenda, e.g., preparing a list of experts and laboratories, improving coordination in planning a response to a terrorist attack, building a comprehensive database on biological incidents

ing terrorists benefiting from transnational organized crimes, and Resolution 2199 (2015) aiming to prevent terrorist groups in Iraq and Syria profiting from trade in oil, antiquities, hostages, and donations. By Resolution 2253 (2015), the Council strengthened its al-Qaeda sanctions framework to focus on ISIS. It devised ways to cut its funding and support channels. Resolution 2331 (2016) was adopted to undermine ISIS's funding from sexual and gender-based violence with or without the involvement of human trafficking. Resolution 2347 (2017) aimed to prevent and counter the illicit trade and trafficking in cultural property originating from armed conflicts and terrorist groups.

Under the U.N. General Assembly Resolution 71/291, the UN Office of Counter-Terrorism (UNOCT) was created in 2017 in order to further consolidate the U.N. efforts toward counter-terrorism and curbing terror financing: CTITF as well as UNCTC were moved out of the U.N. Department of Political and Peace Building Affairs and into the Office of UNOCT.

Sponsored by France, in 2019 the Security Council adopted Resolution 2462 to "combat and criminalize financing terrorists, their activities." It is the first comprehensive U.N. resolution for CFT as opposed to previous piecemeal resolutions. It is binding on all member states and can be enforced by U.N. sanctions.

10.3.3.2 International Money Laundering Information Network (IMoLIN)

In 1998 the U.N., partnering with international organizations involved in anti-money laundering, launched a website IMoLIN (International Money Laundering Information Network) as a research and information resource, most of which grants free access. The URL is https://www.imolin.org. The Global Programme against Money Laundering, Proceeds of Crime and the Financing of Terrorism (GPML) of the UN Office on Drugs and Crime (UNODC) now administers and maintains IMoLIN.[4]

There are eleven partner organizations: the Asia Pacific Group (APG) on money laundering, the Caribbean Financial Action Task Force (CFATF), the Commonwealth Secretariat, the Council of Europe—MONEYVAL, the ESAAMLG, the Euro Asian Group (EAG), FATF, the Financial Action Task Force of Latin America (GAFILAT), the Inter-Governmental Action Group Against Money Laundering in West Africa (GIABA), INTERPOL, and the Organization of American States—Inter-American Drug Abuse Control Commission (OAS/CICAD).

More specifically, IMoLIN serves the global anti-money laundering community by providing information about AML/CFT laws and regulations and contacts for inter-country assistance. It identifies areas for improvement in domestic laws, counter-terrorism measures, and international cooperation.[5]

---

[4] Both GPML and UNODC were established in 1997.

[5] As accessed on December 1, 2021 IMoLIN contains sections: (i) AMLID (The Anti-Money Laundering International Database), (ii) Calendar Events, (iii) Case Law Database, (iv) eLearning Resources, (v) International Norms and Standards, (vi) References, (vii) Related Links, (viii) Technical Assistance, (ix) Training Courses Certificates, (x) About Us, and (xi) Vacancies. All sections except AMLID are unrestricted.

As of 2021, IMoLIN is used widely by law enforcement agencies, lawyers, and policy practitioners, among others.

10.3.4 IMF and World Bank

Large amount of international flow of illegal money has the potential of destabilizing the financial sectors across the world. Illegal transactions are typically associated with massive fraud that can undermine general confidence in the financial system of nations. If large financial institutions are controlled by mafias or criminal entities, it creates monitoring problems for competent authorities. In order to minimize these potential adverse impacts of money laundering and terror financing on national economies and the international economy, the IMF and the World Bank also take measures and work with FATF.

In 2002 and 2003 both IMF and World Bank initiated year-long pilot programs to evaluate national policy measures to detect and control money laundering and terror financing, consistent with the recommendations of FATF. Since 2004 this has become a permanent activity.

In 2011, IMF published its assessment of the effectiveness of AML/CFTmeasures based on a large survey. Out of 161 countries surveyed during 2004–2011, 42.5% largely complied with FATF recommendations, while only 12.3% of cases were in full compliance. The assessment not only focused on whether a country has formally complied with requirements in terms of laws and regulations but also how effectively the standards were being implemented. It acknowledged that compliance to FATF recommendations is costly and time consuming for countries as well as assessors.

Over time, both IMF and World Bank have recommended changes in the approach toward AML/CFT compliance, calling for more targeted and specific tasks to identify country-wise sectors or areas where there is poor compliance and the risks are high (Jackson, 2017).

AMLID is a compendium of analyses of anti-money laundering laws and regulations. A click-on map that takes users to regional lists of national legislations. Eventually, this section will contain the full text or links to the full text of all national AML/CFT legislations and regulations throughout the world. The database now contains legislation from some 163 jurisdictions. AMLID is a secure, multi-lingual database and is an important reference tool for law enforcement officers involved in cross-jurisdictional work.

The Calendar section lists current training events and conferences at national, regional, and international level. Various cases against individuals and other entities and the verdicts are reported in the Case Law Database section. The eLearning Resources section lists various modules that are available for learning. The International Norms and Standard section contains information on UN instruments, model laws for common law and civil law systems, conventions, legal instruments, and other information. The Reference section contains a bibliography and various reports.

The Reference section contains details of the UN's latest research, abstracts of the best new research from governments and international organizations and a bibliography. The Links section that includes links to the websites of related regional organizations active in the field of AML/CFT and financial intelligence units (FIUs).

10.3.5 Egmont Group

The Egmont Group was formed in 1995 by FIUs from various countries, who gathered in the Egmont Arenberg Palace in Brussels. Its headquarters is located in Toronto (as of 2021). The Egmont group membership stood at 167 FIUs as of November 2021 and the membership is distributed over eight regional groups: Americas, Asia and Pacific, East and Southern Africa, Eurasia, Europe I, Europe II, Middle East and North Africa, and West and Central Africa. It is a platform where expertise and financial intelligence are shared securely among the members. Its objective is to provide valuable input to national and international institutions to fight money laundering and terror financing. Egmont Group's governing body decides on membership, structure, and its budget. There are four working groups: Information Exchange on Money Laundering/Terrorist Financing Working Group (IEWG), Membership, Support, and Compliance Working Group (MSCWG), Policy and Procedures Working Group and Technical Assistance and Training Working Group. They meet periodically and report to the governing body.

10.3.6 Measures by the USA

The USA has experienced the most lethal terror attacks till date, the *9/11* disaster. Even before *9/11*, the US individuals, military personnel, and civil and military assets were the targets of many terror attacks around the world. It is thus natural that the USA has been extremely proactive in combating terrorism, including terror financing. Below, we discuss its legislative actions as well as institutions that aim to squeeze terror financing.

10.3.6.1 USA Patriot Act

This was passed in October 2001, barely a month after the *9/11* events. The Patriot Act essentially broadened the scope of many existing laws including immigration, surveillance, search and seizure, and financing in addressing modern terrorism. Title III of the Patriot Act, entitled the "International Money Laundering Abatement and Anti-Terrorist Funding Act of 2001," deals specifically with terror finance.

[a] It requires domestic financial institutions to revise and enhance existing compliance rules and procedures. For instance, it has imposed tighter bookkeeping requirements, particularly transactions involving countries where laundering is a known problem. The financial institutions must install methodologies of tracking and identifying beneficiaries of such accounts, as well as individuals authorized to route funds.

[b] It is mandatory for foreign financial institutions with assets in the USA, which were never before been directly subject to US financial regulation, to accept new anti-money laundering obligations as a pre-condition for doing business in the USA.

[c] It extends the authority of the Secretary of the US Treasury to develop regulations that facilitate effective communication between financial institutions, with an aim of stemming laundering activity and making it harder for launderers to conceal their

identities. The Treasury may deny a merger of two banking institutions if both have historically failed to discourage money laundering with their own internal safeguards. [d] In an effort to control suspicious activity abroad, Title III prevents business with offshore shell banks that are unaffiliated with a bank on the US soil. Banks must also investigate accounts owned by political figures suspected of past corruption. There are greater restrictions on the use of internal bank concentration accounts that fail to effectively maintain audit trails—regarded as a money laundering red flag according to the law.

In brief, Title III of the Patriot Act imposes the most stringent due diligence procedure for any corresponding account that exists in money laundering jurisdictions throughout the world on the part of banks, financial advisors, intermediaries, investors, brokers and dealers, and other financial professionals.

10.3.6.2 Financial Technology Protection Act

In 2018 the House of Representatives passed the Financial Technology Protection Act, which was led by Congressman Ted Budd (R-NC) and Congressman Stephen F. Lynch (D-MA). This legislation aims to address the emerging threat of terrorist and criminal actors relying on digital currencies, including Bitcoin.

The Financial Technology Protection Act envisages a public-private sector task force that would research terrorist and illicit uses of financial technologies, including digital currencies, and develop proposals to counter them. It will also create a grant program to develop tools to detect terrorist and illicit uses of these currencies. It would establish a reward for any person who provides information leading to the conviction of anyone involved with the terrorist use of digital currencies. Finally, the bill requires the government to identify how illicit actors and foreign terrorist organizations evade sanctions, finance terrorism, or launder money by using these currencies and to develop strategies to counter such illicit uses.

As of 2021, this Act was pending in the Senate, which has referred it to Committee on Banking, Housing, and Urban Affairs.

10.3.6.3 Terror Finance Tracking Program (TFTP)

As a result of the Patriot Act, the offices under the Department of Treasury and the Department of State are empowered, among other functions, with the task of combating terror financing.

Shortly after the *9/11* attacks and passing of the Patriot Act, the Office of the Foreign Asset Control within the Office of the Terrorism and Financial Intelligence under the Department of Treasury initiated TFTP secretively. Under the program, the US Treasury Department issues subpoenas to the Society for Worldwide Interbank Financial Telecommunication (SWIFT)—a Belgium-based company with US offices that operates a worldwide messaging system used to transmit financial transaction information—seeking information on suspected international terrorists or their networks. Under the terms of the subpoenas, the US Government may only review information as part of specific terrorism investigations. The program came to the knowledge of the media and the public in 2006. TFTP has accessed millions of international transactions and provided thousands of valuable leads to the USA and other countries that have led to prevention or investigation of numerous terrorist attacks till date.

After its public disclosure in 2006 the program led to serious differences with the European Union. An agreement between the USA and the E.U. was reached in 2010. Since then it has become more collaborative insofar as information on individuals or entities in the E.U. is concerned. Details are spelled in Sect. 10.3.7.

10.3.6.4 Bureau of International Narcotics and Law Enforcement Affairs (INL)

It is one of the three "bureaus" under the Department of State, also entrusted with the task of curbing illegal financial transactions including terror financing. The Bureau of International Narcotics and Law Enforcement Affairs (INL) represents the US Department of State in multilateral processes and organizations, such as the FATF and related regional bodies that develop and evaluate the implementation of international AML/CFT standards. INL also cooperates directly with foreign countries to help national authorities strengthen their AML/CFT regimes in response to traditional and emerging threats, such as kidnapping for ransom, wildlife trafficking, exploitation of the gaming industry, and misuse of non-bank financial products including hawala and other unconventional and emerging payment methods, as well as pursue legal cases, obtain convictions, and confiscate the proceeds of crime.

It supports the State Department's Bureau of Economic and Business Affairs and Bureau of Counter-Terrorism in their work related to countering the financing of terrorism.

10.3.6.5 Bureau of Economic and Business Affairs

The Counter Threat Finance and Sanctions (TFS) division of the Bureau of Economic and Business Affairs is responsible for developing and implementing sanctions to counter threats to national security posed by particular activities, terrorist groups, and countries. TFS advises the Secretary of State on economic sanctions strategies to achieve US foreign policy objectives and works with other agencies to enact such strategies. TFS builds international support for the implementation of economic sanctions, provides foreign policy guidance to the Department of Treasury and Department of Commerce on sanctions implementation, and engages with Congress on legislations that advance US foreign policy goals in these areas.

10.3.6.6 Bureau of Counter-Terrorism

The Bureau of Counterterrorism leads in developing coordinated strategies to defeat terrorism abroad and securing the cooperation of international partners. On behalf of the State Department, it prepares annual country reports on various aspects of terrorism around the world. Addressing terror financing is only a part of its overall function to counter global terrorism and enhance the security of the USA.

10.3.6.7 Terrorist Financing Targeting Center (TFTC)

In 2017, a memorandum of understanding was reached between the USA and the countries of the Gulf Cooperation Council to establish this center co-chaired by the USA and Saudi Arabia. Besides these countries, the other participating countries are: Bahrain, Kuwait, Oman, Qatar, and U.A.E. It happened during President Trump's visit to Saudi Arabia. The aim of TFTC is to "enhance existing tools and cooperation" to counter global terror networks. It does not, however, replace any existing bilateral cooperative initiatives.

In 2017, the member countries "imposed sanctions on several individuals and entities accused of supporting the Islamic State and al-Qaida in Yemen." According to a Press release by the US Department of Treasury dated October 30, 2019, the TFTC jointly designated 25 targets as affiliates of "the Iranian regime's terror-support networks in the region." The designation's focus was on entities supporting Hezbollah which include Iran and Iran's Islamic Revolutionary Guard Corps (IRGC).[6] While not explicitly stated, the Middle East appears to be TFTC's focus region.

10.3.7 European Union

The E.U.'s measures to combat financing of terrorism can be summarized into two areas: (a) various superceding AML/CFT directives over time and (b) The EU-US common Terrorist Finance Tracking Program (TFTP) and the proposed European Terrorist Finance Tracking System (EU TFTS).

10.3.7.1 AML/CFT Directives

Soon after the FATF was instituted in 1989, the first European AML Directive was issued in 1991, providing that financial entities shall apply customer due diligence requirements when entering a business relationship, i.e., identify and verify the identity of clients, monitor transactions, and report suspicious transactions. It applied to banks and financial institutions. Further, it required the member states to criminalize the laundering of profits from drug trafficking (Borlini & Montanaro, 2017). The second AML Directive, introduced in 2001, brought into its ambit legal professionals, casinos, remittance offices, and insurance companies. It was aligned itself with the FATF recommendations. The third Directive, launched in 2005, widened the scope even more by targeting terror financing. It additionally included trusts and company service providers. Risk-based approach (RBA) to customer due diligence (CDD) and the concepts of simplified due diligence (SDD) and enhanced due diligence (EDD) were introduced.

The third Directive was followed by a hiatus over ten years in the E.U.'s legislation to further strengthen AML/CFT. The fourth Directive, implemented in 2017, expanded the E.U. measures to cover business relationships and some e-money products. More specifically, it introduced requirements for the E.U. member countries to record ultimate beneficial ownership (UBO) information in centralized regis-

[6] It coincided with the Middle East visit of the Secretary of the Treasury, Steven Mnuchin.

ters and widened the definition of UBO to include senior management officials. Record-keeping requirements were also introduced for trustees of express trusts. It significantly strengthened criteria for the RBA to money laundering, requiring firms to factor geographic locations, products, services, types of transactions and delivery channels into their customer risk profiles.

Notably, the fourth Directive broadened the category of politically exposed persons (PEPs) by adopting additional provisions on PEPs at the domestic level and those working for international organizations including the E.U.[7] It required the member states to release publicly available functional PEP lists, while the E.U. also published its own EU-level PEP list.

Introduced in 2020, the fifth AML/CTF Directive addressed many areas.

[a] A legal definition of cryptocurrency was introduced, bringing both cryptocurrencies and cryptocurrency exchanges and platforms under the scope of existing AML/CFT regulations. The providers of cryptocurrency services must register with financial authorities. The FIUs of individual states were empowered to obtain the names and addresses of owners of cryptocurrency.

[b] It streamlined the listing of high-risk third countries and introduced a requirement for firms to perform mandatory enhanced due diligence (EDD) on customers from high-risk third countries.[8]

[c] Transaction limit on prepaid cards was reduced from €150 to €50 for online transactions. Transactions from prepaid cards issued outside the EU were prohibited unless they were issued in a territory with EU-equivalent AML/CFT standards.

[d] Traders in high-value goods, such as artwork, became subject to AML/CFT reporting obligations and CDD measures when engaging in transactions of €10,000 or more. Historical, cultural, and archaeological artifacts also fell under the high-value AML/CFT rules.

[e] Centralized UBO registers were made publicly accessible while private UBO registers for bank accounts were required. The E.U. member states must make their UBO lists inter-connected across countries and strengthen their verification mechanisms. These registers were made accessible to FIUs.

The sixth AML/CFT Directive was introduced in 2021, which envisioned the creation of a central authority with the task of coordinating national authorities to correctly and consistently enforce the rules and regulations of the E.U.

10.3.7.2 The EU-US Terrorist Finance Tracking Program (TFTP) and The European Terrorist Finance Tracking System (EU TFTS)

TFTP by the USA is already described. However, since its collected data included transactions from and to the European Union member states, it led to a controversy between the USA and the E.U. on grounds of legality from the E.U.'s perspective,

---

[7] PEPs are "natural persons who are or have been entrusted with prominent public functions." The definition also includes their family members and their associates, as long as they share the beneficial ownership of legal entities or have any kind of close business relationships.

[8] These are designated countries with serious deficiencies in monitoring money laundering and due diligence.

privacy legislations passed by the E.U. as well as the E.U.s objective of transparency toward its citizens. The E.U. questioned "desirability of the [this] Orwellian practices" and asked for proof of the effectiveness of the program in containing terror financing. Civil right groups in Europe and data protection agencies started to investigate if any European or national privacy and data protection laws were violated by such "illegal" transfer of data from SWIFT to the USA. A negotiation between the USA and the E.U. was called for and an agreement was inked in 2010. As per the agreement, ***Europol***, the main law enforcement agency of the E.U., whose goal is a safer Europe for the benefit of all E.U. citizens, would first receive a copy of the data request and it would verify that the US requests meet certain conditions, including that they must be specific enough to minimize the volume of the requested data.

Despite the agreement, many members of European parliament continued to feel dissatisfied (Wesseling, 2014). Since 2010 the Agreement has been reviewed at least five times. The fifth review took place in 2019. However, all reviews have found TFTP to be a very useful source of information and investigative leads. Europol continues to oversee on behalf of the E.U.[9]

After the E.U.-USA agreement in 2010, there was a proposal to institute E.U.'s own terrorist finance tracking system (EU TFTS). The European Commission has considered this possibility. But its value-added and cost-effectiveness continue to be questioned. There was a renewed interest in having a separate European tracking system after terror attacks in Paris in 2015. It is yet to materialize.

10.3.8 OECD's Handbook

It is noteworthy that in 2019, OECD published a Handbook (OECD, 2019) on money laundering and terror financing for tax examiners and auditors for the purpose of increasing their awareness.[10] The recommendations are not mandatory. They are meant to help recognize suspicious transactions, which can be reported to competent authorities.

The Handbook provides a comprehensive list of indicators to suspect money laundering and/or terror financing. For money laundering it divides indicators into ten subject areas and for terror financing there are four. These are

Money Laundering Indicators for:

- individuals
- tax return examination and pre-audit
- businesses
- charities and foreign legal entities
- real estate
- cash
- cryptocurrencies
- international trade
- loans
- professional service provides

[9] Europol received about 600 leads from TFTP on perpetrators of Charlie Hebdo attacks in 2015 and about 900 leads on those involved in the November 2015 Paris attacks. See van Ballegooij and Bakowski (2018).

[10] It is an update of OECD's Handbook published in 2009.

Terror Financing Indicators for:

- individuals
- businesses
- charities and foreign legal entities
- cryptocurrencies

For each category, the Handbook provides a host of identifying situations where transactions may arise suspicion. For instance, indicators for terror financing in business tax filing are grouped into unusual transactions and parties, unusual money flows, unusual business activity, and unusual expenditures. In each category there are several situations that may raise a red flag for close scrutiny. For example, under unusual expenditure there are five items:

- Paying for travel to and from conflict zones or neighboring regions, for another person;
- Large or frequent donations to charities with connections to conflict zones or neighboring regions;
- Assets paid for by the business which cannot be located or verified;
- Advertising, publishing, printing expense invoices located and/or claimed, but not seen used in the business (possibly the creation of propaganda materials, e.g., printers, pamphlets, flags, etc.);
- Personal assets or expenses paid for by the business which do not appear to be used by the business owner.

The Handbook contains a long list of illustrative examples.

10.3.9 Individual Country Initiatives

Many countries other than the USA and the European Union have instituted their own initiatives to combat money laundering and terror financing, consistent with FATF and FATF-like regional organizations. As noted earlier, all 164 members of the Egmont group have their FIUs. The names and the acronyms of these FIUs can be found from the Egmont group's website. FIUs are not just confined to countries that are mostly targets of terror attacks. Some of the countries from where terrorists originate also have FIUs like Afghanistan and Syria.

Many countries have their AML/CFT "regimes," meaning legislations and implementations. As a specific example, Saudi Arabia, from which most of the perpetrators of *9/11* attacks hailed, issued its own AML/CFT legislation in 2003. Some regimes are considered to be weak and some strong. For instance, in a press release dated February 13, 2019, The European Commission prepared a list of 23 jurisdictions where the AML/CFT regimes are weak. These are: Afghanistan, American Samoa, Bahamas, Botswana, North Korea, Ethiopia, Ghana, Guam, Iran, Iraq, Libya, Nigeria, Pakistan, Panama, Puerto Rico, Samoa, Saudi Arabia, Sri Lanka, Syria, Trinidad & Tobago, Tunisia, US Virgin Islands, and Yemen.

10.4 Take-Aways

- In the pre- *9/11* era, the focus was on imposing financial hardships to states considered to be supporting terror such as Libya, Iran, Syria, and Sudan as well as money laundering and crime finance by mafia groups and drug traffickers.
- Explicit mention of intention to curb finances of non-state organizations perpetrating terror began to surface in the late 1990s, especially after terror attacks on the US embassies in Kenya and Tanzania in 1998.
- The U.N. initiated measures to stop the financing of Taliban in the late 1990s.
- The U.N. convention in 1999, *International Convention for the Suppression of Terrorist Financing*, marked the beginning of more comprehensive U.N. efforts to curb money flows to (non-state) terror organizations.
- Soon after *9/11*, the inter-governmental agency Financial Action Task Force (FATF)—that was originally formed in the 1980s to fight money laundering in the global economy—was mandated to make recommendations and evaluations on terror financing (along with its efforts on money laundering).
- FATF (headquartered in Paris) is arguably the most potent international organization now to deal with money laundering and terror financing. It works in collaboration with international organizations like the U.N., IMF, and World Bank as well as many regional FATF-like organizations.
- Measures to combat money laundering and terror financing have acquired an acronym AML/CFT (anti-money laundering and combating financing of terrorism).
- FATF evaluates the effectiveness of each country's AML/CFT measures, covering both developed and developing countries. It designates lists of black-listed and grey-listed countries or jurisdictions where money laundering and/or terror financing combating regulations and checks are lax.
- The U.N., on its own, has developed institutions and programs to fight money laundering and terror financing. It has passed many Security Council and General Assembly resolutions.
- It created the Counter-Terrorism Implementation Task Force (CTITF) in 2005. In order to consolidate functions of different entities with the U.N. to deal with the problem, the UN Counter-Terrorism Centre (UNCTC) was created in 2010. Finally, in 2017, the UN Office of Counter-Terrorism was established into which both CTITF and UNCTC were moved.
- The Global Programme against Money Laundering (GPML), Proceeds of Crime and the Financing of Terrorism of the UN Office on Drugs and Crime maintains a website called IMoLIN (https://www.imolin.org) that contains a vast amount of information on global AML/CFT initiatives.

- IMF and World Bank also run programs to control money laundering and terror financing.
- The Egmont Group is an international body constituted by many Financial Intelligence Units around the world, where ideas are exchanged and co-operative efforts are made to gather information on financial transactions that may be conduits for money laundering or terror financing.
- Shortly after the *9/11* attacks, the USA passed the Patriot Act on the basis of which strong measures were taken to control terror financing. The Act itself requires reporting of transactions involving foreign financial institutions by individuals and businesses.
- As a result of the Patriot Act the USA launched the Terror Finance Tracking Program (TFTP) which accesses data on international financial transactions through SWIFT. With respect to collection of data on entities in the E.U., TFTP requires the participation of Europol.
- There are three bureaus under the Department of State that are also entrusted with the task of curbing illegal financial transactions including terror financing. They are the Bureau of International Narcotics and Law Enforcement Affairs (INL), the Bureau of Economics and Business Affairs, and the Bureau of Counter-Terrorism.
- In 2017 the USA, together with six Arab nations, created the Terror Financing Targeting Center (TFTC). The aim is to enhance the existing tools and cooperation to counter terrorism by restricting financial transactions. Middle East appears to be its focus region.
- The Financial Technology Protection Act has been passed the US Congress that aims to deal with the threat of terrorists and criminals who rely on digital currencies. As of 2021, the bill was pending in the US Senate.
- The European Union has also been active in countering money laundering and terror finance through various "directives" as well as in conjunction with the TFTP initiated by the USA.
- There is a proposal since 2010 to institute E.U.'s own terror financing tracking system but it has not materialized yet.
- In 2019 the OECD has published the second edition of its Handbook on money laundering and terror financing for tax examiners and auditors, which has elaborate instructions and guideline to suspect illicit fund-raising or transferring.
- At least 164 countries and jurisdictions have their own FIUs. Many countries have AML/CFT regimes in place, some of which are robust, while others are not. In 2019 the European Commission prepared a list of 23 countries or jurisdictions where the AML/CFT regimes are weak.

Appendix to Chapter 10

10.A FATF's List of Recommendations

This is based on "International Standards on Combating Money Laundering and the Financing of Terrorism & Proliferation: The FATF Recommendations" adopted in 2012 and updated in June 2019.

Number	Subject Areas
	A—AML/CFTPOLICIES AND COORDINATION
1	Assessing risks and applying a risk-based approach
2	National cooperation and coordination
	B—MONEY LAUNDERING AND CONFISCATION
3	Money laundering offence
4	Confiscation and provisional measures
	C—TERRORIST FINANCING AND FINANCING OF PROLIFERATION
5	Terrorist finance offence
6	Targeted financial sanctions related to terrorism and terror financing
7	Targeted financial sanctions related to proliferation
8	Non-profit organizations
	D—PREVENTIVE MEASURES
9	Financial institution secrecy laws
10	Customer due diligence
11	Record keeping
	Additional measures for specific customers and activities
12	Political exposed persons
13	Correspondent banking
14	Money or value transfer services
15	New technologies
16	Wire transfers
	Reliance, controls and financial groups
17	Reliance of third parties
18	Internal controls and foreign branches and subsidiaries
19	Higher-risk countries
20	Reporting of suspicious transactions
21	Tipping-off and confidentiality
	DESIGNATED AND NON-FINANCIAL BUSINESSES AND PROFESSIONS (DNFBPs)
22	DNFBPs: Customer due diligence
23	DNFBPs: Other measures
	E—TRANSPARENCY AND BENEFICIAL OWNERSHIP OF LEGAL PERSONS AND ARRANGEMENTS
24	Transparency and beneficial ownership of legal persons
25	Transparency and beneficial ownership of legal arrangements
	F—POWERS AND RESPONSIBILITIES OF COMPETENT AUTHORITIES AND OTHER INSTITUTIONAL MEASURES

	Regulation and supervision
26	Regulation and supervision of financial institutions
27	Powers of supervisors
28	Regulations supervision of DNFBPs
29	Financial intelligence units (FIUs)
30	Responsibilities of law enforcement and investigative authorities
31	Powers of law enforcement and investigative authorities
32	Cash couriers
	General requirements
33	Statistics
34	Guidance and feedback
	Sanctions
35	Sanctions
	G—INTERNATIONAL COOPERATIONS
36	International instruments
37	Mutual legal assistance
38	Mutual legal assistance: freezing and confiscation
39	Extradition
40	Other forms of international cooperation

Table 10.1: FATF's List of Recommendations

Questions

10.1 By searching the relevant literature on the internet, list the most recent FATF's grey-list countries. For any five of them, find out the a priori reasons behind such decisions by the FATF.

10.2 By searching the relevant literature on the internet, make an assessment of the efforts of Syria, Afghanistan, Nigeria, Iraq, and Pakistan individually toward curbing the flow of funds to terror groups.

10.3 By searching the relevant literature on the internet, list the names of the FIU's of G-20 nations.

10.4 Write a 2000-word critical essay on the success of the Egmont group toward AML/CFT.

Chapter 11

Security-Deterrence "and" Preemptive Measures

11.1 Introduction

In this chapter we study three models of terrorism. The commonality between them is that they incorporate both defensive and preemptive CT measures, not just one at a time. Needless to say, the countries impacted by terrorism problems pursue some combination of both types of CT measures. However, to keep analytical tractability we will abstract from multiple-target-country interdependence.

In Sect. 11.2 we analyze a terrorist organization as a network and its decision making with respect to size of the network and the degree of communication among the nodes of the network. We use some of the basic concepts of network theory introduced in Chap. 7. It permits us to derive the implications of intelligence and infiltration as CT measures—in particular how they may impact on the *structure* of terrorist networks. Recall from Chap. 1 that intelligence and infiltration contain both defensive and preemptive elements. We only consider the behavior of a terror organization, not the choice of the level of policy measures by a target country.

In Sect. 11.3 we return to the game-theoretic (i.e., strategic) interaction between a terrorist organization and a target country as in Chaps. 8 and 9. A terrorist organization is treated as a unitary entity, rather than a network. In fact, from then on in this chapter and other analytical chapters to come, we shall presume that a terrorist organization is a unitary decision-making entity. We consider a model having one terrorist organization (the Org) and one defending state (the State), but, unlike in Chaps. 8 and 9, the State rationally chooses security and preemptive measures both. Our model thus integrates the analysis of SD measures and preemptive measures studied respectively and separately in section of 8.3 of Chap. 8 and sections 9.3 and 9.4 of Chap. 9. This enables us to understand the implications for both types of CT measures working in tandem.

The analysis of counter-terrorism measures in Chaps. 8 and 9 assumed that a terrorist organization is preoccupied with terrorist activity only with the objective of causing damage to a target country. However, many large terrorist organizations do multi-tasking. Apart from planning and executing terror attacks, they run public and social services and some participate in the political process (see Chap. 2).

S. P. Das, *Economics of Terrorism and Counter-Terrorism Measures*,
https://doi.org/10.1007/978-3-030-96577-8_11

Examples include Hezbollah, Hamas, and Taliban among others. Section 11.4 considers a model that incorporates both terrorist and *non-terrorist* activities of a terror organization. The question posed is, how are SD and preemptive measures expected to affect these activities by influencing the terrorist organization's trade-off between them?

11.2 Intelligence and Infiltration of Terrorist Networks

As said in the Introduction, we analyze how intelligence and infiltration (I&I) impact on a terrorist network's size and density. In a network, size is the number of nodes, which translates into the number of operatives in a terrorist group. Density is a measure of communication among different nodes in a network—in our context, a measure of connectivity among various cells in a terrorist organization.

Toward this end, we follow Enders and Su (2007), who consider a connected network, the Org. A connected network is one in which all nodes have some direct links. Assume that the intelligence and infiltration operations plan to bust or infiltrate one node, the probability of success of which is π. An increase in π captures a more effective I&I strategy as a counter-terrorism measure. Thus, the probability of any particular node being "exposed" is π/N, where N is the number of terrorists or nodes, equal to the size of the network. If a node is exposed or "compromised," those who are directly linked to the compromised node are also assumed to be compromised. Hence, how many are exposed depends on the size and the density of the network. (Refer to Chap. 7 for the definitions of connectedness and density of a network.)

11.2.1 Expected Number of Compromised Nodes/Terrorists

Based on the number of nodes, N, and the probability of success of I&I, we first derive an expression for the expected number of compromised nodes or terrorists, say M, *in terms of size and density.*

Let us group the nodes according to how many other nodes they are directly linked with. Let k_i be the number of nodes in the network having direct link with i number of other nodes. Obviously, i takes values $1, 2, \ldots, N-1$ since the minimum number of direct link will be 1 as long as the network is connected and the maximum is $N-1$. For instance, k_3 is the number of nodes that are directly linked to *exactly* three other nodes. It is possible, for example, that $k_5 = 0$, i.e., there is no node that is directly linked with exactly five other nodes.

The sum of all k_i's must equal the total number of nodes, N, i.e.,

$$\boxed{N = k_1 + k_2 + \cdots + k_{N-1}.} \tag{11.1}$$

Also,

$$\boxed{\text{Total number of direct links} \equiv n = \frac{k_1 + 2k_2 + \cdots + (N-1)k_{N-1}}{2}.} \tag{11.2}$$

For example, k_2 is the number of nodes having two direct links. Hence the total number of such links in a network equals $2 \times k_2$. Likewise, since k_5 is the number of nodes that have five nodes, the total number of these links would be $5 \times k_5$. If we add all these, the sum will be twice the total number of direct links because each link is counted twice.[1] This is why the sum of $k_1 + 2k_2 + \ldots$ is divided by "2" in (11.2).

Next, we derive an expression for M, the expected number of compromised nodes, based on the k_i's, that is,

$$\text{Expected number of compromised nodes} \equiv M = \frac{\pi}{N}(2k_1 + 3k_2 + \cdots + Nk_{N-1}). \tag{11.3}$$

Mark that k_i counts the number of "other" nodes connected to a given a node. Hence the number of nodes (not links) having k_i direct links is $i+1$ and the expected number of nodes of this type being compromised equals the probability of any particular node being compromised ($= \pi/N$) times $(i+1) \cdot k_i$. Summing up over all k_i types gives the expression in (11.3). We rewrite (11.3) as

$$\begin{aligned} M &= \frac{\pi}{N}[(k_1 + k_2 + \cdots + k_{N-1}) + (k_1 + 2k_2 + \cdots + (N-1)k_{N-1})] \\ &= \frac{\pi}{N}(N + 2n), \end{aligned}$$

where we have made use of expressions in (11.1) and (11.2). From Chap. 7, recall that density of a network has the expression $\rho = 2n/[N(N-1)]$. Thus, we can write the above expression of M as

$$M = \pi\,[1 + (N-1)\rho]. \tag{11.4}$$

This is the mathematical expression for the expected number of exposed or compromised nodes in terms of size and density of a network. Based on (11.4),

Result 11.1

The expected count of exposed nodes increases with both size and density of a terrorist network.

Increasing size and density naturally involves more resource costs as operatives have to be economically compensated and more density requires greater cost of maintaining communication. Result 11.1 says there is an additional cost of increasing size and density of a network: that is, *an increasing specter of detection and apprehension, which can pose a serious threat for the members and the organization.*

[1] Consider a direct link between two nodes say A and B. This (one) link is counted twice, once for A and once for B.

11.2.2 Production Function of Terror

In Chaps. 8 and 9, the technology of producing terror (same as terror production function) was indirectly represented by the cost function $C(X)$, where X is the aggregate terror input. Here, we will explicitly model the technology of producing X and costs of inputs that help produce X. In the present context there are two inputs: (1) the number of terrorist operatives (nodes) N and (2) the network density ρ.

Assume for a moment that there is no chance of detection, i.e., $\pi = 0$, so that $M = 0$. Let

$$\boxed{X = F(\underset{+}{N}, \underset{+}{\rho})} \tag{11.5}$$

be the production function of terror. The greater the size of the network, the higher is the terror output. Also, the higher the density, the greater is the output due to enhanced coordination.

Against this background, if $\pi > 0$ and there are compromised nodes, it is reasonable to suppose that the productivity of those nodes will be less compared to those who are not compromised. We may capture this simply by supposing that one compromised node is μ fraction as productive as a non-compromised node. Thus the *effective size* of a terrorist organization is equal to

$$\boxed{N - M + \mu M = N - (1 - \mu)M.}$$

As an example, if the compromised members are captured, they are simply gone and $\mu = 0$ and the effective size is $N - M$. The compromised individuals may be partly hampered, so that $0 < \mu < 1$. In general then, $0 \leq \mu < 1$. Accordingly, we substitute N in (11.5) by $N - (1 - \mu)M$. Thus $X = F(N - (1 - \mu)M, \rho)$. Next, we substitute in it the expression of M from (11.4), leading to:

$$\boxed{X = F\left(\underset{+}{N - (1 - \mu)\pi [1 + (N - 1)\rho]}, \underset{+}{\rho}\right).} \tag{11.6}$$

We reinterpret X as expected terror output. Notice in (11.6) that size and density exert two effects on terror output: direct effects that are positive, and indirect effects that are negative as they tend to increase the expected number of compromised nodes. These negative impacts are, essentially, costs to the Org.

Consider the net marginal impact of size on the terror output. Partially differentiating the expected terror output with respect to size,

$$\boxed{\frac{\partial X}{\partial N} = F_N(\cdot)[1 - (1 - \mu)\pi\rho] > 0 \text{ since } \pi < 1,\ \mu < 1,\ \rho < 1.}$$

Therefore, the net impact of size on terror production is positive. However, the net marginal effect of density is generally ambiguous:

$$\frac{\partial X}{\partial \rho} = -F_N(\cdot)(1-\mu)\pi(N-1) + F_\rho(\cdot) \gtreqless 0.$$

We assume however π is not too high, and hence $\partial X/\partial \rho > 0$, so that there is also a net marginal "positive" effect of density on terror output. How does terror output change with respect to an increase in infiltration probability?

$$\frac{\partial X}{\partial \pi} = -F_N(\cdot)(1-\mu)\left[1+(N-1)\rho\right] < 0.$$

This is expected. In view of the various marginal effects, we can express the terror-producing technology (11.6) as

$$X = F(N-(1-\mu)\pi\left[1+(N-1,\rho\right],\rho) \equiv X(\underset{+}{N},\underset{+}{\rho};\underset{-}{\pi}). \tag{11.7}$$

11.2.3 Damage from Terror: Benefit for the Org

We borrow the expected damage function $D(\underset{+}{X},\underset{+}{s})$ from Chap. 8. For now, we consider security as exogenous and thus ignore the variable s in the $D(\cdot)$ function and write it as $D(X)$ as in Chap. 9. Using (11.7), we can now express

$$D(X) = D(X(N,\rho)) = \bar{D}(\underset{+}{N},\underset{+}{\rho};\underset{-}{\pi}). \tag{11.8}$$

This is the total benefit function for the Org with respect to size and density. We further assume that (a) the marginal benefits of size and density are decreasing with respect to the respective variables as well as with the probability of detection π, and, (b) if the probability of detection increases, the marginal effects of size and density on terror production decrease. Algebraically,

Assumption 11.1.

$$\bar{D}_N > 0 > \bar{D}_{NN};\quad \bar{D}_\rho > 0 > \bar{D}_{\rho\rho};\quad \bar{D}_\pi < 0;\quad \bar{D}_{N\pi} < 0;\quad \bar{D}_{\rho\pi} < 0. \tag{11.9}$$

11.2.4 Resource Costs and Rational Choice of Size and Density

On the cost side facing the Org, let $C^1(N)$ and $C^2(\rho)$ denote the Org's total resource cost functions associated with size and density, respectively.[2] Using the $\bar{D}(\cdot)$ and these cost functions, we have

$$\text{Org's Surplus} = \bar{D}(\underset{+}{N}, \underset{+}{\rho}; \underset{-}{\pi}) - C^1(\underset{+}{N}) - C^2(\underset{+}{\rho}).$$

The Org maximizes this by choosing N and ρ, representing size and density of its network, respectively. The trade-offs are clear, and the respective first-order conditions are

$$N\colon\ \underbrace{\bar{D}_N(N, \rho; \pi)}_{\text{MB from } N} = \underbrace{C^1_N(N)}_{\text{MC of } N} \tag{11.10}$$

$$\rho\colon\ \underbrace{\bar{D}_\rho(N, \rho; \pi)}_{\text{MB from } \rho} = \underbrace{C^2_\rho(\rho)}_{\text{MC of } \rho}. \tag{11.11}$$

The effects of I&I measures are determined by applying comparative statics to these equations with respect to π. Recall Assumption 11.1 that marginal effects of size and density on expected damage from terror decrease with respect to I&I. Without further analytics, intuitive reasoning dictates that both size and density of the network would decrease with I&I. Furthermore, if we associate more complex terror attacks with higher density (as complexity requires a high degree of connectivity), we can also say that higher π implies less complex or sophisticated terror attacks.

Result 11.2

A more effective intelligence-and-infiltration measures lead to a less connected network of terrorists, less number of terrorists as well as less sophisticated terror attacks.

11.2.5 Intelligence and Infiltration as Defensive Measures

Apprehension of terrorists leads to their partial or full neutralization. This is how I&I measures act as preemptive measures. In addition, apprehensions, confessions, and seizure of documents lead to critical information on location and planning of attacks. In turn, this prompts better security arrangements. Thus, I&I serve as defensive measures too. We can understand this role of I&I more exactly by postulating that

[2] More generally, we can specify an aggregate cost function $C(\underset{+}{N}, \underset{+}{\rho})$.

Assumption 11.2. *An increase in the expected number of compromised nodes increases the probability of failure of attacks, say p. That is,*

$$\boxed{p = p(\underset{+}{M}) = p(\pi(1 + (\underset{+}{N} - 1)\rho)).}$$

In order to focus on the defensive role of I&I, let us suppress other forms of security measures as well as the preemptive role of I&I. Accordingly, instead of (11.6), let (11.5) describe the terror production technology. This leads the following expression for the expected damage:

$$\boxed{D = (1 - p)F(N, \rho) = [1 - p(\pi(1 + (\underset{+}{N} - 1)\rho))]F(\underset{+}{N}, \underset{+}{\rho}) = \bar{D}(N, \rho, \pi).} \quad (11.12)$$

Notice the similarity with the earlier model of I&I as preemptive measures. While size and density contribute to the benefit of the Org (via the function $F(\cdot)$), they undermine the benefit by increasing the probability of failure of terror attacks. It is reasonable to suppose that the negative effects of size and density via detection or apprehension are not large enough to fully offset their positive effects on the expected damage. Thus, $D = \bar{D}(\underset{+}{N}, \underset{+}{\rho}, \underset{-}{\pi})$. As long as the impact of π on the *marginal* effects of size and density on expected damage is negative (Assumption 11.1), we obtain the same comparative static results as in the previous model: $dN/d\pi < 0$ and $d\rho/d\pi < 0$. Result 11.2 continues to hold.

Therefore, the qualitative impacts of offensive and defensive elements of I&I on a terrorist organization's choice of size and density of network are similar.

11.2.6 Evidence on the Effect of Intelligence on Terror Attacks

It is hard to statistically measure the impact of I&I measures of terrorist networks per se. However, in an interesting study, Gardeazabal and Sandler (2015) are able to estimate the impact of intelligence on terror *attacks*.

Founded in 1923, INTERPOL, an acronym for International Criminal Police Organization, is an international organization that coordinates law enforcement agencies across the member countries with an aim toward controlling cyber crime, organized crime and terrorism.[3] Headquartered in Lyon, France, it had 194 member countries as of 2020. In 2005, it developed two surveillance networks: FIND (Fixed INTERPOL Network Database) and MIND (Mobile INTERPOL Network Database). By using the INTERPOL databases, these two agencies enable screening of people and their documents as they cross national borders. The number of participating countries in these two databases grew from less than ten in 2005 to 102 in 2011.

[3] Its website, as on November 7, 2021, is https://www.interpol.int/en.

Using data on transnational terrorism from ITERATE in INTERPOL-member countries from 2005 to 2011 and comparing between member countries that use FIND/MIND and those who do not, Gardeazabal and Sandler (2015) estimate that those who use FIND/MIND databases experience, on average, less number of transnational terror attacks than those who do not use: 0.5 fewer annually per 100 million people.[4] It means that a country like France that had a population of nearly 64 million in 2008 would have experienced $0.5 \times 0.64 = 0.32 = 32\%$ fewer transnational terrorist events, a large effect.

It is of interest that according to the estimates by Sandler et al. (2011) "every dollar invested in INTERPOL's counter-terrorism activities, member countries receive $200 in average returns."

11.3 Simultaneous Choice of Security-Deterrence and Preemptive Measures

From now on, we abstract from terrorist network issues and the role of I&I and revert back to thinking of a terrorist organization as a single entity. We focus here on the "simultaneous" choice of security-deterrence and preemptive actions by the state and how it responds to an increase in terrorism in terms of both types of counter-terrorism interventions.

We return to the game-theoretic models of terror attacks studied in Chaps. 8 and 9. Suppose that there is one terror organization (the Org) and one defending country or jurisdiction (the State). Recall that preemptive measures reduce damage from terror by inducing a terror organization to produce less terror, not directly as security-deterrence measures can. Therefore, in Chap. 9 we modeled a two-stage game of interaction between the Org and the State. We retain the same two-stage setting here. The difference is that we incorporate *both* security-deterrence and preemptive measures as choice variables of the State. This is the model of terrorism developed and explored by Das and Roy Chowdhury (2014).

11.3.1 Damage/Fear Function

We begin with the same (expected) damage function introduced in Chap. 8:

$$\boxed{D\Big(\underset{+}{X}, \underset{-}{s}\Big),}$$

where X is the aggregate terror input and s is the level of SD measures. The expected damage increases with the aggregate terror input and decreases with SD measures; thus, $D_X > 0$ and $D_s < 0$. Remember that we are not just talking about physical damages like death, injury, or destruction of property. Damages include the valuation

[4] In the regression analysis, the dependent variable was the ratio of the number of transnational terror incidents in a member country in a year to its population in that year in 100 million.

of the (psychological) sense of fear and insecurity that terror attacks engender. Indeed, let us interpret damage, $D(\cdot)$, as public fear, and let

Assumption 11.3.

$$D_{ss} > 0 > D_{Xs}.$$

The signs of the second derivative and the cross partial, respectively, say that as SD measures increase, the marginal returns or effectiveness of SD measures and the marginal effect of terror on damage/fear both decrease. These are intuitive; see Chap. 8, Sect. 8.3.1 for details.

But, importantly, we now depart from Assumption 8.4(iii) that the *marginal* effect of terror on fear diminishes with an increase in terror (i.e., $D_{XX} < 0$). This assumption says that while fear increases with terror attacks, its incremental effect diminishes. Put differently, while terror attacks increase public's fear of physical danger, they do not trigger a fear psychosis or paranoia that feeds on itself. Instead, let us allow $D_{XX} \lesseqgtr 0$.

Following the terminology of Das and Roy Chowdhury (2014), we differentiate between the two cases of

1. *weak marginal fear*, $D_{XX} < 0$, and
2. *strong marginal fear*, $D_{XX} > 0$.

That is, the "marginal" fear effect of terrorist attacks is weak or strong accordingly as it decreases or increases with the attacks.

11.3.2 Cost Functions and the Sequential Game

The State faces three cost functions: the damage/fear cost $D(X, s)$, the cost of security-deterrence, $T(s)$, and that of preemptive measures, $H(m)$, where m is the level of preemptive measures. In stage 1, the State rationally chooses s and m in order to minimize the sum of all three costs, i.e., its objective is to

$$\text{minimize} \quad \Gamma = D(X, s) + T(s) + H(m) \text{ with respect to } s \text{ and } m. \tag{11.13}$$

However, in doing so, it must take into account how its choices would influence the Org's choice of terror in stage 2. We solve the model by backward induction, starting with stage 2 and then stage 1.

In stage 2, the Org maximizes its surplus, equal to the valuation of damage/fear cost to the State minus the cost of producing terror. We use the same cost functions for the Org as in Chap. 9:

$$\text{Total cost: } C(X; m) = (z + m)X + \frac{1}{2}vX^2$$
$$\text{Marginal cost: } C_X(X; m) = z + m + vX.$$ [5]

[5] Note that these are not independent functions: given one, we can derive the other.

To reiterate what we already know in Chap. 9, an increase in the level of preemptive actions by the State, i.e., an increase in m, increases total and marginal cost functions facing the Org. A decrease in the parameter z reflects an exogenous increase in terrorism or in the potency of the terror organization. It tends to shift down both the total and marginal cost functions.

Our aim is to determine the impact of a decline in z on the counter-terror measures s and m.

11.3.3 Org's Choice of Terror Production in Stage 2

The Org aims to

$$\text{maximize} \quad D(X,s) - C(X;m) = D(X,s) - (z+m)X + \frac{1}{2}vX^2,$$

by choosing X. The first-order condition is

$$\underbrace{D_X(X,s)}_{\text{Org's MB}} = \underbrace{z+m+vX}_{\text{Org's MC}}, \tag{11.14}$$

a generalization of Eq. (9.4) in Chap. 9 in that the marginal damage effect of terror has affected the SD measures s too. Following Assumption 11.3, an increase in s tends to reduce the marginal damage effect or MB of terror ($D_{Xs} < 0$) and would induce less production of terror (the deterrence effect). On the other hand, an increase in preemptive measures m increases MC of producing terror. This also leads to a decline in the production of terror. Hence, both types of CT measures work differently but exert the same qualitative impact. The Org's behavior in stage 2 is summarized as

$$X = g(\underset{-}{s}, \underset{-}{z+m}). \tag{11.15}$$

This is the Org's best response function.

11.3.4 State's Choice of CT Measures in Stage 1

We now turn to the stage 1 decision-making by the State, who anticipates the (best) response of the Org given in (11.15) above. We capture this by substituting (11.15) into the State's objective function (11.13):

$$\Gamma = \underset{+}{D(X(\underset{-}{s}, \underset{-}{z+m}), \underset{-}{s})} + T(\underset{+}{s}) + H(\underset{+}{m}) = \bar{D}(\underset{-}{s}, \underset{-}{z+m}) + T(\underset{+}{s}) + H(\underset{+}{m}). \tag{11.16}$$

We see the direct and indirect negative impacts of SD measures and the indirect negative impact of preemptive measures on damage from terror. These are the benefits to the State. The functions $T(s)$ and $H(m)$ are the cost functions of the respective CT measures. The trade-offs are evident. Minimizing Γ implies two first-order conditions:

$$s:\quad \underbrace{-\bar{D}_s(s, z+m)}_{\text{State's MB}} = \underbrace{T_s(s)}_{\text{State's MC}} \tag{11.17}$$

$$m:\quad \underbrace{-\bar{D}_m(s, z+m)}_{\text{State's MB}} = \underbrace{H_m(m)}_{\text{State's MC}}.[6] \tag{11.18}$$

Note that each equation spells a locus between s and m for any given exogenous level of terrorism z. This is depicted in Fig. 11.1. The curves SS and MM, respectively, represent Eqs. (11.17) and (11.18). Both are downward sloping, reflecting that security-deterrence and preemptive measures are substitutes of each other in that in order to keep the level of terror unchanged; an increase in one would have to be coupled with a decrease in the other. The intersection point E_0 is the equilibrium point for the State, marking the rational choice of s and m indicated by s_0 and m_0.

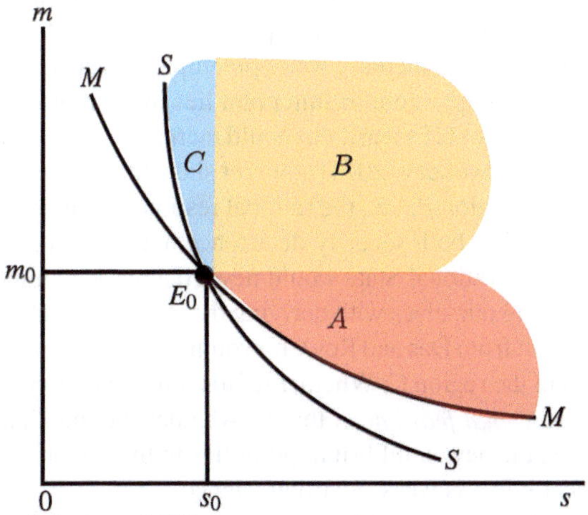

Fig. 11.1: Rational choice of CT measures, and an exogenous increase in terrorism

Even though the CT measures are substitutes we should understand with care that it does *not* mean that in order to counter terrorism, a country would always have to increase security and decrease preemptive actions or vice versa. We can understand this via a completely unrelated example.

Suppose a person's only source of income is his pay from work, \$5000 per month. He can use this amount for consumption (buying goods and service) and

[6] This is same as Eq. (13.3.3) in Chap. 9.

savings for the future. Thus, more consumption means less savings and vice versa: they are substitutes of each other. Suppose the person consumes \$4000 and saves \$1000 per month. Now suppose she gets promoted and her monthly take-home pay jumps to \$6000 per month. The point to note is that consumption and savings are substitutes *only when income is given*. But if income changes, both can change in the same direction. For instance, the person can now consume \$4600 and save \$1400. Hence, compared to the original situation, consumption and savings are both higher.[7]

Keeping this in mind, let us now consider (as in Chap. 9) an exogenous increase in terrorism indicated by a decrease in the parameter z in the marginal cost function facing the Org. The question is how would this impact on the State's choice of s and m?

Turn to the first-order conditions with respect to s and m. It is reasonable to suppose that a decrease in z, via encouraging the production of terror, would increase the marginal benefits from both security-deterrence and preemption in terms of reducing the marginal damage/fear from terror. This implies that as z falls, the State, at any given value of m, would tend to increase s, and, similarly, at any given value of s, it would tend to increase m. This implies that both SS and MM curves in Fig. 11.1 would shift to the right. As a result, the new equilibrium point would lie to the right of both curves.

Which region will the new intersection (equilibrium) point fall in? There are three possibilities: A, B, or C depending the nature of the outward shifts of the two curves relative to each other. If the new equilibrium point falls in the region A, it means that security measures increase while preemptive measures fall. The opposite implication follows if the new equilibrium point lies in the region C. If it falls in the region B, then both types of CT measures should increase—and this is what we would expect. Das and Roy Chowdhury (2014) however show that the new equilibrium point may *not* belong to the region B, i.e., the rational response to an increase in terrorism may *not* entail increasing both security-deterrence and preemptive actions. It is of course obvious that the rational State would never decrease both measures.

Without burdening ourselves with deriving the implications formally, we simply note here a main result from Das and Roy Chowdhury (2014) that the new equilibrium point does not fall in the region C. Whether it falls into the region A or B *depends on the nature of the marginal fear effect*, that is, whether the marginal fear is weak or strong. Specifically, the new equilibrium point lies in the region A or B accordingly as the marginal fear effect is weak or strong. Hence,

Result 11.3

An exogenous increase in terrorism or the potency of a terrorist organization leads the target country to step up its security-deterrence level unambiguously, whereas preemptive measures are to be scaled down or up as the marginal fear effect is weak or strong (Das & Roy Chowdhury, 2014, Proposition 4).

---

[7] It is of course possible, although unlikely, that as income increases a person would consume more and save less or consume less and save more.

It is intuitive that an increase in terrorism calls for more security-deterrence measures. But the state should not necessarily respond with more preemptive actions. The nuanced counter-terrorism implication is that an increase in terrorism may call for more *or less* preemptive action depending on the fear effect. Intuitively, as the terror potency of the organization increases, the terror production will increase. Consequently, preemption will tend to increase. However, we know that security-deterrence is a substitute for preemption *at any given level of terrorism*. As security increases, it will tend to exert a negative substitution effect on preemption. If the marginal fear effect is strong, the substitution effect is dominated and the State would increase preemptive actions also. But if the marginal fear effect is weak, the substitution effect outweighs the independent effect on preemption and a rational State should scale down its preemptive actions.

The upshot is that

Is That So? 11.1: Is Offense the best Defense?

The old adage that offense is the best defense does not hold necessarily. A hawkish approach to combat terrorism may not be always rational.

11.4 Choosing Terror and Non-Terror Activities

We have learned that terrorist organizations do not always engage themselves in planning or executing terror attacks: they multi-task and participate in non-terrorist activities. We have noted in Chap. 2 that many terror organizations like Hezbollah, Taliban, and even ISIS to some extent take part in the political process and/or in providing public and social services. We explicitly consider here a terrorist organization's (Org's) choice of *both* terror and non-terror activities and how counter-terrorism measures weigh on these choices. In this context, the choice of non-terror activities by a terror group is of special significance. If it represents a political process, then it may pave the path toward a permanent solution to the terror problem. If it is social services, it assumes importance in the absence of an administration and a state that cannot adequately provide these services for reasons like corruption, lack of funds, etc. More services mean higher social welfare.

Let's denote the Org's terrorist and non-terrorist activities by T and N, respectively, and, in particular, interpret T as the number or scale of *successful* terror attacks, equivalently expected damage, which we previously denoted by "D." Keep in mind that, given the number or scale of terror attacks, the success of terror attacks partly depends on security measures undertaken by the defending state.

These activities have their own costs or "prices" so to speak. Executing successful attacks T involves resource costs for the Org. So do tasks, N, like cleaning garbage and providing social services. If the relative cost between the two activities changes, a terror organization's participation in these activities would change too—similar to a consumer facing two goods in a market, who changes the mix of demand for the two goods in response to a change in the relative price between the two goods. That is, there is transference, i.e., a redirection toward a substitute product or services.

The model below was developed by Enders and Sandler (1993) and is described in Enders and Sandler (2012, Chapter 5).

11.4.1 Org's Preferences

The behavior of a terrorist organization is similar to that of a rational consumer facing its preference over two goods represented by indifference curves, along with a budget constraint. Basic micro theory comes to play here. Define a utility function for the Org based on successful terrorist attacks and non-terrorist "goods" it provides:

$$\boxed{U(\underset{+}{T}, \underset{+}{N}).}$$

The Org's utility function implies downward sloping and convex-to-the-origin indifference curves, as in Fig. 11.2. (The three panels will be explained later.) Recall that, for a decision-making unit, an indifference curve to the right of a given indifference curve represents higher utility.

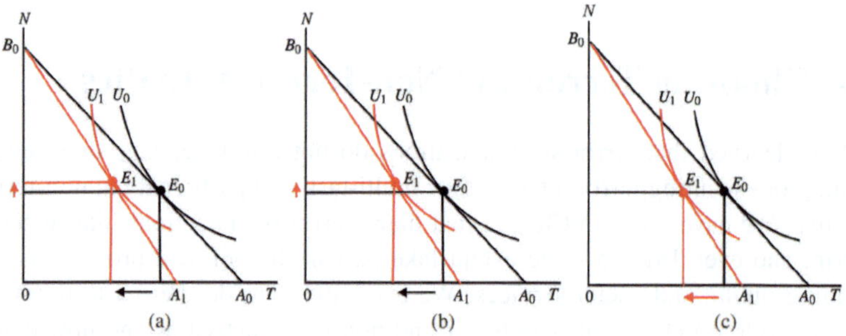

Fig. 11.2: Choice of terror activities (T) and non-terror activities (N): An increase in p_T. (**a**) T decreases; N increases. (**b**) Both T and N decrease. (**c**) T decreases; no change in N

11.4.2 Prices and the Budget Constraint Facing the Org, and The Counter-Terrorism Measures

Let p_T and p_N denote the unit cost or "price" of T and N, respectively. It is important to understand that these "prices" reflect the difficulty and/or resource costs facing the Org, and, in turn, these prices are affected by counter-terror measures. Here are some examples:

(i) An increase in security measures would tend to increase p_T by lowering the probability of a successful terror attack. This is equivalent to saying that with an increase in security, it is more difficult or costly for the Org to carry out a successful terror attack (e.g., getting around an advanced bomb-detecting device and entering some premises).

(ii) Preemptive measures like bombing a warehouse of ammunition would also tend to increase p_T by increasing the cost of producing terror.

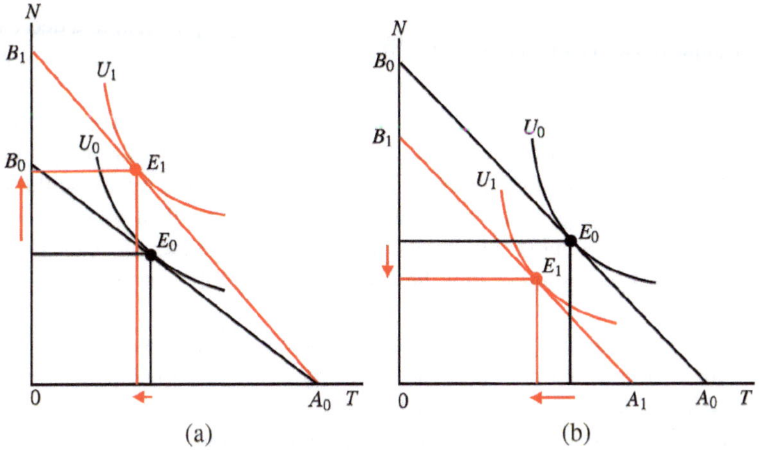

Fig. 11.3: Choice of terror activities (T) and non-terror activities (N): A decrease in p_N and a decrease in total resources. (**a**) T decreases; N increases. (**b**) Both T and N decline

(iii) "Benevolent" counter-terrorism measures like allowing political representation or less severe punishment for renouncing violence lower the price p_N.

The Org's budget constraint is

$$\boxed{p_T T + p_N N = I,} \tag{11.19}$$

where I stands for a *given* amount of total resources at the disposal of the Org. The budget equation (11.19) is shown in all panels of Figs. 11.2 and 11.3. Since prices and total resources are exogenous to the Org, it is a downward sloping straight line. In each graph, A_0B_0 is the original budget line to start with before we consider any variation in the counter-terror measures. The intercept points A_0 and B_0 mark the maximum amount of T or N that the Org can "afford" if it were to carry out one activity only. For example, if it abandons N completely, i.e., chooses $N = 0$, then I amount of resources can support a "quantity" of T equal to I/p_T. This is the point A_0. Similarly, $I/p_N = B_0$.

Notice that a change in p_T and p_N shifts one intercept point only, whereas a change in I shifts both intercept points proportionately. Thus, analogous to elementary consumer theory, a change in costs rotates the Org's budget line and a change in the total amount of resources leads to a parallel shift of the budget line. These are shown in Figs. 11.2 and 11.3.

We have already discussed how counter-terrorism measures (i)–(iii) change p_T or p_N. It follows that an increase in or a more effective security-deterrence measure (that is (i)) or a preemptive measure that specifically reduces the Org's terror-generating capability (that is (ii)) would rotate the budget line inward on the horizontal axis that measures T. These rotations are exhibited in all three panels of Fig. 11.2. Consider the "benevolent" counter-terrorism measures (iii). Being equivalent to a decrease in p_N, it rotates the budget line outward on the vertical axis measuring N. This is shown in Fig. 11.3a.

The model indeed permits a fourth type of counter-terror measures, namely, (iv) a preemptive measure like financial controls, destruction of infrastructures, or killing of personnel used for both types of activities by the Org, which would reduce I without changing any of the prices and thus shift, rather than rotate, the whole budget line inward, as in Fig. 11.3b. Of course, a preemptive measure can affect both the amount of total resources *and* the prices, but for analytical purposes we treat them separately.

We are ready to analyze the impacts of counter-terror measures (i) to (iv) on the choice of terror and non-terror activities by the Org. To begin with, consider the original situation with the budget line A_0B_0 in any of the diagrams. We know from micro theory that has given such a budget constraint, the "consumer"—here the Org—would like to choose T and N so as to maximize its utility or satisfaction $U(T, N)$ and the rational choice is shown at the point of tangency between the budget line and the indifference curve. This is the point E_0. Realize that the model reflects a static and relatively short- or medium-run time horizon where the size of the total resources for the Org is held constant.

11.4.3 A Review of Income, Substitution, and Price Effects

At this point, it will be helpful to recall three concepts from the consumer theory: income effect, substitution effect, and the price effect. Income effect refers to how the quantities demanded of goods change as the consumer's income or total spending changes. In general, if the demand for a good increases as income increases, we call it a "normal" or "superior" good. If it decreases—it can—then we call it an "inferior" good. In the current setting we assume that both T and N are normal goods. Substitution effect is the impact on the demand for goods when the relative price of goods (the ratio of prices) changes with income compensated so that the consumer can afford to buy the original bundle of goods or enjoys the original level of satisfaction. Own substitution effect is unambiguously negative. Note that a price change leads to a rotation of the budget line, which, in turn, entails two things: a change in the price ratio and a shift of the budget line on one axis. Hence a price effect is composed of a substitution effect and income effect:

Price effect = substitution effect + income effect.

From micro theory, we know that in a two-good model (like the current model), an increase in the price of a good, along with the price of other good and income remaining unchanged, increases the relative price of the good in question and thus increases the demand for that good and reduces the demand for the other good. This is the substitution effect. It also tends to reduce the purchasing power or "real income" (as it rotates the budget line inward). This is the income effect. Assuming that both goods are normal, the demands for both goods tend to decline by the income effect.

Defensive or preemptive	CT measure	Impact on terrorist activities T			Impact on non-terrorist activities N		
		S.E.	I.E.	Net	S.E.	I.E.	Net
Defensive	(i) SD Measures	–	–	–	+	–	±
Preemptive	(ii) Destroying terror producing infrastructure or activities	–	–	–	+	–	±
	(iii) Benevolent CT measures	–	+	±	+	+	+
	(iv) Destroying aggregate resources like financial controls and destruction of general infrastructure	0	–	–	0	–	–

S.E.: substitution effect; I.E.: income effect; Net: S.E. + I.E.

Table 11.1: Effects of counter-terrorism measures on terror and non-terror activities

11.4.4 Effects of Counter-Terror Measures

Equipped with the relevant concepts and results from microeconomic theory, we first consider an increase in security deterrence (i) or a preemptive measure that targets terror activities only (ii), both of which tend to increase p_T. This is illustrated in Fig. 11.2, where the budget line rotates clockwise on the N axis from A_0B_0 to A_1B_0. It is analogous to the effect of an increase in price of a good on the demand for goods, a price effect. The equilibrium point for the Org shifts from E_0 to E_1. We can divide the price effect into substitution and income effects. By the substitution effect (as the relative price p_T/p_N increases), T falls but N increases. In addition, an increase in p_T tends to reduce the value of total resources at the disposal of the Org—equivalent to a decrease in income. Given that T and N are normal "goods," both T and N tend to decline by income effect. Thus terror activities (T) decrease unambiguously while non-terror activities (N) may increase, decrease, or remain unchanged. Different possibilities are shown in the three panels of Fig. 11.2. It is likely however that the income effect of a price change is not strong enough to outweigh the substitution effect. Hence, the expected outcome is a decrease in terror activities, combined with an increase in non-terror activities (shown in panel (a) of Fig. 11.2).

A benevolent preemptive measure (iii) reduces the relative price of N. Applying the same reasoning of substitution and income effects, non-terror activities increase unambiguously, while terror activities may increase, decrease, or remain unchanged. One of these possibilities—the most likely one—is shown in panel (a) of Fig. 11.3.

The budget line rotates clockwise on the T axis from A_0B_0 to A_0B_1, and the equilibrium point of choice shifts from E_0 to E_1. Terror activities decline, and non-terror activities increase.

Finally, an increase in preemptive measures that degrade the overall capability of the Org is equivalent to a decrease in I. As shown in Fig. 11.3b, the budget line shifts inward in parallel from A_0B_0 to A_1B_1. The equilibrium point moves from E_0 to E_1. By the income effect, both terror and non-terror activities fall.

The substitution and income effects of the four types of counter-terrorism measures are summarized in Table 11.1. The overall implication is that

Result 11.4

Security-deterrence measures, preemptive measures targeted to terror activities only and benevolent preemptive actions can potentially yield desirable results, but general preemptive measures that can affect both terror and non-terror activities of a terrorist organization would have a negative side effect of decreasing the non-terror activities insofar as the state is not able to provide adequate social and public goods.

11.5 Take-Aways

- Connectivity with a terror network is measured by the (mathematical) concept of density of a network.
- Intelligence and infiltration refer to busting a node (a member in a cell) and those associated with the node in a terror organization.
- More intense or effective intelligence-and-infiltration measures lead to a less connected network of terrorists, less number of terrorists as well as less sophisticated terror attacks.
- From a defending state’s perspective, there is an element of substitutability between SD measures and preemptive actions. An exogenous increase in terrorism or the potency of a terrorist organization calls for more SD measures by the state. But it may not be rational to engage in more preemptive actions. A rational state would increase or decrease the level of preemption accordingly as the marginal fear effect is strong or weak.
- The third and the last model introduces non-terrorist activities into the choice set of a terrorist organization. It analyzes how CT measures impact on terrorist and non-terrorist activities through substitution, income, and price effects. Four types of CT measures are considered: SD measures, and three types of preemptive measures, namely, (a) those that are specific to terror-producing capability, (b) those that destroy or damage resources available to use toward terror and non-terror activities, and (c) “benevolent” CT measures that encourage members to desert terrorist organizations.

- SD measures and type-(a) preemptive measures induce a terror organization to reduce terror activities but may lead to an increase or a decrease in its non-terror activities. Type-(b) preemptive actions that reduce the capability of a terror organization for both terror and non-terror activities lead to less terror and non-terror activities. The latter effect may be an undesirable collateral effect as long as the host state is not able to adequately provide social and public services. Finally, benevolent (type-(c)) preemptive measures increase non-terror activities while discouraging or encouraging terror activities.

Questions

11.1 Each of the two terrorist networks, A and B, has eight members, while the connectedness differs between the two networks. Let the probability of any one node being busted in either group be $\pi = 0.1$, i.e., 10%.

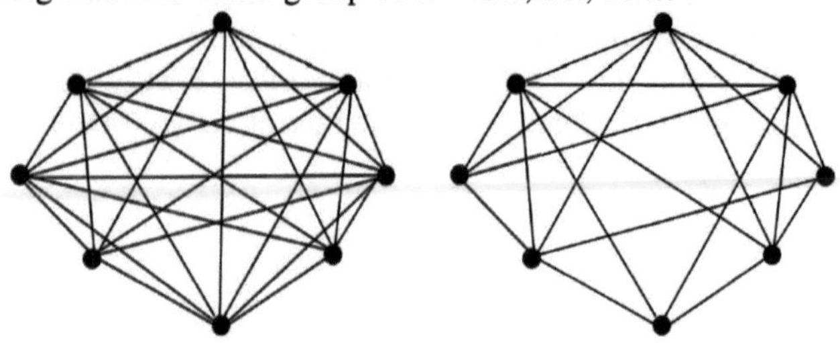

A B

(a) What is the expected number of "compromised" operatives in networks A and B, namely, M_A and M_B? If you get a decimal answer, take the nearest integer.

(b) Can you rationalize the ranking between M_A and M_B?

11.2 In the terror network model, explain in words how an increase in density of the network may affect the production of terror attacks.

11.3 Let the terror-damage function be $D(X, s) = 20X/s$ and the marginal cost function of the terrorist group be $C(X) = z + m + 2X$.

(a) Derive the Org's choice of the terror input as a function of security and preemptive measures denoted by s and m, respectively, that is, the function indicated in (11.15).

(b) In the light of your answer to part (a), by how many units will terror input production increase or decrease per a unit increase in militancy?

11.4 Consider the model of transference where the terrorist organization chooses the level of terror, T, in terms of expected damage, and non-terrorist activities, N. Its utility function is

$$U(T, N) = T \cdot N + T + N.$$

(a) Suppose initially $P_T = 4$, $P_N = 4$ and resources at the disposal of the Org are equal to $I = 240$. What will be the Org's optimal choice of T and N? [You have to use (i) the principle that MRS = price ratio and (ii) the budget facing the Org.]

(b) Let the solutions for part (a) be denoted as T_s and N_s. From this situation, the State wants to reduce the expected damage to $T = 5$ from $T = T_s$, while N remains the same as N_s by using security-deterrence measures (through manipulating P_T) and preemption (through affecting I). How can it achieve its objective by mixing security-deterrence and preemptive measures, i.e., what combination of P_T and I will imply that the Org will choose $T = 5$ and $N = N_s$?

Chapter 12

Hostage-Taking, Ransom, and Negotiations

12.1 Introduction

TERRORISTS engage in hostage-taking missions in order to achieve some short-term goals like passage to a desired destination (e.g., to Cuba during the 1960s), release of fellow terrorists or comrades, securing ransom money, or some combination of the above. Killing, harming hostages, or threatening to do so is used as a means to an end, *not* the primary goal. The *9/11* attacks were a different breed: the terrorists' immediate purpose was to kill everyone aboard including themselves and others on ground and damage national properties. It was not really a hostage situation because there were no quid pro quo demands.

We can group hostage-taking incidents into four types *a la* Enders and Sandler (2012):

(1) Kidnapping
(2) Taking over of ground or water transportation (bus, train, and ship)
(3) Barricade missions, i.e., taking control of a venue or building and seizure of hostages
(4) Skyjacking[1]

There are numerous examples of (1): kidnapping. In 1972, some members of Black September, a violent Palestine group described in Chap. 2, broke into the Olympic village in Munich, killed an Israeli athlete and a coach and abducted nine Israelis. They demanded the release of 200 Arab prisoners held by Israel and safe passage to Tunisia. It ended in an explosion and a gun fight that led to the death of all five terrorists and all nine hostages. In 1975, six terrorists led by the Venezuelan terrorist *Carlos the Jackal* attacked the semi-annual meeting of OPEC.[2]

---

[1] GTD divides hostage-taking into three categories: hijacking, barricade incidents, and kidnapping. Hijacking includes skyjacking and takeover of other means of transport.

[2] The birth name of Carlos the Jackal was Ilich Ramirez Sanchez.

S. P. Das, *Economics of Terrorism and Counter-Terrorism Measures*,
https://doi.org/10.1007/978-3-030-96577-8_12

After killing a policeman, a security officer, and an economist, the terrorists took more than sixty hostages. Negotiations led to the release of hostages and safe passage of the terrorists. In the mid-1980s, Rev. Benjamin Weir, Rev. Lawrence Jenco, and David Jacobsen, among others, were kidnapped in Lebanon by Muslim extremists. The Reagan administration secured their release in exchange for arms delivered to Iran. Thomas Hargrove, an American journalist, was kidnapped in Colombia in 1994 by FARC. He was released in 1995 after a ransom payment. A freelance American journalist James Foley was captured by ISIS in 2012. The captors asked for €100 million as ransom from his family and the USA. It was denied and he was brutally murdered in 2014. A Spanish journalist, Javier Espinosa, and a photographer, Ricardo Garcia Vilanova, were kidnapped by ISIS in 2013. They were released in 2014 in exchange for ransom payments.

As an example of (2)—taking over of ground or water transportation—in 1988, three Arab militants took eleven bus passengers as hostages and killed two of them in Dimona, Israel. The bus was stormed and secured by Yamam, the Israeli special counter-terrorism unit. The event is known as the *Mother's Bus Attack.*

In 2002 Chechen extremists captured Dubrovka theater in Moscow. About 900 people became hostages. The stand-off lasted fifty-seven hours. The Russian special forces pumped narcotic gas into the building that made the terrorists and hostages unconscious. In the counter-attack, about 120 hostages died and all terrorists were either killed or captured. In 2004, twenty-five Chechen and other terrorists held over 1000 people in a school in Beslan, Russia. No concessions were made. In the end, more than 330 people were killed including 186 children, and more than 700 were injured. These are instances of category (3): barricade missions.

Skyjackings, category (4), incidents galore. Here are some prominent examples.

[a] As described in Chap. 2, in 1968, terrorists belonging to PFLP hijacked an Israeli El Al flight from Rome to Tel Aviv and diverted it to Algiers, Algeria. According to the experts, this event signaled the beginning of the modern era of transnational terrorism. The hostage crisis continued for nearly forty days, catching the world's attention. Despite its official policy of not negotiating with terrorists, Israel was forced to bargain. A ransom payment was made and sixteen Arab prisoners were released.

[b] In 1976, an Air France flight from Tel Aviv to Paris via Athens was hijacked by four terrorists who claimed to belong to PFLP and demanded the release of forty Palestine prisoners in Israel and ten outside of Israel (see Chap. 2 also). It landed in Entebbe, Uganda. Israeli commandos raided the plane in a night-time operation and released 102 hostages.

[c] In 1985, the Trans World Airlines flight 847 from Cairo to San Diego via Athens, Rome, Boston, and Los Angeles was hijacked after takeoff from Athens by two Shi'ite Muslim hijackers, apparently members of Hezbollah in Lebanon (although Hezbollah denied it). There were 153 hostages including 85 Americans. The hijackers demanded the release of more than 700 Shi'ite prisoners in Israeli jails. The plane was forced to fly repeatedly to Beirut and Algiers. The ordeal lasted for three days and

ended in Beirut. The Reagan administration's priority was the release of hostages. Pressurized by the USA, Israel released 756 prisoners.[3]
[d] In 1999, an Indian Airlines flight from Kathmandu to New Delhi was hijacked by the militants belonging to *Harkat-ul-Mujahideen*, a Pakistan-based extremist group. The plane was diverted to Amritsar, India, Lahore, Pakistan, Dubai, and finally to Kandahar, Afghanistan. Shortly after the landing in Kandahar, the aircraft was surrounded by Taliban militants, who claimed that their objective was to dissuade the hijackers from killing or injuring the hostage. But the real intent was to prevent an Indian military strike against the hijackers by keeping the hostages under tight vigilance, although in the end no one was harmed. The ordeal lasted seven days, literally bringing the Indian government to its knees. All 176 passengers and crew members were returned in exchange for the release of three militants: Mushtaq Ahmed Zargar, Ahmed Omar Saeed Sheikh, and Maulana Masood Azhar. These terrorists were later implicated in the *9/11* attacks, the kidnap and murder of Daniel Pearl and the 2006 Mumbai terror attacks.

Hostage-taking is a unique situation where the government has to decide, on the spot, whether or not to negotiate and if negotiate how far to concede—while it is an on-going crisis involving the prospect of death of citizens. A highly stressful event, hostage-taking may continue for hours, days, weeks, or longer for all parties concerned. In case of kidnapping, it may be months or years before it is drawn to a conclusion. This is unlike other acts of terrorism *during* which there is little scope for decision making or negotiation except to possibly unilaterally limit the damage.

From the perspective of perpetrators, hostage-taking is a rational decision based on the consideration of benefits and costs including risk. The only conceptual difference with other forms of terror attack is that the benefit from hostage-taking is not just a general fear that a terror organization wants to instill: there can be direct personal non-pecuniary gains, pecuniary benefits in the form of ransom payments or a quid pro quo benefit in terms of release of fellow terrorists.

Among the four forms of hostage-taking, kidnapping is least risky since hostages are typically kept in clandestine locations. We would then expect kidnapping to be most frequent among all forms of hostage-taking. In the GTD dataset that records domestic and transnational terror attacks during 1970–2018, while hostage-taking constitutes about 7.5% of all attacks, among the hostage-taking events 87.5% are kidnappings.

In Sect. 12.2, we theoretically analyze how counter-terror measures may influence hostage-taking behavior. Unlike with respect to other kinds of terror attacks, in a hostage situation the possibility of negotiation and concession to the terrorists comes into play in order to secure the safety of the hostages. Any such negotiation involves some give and take. Terrorists typically demand ransom payments—which

[3] The leader of the two hijackers, Mohammed Ali Hamadei, a Lebanese citizen, was arrested in 1987 at the Frankfurt airport for carrying explosives in his luggage. He was convicted in Germany for murder and handed a life-in-prison sentence. He was however released in 2005.

they need to finance their activities—and/or release of other terrorists from prison. The unfortunate part is that, like blackmail, yielding to these demands in exchange for lives and safety of hostages held can encourage the terrorists to attempt more hostage-taking in the future. It is a tough choice facing the target country. Saving lives in a current hostage situation may lead to the prospect of more lives put in harm's way in the future, but willingness to risk human lives at a given point of time may alleviate this problem in the future. Some countries like the USA, the UK, and Israel have legislated a no-concession policy in order to constrain the negotiators from granting concessions to the hostage-takers. Section 12.2 examines the theoretical rationale behind this policy.

Section 12.3 reviews the empirical evidence on various aspects of hostage-taking incidents such as the impact of direct counter-terror measures and concessions on hostage-taking behavior, determinants of logistic and negotiation success by terrorists, and hostage safety. Details of some specific studies are given in the chapter appendix.

12.2 Counter-Terror Measures and Hostage-Taking: Theory

We consider three types of counter-terror measures with respect to hostage-taking.
General and hostage-specific security measures: Similar to other forms of terror attacks, hostage-taking responds to general security measures like border entry regulations and general law and order within a country, and to hostage-specific security measures like personal security guards and specialized vehicles for VIPs. Many businessmen and high-profile professionals deploy their own security apparatus.
Negotiation policy: It is a counter-terrorism measure that is unique to hostage-taking situations.
Reward schemes: They include granting amnesty and right to engage in civil and legal activities without any severe reprimand. These are not specific to hostage-taking attacks, rather granted in course of negotiation with terror groups toward agreeing to eschew terrorism, surrendering arms, and returning hostages.

There are two types of theoretical models that analyze and predict the terrorists' behavioral changes toward hostage-taking in response to these counter-terror measures. One set of models considers no strategic interaction between terrorists and the target government and focuses on how terrorists respond to *exogenous changes* in policy measures. The other incorporates strategic interaction and thus explicitly accounts for costs and benefits of terrorists *as well as* those associated with the counter-terrorism measures by the state and the state's rational choice of the counter-terror measures.

12.2.1 No Strategic Interaction

In Landes (1978)'s model of sky-jacking decision analyzed in Chap. 8, the objective of the perpetrator was to reach a preferred destination country like Cuba. There was no pecuniary or any other demand. Skyjacking was a binary choice: whether or not to attempt skyjacking. The introduction of metal detectors, which tends to reduce the incentive to attempt a plane hijacking, was represented by an increase in the probability of detection and apprehension.

Subsequent to Landes (1978), Islam and Shahin (1989) developed a model where the number of hostages taken was a continuous variable, say n. In reality, n can take only integer values like 0, 1, 2, and so on, but for analytical simplicity we may assume n to be a continuous non-negative real number. The authors considered three environments surrounding hostage-taking. The target country, i.e., the State (i) does not take any punitive action against the hostage-takers or negotiate with them, (ii) negotiates and concedes at least to some demands, and (iii) take punitive action, i.e., attack the terrorists while they hold hostages. Scenario (i) is more relevant in case of kidnapping than other forms of hostage-taking. For simplicity, we ignore this situation and focus on (ii) and (iii). The authors also included the level of media attention as a choice variable for the terrorists, which we also ignore. We equate terrorists with a terrorist organization, the Org.

Let the respective probabilities of the State negotiating and conceding and not negotiating and taking punitive action be p and $q = 1 - p$. These are probabilities perceived by the Org, based upon the past behavior of the State. In the event of (ii) there are (expected) gains, say $G(n)$, to the Org. Let

$$\boxed{G_n(n) > 0,}$$

capturing that the gains to the Org increase with the number of hostages. The source of gains $G(n)$ to the Org lies in generating a fear psychosis as well as receiving ransoms and/or getting prisoners released. If the State attacks the hostage-takers (scenario (iii)), the Org incurs a loss $L(n)$. Assuming that the scale of retaliation increases with the number of hostages:

$$\boxed{L_n(n) > 0.}$$

Irrespective of the outcome, carrying out a hostage operation costs resources to the Org. Let $X(n)$ denote the Org's resource costs, assumed to increase with the number of hostages, i.e.,

$$\boxed{X_n(n) > 0.}$$

Let the objective function of the Org be to maximize its *expected* net gains or the expected surplus, that is,

$$\boxed{\text{Maximize } pG(n) - (1-p)L(n) - X(n) \text{ by choosing } n.}$$

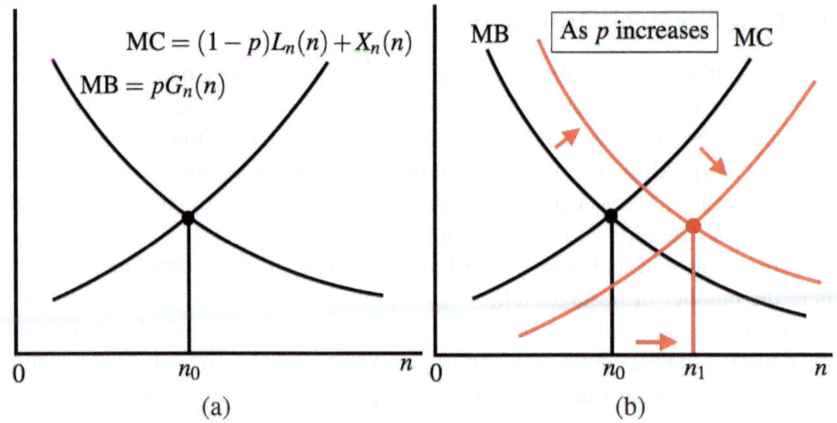

Fig. 12.1: Org's choice of the number of hostages. (**a**) Optimal choice of n. (**b**) Impact of an increase in p

We see that the Org faces one source of gain (if the State negotiates) and two sources of loss (resource costs and costs if the State does not negotiate). The first-order condition is

$$\underbrace{pG_n(n)}_{\text{MB to the Org}} = \underbrace{(1-p)L_n(n) + X_n(n)}_{\text{MC facing the Org}}. \tag{12.1}$$

The solution to this equation spells the rational/optimal choice of the number of hostages taken by the Org. This is depicted graphically in Fig. 12.1a at the intersection of the MB and MC curves.

As a comparative statics, consider a more conciliatory approach of the State in terms of an exogenous increase in p and an equal decrease in $1-p$: that is, the State is more willing to negotiate and less inclined to take any punitive action. We see in Eq. (12.1) that for any given n, the MB to the Org from taking hostages increases and its MC falls. These effects are intuitive. In Fig. 12.1b, the MB curve shifts to the right and the MC curve down. The new rational choice of n (n_1) is greater than the original choice, n_0. Thus, *a more liberal negotiation policy encourages host-taking behavior.*[4]

Along with punitive action by the State, the authors' later work, namely, Shahin and Islam (1992), incorporated a reward policy toward terrorists if they release hostages, defined in terms of amnesty and civil rights being granted that enables the (former) terrorists to participate in legal activities. Thus, it is a punishment–reward, i.e., a carrot–stick model. The authors argued that that a carrot-*and*-stick policy is more effective to combat hostage-taking than a carrot *or* stick policy. However, as Enders and Sandler (2012) point out, the critical assumption underlying this result is that the rewards are unanticipated, which is highly unrealistic. If rewards were

[4] Our model here is a slight deviation from the theoretical setup of Islam and Shahin and yields this outcome in a stronger form.

anticipated, it may very well encourage the terrorists to attempt more hostage-taking attacks, not less.

12.2.2 Strategic Interaction Between Terrorists and the Target Country

A major limitation of the no-strategic-interaction models is that the behavior of the target country is held passive. There is no recognition of the costs and benefits of counter-terror measures or the rational choice of these measures by the target country.

However, keeping in mind the game-theory model of security choice in Chap. 8, we can easily imagine a situation where the Org chooses the attempted number of hostage-taking missions within a time period by weighing its benefits and costs and the State chooses the level of its security measures. We would reach the same qualitative conclusion as we did in Chap. 8: *an increase in security measures will exert a direct and a deterrence effect on hostage-taking.*

Our focus here is on the hostage negotiation policy, a CT measure that is unique to hostage-taking and different from standard security measures or preemption.

12.2.2.1 Negotiate or Not Negotiate

It is obvious to see why a target country would want to negotiate: to save the lives of innocent people. But we have already noted the "price" of granting concessions: it may very well encourage hostage-taking attacks in the future. In view of this, some nations, e.g., the USA, the UK, and Israel, have legislated a *no-concession* or a *no negotiation policy* with regard to terrorists hoping that hostage-takers would anticipate it and therefore will not undertake hostage-taking in the first place. The idea is that the officials in charge of contacting terrorists during a hostage situation can, in principle, proclaim that their hands are tied and they can do very little. If they do stick to this policy and perhaps meet the terrorists' demand in a minimal way at best like a guarantee of a safe passage for the hostage-takers if they release the hostages unharmed, it would act as a deterrence to future hostage-taking attempts regardless of the outcome of an on-going hostage situation.

There are instances of target countries adhering to this policy at the cost of lives—by either using force against the hostage-takers or essentially letting the terrorists execute the hostages. The skyjacking of the Air France Flight in 1976 by PFLP and the seize of a theater in Moscow by Chechen extremists, both described in the Introduction, are examples. Back in 1973, the Palestinian terrorist group Black September seized the Saudi Embassy in Khartoum, Sudan. Foreign diplomats including two Americans were taken as hostages. Just hours after President Nixon pronounced no ransom payment or deal, the two American diplomats and a Belgian citizen were shot dead.

In more recent years, ISIS brutally killed American and British hostages as the respective governments refused to pay ransom. The list includes the American journalists James Foley and Steven Sotloff and American aid workers Kayla Jean

Mueller and Peter Cassig, and British aid workers David Cawthorne Haines and Alan Henning.[5]

There are also instances where the target country has yielded to terrorist demand in exchange for safe return of hostages, e.g., the seize of El Al flight in 1968 by PFLP members, TWA flight in 1985 by Lebanese militants, and Indian Airlines flight in 1999 by Pakistani extremists. Additionally, in an arms-for-hostages deal, the Reagan administration secured the release of Rev. Benjamin Weir, Rev. Lawrence Jenco, and David Jacobsen who were kidnapped by Lebanese militants presumably associated with Hezbollah.[6] These incidents along with the kidnapping and release of an American journalist in Colombia are noted in the Introduction. Indeed, the Reagan administration's arms-for-hostages deal encouraged the terrorists to capture other academics and journalists in Beirut (e.g., Robert Polhill, Allan Steen, Jesse Turner, Mithileshwar Singh, and Roger Augue); see Enders and Sandler (2012, Chapter 7).

In 2004, terrorists in Iraq took citizens of South Korea and the Philippines as hostages and these countries made concessions. In contrast to the American and British governments' response toward hostages held by ISIS, the continental European countries did pay ISIS ransoms and got their citizens freed in exchange, e.g., Italian aid worker Federico Motka, Danish photojournalist Daniel Rye Ottosen, and French journalist Didier François, among others.

The divided approach in dealing with hostage situations entails a negative externality of one country's concession on other countries' pledge for no-concession. This has led to a debate on the effectiveness of the no-concession policy. In what follows, we first understand the theoretical logic behind the no-concession policy and the underlying assumptions *a la* Lapan and Sandler (1988). This would enable us to evaluate whether or how far such a policy can be effective in real situations.

12.2.2.2 Logic of No-Concession Policy

To understand no-concession policy, we first understand how a concession policy plays out in an interactive, strategic framework with two players: a group of terrorists and the government.

Concession Is a Possibility Consider Fig. 12.2a, which depicts a sequential game between the two players. The terrorists move first and decide between two actions: (i) do not attempt a hostage-taking attack or (ii) attempt a hostage-taking attack. If the terrorists choose (i), the game terminates. This is shown as the terminal node A. This scenario is the baseline, where nothing happens so-to-speak. Let the payoffs at node A be $(0, 0)$. Here and later, the first entry of the payoff vector is for the terrorists and the second for the government.

[5] See Yourish (2015) for a pictorial display of who were kidnapped and when by ISIS and who were released or executed and when. A more detailed list is given in Enders and Sandler (2012, Table 7.2).

[6] This encouraged the terrorists to capture other academics and journalists in Beirut.

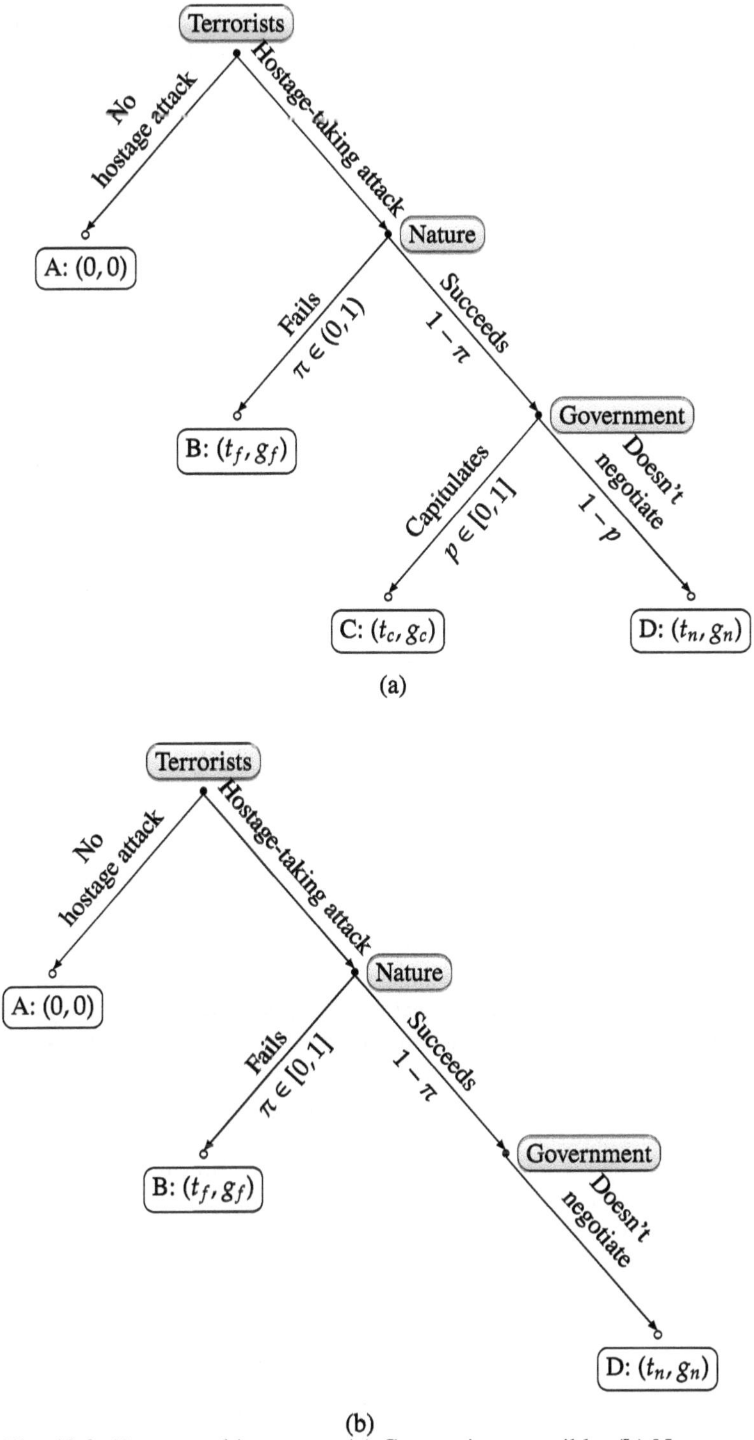

Fig. 12.2: Hostage-taking game. (**a**) Concessions possible. (**b**) No-concession policy

If the terrorists do launch a hostage-taking attack (i.e., choose action (ii)), there are two possibilities: the attack fails or it succeeds. Let the logistic failure or success probabilities be $\pi \in [0, 1]$ and $1 - \pi$, respectively. We can imagine "Nature" as a (third) background player at this stage, whose action is simply to role a dice with two outcomes: Fail or Succeed. To be clear, the probabilities π and $1 - \pi$ are *not* entirely dependent on Nature. They depend also on security measures by the government to deter hostage-taking, e.g., general security measures at airports, highways, etc. and personal security measures for prominent public officials. These measures are undertaken prior to the game and assumed unchanged during the "game." Hence their costs (say K) are sunk for the government. For notational simplicity, we normalize K to zero.[7]

If the attack fails, the game ends. The corresponding terminal node is B and the payoff vector is (t_f, g_f), where t and g, respectively, denote the terrorists and the government. It is likely that $t_f < 0$ as planning an attack and carrying it with failure are costly for the terrorists in terms of resources lost including possibly the lives of terrorists. However, if the terrorists are committed jihadis who value losing their lives, then t_f can be arguably positive. For the government, resources may have to be expended to foil a hostage attack; thus, $g_f \leq 0$.

If the terrorists succeed in the hostage-taking mission, the game continues. They submit their demands, to which the government responds. It has two choices: capitulate, i.e., partially or fully accede to the terrorists' demand or do not negotiate at all. Let p and $1 - p$ be the respective probabilities *as perceived by the terrorists*. The game can end with either choice made by the government. The terminal nodes for capitulating and not negotiating are C and D, respectively. As capitulation by the government leads to gains by the terrorists and a loss to the government, we assume $t_c > 0 > g_c$. There are two potential sources of gain to the terrorists: their demands (release of terrorists held in captivity by the government, money etc.), are met, and the publicity through the media enhances the group's prominence. If the government does not negotiate, hostages are killed or kept in captivity by the terrorists. The government may launch an attack to free the hostages, the outcome of which is uncertain. The payoff to the terrorists, compared to the case of capitulation by the government, must be less and probably negative: i.e., $t_n < t_c$, where it is likely that $t_n < 0$. The payoff to the government, g_n, may be positive or negative. We assume that g_n is random. Let $\bar{g}_n$ be its mean.

Furthermore, not only is $t_c > t_n$, it is obvious that $t_c > t_f$ too, which means that the payoff to the terrorists in the event that the government capitulates exceeds their payoff if their hostage-taking mission fails in the first place. How does t_n compare with t_f? This is not so clear (while both are likely to be negative).

From the preceding discussion, we note the following ranking of the payoffs:

Terrorists:	$t_c > [0, t_n, t_f]$ and it is likely that $t_c > 0 > [t_n, t_f]$
Government:	$0 \geq g_f > g_c \gtreqless \bar{g}_n.$

[7] Otherwise, the payoff vector at node A would have been $(0, -K)$. However, since K does not change, it is immaterial for comparisons.

In a sequential game, we solve the model backwards. Consider the event of success in hostage-taking. Once in this situation, in principle, the government would decide to capitulate or hang tough depending on whether $g_c \gtrless \bar{g}_n$.[8]

Regardless of the action chosen by the government, the terrorists make their hostage-taking choice beforehand. Treating the government's action as a mixed or a probabilistic strategy based on their beliefs on how likely the government may be willing to negotiate—indicated by the probability p—their expected payoff has the expression $pt_c + (1-p)t_n$. Based on this expression and the probability of success or failure of the attack in the previous stage, the terrorists' expected payoff from attempting a hostage-taking attack at the time of deciding whether or not to do so has the expression

$$\begin{aligned} P_{\text{attack}} &= \pi t_f + (1-\pi)\left[pt_c + (1-p)t_n\right] \\ &= \pi t_f + (1-\pi)t_n + \underbrace{(1-\pi)p(t_c - t_n)}_{+}. \end{aligned} \tag{12.2}$$

The first two terms in the right-hand side of the last expression are likely to be negative, whereas the last term is positive. Hence $P_{\text{attack}} \gtrless 0$. The terrorists' payoff from not attacking is $P_{\text{no attack}} = 0$. Thus, their decision rule is

Hostage-taking attack or no hostage-taking attack

$$\text{as } P_{\text{attack}} \gtrless P_{\text{no attack}} \Leftrightarrow \pi t_f + (1-\pi)t_n + \underbrace{(1-\pi)p(t_c - t_n)}_{+} \gtrless 0. \tag{12.3}$$

We have assumed so far that the terrorists' believe that concessions are a possibility, i.e., $p > 0$. Given $p > 0$, the probability of a hostage attack equals the probability that the above inequality holds with "greater than," not "less than," i.e., the probability that

$$\pi t_f + (1-\pi)t_n + \underbrace{(1-\pi)p(t_c - t_n)}_{+} > 0. \tag{12.4}$$

No-Concession Policy Now suppose that the government pledges a no-concede policy that is credible to the terrorists. If so, $p = 0$. Part (b) of Fig. 12.2 is the corresponding game tree. With $p = 0$, the decision rule (12.3) reduces to

[8] However, it is typically hard to assess the cost or the value of damage $\bar{g}_n$ associated with no concession. Although eventually the decision may depend on a single individual (like the president, prime minister, or whosoever is in charge), expert opinions may vary widely on the value of $\bar{g}_n$.

$$\begin{array}{l}\text{Hostage-taking attack or no hostage-taking attack} \\ \textit{\textbf{under no-concession policy}} \\ \text{as } P_{\text{attack}} \gtrless P_{\text{no attack}} \Leftrightarrow \pi t_f + (1-\pi)t_n \gtrless 0.\end{array} \tag{12.5}$$

Hence, the probability that an attack will be undertaken in the no-concession regime equals the probability that:

$$\pi t_f + (1-\pi)t_n > 0. \tag{12.6}$$

Check that the inequality (12.6) is more restrictive than the inequality (12.4). This proves, in principle, that the scope for a hostage attack in the no-concession regime is less than that in a regime where concessions can be contemplated. Look at each term in (12.6), wherein t_f and t_n are the payoffs to the terrorists in the event that the attack fails and in the event that the attack succeeds but there are no concessions. As argued earlier, both terms are negative unless the terrorists perceive a benefit from carrying out the attack as such, apart from the benefit of their demands being fulfilled. Hence *a hostage attack in a no-concession regime is less likely than in a concession regime.* This is the logic of the no-concession policy.

The intuition behind the no-concession policy is simple. If this policy is credible to the terrorists, they would "realize" that their hostage-taking attack would not yield any concession or benefits. Knowing this would deter their attempt to mount a hostage-taking attack in the first place.

The usefulness of the model lies in identifying the underlying assumptions behind the effectiveness of the no-concession policy, so that we can evaluate the assumptions and judge the merit of this policy in reality. Before highlighting the assumptions, note that increased security measures to deter any terror attacks including hostage-taking attacks increase the chance of failure (π in our model) and hence reduce the chance of hostage attacks *even if the government does not have a no-concession policy.*[9] This underscores that standard security measures are important to check hostage-taking attacks too. We now specifically look at the no-concession policy.

(1) Given the level of security measures, a no-concession policy works as long as the terrorists only gain from the concessions, not from attempting an attack per se. Otherwise, if the terrorists gain utility even in the face of sacrificing their lives, they would launch hostage-taking attacks regardless of whether the government may capitulate or not.[10] Thus, terrorists' preference plays a role in the success of the no-concession policy.

(2) If the cost of not conceding ($|\bar{g}_n|$) happens to exceed the cost of conceding ($|g_c|$), then the government would prefer to concede. That is, no-concession policy is not

[9] Technically, the right-hand side of Eq. (12.4) decreases with π. Hence the chances of this inequality being satisfied fall.

[10] In Eq. (12.6) if either t_f or t_n or both are positive so that the left-hand side as a whole is positive, the terrorists would prefer attack to no attack.

a preferred choice. The implication is that if there are high-value VIP hostages (like eminent political or diplomatic figures) or just too many hostages, a no-concession approach may not be wise.

③ *The strongest limitation of the effectiveness of the no-concession policy is its credibility to the terrorists.* If a government has a track record of conceding in the past, a new announcement of a no-concession policy would not be taken seriously by the terrorists, who would continue to mount hostage attacks. Reputation building is thus an important component of any effective no-concession policy. However, reputation building does not happen overnight: it takes time and demonstration of intent. Unfortunately, it means that a country may have to bear the cost of kidnapping and execution of its citizens for some time period before the terrorists come to internalize that the target country is serious about not conceding and thus a hostage-taking attack will not yield results.

These considerations imply that the success of a no-concession policy is as much an empirical issue as it is theoretical.

12.3 Empirical Evidence

Empirical research on hostage-taking covers various aspects of hostage-taking like effectiveness of direct counter-terror measures and concession to hostage takers, factors that significantly explain logistic and negotiation success of host-taking missions, their duration, ransom payments and hostage safety, and, finally, the role of democracy and democratic institutions.

12.3.1 Direct Counter-Terror Measures and Major Policy Initiatives Impacting Skyjacking

In Chap. 8 we studied the estimated impact of installation of metal detectors at airports in the early 1970s—an all-time major technology-based counter-terror measure—on skyjacking, a hostage-taking event. Besides the introduction of metal detectors aside, major policy initiatives and direct counter-terror measures were undertaken by world bodies and the USA to deter terror attacks including skyjacking. By using intervention analysis, Enders et al. (1990a) measured how skyjacking and other forms of terror attack were impacted by a series of U.N. conventions and resolutions in 1977 involving terrorist events (e.g., on crimes against protected persons including diplomatic agents, hostage-taking, and aerial hijackings), and the US retaliatory raid against Libya in 1986 in response to Libya's sponsoring of terrorism against US forces and citizens.[11] However, the impact of U.N. initiatives had no significant impact of skyjacking, whereas the retaliatory strike on Libya was followed by an

[11] In the 1970s and 1980s, Libya reportedly financed terror groups that were anti-American and anti-British. It fired at a US aircraft in 1981 over the Gulf of Sidra that was claimed by Qaddafi to a part of Libyan waters. Five Americans were killed simultaneously at Rome and Vienna airport in 1985. These attacks were believed to be aided by Libya.

increase in terror attacks against the USA and the UK in the short run. Thus, the U.N. sanctions and the US strike against Libya were ineffective.[12,13]

12.3.2 Concessions to Hostage Takers

Pre-9/11 studies found little support for the effectiveness of the no-concession policy, e.g., Poe (1988). The main result and thinking was that less conciliatory or stronger response did not result in significantly fewer hostage-taking events. Brandt and Sandler (2009) is a major study on the impact of concessions on hostage-taking attacks. The attacks are divided into three categories: kidnapping, skyjacking, and the remainder. Negotiation success was their central explanatory variable. For kidnapping, the long-run multiplier of negotiation success was 2.62 additional incidents per quarter. In case of skyjackings, it was 0.59 additional incidents per quarter. The long-run multiplier for other hostage incidents was insignificant. Hence, for kidnappings and skyjackings, the conventional wisdom holds: *giving in to terrorist demands results in more such incidents.*

Over the period 1968–2005 studied by Brandt and Sandler (2009), there were much fewer religious fundamentalist terrorist groups than after 2005. Also, the USA was much less consistent in fulfilling its no-concession pledge prior to 2001 than after.[14] Brandt et al. (2016) is a more recent work on the same issue that overcomes these natural limitations. It, however, confines to kidnappings, which became the lion's share of hostage incidents after *9/11*. Their sample period is 1978–2013, which obviously includes many beheading executions by ISIS and other fundamentalist groups in the Middle East. The authors apply the Brandt–Sandler methodology to three samples: (i) the USA and the UK combined (these countries generally stood by their no-concession pledge), (ii) ten "concessionaire" countries

---

[12] In another study, by also using intervention analysis, Enders et al. (1990b) estimated the impact of metal-detector installation, US strikes against Libya as well as the legislation of the Reagan's "get-tough" laws on terrorism in 1984 and enhanced security for US embassies and personnel. Along with skyjacking, terror attacks against US diplomats and protected persons, US interests and UK interests were analyzed. The same conclusions were reached with regard to metal detectors and US attack on Libya; in addition, Reagan's get-tough laws were ineffective and expenditures to secure US embassies had the desired effect, but it also entailed the unintended effect of putting non-US diplomats at a greater risk.

[13] Enders and Sandler (1993) analyzed the evidence on cross effects—substitutes and complements—among the modes of attack in response to security initiatives. Using quarterly data from 1968 to 1988 and combining intervention analysis with vector autoregression, the authors found strong evidence of both types of cross effects. For example, the installation of metal detectors in airports reduced skyjackings and diplomatic incidents but increased other types of hostage attacks and assassinations. Embassy fortifications decreased barricade missions but increased assassinations. These are substitution effects. Metal detectors not only damped skyjacking but also threats and hoaxes (because they became less credible). These are complementary effects. This study included fifteen types of terror attacks to estimate the cross effects.

[14] During 1978–2000, the USA gave concessions to kidnappers 23.1% of the time, whereas in 2001–2013, its concessions to kidnappers rate declined 10.7% of the time.

together that less frequently adhered to their no-concession policy[15], and (iii) all E.U. countries, except the UK, that also less frequently upheld their no-concession pledge.

The central empirical finding is that making a concession increased the median baseline kidnappings by 64% to 87%, depending on the group of countries considered. Although restricted to kidnapping, the study reaffirms the earlier Brandt–Sandler conclusion.

Is That So? 12.1: Evidence of the Effect of No-Concession Policy toward Hostage-Taking

According to Brandt and Sandler (2009) and Brandt et al. (2016), granting concessions has encouraged hostage-taking.

12.3.3 Is No-Concession Policy a Good Idea?

While empirical work has shown that concessions have encouraged (future) hostage-taking, only a handful of countries including the USA, the UK, and Israel have legislated no-concession policies. Many other countries that have been afflicted seriously by terrorism do not have such a policy mandated by law. We have studied the logic behind how a no-concession policy is *supposed* to work. Judging all this, is a no-concession policy a good idea?

Those who are not in favor argue that having a law but failing to uphold it when a push comes to shove undermines the credibility of a government and thus is unlikely to deter future hostage-taking attacks. That is, having a law against negotiation with or concession to terrorists, in and of itself, is unlikely to be effective. The key lies in the commitment of the government in upholding its no-concession pledge, so that it is deemed credible to the terrorists. Yes, such a commitment does entail a potential of tragic loss of innocent lives in the short run. The Russian government was heavily criticized after many innocent people died in the Moscow theater holdup in 2002. It was again criticized when its talk with Chechen rebels failed during the Beslan school crisis in 2004.

The issue of the no-concession policy boils down to a very painful tradeoff between current and future human lives. In principle, the "best" solution is a collective commitment by countries for not yielding to pressure by the terrorists. However, once a government is in the midst of a hostage situation, the tradeoffs weigh in differently in view of the unpalatable sight of immediate harm to innocent folks, media pressure, and public sympathy. In any event, a collective agreement by countries for a no-concession policy is a far cry at the moment.

Nonetheless, my (the author's) own opinion is that a no-concession policy is the preferred option. All else the same, it plants more doubt, than otherwise, in the minds of the abductors on whether the target country would opt for a settlement.

[15] They are Austria, Belgium, Canada, France, Germany, Italy, the Netherlands, Spain, Sweden, and Switzerland.

12.3.4 Logistic Success, Duration of Hostage-Holding, Negotiation Success, and Ransom Payments

In a series of papers, Sandler and his coauthors, i.e., Sandler and Scott (1987), Atikinson et al. (1987), and Gaibulloev and Sandler (2009a), have uncovered the factors that are significant determinants of the logistical success of hostage-taking (whether the terrorists completed the hostage-taking mission with some success), and, given that it was successful, what variables significantly explain the duration of the events and negotiation success with the target country (defined by whether the terrorists obtained some or all of their demand)—particularly whether any ransom payments were made. Both Sandler and Scott (1987) and Gaibulloev and Sandler (2009a) analyzed logistic success and negotiation success, while Atikinson et al. (1987) were concerned with explaining duration of events and ransom payments.[16]

Atikinson et al. (1987) studied the post-logistic success in bargaining.[17] The explained variables were the ransom paid and the duration of the hostage incidents. Some explanatory variables were relevant for both outcomes, whereas others were specific.

A number of hypotheses were considered. Greater terrorist demands are expected to lead to larger ransom payments and longer incidents. Bluffing by terrorists (in the form of allowing a deadline to pass uneventfully, e.g., a threat to kill some hostage not being executed) is likely to reduce ransom payments and duration (as it signals lack of terrorists' resolve). Sequential actions by the terrorists in releasing hostages indicate a willingness on the part of both parties to negotiate, and this should result in greater ransoms being paid and a longer incident. The number of hostage nationalities likely increases the amount of the concession (as more nations are involved). The greater the number of terrorists wounded, the shorter is the duration. The duration is longer if it is a kidnapping event (as location is typically unknown) or if hostages are American (given the no-concession policy of the USA). Finally, the magnitude of the proposed ransom payment itself can impact the duration: the larger the payment, the longer is the incident.[18]

The results show that ransom demanded and terrorists allowing sequential release of hostages were significant determinants of both ransom paid and the duration of the event, each having positive effects on both outcome variables. In addition, the number of nationalities among hostages and bluffing had significant (respectively,

---

[16] We ignore Sandler and Scott (1987) as the same issues were analyzed later by Gaibulloev and Sandler (2009a) who worked with more recent data and more refinements in the choice of explanatory variables.

[17] They enlist five stages of hostage events that involve bargaining: initiation of the hostage-taking act, presentation of demands, bargaining, completion of bargaining (e.g., ransom paid or prisoners released, etc.) and cessation of the incident at which time terrorists depart and hostages are freed.

[18] The economic rationale for these determinants lies in how they affect the bargaining cost of the two parties involved. For instance, more injuries and fatalities among hostage takers increase their bargaining cost and hence imply shorter duration. The larger the number of countries whose citizens are hostages, the greater is the pressure on the negotiating country, which means a higher bargaining costs; this would imply more concessions granted to the terrorists. Chapter Appendix 12.A describes the data and the estimation method.

positive and negative) impacts on ransom paid. Ransom paid and the hostages being American had a significantly positive effect and the number of terrorists had a significantly negative impact on duration of hostage-holding.

Gaibulloev and Sandler (2009a) were concerned with logistic success and negotiation success.[19] They reasoned that the probability of logistic success increases with the resources in the hands of the terrorists (like manpower and weapons), decreases with the multiplicity of terrorists' nationalities (as this may create communication, language, and coordination problems), and increases with the vulnerability of the target hostages.[20] Among all forms of hostage-taking, hostages are most vulnerable in kidnapping situations as terrorists have control over the venue and face less risk of passing through metal detectors and other security checks. Thus, compared to non-kidnapping, kidnapping should be associated with a higher probability of logistic success. A larger number of intended hostages may increase the vulnerability of a hostage target and, thus, increase the terrorists prospects of logistical success.[21] Target fortification is another factor behind vulnerability. It tends to limit vulnerability, thereby reduce logistical success.[22]

Negotiation success by the terrorists should increase with the number of captured hostages (as more non-terrorist deaths imply less lives are "hung in balance" reducing the bargaining power of the terrorists) and decrease with casualties among the perpetrators and hostages.

The authors utilize the ITERATE dataset over the period 1978–2005, recording 413 host-taking incidents.[23] Among the plausible determinants of logistic success, terrorist nationalities, the number of hostages taken, whether the hostage-taking is by kidnapping and the number of terrorists wounded or killed are significant determinants and their directional (qualitative) effects are consistent with the hypotheses. For example, kidnapping has a positive impact and the number of terrorists wounded or killed exerts a negative impact on the probability of logistic success in hostage-taking.

In estimating the negotiation success of the perpetrators, separate regressions were run for kidnapping and non-kidnapping incidents. In both regressions the number of hostages and the number of non-terrorists killed are highly significant and

[19] Logistic success and negotiation success can be seen in the game tree depicted in Fig. 12.2 along the respective arms "Succeeds" and "Capitulates."

[20] Sandler and Scott (1987) had argued the opposite: the more the number of nationalities, the greater will be the funds available to the terrorists and hence the greater is the likelihood of logistic success.

[21] There are two reasons. First, the probability of securing some hostages is higher while others may escape. Second, when the number of hostages taken is large, the authorities are likely to be more reluctant to use lethal force, thereby making such targets more vulnerable at the abduction stage.

[22] In addition, "Protected persons" like diplomats, military officials, and government personnel are likely to be accompanied by bodyguards and using armor-plated cars and other protections and thus their vulnerability to be captured as hostages are less compared to other people or professionals like journalists, social workers, etc.

[23] Logit regression (see General Appendix B, Sect. B.4.2) is used since the outcome variables are binary: either logistic success or failure and either negotiation success or failure.

respectively exert positive and negative effects. The number of terrorists wounded or killed has somewhat weaker effects on negotiation success. Interestingly, the demand for ransom money has a significant and *negative* impact on negotiation success. The magnitude of these marginal impacts sharply differed between kidnapping and non-kidnapping attacks. For example, the negative impact of demand for money is much stronger in case of non-kidnapping incidents than for kidnapping incidents. Duration (measured by hours in case of non-kidnapping and days for kidnapping incidents) has a mildly positive impact on negotiation success in non-kidnapping situations and a stronger positive effect on negotiation success of terrorists in kidnapping situations. Hence, prolonging a hostage-taking event is not a good idea.

12.3.5 Hostage Safety

In an interesting paper, Yun and Roth (2008) explored the determinants of the fate of hostages: whether a hostage is killed or not.[24] The authors alluded to ***script theory*** in psychology, which posits that human behavior is not random. It follows a pattern similar to a written script. Individuals are *schema carriers* and schemata depends on various sources. The hostage-takers' schemata draws from three sources: a preexisting schemata before the hostage-taking mission, inputs from the bargaining situation itself, and exogenous factors.

Pre-existing schemata is captured by a binary variable: whether the group is Islamic or not. The presumption is that Islamic fundamentalist groups are innately more inclined to execute their hostages than non-Islamic groups. Bargaining situation schemata is derived from the length of captivity and whether the hostage is foreign or domestic. A foreign hostage would have a higher trading or exchange value than a domestic hostage and hence a greater chance of being released. Exogenous sources affecting schemata are proxied by a contagion effect of executing hostages: whether execution has become more common. This is modeled by a time dummy, pre-Iraq war versus post-Iraq war era. The latter period is indicative of the contagion effect as executing hostages became more common in this era. Exogenous factors also included the length of hostage captivity; the longer a hostage is held, the higher are the chances of release.[25]

Logit regression yielded that

[24] The authors used 764 cases of terrorist hostage-taking and kidnapping data originally collected by the Institute for the Study of Violent Groups (ISVG) at Sam Huston State University, of which 234 cases were finally selected for the analysis. There is no mention of the sample period however. ISVG aims to build a comprehensive terrorism database of terrorist events by collecting and analyzing various open-source material like books, magazines, court documents, etc.

[25] But one may argue that the length of captivity is not an exogenous factor; instead, it proxies bargaining situation schemata.

Is That So? 12.2: Hostage Safety

Whether or not the group is Islamic and whether a hostage is domestic or foreign were significant predictors of the safety of hostage. A group being Islamic and hostages being domestic rather than foreign tend to increase the chances of execution. However, the effect of length of captivity and the contagion effect of executing hostages were not significant.

12.3.6 Democracy and Hostage-Taking

Which type of governments are more susceptible to hostage-taking attacks? Does democracy encourage hostage-taking because a more democratic government will be more inclined to negotiate, compared to a less democratic regime, because of greater freedom of press and thereby higher pressure to negotiate and higher valuation of human lives? Does democracy, by legislation, impose constraints on the government representatives, binding their hands in negotiating with terrorists?

These issues were examined by Lee (2013), who used the data on hostage events from 1978 to 2005. During this period, the top five countries in terms of the number of hostage victims were: the USA, Colombia, France, Yemen, and the Philippines. There were four principal explanatory variables: (i) civil liberty (measuring the importance of personal freedom and human life), (ii) press freedom, (iii) executive constraints, and (iv) time to election. The results indicate support for the hypotheses that

Is That So? 12.3: Democracy and Hostage-Taking

Democracy in the form of civil liberties encourages hostage-taking terror attacks, whereas executive constraints exert a negative effect on hostage-taking incidents.

12.4 Take-Aways

- Hostage-taking is different from other forms of terror attacks in the sense that lives can be saved by non-violent means if the target country negotiates and at least partly accedes to the demand of the terrorists.
- The flip side of negotiation and concessions is that they may encourage hostage-taking missions in the future.
- Hostage-taking incidents can be grouped into four types according to the mode of attack: kidnapping, taking over of ground and water transportation means like bus, train, or ship, barricade attacks, and skyjacking.
- Among these types, kidnapping is the least risky for the perpetrators—as the hostages can be moved to places of hiding suitable to the terrorists—and hence the most frequent among all types of hostage-taking attacks.

- General and hostage-taking-specific security measures work in the ways described in Chap. 8, while negotiation or no negotiation is a different kind of counter-terror measure, unique to hostage-taking situations.
- There is a theoretical justification for no-concession policy in that if this is credible and thus anticipated by the terrorists, then there is no benefit from taking hostages in terms of ransom payments or other demands.
- A no-concession policy has been strongly advocated by many experts, but only a few countries have legislated this.
- Empirical studies show that concessions tend to be associated with more hostage-taking incidents in the future and hence are supportive of the effectiveness of no-concession policy.
- Empirical work has uncovered significant determinants of various aspects of hostage-taking like logistic success, duration of negotiation, negotiation success, and whether ransom payments are made. For example, bluffing by terrorists tends to reduce both duration of the event and ransom payments granted to the terrorists, whereas sequential actions by hostage-takers implies a longer duration and higher ransom payments. Negotiation success by the terrorist increases with the number of hostages captured and duration, while it is negatively related with death and injuries to hostage-takers and victims.
- Compared to non-Islamic hostage-takers, there is less hostage safety if the hostage-takers are affiliated with Islamic groups.
- In a democracy, civil rights on the one hand and executive constraints on the other hand are, respectively, positively and negatively associated with hostage-taking attacks.

Appendix to Chapter 12

12.A Details of Atikinson et al. (1987)

The authors used ITERATE dataset from 1968 to 1977. There were 387 incidents that involved negotiation. But not all incidents were followed (in the data description) till the end of the event. Finally, 122 incidents were selected for which data on both duration and ransom (if ransom was demanded, and if yes, whether any ransom was paid, and if yes, how much) were available. In forty-two of the 122 incidents, ransom was demanded. Among these, no ransom was paid in twenty cases. The ransom paid was less than or equal to the terrorists' initial demand with a cluster at 0. This motivated the use of Tobit regression (see General Appendix B, Sect. B.4.2) by using data on the forty-two observations just described.

Time-to-event regression models (see General Appendix B, Sect. B.21) were used to estimate the duration equation.

12.B Details of Poe (1988)

The author used ITERATE dataset, from which he generated a target-country "response strength" variable taking values from 1 to 5. Capitulation by the target country is accorded a value 1. Stalling with eventual compromise on demand was assigned 2. ***Bankok solution***, meaning safe passage for terrorists in return for hostages and withdrawal of demands, was given value 3. No compromise and yet no shoot out was assigned 4, and finally no compromise and shoot out was accorded a value of 5. Multiple regression was used with the number of hostage-taking events as the dependent variable. The independent variables include response strength as well as dummy for being a developed or a developing country and regional dummy as control variables.

12.C Details of Brandt and Sandler (2009)

It uses the ITERATE dataset on international hostage incidents during 1968–2005 was used, to which a Poisson regression model (General Appendix B, Sect. B.19) was applied. For each of the three time-series on kidnapping, skyjacking, and the rest, the authors first identified "change points" in time—introduction of major counter-terror measures or initiative—from the data rather than exogenously imposed them as did earlier studies like Landes (1978), Enders et al. (1990a,b), and Enders and Sandler (1993). Each hostage series exhibited a different change point caused by a variety of circumstances. For instance, the kidnapping data contained ten change points. These are in February 1970, October 1977, July 1983, July 1988, May 1993, January 1998, December 1998, October 2000, April 2004, and November 2004. Each change point was linked to some exogenous changes. For example, November 2004 was associated with a decline in kidnappings in Iraq.

Three explanatory variables or covariates were considered: negotiation success, response of the target and death, each being a binary variable. Negotiation success took value 0 if some terrorist demands were met or 1 otherwise; response of the target was 0 if there is no shoot out or 1 otherwise; and death was equal to 0 if there are no deaths or 1 otherwise. While negotiation success was the primary variable of interest, the other two variables were included to estimate whether violent endings or deaths can predict immediate and future hostage-taking occurrences. The model included a lag structure for the number of hostage-taking incidents as well as other covariates, which, as we saw in Chap. 8, enables the estimation of short-run and long-run effects.

12.D Details of Lee (2013)

ITERATE was the data source on hostage terrorism. The data on civil rights, political rights, and press freedom were obtained from Freedom House, which provides scores on political rights and civil liberties. The author used the data on civil rights, not political rights on the ground that the former measures the degree of democratic values, which are more important than political rights enjoyed by the public. The index ranges from 1 to 7 with 1 as the highest level of civil liberties. This is reversed. Press freedom is indicated by numbers 1, 2, and 3 representing "not free," "partly free," and "free." The data on executive constraints was taken from Policy IV dataset. This index is from 1 to 7 with 7 being the most limitations on the executive leaders.

A long list of control variables were included, e.g., the level of real GDP, the growth of real GDP, land area, population, and number of involvements in foreign crises and variables are lagged by one year except *time to election.*. Poisson regressions for panel data were used. That is, it was assumed that $y_{it} \sim \text{Poisson}(\lambda_{it})$, where y_{it} is the number of hostage-taking events in country i during year t.

Questions

12.1 Consider the following deterministic sequential game. There is no chance mechanism like nature deciding if a mission fails or succeeds, and there is no probability attached to any action taken by the terrorists or the government. The left (right)-hand entry at the terminal nodes represents the payoff of the terrorists (government).
(a) What is the solution of the game, that is, given the payoffs, will the firm attempt kidnapping?
(b) Suppose, the government announces a no-concession policy and it is credible to the terrorists. Will they still attempt to kidnap?
(c) Suppose the payoff vector at node R was $(0.5, -1)$. How would the answers for parts (a) and (b) change?

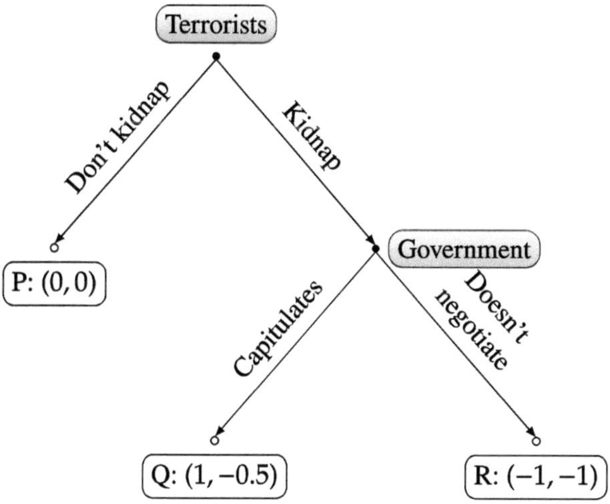

12.2 From reading Yun and Roth (2008), determine by how much hostage safety is impacted if a group is Islamic vis-à-vis not being Islamic.

12.3 "A democratic government as opposed to an autocratic regime is more likely to invite hostage-taking by terrorists." Defend or refute.

Part V

Addressing Fundamental Causes of Terrorism

Chapter 13

Combining Preventive Measures with Preemptive Measures[1]

13.1 Introduction

In the preceding chapters we have assumed that a terrorist organization derives direct utility from the expected damage it causes to the target nations by means of producing and unleashing terror. While the models based on this assumption generated reasonable predictions on the behavior of terror organizations and reasonable conclusions on how security and preemptive measures "work," they did *not* capture terrorism as a means to a long-term end. Remember that terrorism as a form of violence is defined as the use of terror to instill public fear *in order to achieve some long-term political, religious, or socio-economic goal.*

While ideological goals cannot/shouldn't be accommodated at any cost, other types of goals could be arguably deemed as legitimate. For instance, IRA in Northern Ireland wants more political participation and complete independence of Northern Ireland from England—which is very different from ISIS's goal of global caliphate. Even Hamas's goal of a separate Palestinian state has some legitimacy. In general, withdrawal of outside armed troops from the ground or removal of an oppressive regime supported by a major world power can be regarded as a "legitimate" goal.

In this chapter we incorporate such a long-term objective of a terror organization into our analysis. Doing so adds an important and extra dimension to the array of counter-terrorism (CT) measures. Meeting the long-term legitimate demands of a terror organization or the population it represents amounts to *preventive counter-terror measures*. CT measures like security, preemption, and intelligence-and-infiltration studied in previous chapters are *direct* means to "fight" terrorism. We can compare these measures to medicines or procedures to combat a disease in the field of medical science. Redressal of legitimate grievances of communities from which terrorist organizations emerge is akin to a preventive care for a disease.

Right after *9/11*, the U.S. President George W. Bush declared a global "war on terror" (WoT), which meant cracking down of terrorists, terrorist leaders, and their bases along with increased measures of security. Two decades later (at the time of writing this chapter), terrorism still continues as a major global problem.

[1] This chapter is based on Das and Lahiri (2021).

S. P. Das, *Economics of Terrorism and Counter-Terrorism Measures*,
https://doi.org/10.1007/978-3-030-96577-8_13

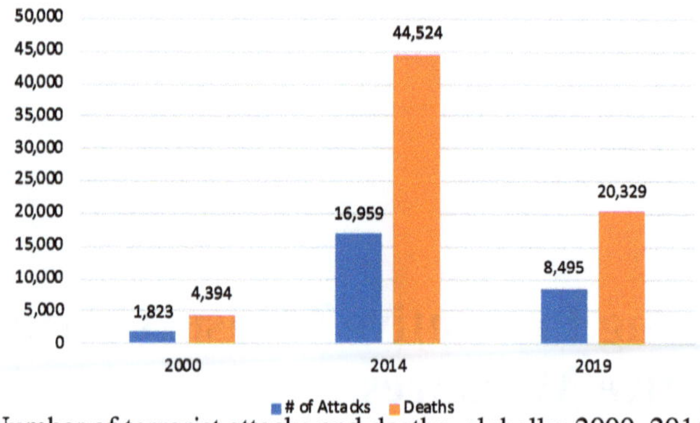

Fig. 13.1: Number of terrorist attacks and deaths, globally: 2000, 2014, and 2019. *Source:* GTD

While the likelihood of spectacular attacks such as *9/11* has receded—thanks to the deployment of comprehensive security measures across many countries, strikes on terrorist havens, scrutiny of movement of funds, larger volume of intelligence gathering, and the like—the number of terror attacks and the number of human lives lost by these attacks have increased globally. Notice in Fig. 13.1 (consistent with Fig. 3.1 in Chap. 3) that in the year 2000, there were 1823 recorded terrorist attacks globally, claiming 4394 lives. The situation became worst during 2014 (16,959 attacks and 44,524 deaths). Since then the number of incidents and fatalities have declined. In 2019, 8495 terror attacks were recorded and 20,329 were dead on account of these attacks. However, compared to the pre-*9/11* years, terrorism is a far bigger issue. In this sense, winning the WoT remains distant.

If a lasting solution to the problem of terrorism is the objective, we must realize that WoT is not just about raising security, killing or capturing terrorists, squeezing the flow of funds or destroying their bases, infiltrating their organizations, etc. Furthermore, poverty and lack of education may be a contributing but may or may not the primary factor behind the rise of terrorism. The key is to heed what the terrorist organizations really want or what their ultimate goal may be. There is already a recognition of the need to redress some of terror organizations' grievances as a part of a holistic approach to deal with terrorism. Painstaking collection of quality data by Pape and Feldman (2010) suggests that direct and indirect control or occupation by foreign armed forces is a primary cause of suicide terrorism. The lack of political and religious freedom and failed states provide a breeding ground of terrorists and terrorism (Krueger (2007), Berman & Laitin (2008), and Berman (2009)). Krueger (2007) capsules these factors as "geopolitical *grievances.*"[2]

[2] A broader list of geopolitical grievances or fears of the population from which terrorist organizations emerge is provided by Hegghammer (2009).

David Sedney, the Deputy Assistant Secretary of Defense for Afghanistan, Pakistan, and Central Asia from 2009 to 2013 and the Deputy Assistant Secretary of Defense for East Asia from 2007 to 2009, writes

> Our singular focus on killing, without any serious attempt to ameliorate basic societal problems—and the absence of a moral core for our actions—have led huge swathes of the world to see us as the evil doers. Extremists today seek revenge for those we have killed, to punish us for abuses they suffer, and to end our support for abusive, corrupt rulers. (Sedney (2015))

In the White House Summit on Countering Violent Extremism in 2015, President Obama voiced that "we have to address grievances terrorists exploit."

One of the notable success stories in more or less eliminating terrorism and conflict is the Northern Ireland case. The main grievance of the nationalists (Sinn Fein and the Irish Republican Army) was the lack of representation of the Catholics in actual policy-making, and the main tenet of the Easter Peace Agreement (1998) has been power-sharing by all the groups in the Northern Ireland administration. Recent negotiations between the Colombian government and FARC at the behest of the United Nations that have ended more than fifty years of violence and terrorism include redressing the longstanding grievances of the rebels in terms of government's promise of large-scale investments in rural areas, which, historically, have been neglected in Colombia.

This chapter argues that combining preventive measures in terms of ("legitimate") grievance redressal with direct measures can deliver better outcomes in the War on Terror (WoT) and offers an understanding of the mechanism behind it. To keep our analysis in perspective, I, as the author, take the position that major instances of terrorism perpetrated by ISIS and modern al-Qaeda are driven more by a global agenda of spreading extreme ideology, and such objectives are *not* aligned with eventuating redressal of geopolitical grievances. They are unacceptable.

Authors such as Kagan et al. (2016) strongly warn that extreme ideological goals pose an existential threat—effectively a WoT of a very complex kind—to liberal democracies and hence require non-conventional, out-of-the-box, innovative counter-terror strategies. Iannaccone and Berman (2006) recommend instituting religious competition in order to deter the emergence and growth of religious extremism. Dealing with ideological goals or religious freedom would, however, require a very different set of preventive CT measures, the analysis of which is outside the scope of this chapter.

We did investigate the issue of winning WoT in Chap. 9, where, by assumption, direct (preemptive) measures were the only kind of CT measures at the disposal of the State. This chapter builds upon the framework of analysis in that chapter, a recap of which at this point is a good idea.

Recall the definition of losing or winning WoT. It is "lost" if, in response to an exogenous increase in militancy or terrorism, the State steps up its CT measures but *not* sufficiently enough, with the outcome that the new equilibrium level of terror is higher despite higher intervention by the State. WoT is said to be won if CT measures are enhanced to an extent such that terror is reduced or at least not increased. The principal insight from our analysis in Chap. 9 is that it is impossible to win WoT by direct measures only as long as the marginal cost of direct measures is increasing. Thus direct measures to confront terrorism are essential, but insufficient. In continuation of this, we will learn in this chapter that *the possibility of winning WoT opens up even in the presence of increasing marginal cost of direct measures if these measures are integrated with preventive measures.* As in Chap. 9, we will assume for simplicity that preemption is the only direct CT measure. Incorporating security does not counter the spirit of our conclusions.

Section 13.2 builds the analytical framework. A key feature of our analysis will be that the expected damage from terror is *not* directly utility enhancing for the Org. Instead, grievance redressal increases the Org's utility. It is articulated that the Org uses terror against the State in order to induce the State to grant this. The game theoretic model is laid out and "solved" in Sect. 13.3. We first focus on preemptive measures only (similar to Chap. 9). Next, preventive measures in terms of meeting the long-term goal of a terror organization are embedded. Characterizing a full solution of these measures is technically demanding however. Instead, preventive measures are introduced exogenously. However, our analysis is sufficiently illustrative of how they work. We will see clearly that combining preventive measures with preemptive actions can yield a better outcome and increase the odds of winning the WoT.

One may argue that granting partial redressal may encourage terror organization to step up terror attacks thinking that they "work." In other words, preventive measures may invite more terror attacks. Section 13.4 addresses the validity of this concern. It will be argued that these considerations may somewhat weaken but does not eliminate the scope of preventive measures. The other side of the coin is that not addressing the legitimate concerns may not increase the odds of "victory" on WoT.

13.2 Analytical Environment

There are two players in a game: a terror group, the Org, and, a target state, the State. The population that the Org represents lives in a socio-economic-political environment that is partly dictated by the State, toward whom the population and the Org feel resentful. It could be due to occupation by armed forces of the State, a regime abhorred by the population but supported by the State, or a failed state as a result of prior policies of the State. Improving this environment is tantamount to a preventive strategy of redressing the population's grievances.

Let grievance redressal be measured in a single (composite), continuous dimension, g. An increase in g stands for more grievance redressal. We consider g as a unilateral concession, not an outcome of a bargaining process. The upper limit on g is $\bar{g}(>0)$ and achieving it is the primary goal of the Org. Both the State and the Org inherit the problem of terrorism, which is captured by the initial g, say 0. Thus, any $g>0$ signifies *grievance redressal.*[3] We call $\bar{g}-g$ the *grievance redressal deficit.* The Org obtains utility from grievance redressal, say $U(g)$. Let $U(\bar{g})-U(g)$ be called the *utility deficit.* The Org's goal is to achieve $\bar{g}$ and enjoy utility $U(\bar{g})$. Figure 13.2

[3] It is worth stressing again that g is intended to capture terrorist demands that have some justification or legitimacy—not goals like political, cultural, or religious subjugation of the target countries.

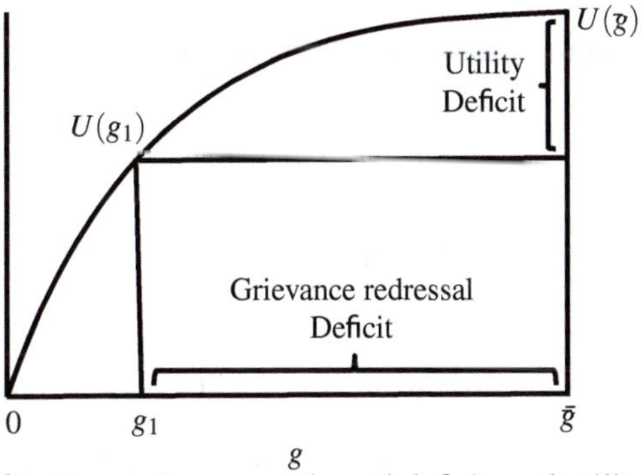

Fig. 13.2: Utility function, grievance redressal deficit, and utility deficit facing the Org

illustrates the utility function, the grievance redressal deficit, and the utility deficit at $g = g_1$.

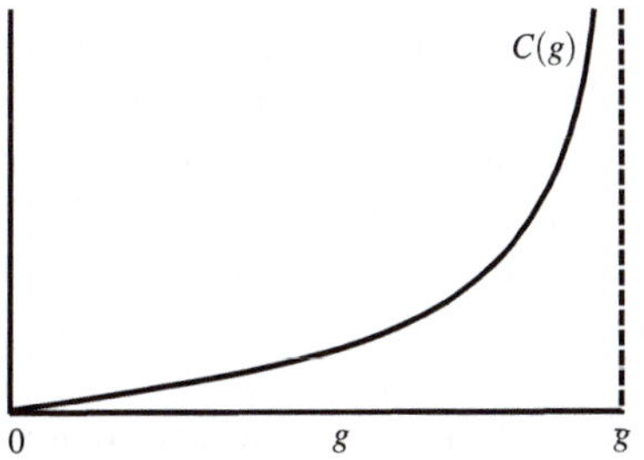

Fig. 13.3: Cost to the state from granting grievance redressal

From the State's perspective, redressing the grievances of the Org, i.e., granting g, is costly. Let $C(g)$ denote the grievance redressal cost to the State like the cost of potential loss of its security and strategic interests. This is exhibited in Fig. 13.3. Apart from grievance redressal, the State undertakes preemptive measures, the scale of which is denoted by m as in Chaps. 9 and 11. An increase in m tends to increase the Org's MC of producing terror. As mentioned earlier, for the sake of simplicity, we abstract from the choice of security measures by the State and hence assume an exogenous level of security.

The State and the Org choose their strategies or actions sequentially. Consider a three-period setting where 0 is end of period 0 or the beginning of period 1. We have $g_0 = 0$, where the subscript denotes the respective period. During period 1, the State chooses its strategies: the scale of preemptive measures (m) and the extent of preventive measures (g_1) between 0 and $\bar{g}$. If the State chooses $g_1 = \bar{g}$, the terrorists' demands are met and (by assumption) the terrorism problem is solved. There is no need to engage in direct CT measures and $m = 0$. If the State chooses $g_1 < \bar{g}$, possibly 0, the problem of terrorism continues. The *choices of m and g by the State, respectively, determine the Org's utility deficit and marginal cost of producing terror.*

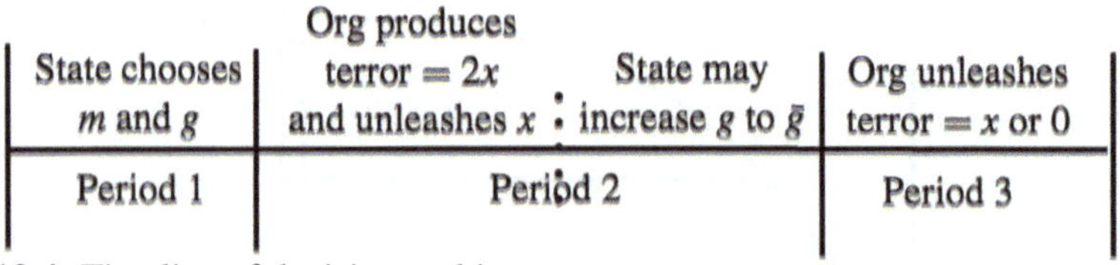

Fig. 13.4: Timeline of decision making

Let us divide period 2 into two parts. In the first part, say 2a, the Org produces planned attacks or terror input 2X, which translates into a random flow of potential damages to the State. Half of it, X, is executed in period 2a, and the remainder is reserved for period 3. (More generally, a fixed proportion of the total terror input produced in period 2a is allocated between period 2a and period 3.) Let the expected damage from terror to the State in period 2a, say D, be proportional to the terror input X, i.e., $D = \beta X$, where $\beta > 0$. The magnitude of β would depend, among other factors, on the security level chosen by the State, which we treat as exogenous. Hence β is constant for our purpose here.

After the unleashing of terror input equal to X against the State in period 2a, in the second half of period 2, say period 2b, the State reconsiders whether to grant further redressal—keeping in mind the terror threat in period 3 equal to X. Thus, terror attacks by the Org in period 2a are used as a credible signal of the magnitude of terror to come in the future, unless grievances are met. This setting is constructed so as to capture the notion that *terror is used by the Org as a threat or a means to an end; it does not provide direct utility to the Org.*

With regard to the State's decision on grievance redressal in period 2b, assume for simplicity that the State faces a binary choice situation: either do not increase g further or grant full redressal, i.e., $g_2 = g_1 < \bar{g}$ or $g_2 = \bar{g}$. Further, it cannot reverse its choice of grievance redressal, i.e., cannot choose $g_2 < g_1$, reflecting commitment on the part of the State, or that rolling back on concessions is too costly for the State in terms of reputation and credibility. Moreover, if g relates to military occupation with supporting military hardware and logistics, the resource cost in reversing a pullback may be quite high. If $g_2 = \bar{g}$, the game ends in period 2b. Otherwise, if $g_2 = g_1 < \bar{g}$, in period 3 the Org unleashes the terror input equal to X, produced earlier.

The timeline of strategies and actions is illustrated in Fig. 13.4. The State and the Org choose their strategies based on their payoffs. Since there are multiple periods of time, they would consider the discounted value of payoffs. For simplicity, we assume that the discount rate is zero. Nothing qualitative hinges on this simplifying assumption.

13.3 Solving the Model

We need to clearly understand the MBs and the MCs facing the Org and the State. Note that the strategy choices being sequential, the MB to the State in period 1 from preemptive and preventive measures would depend on the anticipated behavior of the Org in period 2. In turn, in period 2a the MB to the Org from choosing the terror input depends on its anticipation of State's behavior with regard to grievance redressal in period 2b. Such interdependence makes the model fairly intricate.[4]

Being sequential, the game is solved backward. Beginning first with the last period 3, we note that there is no fresh decision making in this period by either player. The Org either simply disposes x off freely if grievances are fully met or executes it otherwise.

13.3.1 The State's Decision Making in Period 2b

In period 2b, the State inherits its own choice g_1 from period 1 and the Org's reserve of terror input X for period 3. By assumption, it faces two choices: grant full redressal, i.e., $g_2 = \bar{g}$, or keep the status quo, i.e., $g_2 = g_1$. The general expression of expected total cost of the State in period 2b is $C(g_2) + D = C(g_2) + \beta x$. If the State grants full redressal, the expected total cost is $C(\bar{g})$, since the Org would not use terror in period 3. If the State maintains status quo, i.e., chooses $g_2 = g_1$, it is $C(g_1) + \beta X$. What will be the State's choice? Comparing the two total cost expressions, the State's choice rule is

$$g_2 = \begin{cases} g_1 \ (< \bar{g}) & \text{if } C(g_1) + \beta X < C(\bar{g}) \\ \bar{g} & \text{otherwise.} \end{cases} \tag{13.1}$$

Note that an increase in terror tilts the State's choice toward full redressal, which underscores the role of terror by the Org as a means to an end.

13.3.2 The Org's Decision in Period 2a

After observing $g = g_1$ granted by the State and its preemptive action m that determines the level of its cost function, the Org decides the production level of terror. Assume that the Org does not have full information on the State's cost of granting g, that is, $C(g)$. For instance, the Org may be unsure about the political willingness of the State toward granting redressal, which may depend on political pressure groups' preferences facing the State. Thus, the Org does not know for sure whether $C(g_1) + \beta X \gtreqless C(\bar{g})$ for any given terror output it chooses, whereas the State knows its own cost of g, i.e., *there is asymmetric information.*[5] Given the anticipated choice rule by the State, the choice of terror output by the Org generates a probability of full redressal from the Org's perspective. A higher X implies a better chance that

[4] A full solution is worked out in Das and Lahiri (2021).

[5] Likewise, the State may not have full knowledge of the Org's utility function $U(g)$. But this is not critical to our analysis.

$C(g_1) + \beta X \geq C(\bar{g})$ and hence a higher probability of full redressal. Letting p denote the probability that the State would grant full redressal, we have

$$p = p(X), \quad p' > 0.$$

We further assume $p''(X) < 0$, i.e., the marginal effect of terror on the probability of full redressal is positive but diminishing.[6] Given the function $p(X)$ and noting that the Org derives utility $U(\bar{g})$ in case of full redressal and $U(g_1)$ in case of partial or no redressal, the total expected utility or benefit from using terror is: $p(X)U(\bar{g}) + (1 - p(X))U(g_1)$. We can rewrite it as:

$$U(g_1) + \underbrace{[U(\bar{g}) - U(g_1)]}_{\text{utility deficit}} \cdot p(X), \tag{13.2}$$

which is easy to interpret: the higher the utility deficit, the greater is the benefit from increasing terror. If the utility deficit is zero, there is no gain to the Org from producing terror. The expected benefit expression (13.2) implies that the marginal benefit to the Org from using terror being equal to:

$$\text{MB}_{\text{terror}} = \underbrace{[U(\bar{g}) - U(g_1)]}_{\geq 0} \cdot p'(X) \geq 0.$$

Note that the MB to the Org from terror depends on the *change* in p, i.e., how the odd changes, *not* on p or the odd itself. Our assumption of $p''(X) < 0$ implies that the MB from producing terror diminishes with the amount of the terror input produced. This is exhibited in panel (a) of Fig. 13.5.

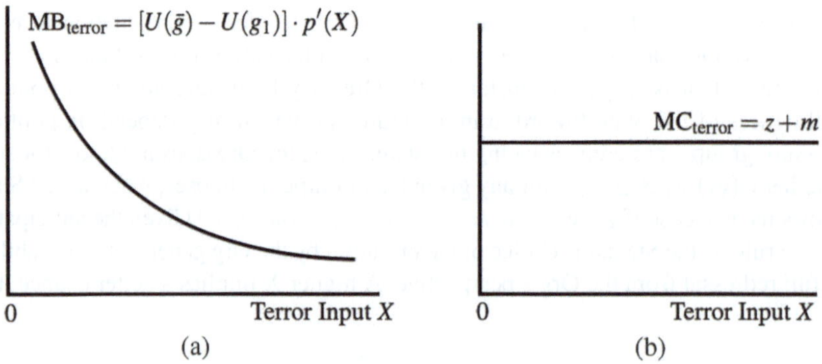

Fig. 13.5: Org's marginal benefit and marginal cost functions. (**a**) Org's marginal benefit from terror. (**b**) Org's marginal cost of producing terror

[6] Here are a couple of examples of the p function that satisfy $p' > 0 > p''$: (a) $p(X) = 1 - e^{-X}$ and (b) $p(X) = 1 - (1 + X)^{-a}$.

Turning to the cost side of producing terror, let the total cost function facing the Org be linear in the terror input produced:

$$b \cdot (z + m) \cdot (2X), \quad b > 0,$$

where b, a positive constant, is a technology parameter. As in Chap. 9, a decrease in z is interpreted as an exogenous increase in militancy or terrorism. An increase in preemptive measures m tends to raise the MC of producing terror. Remember that the Org produces $2X$ amount of terror for periods 2 and 3 together. The MC of producing terror is $2 \times b \cdot (z+m)$. For convenience of notation, let us choose $b = 1/2$, which does not change any qualitative results. Thus

$$\text{MC}_{\text{terror}} = z + m. \tag{13.3}$$

Panel (b) of Fig. 13.5 shows the MC curve facing the Org.

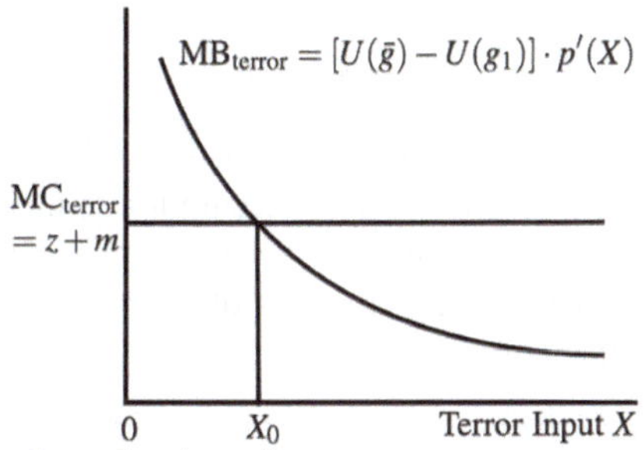

Fig. 13.6: Org's optimal production of terror

Realize that the State's choice of preemptive and preventive measures in period 1 determines the positions of the MB and MC curves of the Org in period 2a. Given these schedules in Fig. 13.5, the rational production level of terror is governed by the first-order condition that the MB from terror = the MC of producing terror. That is,

$$[U(\bar{g}) - U(g_1)] \cdot p'(X) = z + m. \tag{13.4}$$

In Fig. 13.6 this condition is met at a point like X_0, which defines the optimal or rational level of production of the terror input. It is noteworthy that an increase in grievance redressal reduces the MB (shifts MB curve in) from using terror and hence leads to a decline in the quantity produced of terror at any given level of MC. Preemptive measures work differently: they shift up the MC function of producing terror and tend to reduce terror at any given level of MB. Hence, combining the two constitutes a two-pronged counter-terror intervention/measure to contain terrorism. Algebraically,

$$X = X(\underset{-}{g}, z \underset{-}{+} m). \tag{13.5}$$

Compare this with Eq. (9.5) in Chap. 9, which is reproduced below:

$$X = X(z + m). \tag{9.5a}$$

We see that Eq. (13.5) is a generalization of Eq. (13.3.2) in that terror production declines with grievance redressal too.

13.3.3 The State's Choice of CT Measures in Period 1

In view of (13.5), we have the damage-deterrence function

$$D(X) = D(X(g, z + m)) \equiv \bar{D}(\underset{-}{g}, z \underset{-}{+} m). \tag{13.6}$$

This is a generalization of the same function in Chap. 9, namely, Eq. (9.7), which is reproduced below for quick reference:

$$\bar{D}(z + m). \tag{9.7a}$$

Recall the cost function of preemptive measures $H(m)$, $H_m > 0$ from Chap. 9. We assume here that the marginal cost of preemption is increasing, i.e., $H_{mm} > 0$. The rational State is assumed to minimize the sum total of all costs: cost of granting redressal, that from terrorist acts and the cost of preemptive measures. In symbols, the State's objective is to

$$\text{Minimize} \quad C(\underset{+}{g}) + \bar{D}(\underset{-}{g}, z \underset{-}{+} m) + H(\underset{+}{m}) \text{ with respect to } m \text{ and } g.$$

Notice that the trade-off in choosing the level of preemption m is exactly same as in Chap. 9: an increase in it reduces the damage cost but increases its own cost. The trade-off in choosing g is new, yet intuitive. On one hand, granting grievance redressal tends to reduce the political and other benefits to State. These are costs, summarized by the $C(\cdot)$ function. On the other hand, it offers a benefit to the State in terms of reduced terror as it induces the Org to produce less terror.

The first-order conditions are

$$m: \quad \underbrace{-D_m(z + m)}_{\text{State's MB from } m} = \underbrace{H_m(m)}_{\text{State's MC of } m} \tag{9.10a}$$

$$g: \quad \underbrace{-\bar{D}_g(g, z + m)}_{\text{State's MB from } g} = \underbrace{C_g(g)}_{\text{State's MC of } g} . \tag{13.7}$$

The first-order condition (13.3.3) is exactly same as Eq. (9.10) in Chap. 9. It should, since at any given level of redressal g, the trade-off in choosing the optimal level of preemption is the same. Eq. (13.7) is new here. However, a full analysis of the choice of both m and g, i.e., preemptive and preventive CT measures, is rather complicated and skipped here.

Instead, we will revisit, at the cost of some repetition, the optimal choice of m as in Chap. 9 and its inadequacy in winning WoT if the marginal cost of preemption is increasing—and augment it with an intuitive argument of how an *exogenous* increase in grievance redressal as a preventive measure expands the scope of winning WoT.

13.3.4 The State's Choice of Preemptive Measures Only

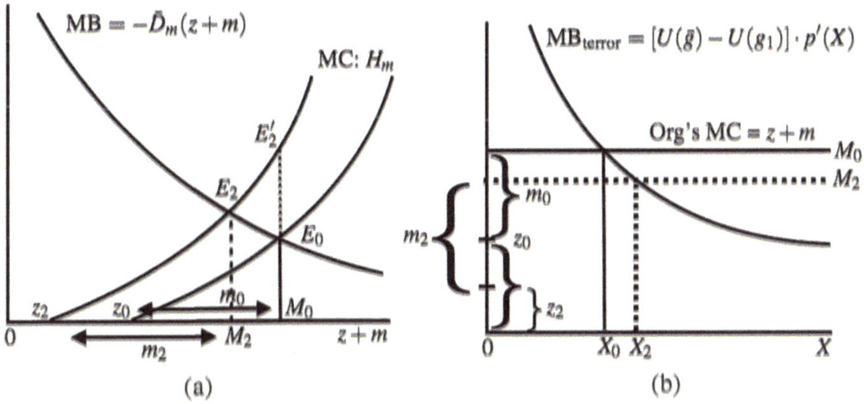

Fig. 13.7: State's choice m and Org's choice of X. (**a**) State. (**b**) Org

Refer to Fig. 13.7a, which is same as the top quadrant of Fig. 9.8b in Chap. 9. The upward sloped lines are the MC functions of preemption, which increase with the level of preemption and whose horizontal intercepts are determined by the value of z.[7] Initially, $z = z_0$ and the MC of preemption (m) starts at point z_0. See that it intersects with the State's MB curve at E_0. The equilibrium MC of the Org is $M_0 \equiv z_0 + m_0$, where m_0 is the rational choice of preemption by the State. The Org's choice of terror is depicted in panel (b). With the level of the MC function given at M_0, the Org weighs its MB against MC. Its rational choice of terror production is X_0.

As militancy increases, so that z falls from z_0 to say z_2, the upward sloping MC curve of preemption for the State moves to the left. The new equilibrium point is E_2, the new equilibrium level of preemption is m_2, and the new MC of the Org is at $M_2 \equiv z_2 + m_2$. However, $M_2 < M_0$ means that MC facing the Org is lower than before, *even after enhanced preemptive measures undertaken by the State.* The optimal choice of terror by the Org is X_2. Since $X_2 > X_0$, the State does not win the WoT. If the State did fully offset the increase in militancy by increasing m from m_0 such that the new M for the Org remains unchanged at M_0, the MC of preemption

[7] This is explained in more detail in Chap. 9.

would be E_2', which is higher than MB = E_0. Therefore, the rational State would *not* step up m to that extent—"thanks" to the *increasing* MC of preemption, reflected by the upward sloping MC curve for the State. This was our main point in Chap. 9.

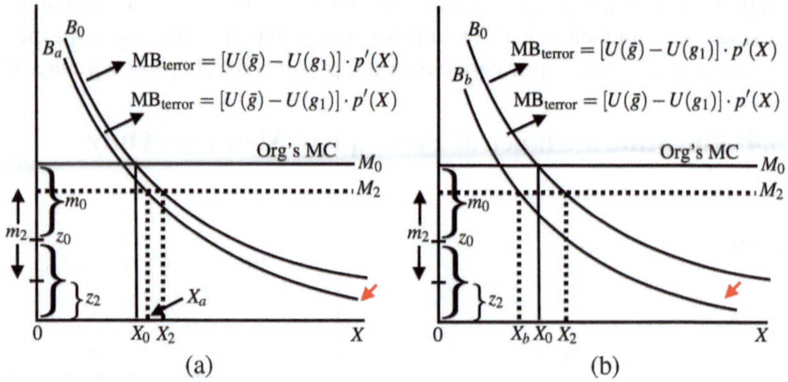

Fig. 13.8: Preventive measures and Org's choice of terror. (**a**) WoT is still lost. (**b**) WoT is won

13.3.5 Grievance Redressal

We now bring in grievance redressal, which lowers the MB of the Org from terror. Suppose the State is open toward offering grievance redressal. Consider panel (a) of Fig. 13.8, which graphs the choice of terror by the Org. The original situation is described by (z_0, m_0, g_0, X_0) and the original MB curve facing the Org is B_0. If, as before, militancy increases so that z falls to z_2, and the State provides a relatively modest redressal so that the new MB curve of the Org is B_a (somewhat very close to the original curve B_0), the equilibrium terror production is X_a. But, notice that $X_a > X_0$. Hence WoT is still "lost. " However, the outcome in terms of terror production and expected damage from terror is still better than if there were no grievance redressal.

Figure 13.8b illustrates a situation where the State grants more grievance redressal so that the inward shift of the Org's MB curve is greater. The new MB curve is B_b. The equilibrium terror production is now X_b, which is *less* than X_0. As a consequence, WoT is won. Das and Lahiri (2021) show that such an increase in g leading to less equilibrium terror production can be a rational choice of the State, rather than exogenous.

Hence, the upshot is that *combining preemptive and preventive measures is likely to yield a better solution than just using preemptive measures only and has the potential of winning the WoT.*

It is important however to note that *preemptive and preventive measures are not substitutes.* Rather, they work in tandem with each other: while preemptive measures enhance the Org's MC of producing terror, preventive measures curtail the Org's MB from producing terror.

13.4 Partial Redressal May Encourage the Terror Organization to Produce More Terror

It may be argued that granting partial redressal would lead the Org to think that the State is soft liner and "terror works on the State. " Partial redressal would thus encourage terror instead. We can call this an *expectations revision effect* in that partial redressal leads the Org to revise its estimation of the $p(\cdot)$ function. There are two counter-arguments however.

First, let the Org's expectations revision because of partial redressal be reflected in a more general p-function, $p = p(\underset{+}{X}, \underset{+}{g_1})$, where the partial $\partial p/\partial g_1 > 0$ means that a partial redressal leads to the Org to believe that the State is more likely to offer full redressal at any given level of terror X.

Does it necessarily imply that the Org will produce more terror? Recall the terror output choice rule:

$$\underbrace{[U(\bar{g}) - U(g_1)] \cdot p_X(X, g_1)}_{\text{MB to the Org}} = \text{MC of producing terror,}$$

and note importantly that the terror output choice does *not* depend on p itself. Instead, it depends on p_X: how p changes (i.e., the odds change) with respect to an increase in terror. It is possible that even if $p = p(\underset{+}{X}, \underset{+}{g_1})$, p_X may be independent of g_1. For example, suppose

$$p = \frac{X}{1+X} + \gamma g_1. \quad \gamma > 0.$$

It is easily checked that p_X is independent of g_1. Hence if the p function is one like the above, terror production is *not* affected by any revision of belief by the Org. The expectations revision effect does not lead to more terror production.

Second, even if the $p(X, g_1)$ function is such that the expectations revision effect implies more terror production, it does not wash away the utility deficit-reducing effect. The latter effect is likely to be stronger if the grievance redressal is not relatively minor. To see this, consider the following example:

$$p = \frac{\gamma g_1}{1+\gamma g_1} \cdot \frac{X}{1+X}.$$

In this case,

$$p_X = \frac{\gamma g_1}{1+\gamma g_1} \cdot \frac{1}{(1+X)^2},$$

which increases with g_1. This is the expectations revision effect. Accordingly, the choice rule for terror production is

$$[U(\bar{g}) - U(g_1)] \cdot p_X = \underbrace{[U(\bar{g}) - U(g_1)]}_{\text{utility deficit reducing effect}} \cdot \underbrace{\frac{\gamma g_1}{1+\gamma g_1} \cdot \frac{1}{(1+X)^2}}_{\text{expectations revision effect}}$$
$$= \text{MC of producing terror.}$$

Notice that an increase in grievance redressal (g_1) has two effects on the MB of the Org from terror: a utility deficit effect as earlier and an expectations revision effect. It is *not* necessary that the latter outweighs the former.

The model anticipates that a conditional grievance redressal—as opposed to a unilateral concession—will dissuade the Org from "irrational exuberance" and minimize the expectations revision effect.

In sum, the message is that combining direct and preventive counter-terrorism measures can deliver a better outcome for the state.

13.5 Take-Aways

- Preventive measures reduce the terrorists' demand for engaging in terror as a means to achieve their end, whereas (as we have learned in previous models) preemptive measures tend to reduce or limit the capability of terror organizations to produce terror.
- As long as the *marginal* cost of preemption is increasing, in the face of an increase in militancy or threat of terrorism, the State will *not* enhance its preemptive measures to the extent that will fully counter the increase in militancy. As result an increase in preemption will be associated with an increase in terror. In this sense, winning the war on terror (WoT) by preemptive measures only is impossible. However, combining direct counter-terror measures like preemption with preventive measures is more effective in combating terrorism and can win the WoT while the marginal cost of preemptive measures to the State is increasing.
- Granting partial redressal, it may be argued, can lead a terror organization to think that the State is soft liner; this may lead to more terror instead. This is termed as an expectations revision effect. There are two counter-arguments however. First, equilibrium terror attacks depend on the *change* in the odds of the state granting redressal, not on the level of odds itself. Hence as long as granting partial redressal as a commitment by the targeted state does not change the odds of further redressal in the future, and this is rationally anticipated by the terror organization, there is not incentive for the terror organization to increase terror. Second, even if the terror

organization has an incentive to step up terror because of its expectation that the target country is a soft liner, the very fact that the utility gain from engaging in terror is less may be the dominating factor. Thus the role of preventive measures remains the same qualitatively.

- A conditional grievance redressal will minimize the expectations revision effect.

Questions

13.1 Assume that the State is unwilling to provide any grievance redressal, i.e., $g_1 = 0$. Let the State's marginal benefit function with respect to preemptive actions be

$$\text{MB from preemption} = 110 - (z + m).$$

The total cost of terror production by the Org is $(z + m)X$, so that the marginal cost of terror production is $z + m$. Notice that an increase in preemption m increases the marginal cost of producing terror. Let the initial value of z be $z_0 = 10$. A decrease in the value of a would reflect an increase in militancy or terrorism.

Suppose the total cost function of preemption is $C(m) = 90m$, so that the marginal cost of preemption is constant, equal to 90.

(a) What preemption level will be chosen by the State? What is the Org's equilibrium level of marginal cost producing terror?

(b) Suppose there is an increase in militancy or terrorism in terms of a decrease in the value of z from $z_0 = 10$ to $z_1 = 0$ (an extreme case). What will now be the optimal level of preemption for the State and what would be the Org's equilibrium marginal cost of producing terror?

(c) Compare your answers to parts (a) and (b) and provide an intuitive reason.

13.2 Consider the decision making by the Org in period 2 now. The probability of success in securing full grievance redressal is given by the function

$$p(X) = \frac{X}{1 + X}.$$

Check that as long as $X \geq 0$, p lies between 0 and 1; further, it increases with X at a decreasing rate, i.e.,

$$p'(X) = \frac{1}{(1 + X)^2} > 0 \quad p''(X) = -\frac{2}{(1 + X)^3} < 0.$$

Recall that g varies from 0 to $\bar{g} = 1$. The Org's objective is to achieve $g = \bar{g} = 1$. Let the Org's utility function from grievance redressal be

$$U(g) = 980\sqrt{g}.$$

(a) If the State is unwilling to grant any redressal, so that $g_1 = 0$, what is the utility deficit facing the Org?

(b) What will be the Org's choice of terror X when $z = z_0 = 10$?

(c) What will be the Org's choice of terror X when z falls to $z_1 = 0$?

(d) Compare your answers to parts (b) and (c) and very briefly describe why the answers may be different or the same.

13.3 Suppose, instead, that the cost function of engaging in preemptive measures is $C(m) = 9m^2/2$, implying that the marginal cost of preemption is $9m$, which increases linearly with preemption.

(a) Answer part (a) and part (b) of Question #13.2.

(b) Briefly discuss in words why you get different results for part (b).

(c) Computer the levels of terror X that will be chosen by the Org when $z = z_0 = 10$ and when $z = z_1 = 0$.

(d) Is the State winning the war on terror or militancy when there is such an increase in terrorism or militancy? Why or why not?

13.4 Continue to assume that the marginal cost of preemption is increasing and equal to $9m$. Suppose that in response to an increase in militancy or terrorism, the State is now willing to grant redressal. What is the level of grievance redressal needed so that the equilibrium terror at $a = 0$ is same as that when $a = 10$?

13.5 "Acceding to the demand of terrorist would only serve to encourage terrorists and terrorist attacks." Defend or refute.

Chapter 14

Religious Orthodoxy and Terrorism

14.1 Introduction

RECALL from Chap. 2 Rapoport's fourth and "latest" wave of terrorism, which is based on religion. Most of the deadly terrorist organizations in recent decades are linked to religious fundamentalism, extremism, or radicalism. However, the vice versa is *not* true. Many extreme religious groups and sects that practice religion by imposing prohibitions, sacrifices, rigorous prayer norms, and rituals are non-violent. Prohibitions include various combinations of diet restrictions, unusual clothing, celibacy, geographic isolation, Sabbath laws, etc. For example, Hare Krishna devotees shave their heads and wear saffron colored robes. For Mormons, consuming tobacco and caffeine is forbidden. Orthodox Jews wear yarmulkes and side curls and do not do business on the sabbath. Orthodox Muslims offer prayers a certain number of times in a day. The list goes on.

Besides prohibitions, joining an orthodox group typically requires an initiation process involving irreversible sacrifices. They include various combinations of membership fee, qualifying serving time, circumcision, destruction of resources, surrender of possessions, burnt offerings, etc.[1]

In this chapter we try first to understand religious orthodoxy through the lens of economics and, next, how it may be linked to terrorism. On purpose, I use the word "orthodoxy" instead of "fundamentalism" or "extremism", since these (last two) words are often associated with violence, whereas orthodoxy is not.

Is That So? 14.1: Orthodox Religious Groups

In reality, only a small fraction of orthodox religious groups/sects are or become violent. Most are non-violent.

In any event, given the dominance of Islamic fundamentalist terror groups in the last two/three decades, many people equate Islamic fundamentalism with terrorism implying that religious fundamentalism is a root cause of terrorism. This is debatable since there is evidence to support that religion is used by at least some Islamic terror-group leaders as a means to achieve an end. In and of itself, it is not a cause of

[1] Burnt offerings mean burning of material possession including burning of animals in communal meals.

S. P. Das, *Economics of Terrorism and Counter-Terrorism Measures*,
https://doi.org/10.1007/978-3-030-96577-8_14

terrorism. As we have discussed in Chap. 2, it is Osama Bin Laden who distorted the meaning of jihad the true meaning of which is inner self-cleansing, not killing the non-believers. We may remember that the one of the main stated goals of Bin Laden was that US troops must leave the Arabian peninsula. This is *not* an ideological demand. But in order to achieve this and other demands, he created a rally around the notion of religion and distorted the meaning and practice of jihad. At the same time, there is no denying that the objective of organizations by ISIS and Boko Haram is purely ideological and fundamentalist. Global jihad, establishing a caliphate or shunning western education and culture is *not* a political objective. The point is that *Islamic fundamentalism does not match one-to-one with global jihadism.*

Our objective in this chapter is to understand:

1. The economic basis of religious orthodoxy
2. How it may provide a platform for terrorism: in other words how *some*, not most, orthodox religious group may become violent

Section 14.2 is central. It introduces the kind of practices that define orthodoxy and develops economic rationales behind such practices, which may otherwise be thought as an unconventional, or, what some may think, strange preferences. In Sect. 14.3, we discuss the basis of how some orthodox organizations may be inured to organized violence, while Sect. 14.4 briefly outlines an economic model of "joint production" of religion and terror.

14.2 Religious Orthodoxy as Rational Behavior: Iannaccone's Model

We will first understand the economic logic behind orthodoxy without considering any inclination toward violence. In his pioneering work, Iannaccone (1992) developed an economic theory where orthodoxy results from rational, welfare improving behavior *as long as individuals value organized religion.*[2]

Iannaccone's theory views religious participation as a *voluntary private club activity*, hence called the *club theory of religion. Organized religion* is a group or club activity, which offers a collective utility that is enjoyed by all members. Utility from organized religion for one member does not reduce utility for another. Hence, it is a *"local" public good.* In economics, a public good is defined as a product or service, which has two characteristics: it is (a) non-rivalrous and (b) non-excludable. Non-rivalry means your consumption of it does not reduce the consumption of the same good by another individual. A public park is a good example. Your enjoyment from strolling in the park does not depend on use of the park by others (unless of course there is an overcrowding). Non-excludability means that your use does not prevent or exclude use by others. For instance, a public park is open for all. "Local" public good has the property of being non-rivalrous but does not satisfy non-excludability in that the public good is available only to a certain section of the community. Private beaches maintained by waterfront hotels are examples: only

---

[2] This insightful research has earned Laurence R. Iannaccone, an informal title of being the Father of the modern economics of religion.

residents of the hotel are permitted to use them. Similarly, organized religion is a local public good, only available to the respective members. We term it as *religion public good,* which does not just mean religious discourse and rituals but also engagement in social interaction and public services. The collective utility from the religion public good results from social interaction.

In order to understand the economic rationale behind religious orthodoxy, we first note that there are two generic problems associated with any collective activity that is *voluntary*, namely, *moral hazard* and *adverse selection*, the two most familiar terms in the economics of information. As described in Chap. 7, the former refers to incentive problems when one's action cannot be perfectly observed, monitored, or enforced. For instance, if a manager delegates a certain task to a worker and cannot monitor it, the worker may have an incentive to shirk. In the case of religion activity, from an individual's perspective, if others participate more, it tends to increase group activity and enhance the utility of everyone irrespective of the extent of any single member's participation. This creates an incentive to shirk and free ride on others as long as effort is costly in terms of mental and physical strain as well as opportunity cost for working elsewhere for money.

The adverse selection problem, also introduced in Chap. 7, is the following. Suppose different people have different opportunity cost of time. Some prefer to devote a lot of time for the club or religion-related activity and others do not. Those with low levels of participation will be tempted to free ride off those with higher levels as both types derive utility from the religion club good. This would imply that the average time spent on the religion public good, which can be interpreted as its quality, will be relatively low due to the participation of those who are not very motivated. The problem arises when a religious organization cannot distinguish between "good" (more dedicated) and "bad" (less dedicated) prospective members and ends up offering membership to both types. Consequently, the quality of services will be worse compared to what it would have been if all were very dedicated. Put differently, adverse selection arises as an asymmetric information problem in the presence of a heterogeneous population. The religious organization would not know for sure who will turn out to be dedicated and who will not—whereas an individual knows which kind she/he is.

Going back to the moral hazard issue, we can say that no one is perfect. By and large people are inherently opportunistic. *Moral hazard is an across-the-board low participation problem, while its degree may vary from one person to another*. In contrast, *adverse selection is a bad-composition problem.*

As discussed earlier, we define orthodoxy in terms of two sets of practices: prohibitions and initial irreversible sacrifices. Quite interestingly and insightfully, Iannaccone shows that prohibitions tend to address the moral hazard problem, while initial sacrifices tend to solve the adverse selection problem. Figure 14.1 is a schematic view of how these practices work.

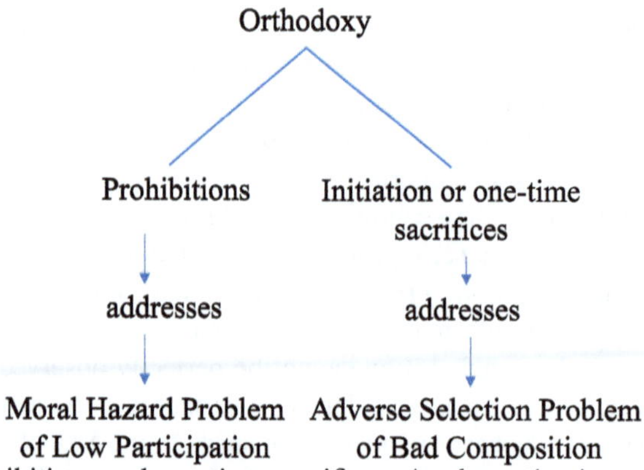

Fig. 14.1: Prohibitions and one-time sacrifices: A schematic view of their economic roles in religious orthodoxy

14.2.1 Prohibitions Solving the Moral Hazard Problem of Low Participation

In reality, a religion club would have many members. For simplicity, assume that it has two members, 1 and 2.[3]

Assumption 14.1. *A member derives utility or satisfaction from two kinds of goods/activities: (i) a religion public good or simply religious participation or interaction and (ii) goods and services for private consumption such as one's normal purchase of those from the market.*

For simplicity, let the market-provided goods and services be lumped together as a basket of what Iannaccone calls the ***secular good***, as opposed to the ***religion good***. In other words, *a member obtains utility from consuming a secular good and a religion good.* Let $u(s_i)$ denote member i's utility from consuming the secular good. We assume a simple $u(\cdot)$ function:

Assumption 14.2. *The utility from the consuming the secular good is linear:*

$$u_i(s_i) = a_i s_i, \ a_i > 0. \tag{14.1}$$

Thus the marginal utility from consuming secular good is constant and equal to a_i.

With regard to the religion good or activity:

Assumption 14.3. *For each member, the utility (v_i) from the religion, a local public good or activity, depends on the quality of this activity, where quality is proportional to the average quantity of participation in terms of time.*

[3] It is straightforward to extend our analysis to many members but that is beyond our scope here.

If z_i denotes the time volunteered by member i to the religion club, the average is $(z_1 + z_2)/2$.[4] Thus, we can express $v_i = \tilde{v}_i((z_1 + z_2)/2)$. For simplicity, we write it as

$$v_i = v_i(z_1 + z_2).^5 \tag{14.2}$$

The average per se does not play any role here, but it will in our adverse selection model later.[6] We impose

ASSUMPTION 14.4.

$$v_i'(z_1 + z_2) > 0 > v_i''(z_1 + z_2),$$

meaning positive but diminishing marginal utility for any member from consuming the religion public good. Assumption 14.4 implies two things.

(1) Any member's total utility from the religion good increases with own participation or effort as well as on participation by other member(s). That a given member's utility increases because of participation by another member is a *positive externality effect.*

(2) However, his/her marginal utility from the religion good declines with own participation or that by other member(s).

Assumption 14.4 and the two implications for member 1 are illustrated in Fig. 14.2, while similar implications hold for member 2. Panel (a) is simply a direct graphical illustration of Assumption 14.4: the total utility curve has a positive slope (i.e., $v_1'(z_1 + z_2) > 0$), while the slope itself declines with group effort (i.e., $v_1''(z_1 + z_2) < 0$). His/her marginal utility (MU_1) from the religion good at a given level of participation by member 2 ($z_2 = z_2^0$) is exhibited in panel (b). At a given value of z_2, an increase in z_1 implies an increase in the group effort $z_1 + z_2$, which tend to diminish the marginal utility for member 1. Panel (c) depicts the same at two values of z_2. A change in z_2 affects MU_1 at any given value of z_1. Hence, there is a shift of the MU_1 curve. At a higher value of z_2, $z_1 + z_2$ is higher for any given z_1 and hence MU_1 is lower. Put differently, an increase in z_2, say from z_2^0 to z_2^1, implies a downward shift of the MU_1 curve. Intuitively, since one member's utility depends on the *total* group participation in religion, if the others provide more, the marginal gains from one's own participation in the club activity decline. This leads to what is called a *free-rider problem*, an incentive to take advantage of the efforts or contributions from other members in a society and participate relatively less. As

---

[4] If there are n members, the quality of the religion public good has the expression:

$$\frac{z_1 + z_2 + \cdots + z_n}{n}.$$

[5] Note that this is function $v_i(\cdot)$, not $\tilde{v}_i(\cdot)$.

[6] More generally for any many individuals N, Iannaccone (1992) defines $v_i = v_i(z_i, \left(\sum_{j \neq i} z_j\right)/(N-1)\big)$. It means that member i utility from religion depends on one's own level of participation (z_i) as well as the average participation or effort by others, which defines quality of the religion good. Our specification is simpler.

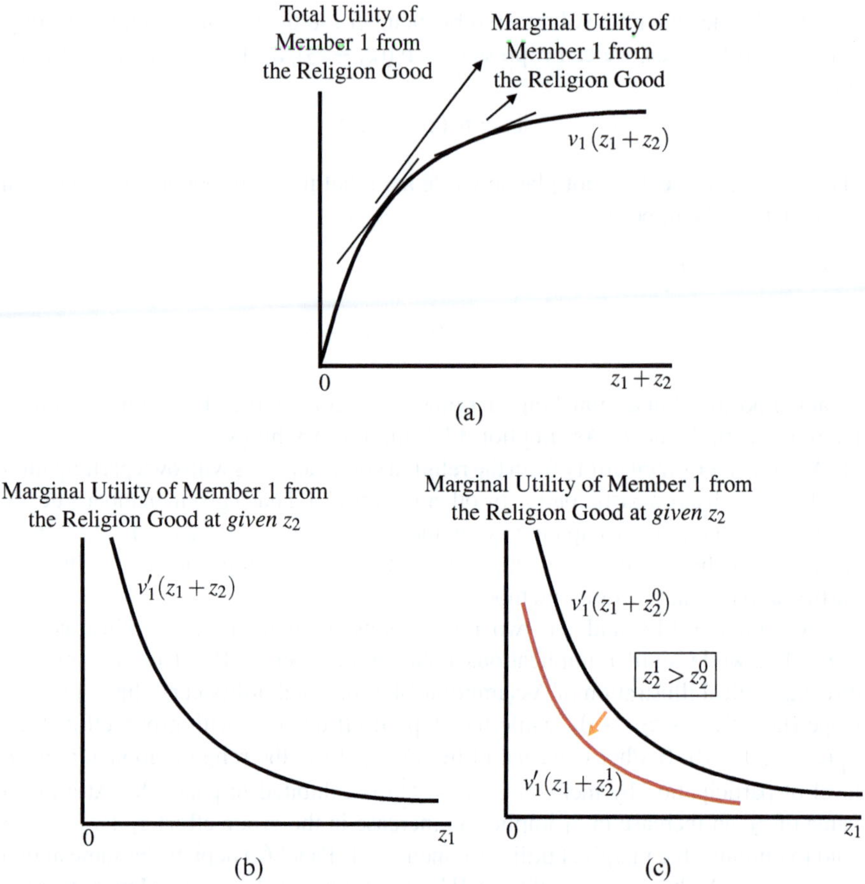

Fig. 14.2: Total utility and marginal utility from the religion good. (**a**) Total and marginal utility of Member 1 as group effort varies. (**b**) Marginal utility of Member 1 as z_1 varies, when $z_2 = z_2^0$. (**c**) Marginal utility of Member 1 as z_1 varies, when $z_2 = z_2^0$ and $z_2 = z_2^1$

we shall see later, in equilibrium every member would tend to participate less than what is collectively optimal.

To grasp this better, we need to first understand a member's own rational choice of effort or participation. Let U_i denote the "grand-total utility" enjoyed by member i from the secular good and the religion good. This will depend on the sub-utilities obtained from these goods. We can express it as $U_i = U_i(u_i, v_i)$. For simplicity of exposition, we suppose the following:

ASSUMPTION 14.5. *The grand-total utility is linear in total utilities from the secular good and the religion good, i.e.,*

$$U_i = a_i s_i + v_i(z_1 + z_2). \tag{14.3}$$

This is an example of what is called a "quasi-linear utility function," since it is linear in the secular good but non-linear with respect to the religion good.

The question is: What is the optimal choice with regard to the secular good and the religion good by a particular member?

To answer this, we have to bring into consideration a member's budget constraint. Let p denote the price of the secular good (a basket), w_i the market wage rate per hour for member i, and T_i the total time available for work and participating in the religion club activity together.[7] We can write member i's budget constraint as:

$$\underbrace{ps_i}_{\text{Spending on the secular good}} = \underbrace{(T_i - z_i)w_i}_{\text{Total earnings}}. \tag{14.4}$$

This is self-explanatory. The left-hand side expression is a member's spending on the secular good (price times quantity). The time available for work equals total time (T_i) minus time spent on the religion club activity (z_i). The right-hand side is the expression of total earnings. A person's savings are ignored for simplicity.

The budget yields the following expression for the amount consumed of the secular good:

$$s_i = \frac{(T_i - z_i)w_i}{p}. \tag{14.5}$$

Notice that s_i and z_i are negatively related, that is, within a budget, the secular good and the religion good are substitutes of each other.

Now plug this expression into the grand-total utility function (14.3) and eliminate s_i. We get

$$U_i = \underbrace{\frac{a_i w_i T_i}{p}}_{\text{Maximum possible consumption of the secular good}} + \underbrace{v_i(z_1 + z_2)}_{\text{Utility from consuming religion good}} - \underbrace{\frac{a_i w_i z_i}{p}}_{\text{Opportunity cost of consuming the religion good}}. \tag{14.6}$$

Eliminating s_i enables us to focus on the choice of the religion good.[8] We can interpret (14.6) as follows. Given the budget constraint, more of one good can be

---

[7] For simplicity, there is no time involved in consuming the secular good.

[8] Eliminating s_i from the grand-total utility this way was possible because (a) the utility from the secular good is linear in secular-good consumption and (b) the grand-total utility function is also linear in total utilities from the secular good and the religion good.

obtained by sacrificing some of the other. Hence grand-total utility equals maximum consumption of the secular good possible *plus* utility from consuming the religion good *minus* the opportunity cost of consuming the religion good in terms of the secular good. (If one extra hour is spent on the religion good, the foregone earnings equal the wage per hour (w), which would have bought w_i/p amount of the secular good. Thus z_i hours spent on the religion good entail a sacrifice of $w_i z_i/p$ amount of the secular good.)

How do members 1 and 2 choose z_1 and z_2, respectively? Note that the marginal utility for a member from the religion good does not depend on his/her own choice or "strategy" only. It depends on the other member's choice of action or strategy. Hence we use game theory and Nash equilibrium. Indeed, the scenario is similar to the choice of preemption by target countries in a multiple-target-country situation, analyzed in Chap. 9, Sect. 9.6.

In Nash equilibrium, each player chooses her action such that it is the best choice given the action of other players (so that no player has an incentive to unilaterally deviate from his chosen action). This amounts to member 1 maximizing U_1 with respect to z_1 at a given value of z_2 and member 2 maximizing U_2 with respect to z_2 at a given value of z_1. In view of the grand-total utility function (14.6), the first-order conditions for choosing z_1 and z_2, respectively, by members 1 and 2 are

$$z_1\colon \underbrace{v_1'(z_1+z_2)}_{\text{MU}_1} = \underbrace{\frac{a_1 w_1}{p}}_{\text{MOC}_1} \tag{14.7}$$

$$z_2\colon \underbrace{v_2'(z_1+z_2)}_{\text{MU}_2} = \underbrace{\frac{a_2 w_2}{p}}_{\text{MOC}_2}, \tag{14.8}$$

where MUs are the marginal utilities from the religion good for respective members and MOC denotes the marginal opportunity cost.

These first-order conditions lead the respective best response functions, which are the loci of the optimal choice of participation by one member at different levels of participation by the other. Consider member 1. As z_2 increases, the marginal utility for member 1 from participation in the religion club falls, and, as a result, member 1 chooses a lower level of participation, z_1. Thus, a higher z_2 is associated with a lower level of z_1, reflective of the free-rider problem discussed earlier. The same is true for member 2. As shown in Fig. 14.3, the best response functions are negatively sloped (they are drawn as straight lines only for simplicity).

We have argued that moral hazard in voluntary participation is an inherently individualistic problem cutting across all rational individuals. Hence, at this point, for simplicity, we assume that all members are alike:

ASSUMPTION 14.6. *The population that values organized religion is homogeneous in terms of preferences and economic opportunities.*

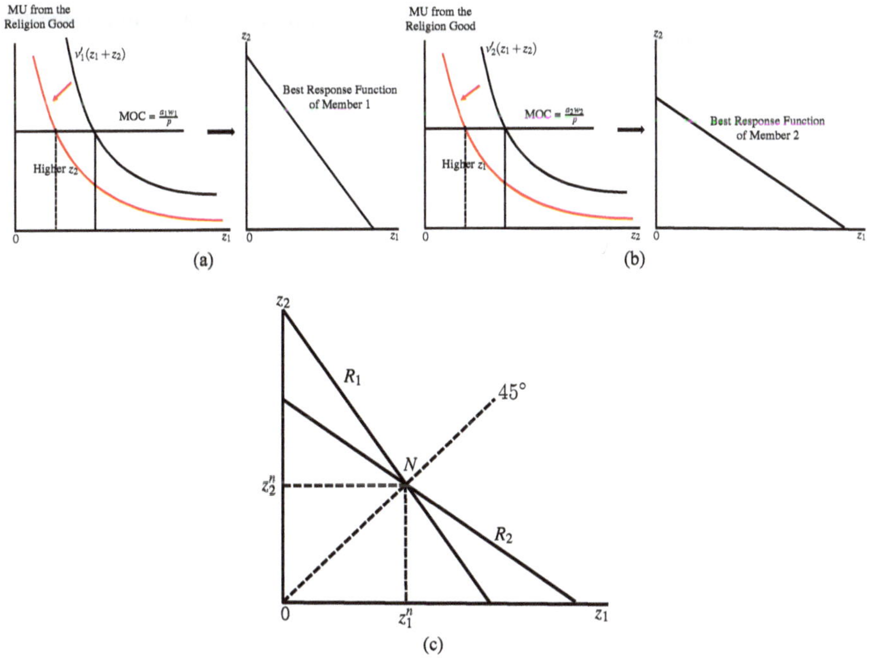

Fig. 14.3: Best response functions and Nash equilibrium in terms of participation in the religion club. (**a**) Member 1. (**b**) Member 2. (**c**) Nash equilibrium in the symmetric case

Thus, in the present two-member context, $a_1 = a_2$, $v_1(z_1+z_2) = v_2(z_1+z_2)$, $T_1 = T_2$, and $w_1 = w_2$.

As a consequence, the best response functions are symmetric, shown together in Fig. 14.3c as R_1 and R_2. The intersection point N (which falls on the 45° line since R_1 and R_2 are symmetric) defines the Nash equilibrium and solves the equilibrium choice of participation in the religion club. Member 1 chooses z_1^n level of participation and member 2's equilibrium choice is z_2^n. Of course, symmetry implies $z_1^n = z_2^n$.

14.2.1.1 Prohibitions

We are now ready to understand how prohibitions affect consumption of the secular good and religion club activity. The important point to realize is that *prohibitions are equivalent to a (sales) tax on consuming the secular good.* Fasting, for example, is equivalent to a tax on food. Growing a long beard is equivalent to a tax on hair cutting in the market and so on. Once we understand this, it follows that, like a sales tax, *the prohibitions effectively increase the price of the secular good facing the members* and this tends to reduce the members' consumption of the secular good. That is, members effectively pay a price $p + \tau$, where τ is the implicit tax, representing prohibitions. What does it do to the opportunity cost of time devoted to religion club? Without prohibitions, it was w/p, where w is the same wage for both members. With prohibitions, it is $w/(p + \tau)$. That is, *prohibitions reduce the opportunity cost of participating in religion.*

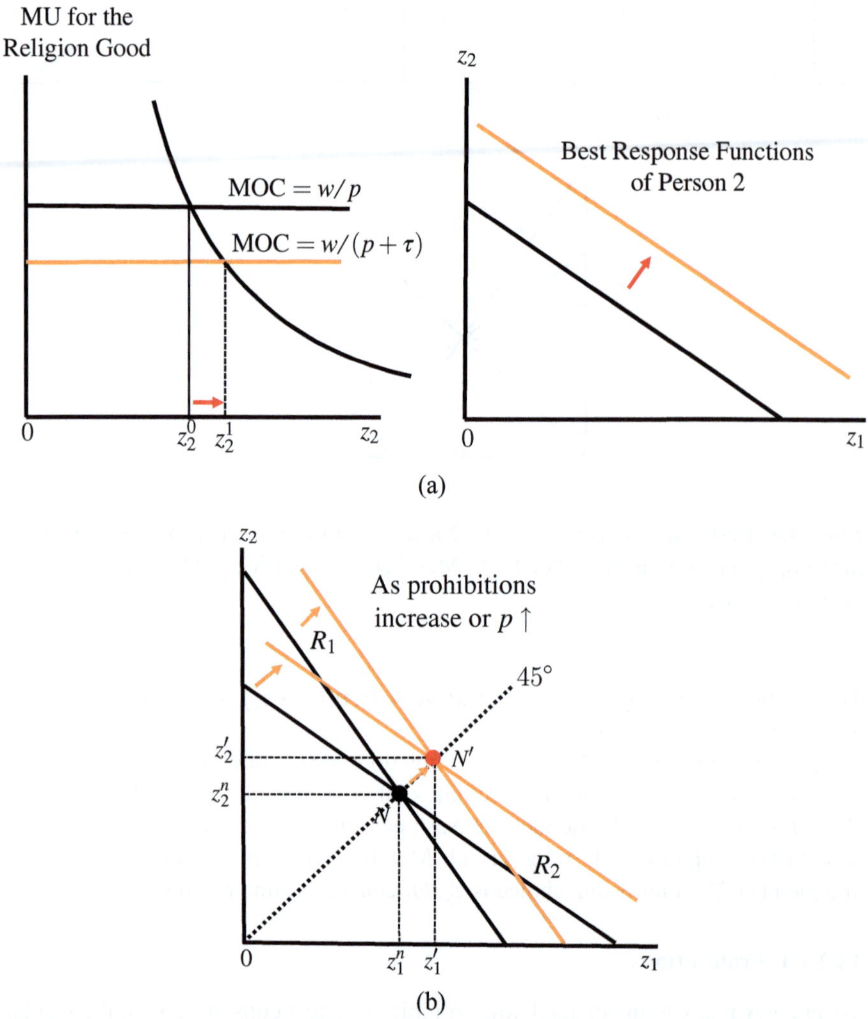

Fig. 14.4: Impact of prohibitions on participation by the members and the Nash equilibrium. (**a**) Shift of best response functions. (**b**) Effect on the Nash equilibrium

How does it affect the behavior of the members? Turn to Fig. 14.4a. Consider member 2, for example. Because the opportunity cost of participating in the religion activity is less in the presence of prohibitions or a consumption tax, he/she would choose a higher z_2, z_2^1 as opposed to z_2^0, at any given level of z_1, i.e., participate more in the club activity—as shown in left panel. This implies that the best response function or curve of member 2 shifts out (see the right panel). An outward shift of the best response function applies to member 1 also. That is, prohibitions lead to outward shifts of the best response functions of both members. As shown in Fig. 14.4b, the Nash equilibrium shifts from a point such N a point like N' along the 45° line to the right. The implication is that both individuals participate more in the religion club activity.

Result 14.1

By reducing the opportunity cost of participation, prohibitions induce members to participate more in religion.

While prohibitions force members to devote more time for club/religion activity, do they increase their welfare? If yes, that would be an economic basis for prohibitions; we cannot say that prohibitions are only a reflection of uncommon preferences.

14.2.1.2 Cooperative Behavior and Welfare

As it turns out, an analytical path toward understanding how individuals may be better off due to prohibitions opens by first determining how the two members would choose their participation if they were to decide jointly in a spirit of cooperation and collective welfare.

Imagine a social planner choosing or "dictating" z_1 and z_2 for respective individuals, keeping in view the joint welfare of the two members together. Let us define joint welfare as the sum of utilities accruing to both members; that is,

$$\begin{aligned}\mathcal{W} &= \frac{awT}{p} + v_1(z_1+z_2) - \frac{awz_1}{p} + \frac{awT}{p} + v_2(z_1+z_2) - \frac{awz_2}{p} \\ &= \frac{2awT}{p} + v_1(z_1+z_2) + v_2(z_1+z_2) - \frac{awz_1}{p} - \frac{awz_2}{p}. \end{aligned} \tag{14.9}$$

This follows from the grand-total utility expressions (14.6). In writing this expression, note that we write $v_1(\cdot)$ and $v_2(\cdot)$ separately, although $v_1(\cdot) = v_2(\cdot)$. This is done on purpose in order to better illustrate the qualitative difference between the non-cooperative and the cooperative outcomes.

The social planner's choice of z_1 and z_2 that maximizes $\mathcal{W}$ is the cooperative solution. In view of (14.9), the respective first-order conditions are

$$z_1: \quad \underbrace{\underbrace{v_1'(z_1+z_2)}_{\text{private marginal benefit}} + \underbrace{v_2'(z_1+z_2)}_{\text{positive externality effect}}}_{\text{social marginal benefit}} = \frac{aw}{p} \tag{14.10}$$

$$z_2: \quad \underbrace{\underbrace{v_1'(z_1+z_2)}_{\text{positive externality effect}} + \underbrace{v_2'(z_1+z_2)}_{\text{private marginal benefit}}}_{\text{social marginal benefit}} = \frac{aw}{p}. \tag{14.11}$$

These are two equations with two variables, z_1 and z_2, the solutions of which constitute cooperative equilibrium, the social optimum or the efficient solution. Notice that the two equations are exactly the same because the opportunity cost of participating in religion is the same for both members.

It is important to note that, compared to the first-order conditions (14.7) and (14.8), each equation has additional term representing the positive externality effect—that is, more participation by one member tends to increase the utility of other members from religion (besides increasing own utility). It means that the positive externality effect of member 1s participation on member 2 and that of member 2s participation on member 1 are recognized and "internalized" in the cooperative solution. The entire left hand of each equation is the *social marginal benefit* from a member's participation in the religion club. This is different from the individual or *private marginal benefit*, respectively, equal to $v_1'(z_1+z_2)$ and $v_2'(z_1+z_2)$ for the members 1 and 2.

The difference between the social and the private marginal benefit is the positive externality effect, implying that the social marginal benefit is greater than the private marginal benefit (as both members gain from each other's participation). The implication is that in cooperative equilibrium each member will be called upon to offer more participation, compared to the non-cooperative Nash equilibrium. It is illustrated in Fig. 14.5a at a point like C, which marks the cooperative or the efficient solution. This is the intersection point of two lines that represent the first-order conditions of maximizing the joint welfare $\mathcal{W}$. Compared to the Nash equilibrium, the participation levels, z_1^e and z_2^e, are higher. Consequently, there is a higher output of the religion public good. Notice also that, at the efficient point, each member's utility or welfare must be greater, because the members being alike, maximizing joint welfare maximizes individual welfare too. Hence,

Result 14.2

Compared to the non-cooperative Nash solution, in the cooperative equilibrium, there is more participation by and higher welfare for all the members.

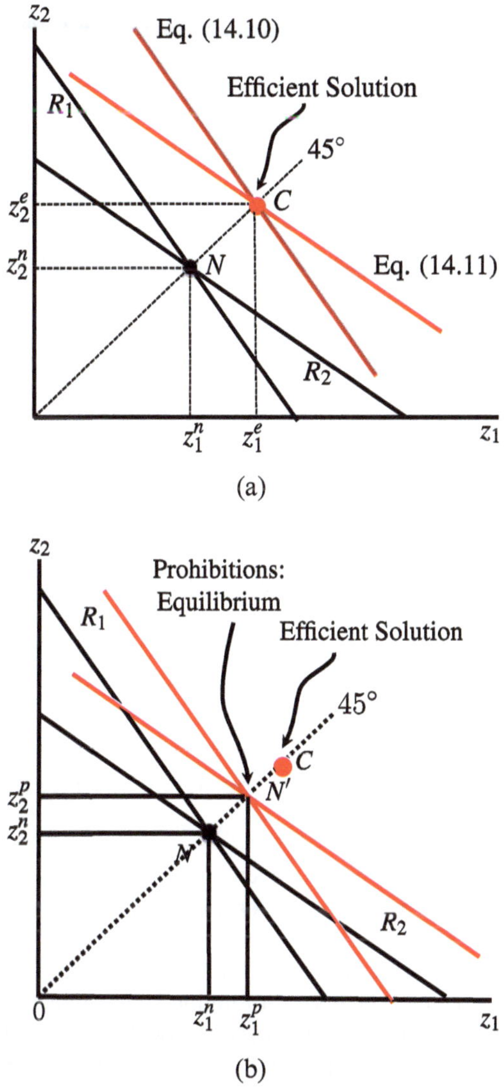

Fig. 14.5: Cooperative equilibrium and prohibition. (**a**) Cooperative equilibrium. (**b**) Prohibition moving the equilibrium point toward the cooperative solution

Put in reverse, compared to the efficient solution, in Nash equilibrium there is under-provision of the religion club good. This is due to the positive externality effect that leads to a free-rider problem.

14.2.1.3 Approaching the Efficient Solution

The next question is how can the equilibrium be moved from the Nash equilibrium point like N toward the efficient point such as C. This is where prohibitions come to play. Turn to Fig. 14.4b and recall that prohibitions shift out the best response functions from a point like N to another like N'. Note simply that it is similar to moving from N to C. This effect is shown in Fig. 14.5b. As long as the prohibitions are not too prohibitive (pun intended), so that the point N' is not to the right of and too distant from C, they must be welfare-improving. We can hence say that

Result 14.3

Prohibitions tend to move the Nash equilibrium close to the efficient point and benefit the club members.

This is the upshot. In sum, religious services or club efforts by other members exert a *positive externality* and members would tend to free ride on them. As a result, the group effort would be low. Equivalent to a consumption tax, prohibitions tend to limit consumption of secular goods. This substitution effect motivates members to devote more time for the religion club activity. In the process they gain more utility, because in the absence of it their participation was low from what is best for them as a group.

Observe interestingly that members are coerced to do something, but it increases group activity and, in the process, each member is better off. It is like you are being forced to exercise more—something you may not do on your own—but, after exercise, you feel better and enjoy good health. This is the economic rationale behind the practice of the prohibitions.

14.2.2 Initial Sacrifices Solving the Adverse Selection Problem of Bad Composition

Analogous to prohibitions being equivalent to a consumption tax, one-time initial sacrifices for becoming a member of an orthodox club is equivalent to an entrance or a one-time membership fee.

Let us now deviate from our assumption that all members are homogeneous and recognize that potential members of religion clubs are heterogeneous in terms of levels of participation due to either different preferences or different economic opportunities, or both. For simplicity, let us consider two types of potential members: high-participation type G (good) and low-participation type B (bad), with participation levels z_G and z_B in terms of time, respectively. The two types are distinguished by:

Assumption 14.7. $z_G > z_B.$

If μ and $1 - \mu$ are the proportions of G and B types in a club, the quality of the religion good is $\mu z_G + (1 - \mu)z_B = z_G - (1 - \mu)(z_G - z_B)$. Given Assumption 14.7, i.e., $z_G > z_B$, the quality of organized religion attains maximum if $\mu = 1$, i.e., there are no B-type members. To ensure this is the aim of an orthodox club.

However, there is a problem. Presuming that a rigorous screening process, which can correctly distinguish between the G and the B types is too costly, the club management cannot know who is of which type. All potential members, irrespective of their type, would wish to join the orthodox club (proclaiming themselves to the G type if asked) in order to enjoy the high quality of the religious-cum-social-interaction service. It is a situation of asymmetric information where the individual knows his type but the club management does not.

How would then an orthodox club be able to screen out the B-type without actually rigorously screening potential members to discover their types? As will be argued below, the solution lies in the initial one-time sacrifices. They act as a screening device through which potential members self-signal their own type *voluntarily* to effect the entry of only the G type individuals to an orthodox club. Fully working out the analytical solution is however technically demanding. Instead, we will touch upon the key elements of the argument that will be sufficient for us.

Suppose that the potential religion club members, both G and B types, face two choices: a "secular club" where the quality is less, equal to q, and an orthodox club that promises a higher quality, Q ($> q$). Let $U_G(q)$ and $U_G(Q)$ denote the utility associated with the respective club for the G type. The utility expressions for the B are analogous: $U_B(q)$ and $U_B(Q)$. Since $Q > q$, we have

$$\Delta U_G \equiv U_G(Q) - U_G(q) > 0; \quad \Delta U_B \equiv U_B(Q) - U_B(q) > 0, \tag{14.12}$$

where ΔU is utility gain from joining the orthodox club, compared to the secular club.

14.2.2.1 Heterogeneity in Preferences

We first consider a scenario where the G and the B types are defined in terms of their preferences toward the religion good:

$$\Delta U_G > \Delta U_B; \tag{14.13}$$

that is, the G type are those whose utility gains from the joining the orthodox club are greater.

Consider the opportunity cost of joining the orthodox club relative to joining the secular club. Assume that both types face the same market wage and being a member of the orthodox club demands the same number of additional hours, compared to the secular club. Thus, the opportunity costs for both types are the same, say equal to c. Consequently, the *net* utility gain is higher for the G type. This is illustrated in the left panel of Fig. 14.6a.

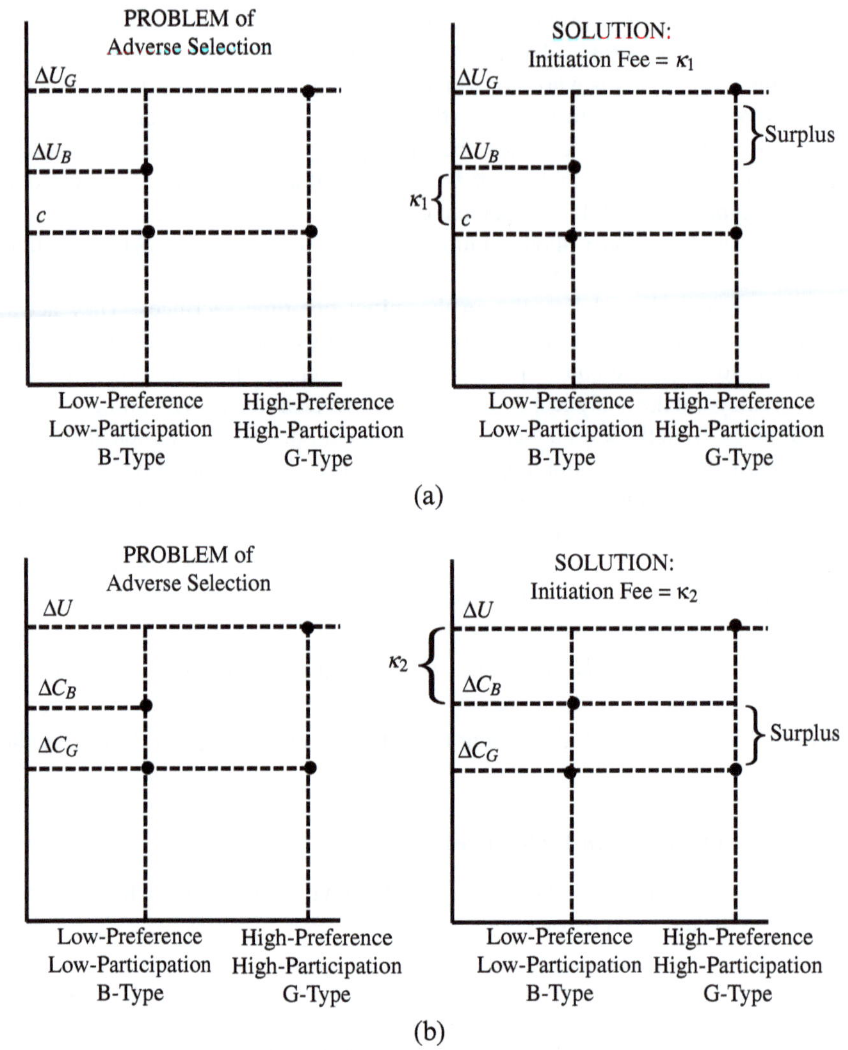

Fig. 14.6: Adverse selection problem of bad composition. (**a**) Heterogeneity in preferences. (**b**) Heterogeneity in economic opportunities

The question is how will the orthodox club be able to deter the B type from joining the club? The left panel offers a solution: that is, *charge an initiation fee marginally higher than* $\Delta U_B - c \equiv \kappa_1$ *to anyone who wishes to join the orthodox club.* This is shown in the right panel of Fig. 14.6a. The net after-fee utility gain for the B-type (after paying the initiation fee κ_1 plus a minimal marginal amount) is negative. Hence they voluntarily choose not join the orthodox club. Notice importantly that κ_1 is not high enough to deter the entry of the G-type, because their net before-fee utility gain from joining the orthodox club is greater (equal to $\Delta U_G - \Delta U_B$).

More generally, there is a whole range of the initial fee κ to enter the orthodox club, $\Delta U_B - c \leq \kappa < \Delta U_G - c$, which the G type would be willing to pay but the B type would not. The orthodox club would charge the lower bound of this range, equal to κ_1 defined above, to keep the B type away while keeping the G types in without overly penalizing them.

The upshot is that initial sacrifices work as a screening device for the orthodox group. The low-participation types voluntarily decide to keep themselves out. The bad composition problem is solved.

14.2.2.2 Heterogeneity in Economic Opportunities

The same qualitative solution follows if the two types differ in the economic opportunities available to them. Suppose one group is the high-wage cum low-participation type B, and the other is the low-wage cum high-participation type G. Assume $U_G = U_B$, so that their preferences toward the religion good are identical. That is,

$$\Delta U_G = \Delta U_B = \Delta U = U(Q) - U(q) > 0.$$

Assume further that, although the time contribution to a religion club differs between the two types, both types would contribute more time if allowed a membership in the orthodox club (because the marginal utility from joining an orthodox club is higher) than if they were members of the secular club. Let I_B and i_B be the total wage earnings (wage × hours worked in the market) of a high-wage individual if he/she goes to the secular or the orthodox club, respectively. We have

$$\Delta C_B \equiv \underbrace{I_B}_{\substack{\text{if member of the}\\\text{secular club}}} - \underbrace{i_B}_{\substack{\text{if member of the}\\\text{orthodox club}}} > 0.$$

Similarly, for the G type, let I_G and i_G denote total wage earnings if he/she goes to the secular or the orthodox club, respectively. Thus, $\Delta C_G \equiv I_G - i_G > 0$. The expressions ΔC_B and ΔC_G are equal to the respective opportunity costs of the two types of individuals for having a membership in the orthodox club as opposed to the secular club.

Given these expressions, the net utility gains to B-type and G-type from joining the orthodox club are $\Delta U - \Delta C_B$ and $\Delta U - \Delta C_G$, respectively. Let ΔU be high enough such that both prefer orthodox club, i.e., both $\Delta U - \Delta C_B$ and $\Delta U - \Delta C_G$ are positive. A critical and relevant assumption is that

Assumption 14.8. *The wage difference between the two types is high enough such that*

$$\Delta C_B > \Delta C_G. \tag{14.14}$$

That is, the opportunity cost in terms of earnings in joining the orthodox club is higher for the high-wage B type than for the low-wage G type.

It essentially says that the high-wage B types stand to lose more earnings from becoming a member of the orthodox club than do the low-wage G types.

The above scenario is depicted in Fig. 14.6b. The left panel shows that both types prefer to be the members of the orthodox club, i.e., $\Delta U - \Delta C_B > 0$ and $\Delta U - \Delta C_G > 0$, while the benefit, net of the opportunity cost, is greater for the low-wage G type, i.e., $\Delta U - \Delta C_G > \Delta U - \Delta C_B > 0$. The last inequality follows from Assumption 14.8.

The left panel lends itself to a solution that is depicted in the right panel. *Charge an initiation fee marginally higher than* $\kappa_2 \equiv \Delta U - \Delta C_B$. It works because the after-fee net utility gain for the B type is negative, so they voluntarily opt out. The same for the G type is positive however, i.e., they still enjoy a surplus approximately equal to $\Delta C_B - \Delta C_G > 0$. Hence, they join the orthodox club voluntarily.

An interesting aspect of this scenario is that it is the relatively low-wage individuals who are willing to pay the initial fee, while the high-wage individuals are not.

14.2.2.3 Overall Implication

The commonality between the two settings considered above is that

Result 14.4

Between two groups of potential members, the members of the group who either value religion less or whose opportunity costs are higher experience a net utility gain from joining an orthodox club relative to joining a secular club (over and above the opportunity cost) that is less compared to the other group. Hence there exists a range of initiation fees or initial sacrifices such that the former group that is less motivated are blocked effectively from joining the orthodox club, while the more motivated group finds it worthwhile to join.

The bad composition effect is eliminated by the initial sacrifice scheme. The quality of the orthodox group's religion activity is kept high. In effect, the initiation or the one-time sacrifice helps screen out those who are not motivated. The orthodox club is constituted by highly motivated members only.

The theory of orthodoxy espoused above is not just a matter of intellectual curiosity. Its predictions are supported by data. For instance, Iannaccone (1992) analyzed two sets of data on different Christian denominations in the USA, one based on a 1963 survey of nearly 3000 church members in the Bay area, California, and the other from the National Opinions Research Center's 1984–1987 General Social Surveys. Within the Christian faith, a four-way classification was made on the basis of the stringency of demand by organized religion: most Church-like, Church-like, sect-like, and sect. Averages of household income, Church contributions, Sunday and evening attendances, etc. were compared across these four categories. The data revealed, for example, that the average household income declines and the average

Church contributions increase as we move from the most Church-like to the sect—which agrees with the model's prediction. In a study on ultra-orthodox Jews in Israel, Berman (2000) found strong evidence of voluntary religious activity and group insurance.

14.3 Orthodoxy Leading to Violence and Terrorism

Iannaccone's work precedes *9/11* attacks by almost a decade. It was not meant to explain how religious orthodoxy may give rise to organized violence or terrorism. The connection was explored in subsequent research, namely, Iannaccone and Berman (2006), Berman and Laitin (2008), and Berman (2009).

The causal link between orthodoxy and terrorism runs as follows. Iannaccone's theory of religious orthodoxy implies an orthodox religious group to be a collection of relatively homogeneous people with coherence, bonding, and commitment who value the group activity highly. And these are the traits needed for successfully producing organized terror attacks too. Hence, if (mis)guided and exploited by extremist leaders, such groups may become violent. This is *not* to say that most orthodox groups are violent. On the contrary, only a few are. Our purpose is to understand how this may happen to *some* orthodox groups.

To see the process more clearly, let us first recognize that successful production of a terror attack by a group requires combining a chain of interrelated tasks with high probability of successful execution of each task. In the extreme form if one task fails, it has the potential of undermining the entire mission. Imagine one of the operatives in the *9/11* attacks failing to do what he was supposed to do or getting arrested at the airport for whatever reason. It would have jeopardized the entire operation. Remember the space shuttle Challenger disaster on January 28, 1986. Such a complex rocket launching project failed spectacularly due to the malfunctioning of a very small set of ordinary components, namely, O-ring seals that could not withstand extreme cold. Organizing a major terror attack is similar. Each task is important no matter how small it is and whether it is simple or complicated. In essence, *a successful major terror attack is as good as its weakest link.*

In order to "capture" or model this central characteristic of a successful terror mission, let us deviate from the way the terror production technology was introduced in Chap. 8 through a producer cost function as in standard micro theory. Instead, let us think of terror production as a product of the probability of success of each task led by a group of people. Think of the simplest case of a two-task terror mission with two terrorists. Terrorist 1 is assigned to task 1 and terrorist 2 is in charge of task 2. Let p_1 and p_2 denote the respective probability of success. We define the expected terror output as

$$X = Ap_1p_2. \tag{14.15}$$

Because the probabilities appear multiplicatively, note that if any of these tasks fails, i.e., if either p_1 or p_2 is zero, the expected output is zero, i.e., the mission fails. This characteristic becomes starker if there are many, say n number of tasks, in which case the technology will be $X = Ap_1p_2 \ldots .p_n$. If any one of these probabilities approaches zero, the expected output approaches zero. A technology like (14.15) or $X = Ap_1p_2....p_n$ captures the idea of a project being as good as its weakest link.

In regard to the two-task technology, assume further that p_1 and p_2 depend on the level of commitment of the assigned individual. If both are equally committed, then $p_1 = p_2 = p$ and the expected output is equal to

$$\tilde{X} = Ap^2. \tag{14.16}$$

Compare this with what the expected output would be if the two members were not alike in terms of their commitment and dedication. Let

$$p_1 \equiv p - b, \; p_2 \equiv p + b, \; 0 < b < p + b \leq 1, \tag{14.17}$$

so that both probabilities are bound between 0 and 1. The parameter b measures the degree of heterogeneity between the two individuals. What is the expected output? We have

$$X^* = A(p - b)(p + b) = A(p^2 - b^2). \tag{14.18}$$

We know that for any $b \neq 0$, $X^* = A(p^2 - b^2)$ is always less than $\tilde{X} = Ap^2$, that is, the expected output is smaller. This is the main point: *homogeneity improves the outcome of technologically or operationally complicated tasks.* It implies that if some operatives “chicken out” or “sell out” to outside bribes (as put by Iannaccone & Berman (2006)) such that p_1 or p_2 is small, the mission's chance of success is pulled down considerably. In the extreme case if $p_1 \simeq 0$, then $X \simeq 0$ no matter how high p_2 is. On the other hand, the chance of this happening is small and terror attacks are likely to succeed if both p_1 and p_2 are close to each other and far away from zero. This is likely to be case if members are homogeneous and committed—the same attributes that are associated with religious orthodoxy.

The above model illustrates how religious orthodoxy may be linked to terrorism, providing a rational framework within which to understand the emergence of Islamic fundamentalist terror groups. It is worth emphasizing however that much depends on the ability of leadership to rally the members in the name of religion. Our model illustrates how a homogeneous and committed bunch of people without much scope for economic opportunities in the market place—like members of an orthodox religious group—may be led to embrace violence.

14.4 Economies of Scope and Joint Production of Religion and Violence

Our discussion in Sect. 14.3 does *not* imply that orthodox groups once formed and later exploited by leaders to engage in terrorism abandon religious activities. Instead, both activities coexist. Islamic terror organizations promote religious fundamentalism *and* produce terror simultaneously. This is achieved by allocating common resources between the two activities. We take a deeper look at this process here.

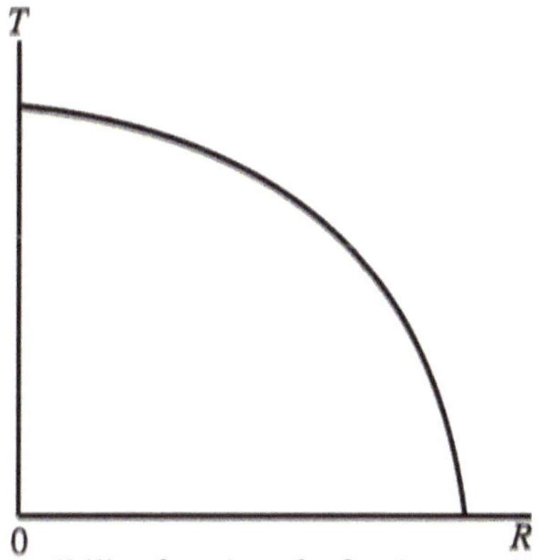

Fig. 14.7: Production possibility frontier of a fundamentalist terror organization or militia

Remember the notion of the production possibility frontier (PPF) of an economy from Economics 101, which, in a two-good context, shows the maximum amount produced of good A for any given amount produced of good B from given amounts of resources (like labor, capital, etc.) and given technologies. It is typically concave to the origin due to increasing marginal opportunity cost of one good vis-à-vis another.

Analogously, we can say that a religious-cum-terror organization produces a religion good R and terror T from the resources available to it, where resources include manpower, raw material, capital, etc. If we club together all resources into a composite, say K, which can produce either R or T, the relationship between the two production activities of the organization can be capsuled by:

$$K = F(\underset{+}{R}, \underset{+}{T}). \tag{14.19}$$

This defines the organization's PPF. The positive sign of the partials means that higher production of either R or T requires more resources, K. Hence the endowment of K remaining constant, more production of R implies less production of T and conversely. The organization's production possibilities are exhibited by the PPF drawn in Fig. 14.7.

Even though the PPF in Fig. 14.7 looks concave or bulging out similar to a "standard" PPF representing production possibilities for an economy, the reason for the concavity in the present context is special however. The complementarity between the production of religion activities and terror using the same resources amounts to what is called the ***economies of scope*** that defines a multi-product technology such that the total cost of producing multiple goods (two, in our case) jointly is less than that of producing each good separately. That is, religious activities and terror can be jointly produced with less total cost than if they were produced separately. Algebraically, it translates to

$$F(R,T) < F(R,0) + F(0,T), \tag{14.20}$$

where the left-hand side is the joint total cost of producing religion activities and terror and the right-hand side is the total cost of producing them separately. The inequality (14.20) spells the definition of economies of scope, and we assume that it holds for the religion-cum-terrorism joint production spelled in Eq. (14.19). It is the economies of scope between religion and terror, which imply increasing marginal cost of producing one activity vis-à-vis the other and thus explains the bulging out or the concavity shape of the production possibility frontier in Fig. 14.7. The algebraic proof of this exists but is beyond our scope.

Such a joint-production technology can be analytically incorporated along with the specifications of subjective valuations of the religious and terror activities to determine how much of these activities an organization would produce in equilibrium. This is something we do not however pursue here. Our purpose is to understand that *complementarity between religious and terror activities offers economies of scope, which form the basis of their joint production.*

In closing, we may note that, besides religious activities and terrorism, some fundamentalist terror organizations provide public services, engage in fund-raising activities, both quasi-legal and illegal, etc. (This includes ISIS too.) These services can be accommodated in this framework by introducing them as additional goods or services besides R and T.

14.5 Take-Aways

- Religious orthodoxy is characterized by two types of practices: prohibitions and one-time initial sacrifices.
- These practices are not necessarily idiosyncrasies. They have a rational foundation.
- Prohibitions are equivalent to a consumption tax on the secular goods.
- Prohibitions address the moral hazard problem of low participation, whereas one-time initial sacrifices serve as a screening device that blocks

the entry of low-participation types into an orthodox organization and thus solve an adverse selection problem.
- Organized religious orthodoxy can be welfare-improving.
- By virtue of practicing orthodoxy, orthodox groups become a collection of highly committed individuals with a strong communal bond.
- The causal link between orthodoxy and terrorism is that an orthodox religious group is a collection of relatively homogeneous people with coherence, bonding, and commitment who value the group activity highly. These are also the traits needed for successfully producing organized terror attacks that are inherently risky. Hence, if (mis)guided and exploited by extremist leaders, such groups may become violent terror organizations.
- A successful major terror attack is as good as its weakest link. Hence homogeneity among the members is a factor toward successful execution of terror attacks.
- A fundamentalist terror organization promotes religious orthodoxy and at the same time engages in terrorism by exploiting the economies of scope in using the resources available to it.

Questions

14.1 Differentiate between secular goods and organized religion as a local public good, i.e., a private club activity.

14.2 Explain in words how various religion-related prohibitions work like a consumption tax on secular goods and solve the moral hazard problem of participating in religion.

14.3 Various prohibitions are involuntary and hence cannot increase in an individual's welfare. Do you agree or disagree? Give reasons.

14.4 Consider Iannaccone's model of religious orthodoxy in terms of prohibitions on the consumption of secular goods. All members of the orthodox organization have same preferences and earnings, and, for simplicity, there are only two members. Each member's utility function is quasi-linear in secular goods and religion good as in (14.3). In addition, let $v_i(z_1+z_2) = a\cdot(z_1+z_2)-(z_1+z_2)^2/2$, where $a = 20$. Further, let $T = 20$, $w = \$40$ and $p = \$5$.

(a) Begin with a situation of no prohibitions. Assuming Nash equilibrium, how many hours will each member contribute to religion, what will be his/her consumption of the secular good and his/her equilibrium level of utility U_i?

(b) Consider prohibitions by the religious organization that limit the consumption of secular good by each member, s_i, to 100. How many hours will each member contribute to religion and what will be his/her equilibrium level of utility U_i? Comparing your answer to part (a), is a member better or worse off in terms of utility?

14.5 Consider two groups of potential entrants to a religious club: less committed who are rich and whose opportunity of time is higher, and, the more committed, who are poor and whose opportunity of time is lower. However, the club does not have information on who are more committed and who are less. Compared to a secular club, each entrant will gain additional utility, which is worth \$100 and lose *two* hours of work by joining an orthodox club. Suppose the hourly wage earnings of the less committed and the more committed are, respectively, \$30 and \$20 per hour.
(a) What (minimum) initiation fee the orthodox club may charge so that the less committed group will not join the orthodox religious club but the more committed group will? Explain the steps toward arriving your answer.
(b) Because of adverse economic conditions, the wage earnings of both types fall by 20%. What will be the new initiation fee? Also explain your answer intuitively.

Chapter 15

Root, Breeding, and Propagative Causes of Terrorism

15.1 Introduction

This is the final, "So What" chapter. At the end of the day, what are the *data-based* "deep" causes of terrorism, so that we properly identify the underlying factors and hopefully deal with the problem successfully? In Chap. 1, Sect. 1.15, we had grouped fundamental causes of terrorism into three categories: (1) root, (2) breeding-ground, and (3) propagative.

"What are the root causes of terrorism?" became a central question immediately after the *9/11* attacks. The question has been wrestled by scholars in economics, political science, and other social sciences. The studies on this are based upon opinion polls, profiles of terrorists, correlates of terror attacks with surrounding geopolitical issues, recovery of data on recruits from the records of ISIS as well as cross-region and cross-country data.

The commonly analyzed root causes of terrorism include foreign occupation, poverty and state of the economy, lack of educational opportunities, and lack of political and religious freedom. As economists, it is natural to think that economic and educational deprivation is expected to drive young folks to terrorism. Soon after the *9/11* attacks, George W. Bush said that "We fight against poverty"...."because hope is an answer to terror." He was referring to the role of poverty in attracting young people to acts of terror. The First Lady Laura Bush said in 2002 that "A lasting victory in the war against terror depends on educating the world's children because educated children are much more likely to embrace the values that defeat terror."[1]

---

[1] James Wolfensohn, former President of World Bank, said, "The war on terrorism will not be won until we have come to grips with the problem of poverty and thus the sources of discontent." Richard Armitage, the deputy secretary of state from 2001 to 2005 said the following in *New York Times* on Pakistan's problem with terrorism: "General Musharraf has shown that he understands the seriousness of dealing with the *root* cause of extremism, making real efforts to improve economic and educational opportunities." Within the Muslim community, a distinguished group of 39 imams and ulama (religious leaders and scholars) said in reference to the terror attacks in London "The tragedy of 7th July 2005 demands that all of us... confront together the problems of Islamophobia, racism, unemployment, economic deprivation and social exclusion—factors that may be alienating our children and driving them toward the path of anger and desperation." The Nobel laureate

S. P. Das, *Economics of Terrorism and Counter-Terrorism Measures*,
https://doi.org/10.1007/978-3-030-96577-8_15

It is also not difficult to imagine that the inability to freely express political opinion and practice one's religion, as long as they do not interfere with security, social harmony, or confront individual justice, is likely to push people to organized violence including terrorism.

This chapter begins with foreign occupation as a causal factor (in Sect. 15.2). Research by Robert Pape and James Feldman (see below) is strongly indicative that suicide terrorism in particular is prompted by foreign occupation. They advance as the strategy of "off-shore balancing" to counter suicide terrorism. This is explained in Sect. 15.2. The evidence on how economic factors like poverty, unemployment, per-capita income, and education are related to terrorism is laid out in Sect. 15.3. The results are based on interviews, opinion polls as well as econometric analysis. Section 15.3 includes, among other studies, econometric micro studies on two particular terrorist organizations, namely, Hezbollah and ISIS. The link between political and civil rights on one hand and terrorism on the other is explored in Sect. 15.4. Economic inequality as a causal factor of terrorism is studied in Sect. 15.5. Section 15.6 discusses the evidence of minority discrimination and Islamophobia as factors behind propensity of individuals to lean toward fundamentalism and terrorism. Section 15.7 outlines evidence showing that pre-existing conflicts are a contributing factor toward terrorism. Finally, in Sect. 15.8 we evaluate whether globalization has contributed significantly to transnational terrorism.

15.2 Foreign Occupation and Suicide Terrorism

What do we mean by foreign occupation being a root cause of terrorism? In their study, Pape and Feldman (2010) discovered a pattern that suicide attacks have occurred where and when foreign occupation was present *in the sense of foreign troops being deployed on the ground.* For instance, suicide attacks in Iraq started only after the American and allied troops marched into the country in 2003.

The logic is that the "physical" presence of foreign troops provokes a strong nationalist sentiment. Domestic residents fear losing their ability to "perpetuate [their] political, social, economic and religious institutions" (Collard-Wexler et al., 2013) and chart their own destiny so to speak. This motivates suicide attacks as a last resort to force out foreign forces off the home soil. Pape and Feldman also emphasized that it is not the presence of foreign troops of "any" country but those of *liberal democracies* like the USA and countries in Europe that invite suicide terrorism. It is because these countries are typically averse to casualties and therefore more coercible toward withdrawing troops, compared to troops from autocratic regimes. Occupation of Afghanistan by the former Soviet Union is a classic example of the latter. Additionally, the militants know that liberal democracies are constrained to honor human rights and public opinion and thus would refrain themselves from mounting severe reprisals lest they should cause massive collateral damage and loss

---

Mohammad Yunus of Bangladesh said in 2006 it was essential to put "resources into improving the lives of the poor people" to end the root cause of terrorism.

of international goodwill. In the words of Robert Pope, terror groups use suicide attacks because they work.

Pape and Feldman also argued importantly that religious differences between the occupier and the occupied is a factor in the sense that such differences are utilized to demonize the occupiers in the name of religion and glorify death by suicide attack as martyrdom. Thus, religious radicalism becomes an appealing and effective means to an end, not the cause of terrorism per se. In Chap. 14 we have studied how terrorism can be rallied around people who have embraced religious orthodoxy.

15.2.1 Evidence by Pape, and Pape and Feldman

Pape (2005) cited a series of international instances mostly in the pre-*9/11* era to support his foreign occupation hypothesis, whereas Pape and Feldman (2010) analyzed both pre- and post-*9/11* period up to the end of 2009. Examples as well as simple yet compelling data analysis are presented on a country-by-country or region-by-region basis focusing on prominent terrorist organizations involved. Limited formal statistical/econometric analysis is contained in Pape (2005).

Foreign occupation is broadly interpreted to include direct occupation (like USA in Afghanistan and Iraq), uprising of a major minority group against a majority government (e.g., Tamils in Sri Lanka) as well as pressure by a foreign democracy like the USA to reorient another country's military away from its own strategist interest. The last category is termed as *indirect occupation* with Pakistan being the reference country.[2]

Indeed, the highest number of suicide attacks in the pre-*9/11* period was perpetrated by LTTE, a secular Hindu Marxist-Leninist terrorist group, aiming for separate homeland or at least more autonomy within Sri Lanka, which is dominated by the native Sinhalese population. Figure 15.1 graphs the number of suicide attacks in various countries from 1981 to 2019. The top-left diagram depicts Sri Lanka where LTTE is the only active group that carried out suicide attacks. We see that these attacks continued till almost LTTE's surrender to the Sri Lankan forces in 2009.[3]

Hezbollah is credited with the first ever major suicide attack. In 1983 a one-person suicide mission killed 241 US service men in a marine barrack in Beirut. The US Marines were there as a part of a multinational peacekeeping force. Four months later, the US forces left Lebanon almost completely. From hindsight, Pape argues, it was a huge tactical error, because it established suicide terrorism as an effective means to an end.[4] The principal cause of suicide terrorism in Lebanon was foreign military occupation.[5] In 1986, Israel scaled down its military presence in

[2] As noted by Pape and Feldman (2010), following the American occupation of Afghanistan starting in 2001, Pakistan was pressured to shift its strategic focus away from India to the Western front bordering Afghanistan. This created a resentment against the USA and is interpreted as indirect occupation. In general, Pape broadly defines occupation as "the exertion of political control over territory by an outside group."

[3] It is interesting that LTTE learnt the "art" of suicide terrorism from Hezbollah.

[4] Earlier to this, Israel invaded southern Lebanon in June 1982 with 78,000 soldiers and 3000 tanks and army vehicles and Hezbollah was born a month later.

[5] According to Hezbollah's written communications, its "great and necessary objectives" were "to put an end to foreign occupation and to adopt a regime freely wanted by the people of Lebanon"

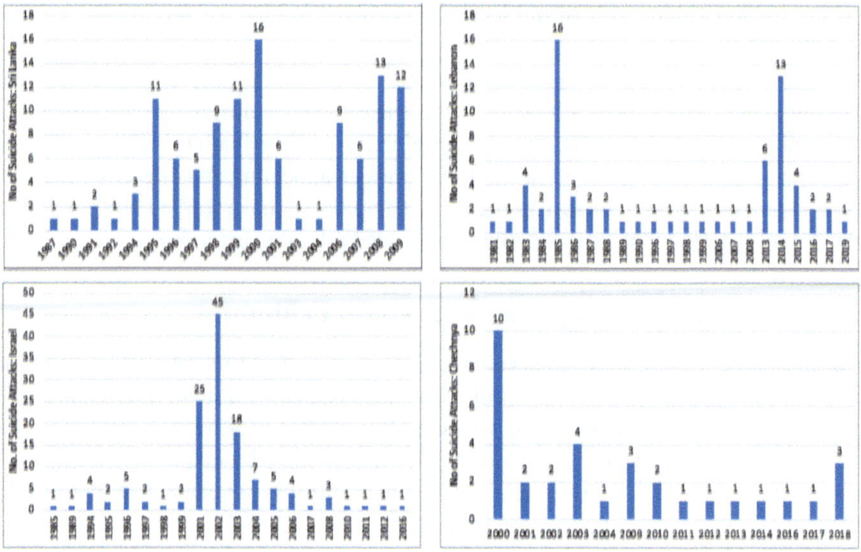

Fig. 15.1: Suicide attacks in selected countries: 1981–2019.
Source: GTD

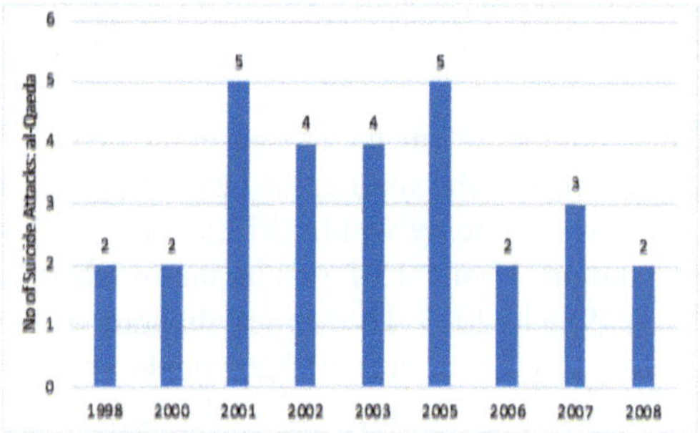

Fig. 15.2: Al-Qaeda attacks: 1998–2008.
Source: GTD

southern Lebanon (and withdrew its troops entirely from Lebanon in 2000). After the mid-1980s, the outside military presence in Lebanon has been rather very limited and we see from Fig. 15.1 that the suicide attacks in Lebanon became somewhat less incident after the mid-1980s. In Lebanon, Hezbollah is the main perpetrator of suicide attacks in the 1980s. Notice the resurgence of suicide attacks in Lebanon since 2013. These attacks are however mostly committed by ISIS, not Hezbollah, and they coincide with the rise and fall of ISIS—very different in nature from the situation in the 1980s.

and "to expel the Americans, the French and their allies definitely from Lebanon, putting an end to any colonialist entity on our land."

Consider the Palestine–Israel conflict and Palestinian suicide terrorism against Israel. Notice from Fig. 15.1 that Israel began to face discernible suicide terrorism in the 1990s, which escalated dramatically between 2001 and 2003 (after which it declined gradually). Pape's rationale for suicide terrorism in Israel in the 1990s is that the "ordinary" Palestinian violence against Israel ended with the Oslo Accord signed between Israel and the PLO, according to which Israel granted concessions. This encouraged suicide terrorism aimed at coercing Israel to roll back its occupation policies. Suicide attacks in Israel became particularly frequent and severe during the Second Intifada (between 2000 and 2005), also called the Al-Aqsa Intifada. It was triggered by the perceived failure of the Oslo peace process as a result of the Camp David negotiations in August 2000. Abdel Karim, a leader of the al-Aqsa Martyrs Brigades, said that the goal of his group was "to increase losses in Israel to a point at which the Israeli public would demand a withdrawal from the West Bank and Gaza Strip." The al-Aqsa Intifada came to an end with Israel's unilateral disengagement plan, announced by Ariel Sharon in 2003.[6] The relative calm after 2005/2006 coincided with the Israeli disengagement from Gaza and large parts of the West Bank.

Chechnya started to experience suicide terrorism in 2000, one year prior to the *9/11* attacks. This was also the year that witnessed the largest number of suicide attacks. It began on July 7, 2000, approximately six months after the beginning of the Second Russo-Chechen War, in response to Russian occupation and counter-terrorism operations. You may refer to Chap. 2 and find that Chechnya's conflict with Russia has a long history. But suicide attacks did not occur until the brutal Russian occupation of 2000.[7] Suicide attacks became relatively insignificant since 2010, which coincided with the end of the Second Chechen War in 2009 that brought Ramzan Kadyrov to power.[8,9]

A principal objective of Osama bin Laden was the expulsion of American troops from the Persian Gulf and a reduction of Washington's power and influence in the region, especially in Saudi Arabia. During the period around Kuwait war in 1991, the size of American troops in Persian Gulf exceeded 300,000. It declined sharply to less than 2000 immediately after the war but steadily increased throughout the late 1990s, reaching over 13,000 in 2000 and over 12,000 in 2001 (Pape, 2005). This build-up roughly matches with the heydays of al-Qaeda. Observe in Fig. 15.2 that

[6] According to Sharon, "It is not in our interest to govern you. We will not remain in all the places where we are today."

[7] In December 2003, Chechnya's rebel commander, Abu al-Walid al-Ghamidi, said, "As you have seen and noticed, most of the suicide attacks were carried out by women ... These women, particularly the wives of the mujahedin who were martyred, are being threatened in their homes, their honour and everything are being threatened. They do not accept being humiliated and living under occupation."

[8] Although Kadyrov is an avid supporter of Putin and Kremlin, he is highly autocratic and a supporter of Sharia law.

[9] As a small note, the USA established an airbase in Uzbekistan in 2001, which housed 1500 troops. As a country with no previous history of suicide attacks, it experienced four such attacks three years later (in 2004).

the number of suicide attacks by al-Qaeda was not large, but they were generally spectacular in terms of high-value and high-profile targets.

15.2.1.1 Major Suicide-Attack-Afflicted Nations After *9/11*

Suicide terrorism in the post *9/11* era is blatantly visible in Afghanistan, Pakistan, Iraq, and Somalia. This is illustrated in Fig. 15.3. Afghanistan is the best post-*9/11* evidence supporting Pape's theory. Suicide terrorism began mildly in 2002 and exploded in the 2010s. Although we see a decline since 2014, it is not close to the early 2000s. We also see how it correlates with the size of allied troops over the period 2001–2018 (top right). A point to note is that the top-right chart indicates the annual numbers, not the *persistence* of foreign occupation through decades. We must not lose sight that in Afghanistan Russian troops were physically present from 1979 to 1989 and the US and the applied forces were on the ground from 2001 onward till August 2021. In view of this long period of foreign occupation it is not surprising that the number of suicide attacks remained high even in the latter half of 2010s when the size of the allied forces was small compared to earlier years.

Iraq is another prominent post-*9/11* example that fits Pape's theory. Its experience is somewhat similar to Afghanistan. Before 2003, there was only one recorded incident of suicide attack. But after the American and allied troops marched in, it was a different story. There were far more suicide attacks in Iraq than in Afghanistan. One should discern that while Muslim Shi'ites constitute about 2/3rd of the population, most suicide attacks are perpetrated by Sunni groups, as they felt most threatened by American occupation. It is remarkable that Iraq witnessed a drastic decline in suicide attacks in subsequent years.

We have already noted how suicide attacks in Pakistan are also consistent with Paper's theory if we interpret the USA's pressure on Pakistan as indirect occupation. Pakistani Taliban spokesman Maulvi Umar once called the US government and the NATO alliance "the real enemy" and said that once international forces withdrew from Afghanistan, "the mujahideen would return to their homes." But, if Western forces fail to withdraw, the Tehreek-i-Taliban Pakistan would launch suicide terrorism.

Finally, Somalia is another country where suicide terrorism has a strong presence, although it is not as familiar to us as Afghanistan, Pakistan, or Iraq. With the help of US forces, the army of Ethiopia attacked Somalia in 2006, and this is when the country started to witness suicide attacks. Since then, it became increasingly worse till 2017. The US troops in Somalia have trained Somalian military and conducted air strikes to contain al-Shabaab.. In his last days in office in the late 2020, President Trump ordered the withdrawal of American troops (about 700) from Somalia. However, Horton (2020) cites Pentagon saying while troops are out of Somalia, "cross-border operations" in Somalia will continue.

According to Pape and Feldman, a vast majority of suicide attacks is explained by military occupation.

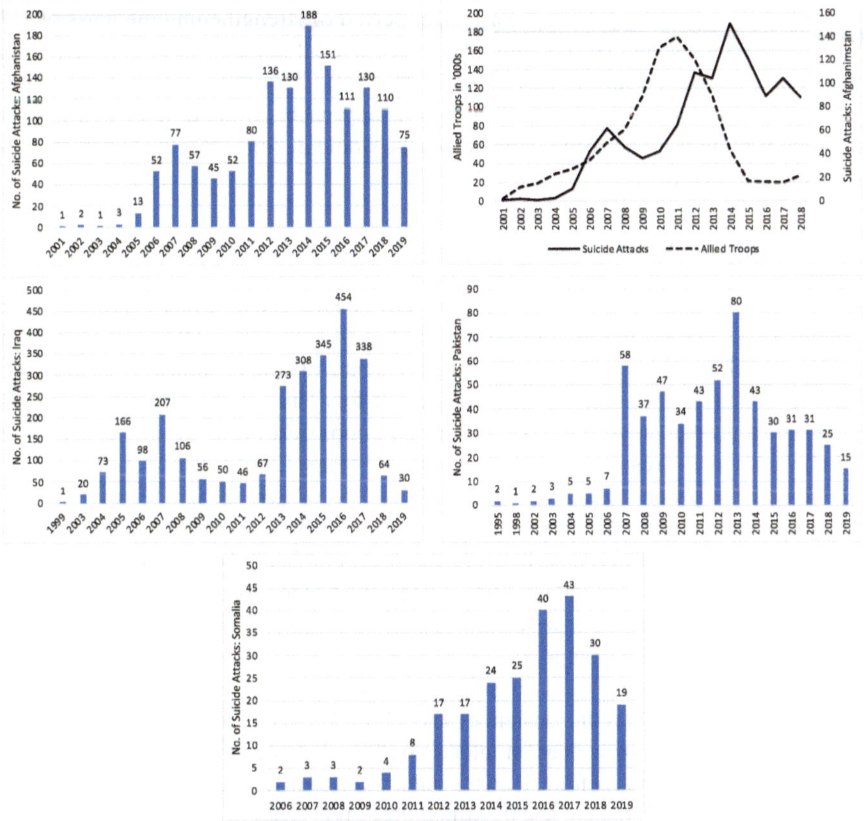

Fig. 15.3: Suicide attacks in Afghanistan, Pakistan, Iraq, and Somalia.
Source: GTD

15.2.2 Policy of Off-Shore Balancing

Based on case-study evidence, Pape and Feldman have proposed a fundamental counter-terror strategy: ***off-shore balancing***, meaning a strategy of removing American troops from the Eurasian land mass and maintaining "over the horizon" marine and naval forces for occasional intervention to maintain the supply of oil. In other words, Pape and Feldman recommend desisting from massive boots on the ground while maintaining the capability of selective intervention being launched from neighboring space.

Importantly also, the authors recommend offshore balancing being supplemented by a safeguard of local ways of life by "providing political, economic and military wherewithal."

It is striking that the US defense and military establishment has taken heed of Pape's analysis and recommendation. The massive pull-back of American forces from Afghanistan and Iraq by the Obama administration is consistent with the offshore balancing strategy. Except for a brief period of strengthening the mass of US forces in Afghanistan, Trump administration's overall strategy in Afghanistan and Iraq was consistent with off-shore balancing. The total withdrawal of forces under Biden administration is a continuation of this approach. At the time of writing this chapter, it remains to be seen if suicide attacks would decline after the exit of the US and allied troops in 2021.

15.2.3 Pape's Statistical Test

There is no straightforward way of case-study-based cause–effect evidence to be framed in a standard regression framework. For instance, the same level of foreign occupational forces may lead to a varying incidence of suicide attacks over time due to many other factors that are hard to account for. Thus, if the number of suicide attacks is regressed against the size of foreign troops over the same period that has a small variance, the results are bound to be poor.[10] Pape (2005) tested a more focused version of the theory, entitled, *nationalist theory*, which recognizes that suicide attacks against foreign occupation are more effectively motivated and organized by exploiting religious differences between the "occupier" and the "occupied." Further, any pre-existence of a general rebellion against the occupation or a regime supported by a foreign democracy is more conducive to the choice of suicide attack as a tactic of last resort to effect a change.

Accordingly, Pape (2005) considered two independent variables, existence of religious differences and the existence of rebellion between the foreign occupier and the local community, as well as an interaction term between them.[11] The nationalist theory predicts that the coefficient on the interaction term be positive (and statistically significant). Pape's statistical test identified fifty-eight cases of foreign occupation by democratic states. The dependent variable is a dummy, equal to 1 for these nine cases and zero otherwise. Suicide attacks occurred in nine out of the fifty-eight cases.[12] Logit regression is used, where the right-hand variables included an indicator of religious difference, an indicator of prior rebellion, *and* an interaction term between the two.[13]

The results showed that religious differences and prior rebellion were both significant at the 5% level, whereas the interaction term was significant at the 0.1%

---

[10] As mentioned earlier, Pape and Feldman (2010), which contains a more comprehensive case-study evidence over time and regions than Pape (2005), did not present any statistical test of the foreign-occupation-by-a-democracy theory.

[11] Rebellion is defined as any organized resistance by militant group beyond political protests or other forms of nonviolent civil disobedience.

[12] Of the fifty-eight data points, fourteen were marked by rebellion and religious differences, nine associated with rebellion but no religious difference, fifteen cases where there was no rebellion but religious difference and the remaining twenty cases having no rebellion or religious difference. Seven of nine suicide terrorism occurred among the fourteen cases that had rebellion and religious differences, one of nine associated with rebellion but no religious difference and the remaining one was associated with no rebellion but religious difference.

[13] The concepts of logit regression, dummy variable, and the interaction terms are in the General Appendix B, Sects. B.4.2, B.4.1, and B.6, respectively.

level, demonstrating that the interaction of religious difference and prior rebellion has a clear effect beyond the independent effect of each, thus supporting the nationalist theory.[14]

15.2.4 Subsequent Tests: Hardening Theory

Pape's thesis and his statistical work have been criticized. The notion of indirect foreign occupation has been questioned. If we focus on explicit foreign occupation by democracies as an explanation, then suicide terrorism in Pakistan and Yemen are counter-examples. Scholars have taken issue with Pape's claim that al-Qaeda's principal objective was the removal of US occupying forces from the Arabian Peninsula since it is unclear that the USA's presence in the region should be conceptualized as occupation. Where suicide attacks did occur in the context of occupations such as in Iraq or Afghanistan, they targeted co-nationals as often as foreigners. A dataset with fifty-eight observations is rather small; hence, any results based on them are likely to be unreliable.[15]

Using a larger dataset including both suicide and other forms of terror attacks, Piazza (2008) does *not* find supporting evidence of foreign occupation by democratic states in particular being a significant factor in explaining suicide terrorism. But foreign occupation in general has a significant explanatory power, thus partially supporting Pape's theory.[16]

A more definitive empirical work testing Pape's theory of suicide terrorism being linked to foreign occupation is due to Collard-Wexler et al. (2013), who differentiated between foreign occupation and domestic occupation. The former refers to a situation where one country invades and occupies another, while domestic occupation describes a situation where a minority group perceives itself as under occupation and seeks autonomy or independence. The distinction is important because foreign and domestic occupations require different policy responses.

The authors went one step further and proposed a *hardening theory*, emphasizing that hard-to-penetrate targets are more likely to encourage suicide attacks. This is

---

[14] The estimation correctly predicts forty-eight out of fifty-eight cases. All seven cases of suicide terrorism out of fourteen, which had both rebellion and religious difference are predicted by the estimated equation. The two positive cases of suicide terrorism campaigns that are not predicted by the interaction of the independent variables are the Kurdistan Workers' Party (PKK) in Turkey and al-Qaeda.

[15] Pape's work has also been criticized on methodological grounds. Since all fifty-eight cases are democratic occupiers—and there are no cases where occupation and democracy can take different values—the regression exercise cannot test whether the occupier being a democracy is a factor: this is a selection bias (see General Appendix B, Sect. B.5.3).

[16] His study examines the effect of foreign occupation as well as supply-side factors on suicide terrorism. These factors include, among others, how democratic a country is, where suicide terrorism occurs. The hypothesis is that the more democratic is a country, the more opportunities and platforms are available for venting grievances and hence the less will be the incentive to engage in extreme forms of violence like suicide attacks. The dependent variable is a dummy taking value one for a suicide attack and zero for other forms of attacks. Logit regression models are used on a database of 4660 incidents of terrorism over the period 1998–2005. The data source is RAND-MIPT (see Chap. 3, Sect. 3.2), which includes both domestic and transnational terror incidents.

relevant for analyzing foreign and domestic occupation, because foreign and domestic occupations generally involve different degrees of hardening. Generally speaking, the bases and camps housing foreign forces are heavily fortified, while domestic institutions and infrastructure are not fortified as much. Details of the authors' econometric estimation are outlined in chapter Appendix 15.A.

The principal findings of Collard-Wexler et al. (2013) are that the coefficients on foreign occupation and the measure of foreign-target hardening are significant predictors of suicide attacks, whereas domestic occupation does not exert any significant impact.[17] In sum,

Is That So? 15.1: Foreign Occupation and Suicide Terrorism

Foreign occupation, not indirect occupation/influence or domestic occupation, is a significant predictor of suicide terrorism.

15.3 Poverty, Unemployment, Economic Well-Being, and Education

Pape noted that suicide terrorism has occurred in countries, many of which are not very poor. This was to buttress his point that foreign occupation was the overriding factor, not poverty.

However, it is natural to think of the role of economic factors like poverty and lack of economic opportunities, well-being, and education in the rise of terrorism. This is similar to the role of these factors in explaining crimes. The economic theory of crime and punishment posits normal gainful legal economic activities and gainful illegal activities like crime as economic choices. Taking into considerations the risks and payoffs involved in illegal activities and comparing them to payoff from legal activities, a rational individual would allocate time to illegal activities, if at all. If economic conditions worsen, the relative payoff from crime increases and we would expect to see more crimes. The same applies to engaging in terror activities.

However, the earlier pre-*9/11* literature on terrorism viewed, on the whole, that these factors are *not* important.[18] Furthermore, recall from Chap. 3 that the list of countries seriously affected by terrorism starkly differs between the pre-*9/11* era and the post-*9/11* era: compare Fig. 3.12 with Fig. 3.13. Two relatively developed countries, namely, the U.K. and Spain, figure prominently in the pre-*9/11* era, but

[17] According to one set of regression, all else the same, foreign occupation leads, on average, to six to seven additional suicide terror attacks per year and a unit increase in armored vehicles (per 100 soldiers) possessed by the occupier is associated with one to two additional suicide attacks per year.

[18] As noted by Krueger and Malečková (2002), Taylor (1988) argued that "neither social background, educational opportunity or attainment seem to be particularly associated with terrorism." The Library of Congress Report "The Sociology and Psychology of Terrorism: Who Becomes a Terrorist and Why," which was prepared for CIA in 1999 (and which actually anticipated *9/11* type attacks by al-Qaeda) observed that "terrorists in general have more average education."

there are no developed countries facing serious problems in the post-*9/11* period. So we should expect the role of per-capita income on terrorism to be different between the two eras.[19]

Our focus below will be to understand the role of economic factors in the post-*9/11* years.

15.3.1 Case Studies and Opinion Polls

In-depth, early post-*9/11* studies on the role of economic well-being and education in suicide terrorism were led by Alan Krueger and his coauthor (Krueger & Malečková (2002; 2003) and Krueger (2003, 2007)) as well as Berrebi (2007). Their general findings are similar. Poverty, low per-capita income, or lack of education are *not* significant predictors of terrorism. In what follows we review the methodology and conclusions reached in different contexts.

15.3.1.1 *Gus Emunim*: An Israeli Jewish Underground Group

This was the leading terror group in Israel in the late 1970s and early 1980s that targeted Palestinians. The ideological outlook of Gus Emunim was a mix of being messianic, theocratic, and right-wing. It attempted to kill Palestinian mayors of the West Bank and blow up the Dome of the Rock mosque, killed 23 Palestinians, and injured nearly 200 of them. Krueger and Malečková analyzed the profile of 27 members of this group, many of whom were professionals like engineers, teachers, etc. One was a combat pilot. Three of the members of Gus Emunim, who were convicted of murder, were well educated as well as religious. Obviously, poverty or lack of education did not drive the members of this group to terrorism.

15.3.1.2 Nasra Hassan's Interview-Based Study of Palestinian Militants

In 2001 Nasra Hassan, a U.N. relief worker in West Bank and Gaza, published an insightful article in *New Yorker*, in which she described her interview with 250 militants involved in the Palestinian cause in the late 1990s and their associates including failed suicide bombers, the families of decreased bombers, and those who trained and prepared suicide bombers for their missions. She found none were uneducated, abjectly poor, simple minded, or depressed. In fact, many were middle class, and some held high paying jobs. Two were sons of millionaires. One Hamas leader told her, "Our biggest problem is the hordes of young men who beat on our doors, clamoring to be sent on suicide missions. It is difficult to select only a few." A senior member of the al-Aqsa Martyrs Brigades told Nasra Hassan that "The selection process is complicated by the fact that so many wish to embark on this journey of honor. When one is selected, countless others are disappointed."

[19] For example, one of the findings of Blomberg et al. (2004b), who analyze the effect of the state of the economy on terrorism during 1968–1991, is that high-income and democratic countries tend to be afflicted by terrorism more than relatively low-income or non-democratic countries.

15.3.1.3 Opinion Polls Among Palestinians by Palestinian Center for Policy and Survey Research (PCPSR)

An independent non-profit research organization in Ramallah (West Bank), PCPSR, conducts policy analysis and economic research in the West Bank and Gaza. In December 2001 it conducted a public opinion poll (through personal interviews) of 1357 Palestinians, eighteen years or older, in West Bank and Gaza, covering topics including the participants' views toward *9/11* attacks, their support for Israel–Palestinian peace agreement, and their opinions about armed attacks against Israel.[20] Although public opinion polls are subject to multiple interpretations, they can provide indirect information about which segments of the population support terrorist or military activities.

The poll results are revealing. There was wide support for armed attacks against Israeli targets—although support in an opinion poll and actual or active support for such attacks are quite different.[21]

The role of poverty and education can be seen from the responses to one of the many questions illustrated in Fig. 15.4. The question is on the opinion toward armed attacks against Israelis among people of different professions and educational attainment levels. As shown in panel (a), the percentage of those who supported or strongly supported is actually the lowest for the group of the unemployed compared to students; laborers, craftsmen, and employees; housewives; and merchants, farmers or professionals. This is an indication that adverse economic conditions may not be a strong incentive for participating in terror activities. Panel (b) shows that support for attacks was stronger among the more educated groups.

15.3.1.4 Profiles of Palestinian Militants

Berrebi (2007) constructed a sample out of biographies of 285 *shahids* (those who have lost their lives for a cause) that were published in the magazines of Hamas, Palestinian Islamic Jihad, and the Palestinian National Authority during the period 1987–2002, in which the majority of the terrorist acts were committed between 2000 and 2002.[22] Figure 15.5 presents some of his results. It compares the percentage of poor and the percentage of different level of education among the suicide bombers vis-à-vis those of the Palestinian population.[23] Observe that only 13% of suicide bombers were poor as opposed to 32% in the population, and suicide bombers were more educated, on average, compared to the population average.[24]

[20] The results of these polls were provided in a tabular form to Krueger and Malečková.

[21] Majority believed that armed attacks against Israel yielded more for Palestinian rights than did negotiations. They did not consider suicide attacks as terrorist activities. Even 53.1% did not think *9/11* events in the USA as terrorist attacks and many even doubted Bin Laden's role in the *9/11* attacks.

[22] See Chap. 2, Sect. 2.8.13 for a description of the Palestinian Islamic Jihad.

[23] A person is considered poor if the wages earned are less than 18% of the average wage earned in Israel.

[24] The same results were confirmed by logit regression, where the dependent variable is a dummy, equal to one if the individual participated in the Hamas or PIJ terrorist activities and zero otherwise

15.3.1.5 Profiles of Hezbollah Militants

Hezbollah used to have a website and publish a Newsletter, *Al-Ahd*. (It is unclear whether the website and the Newsletter are operative currently.) It is interesting that Eli Hurvitz of Tel Aviv University was able to assemble biographies of 129 decreased Hezbollah militants that were published in *Al-Ahd*, which was obtained subsequently by Krueger and Malečková. These militants died in action mostly in the

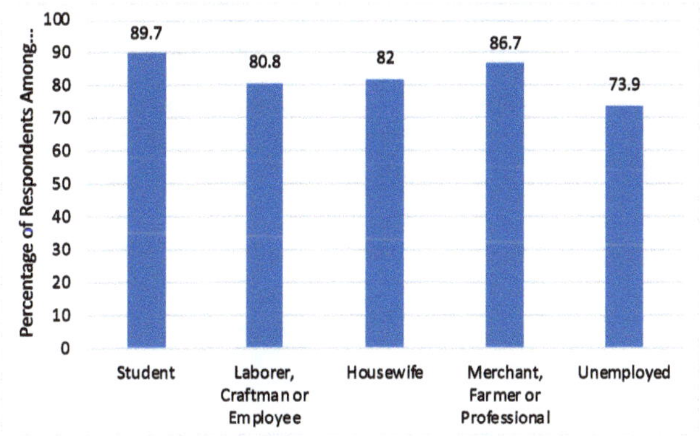

(a)

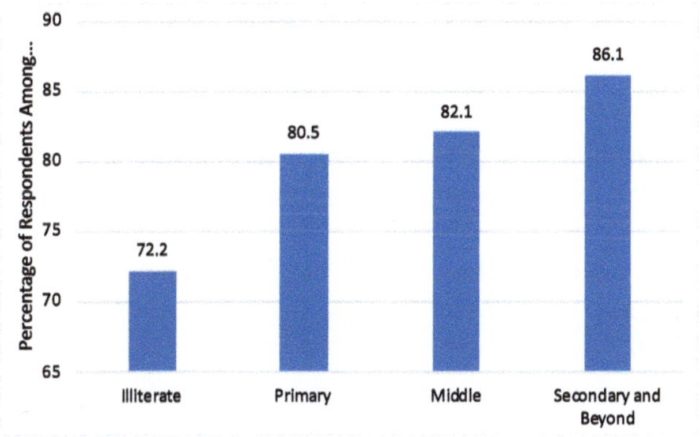

(b)

Fig. 15.4: Results of opinion poll among Palestinians asking if they support armed attacks on Israeli targets.
The question is: Concerning armed attacks against Israeli targets, I "support or strongly support" [as opposed to "Oppose or Strongly Oppose" and "No Opinion"].
(**a**) According to occupation. (**b**) According to the level of education.
Source: Krueger and Malečková (2003)

---

and the independent variables included the age, the martial status, and the region of residence (West Bank or Gaza), among others.

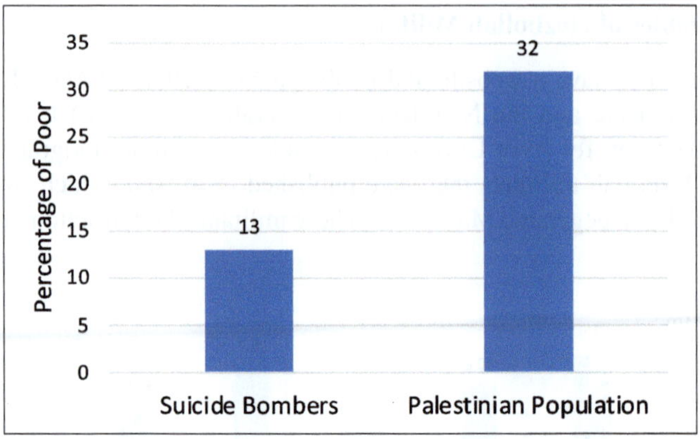

(a)

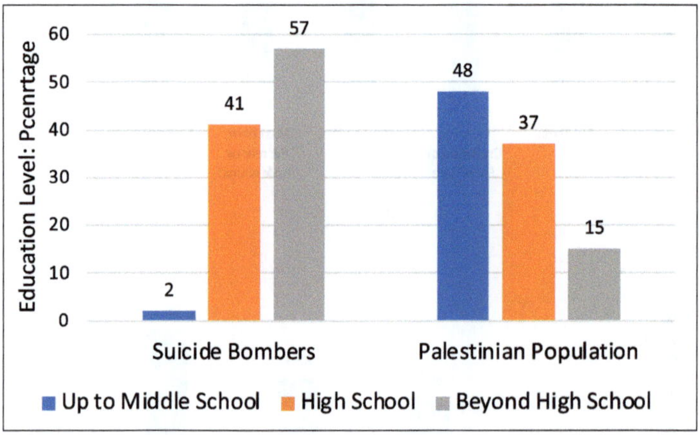

(b)

Fig. 15.5: Palestinian suicide bombers versus Palestinian population. (**a**) Poverty. (**b**) Levels of education.
Source: Berrebi (2007)

late 1980s, some while fighting, some in suicide attacks, and some while planting booby traps. Their profiles were compared with those of a random sample of 121,000 young people in the Lebanese population, which were obtained from the Lebanese Population and Housing Survey conducted in 1996. This is illustrated in Fig. 15.6.[25]

Notice that the poverty rate is less among the decreased militants than among the Lebanese population. There were no illiterates among the militants as opposed to 6% of illiterate in the population. Overall, the decreased militants were more educated on average, compared to the Lebanese population.

[25] Depending on the information available, the sample size of Hezbollah militants was 50 for poverty and 78 for education.

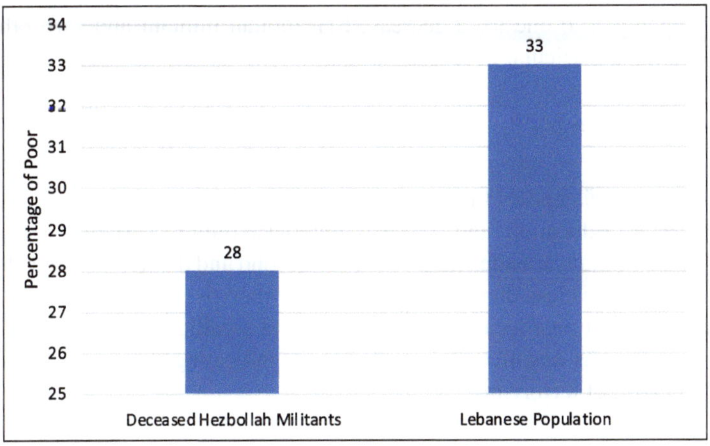

(a)

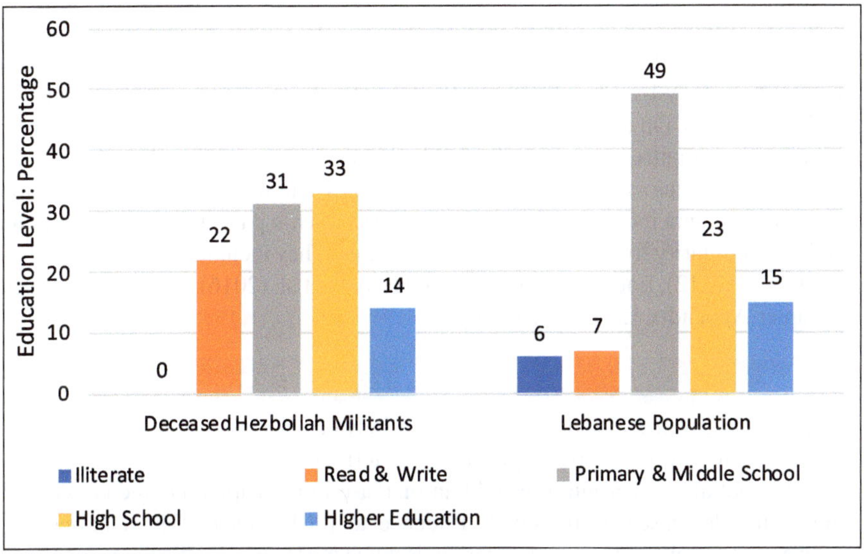

(b)

Fig. 15.6: Decreased Hezbollah militants versus Lebanese population. (**a**) Poverty. (**b**) Level of education.
Source: Krueger and Malečková (2003)

15.3.2 Regression-Based Studies

Regression-based studies show mixed effects of poverty or per-capita income on terrorism. Krueger and Malečková (2003) combined the data on decreased militants with the Lebanon's Population and Housing Survey (PHS) data and ran a logit regression (see General Appendix B, Sect. B.4.2), where the dependent variable (Y_i)

is a dummy, equal to one for a decreased Hezbollah militant and zero otherwise, with i denoting a particular deceased militant.[26] The regression equation was

$$Y_i = a + b_1 \cdot \text{Education}_i + b_2 \cdot \text{Poverty}_i + \boldsymbol{\beta} \mathbf{Z}_i + u_i, \tag{15.1}$$

where the vector **Z** denotes the set of control variables (see Eq. (B.14) in General Appendix B).[27] "Education" and "Poverty" entered as dummy variables. "Education" equals 1 if the militant attended high school or beyond and 0 otherwise and "Poverty" equals 1 if income is less than a threshold and 0 otherwise.

The coefficient on education was positive and significant statistically, whereas that on poverty was negative and insignificant, indicating that poverty was *not* a significant cause of terrorism.[28]

15.3.2.1 Non-Linear Relation

However, these studies as well as those covering the pre-*9/11* era did not a priori allow the existence of a non-linear relation between per-capita income and terrorism. It is intuitive that if the population is very poor, they would be pre-occupied with earning their daily livelihood and not be thinking about achieving any political or ideological goals. On the other side of the spectrum, the populations of the high per-capita income countries are generally fulfilled in their economic needs and would be averse to engage in organized violence. This suggests an inverted U-shaped relation between per-capita income and terrorism. Indeed, such a pattern has emerged as an empirical regularity from various post-*9/11* studies. They include Lai (2007), Enders and Hoover (2012), Enders et al. (2016), and Enders et al. (2016), which are outlined in chapter Appendix 15.B. In summary,

Is That So? 15.2: Per-Capita Income (Poverty) and Terrorism

There is an inverse U-shaped relationship between per-capita income and terrorism: at low levels of per-capita income, terrorism increases with per-capita income, but after a certain threshold an increase in per-capita income is associated with a decrease in terrorism. As Enders et al. (2016) noted, "The relationship between per-capita income and terrorism is much more nuanced than presupposed by political leaders, the media and researchers."

---

[26] Because the data on Hezbollah fighters is not random, the data from the two sources had to be weighted appropriately, so that the estimates are statistically consistent.

[27] The control variables included age of a militant and regional dummies representing whether or not the militant hailed from Beirut and whether or not he is from South Lebanon.

[28] In their meta-study that used 13.4 million different regressions with various combinations of 65 explanatory variables considered in 43 studies over various periods between 1980s and 2000s, Gassebner and Luechinger (2011) also did not find any statistically significant link between per-capita income and terrorism.

15.3.3 Unemployment, Transport Costs, and Recruitment

Interestingly, at some time in the mid-2010s, ISIS's personnel records reached the hands of a number of news outlets including Syria's Zaman al Wasl (who in turn shared the data with the World Bank), Britain's Sky News, and NBC News in the USA—presumably from an ISIS (Daesh) defector.[29] The data contains information on 3965 foreign recruits from 59 countries, including their age, education, country of residence, and country of citizenship. Dodwell et al. (2016) corroborate 98% of the records with data maintained by the US Department of Defense and estimate that this data accounts for approximately 30% of the total number of foreign recruits who entered Syria between early 2013 and late 2014.

Using this unique data, Brockmeyer et al. (2018) have studied how economic opportunities in different countries and migration costs to Syria or Iraq interacted in explaining the spatial pattern of foreign participation in transnational terrorist organizations like ISIS. Country-wise unemployment rate representing economic opportunity costs is the main explanatory variable. The core question posed by Brockmeyer et al. (2018) is how are the number of Daesh recruits of different education levels from individual countries explained by unemployment rate faced by workers in the same country with similar level of education? Their estimated equation is

$$\ln N_{ie} = a + b_1 U_{ie} + b_2 (U_{ie} \times D_i) + \boldsymbol{\beta} \mathbf{Z} + u_{ie}, \tag{15.2}$$

where N_{ie} is the number of Daesh recruits from country i with education level e and U_{ie} is the rate of unemployment in country i among those having an education level e. Education level is classified into primary, tertiary, and secondary. The variable D_i is the distance of the country from the *Mashriq region*.[30]

Theoretically, unemployment has an ambiguous effect on foreign terrorist recruitment. On the one hand, unemployment lowers the economic opportunity cost of participation in terrorist activities and should have a positive impact on recruitment. It is a push factor. On the other hand, individuals may face liquidity constraints that can hamper their ability to travel to the Mashriq region, a pull factor. This mechanism is expected to be more relevant in faraway countries from where travel costs are very high. In general then, the marginal impact of unemployment is dependent on the distance of the countries from where ISIS recruits come. This is captured by the product term $U_{ie} \times D_i$.

Finally, the control variables $\mathbf{Z}$ include unobserved country-specific and education-level-specific (fixed) effects, size of the labor force in the country-

---

[29] In Arabic, Daesh is a derogatory word. ISIS strongly resents being addressed by this word by its detractors.

[30] It refers to the eastern part of the Arab world, comprising Bahrain, Egypt, Iraq, Jordan, Kuwait, Lebanon, Oman, Palestine, Qatar, Saudi Arabia, Sudan, Syria, the United Arab Emirates, and Yemen.

education cell, and average wage in each country-education cell where "cell" refers to the respective group.[31]

To disentangle the opposing effects of unemployment on terrorist recruitment, the authors first considered countries in the neighborhood of Iraq and Syria where there is a minimal role for travel costs. For this sample of countries, higher unemployment rates pushed more recruits to join Daesh, with a semi-elasticity of 0.16. This estimate implies that 1200 fewer recruits would have joined Daesh if the unemployment rate had been 1 percentage point lower in all countries in the sample. As more distant countries are added to the analysis, the estimated elasticities drop until they become close to zero for countries at the median distance from Iraq and Syria.

Furthermore and interestingly, among countries located farther than 2500 miles away from Iraq and Syria, unemployment rates negatively affected Daesh recruitment, with a semi-elasticity of −0.15, implying that for these countries travel costs became binding constraints for unemployed individuals who wanted to join Daesh.

Is That So? 15.3: Unemployment, Distance, and Recruitment by ISIS from Abroad

ISIS recruitment from countries relatively near to (respectively, distant from) Iraq or Syria was positively (respectively, negatively) related to unemployment in the source countries.

15.4 Political and Civil Rights

Unlike economic status-related factors like poverty or per-capita income, the role of political and civil rights on terrorism has received a more definitive empirical support. Political and civil rights are similar in their nature in terms of freedom of expression and choice, but there are differences. Political rights refer to the electoral process and participation, etc., whereas civil rights are about individual and organizational rights and freedom of belief and expression.

Under autocracy, any form of dissent or alternative opinion is trampled, leaving little scope for organized non-state violence like terrorism. Granting political and civil rights opens the door for dissenting views and taking up acts of terrorism to pressurize the government. According to the "strategic" school, a term coined by Gaibulloev and Sandler (2019), political and civil rights encourage terrorism in this sense. On the other hand, when political and civil rights are available liberally without undue restrictions, there will be little incentive to engage in violence to bring about changes that a group of people may want to see as long as they do not impinge on the overall harmony of a nation. This is the "political access view," which asserts that political and civil rights are expected to reduce terrorism. There is also a

[31] ILOSTAT data (a database maintained by the International Labor Organization) is used to construct education-level-specific unemployment rates for individual countries. Altogether the data includes 177 country × education-level observations (cells). Distance is introduced interactively with unemployment, i.e., there is a product term: unemployment rate × distance. Panel regression is used.

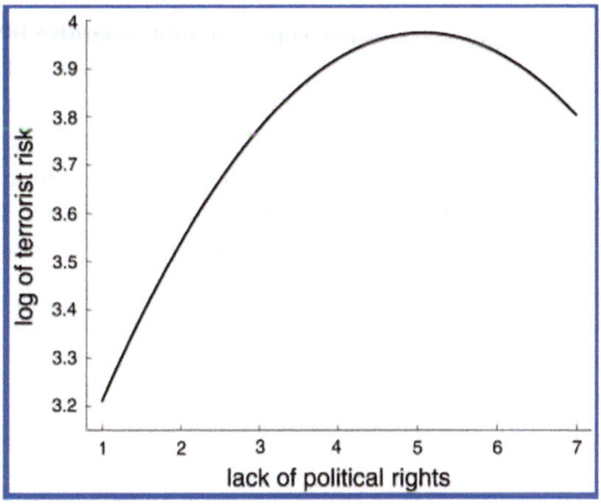

(b)

Fig. 15.7: Political or civil rights, and terrorism: An inverse U-shaped relation hypothesis. (**a**) Theoretical relation. (**b**) Estimated relation. (**b**)
Source: Abadie (2006, Figure 1); Permission to reproduce by the author and the American Economic Association is thankfully acknowledged

"democracy protection view" arguing that liberal democracies are expected to take strong actions against terrorism in order to maintain the virtues and legitimacy of the freedom and political and civil rights. This implies a negative causal link from political and civil rights to terrorism.

There are empirical studies such as Eubank and Weinberg (1994, 2001), Li and Schaub (2004), and San-Akca (2014), among others, which support the strategic view, i.e., a positive link between political or civil rights and terrorism. There are also studies attesting that political or civil rights tend to reduce the incidence of terrorism, favoring the political-access-cum-democracy-protection. For instance, Krueger and Malečková (2003), referred to earlier, also considered civil liberty.[32] Assembling a country-level dataset on transnational terror events over the period 1997–2003 and ascribing each event to the country of origin of the perpetrators, their cross-country regression analysis yielded that if country-wise indicators of civil rights are not included, relative poverty of a nation vis-à-vis others exerts a positive and significant effect on terrorism.[33] But once the country-level civil rights scores are accounted

[32] Civil liberty scores are obtained from Freedom House organization, which defined civil liberty as "freedom to develop view, institutions, and personal autonomy without interference from the state."

[33] In case of transnational terrorist attacks that are perpetrated by individuals from different countries, the number of attacks apportions the country of origin of the perpetrators in proportion to the number of terrorists from the respective countries.

for, the impact of relative poverty or per-capita income becomes insignificant, while the effect of civil rights on terrorism is statistically significant and *negative*.[34,35]

The important point is that relatively poor countries also tend to be poor in the scale of civil rights, whereas it is the absence of civil rights, not poor economic status per se, that contributes to terrorism. In the authors' words, "Once one accounts for the fact that poorer countries are less likely to have basic civil liberties, there is no difference in the number of terrorists springing from the poorest or the richest countries."

Similar conclusion is reached by Piazza (2008), who studied suicide terrorism and used Freedom House's rating of countries on political rights. He found a negative relation between democracy and suicide terrorism, that is, "democracies are significantly less likely to produce terrorists who go on to commit suicide attacks."[36]

15.4.1 Inverse U-Shaped Relation Between Political/Civil Rights and Terrorism

It is not hard to imagine that if, hypothetically, a country moves from an autocratic regime to an anocracy (a mix of autocratic and democratic elements) and from that regime to a liberal democracy, in the initial phase hitherto suppressed groups would tend to raise their voices through violence including terrorism, because there will be lesser scope for practices like surveillance of "potential" terrorism, easier mobilization to organize terror, and greater scope for publicity by freer press. This is the strategic view. But after a threshold, this would decline as the political-access-cum-democracy-protection factor would tend to dominate. The overall scenario will be a non-linear and more specifically an inverse U-shaped relation between political and civil rights (or lack thereof) and incentive to engage in terrorism as depicted in Fig. 15.7a.

To fix ideas, we can think of a model akin to the one developed in Chap. 13, in which there is one terror organization (or a group of terror organizations as one entity), the Org and one target country, the State. As long as terrorism originates fundamentally from lack of some grievance redressal, starting from an autocratic regime where political and civil liberties are scarce, as liberties are available on a limited scale, on one hand grievance redressal (g) increases from 0 in terms of the model in Chap. 13, but on the other, the marginal cost of producing terror begins to decline from an inordinately high level. These are respectively marginal-benefit-

[34] The data on transnational terror occurrences and countries of origin of the terrorists is obtained from the US State Department's annual list of "significant international terrorist incidents." Each data point refers to a particular country: number of terror incidents emanating from it, its population, an indicator of a country's per capita GDP relative to other countries, civil liberty index, literacy rate, and proportions of Muslims, Christians, Buddhists, and Hindus. A country's per capita GDP position is captured by three dummy variables: whether it is in the bottom quartile, second to bottom quartile, or second to top quartile. The estimation is done by negative binomial regressions.

[35] Similar conclusion is reached by Krueger and Laitin (2008). Lack of political rights, rather than per-capita GDP in the perpetrators' home countries, is positively linked to transnational terrorism.

[36] Similar conclusion is reached by Eyerman (1998) pertaining to the pre-*9/11* era.

reducing (i.e., demand-reducing) and supply-increasing or marginal-cost-decreasing factors behind terrorism. The supply-increasing effect is likely to dominate the demand-reducing effect if g is not too far from zero. In equilibrium terrorism will increase. Thereafter, as more political and civil rights are granted and g gets closer to its maximum value, the opposite will begin to take hold. The fall in the marginal benefit from or demand for terrorism will be the dominating factor. The equilibrium level of terrorism will fall. Gaibulloev et al. (2017) outline a different theoretical scenario with security measures rather than preemption, but it is similar in spirit to what is just described.

Empirically speaking, Abadie (2006) was the first, or one of the first, to discover an inverse U-shaped relation between political rights (not civil rights) and terrorism. He used a measure of terror risk across 186 countries during the period 2003–2004 as the dependent variable.[37] The regression equation was

$$\ln(\text{Terrorism Risk})_i = a + b_1 \ln y_i + b_2 X_i + b_3 X_i^2 + \boldsymbol{\beta} \mathbf{Z} + u_i, \tag{15.3}$$

where y_i is the per-capita GDP of country i and X_i is the measure of lack of political rights and the vector **Z** represents the control variables. Note that the political-rights variable enters in quadratic form, which captures non-linearity.[38] The relationship is U-shaped or inverse U-shaped according as $b_2 < 0 < b_3$ or $b_2 > 0 > b_3$. Control variables include human development index, GINI coefficient of inequality and fractionalization (a measure of diversity in a population), and geographical and climatic measures of a country.[39]

The estimation results show that per-capita GDP—representing poverty—is *not* a significant predictor of terrorism, but political rights are, and the impact of political freedom is inverse U-shaped. The estimated relationship between political rights and terrorism is shown in Fig. 15.7b. Since it measures lack of political rights in the horizontal axis it is a sideways mirror of Fig. 15.7a.[40]

The inverse U-shaped relation is firmly established by Gaibulloev et al. (2017), a more comprehensive study than previous works. It incorporated many control variables. Civil rights were not included, because there might be a reverse causality from terrorism to civil rights. Only the variables pertaining to political rights were taken as explanatory variables.[41] The hypothesis of an inverted U-shaped relation be-

[37] Country-level terrorist risk indices were prepared by the World Market Research Center based in London (which does not seem to exist any longer).

[38] Political-rights data are sourced from the Freedom House's Political Rights Index (PRI). The PRI has a 1–7 range, with high values representing greater absence of political rights.

[39] Fractionalization is typically defined and computed for linguistic, ethnic, or religious diversity.

[40] The already noted study by Bandopadhyay and Younas (2011) on developing countries finds that political freedom has a significantly non-linear effect on domestic terrorism but no significant effect on transnational terrorism. Also see Drakos and Gofas (2006) and Chenoweth (2013).

[41] Details of this study are outlined in chapter Appendix 15.C.

tween political freedom and terrorism was borne out robustly. The average predicted number of terrorist events peaks when the normalized Polity2 score is 0.6.

Is That So? 15.4: Politico-Civil Liberty and Terrorism

Terrorism bears an inverse U-shaped relation with politico-civil liberty. An important policy implication is that an endeavor to effect a change from an autocratic regime to limited democracy runs the risk of more violence and terrorism in the initial phase.

15.5 Income Inequality and Domestic Terrorism

The third-wave terrorism, the new left, is founded on the notion and existence of large economic chasm between the rich and the poor, a manifestation of gross *relative* deprivation or economic inequality. Remember that all major terror groups in Latin America were extreme leftwing. Theoretically, inequality is related to crime and violence on the basic argument that increasing disparity between the rich and the poor reduces the opportunity cost for the poor to engage in violence and increases the expected return from violence (e.g., McAdams (2010)). As noted by Krieger and Meierrieks (2019), Pope Francis in 2013 voiced that "until exclusion and inequality in society and between peoples are reversed, it will be impossible to eliminate violence." The same logic can be extended to argue that *relative* economic deprivation leads the relative poor to seek political and economic rights by resorting to terrorism. In more recent decades, the Naxalite groups in India form an example of this. In addition, economic inequality can undermine the quality of social, legal, and political institutions, allowing terror groups to germinate and flourish. These considerations imply that economic inequality can potentially increase domestic terrorism, not transnational terrorism.

It is noteworthy that most empirical works on the causes of terrorism that include indices of inequality treat it as one of the control variables, *not* as a primary explanatory variable.[42] Krieger and Meierrieks (2019) is an exception. They focus on inequality as a main causal factor of terrorism, whereas control variables include civil war dummy, various economic and demographic variables, regional and year dummies as well as indices of political freedom. As results, several insights emerge. The authors also analyze transmission channels through which inequality may impinge on domestic terrorism, such as rules of raw, corruption, domestic investment, education, etc. One of their findings is that inequality directly impacts on domestic terrorism and also via the weakening quality of institutions.

If inequality is a factor behind domestic terrorism, then redistributive measures should reduce domestic terrorism. The authors do find that, all else the same, countries that have more redistributive programs experience less domestic terrorism.[43]

[42] Economic inequality as a control variable and having a positive impact on terrorism shows up in Lai (2007), Piazza (2011), and Enders and Hoover (2012), among others.

[43] Details of this study are outlined in chapter Appendix 15.D.

15.6 Minority Discrimination and Islamophobia

Economy-wide inequality indices capture lack of opportunity for a class of people irrespective of their social characteristics. Discrimination against specific minority groups who do not typically possess a strong political voice can drive individuals to extremism and violence including terrorism. In what follows, we discuss minority discrimination and Islamophobia as root causes of terrorism.

15.6.1 Minority Discrimination

Minority discrimination has been recognized as a cause of domestic terrorism; see Whittacker (2001) and Bradley (2006), among others. However, the discussion by these authors is qualitative. Piazza (2011) undertook a formal empirical analysis and found that, vis-à-vis general level of economic development, minority economic discrimination was a strong and substantive predictor of *domestic terrorism.* Two main results of his study are the following. First, discrimination mattered. Countries in which minority groups were subjected to discrimination were vulnerable to domestic terrorism in a major way. Second, the overall economic status of the country had a smaller effect on terrorism than did economic status of a country's minority groups.[44]

Theoretically, economic discrimination against minorities, which typically manifests in some combination of employment discrimination, unequal access to government health, educational, or social services and lack of economic opportunities, provides an impetus for minority group grievances, directed against the state, the status quo, and the majority population. However, if minority discrimination is being addressed, these groups are less likely to be radicalized and take up terrorism. As examples, it has been documented that the poor economic status of specific groups within the population, instead of overall economic climate, was crucial in fueling terror group recruitment and activities for Red Brigades in Italy, Tupamaros in Uruguay and EOKA in Cyprus (Hewitt, 1984).

15.6.2 Home-Grown Terrorism in the West

From 2001 onward, the threat of "home-grown" extremism, especially among the Muslims in the western countries, has expanded. London bombings of 2005 were reportedly carried out by four bombers, Muslims by religion and characterized as "ordinary British citizens." According to Altunbaķ and Thorton (2011), in the USA, seventy-seven resident Muslim individuals were either convicted of terror acts or died while carrying out terror attacks during 2001–2009. Terrorist attack in Paris in November 2015 that killed 130 people and injured more than 350 was led by Abdelhamid Abaaoud, who was born in Belgium; these attacks were carried out by people who were Muslims and inspired by ISIS. Such threats in the USA exist and but are less compared to Europe (see Brooks (2011) and MacFarquhar (2020)). Boston marathon bombings were carried out by two brothers of Chechen Muslim origin.

[44] See chapter Appendix 15.E for details on Piazza's empirical exercise.

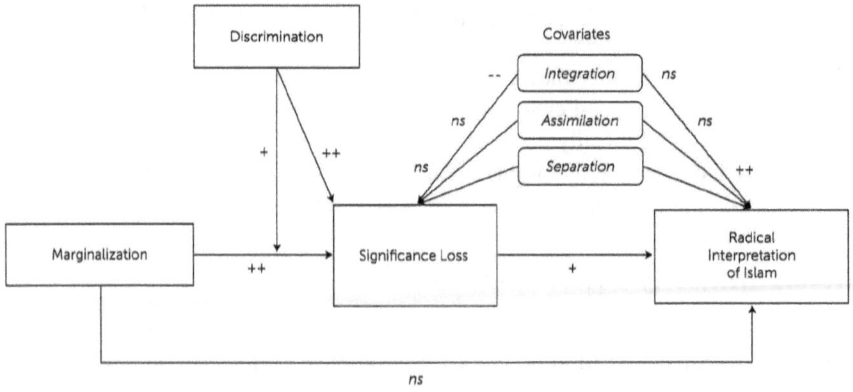

ns = the relationship between the variables was not significant; + = a significant positive relationship at the $p < .05$ level; ++ = a highly significant positive relationship at the $p < .001$ level. -- = a highly significant negative relationship.

(a)

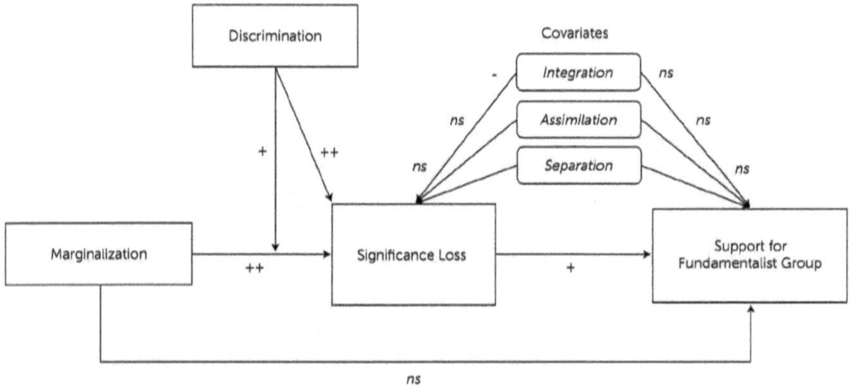

ns = the relationship between the variables was not significant; + = a significant positive relationship at the $p < .05$ level; - = a significant negative relationship; ++ = a highly significant positive relationship at the $p < .001$ level.

(b)

Fig. 15.8: Results from the moderated median analysis based on survey of 198 muslim individuals in the USA. (**a**) Inclination toward radical interpretation of Islam. (**b**) Inclination toward support for a fundamentalist group.
Source: Lyons-Padilla et al. (2015); permission to reproduce from Sarah Lyons-Padilla as well as the Behavioral Science and Policy Association is thankfully acknowledged

The younger brother was a naturalized citizen, while the older brother had passed the tests to become a US citizen. The mass shooting in San Bernardino, California, in 2015 was perpetrated by a husband–wife duo. The husband, Rizwa Farooq, was an American-born citizen who grew up in California and the wife, Tashfeen Malik, was an immigrant of Pakistani origin from Saudi Arabia since 2014.

In general, violent Muslim terror organizations have tried to recruit or inspire ordinary Muslims throughout the world via social media. While majority of Muslims ignore these "calls," as noted by Lyons-Padilla et al. (2015), an estimated 5000 recruits from the USA and Europe went to Iraq and/or Syria to join ISIS and other extremist groups, got radicalized, and returned to their countries after being trained to carry out terror attacks. However, religion is *not* the prime motivator for joining organizations like ISIS. Research on the characteristics of violent extremism suggests that many are religious novices or converts. For example, two young British men jailed in 2014 on terrorism charges had ordered *Islam for Dummies* and *The Koran for Dummies* before going to fight in Syria. Instead, religion is used to legitimize personal and collective frustrations and justify violent ideologies.

In what follows, we discuss in fair detail Lyons-Padilla et al. (2015), a pioneering research on cultural identities and attitudes toward extremist Muslim youth in the USA based on a survey of 198 Muslims. The central thesis is that

Is That So? 15.5: Radicalization in the West

The study by Lyons-Padilla et al. (2015) on Muslim youth in the USA finds that a person's cultural identity plays a vital role in radicalization. More precisely, a sense of marginalization in the society leads a feeling of significance loss, which, in turn, leads to radical consideration of Islam as a religion and joining a radical terrorist organization. Social discrimination exacerbates this thinking and attitude. Social integration, on the other hand, tends to attenuate the sense of significance loss.

Immigrants who do not identify with their heritage culture or the culture they are living in feel marginalized and insignificant. Insignificance or significance loss results from humiliation and anticipation of maltreatment by the society. Recruitment material from groups like al-Qaeda affiliates and ISIS do invoke humiliation and suffering faced by Muslims in the world and promise the recruits a sense of meaning, belonging, pride, and purpose in life.

In more detail, the authors uncovered that it is marginalization that leads to an inclination toward radicalism, while this cause–effect process is fed by other factors. Support from radicalism is measured in two ways: (a) radical interpretation of Islam and (b) how strongly the respondents thought that people in their social circle would support a hypothetical group having attributes of a violent organization. These are two outcome variables and the processes involved are the following:

(1) A feeling of marginalization leads to a radical interpretation of Islam or support for a fundamentalist group both directly and via a sense of significance loss.

(2) Discrimination is a direct factor of significance loss and it also affects how marginalization impacts on significance loss.

(3) In turn, significance loss directly affects the outcomes, while the marginal effect of significance loss on outcomes depends on one's sense of assimilation, integration, separation, and being marginalized within the host culture.

What do the terms like assimilation, integration, etc. exactly mean? Immigrants who feel belonging to the host-country culture but do not cultivate linkage with their heritage culture are considered "assimilated." Those who are at home and identify with both cultures are "integrated." Thus assimilation is like a melting pot and integration is like a tasty salad bowl with different ingredients. Those who are unable to adopt to the culture of the host country yet continue to identify with their heritage culture are considered "separated." Finally, those who do not fit into either culture are considered to be "marginalized."[45] The feelings of marginalization, assimilation, separation, integration, discrimination, and significance loss were assessed by scaled responses to various questions in a survey questionnaire.

The processes of how marginalization affects fundamentalism are depicted in Fig. 15.8, in which arrows show the nature of cause–effect relations. Moderated mediation analysis is the statistical method used to estimate the relationships.[46] Statistical significance is indicted by "+" and "−" signs; "++" represents highly significant positive relationship with p value less than 0.001, whereas + means significant and positive relation with p value less than 0.05 and so on; "ns" means no statistical significance. We see that marginalization has no significant direct effect on radicalism or fundamentalism, whereas it has a strong positive effect on significance loss, which is also affected positively by discrimination and negatively by the sense of integration.[47] Discrimination exacerbates the marginal impact of marginalization on significance loss. In turn, significance loss leads to a leaning toward radicalism and fundamentalism. Integration, assimilation, or separation does not generally affect the outcome variable significantly except that separation has a significant impact on radical interpretation of Islam. Furthermore,

Is That So? 15.6: Integration and the Sense of Loss of Significance

According to the study by Lyons-Padilla et al. (2015) on young Muslims in the USA, it is their feeling of integration, not assimilation or separation, which significantly mitigates their sense of significance loss.[a]

[a] Similar results were found by Doosje et al. (2013) in the context of Muslims in the Netherlands.

The results of Lyons-Padilla et al. (2015) are only suggestive since the study is based on self-reporting survey on mental inclination, not actual actions or decisions undertaken. Further, it was a one-time survey and had a rather small sample size. Nonetheless, the socio-political message coming from studies such as Lyons-Padilla et al. (2015) is that "better safe than sorry approach," Islamophobia and anti-Muslim rhetoric encouraging suspicion of Muslims for any unusual occurrences or limiting

[45] Integration was measured by the response on a scale to the statement "I wish to maintain my heritage culture values and also adopt key features of American values". Corresponding statements for assimilation, separation, and marginalization were "I wish to give up my culture heritage values for the sake of adopting American values," "I wish to maintain my heritage culture customs rather than adopt American customs," and "I do not wish to maintain my heritage culture values or adopt American values as I feel uncomfortable with both types of values."

[46] This is explained in General Appendix B, Sect. B.18.

[47] There were eight questions to measure discrimination, two of which are "Have you ever experienced hostility or unfair treatment because of your religion?" and "Have you ever experienced hostility or unfair treatment because of your cultural background?"

their activities and movements is likely to be counter-productive. There are more than three million Muslims in the USA and more than thirty million in Europe. Prevention of radicalization is likely to succeed if the nations focus on their assimilation rather than alienation.

15.7 Pre-Existing Conflict

It is also important to understand the surrounding environment in which a problem can grow and fester. We all know mosquitoes are the root cause of malaria, and they grow in stale water and swamp. Besides mosquito-killing chemical agents, cleaning water and draining swamps are preventives of malaria and other mosquito-caused illnesses too. In the similar vein, we can ask: what is the surrounding environment in which terrorists and terrorism originate and flourish? The obvious answer is a failed, conflict-ridden state, in which law and order are relatively ineffective. Situations in Afghanistan, Iraq, and Syria are obvious examples.

Empirical work on terrorism has considered pre-existing conflict as one of the causal factors. Typically, measures of conflict are included as control variables, not variables of central interest or hypothesis. See, for example, Drakos and Gofas (2006), Lai (2007), Savun and Phillips (2009), Chenoweth (2010), Gassebner and Luechinger (2011), Collard-Wexler et al. (2013), Gaibulloev et al. (2017), and Krieger and Meierrieks (2019). The result is clear-cut: pre-existing conflicts have significant and positive coefficients, and, in some studies (e.g., Drakos & Gofas (2006), Lai (2007), and Chenoweth (2010)), a country's engagement in external warfare is also related to terrorism. Thus pre-existing conflicts are a significant contributor toward the presence of terrorism.

15.8 Globalization

Globalization, in and of itself, may not be the root cause of terrorism, but it magnifies and propagates the problem, making it worldwide and more potent. As Li and Schaub (2004) noted, globalization reduces the cost of producing terror by facilitating movement or transfer of people and funds, increases the spillover of grievances, and leads to demonstration effect of major events across the world. In their empirical analysis, globalization is proxied by a country's openness to trade, foreign direct investment (FDI), portfolio investment, the level of economic development, and the development of its top economic partner countries.[48] However, the main finding—robust to alternative model specifications and statistical estimators—is that globalization is *not* significant in explaining transnational terrorism. More precisely, international trade, FDI, and financial capital flows of a country have no direct positive effect on the number of transnational terrorist incidents initiated within the country. But,

[48] The dependent variable is the number of transnational terror events in a country within a year and the dataset on terror events spans 112 countries from 1975 to 1997. The authors employ dynamic panel analysis and include control for country size, level of democracy, government capability, interstate conflict, regional variations, etc.

the economic development of a country and its top economic partners reduces the number of transnational terrorist incidents within the country. Thus, to the extent that trade and FDI promote economic development, economic globalization has an indirect *negative* effect on transnational terrorism.

Gassebner and Luechinger (2011) applied a modified extreme bound analysis (see General Appendix B, Sect. B.20) to a host of possible determinants of transnational terrorism, including globalization, based on Dreher's (2006) KOF index of globalization.[49] Among other results, the authors showed that globalization was *not* a robust determinant of transnational terrorism in the various estimations based on venue country, victim country, or perpetrators' origin.[50]

In their review article, Gaibulloev and Sandler (2019) aptly observe that the studies that aim to find if globalization affects terrorism are typically subject to endogeneity issues. That is, terrorism may affect variables that proxy globalism such as FDI, a country's openness to trade, etc. Without accounting for endogeneity, it is difficult to obtain reliable estimates either supporting or rejecting the hypothesis that globalization has indeed significantly contributed to terrorism. Hence it remains an open issue.

15.9 Take-Aways

- Robert Pape and James Feldman have shown that foreign occupation by democracies, e.g., American and European occupation of Afghanistan and Iraq and Israel's occupation of Arab areas, is the principal factor behind suicide terrorism.
- To deal with suicide terrorism, the authors advocate "off-shore balancing," meaning withdrawal of forces from the grounds of foreign countries while maintaining over-the-horizon marine and naval forces for occasional intervention when special situations arise.
- Subsequent literature distinguishes clearly between foreign occupation and domestic occupation (which is defined as a situation where minority groups perceive themselves as under occupation). The results indicate that while suicide attacks are explained (partly) by foreign occupation, domestic occupation does not explain suicide terrorism.

[49] KOF stands for Konjunkturforschungsstelle, a German word, meaning Economic or business cycle research institute. The index is constructed by using three criteria: economic, social, and political. The KOF index of globalization is widely used in applied work.

[50] Other studies use globalization indices as controls whereas the main variable of interest is different. For instance, the main aim of Gaibulloev et al. (2017) is to measure how regime type, i.e., how dictatorial or liberal a country is in terms of political and civil rights impacts terrorism. As controls the study includes, among other variables, indices of economic globalization and political globalization. These indices are taken from Dreher (2006) and Dreher et al. (2008). Both variables are however generally insignificant in explaining terrorism.

- Studies before *9/11* attacks and early studies after *9/11* attacks do not find evidence of poverty or low-income and lack of education as significant factors behind individuals joining terror groups. More recent studies find a non-linear inverse U-shaped relation between real per-capita income and terrorism, meaning that very poor and rich countries are not conducive for terrorist groups to flourish. Terrorism emerges largely from middle-income countries.
- A leaked-out cache of records kept by ISIS having data on foreign recruits and their educational level, country of residence, and country of citizenship has been subject to econometric analysis. It shows that unemployment in origin countries was a significant for traveling to Iraq or Syria to join ISIS, unless the origin countries are very far off from Iraq or Syria.
- There is an inverse U-shaped link between political rights and terrorism. That is, terrorism is a less serious issue where there is little or ample political rights to protest and voice opinions compared to regimes of anocracy.
- Income inequality is a significant factor of domestic terrorism.
- Minority discrimination in a country contributes toward domestic terrorism.
- Home-grown terrorism in the West, particularly among Muslims, in terms of fundamentalist belief and inclination to join radical and violent groups like ISIS and al-Qaeda is linked not to religion per se, but to a sense of marginalization and loss of significance of life in the West, and that is exacerbated by discrimination. Groups like ISIS take advantage of such psychological feeling to attract recruits from the West.
- Pre-existing conditions of conflict are linked to terrorism.
- Somewhat surprisingly, globalization in terms of free trade, FDI, etc., does not show up as a significant causal factor of transnational terrorism. This could be due to methodological issues associated with estimation. Thus, the effect of globalization on terrorism remains an open issue.

Appendix to Chapter 15

15.A Details of Collard-Wexler et al. (2013)

The empirical model includes several explanatory variables and interaction terms. The authors consider cross-country data from 1981 (the year prior to the first suicide attack) to 2007. There are 145 to 154 countries in the sample, depending on the availability of individual, independent variables. The dependent variable is the number of attacks against a target state per year. All data on suicide attacks, including their targets, are drawn from the CPOST (see Chap. 3, Sect. 3.2, for a description of the CPOST dataset). The authors use negative binomial regression (see General Appendix B, Sect. B.19).

There are three main explanatory variables that capture foreign occupation, domestic occupation, and target hardening. Foreign occupation is represented by a dummy variable "Occupier," which takes value 1 if there are foreign forces present in a country's territory within a particular year and 0 otherwise. Target hardening of the occupation forces is measured by an index of the occupier country's military hardware: the natural log of the number of armored vehicles per 100 soldiers for the occupier country, named, "Log Mech." Log Mech. enters through interaction with the dummy variable Occupier. That is, Occupier × Log Mech. is the interaction variable. In the spirit of Pape's theory there is another interaction term associated with the variable Occupier: namely, a dummy capturing whether or not the occupier and the target country's principal religions are different. Finally, domestic occupation is captured by a *separatism index* available for various countries. Several control variables are included to represent a country's general state of conflict, the economy, and demographic characteristics—one of which is the share of Muslims in the total population.

15.B Details of Lai (2007), Enders and Hoover (2012), Enders et al. (2016), and Enders et al. (2016)

Lai (2007) was probably the first study to discover this pattern.[51,52] More definitive analysis and results were furnished by Enders and Hoover (2012) and Enders et al. (2016).

Enders and Hoover (2012) used data from GTD and examined separately how domestic and transnational terrorism varied with economic well-being. All variables were country averages by use of as many years as possible during the 1998–2007 period. Simple "linear" regression models led to the standard result that per-capita real GDP had no influence on terrorism. But classifying the 172 countries in the sample into four per-capita income groups following World Bank's Low

[51] It used ITERATE data and transnational terrorism data in the sample period 1968–1998 (in the pre-*9/11* era).

[52] In the context of data from 125 developing countries over the period 1998–2007, Bandopadhyay and Younas (2011), who did not allow for non-linearity, found a significant and positive effect of per-capita real GDP on transnational terrorism, but not on domestic terrorism. This can be viewed as consistent with the non-linearity hypothesis, which implies that terrorism is expected to increase with per-capita income in a lower range of per-capita incomes.

Income, Lower Middle Income, Upper Middle Income, and High Income categories as of 2007 led to non-linear effects on both domestic and transnational terrorism. Smooth transition regression (STaR) estimation technique, rather than a quadratic form, was used for allowing a non-linear relationship between terrorism and poverty.[53] As nations develop, the level of domestic terrorism they experience is likely to decline once their real per capita GDP passes a threshold of about $1000. If development is accompanied by an increase in income inequality, however, domestic terrorism could increase. On transnational terrorism, economic development was predicted to increase the number of transnational incidents until per capita GDP reached a threshold of about $2215. One policy implication is that nations providing development assistance need to be aware that their efforts might actually increase the number of attacks directed at their interests. Furthermore, it is especially important to be concerned about constructing a development plan that does not exacerbate income inequality.

Enders et al. (2016) differed from Enders and Hoover (2012) in that it utilized a much longer sample period running from 1970 to 2010, more controls, and two datasets, ITERATE and GTD. The longer time frame allowed them to ascertain changes, if any, in the non-linear income–terrorism relationship for two important sub-periods, 1970 to 1992 and 1994 to 2010, that correspond to the greater dominance of the leftist and fundamentalist terrorist groups, respectively. It provided predictions on eight measures of terrorism distinguishing between location of attacks and the nationality of the perpetrators and whether attacks were domestic or transnational. Like Enders and Hoover (2012) a flexible non-linear STaR estimation method was applied.

Non-linear relations emerged between per-capita real GDP and eight measures of terrorism. Further, the nature of non-linearity differed between years prior to and after 1993. The peak per-capita GDP for which terrorism was at the maximum varied between the two time periods, occurring at a relatively high intermediate GDP per capita when the leftist terrorists were proactive in the pre-1993 era, and at a relatively low intermediate GDP per capita when terrorists embracing religious fundamentalism dominated in the post-1993 era.

15.C Details of Gaibulloev et al. (2017)

The authors use a panel dataset covering 159 countries over nine periods, 1970–1974, 1975–1979, 1980–1984, 1985–1989, 1990–1994, 1995–1999, 2000–2004, 2005–2009, and 2010–2012 where the explanatory variables are averaged within each period.[54] Since regime-type variables change slowly over time, grouping years into periods allows the authors to obtain more accurate within-estimates of these variables. Fixed-effect estimation is implemented for most of the analysis. The authors use a variety of measures for political rights obtained from two datasets: Freedom House as well as the Polity dataset initiated by Ted Robert Gurr and Monty G. Marshall (sponsored by the Political Instability Task Force, which, in turn, is funded by CIA). Policy scores are assigned to different countries annually taking into account competitiveness and openness of executive recruitment, constraints on the chief executive, competitiveness in political participation, etc. They range from -10 to 10. The sub-ranges $[-10, -6]$, $[-5, 5]$, and $[6, 10]$ represent autocracy, anocracy (a mix of autocratic and democratic features); and democracy. The authors use Polity2, which is a combined score on the regime type.

The counts of domestic and transnational terror incidents are separately culled from two datasets, ITERATE and GTD. Hence there are four measures of terrorism and hence four dependent variables covering both datasets. One set of regressions simply uses terror incidents occurring in countries that are regressed against explanatory variables pertaining to the respective venue countries. Quite notably, some regressions that consider transnational terrorist events use the explanatory variables for the country or countries of origin of the perpetrators; this directly estimates

[53] STaR estimation is briefly explained in General Appendix B, Sect. B.22.

[54] This constitutes a far more comprehensive dataset compared to Abadie (2006) or Bandopadhyay and Younas (2011), for example.

which factors may be responsible for spawning terrorists whether terror attacks are domestic or transnational.

15.D Details of Krieger and Meierrieks (2019)

The data covers 113 countries from 1984 to 2012, sourced from GTD. Negative binomial regressions are used as the estimation method. It is possible that terrorism itself affects economic inequality, i.e., there are potential endogeneity issues. To deal with this, the authors use instruments such as 10-year lag values of inequality indices and value added in agriculture, the reason being that agricultural output and the level of inequality are inversely related. The main result is robust to different model specifications, different measures of the dependent variable, and different measures of income inequality (Gini and Theil indices).

The authors' procedure to analyze transmission channels through which inequality may affect domestic terrorism, such as rules of raw, corruption, domestic investment, education, etc. is the following. First, potential transmission variables are regressed against measures of inequality and other controls using ordinary least squares. If the results of first regression are poor, then the transmission mechanism is not valid. Assuming that the first regression yields significant coefficients, in the second regression, the measure of terrorism is regressed against the inequality measure, control variables, and the transmission variables using instruments. If the coefficients on inequality and transmission variables are significant, then part of the effect of inequality on terrorism works through the transmission variables. The coefficients on relevant variables in both regressions in the study were indeed significant.

15.E Details of Piazza (2011)

Piazza's empirical exercise uses country-year data for 172 countries over the period 1970 to 2006. The count of domestic terror attacks is the outcome variable. Minority discrimination data is obtained from Minorities at Risk (MAR) Project housed at the Center for International Development and Conflict Management at the University of Maryland. It is called the ECDIS/Economic Discrimination Index. It measures the degree to which members of groups designated as MARs face economic discrimination on a 0 to 4 point scale, 0 for countries exhibiting no discrimination against minorities. Control variables include per-capita real GDP, human development index, Gini measure of income inequality, national population, geographic area, etc. Negative binomial regression is the estimation method.

Questions

15.1 What is considered as the main cause of suicide terrorism and why?
15.2 Briefly explain the concept of "offshore balancing" by giving examples.
15.3 How is hardening theory of suicide attacks related to foreign versus "domestic occupation"?
15.4 "Poverty drives people to crimes including terrorism." Defend or refute.
15.5 "Political freedom would tend to lessen the problem of terrorism." Defend or refute.
15.6 What are the mechanisms behind greater inequality being associated to a greater incidence of domestic terrorism?
15.7 In terms of the model by Lyons-Padilla et al. (2015), describe in your own words how Islamophobia may encourage terrorism.

General Appendices

Chapter A

General Appendix A: Theory

This appendix chapter cover two topics: compensating surplus (also called compensating variation in income) and some basic elements of game theory.

A.1 Compensating Surplus

This is a concept from micro theory that is used in Chap. 6. Suppose an individual uses his total income (same as total spending or expenditure) I^0 on purchasing goods a and b, whose respective initial prices are p_a^0 and p_b^0. The amounts bought of goods a and b are consumed, providing utility or welfare to the individual. Consider the steeper budget line in Fig. A.1; I^0/p_a^0 and I^0/p_b^0 mark the maximum quantity of goods a and b that can be purchased and consumed if the entire spending is used for one good only. The equilibrium consumption point is E^0 where the indifference curve is tangent to this budget line and the utility level is U^0. Suppose the price of good b increases from p_b^0 to p_b^1 while that of good a remains unchanged. The new equilibrium point is E^1 and the new equilibrium utility or welfare level is U^1, which is less than U^0. This is intuitive: the increase in the price of good b is detrimental to the welfare of the individual as long as his total income remains the same. It is because higher prices along with given income reduce a person's real purchasing power.

The following question underlies the concept of *compensating surplus*, also called *compensating variation in income*: *how much extra income can the individual be compensated with, so that she/he is able to enjoy the old level of welfare at the new prices?*[1] Now turn to panel (b) of Fig. A.1. See that if the new (flatter) budget line shifts in parallel to the right from by a particular magnitude, i.e., the individual is compensated by a particular amount, she can reach the point E' and be able to maintain her original standard of living or welfare, U^0. This amount of extra income is the compensating surplus or compensating variation in income. Note that GH *is equal to the compensating surplus in terms of good* a. As a specific example, if $p_a = \$10$ and horizontal segment GH is equal to 15 units of good a, then $p_a \times GH = \$150$ is the compensating surplus in dollars.

[1] In many countries, government employees are paid dearness or inflation-adjustment allowances which are intended to offset the decline in the real purchasing power due to inflation. The idea behind such schemes are the same.

S. P. Das, *Economics of Terrorism and Counter-Terrorism Measures*,
https://doi.org/10.1007/978-3-030-96577-8

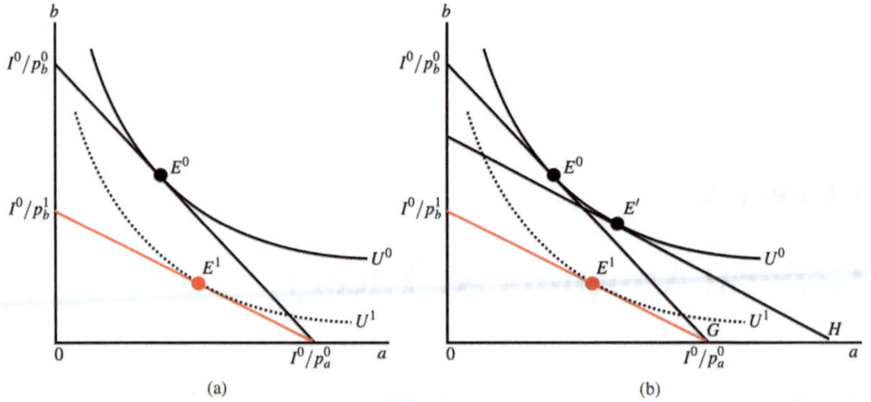

Fig. A.1: Compensating surplus or compensating variation. (**a**) Increase in p_b. (**b**) Compensating surplus

Algebraically we can express utility (such as U^0 and U^1 in Fig. A.1) in terms of prices and income: $U = V(p_a, p_b, I)$, called the *indirect utility function*. Suppose in the original situation p_a, p_b, and I are equal to p_a^0, p_b^0, and I^0, respectively, so that the original level of utility or welfare equals $V(p_a^0, p_b^0, I^0)$. Let the new prices be p_a^1 and p_b^1 (in our example, $p_a^1 = p_a^0$ and $p_b^1 > p_b^0$, i.e., there is a change in the price of good b only). If we consider a new level of income, say I^1, then the new level of welfare is $V(p_a^1, p_b^1, I^1)$. Let I^1 be such that

$$V(p_a^0, p_b^0, I^0) = V(p_a^1, p_b^1, I^1). \tag{A.1}$$

That is, the new income I^1 enables the individual to maintain the old level of utility or standard of living at the new prices. Therefore, the absolute difference between I^0 and I^1, equal to $|I^1 - I^0|$, is the compensating surplus or compensating variation in income. Given that we have information on old prices, new prices, and old income, we can solve I^1 from Eq. (A.1) and calculate $|I^1 - I^0|$.

A.2 Game Theory: Some Preliminaries

A.2.1 Introduction

Our economic theorizing and analysis of terrorism and counter-terror measures use some basic concepts and results of *game theory*. We delve into it to the extent we will need.

In many real-world game situations, one person or a team wins and the other loses, e.g., tennis, baseball, basketball, football, cricket, and wrestling. As winning and losing cancel out in some sense, such games are called *zero-sum games*. In regular warfare when one party or country wins and the other loses, one may be tempted to think that it is zero-sum game. But if we take into consideration the value of resources used or lost in war, it is a negative-sum, *not* a zero-sum game. To see it suppose that the party A wins and the party B loses in a war. Let the values of winning and losing be T and $-T$, respectively, measured in dollars. War is costly in terms of resources, lives lost, injuries, etc. Let these costs be C_A and C_B, respectively. Thus the (net) payoffs to parties A and B are, respectively, $T - C_A$ and $T - C_B$, and both add up to $\not{T} - C_A - \not{T} - C_B = -(C_A + C_B) < 0$. It is a negative-sum game, and, more generally, a *non-zero-sum game.*

Most game situations in the context of economics and all game situations analyzed in this book are non-zero-sum games.

A.2.2 Defining a Game and the Central Question

A game is defined by three elements:
① A set of players, say from 1 to P;
② A set of strategies or actions available to each player. We can call them $\{z_1\}$, $\{z_2\}$, $\ldots \{z_P\}$;
③ An expression of payoff of each player which depends on strategies chosen by himself *and* other players.

It is crucial that payoffs of any particular player must depend not only on that player's strategy or action alone but also on at least one other player's strategy. Otherwise, there is no strategic interaction and no "game" between that player and others.

In a two-person or two-party (hypothetical) game, say between the USA (player 1) and N. Korea (player 2), we can think of the strategies for USA as z_1 = {status quo, bomb, impose sanctions} and those for N. Korea as z_2 = {status quo, bomb}. With three strategies for the USA and two for N. Korea, there are altogether six combined-strategy outcomes. Plus, we need to be given the expressions or numbers representing payoffs to both the USA and N. Korea associated with each possible outcome. Here is an example.

Strategies		Payoffs	
The USA	N. Korea	The USA	N. Korea
Status quo	Status quo	0	0
Status quo	Bomb	−100	0
Bomb	Status quo	0	−100
Bomb	Bomb	−100	−100
Sanctions	Status quo	0	−20
Sanctions	Bomb	−100	−20

Note that the same numbers for the USA and N. Korea may not mean the same magnitudes of payoffs, because their units may be different, e.g., US$ for the USA and "won" for North Korea (its currency).

In the above example, strategies are discrete. Depending on the situation, they may be continuous. In a duopoly market with two firms, 1 and 2, for instance, their strategies may be the outputs they sell in a given period, z_1 for firm 1 and z_2 for firm 2, where outputs are measured on a continuous scale like wheat in tons or electricity in kilowatt. In this case, the *strategy space* of each player is infinite: 0 to ∞.

In another dimension, the strategies could be *deterministic* (as in our preceding example and examples to come) or *random*. As an illustration of random strategies, consider a penalty shootout in soccer or football with two players, the striker and the goal-keeper. Each has three strategies with some probability distribution. For the goal-keeper they are: dive to the left with some probability, dive to the right with some probability, or hold still with some probability. For the striker, it would be to shoot left with some probability, shoot right with some probability, or shoot straight with some probability. The probabilities must add to one for each player. When strategies are deterministic, they are called *pure strategies* and when they are probabilistic, they are called *random strategies.*

The central question that game theory seeks to answer is: *which strategies will the players choose?* Put differently, what is the solution concept that defines the *equilibrium choice* of strategies. The most widely used equilibrium concept is the *Nash equilibrium*, which will be introduced in the first example below. Altogether, we will analyze three game situations, which should suffice for our purpose.

A.3 Prisoner's Dilemma Game

It is a classic example. Imagine two prisoners, A and B, who are suspects in a crime committed together. Both are interrogated separately and simultaneously without any contact with each other. Each has two choices or strategies: {confess, hang tough}. There are four strategy combinations. Table A.1 summarizes the anticipated years in jail in different scenarios. The negative signs reflect that the payoffs are negative. In each cell, the left-hand number is for A and the other for B. If both confess, they will be sentenced five years each. If both hang tough, they will get two years. As an incentive for confessing, they are offered a deal that if one confesses and the other does not, the person who confesses gets a much reduced sentence, half year in prison, whereas the person who hangs tough and does not confess is handed out a stiff ten-year sentence. The 2×2 matrix is called the *payoff matrix*.

		Player B: Confess	Player B: Hang tough
Player A	Confess	(−5,−5)	(−0.5,−10)
	Hang tough	(−10,−0.5)	(−2,−2)

Table A.1: Prisoner's dilemma game

Of course, if both prisoners deny and hang tough, they get the best deal jointly. But the problem is that they cannot communicate (cannot meet or use telephone, mobile phone or email) and hence there is no scope for them to cooperate. That is, they are pretty much on their own. A does not know for sure whether B will hang tough and vice versa. The question is, *which strategy will they rationally choose on their own*? We need to use a reasonable equilibrium solution notion. The classic one is Nash equilibrium or Nash-strategy, named after John Nash, a Nobel prize winner in economics.

Formally put, in a P-person game, strategies $\{z_1^N, z_2^N, \ldots, z_P^N\}$ constitute Nash equilibrium if for any player, say player p, z_p^N is the best, i.e., the payoff maximizing strategy, *given the strategies by all other players*, $\{z_1^N, \ldots, z_{p-1}^N, z_{p+1}^N, \ldots, z_P^N\}$. Differently put, Nash equilibrium strategies are such that they are individually rational for each player in the game. The underlying notion of rationality is what makes the concept of Nash equilibrium attractive, particularly to economists.

In the Prisoner's Dilemma, intuitively, a strategy-choice combination constitutes Nash equilibrium if, given the strategy of player A (respectively, player B), player B (respectively, player A) has no incentive to deviate from his/her own strategy. Let us see whether the strategy combination {confess, hang tough} is a Nash equilibrium. One can easily see that it is not—because, given "confess" chosen by A, prisoner B would like to deviate from "hang tough" to "confess" which reduces his sentencing from ten to five years. By similar logic, {hang rough, hang tough} and {hang tough, confess} are not Nash equilibrium. In fact, {confess, confess} is the only Nash equilibrium—since if player A deviates from it, his payoff is −10, which is a worse proposition and likewise for player B. Note the following.

[a] Nash equilibrium is also called a *non-cooperative equilibrium* in the sense that the players decide their strategies on their own without coordinating or cooperating with others.

[b] Prisoner's Dilemma is a two-person, two-strategy game. In general, there can be game situations with more players. In the auto market, for example, there are many firms like General Motors, Ford, Toyota, Honda, and Volkswagen among others, whose choose strategies in terms of different models and the number of vehicles produced, etc.

[c] There can be more than two strategies. In the auto example, the number of product lines (models) can be a strategic variable and it can exceed two. Further, the number of different models can vary from one manufacturer to another.

[d] The number of strategies available for a player can be (technically speaking) infinite, e.g., annual production level of a commodity by a firm in a continuous scale, starting from zero upwards.

		Player B	
		Head	Tail
Player A	Head	(1,−1)	(−1,1)
	Tail	(−1,1)	(−1,1)

Table A.2: Coin matching game

[e] In some game situations, there may not be any Nash equilibrium. The *coin matching game*, shown in Table A.2, is an example, where both players have coins inside their palms and they open their palms to show head or tail to each other simultaneously. If both coins match (show head or tail), player A wins and obtains \$1 from player B, and if the coins do not match, player B wins and gets \$1 from player A. Notice that it is a zero-sum game. You can check that none of the four outcome satisfies the definition of Nash equilibrium.

		Nathan	
		Opera	Boxing match
Patrice	Opera	(2,1)	(0,0)
	Boxing match	(0,0)	(1,2)

Table A.3: Battle of sexes

[f] Similarly there are games, e.g., *battle of sexes*, where there are more than one Nash equilibrium. Nathan and Patrice love each other's company. There are two options available to them on a Saturday night: go to an opera or a boxing match. If one goes to the opera and the other to the boxing match separately, each obtains zero utility. However, if they go to an event together, Patrice prefers opera to boxing match, whereas Nathan prefers boxing match to opera. The utility payoffs are illustrated in Table A.3. You can check that there are two Nash equilibria in this game: {opera, opera} and {boxing match, boxing match}.

Nash equilibrium is a useful concept for two reasons. First, it defines equilibrium in a non-cooperative situation which is natural and intuitive. Realize that since the two prisoners are being interrogated in separate cells and they have no means to communicate, coordinate, or cooperate, they make choices on their own—i.e., choices are individually rational. Secondly, we can compare Nash equilibrium to what the outcome will be in a cooperative environment. Notice in Table A.1 that if the prisoners could somehow cooperate or collude and maximize their joint gains so to speak, they would both choose "Hang Tough," i.e., deny the crime and their gains will be three less number years in prison (from five to two).

A.4 Dormitory Game: A Case of Negative Externality

Unlike the Prisoner's Dilemma where each player had two distinct (discrete) strategies to choose from, in this game as well as the next, players choose the level of their strategies, which is continuous. Imagine two adjacent rooms in a dormitory. Sandy stays in one and John is her neighbor, sharing a common wall which is not adequately sound-proof. Both love to play music and at the same time of the day. Music volume or loudness is the choice variable or strategy of each "player." Assuming that the volume can be raised continuously from zero to very loud, the number of strategies available to each player is infinite like points on a line, i.e., the strategy level is a continuous variable. Accordingly, the Nash equilibrium will be determined in a different way, although the concept of Nash equilibrium remains exactly the same: it is that combination of strategies such that no single player has any incentive to deviate.

Let the volume chosen by Sandy and John be denoted by v_S and v_J, respectively, and let the utility functions from one's own music be

$$U_S = U_S(\underset{\pm}{v_S}, \underset{-}{v_J}); \quad U_J = U_J(\underset{-}{v_S}, \underset{\pm}{v_J}). \tag{A.2}$$

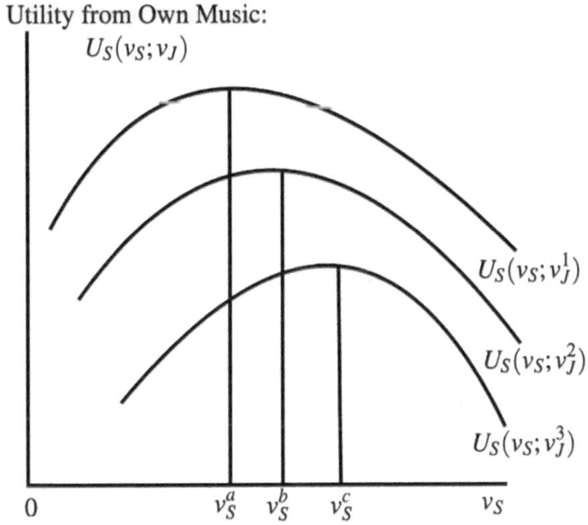

Fig. A.2: Sandy's utility from playing own music

The sign beneath each argument of the respective function indicates the nature of the cause–effect relation. The "±" sign below v_S in the $U_S(v_S, v_J)$ function means that, John's music volume remaining the same, Sandy's utility from the volume of her own music first increases and then falls. The "−" sign below v_J reflects that, for any given volume chosen by Sandy, an increase in volume set by John negatively affects Sandy's utility. This is a case of *negative externality*. The utility function of John has similar properties.

At different volumes set by John, Sandy's utility functions are exhibited in Fig. A.2. It graphs three sound levels by John: v_J^1, v_J^2, and v_J^3 where $v_J^1 < v_J^2 < v_J^3$. For any given volume played by John, Sandy's utility from the volume of her own music first increases and then falls. Notice the higher the volume played by John, (a) the less is the utility for Sandy from the same volume she plays (reflecting negative externality) and (b) the higher is her own optimal volume (since her optimal volume is louder). Figure A.2 implies that in order to counteract the negative externality, the louder John's volume, the louder plays Sandy.

John's utility function exhibits similar patterns. Further, in the above depiction we implicitly assume that the music volume set by either is not too unbearably loud for the neighbor so as not to play music at all.

Recall the definition of Nash equilibrium: it refers to those strategies such that no player benefits by deviating from his/her respective strategy. In the present context, Nash equilibrium translates to volume levels v_S^N and v_J^N such that, given v_J^N, v_S^N is the best strategy for Sandy, and, given v_S^N, v_J^N is the best strategy for John.

Turning again to Fig. A.2, if John chooses volume v_J^1, v_J^2, or v_J^3, the best volume chosen by Sandy is v_S^1, v_S^2, and v_S^3, respectively. But in order to determine Nash equilibrium, we would need to assess Sandy's best volume selection at each possible volume chosen by John as well as vice versa. Toward this end, let us graph each

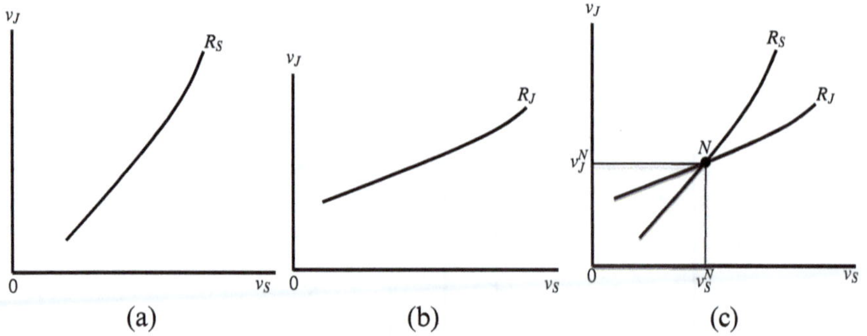

Fig. A.3: Best response functions and Nash equilibrium in the music playing game. (**a**) Sandy. (**b**) John. (**c**) Nash equilibrium

player's best music volume level, given different volumes chosen by the neighbor. This is called the *best response function*. Generally speaking, the best response function in a two-person or two-player game is a graph of one player's optimal strategy against different strategies chosen by the other. In this example, since each player plays his/her music louder as the neighbor plays louder (see Fig. A.2 once again), their best response functions will be upward sloping. These are shown in panels (a) and (b) of Fig. A.3, where R_S is the best response function of Sandy and R_J is the same for John. It is normally the case that the best response function of the player whose strategy is measured along the horizontal axis will be steeper than that of the player whose strategy is measured along the vertical axis. Hence R_S is drawn steeper than R_J.

The best response functions are drawn together in panel (c) of Fig. A.3. They intersect at point N, where the two-strategy levels are $\{v_S^N, v_J^N\}$ for Sandy and John, respectively. Realize that these strategies must constitute the Nash equilibrium, because the intersection point lies on both best response functions. By the definition of a best response function, at volume v_S^N chosen by Sandy, John's best choice is v_J^N, i.e., he has no incentive to deviate from v_J^N, and, similarly, given v_J^N, Sandy has no incentive to deviate from v_S^N. The choices $\{v_S^N, v_J^N\}$ are consistent with each other in some sense and satisfy the definition of the Nash equilibrium.

It may actually be easier to understand Nash equilibrium through equations. Going one more time back to Fig. A.2, notice that the best strategy selection points of Sandy are such that the partial $\partial U_S/\partial v_S = 0$, a first-order condition. The same will hold for John as well. Hence

$$\text{Sandy: } \frac{\partial U_S}{\partial v_S}(v_S, v_J) = 0; \quad \text{John: } \frac{\partial U_J}{\partial v_J}(v_S, v_J) = 0. \tag{A.3}$$

These are two equations in two variables. Each equation spells the respective best response function. The simultaneous solutions of the two equations are the Nash equilibrium solutions—same as v_S^N and v_J^N in Fig. A.3. The important point to note is that when Sandy and John decide their music volumes independently or non-cooperatively, the negative externalities they cause on each other—reflected by the terms $\partial U_J/\partial v_S$ and $\partial U_S/\partial v_J$—are *not* "internalized" or taken into consideration.

Two points may be noted. First, it is possible that the two best response functions do not meet; if so, there is no Nash equilibrium. Alternatively, they may meet at more than one point and in this case there are multiple equilibria. We ignore these possibilities since they are not of central interest to us. Second, negative externalities do not mean upward sloping best response function always. It depends on the nature of the game.

Like in the prisoner's dilemma case, we now ask what music volumes Sandy and John will choose if they cooperatively decide. In general, any cooperative decision aims to maximize some measure of joint gains or utility to all. In our context it seems reasonable to suppose that if Sandy and John sit down cordially over coffee to decide the volumes they will choose, they will set the sum of their utilities, $U_S(v_S, v_J) + U_J(v_S, v_J)$, as the collective objective function, which they would wish to maximize by choosing v_S and v_J.

The respective first-order conditions of maximizing this collective and cooperative objective function will be the respective choice rules:

$$v_S\colon \frac{\partial U_S}{\partial v_S}(v_S, v_J) + \underbrace{\frac{\partial U_J}{\partial v_S}(v_S, v_J)}_{\text{negative externality}} = 0 \tag{A.4}$$

$$v_J\colon \frac{\partial U_J}{\partial v_J}(v_S, v_J) + \underbrace{\frac{\partial U_S}{\partial v_J}(v_S, v_J)}_{\text{negative externality}} = 0. \tag{A.5}$$

We must understand Eqs. (A.4) and (A.5). At any given level of v_J, the best possible level of v_S that maximizes the joint gains $U_S(v_S, v_J) + U_J(v_S, v_J)$ must satisfy the marginal condition Eq. (A.4). Similarly, Eq. (A.5) is the condition that the cooperative solution of v_J must satisfy at a given level of v_S. The cooperative solutions, say v_S^C and v_J^C, are obtained by solving these two equations simultaneously.

Note importantly that unlike the non-cooperative Nash equilibrium, the negative externality effects, namely the negative effect of music volume set by Sandy on John (i.e. $\partial U_J/\partial v_S$) and that set by John on Sandy's utility, (i.e. $\partial U_J/\partial v_S$), are included in Eqs. (A.4) and (A.5), thus *internalized* in the cooperative decision making. This has a significant implication. That is, at any given v_J, the cooperative choice of v_S will be smaller, i.e., Sandy should choose a lower volume, than what she would if Sandy and John did not cooperate. Equivalently, the cooperative choice of v_S at different levels of v_J will lie to the left of the line R_S in panel (a) of Fig. A.3. This is shown by the line in panel (a) of Fig. A.4, marked R_S^c. The same applies to the cooperative choice of v_J at different levels of v_S, marked by R_J^c in panel (b) of Fig. A.4. We can call these lines as *cooperative response functions*. Compared to Nash behavior, they exhibit lower volume levels for each player given the volume choice of the other. In panel (c), the intersection of the cooperative response functions defines the cooperative equilibrium. The cooperative solutions are v_S^C and v_J^C.

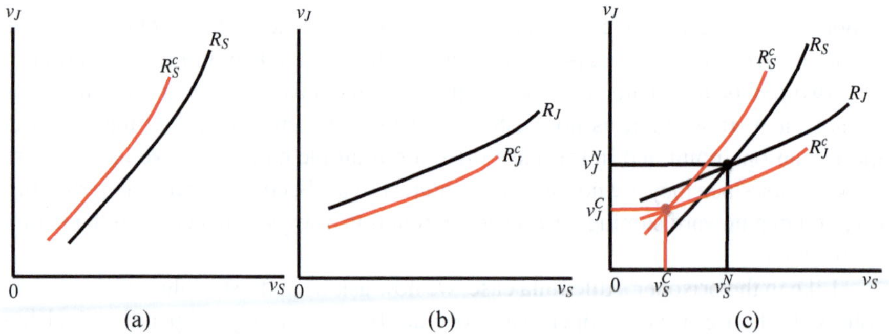

Fig. A.4: Cooperative Response Functions versus Best Response Functions and Cooperative Equilibrium versus Non-cooperative Equilibrium. (**a**) Sandy's music volume. (**b**) John's music volume. (**c**) Cooperative equilibrium

The conclusion is that, compared to the non-cooperative Nash equilibrium, under cooperation each player would use less volume. Equivalently, compared to the cooperative equilibrium, i.e., what is jointly the best strategies, under non-cooperation, each player would play music more loudly. This is because the negative externality is internalized in the cooperative equilibrium, not in the non-cooperative equilibrium. You can check that the dormitory game is analogous to the game model of security as a counter-terror measure, analyzed in Chap. 8, Sect. 8.4.

A.5 Firecrackers Contribution Game: A Case of Positive Externality[2]

Unlike the dormitory game, this an example where the action of one player exerts a positive effect on the welfare or payoff of other players. Imagine a neighborhood trying to raise funds *voluntarily* to buy fire crackers for the Independence Day celebration. If, for example, member A contributes more to the common fund, more fire crackers can be purchased which would bring more enjoyment to member B as well. Hence members would tend to free ride on others: there is a free-rider problem. Accordingly, the implication is the opposite of what it was true for the dormitory game: Nash equilibrium will be characterized by less provision of fire crackers than what is best for all members combined in a cooperative environment.

To see this clearly, suppose there are only two members, A and B. Let their voluntary contributions be m_A and m_B, respectively, both continuous, ranging from zero to infinity. The common pool of funds is $m_A + m_B$, which translates into a volume of fire crackers that provide utility to both. Let

$$U_i = U_i(m_A + m_B),\ U_i'(m_A + m_B) > 0, \text{ where } i = A, B,$$

[2] This model is analogous to preemption game model laid out in Chap. 9, Sect. 9.6.

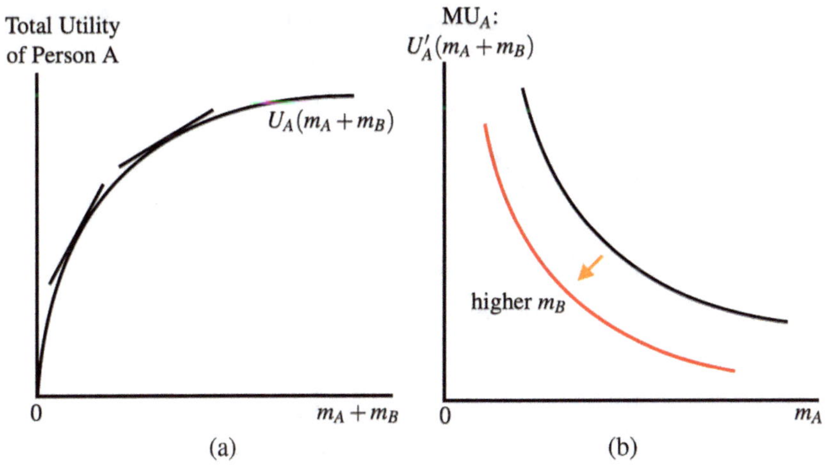

Fig. A.5: Total utility and marginal utility of member A at any given m_B . (**a**) Total utility of A. (**b**) Marginal utility of A

be the respective utility functions. Consider A's utility, for instance. Her contribution remaining the same, if B contributes more, the total contribution toward fire crackers is higher and it enhances A's utility; in this sense there is a *positive externality* from one player's strategy or action to another's utility.

Further, let $U_i''(m_A+m_B) < 0$. It implies (i) diminishing marginal utility *and* that (ii) if, for example, B increases m_B, it reduces the marginal utility of A's contribution at any given level of m_A. Thus, an increase in the contribution by one member leads to an inward shift of the marginal utility curve of the other. Panels (a) and (b) of Fig. A.5 graph the behavior of total and marginal utility curves of person A. Similar patterns hold for Member B.

When a person contributes some money for fire crackers, there is a loss of utility from the contribution itself in terms of foregone consumption of other goods. Let the own utility loss associated with a contribution of m_A by Member A be

$$\frac{1}{2} \cdot c_A \cdot m_A^2, \quad c_A > 0,$$

so that the marginal utility cost of contribution is $c_A m_A$. Hence the higher the contribution, the greater are its total and marginal utility cost. Similarly, let

$$\frac{1}{2} \cdot c_B \cdot m_B^2, \quad c_B > 0$$

be the total utility cost for Member B. In general, $c_A \gtreqless c_B$. The payoff or net utility of member i can then be expressed as

$$P_i \equiv U_i(m_A + m_B) - \frac{1}{2} \cdot c_i \cdot m_i^2.$$

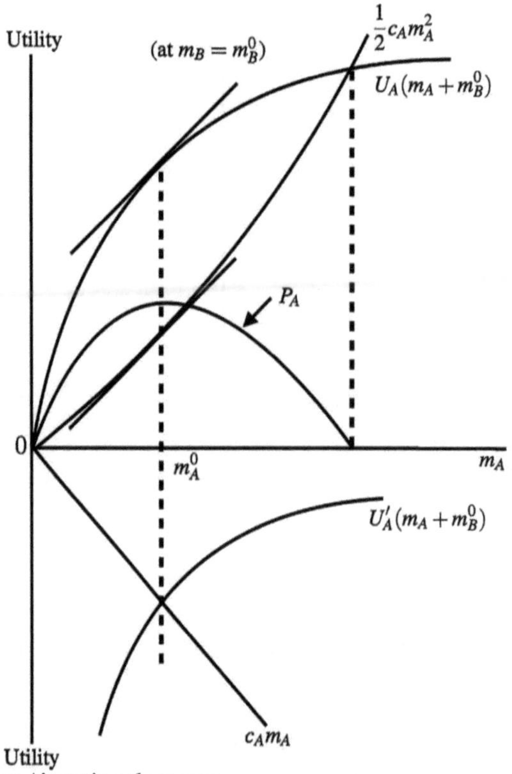

Fig. A.6: Member A's rational strategy

Nash equilibrium refers to that pair of strategies (m_A^N, m_B^N) such that A would maximize her payoff P_A with respect to m_A at m_A^N, given that B chooses m_B^N. Likewise, B would maximize her payoff P_B at $m_B = m_B^N$ given that A chooses m_A^N—so that there is no incentive to deviate from own strategy given the strategy of other player.

Refer to Fig. A.6, which depicts Member A's rational strategy when Member B's contribution is m_B^0. The upper quadrant depicts A's total utility from the firecracker show as a function of her own contribution m_A at Member B's contribution equal to m_B^0 and the total utility cost associated with her contribution. The difference between A's total utility from firecracker and her total utility cost of contribution is the curve P_A. This is A's payoff. Observe that when B contributes m_B^0, A maximizes her payoff by choosing a contribution equal to m_A^0. This is where the slope of her total utility curve, the marginal utility, is equal to the slope of her total cost line, equal to the marginal opportunity cost. The bottom quadrant illustrates A's rational choice in terms of marginal utility and marginal cost.

Algebraically, the individually rational choices, i.e., Nash equilibrium strategies, are governed by the respective first-order conditions of maximizing the payoff P_i with

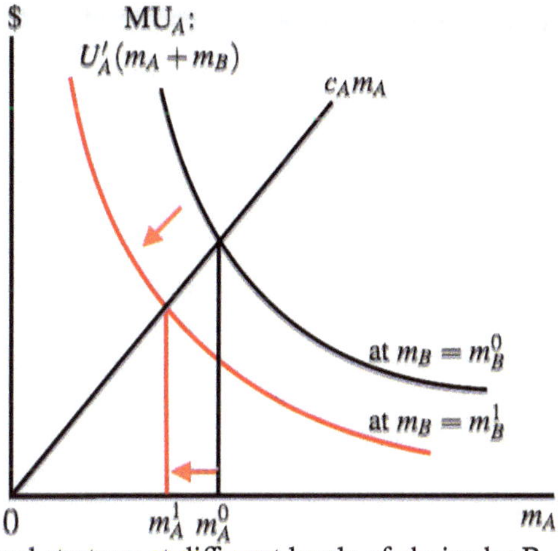

Fig. A.7: A's rational strategy at different levels of choice by B

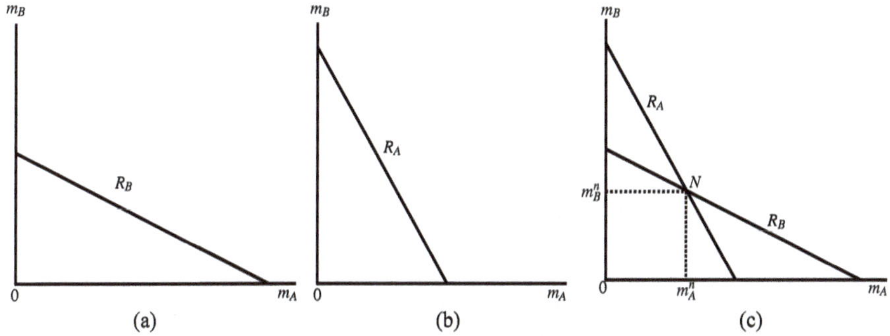

Fig. A.8: Best response functions and Nash equilibrium in the firecracker contribution game . (**a**) A's best response function. (**b**) B's best response function. (**c**) Nash equilibrium

respect to m_i. These are:

$$\text{A's choice rule for } m_A: \quad \frac{\partial U_A}{\partial m_A} = \underbrace{U'_A(m_A + m_B)}_{\text{MU}_A} = \underbrace{c_A m_A}_{\text{MC}_A} \tag{A.6}$$

$$\text{B's choice rule for } m_B: \quad \frac{\partial U_B}{\partial m_B} = \underbrace{U'_B(m_A + m_B)}_{\text{MU}_B} = \underbrace{c_B m_B}_{\text{MC}_B} . \tag{A.7}$$

The solutions for m_A and m_B from these two equations constitute the Nash solution.

As in the previous example, it will be instructive to derive the best response functions and see the Nash equilibrium graphically. We begin with the rational/optimal choice (contribution) of Member A. Panel (a) of Fig. A.7, a continuation of the lower quadrant of Fig. A.6, depicts optimal choice of m_A at two levels of m_B: m_B^0 and m_B^1 where $m_B^1 > m_B^0$. We see that $m_A^1 < m_A^0$. Recall that at an increase in m_B implies an inward shift of the marginal utility curve of Member A. Hence the marginal utility curve of A at $m_B = m_B^1$ lies to the left of that at $m_B = m_B^0$. As a result, the rational contribution by A is less when $m_B = m_B^1$ than when $m_B = m_B^0$.

The best response function of A, R_A, is thus downward sloping, shown in panel (a) of Fig. A.8. Similarly, the best response function of B, R_B, is downward sloping also; see panel (b).[3] The downward slope of the best response functions follows from the positive externality of one member's contribution toward the utility of the other, as a result of which if one member contributes more, the other tends to free ride. As we learned in the previous example, Nash equilibrium is where the two best response functions intersect: at point N in panel (c).

The central qualitative feature of the Nash non-cooperative equilibrium in this example is that there will be an *under-provision* of contributions since each member has an incentive to shirk and free ride. We can see this by analyzing the cooperative solution and comparing it with the non-cooperative Nash solution. As before, we suppose that when members cooperate and jointly decide the individual contributions, the objective is to maximize the sum of payoffs to all members. In the present context of two members, it is equal to

$$\mathcal{P}(m_A + m_B) \equiv P_A + P_B = U_A(m_A + m_B) - \frac{1}{2}c_A m_A + U_B(m_A + m_B) - \frac{1}{2}c_B m_B. \quad \text{(A.8)}$$

Notice how the marginal impact of m_A or m_B on collective payoff under cooperation differs from that on own welfare. The beneficial effect of m_A (or m_B) on Member B's (Member A's) welfare is now "internalized" in the sense that such positive externalities are taken into consideration under cooperative behavior. This was not the case when members choose their strategies independently keeping in mind their own welfare or payoff only. The following first-order (marginal) conditions define the respective cooperative response functions and govern the cooperative choice of strategies:

$$\text{Cooperative choice of } m_A\text{:} \quad \frac{\partial U_A}{\partial m_A} + \frac{\partial U_B}{\partial m_A} = U_A'(m_A + m_B) + \underbrace{U_B'(m_A + m_B)}_{\text{positive externality}} = c_A m_A \quad \text{(A.9)}$$

$$\text{Cooperative choice of } m_B\text{:} \quad \frac{\partial U_B}{\partial m_B} + \frac{\partial U_A}{\partial m_B} = U_B'(m_A + m_B) + \underbrace{U_A'(m_A + m_B)}_{\text{positive externality}} = c_B m_B. \quad \text{(A.10)}$$

The solutions of these equations, say m_A^C and m_B^C, are the cooperative solutions of strategies. These are illustrated and compared with the non-cooperative solutions in Fig. A.9. Since the positive externality of one member's contribution on the other's utility is internalized, the cooperative choice of contribution by any member will be

[3] For simplicity, the R_A and R_B lines are shown as straight lines, but they need not be.

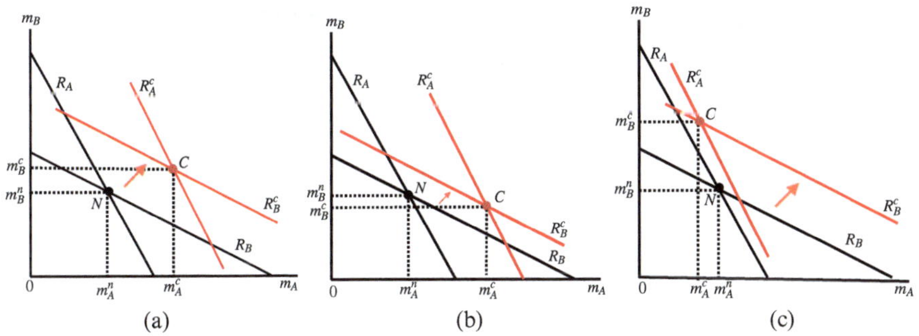

Fig. A.9: Nash non-cooperative versus cooperative equilibria in the fire cracker contribution game . (**a**) Greater contribution by both A and B. (**b**) Greater contribution by A and less by B. (**c**) Greater contribution by B and less by A

higher at any given level of contribution by the other. Accordingly, the cooperative response functions R_A^c and R_B^c lie to the right or above the best response functions under non-cooperation. This is exactly the opposite of what was true for the dormitory game. The cooperative equilibrium is indicated at point C where the two cooperative response functions intersect. Depending on how far apart the cooperative response and the (non-cooperative) best response functions are, the cooperative contributions by both members may be higher or that by one member is higher while that by the other is less. If only the members total utility and total cost functions are very different from each other, possibilities (b) or (c) will occur; otherwise it will be (a), where both members are urged to contribute more. Regardless of whether one member or both would be contributing more, it can be shown that the total contribution is always greater under cooperation than under non-cooperation.

The general conclusion is that, in this firecrackers contribution game, compared to the non-cooperative equilibrium, in the cooperative equilibrium, at least one member will contribute more and total contributions will be greater.

A.6 Other Forms of Games: Sequential and Multi-Stage Games

The games considered in preceding sections are simultaneous games in which players choose their actions simultaneously. There are game situations where some players choose their actions first and others make their choices subsequent to the actions of the first set of players. We can think of the government and the private sector as two players in which the government first announces a general economic policy and then the private sector reacts in terms of expanding business, new investment, etc. This is a *sequential game*, defined as one in which players choose their actions in turn or at different times. The (actual) game of chess is a sequential game. Sequential game concepts are used in Chaps. 9, 12, and 13.

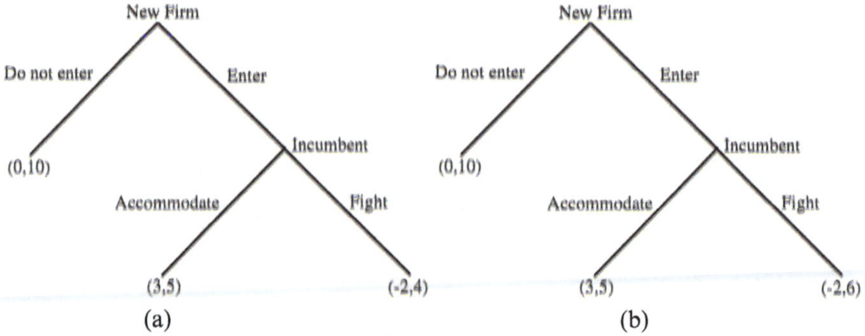

Fig. A.10: Market entry game. (**a**) *Solution:* Entry by new firm; The incumbent accommodates. (**b**) *Solution:* No entry

Figure A.10 depicts a market scenario where there is a pre-existing monopoly in the market for a good and a new firm from outside is contemplating to enter the market. There are two actions facing the potential entrant: Enter or Do not Enter. If it enters, the monopolist has two choices: Fight or Accommodate. Let "Fight" mean reducing the price to an extent such that the new entrant firm cannot make any profit, i.e., cannot survive in the market. Entry is effectively blocked. This is called *predatory pricing*, as the incumbent monopolist behaves like a predator. Let "Accommodate" means no such predatory pricing, the entrant survives and both the incumbent and the new firm produce and sell in a duopoly market. This ends the game. If the potential entrant decides not to enter in the first place, the game ends at that point of time itself. The players obtain their respective payoffs at the end of the game.

Payoffs are indicated at the terminal or ending nodes in the "market entry" game shown in Fig. A.10. There are three possible endings: (1) the new firm decides not to enter, (2) the new firm enters and the incumbent accommodates, and finally (3) the new firm enters and the incumbent fights. The left entry of a payoff vector is the payoff of the new firm or the entrant and right entry is that for the incumbent, e.g., $(3, 5)$ indicates 3 units of profits for the new firm and 5 for the incumbent firm. Notice that the difference between the two panels lies in the payoffs. In fact, there is only one difference: the payoff for the incumbent in the event of (Entry, Fight) is 4 in panel (a) and 6 in panel (b). It is presumed that the players know, i.e., correctly anticipate, what the payoffs are.

Notice there are two time periods or stages in this sequential game. In stage 1, the new firm plays or chooses its action (enter or do not enter) and in stage 2 it is the incumbent firm which chooses its action (accommodate or fight). In general, there can be two or more stages.

A sequential game is solved backward: stage 2, the last stage, first, depending, i.e., conditional on the action chosen in stage 1. Stage 1 is solved next knowing or anticipating what the stage 2 conditional solution would be. The logic is straightforward. Consider panel (a) and stage 2. If the new firm has entered, the incumbent expects a higher payoff by accommodating (equal to 5) than by fighting (equal to 4); hence the incumbent would accommodate. Now consider the decision of the new firm at the outset or stage 1. It knows that if it enters, the incumbent would play "Accommodate" and her (the new firm's) payoff would be 3. If it does not enter, it gets 0. Hence the new firm would enter. The solution of the game is "Enter" by the new firm and "Accommodate" by the incumbent.

Consider panel (b) where fighting is not so harmful for the incumbent: it makes a profit equal to 6, as opposed to 5 if it accommodates. Hence its rational choice in stage 2 is Fight, if the new firm enters. The new firm calculates in stage 1 that if it enters, the incumbent would play "Fight" and its payoff will be −2. If it does not enter, its payoff is zero. Hence its rational choice is "Do Not Enter," which is the solution of the game and which ends the game.

Remarks.
[a] Notice that in a sequential game the player who moves *after* the other player has information about the past actions by the other player. But it does not necessarily mean that the player who has more information has an advantage. It is because the player who moves first (the new firm in our example) anticipates what the future moves of the other player will be (depending on the payoffs) and its choice of action sets the future course of the actions of the other player. The first mover "leads" the game by definition, and being the first mover can be advantageous in that it influences the behavior of the other, not vice versa.
[b] In the market entry game there are two stages: first, when the new firm decides whether to enter or not, and, second, when the incumbent firm chooses its action: fight or accommodate. As said earlier, there are sequential game models having more than two stages.
[c] While a sequential game has two or more stages, *a multi-stage game may or may not be sequential*, i.e., players may not choose their actions one at a time. For instance, suppose two firms A and B are trying to do business in an outside market, e.g., in a foreign country. In doing so, they have to first invest in terms of setting up plants and infrastructure. This is stage 1. When they are ready to sell similar products, in stage 2 they would compete with each other in setting prices or quantities. Hence there is a simultaneous Nash game in stage 1 in investment levels and another simultaneous Nash game in stage 2 in setting prices, for example. It is *not* sequential as both players choose their actions in both stages, not in sequence.

Chapter B

General Appendix B: Statistics and Econometrics

This general appendix introduces and intuitively explains most of the statistical and econometric concepts that are made use of in various chapters in the text.

B.1 Correlation Coefficient

It indicates the direction and measures the strength of a linear relationship between two random variables. If we have data on annual income and the number of restaurant dining in the pre-Covid-19 era of a sample of adult individuals in a region and plot the data points in a graph it will look something like Fig. B.2a in Sect. B.3.2. This is called a *scatter diagram* or a *scatter plot*. We can think of X as income and Y as the number of dining in restaurants. We see that they are positively correlated, i.e., they tend to move in the same direction. Instead, if we plot data on height of a place above the sea level and the average annual temperature across different locations, we are likely to find a scatter plot showing that the temperature tends to go down as we move to the right along the horizontal axis measuring height.

Correlation coefficient, say ρ, is a statistical formula that quantifies the concept of bilateral association between two variables such that $\rho \in [-1, 1]$; $\rho = 1, -1$, or 0 means that the two variables are perfectly positively correlated, perfectly negatively correlated, and not correlated. Suppose we have N pairs of observations on two variables X and Y. Then

$$\text{Correlation Coefficient}_{XY} \equiv \rho_{XY} = \frac{\text{Cov}(X, Y)}{\sqrt{\text{Var}(X) \cdot \text{Var}(Y)}},^{1} \qquad \text{(B.1)}$$

[1] It can be proved that this expression is bounded between −1 and 1.

S. P. Das, *Economics of Terrorism and Counter-Terrorism Measures*,
https://doi.org/10.1007/978-3-030-96577-8

where "Cov" and "Var" stand for covariance and variance. Recall that

$$\text{Cov}(X, Y) = \sum_{i=1}^{N} (X_i - \bar{X})(Y_i - \bar{Y}),^{2} \tag{B.2}$$

where $\bar{X}$ and $\bar{Y}$ are the respective means. We see that $\rho \gtreqless 0$ according as $\text{Cov}(X, Y) \gtreqless 0$.

B.2 Hypothesis Testing or Statistical Inference

Hypothesis testing in statistics refers to testing a hypothesis or a reasoned supposition on a population parameter or population parameters. For instance, suppose that a battery manufacturer claims that its battery for a hand-held vacuum cleaner works, on average, for three hours if fully charged. We want to test whether the claim is supported by evidence. More precisely put, we want to test the hypothesis that the battery life is three hours, or if it is different from—i.e., greater or less than—three hours. This is an example of *hypothesis testing* or *statistical inference* of a population mean, where the population mean is $\mu = 3$ (measured in hours). We have two hypotheses before us:

Null Hypothesis (H_0): It is a claim about the population that is assumed true, unless proven otherwise by reasonable doubt. In our example, $H_o: \mu = 3$.

Alternative Hypothesis (H_a): It is a claim that rejects the null hypothesis. This is, $H_a: \mu \neq 3$.

One can pose an alternative hypothesis of $H_a: \mu < 3$ if the manufacturer's claim appears to be too tall. For now, we stick to the alternative hypothesis of $H_a: \mu \neq 3$.

To test the manufacturer's claim, suppose that an industry specialist obtains a random sample of 26 new batteries, tries each of them, and notes down the hours of operation after they are fully charged. So we have 26 sample data points or observations, e.g., 3.1, 2.98, 3.0, 3.01, 2.97, 2.99, and so on.[3] If we denote the observations by X_i's (there are 26 in our sample), then the sample mean is given by the formula:

$$\bar{X} = \frac{\sum_{i=1}^{N} X_i}{N} = \frac{X_1 + X_2 + \cdots + X_N}{N}, \tag{B.3}$$

where N, the sample size, is 26 in our example. Suppose in our sample $\bar{X} = 2.97$ and the standard deviation of the observations is 0.0495. Statistical measures associated with a sample are generally called *sample statistic*. A sample mean, standard deviation, or mode is a sample statistic. Can we then say with confidence that the manufacturer's claim of the population average/mean being equal to 3 is false? Or is it doubtful? Of course, if the sample mean is too far away from the claimed population mean, you will be more confident that the claim is incorrect. Further, even when the sample mean is very different from the claimed population

[2] The covariance Cov(X,Y) reduces to variance of say X if $Y = X$. Similarly Var(Y)=Cov(X, Y) when we substitute X for Y.

[3] Time is expressed in decimals, not minutes, e.g., 3.1 means 3 h and 6 min.

mean under the null hypothesis, if the standard deviation is very high, there is also a reason to doubt that the null hypothesis is false since high standard deviation means more variability of data and hence less reliability of the sample mean as an indicator of true population mean. Hypothesis testing makes these intuitive notions precise.

The underlying idea behind hypothesis testing is to pose this question: if the true (i.e. population) mean is what it is claimed in the null hypothesis, how large is the probability that the obtained sample mean is 2.97? The most common norm is that if this probability (say p) is less than 5%, i.e., $p < 0.05$, we reject the null hypothesis with "confidence." In fact, we can quantify this confidence level and say that we are rejecting the null hypothesis with a level of confidence equal to $1 - 0.05 = 0.95$ or 95%. When the confidence level is 95%, the remainder 5% is called the *level of significance*. We can equivalently say that we reject the null hypothesis at 5% level of significance.

If we consider, say, $p < 0.01$, it amounts to a 99% level of confidence or a 1% level of significance. Note that if the null hypothesis is rejected at 1% (or 5%) level of significance, it is rejected at any level of significance greater than 1% (or 5%).

To determine the value of sample statistic associated with a given level of significance or equivalently a level of confidence, we must rely on a probability distribution of the sample mean. What do we mean? Although we have only one (random) sample at our disposal, realize that the depending on chance, we could, theoretically, have had a different sample of 26 observations on batteries with a different mean say 3.02 instead of 2.97. The number of potential random samples of a given size from the same population is numerous. Hence, the number of potential sample *means* is also numerous. This implies a theoretical existence of a probability distribution of the sample mean. As you can guess, this would depend on the distribution of the observations in the population itself. Statisticians have derived what the probability distribution of the sample mean may look like depending on what the population mean is.

Let s_X denote the standard deviation of the sample observations (just as $\bar{X}$ is the sample mean). Theoretically, the number of random samples can be many, each having a pair of $\bar{X}$ and s_X. Now define a variable, $t \equiv (\bar{X} - \mu)/(s_X/\sqrt{N})$, where recall that μ is the population mean and N is the sample size. An important theoretical result is that t has a *Student's t-distribution*.[4] The Student's t-distribution has a complicated probability density function which we do not need to know. However, t varies continuously from $-\infty$ to ∞ and its distribution is bell-shaped and symmetric around 0—very similar to a normal distribution with mean 0; see Fig. B.1a. The total area under the curve is 1 (since probabilities must add up to one). In Fig. B.1a, we read that the area A equals the probability that $t \leq t_1$, the area $B + C + D$ measures the probability that $t \geq t_1$, area $A + B + C$ is the probability that $t \leq t_2$ and the area D equals the probability of $t \geq t_2$. Mathematically the Student's t-distribution approaches normal distribution as the sample size increases. That is, for large values of N, the differences between Student's t and normal distribution are negligible.

[4] Student's t-distribution was discovered by Sealy Gosset of England in 1908. By contract, he could publish his papers only in his pseudonym, which was "Student."

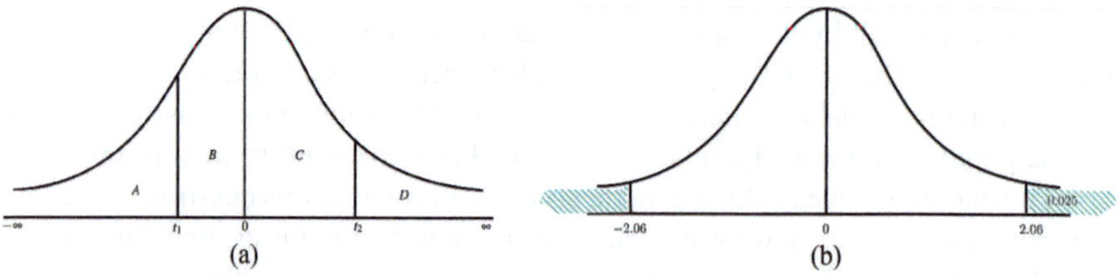

Fig. B.1: Student's t-distribution. (**a**) Shape. (**b**) Critical values

Student's t-distribution table is readily available for different sample sizes. It tells us different values of t corresponding to different probabilities. For instance, for a sample size of 26 observations, the probability that $t \geq 2.06$ or ≤ -2.06 is 0.05 or 5%. Equivalently, the probability that $t \in (-2.06, 2.06)$ equals $1 - 0.05 = 0.95$ or 95%. This is illustrated in Fig. B.1b. Notice that the area in each tail is 0.025 and the two areas add up to $2 \times 0.025 = 0.05$ or 5%.

The very last observation can be interpreted as saying that there is a 95% chance that the t-value or the t-score will lie between −2.06 and 2.06. Using the definition of the $t \equiv (\bar{X} - \mu)/(s_X/\sqrt{N})$, the right hand of which is called the *t-statistic*, we can say that there is a 95% chance that

$$-2.06 \leq \frac{\bar{X} - \mu}{s_X/\sqrt{N}} \leq 2.06,$$

which is equivalent to

$$\mu - 2.06 \times s_X/\sqrt{N} \leq \bar{X} \leq \mu + 2.06 \times s_X/\sqrt{N}.$$

Now turn to the example of hand-held vacuum cleaner. We know that the standard deviation of the observations in the sample is $s_X = 0.0495$, whereas the sample size is $N = 26$. Hence $s_X/\sqrt{N} \simeq 0.0097$. It follows that if *the null hypothesis were true*, i.e., if the population mean is $\mu = 3$, the preceding inequality simplifies to $2.98 \leq \bar{X} \leq 3.02$. That is, there is a 95% chance that $\bar{X} \in [1.98, 2.02]$ if the null hypothesis is correct. This is called a 95% *confidence interval* for $\bar{X}$. Equivalently put, there is only a 5% chance that $\bar{X}$ will have a value outside this interval. Recall that the actual sample mean is 2.97, which is outside this range. Hence our hypothesis testing concludes that *the null hypothesis of $\mu = 3$ against $\mu \neq 3$ is rejected at 5% level of significance* or with a confidence level of 95%.

An alternative method to achieve the same is to first compute the value of t-statistic from the sample under the null hypothesis. Applying the expression of the t-statistic, $(\bar{X} - \mu)/(s_X/\sqrt{N})$, the sample $t = (2.97 - 3)/(0.0495/\sqrt{26}) = -0.03 \times \sqrt{26}/0.0495 = -3.09$. This is less than the critical value of −2.06 from the Student

t-distribution table. In Fig. B.1b, the sample t falls in the shaded area in the left-hand tail, leading to the rejection of the null of $\mu = 3$ vis-à-vis the alternative hypothesis of $\mu \neq 3$. In fact, this computation is simpler than first which determines the confidence interval and then checks if the sample mean falls inside or outside of this interval. This leads to a simple *general procedure of any hypothesis testing: compute the sample statistic and compare with the critical value.*

Notice that the higher the standard deviation or the lower the level of significance, the larger is the confidence interval and hence the smaller are the chances of the null hypothesis being rejected.

B.2.1 Two Tailed and One-Tailed Tests

It is also important to note that in our example the alternative hypothesis is simply the negation of the null: $\mu \neq 3$ vis-à-vis $\mu = 3$. That means we allow the alternative to be on both sides of the null: greater or less than 3. This is why the level of significance equals to sum of the areas in the left-hand and right-hand side tails of the distribution—as in Fig. B.1b. Accordingly the example falls in the category of what is called *a two-tailed test of hypothesis*.

However, as noted earlier, we can pose an alternative hypothesis of $\mu < 3$ against the same null of $\mu = 3$ if we believe that the manufacturer's claim of $\mu = 3$ appears unusually high. In this case, we have to look at only the left tail of the distribution in Fig. B.1b. If we are to do hypothesis testing at 5% level of significance we must look at that value of t in the left-hand tail such that the area to the left of it is 0.05 (*not* 0.025). The critical value of t for this from the Student's t table for $N = 26$ is -1.717. Since the sample $t = -3.09$, the null is rejected. This is an example of a *one-tailed test of hypothesis.*

Hypothesis testing is not restricted to the testing of population mean only. We can test hypotheses on population standard deviation, whether the means of two populations are significantly different from each other or not, and so on. For instance, we may be interested in comparing the average SAT test scores of 12th grade students in public schools and private schools and see if the difference is significant. Let populations 1 and 2 refer to 12th grade students in public and private schools, respectively. Let the mean SAT score of populations 1 and 2 be denoted as μ_1 and μ_2. Here the null hypothesis is $\mu_1 = \mu_2$, while alternative hypothesis would be $\mu_1 \neq \mu_2$ if we have reasons to believe that the public schools may be better or the private schools may be better in terms of SAT score. A two-tailed test is called for. If, otherwise, the researcher believes that the SAT scores by the 12th graders in public schools may be worse or at best as good as but not better than by the 12th graders in private schools, the alternative hypothesis will be $\mu_1 < \mu_2$, which would require a one-tailed test. The appropriate test statistic is also Student's t but the expression of the t-statistic is different from that in the case of hypothesis testing on the mean of one population only.

Finally, note that depending on the population parameter, the relevant sample statistic may *not* be the Student's t. For example, in order to test a hypothesis on the magnitude of population variance, the relevant sample statistic is *chi-square*.

B.2.2 *p*-Value

The term p-value is intimately related to the concept of the level of significance. *It is the minimum of the significant levels at which a null hypothesis can be rejected or barely accepted.* Consider the example of the battery life time of hand-held vacuum cleaners. In a sample with 26 observations, a mean of 2.97 hours and a standard deviation of 0.0495 hours, we had the t-statistic equal to −3.09. For the two-tailed test with H_o: $\mu = 3$ vis-à-vis H_a: $\mu \neq 3$, the p-value associated with −3.09 is twice the area that is associated with the point −3.09 in Fig. B.1b. It is equal to 0.0048.[5] A p-value of 0.0048 means that the null hypothesis can be rejected at any significance level higher than 0.48%, certainly 1% or 5%. This means that the chances of the null hypothesis being true is less than even 0.5%, so that the null hypothesis is strongly rejected.

B.3 Basics of Regression

Typically, theoretical predictions on cause–effect relations in economics and many other disciplines are tested by using a statistical/econometric method called *regression*. *Simple regression* analyzes how, from data on two variables, say, X and Y, one variable, say Y is explained by the other, X. For example, if we have data on earnings of individuals and their years of education in a region or country, we may want to understand how earnings are related, *quantitatively*, to educational attainment by using simple regression.

Multiple regression is one where a variable Y is explained by two or more variables like X_1, X_2, and so on. For instance, with available data on wage earnings of various individuals and their personal characteristics in a given economy, we may want to learn how wage earnings (Y) are related not just to a person's education (X_1) but also to gender (X_2), age (X_3), etc., at a given point or over an interval of time.

The variable Y has several generic names like a dependent variable, an explained variable, a predicted variable, a response variable, an outcome variable and regressand. Similarly, an X is called an independent variable, an explanatory variable, a regressor, or a covariate.

B.3.1 Cross-Sectional, Time-Series, and Panel Data

Data on dependent and independent variables are available in three formats. Cross-section data refers to a situation where X's and Y are variables defined for a single point or over an interval of time. Consider the above example of the dependence of wage earnings on education, gender, etc. Suppose we use the data on these variables within a given year for different individuals, say for the year 2021 and for 10,000 individuals in a particular country or region. Such data across individuals or units at a given time or within a single time period is called *cross-sectional data*. The

[5] There are free calculators available on the internet where you provide the t score, the "degrees of freedom" (equal to the sample size minus 1) and whether you want a two-tailed or one-tailed test. The p value comes up once you hit the "calculate" button.

Dependent variable	Independent variables		
Annual wage earnings ($)	Education (Years of schooling)	Gender	Age (Years)
25,000	13	Female	22
27,500	12	Male	22
31,260	15	Male	30
60,000	20	Female	55
65,000	20	Male	56

Year: 2021

Table B.1: A hypothetical example of cross-section data

	Dependent variable	Independent variables	
Year	Real consumption expenditure Billions of $ (in 2013 prices)	Real GDP Billions of $ (in 2013 prices)	Rate of unemployment In percentage
2015	25.3	35.6	6.7
2016	26.5	37.2	6.0
2017	28.1	38.5	6.5
2018	30.3	41.0	5.4
2019	32.5	42.8	4.6

Table B.2: A hypothetical example of time-series data

time period could be daily, weekly, monthly, quarterly, yearly, or even an interval of multiple periods, e.g., five years together like 2017–2021.[6]

Time-series data refers to data on a variable over time, e.g., annual or quarterly GDP of the USA or any other country during 2000–2021.

Panel data tracks cross-sectional data over time for *the same units of observation*. It has both cross-sectional and time-series elements. For instance, we may have annual record of wheat production, rainfall and acreage devoted to wheat production in different states of a country. For any given year, it constitutes cross-sectional data across different states. But over multiple periods of time, the whole dataset is called *panel data* or *longitudinal data.*

Tables B.1, B.2, and B.3, respectively, present hypothetical examples of cross-section, time-series, and panel data.

B.3.2 Simple "Linear" Regression

Regression analysis is best understood by analyzing cross-sectional data. As stated earlier, simple regression refers to the simple case with only one explanatory variable, i.e., one X. If, for example, we want to know how wage earnings (Y) are explained by education level (X) only, we first have to have a sample of data on various individuals.

[6] *Repeated cross-sectional data* refers to surveys administered on new cross-sectional units at successive points of time.

Year	Cities	Dependent variable Murder rate (per 100,000 population)	Independent variables Population density (per square mile in '000s)	 Size of police force (in '000s)
2014	A	10.1	15.4	10.3
2014	B	11.3	16.4	9.6
2014	C	13.5	18.2	9.0
2015	A	12.2	16.5	10.7
2015	B	12.3	17.1	10.9
2015	C	14.6	18.0	8.9
2016	A	12.0	16.4	10.9
2016	B	14.5	17.7	9.8
2016	C	13.0	18.2	11.0
2017	A	11.9	15.9	11.0
2017	B	13.3	17.7	10.7
2017	C	13.0	18.0	11.2
2018	A	10.5	16.3	11.3
2018	B	13.0	17.0	11.0
2018	C	13.5	17.9	11.5
2019	A	9.3	16.6	12.0
2019	B	9.5	17.0	12.3
2019	C	12.0	18.1	9.6

Table B.3: A hypothetical example of panel data

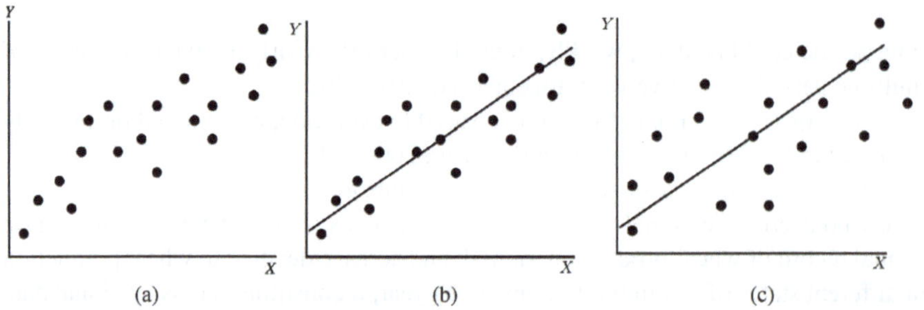

Fig. B.2: Scatter diagram and regression line: Simple regression. (**a**) Scatter plot. (**b**) Regression line 1. (**c**) Regression line 2

Suppose we do have data on wage earnings and the years of education measuring education level. If we plot the (X, Y) data we will get a graph resembling that in panel (a) of Fig. B.2, which is a scatter diagram. We can see that the relationship between X and Y is positive, that is, overall, higher X is associated with higher Y—as one would expect. The idea behind regression is to find a line, called the *regression line*, that best fits the data in a scatter diagram.

In many situations, the regression line is assumed to be linear or a straight line. Accordingly, it is called *linear regression*. Unless otherwise stated, by regression we will mean "linear" regression. Panel (b) of Fig. B.2 shows how a regression line will look like for the scatter plot in panel (a). (Ignore panel (c) for now.) Algebraically, it fits a linear equation, say, $Y = a + bX$, to the data, where a is the intercept coefficient and b is the slope coefficient. The aim is to find the estimates of a and b which fits the data the best. Let the estimates be distinguished by a "hat," i.e. let $\hat{a}$ and $\hat{b}$ denote the estimates of parameters a and b, respectively.

We must specify a criterion for the "best fit." The most common criterion is to choose $\hat{a}$ and $\hat{b}$ such that *the sum of squares of the deviations between the actual and fitted values of Y over all observations in the data is minimized.* If we have, say N observations (e.g. data on education levels and wage earnings of N individuals) like (X_1, Y_1), (X_2, Y_2),..., (X_N, Y_N), then $\hat{a}$ and $\hat{b}$ are such that they minimize

$$\sum_{i=1}^{N} (Y_i - a - bX_i)^2 = (Y_1 - a - bX_1)^2 + (Y_2 - a - bX_2)^2 + \cdots + (Y_N - a - bX_N)^2 .$$

Each term in the right-hand side is the square of the vertical distance between the scatter point and the fitted line, so that *the fitted line passes through the middle of the scatter diagram in some sense.*

More formally, we assume that the *true* or the population relationship between X and Y is given by a *statistical equation*, meaning an equation or a relationship that has a random component or an error term. Linear regression postulates a linear relation like:

$$Y_i = a + bX_i + u_i, \quad E(u_i) = 0, \ i = 1, \ldots, N, \tag{B.4}$$

where u_i is an error term for each observation i and $E(\cdot)$ stands for statistical expectation or mean. The presence of the error term makes the equation statistical rather than "deterministic." The expectation of the error term u_i being equal to 0 is a normalization.

Minimizing $\sum_{i=1}^{N} \left(Y_i - \hat{a} - \hat{b}X_i\right)^2$ amounts to minimizing the sum of the squares of the error terms, $\sum_{i=1}^{N} u_i^2$. The corresponding $\hat{a}$ and $\hat{b}$—which minimize the above sum of squares—are called the *least squares* or *ordinary least squares* (OLS) estimates. As you would expect, $\hat{a}$ and $\hat{b}$ will be dependent upon the data on X and Y in particular ways, i.e., through formulas. We do not, however, specify those formulas here. An interested reader would find them in any elementary book on statistics.

An important assumption is that

Assumption B.1. *There is no correlation between X_i and u_i. More generally speaking, there is no correlation between the explanatory variables and the error term.*

There are other assumptions, for instance, that, for any two observations i and j, $\text{Cov}(u_i, u_j) = 0$.

It important to understand why we need the error term to be uncorrelated with X, because, otherwise, minimizing the sum of the squares of the error terms does not really filter out all effects of X on Y, and, as a result, $\hat{a}$ and $\hat{b}$ would be "poor" or "unreliable" indicators of what the true respective values are. In the language of statistics and econometrics, if X and u are correlated, the least square estimates of a and b will be *inconsistent*.

Suppose that Y is the annual wage earnings in thousand dollars and X is the number of years of education and we find that $\hat{a} = 3.12$ and $\hat{b} = 4.30$, respectively. These numbers mean that (i) the average wage earnings of someone who has had 12 years of education are: $(3.12 + 4.30 \times 12) = $54.72, which translates to annual earnings equal to $54,720 and (ii) one extra year of education brings $4300 extra annual wage earnings. This is a hypothetical example.

B.3.2.1 Hypothesis Testing

Notice that the estimate of b is of central interest to us if we want to learn whether and how X impacts on Y. Whether X impacts on Y is same as asking whether b is different from zero. Although from the data we found $\hat{b}$ to be positive (= 4.30), it is based on one sample only. How confident should we be to conclude from this that the true value of b is different from zero, i.e., education significantly affects wage earnings? It depends on how scattered the actual values are around the fitted regression line. If they are very close to the fitted values and the slope is positive, we should be confident. Otherwise, if the variation of Y around the regression line is high (e.g. panel (c) of Fig. B.2 in comparison to panel (b) [given that scatter diagrams in (b) and (c) yield the same regression line] then, because of high variability, we cannot be confident that $\hat{b} = 4.30$ means that the true b is non-zero. Hence, we cannot conclude that X affects Y significantly even if we find the sample estimate of b equal to 4.30. This is where hypothesis testing plays a critical role.

Let the null and the alternative hypotheses be $H_o\colon b = 0$ and $H_a\colon b \neq 0$. Depending upon the value of the coefficient estimate and other characteristics of data, we can infer, for example, whether the parameter b is different from zero at 10%, 5%, or 1% level of statistical significance. The lower the level of significance, the higher is the level of confidence that the coefficient of interest significantly differs or does not significant differ from zero. The relevant sample statistic to test the null hypothesis of $b = 0$ (or more generally b being equal to any given number) turns out to be Student's t.

Although there is no hard and fast rule, we normally accept a coefficient to be (statistically) "significant" if the associated level of significance is between 5% to 1%, "highly significant" if the level of significance is 1% or less, and "marginally significant" if it is between 10 and 5%.

Testing a cause–effect prediction of a theory amounts to whether the corresponding coefficient estimate is statistically significant *and* it has the right sign. If we get the wrong sign of the coefficient (for instance, if $\hat{b}$ were equal to −2.50 instead of 4.30), then we can safely think that something is seriously wrong: either the theory is bad, there is something wrong with the data, or the estimation procedure is unsound.

B.3.3 Multiple Regression

Ideas behind simple regression extend to multiple regression, while multiple regression brings its own extra dimensions and is algebraically more complicated. If we want to explain variable Y by, say, K variables (X_1 through X_K), we posit a linear statistical equation like:

$$Y_i = a + b_1X_{i1} + b_2X_{i2} + \cdots + b_KX_{iK} + u_i, \quad E(u_i) = 0,\ i = 1,2,\ldots N, \qquad \text{(B.5)}$$

assuming that we have data on the K explanatory variables and the explained variable Y. As in case of simple regression, Assumption B.1 saying that *the error term u and none of the X are correlated*, is very important. Equation (B.5) is a more general version of (B.4). The least squares estimates, $\hat{a}$, $\hat{b}_1, \ldots, \hat{b}_K$, are obtained by minimizing the sum of squares:

$$\sum_{i=1}^{N} u_i^2 = \sum_{i=1}^{N} (Y_i - a - b_1X_{i1} - b_2X_{i2} - \ldots b_KX_{iK})^2 .$$

The formulas for the OLS estimates $\hat{a}$ and $\hat{b}$'s are complicated and typically expressed in matrix notation. However, similar to simple regression, the objective of multiple regression is to estimate, and evaluate or test the hypotheses on the effects of two or more variables on whatever variable we want to explain. After estimating the coefficients, for the coefficient on each explanatory variable, we first check the statistical significance (typically 5%, 1%, or 10%), and, if significant, whether the coefficient has the correct sign. Statistical inference (same as hypothesis testing) may not support all, some or none of the variables being significant.

B.4 Quantitative and Qualitative or Categorical Variables, and Introduction of Dummy Variable

There are two types of explanatory and explained variables: (a) quantitative and (b) qualitative or categorical. Quantitative variables are described by integers or measurements on the real line, e.g., years of education of an individual, his/her age, GDP of a nation, a family's expenditure on clothing, and so on. Such quantitative variables are easy to incorporate in the regression analysis.

Suppose we want to understand how earnings of an individual are explained by the person's education, work experience, gender, and ethnicity. Notice that a person's education and work experience are quantitative variables: they can be measured, say, in years. But the last two "factors" (which reflect discrimination in the labor market) are qualitative or categorical variables—that are identifiable but cannot be measured numerically. Such variables represent states, attributes, or qualitative features. Gender will normally take two values: male or female. Depending on the context, ethnicity can be white, black, or Hispanic. We can think of many other categorical variables in the context of a cause-and-effect relation. For instance, we may want to investigate how location of a house in a metropolitan area may affect its sale price, where locations could be East, West South, North, Center, North Central, etc.

Instead of duration in education (number of years in school and college), we may be interested in the impact of education *level* on earnings, where we can categorize the education level into low-, middle-, or high-education people based on some criteria. Hence depending on what we may be interested to learn, the same variable can be quantitative or qualitative.

Thus far, we have introduced several qualitative variables as explanatory or independent (X) variables so far. The dependent variable can be qualitative too. Here are some examples.

[a] We may want to learn how class attendance affects whether a student would pass or fail. Here pass/fail is a Y variable, i.e., the dependent variable is categorical.

[b] If we are interested to learn how class attendance affects the letter grade of students, the dependent variable is categorical with states or outcomes like A, B, C, etc.

[c] Suppose we are interested in predicting how SAT scores and parental income of students affect whether a student gets admission into an ivy-league school. The dependent variable is qualitative: admission into an ivy-leagues school and no admission into an ivy-league school.

[d] We want to learn how age, education, and work experience of individuals affect their opinions on a particular government policy. One can conduct a survey in which individuals are asked to furnish information on their age, education, and work experience (with privacy being protected or promised) and they would have to "rate" the government policy as "bad," "good," and "very good." Here the dependent variable, the respondents' opinion, assumes three qualitative values: bad, good, and very good.

The question is, how do we incorporate qualitative variables in the regression analysis?

B.4.1 Qualitative Independent Variable

Suppose it takes only two values, i.e., has two states or attributes, e.g., male or female. There is a simple yet ingenious method to incorporate a qualitative independent variable: assign 0 to one attribute or state and 1 to the other, e.g., assign Male = 0 and Female = 1. It does *not* matter, which of the two is assigned 0 or 1. A variable which can take two values, 0 or 1, is called a *dummy variable* or a *binary variable*.

In the gender example, suppose we want to learn the magnitude of gender bias in the labor market in terms of wage earnings. We begin with by assigning the number 0 to one of the categories, say for male. Then female is assigned value 1. (As said earlier, it does not matter which category is assigned 0.) Next we create a variable say "GENDER", and let it be the Kth variable in Eq. (B.5). Then, if the ith observation is a female, then $X_{iK} = \text{GENDER}_i = 1$. If another observation, say j, is a male, then $X_{jK} = \text{GENDER}_j = 0$ and so on. The estimate of $\hat{b}_K$ reveals the gender bias. Almost surely, the value of $\hat{b}_K$ will be negative, meaning that, compared to male workers, female workers are paid less, on average, all other factors remaining the same, i.e., there is a gender discrimination against female workers. Had we assigned male = 1 and female = 0, then we would obtain the $\hat{b}_k$ to be positive with the same magnitude. This should be read as how much more men are paid compared to women on average, all else the same.

More specifically, in Eq. (B.5), let X_K be the gender dummy, 0 for male and 1 for female and let the least square estimate $\hat{b}_K$ be equal to \$−10.5. We have

$$\hat{Y}_i = \begin{cases} \hat{a} + \hat{b}_1 X_{i1} + \hat{b}_2 X_{i2} + \ldots & \text{if } X_{iK} = 0 \\ \hat{a} + \hat{b}_1 X_{i1} + \hat{b}_2 X_{i2} + \cdots + \hat{b}_K & \text{if } X_{iK} = 1, \end{cases} \tag{B.6}$$

implying that the difference between $\hat{Y}_i$ when $X_{iK} = 1$ and $\hat{Y}_i$ when $X_{iK} = 0$ is $\hat{b}_K$. Hence, $\hat{b}_K = -10.5$ means that, all else the same, on the average, a female worker earns \$10, 500 less than a male worker (assuming that Y_i is measured in thousands of dollars).

How do we incorporate a qualitative explanatory variable with more than two attributes or states? Suppose one of our explanatory variables is ethnicity, which can be one of the three states: white, black, or Hispanic. In this case we can use two (0-1) dummy variables, say D_1 and D_2, with D_1 taking value 1 if the person is black and 0 otherwise and D_2 taking value 1 if the person is Hispanic and 0 otherwise. *There is no need to define a dummy variable with respect to a person being white.* Here is how it works. Suppose the ith observation corresponds to a person who is black. Then $D_1 = 1$. Since he/she is not Hispanic, $D_2 = 0$. Likewise, if the person is Hispanic, then $D_1 = 0$ and $D_2 = 1$. Finally, if the person is white, then $D_1 = D_2 = 0$. Hence, all three ethnicities are represented through two dummy variables. It does not matter whether the two dummy variables are defined with respect to (black, Hispanic), (white, black), or (white, Hispanic).

How do we interpret the coefficients? Suppose the regression equation is

$$Y_i = a + b_1 X_{i1} + c_1 D_{i1} + c_2 D_{i2} + u_i, \quad E(u_i) = 0, \tag{B.7}$$

where $D_{i1} = 1$ or 0 if the person is black or not black and $D_{i2} = 1$ or 0 if the person is Hispanic or not Hispanic. Let the corresponding estimated equation be:

$$\hat{Y}_i = \hat{a} + \hat{b}_1 X_{i1} + \hat{c}_1 D_{i1} + \hat{c}_2 D_{i2}. \tag{B.8}$$

Thus,

$$\hat{Y}_i = \begin{cases} \hat{a} + \hat{b}_1 X_{i1} + \hat{c}_1 & \text{if the person is black} \\ \hat{a} + \hat{b}_1 X_{i1} + \hat{c}_2 & \text{if the person is Hispanic} \\ \hat{a} + \hat{b}_1 X_{i1} & \text{if the person is white.} \end{cases} \tag{B.9}$$

Suppose the estimated coefficients on dummy variables are $\hat{c}_1 = -5.5$ and $\hat{c}_2 = -6.2$, respectively. It then means that, on average and all else the same, a black worker and a Hispanic worker, respectively, earn \$5500 and \$62,000 dollars less than a white worker.[7]

[7] If, instead the estimated coefficient on the black worker is positive, it means a black person earns more than a white person, on the average. However, in an actual regression situation with real data, both coefficients will almost surely be negative.

We can now generalize and say that if there are d categories or states of a categorical explanatory variable, we create $d - 1$ dummy variables to capture the effect of d categories on the dependent variable.

Other Uses of Dummy Variable Dummy variables are used extensively in the regression analysis to capture various types of qualitative effects. Here are some additional examples. Suppose we want to explain how, among other factors, residence in a rural area as opposed an urban area, affects, earnings. We can create a dummy, say, URBAN, which takes values 0 or 1 according as the individual resides in a rural or an urban area. Suppose that our sample of earnings and personal-level information like education, sex, work experience, etc. covers individuals across various states of the USA. We can argue that different states offer different earnings opportunities because of state-specific policies, geography, etc. We can capture the state-specific effects by creating state-level dummies, say, STATE1, ..., STATE49, given that there are fifty states.

Monthly and sometime quarterly data contain seasonal effects. For example, if we want to explain the volume of monthly mail deliveries of a post office, we will invariably see a jump in numbers in holiday months, say December and January. If we want to explain monthly data on new air-conditioning units sold in a city or a state, there will be a lot more sold in summer months compared to non-summer months. In general, we can estimate seasonal effects by using *seasonal dummies*. For monthly data, we can create eleven dummies to represent twelve months of a year. If we are dealing with quarterly data and we believe that there may be seasonal effects, then we can use three dummies to capture four quarters.[8]

Annual data does not show seasonality. Yet, in time-series data dummies are used extensively to capture special effect of events specific to certain time periods. Put differently, dummies are used for different time periods if we believe that the time periods are intrinsically different based on some structural variations. In terrorism, we can differentiate between pre-9/11 era and post-9/11 era by introducing a "9/11" dummy. Time period related dummies will be discussed in more detail in Sect. B.13.2.

B.4.2 Qualitative Dependent Variable: Logit, Probit, and Tobit

We have already noted a few examples where the dependent variable is qualitative: pass/fail, letter grade, admission into ivy schools and outcomes of opinion poll on government policy. Different categories or states of a qualitative *dependent* variable are commonly referred to as *outcomes*.

If the dependent variable has binary outcomes, we can define it as a 0-1 dummy. For instance, in the ivy school admission example, if the student gets admission into an ivy school, $Y = 1$; if he/she does not, then $Y = 0$. There is, however, a problem with "linear" regression if the dependent variable is qualitative. Continuing with the example of ivy school admission, suppose that we specify the standard linear

[8] Alternatively, there are methods to "de-seasonalize" data, which we do not discuss here.

regression model as:

$$Y_i = a + b_1 X_{i1} + b_2 X_{i2} + u_i, \quad E(u_i) = 0, \tag{B.10}$$

where X_1 and X_2 denote SAT score and parental income, respectively, and $Y = 0, 1$ according as the student does not get or does get admission into an ivy-league school. By definition then,

$$\begin{aligned} E(Y_i) &= 0 \times \text{Probability of no admission into an ivy school} \\ &\quad + 1 \times \text{Probability of the admission to an ivy school} \\ &= \text{Probability of admission into an ivy school.} \end{aligned}$$

On the other hand, given the values of X_1 and X_2, the expected Y_i in our regression model (B.10) has the expression:

$$E(Y_i) = a + b_1 X_{i1} + b_2 X_{i2} + E(u_i) = a + b_1 X_1 + b_2 X_2, \tag{B.11}$$

since, by definition $E(u_i) = 0$. Now equate the expressions of $E(Y_i)$ in the two mathematical equations above. We have

$$\text{Probability of admission into an ivy school} = a + b_1 X_{i1} + b_2 X_{i2}.$$

The difficulty is that the left-hand side of the above equation should be a real number bounded between 0 and 1 (since it is a probability), whereas the right hand, being linear in X_{i1} and X_{i2}, *can* be negative or positive exceeding one depending on the values of X_{i1} and X_{i2} and their estimated coefficients. This is not acceptable.

This problem is avoided by specifying *a probability model*, rather than a standard regression model, which assigns the probability of Y_i taking different possible values (two possible values here, 0 and 1) to a *non-linear function* of $a + b_1 X_{i1} + b_2 X_{i2}$:

$$\begin{aligned} P(Y_i = 1) &= \frac{\exp(a + b_1 X_1 + b_2 X_2)}{1 + \exp(a + b_1 X_1 + b_2 X_2)} \\ P(Y_i = 0) &= 1 - \frac{\exp(a + b_1 X_1 + b_2 X_2)}{1 + \exp(a + b_1 X_1 + b_2 X_2)} \\ \Rightarrow E(Y_i) &= \frac{\exp(a + b_1 X_1 + b_2 X_2)}{1 + \exp(a + b_1 X_1 + b_2 X_2)}, \end{aligned} \tag{B.12}$$

where $\exp(\cdot)$ is the exponential function. Note that irrespective of the sign and magnitude of X_1 and X_2, in the first two equations in (B.12), the probability lie between 0 and 1, as it should. Since Y_i can take two values 0 and 1, $E(Y_i)$ must be between 0 and 1, confirmed by its expression (B.12). The trick is that probability distribution is made such a non-linear function of X_1 and X_2 that the individual probabilities are bounded between 0 and 1. The parameters of this probability model, namely a, b_1, and b_2, are estimated by a maximum likelihood method (see Sect. B.11 below).

The non-linear model specified in (B.12) is called the *logit model*. The *probit model* is a different non-linear specification of the probabilities that we do not specify here. The general point is that *linear regression does not make sense if the dependent value is categorical. Instead, we must specify a non-linear regression or probability model.*

What if the dependent variable takes more than two qualitative states or outcomes like "bad," "good," and "very good" in the public opinion example? Unlike in case of an independent qualitative variable taking more than two values, it does not make sense to create multiple dummy *dependent* variables because, by definition, the dependent variable must be unique. Instead, different qualitative states are represented by numerics 0, 1, 2,. . . . In the public opinion example, we may define $Y_i = 0, 1, 2$ according as the outcome is bad, good, or very good. If credit rating (not numerical scores) is the qualitative variable, we may consider several categories like very bad, average, good, very good, etc. Note that these outcomes are ordinal, that is, they are ordered in some way, while they are not measured numerically. Non-linear regression method is used—and the standard estimation methods are *ordered logit* or *ordered probit*.

There are situations when we want to explain a categorical variable with more than two types but they are *not* ordinal, i.e., they cannot be ranked, e.g., choice of mode of long-distance travel with say three alternatives (bus, train, or private vehicle) and educational field choice (hard science, health science, social science, or humanities). Again, non-linear regression comes into play and this class of models is known as *multinomial logit* or *multinomial probit*.

While logit and probit models have two mass points of the dependent variable (at $Y = 0$ and $Y = 1$), the so-called *Tobit* model (named after James Tobin, a Nobel Laureate in economics) is a useful specification to account for mass points in a dependent variable that is otherwise continuous. That is, the Tobit model is used when Y is continuous but for one mass point, in many situations at value 0. In this sense, it is similar to logit or probit models. As an example, suppose we want to estimate an equation of expenditure on air travel within a time period over a cross-section of individuals in a region or country. The data will almost surely include many observations where an individual has not traveled by air. The same will be true for demand for housing (owning a home). In these cases the dependent variable has a big mass at 0 but otherwise continuous. Hence the Tobit model can be used.

B.5 Data Issues

In some situations, data may be available on the exact variables incorporated in a theory. For instance, suppose one formulates a theory that crime increases with unemployment and economic inequality. For many countries, data on crime, unemployment as well as income inequality are readily available. In these situations we simply use the available on the variables and choose the appropriate estimation method. For instance, one can perform what is called *a cross-country regression analysis*.[9]

However, in general, there may be different data issues. We discuss three of them below.

B.5.1 Proxy Variables

In some situations, data on the exact variables of interest may not be available. For instance, wage earnings would depend, besides education and other variables, on one's innate ability, but innate ability is something that cannot be directly measured. However, if data is available on IQ of individuals in the sample, it can be used as a proxy for innate ability. Thus, the IQ score is a *proxy variable.*

It is also possible that there can be more than one proxy for a single variable. For instance, in the field of international trade, there are predictions based on differing economy size across countries. How do we measure the "size" of an economy? One proxy would be the real GDP. However, by definition, it includes quantities *and* price terms, which may not be satisfactory. Another proxy used for the economy size is the size of a country's labor force. In such situations, different proxies are used for the same variable to check robustness of the theory. If a prediction holds up when one proxy is used, but does not when another reasonable proxy is included in order to represent the same variable, then the robustness of the impact of the variable is questioned.

For instance, think about the variable wealth gap in Landes's model in Chap. 8. It is generally hard to obtain data on W_i and W_j. In such a situation the next best alternative is to find another variable that is measurable and likely to be strongly correlated with the true variable. Landes used the rate of unemployment and the per-capita expenditure in the USA as the proxies of the wealth gap. The intuitive logic is that the higher the rate of unemployment the greater will be the wealth gap and the higher the per-capita expenditure, the smaller will be wealth gap. Hence in the regression analysis, we should expect to find a positive coefficient of the unemployment rate and a negative coefficient of the per-capita expenditure where some index of the incidence of plane hijacking is the dependent variable.

B.5.2 Omitted Variables Bias and Control Variables

Whereas the real world is complex and many factors can plausibly cause changes in a variable one seeks to explain, any theoretical model can only hope to focus on a few of all plausible relevant variables. That does not mean that in order to test a theory we can and should restrict ourselves only to variables incorporated in the particular theory. Indeed, excluding other relevant variables in the regression poses statistical problems if they are correlated with the explanatory variables one is directly interesting in.

[9] In fact, more detailed data on crime may be available, e.g., homicide, armed robbery, etc. and the impact of unemployment and inequality on homicide and armed robbery will very likely be quantitatively different.

As an example, return to wage earnings regression equation. As said earlier, one's wage earnings will be related not only to education, age, gender, etc. but also to innate ability. Note that education and innate ability is likely to be positively correlated. So if the index of innate ability, say IQ, is ignored in the regression, then the coefficient of education will partly capture the effect of innate ability too and will hence over-estimate the impact of education on wage earnings. This is called the *omitted variables bias*. Therefore, other relevant explanatory variables are typically included in regression even though the theoretical model may not include them. These are called the *control variables* or simply *controls* in the sense that we focus on the impact of one variable or one set of variables of a particular interest on a dependent variable of a particular interest, *while controlling for other determinants.*

It is, of course, not possible to include *all* plausible control variables. First of all, data on all relevant explanatory variables or their proxies may not be available. Secondly, even if data may be available, the inclusion of too many variables causes other statistical problems. Omitted variables bias is inherent in almost any regression analysis—it is a matter of degree. The choice of inclusion of "other" relevant variables is constrained by the availability of data and it is a matter of judgment: how forceful or plausible the marginal contribution of an omitted variable is.

If there are M main variables of interest X_m ($m = 1, 2, \ldots, M$) and R control variables Z_r ($r = 1, 2, \ldots, R$), we can write a linear regression model as

$$Y_i = a + \sum_{m=1}^{M} b_m X_{im} + \sum_{r=1}^{R} \beta_r Z_{ir} + u_i. \tag{B.13}$$

For notational simplicity, in the main text we have denoted control variables in the regression equation in the vector form $\boldsymbol{\beta Z}_i$, where $\boldsymbol{\beta Z}_i \equiv \sum_{r=1}^{R} \beta_r Z_{ir}$. If we ignore the subscript i, we can write Eq. (B.13) a bit more simply as

$$Y = a + \sum_{m=1}^{M} b_m X_m + \boldsymbol{\beta Z} + u. \tag{B.14}$$

B.5.3 Selection Bias

It arises when randomization of the sample is not achieved. Suppose the aim is to determine whether socioeconomic status of women is related to the incidence of breast cancer in a region. Suppose that the researchers obtained, with permission, from hospitals in the region, the names and addresses of a large sample of women who had breast cancer. They were surveyed and asked questions on their socioeconomic status like education, employment, etc. This is the *exposed group*—individuals who were "exposed" to the outcome. To obtain reliable estimates, the research team must, however, find "observations" that are not exposed. In order to do so, suppose that the team conducts door-to-door visits between 9am and 5pm and second-round visits if women were not present at home. The same questionnaire was submitted. Some of the women had breast cancer and others were not.

If these two sets of observations, hospital-provided contacts of patients and door-to-door survey, constitute the dataset for the study, it is likely to contain selection bias, i.e., the sample is not likely to be random. The reason is that women who were at home during 9am to 5pm are likely to be relatively less educated and/or unemployed. Thus the sample is biased toward the presence of women with relatively low socioeconomic status. As a result, the regression estimates will not be unbiased.

There are two common ways to deal with selection bias. One is improving the sample to make it more random. The other is to apply a two-step estimation procedure due to James Heckman, a Nobel laureate in economics. Named after him, it is called *Heckit*.

B.6 Interaction Effect

In some situations we may not just be interested in estimating the *separate* marginal impacts of two variables, say X and H, on a dependent variable Y, but also how the marginal impact of one variable (say X) is affected by the other (H). Suppose we have cross-sectional data on wage earnings on individuals (W) along with information of their gender and years of experience (H). If we posit

$$W_i = a + bH_i + cD_i + u_i, \tag{B.15}$$

where i stands for the individual, H_i is his/her years of experience in years, and D_i is a dummy variable, 0 for a man and 1 for woman, the estimates $\hat{b}$ and $\hat{c}$ tell us the marginal impact of experience and gender on wage earnings. We expect $\hat{b} > 0$ and $\hat{c} < 0$. However, it is possible that the impact of experience on wage earnings may depend on gender and the impact of gender on wage earnings may depend on experience. Keeping this mind, we many introduce a third term in the right-hand side of Eq. (B.15):

$$W_i = a + bH_i + cD_i + d \cdot (D_i \times H_i) + u_i. \tag{B.16}$$

If women are discriminated in the labor market, we expect $\hat{d} < 0$ too (besides $\hat{c}$ being negative), where "hat" denotes the sample estimates. Note that in this regression model, the marginal impact of experience for a man is $\hat{b}$ and that for a woman is $\hat{b} + \hat{d}$. The marginal effect of discrimination against women equals $\hat{c} + \hat{d}H_i$, which is dependent on the years of experience.[10]

We can indeed divide explanatory variables into three types:

• main variables • control variables • interaction variables.

[10] For a man, $D_i = 0$; hence $\partial W_i / \partial H_i = \hat{b}$. For a woman, $D_i = 1$ and thus $\partial W_i / \partial H_i = \hat{b} + \hat{d}$. The marginal impact of discrimination is $\partial W_i / \partial D_i = \hat{c} + \hat{d}H_i$.

B.7 Interpreting Coefficients: Standardizing Changes in Variables in Terms of Standard Deviation

Unless a regression coefficient is an elasticity, a marginal effect of a regressor is unit-dependent. Therefore, the marginal effects of different regressors, unless expressed in the same unit, cannot be compared. Suppose we have two explanatory variables X_1 and X_2 (possibly among other explanatory variables) and these are not in terms of natural log. Then it does not make any sense to compare $\partial Y/\partial X_1 = \hat{b}_1$ with $\partial Y/\partial X_2 = \hat{b}_2$. For example, if $\hat{b}_1 = \hat{b}_2$, we cannot say that the marginal impacts of X_1 and X_2 on Y are close to each other.[11] Even if X_1 and X_2 have the same unit, a unit increase in each may mean something quite different. Suppose we have a regression equation explaining income of an individual and the explanatory variables include years of education, years of work experience, etc. One extra year in school has a very different connotation than one extra year of job experience.

The solution is to standardize and scale the variables such that changes in magnitude become comparable. Standardization typically involves converting the observations from the raw data to their "z-scores," where for a variable, say, X with sample mean $\bar{X}$ and sample standard deviation s_X, $z \equiv (X - \bar{X})/s_X$. Instead of measuring a variable directly, *we measure the variable in terms of deviation from the mean as a multiple of its standard deviation.* The z of X is the scaled variable. We have $dz = (1/s_X)dX$ A one standard deviation increase means $dz = 1$, and hence $dx = s_X$. Suppose the estimated coefficient in a regression is $\hat{b} = 1.5$ and in the sample $s_X = 0.75$. Then the marginal impact of one-standard-deviation increase in X on Y is: $1.5 \times 0.75 = 1.125$.

Although this idea is typically used for a regressor, the dependent variable can be standardized too. The marginal impact of one-standard-deviation increase in x on standardized Y is:

$$\frac{d\left(\dfrac{Y-\bar{Y}}{s_Y}\right)}{d\left(\dfrac{X-\bar{X}}{s_X}\right)} = \frac{dY}{dX}\cdot\frac{s_X}{s_Y} = \hat{b}\cdot\frac{s_X}{s_Y}.$$

We may also want to know

$$\frac{d\left(\dfrac{Y-\bar{Y}}{s_Y}\right)}{dX},$$

i.e., the impact of a marginal change in X on standardized Y.

Thus standardized marginal impacts can be computed by using the standard deviation of a variable.

[11] If the explanatory variable is in its natural log, then its regression coefficient would approximate a proportional or percentage change and this is unit independent. More precisely, if $Y = a + b\ln X + u$, then $dY/dX = b/X$ implying $b = dY/(dX/X)$, where dX/X measures a "proportionate" change in X. Thus, $\hat{b}$ measures the marginal effect of a proportionately change in X, which is unit independent.

B.8 Variables in (Natural) Log

In many regressions, some or all variables are used in their natural logs. Doing so offers some advantages. For example, if the dependent variable is expressed in log, i.e., it is $\ln Y$, then a change in it equals

$$\frac{d \ln Y}{dY} = \frac{dY}{Y},$$

where we have applied the formula for the first derivative of a logarithmic function. Note that the expression dY/Y measures a proportional change. Hence, the estimated coefficient of an explanatory variable multiplied by 100 gives us its marginal impact on the dependent variable in percentage. This is intuitive and appealing.

In addition, if the explanatory variable is also expressed in log, then the estimated coefficient denotes the percentage change in Y with respect to a percentage change in X—which is same as the elasticity of Y with respect to X. Elasticity is independent of units and widely used in applied economics.

Another benefit of using a variable in log is that, because $\ln Z < Z$ as long as $Z > 1$ where Z may be the dependent or an explanatory variable, using $\ln Z$ instead of Z reduces its variability, which tends to reduce certain econometric problems in the estimation of regression coefficients.

Furthermore, we will see in Sect. B.9 that by using logs of variables, non-linear equations can be converted to linear equations in parameters.

It does not mean, however, that all variables should be measured in logs in regression. If a variable can take value 0 or negative values, its natural log does not exist. Even in situations where a variable can take positive values only, taking its natural log in regression may not be appropriate.

B.9 Non-Linearity

Suppose the relationship between X and Y is non-linear and either increasing or decreasing but not both; briefly put, the relationship is non-linear and "monotonic." Then the scatter diagram will one of the four types shown in Fig. B.3. Obviously, a straight line is not a good choice to represent the data. We should specify a non-linear equation. For any of the relationships, there is, however, no single representative non-linear equation. We have a choice based on simplicity of interpretation and estimation. Here are some examples in reference to Fig. B.3.

Panel (a): (i) $Y = aX^b$, $a > 0$, $b > 1$; or (ii) $Y = ae^{bX}$, $a > 0$; $b > 0$; (B.17a)

Panel (b): (iii) $Y = aX^b$, $a > 0, 0 < b < 1$; or (iv) $Y = A - ae^{-bX}, A > 0$, $a > 0$, $b > 0$ (B.17b)

Panel (c): (v) $A - aX^b$, $a > 0$, $b > 0$; or (vi) $Y = A - ae^{bX}$, $A > 0$, $a > 0$, $b > 0$[12] (B.17c)

Panel (d): (vii) $Y = aX^{-b}$, $a > 0, b > 0$; or (viii) $Y = ae^{-bX}$, $a > 0$; $b > 0$, (B.17d)

[12] If Y can only take non-negative values, then we have to specify an upper limit of X to ensure $Y \geq 0$.

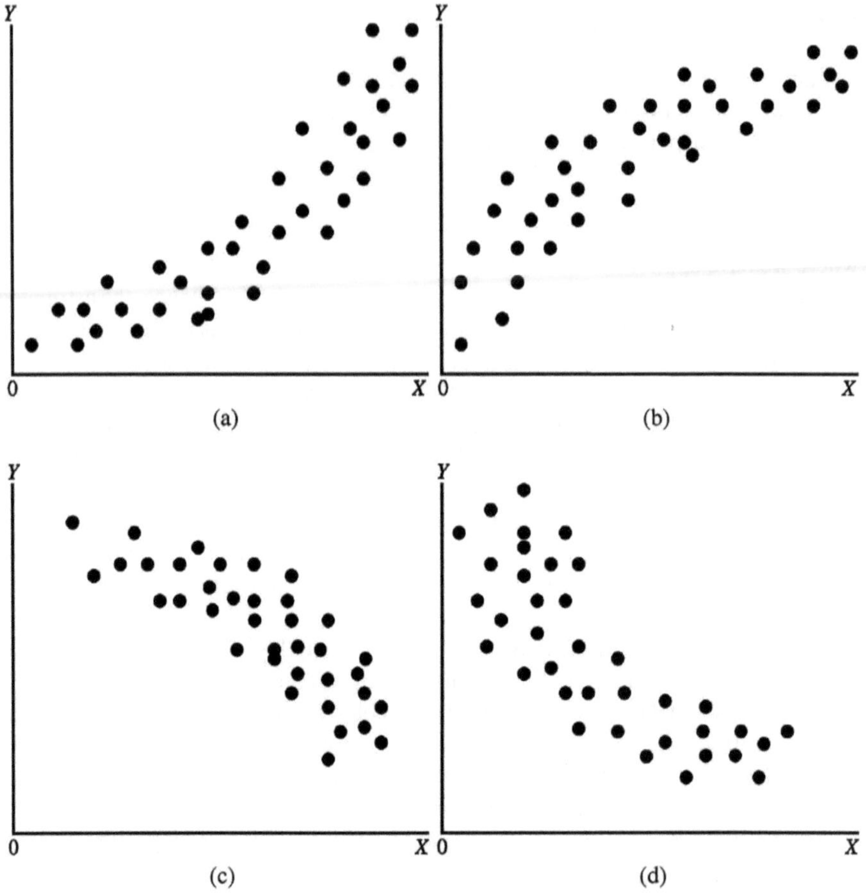

Fig. B.3: Monotonic non-linear relations. (**a**) Increasing at an increasing rate. (**b**) Increasing at a decreasing rate. (**c**) Decreasing at an increasing rate. (**d**) Decreasing at a decreasing rate

where "*e*" is the exponential function. These functions are shown in Fig. B.4.

How do we estimate a regression equation whose predicted part is given by any of the functions from (i) to (viii)? It turns out it is actually easy to accommodate functions (i), (ii), (iii), (vii), or (viii) but not (iv), (v), and (vi). All we need to do is to apply natural log to both sides of any of these five equations and the resulting equation is linear in parameters, so that linear regression applies. More specifically, we have

$$\text{(i')}: \ln Y = \ln a + b \ln X; \quad \text{(ii')}: \ln Y = \ln a + bX$$
$$\text{(iii')}: \ln Y = \ln a + b \ln X; \text{(vii')}: \ln Y = \ln a - b \ln X$$
$$\text{(viii')}: \ln Y = \ln a - bX.$$

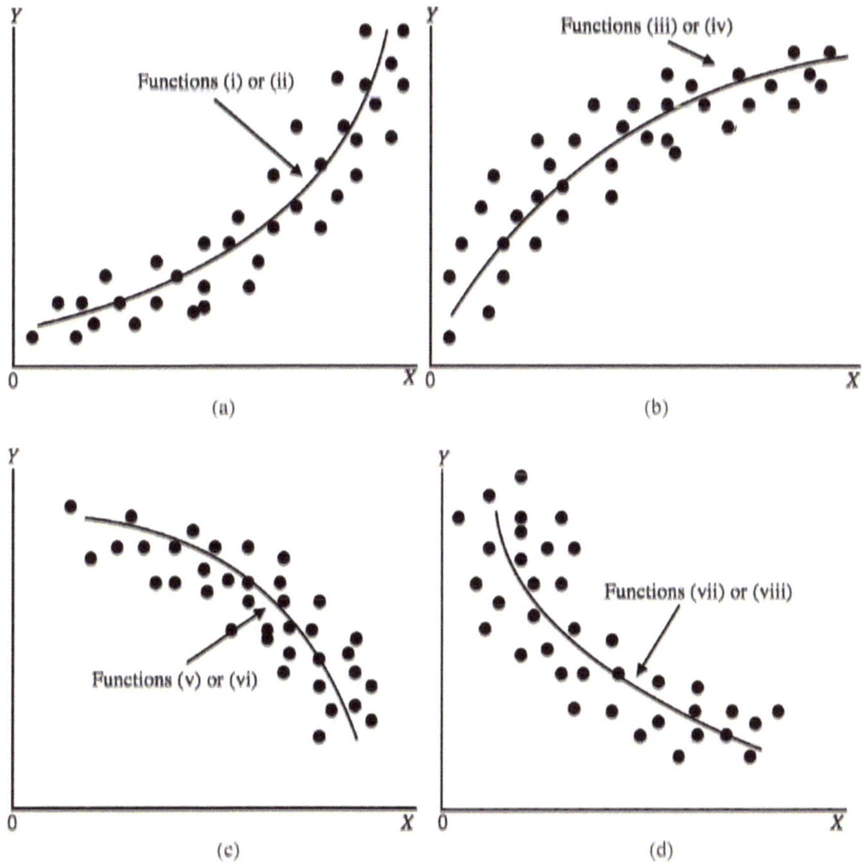

Fig. B.4: Monotonic non-linear relations with fitted equations. (**a**) Increasing at an increasing rate. (**b**) Increasing at a decreasing rate. (**c**) Decreasing at an increasing rate. (**d**) Decreasing at a decreasing rate

We can add an error term to these equations and treat $\ln Y$ as the dependent variable. Note that the right-hand side variable is either X or $\ln X$. It is presumed that the variable that is represented by its natural log in the regression equation must take positive values only (since natural log is not defined for negative numbers). Thus, if a scatter plot or a relationship looks like that in panel (a), (b), or (d) of Fig. B.3 or Fig. B.4, we can apply linear regression. All we need to do is to transform the variables, Y and X both or Y only, to their natural log.

The general point is that *as long as the regression equation is linear with respect to the "parameters," linear regression applies and non-linearity is not a big issue.*

However, there are situations where it is not possible to transform variables so that the resulting equation becomes linear in parameters, e.g., function (iv) for panel (b) and functions (v) or (vi) for panel (c) in Fig. B.3. For these equations and many others, non-linear regression techniques are available, which we shall not cover.

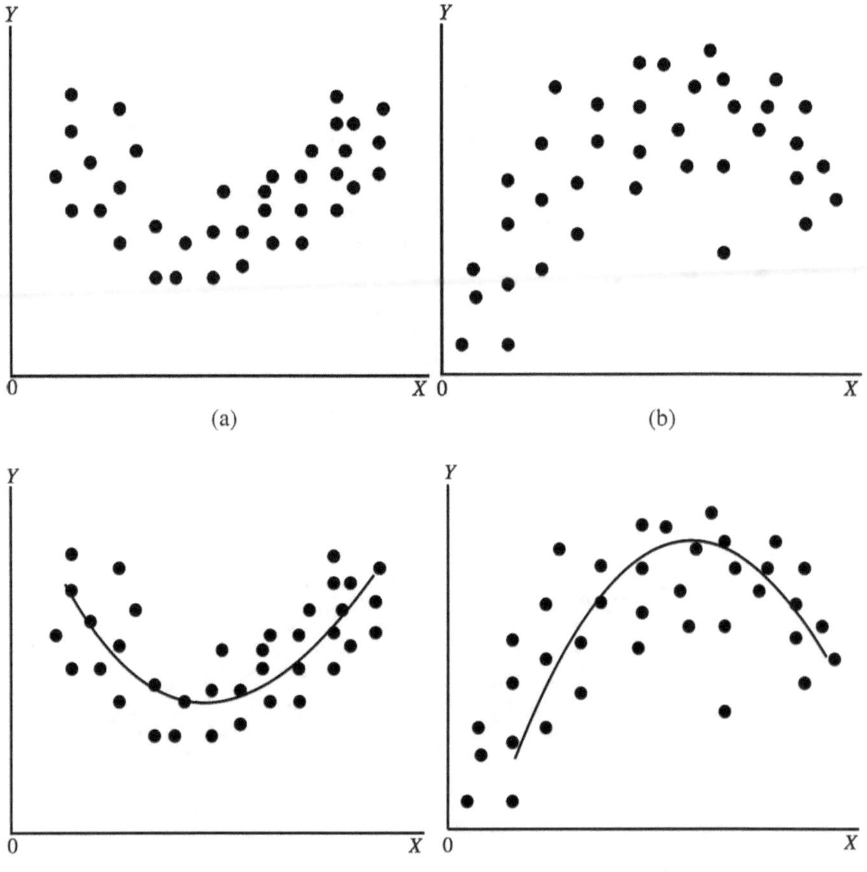

Fig. B.5: Non-monotonic relationships. (**a**) U-shaped. (**b**) Inverse U-shaped. (**c**) U-shaped. (**d**) Inverse U-shaped

So far we have discussed non-linear relations that are monotonic. Consider Fig. B.5 where Y is not monotonic with respect to X. In panels (a) and (c), Y first decreases and then increases with X, i.e., there is U-shaped relation, where in panels (b) and (d) it is just the opposite.

As an example, we may recall the typical shape of the unit or average cost function of a firm studied in micro theory. This is U-shaped. Suppose we have firm-level data on unit cost and volume of output for different output levels within a given time period. To estimate the parameters of the unit cost function, we may posit a relationship such as in panel (a) or (c) of Fig. B.5.

Here is an example from studies on terrorism that aim to learn the impact of political rights and incidences of terror events (Chap. 15). It can be argued that when political rights in a country are minimal like in a dictatorial regime, terrorism will *not* be a major problem as it is likely to be suppressed ruthlessly by the state.

However, if regulations are relaxed and political rights become moderately available, people can form groups and group opinion and express their grievances against some policies. If the government does not address these issues, terror groups can form and terrorism can grow. In the other extreme, we can imagine that in a liberal democracy where most political rights are liberally available, people can express their grievances with effectiveness and there is greater chance of grievances being redressed without having to resort to violence including terrorism. Terrorism is not likely to be a major issue. Now, if X is some index of political rights and Y an index of terrorism (e.g. annual number of terror events), the above description amounts to hypothesizing an inverse U-shaped relation.

It turns out that there is a certain class of non-linear functions that can represent a U-shaped or an inverse U-shaped relation. That is,

$$Y = a + b_1 X + b_2 X^2. \tag{B.18}$$

If we differentiate it, the slope has the expression $dY/dX = b_1 + 2b_2 X$. Suppose $b_1 < 0$ and $b_2 < 0$. Then the slope is positive or negative as $X \lesseqgtr b_1/(-2b_2)$. This yields a U-shaped curve. If $b_1 > 0$ and $b_2 < 0$, then we have the opposite: the slope is negative or positive as $X \lesseqgtr -b_1/b_2$, implying an inverse U-shaped function.

Notice, however, that, although non-linear in X, Y is *linear* in parameters b_1 and b_2 in Eq. (B.18). All we have to do is to create another explanatory variable X^2 which is the square of the original data X and regress Y on X and X^2 by postulating

$$Y_i = a + b_1 X_i + b_2 X_i^2 + u_i. \tag{B.19}$$

If the objective is to test, for example, the existence of an inverse U-shaped effect, we would test an alternative (joint) hypothesis of $b_1 > 0$ and $b_2 < 0$. In Chap. 15 we refer to studies that indeed find $\hat{b}_1 > 0$ and $\hat{b}_2 < 0$ where X is an index of political rights and Y measures terrorism.

Some theoretical models yield relationships that are non-linear in some of the parameters of the model and these non-linearities manifest in many other functional forms than the ones we have considered as examples. In general, non-linear regression techniques are used to estimate the parameters of such models.

B.10 Instrumental Variables

We have noted earlier that if an explanatory variable is correlated with the random term, the estimated least squares coefficient of that variable is not reliable. In some situations, we want to learn about the coefficient of a variable *but* there are reasons to believe that it is correlated with the error term. This is problematic. A couple of examples are in order.

B.10.1 Examples

Example 1 Suppose we want to learn the determinants of wage earnings and our cross-section model is:

$$\ln \text{wage}_i = a + b_1 \text{education}_i + b_2 \text{ability}_i + u_i, \tag{B.20}$$

where the left hand is the natural log of wage. We have data on individuals' education measured in years in school and college. However, ability is innate, not observable. Suppose we simply ignore ability and want to measure the impact of education on wage earning by estimating

$$\ln \text{wage}_i = a + b_1 \text{education}_i + \epsilon_i. \tag{B.21}$$

Note, however, that $\epsilon_i \equiv b_2 \times \text{ability}_i + u_i$ if the relation (B.20) is true. Given that ability and education are positively correlated, we then have the error term ϵ_i correlated with education. Assumption B.1 is violated, implying that the least squares estimates of Eq. (B.21) will be unreliable.

Example 2 Suppose we want to know the effect of the size of police force on crime by a cross-section regression model $Y_i = a + bX_i + u_i$, where Y is some available index on crime and X is an index of the police hiring or police force. Suppose the data refers to different cities in a country in a given year. We would expect $\hat{b} < 0$: police presence would tend to reduce crime. However, we can also argue that more police is hired *because* the crimes are greater in number, indicating positive relationship. This is a situation where not only Y depends on X but X also depends on Y. This is called an *endogeneity problem* where the explanatory variable is endogenous in the sense that it is dependent on Y and therefore not exogenous. The problem is that since X_i depends on Y_i, and, in turn, Y_i varies with the error term u_i at any given X_i, X_i will vary with u_i. This is a violation of Assumption B.1. As a result, a simple least squares regression of Y against X will not deliver a reliable estimate of the parameter b.

Generically speaking the problem is that we want to obtain a reliable estimate of the coefficient b in a regression equation like

$$Y_i = a + bX_i + u_i, \tag{B.22}$$

but $\text{Corr}(X_i, u_i) \neq 0$. What do we do?

B.10.2 Way Out

The idea is to use another variable, say H, which is (i) correlated with X, but (ii) not correlated with u. This "outside" variable is called an *instrumental variable*, i.e., "X is instrumented by H." Condition (i) is called *instrument relevance* which is formally stated as $\text{Corr}(H, X) \neq 0$. Condition (ii), called *instrument exogeneity* or *exclusion restriction*, is stated as $\text{Corr}(H, u) = 0$.

Before discussing why or how an instrumental variable works, in the two example above, let us see which outside variables may satisfy conditions (i) and (ii) so that they can qualify as instruments.

In Example 1, if we have data on an individual's mother's education, then it may be used as an instrument of the individual's own education. A person's education and his/her mother's education are likely to be correlated, especially in relatively poor countries. So condition (i) is met. Moreover, it is highly unlikely that mother's education will affect wage earnings of an individual independently of the individual's education. If the mother's education were related with the error term it would have affected wage earning at any given level of the individual's income. Since the latter implication is highly unlikely, it is also highly unlikely that the mother's education is correlated with the error term. Thus condition (ii) is met.

Consider Example 2. In a study on the effect of police crime in the USA across 59 cities, Levitt (1997) has used mayoral and gubernatorial election years as instruments for the size of the police force, since in these electoral years the hiring of police personnel is disproportionately high relative to other years. Condition (i) is met as these election years and the size of the police force are correlated. Moreover, crime is not directly affected by the electoral years, independent of the size of the police force. So condition (ii) is also met.

Now how does the instrumental variable solve the problem of $\text{Corr}(X_i, u_i) \neq 0$ in Eq. (B.22)? Note that X is related to Y, which is problematic, whereas X is related to H which is unrelated to the error term and hence *not* problematic. Thus, X has a problematic component and a non-problematic component. If we can filter out the problematic part, we can use the remainder to predict Y. The resulting estimate of the coefficient b will be reliable. This is the underlying idea.

How is it operationalized? Simply put, we first regress X against Z and collect the predicted part say $\hat{X}$. This is the non-problematic component. Next, in place of X we use $\hat{X}$ in Eq. (B.22) and obtain the least squares estimate of b. This is a two-stage regression procedure, called a *two-stage least squares method* or simply 2SLS.

More generally, if there are other relevant (control) variables in the regression equation, they need to be included in regression in both stages. Also, one can use more than one variable to instrument a single explanatory variable like X in Eq. (B.22) if they satisfy instrument relevance and instrument exogeneity conditions.

B.11 Maximum Likelihood Estimation (MLE)

This is an alternative to least squares estimation. It is built on the notion of maximizing the likelihood or probability of obtaining all observations of a sample of a given size. What does it mean? Refer back to the simple regression equation (B.4). Let a^* and b^* denote the estimated a and b by some method. Consider observation 1, (X_1, Y_1) and ask, what is the probability of obtaining the observation (X_1, Y_1) from the population if $a = a^*$ and $b = b^*$? Since $Y_1 = a^* + b^*X_1 + u_1$, the probability of the realization of the observation (X_1, Y_1) is equal to the probability that $u = Y_1 - a^* - b^*X_1$. Let us denote this probability (of u) by p_1. Similarly with $a = a^*$ and $b = b^*$, let the probability of observation 2 be p_2, equal to the probability that $u = Y_2 - a^* - b^* X_2$. Hence, assuming that the observations are independent of each other, the joint probability of obtaining all sample observations is equal to $L \equiv p_1 \cdot p_2 \cdots p_N$, where N is the sample size or the number of observations in the sample. This is the likelihood of obtaining the sample and $L(\cdot)$ is called *likelihood function*.

Thus if we postulate a distribution of u (usually a normal distribution), then we have an expression for the likelihood L in terms of all the observations and parameter values a^* and b^*. The idea behind maximum likelihood is to choose a^* and b^* such that the likelihood function is maximized. Since the function $L(\cdot)$ is in the multiplicative form, taking log, we have

$$\mathcal{L} \equiv \ln L = \ln p_1 + \ln p_2 + \cdots + \ln p_N \equiv \sum_{i=1}^{N} \ln p_i, \tag{B.23}$$

called a *log-likelihood function*. Maximizing any function is equivalent to maximizing the natural log of a function. Typically, the log-likelihood function, rather than the likelihood function per se, is maximized with respect to the parameters because of computational simplicity.

This maximization exercise typically leads to some algebraic function or formula for a^* and b^* in terms of the X_i's and Y_i's in the sample. These are the *maximum likelihood estimates* of the parameters a and b in the regression equation (B.4).

While the least squares estimates are derived from minimizing the sum of squares, i.e., minimizing $\sum_{i=1}^{N} u_i^2$, the maximum likelihood estimates are obtained by maximizing the joint probability of obtaining all observations of a sample, *assuming a given form of distribution of the error term* u_i.

A classic result is that if it is a linear regression equation—whether simple or multiple—the least square estimators of the coefficients are same as the maximum likelihood estimates if the error terms u_i's are independently and normally distributed around mean zero and the same variance, that is, $u_i \sim N\left(0, \sigma^2\right)$ where σ^2 is the common variance.

Maximum likelihood is a general method of estimation which is applicable in a large variety of situations, not just linear regression.

B.12 Basics of Simultaneous-Equations Estimation

This refers to estimation of a *system* of equations, rather than just one equation, where the "system" refers to interrelation among variables. Consider, for instance, the demand-supply model for a product:

$$\text{Demand Function: } q_d = a_1 + b_1 p + c_1 y + u_1 \tag{B.24}$$

$$\text{Supply Function: } q_s = a_2 + b_2 p + u_2, \tag{B.25}$$

$$\text{Equilibrium: } q_d = q_s, \tag{B.26}$$

where q_d and q_s stand for quantity demanded and quantity supplied, respectively, p is the market price and y is income. We may eliminate the last equation by simply writing q in place of q_d and q_s and interpreting q as equilibrium, observed, quantity transacted. That is,

$$q = a_1 + b_1 p + c_1 y + u_1; \quad q = a_2 + b_2 p + u_2. \tag{B.27}$$

These two equations are called *structural equations*, containing two *endogenous* or *jointly determined* variables p and q. In equilibrium, both variables will be functions of y *and* the error terms u_1 and u_2, i.e.,

$$p = \frac{a_1 - a_2}{b_2 - b_1} + \frac{c_1}{b_2 - b_1} + \underbrace{\frac{u_1 - u_2}{b_2 - b_1}}_{\text{error term}} \tag{B.28}$$

$$q = \frac{a_1 b_2 - a_2 b_1}{b_2 - b_1} + \frac{b_2}{b_2 - b_1} + \underbrace{\frac{b_2 u_1 - b_1 u_2}{b_2 - b_1}}_{\text{error term}}. \tag{B.29}$$

These are called *reduced-form equations*.

Suppose our objective is to estimate the demand function (B.24), i.e., estimate the coefficients b_1 and c_1. Can—or rather—should we apply OLS estimation for Eq. (B.24)? The problem is that Assumption B.1 is violated since the regressor p is correlated with the error term (see Eq. (B.28)). The OLS estimates will be inconsistent.

The econometrics of simultaneous equations revolves around how to circumvent this problem. In general, there are two ways to estimating simultaneous equations: *full information method* and *limited-information method*. The first refers to estimating the whole system. We shall not discuss this here. A common limited-information method of obtaining consistent estimates is the instrumental variable approach discussed in Sect. B.10. In our example, it boils down to finding an instrument for equilibrium price in the demand equation. If it is an agricultural product, rainfall may be a good instrument. In any event, finding an appropriate instrument is a separate issue.

B.13 Basics of Time-Series Analysis

Instead of the cause–effect type of regression analysis where the left-hand side of a regression equation has one variable and the right-hand a list of other variables (respectively, explained and explanatory variables), there is another kind of regression analysis, called the *time-series analysis*. This is applicable only to *time-series data* that traces one variable or many variables over an interval of time. Examples are quarterly (macro) data of US real GDP, inflation, etc. It could be micro-level data too, e.g., the daily price of the Apple stock from say January 1, 2011 to December 31, 2022. Many time-series graphs related to terrorism are presented in Chap. 3. Figure B.6a plots a time-series on the number of plane hijackings globally over the

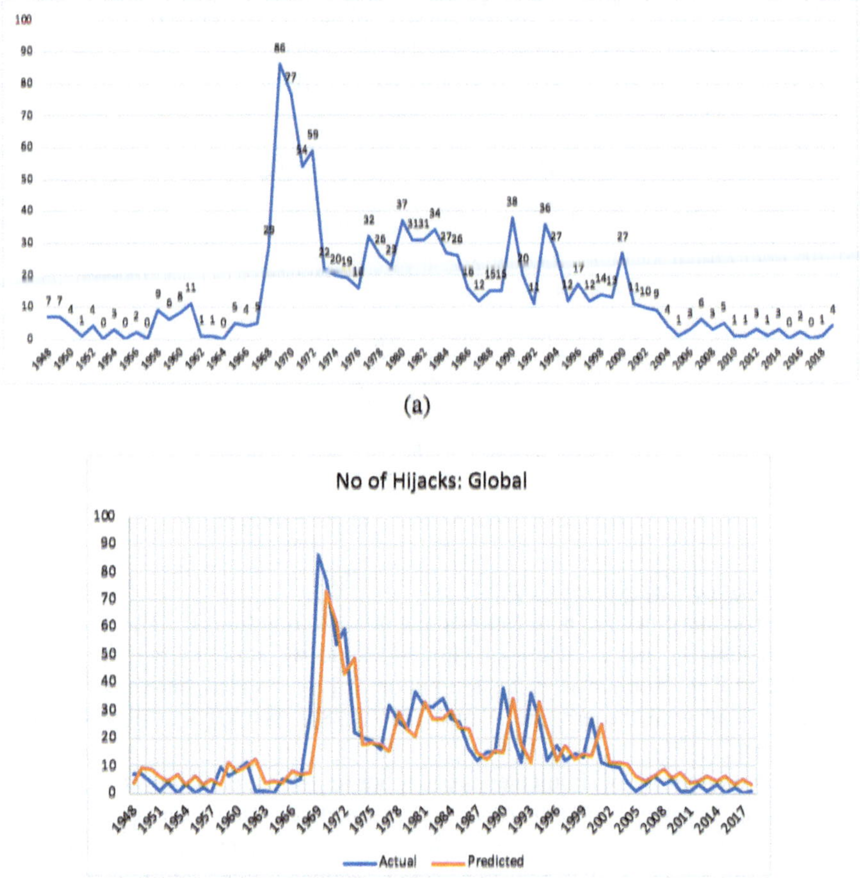

Fig. B.6: Time-series of plane hijacking. (**a**) Data. (**b**) A time-series model. *Source:* (**a**) Aviation Safety Network, https://aviation-safety.net; it is a private independent initiative, founded by Harro Rantoer and Fabian I. Lujan; permission to reproduce obtained, with thanks

period 1945 to 2018 (see Chaps. 3 and 8). A time-series of variable X is sometimes written compactly as $\{X_t\}$, where there is a beginning date and an end date.

In virtually any time-series data, we notice some sort of a pattern over time, The plots do not look completely random or zigzag. This is reflected in two ways. First, some time-series data have a trend—in many cases, a positive trend, e.g., real GDP of a country. But all time-series data do not exhibit a trend, e.g., the rate of unemployment in an economy. Second, whether or not a time-series data has a trend, there is some kind of a dependence of present realization of a variable on its own past realizations.

The hallmark of the time-series analysis is that it primarily views a time-series data as a function of time (if has a trend) and its past values. Accordingly, a time-series model is commonly specified by a regression equation, like

$$Y_t = a + bt + c_1 Y_{t-1} + c_2 Y_{t-2} + \cdots + c_g T_{t-g} + u_t, \tag{B.30}$$

where Y_t could be annual, quarterly, monthly, or daily data and g is the time-lag length. The coefficient b captures the trend, the estimate of which should be positive or negative depending on the direction of the trend. If we are assured that the data does not have a significant trend, we may set $b = 0$ to begin with and specify

$$Y_t = a + c_1 Y_{t-1} + c_2 Y_{t-2} + \cdots + c_g T_{t-g} + u_t. \tag{B.31}$$

Of course, we may not have prior knowledge of the lag length, but various statistical criteria can tell us what would be a statistically appropriate lag length for a particular time-series model.

The advantage of the time-series analysis is that the future course of a variable can be predicted from its past values. We do not "need" to have information on a lot of other factors that can potentially influence the variable and what their predicted future values may be. Time-series analysis is thus very handy for predictive purposes.

As a hands-on example, consider the data on plane hijacking in Fig. B.6. Ignoring any time trend and using a lag length of two years, the underlying data from 1948 to 2018 leads to the following OLS-estimated time-series equation:

$$\hat{Y}_t = 3.680 + 0.838 Y_{t-1} - 0.076 Y_{t-2}. \tag{B.32}$$

Figure B.6b plots the actual and the predicted data. As we see, the time-series model gives a fairly good fit. We are of course not discussing here whether this is the best time-series model to describe the data. It is meant to be illustrative only.

B.13.1 Various Components of a Time-Series Data

In general, a time-series is thought of having four components: trend, cyclical, seasonal, and random. Seasonal elements are present in certain types of time-series data which are more frequent than annual data, e.g., monthly volume of mail handled by a post office, which peaks during winter holiday months of every year. By definition, there will be no seasonal elements in annual data or data with less frequency than annual. Before conducting any time-series analysis, the data is first de-seasonalized if seasonality is present. There are standard methods to do this. Seasonality is not observed in any time-series data on terrorism. We can thus ignore it and focus the trend, cyclical and random components.

Go back to Eq. (B.30). We re-write it here, with the three elements segregated.

$$Y_t = a + \underbrace{bt}_{\text{trend}} + \underbrace{c_1 Y_{t-1} + c_2 Y_{t-2} + \cdots + c_g T_{t-g}}_{\text{cyclical}} + \underbrace{u_t}_{\text{random}}. \tag{B.30a}$$

Formally, Eq. (B.33) is called an *auto-regressive* time-series model, briefly an AR model with a trend, where the term "auto-regressive" refers to a lag structure of a dependent variable.

There are many variations of this basic time-series model. *Remarks.*

[a] The error or random term itself may have a lag structure of its own—such as

$$u_t = \rho_0 + \rho_1 u_{t-1} + \cdots + \rho_m u_{t-m}. \tag{B.33}$$

This is called a *moving average (MA) model*. It is relevant when shocks are believed to have a more than one-period impact. For instance, consider daily newspaper sale. Among other factors, if an interesting, investigative headline appears on a day (but not on subsequent days), it could still have a ripple effect on readership for the next few days.

A more general model will be an auto-regressive, moving average model, a generalization of Eq. (B.33):

$$Y_t = a + bt + c_1 Y_{t-1} + c_2 Y_{t-2} + \cdots + c_g T_{t-g} + \rho_1 u_{t-1} + \cdots + \rho_m u_{t-m}, \tag{B.34}$$

which is called an *Auto-regressive moving average* or an *ARMA model* (with a trend). For our purposes, however, we limit our discussion to AR models only.

[b] Consider a temporary shock to a time-series in terms of an increase in u_t. We see that this information affects Y_t and it propagates into future time periods through Eq. (B.30). A hallmark of time-series analysis is that *temporary shocks would have ripple effects over time*.

[c] A time-series model like Eq. (B.30) does not mean that other explanatory variables affecting Y_t are always excluded. Suppose we have time-series data on another variable, say X, which, we believe to be important in explaining Y_t beside Y's own history. We may then postulate a generalized version of Eq. (B.30):

$$Y_t = a + bt + c_1 Y_{t-1} + c_2 Y_{t-2} + \cdots + c_g T_{t-g} + dX_t + u_t. \tag{B.35}$$

If we further believe that Y_t may be influenced by past X_t's up to, say, the previous two periods, we would specify

$$Y_t = a + bt + c_1 Y_{t-1} + c_2 Y_{t-2} + \cdots + c_g T_{t-g} + d_0 X_t + d_1 X_{t-1} + d_2 X_{t-2} + u_t. \tag{B.36}$$

[d] Another generic situation where an exogenous factor may affect the time-series of a dependent variable is where there is a permanent and major policy initiative or technology shock that can permanently impact upon *outcome variable*, (same as the dependent variable). An example will be how highway accidents may change because of a change in the speed limit. Another example will be how agricultural production may be affected by an introduction of a new fertilizer or seed.

These deliberately introduced shocks are called *interventions*. An analysis of the impact of interventions on a time-series is called the *intervention analysis*.[13]

[13] This was developed by Box and Tiao (1975).

B.13.2 Intervention Analysis[14]

This is explained through two examples. In Chap. 8 we have discussed an application of the intervention analysis to the problem of plane hijacking as a means of terrorism.

B.13.2.1 Structural Macro Policy Changes

Consider the (real) GDP growth rate of a country over time, say from 1971 to 2020. Suppose that during this fifty-years period, massive macro policy reforms were undertaken during the year 1990 which are believed to have exerted permanent positive effects on the functioning and therefore the growth rate of the economy. Our task is to estimate the effect of this structural change on the country's DP growth rate.

Of course, the GDP growth rate may be affected by many factors such as the rate of investment, growth of population, fiscal deficit, etc. Suppose we want to explain the GDP growth rate (Y_t) by two growth-contributing variables X_{1t} and X_{2t} *and* the structural changes that occurred in 1990. We have, say, annual data on Y, X_1, and X_2 from the 1970 to 2020. However, policy reforms are multidimensional and hard to quantify. But there is a way out to represent the reform or the structural change: create a dummy variable, say, STRUC-DUM, and assign it the value 0 for each year during 1971–1989 and 1 for each year during 1990–2020.

Our regression equation is thus:

$$Y_t = a + b_1 X_{1t} + b_2 X_{2t} + c \cdot \text{STRUC-DUM}_t + u_t, \quad \text{where} \tag{B.37}$$

$$\text{STRUC-DUM}_t = \begin{cases} 0 & \text{for } t = 1970,\ldots, 1989 \\ 1 & \text{for } t = 1990,\ldots, 2020. \end{cases}$$

The estimate of the parameter c captures the effect of the macro structural change that occurred in 1990. Intervention analysis assumes typically that the time of the intervention is known.

This example of intervention analysis illustrates how a dummy variable can be constructed to represent a permanent policy intervention which is introduced at a given point of time.

B.13.2.2 A Traffic Example

This is a more detailed example. Suppose we have quarterly data on the number of traffic accidents on interstate highways from 2000Q1 to 2021Q4. Until 2013Q4, the speed limit was 65 miles an hour and from 2014Q1 it has been raised to 75 miles an hour (this is hypothetical). Increasing the speed limit is an intervention. The question is whether this intervention has led to a significant increase in accidents and if yes by how many.

Suppose there were no change in the speed limit. We may model accidents on interstate highways via Eq. (B.30) for t = 2000Q1 to 2021Q4. Against this

[14] See, for example, Enders (2015, Chapter 5).

background, we now think of the increase in the speed limit as a regime or structural change and represent it as a dummy which takes value 0 for each period before the intervention and 1 afterwards. Accordingly, instead of Eq. (B.30), we postulate:

$$Y_t = a + bt + c_1 Y_{t-1} + c_2 Y_{t-2} + d\text{DUM} + u_t, \quad \text{where} \tag{B.38}$$

$$\text{DUM} = \begin{cases} 0 & \text{for } t \leq 2013\text{Q4} \\ 1 & \text{for } t \geq 2014\text{Q1}. \end{cases}$$

We may estimate the coefficients a, b, c_1, c_2, and d by OLS. Almost surely, we will find $\hat{d}$, the estimate of d, to be positive. This, however, does not automatically imply that increasing speed limit has caused more accidents. We have to check the statistical significance of the estimated coefficient $\hat{d}$.

Assume that $\hat{d}$ is statistically significant. We can then interpret its magnitude as the average increase in Y (the number of accidents) at the time when the intervention is introduced, say at time T (e.g. 2013Q4). Hence $\hat{d}$ is called the *impact effect*.

Over time, the impact effect on Y_t at $t = T$ feeds itself because of its own lag effects through changes in Y_{t-1} and Y_{t-2}. What is then the total incremental effect in the long run? Suppose we obtained $\hat{a} = 59.6$, $\hat{b} = 0.14$, $\hat{c}_1 = 0.40$, $\hat{c}_2 = -0.10$, and $\hat{d} = 1.25$. Letting a change denoted by Δ, we have

$$\begin{aligned}
\Delta Y_T &= \hat{d} \\
\Delta Y_{T+1} &= \hat{c}_1 \hat{d} \\
\Delta Y_{T+2} &= (\hat{c}_1^2 + \hat{c}_2)\hat{d} \\
\Delta Y_{T+3} &= \left[(\hat{c}_1^2 + \hat{c}_2)\hat{c}_1 + \hat{c}_1\hat{c}_2\right]\hat{d} \\
\Delta \hat{Y}_{T+4} &= \left\{\left[(\hat{c}_1^2 + \hat{c}_2)\hat{c}_1 + \hat{c}_1\hat{c}_2\right]\hat{c}_1 + (\hat{c}_1^2 + \hat{c}_2)\hat{c}_2\right\}\hat{d} \\
\ldots &= \ldots \\
\ldots &= \ldots
\end{aligned}$$

Adding these increments to time infinity, the long-run effect equals the sum of a geometric series:

$$\Delta Y = \left[1 + (\hat{c}_1 + \hat{c}_2) + (\hat{c}_1 + \hat{c}_2)^2 + \ldots\right]\hat{d} = \frac{1}{1 - \hat{c}_1 - \hat{c}_2} \cdot \hat{d},$$

assuming that the magnitude of $\hat{c}_1 + \hat{c}_2$ is less than unity, that is, $|\hat{c}_1 + \hat{c}_2| < 1$.

Check that in the numerical example, $|\hat{c}_1 + \hat{c}_2| = 0.70 < 1$. Hence, the long-run effect equals

$$\Delta Y = \frac{1.25}{1 - 0.80 + 0.10} = \frac{1.25}{0.30} = 4.17.$$

Our assumption that $|\hat{c}_1 + \hat{c}_2| < 1$ will be met almost surely, because we would normally expect the dynamic effects over time to be smaller.

To summarize, in our numerical example, the impact effect is 1.25 and the long-run effect is 4.17. It means that if accidents are measured in 000's, the impact effect of the speed limit increase is an increase of 1250 and 4170 in accidents initially and in the long run, respectively.

Going back to Eq. (B.35), it is worth noting that we may include other explanatory variable in the right-hand side, depending on what we are trying to explain and the availability of data. For instance, the number of traffic accidents in a locality may be dependent on the intensity of random checks, which, in turn, would depend on the size of the law enforcement. We may thus specify

$$Y_t = a + bt + c_1 Y_{t-1} + c_2 Y_{t-2} + d.\text{DUM} + g.\text{LSIZE}_t + u_t, \tag{B.39}$$

where LSIZE is a measure of the size of police force for highway patrol.

B.13.3 Granger Causality

For a particular country, suppose that we have data on terrorist incidents (X_t) and the growth rates of its GDP (say y_t) for over 100 quarters (twenty-five years). We want to test if terrorism has impacted on the country's growth rate over time. Let the magnitude of terrorism be measured by the number of fatalities, i.e., let X_t be the number of people killed during time t (a particular quarter) from terror attacks. Granger causality—named after Clive Granger, a Nobel laureate in economics—poses the question of *whether the time-series $\{X_t\}$ has influenced or "caused" the time-series $\{y_t\}$*. If yes, we say that X Granger-causes Y or, alternatively put, X is a causal factor of variable Y. Thus Granger causality contains the notion that "X causes Y" if the time-series of X contributes to forecasting of Y or equivalently if the time-series of X has sufficient information in improving the prediction of Y.

In precise terms, let us posit a time-series equation

$$Y_t = a + \sum_{s=1}^{p} b_s Y_{t-s} + \sum_{s=1}^{p} c_s X_{t-s} + u_t. \tag{B.40}$$

Granger causality test refers to testing of whether all estimated "c" coefficients are zero, i.e.,

$$\hat{c}_1 = \hat{c}_2 = \cdots = \hat{c}_p = 0. \tag{B.41}$$

If yes, we reject the hypothesis that X causes Y. Otherwise, if all c coefficient estimates are not jointly zero, we say that X *Granger-causes* Y.[15]

We must note that X causing Y does not preclude Y causing X. Applying the definition, Y would cause X if the estimation of the equation:

$$X_t = \alpha + \sum_{s=1}^{q} \eta_s Y_{t-s} + \sum_{s=1}^{q} \gamma_s X_{t-s} + u_t \tag{B.42}$$

[15] Usually, an F test is used for the purpose.

leads to all $\hat{\gamma}$'s not equal to zero. Hence, it is possible that X Granger-causes Y and vice versa, i.e., the time-series of X contributes toward prediction of the time-series of Y and vice versa.

B.13.4 Vector Auto Regression (VAR) Analysis

When the time-series of two or more variables influence each other, we can posit what is called *Vector Auto-Regression (Auto-Regressive)* or a *VAR* system. For instance, a two-variable VAR can be written as

$$\begin{aligned} X_t &= a_x + \sum_{s=1}^{p} b_{xxs} X_{t-s} + \sum_{s=1}^{p} b_{yxs} Y_{t-s} + u_{xt} \\ Y_t &= a_y + \sum_{s=1}^{p} b_{xys} X_{t-s} + \sum_{s=1}^{p} b_{yys} Y_{t-s} + u_{yt}. \end{aligned} \tag{B.43}$$

This is a VAR(p) model or p-th order VAR with two variables.

B.14 Panel-Data Analysis

Recall from Sect. B.3.1 that panel data refers to data that has both cross-sectional and time-series elements. An example is given in Table B.3, which records the murder rate across three cities over six consecutive years and the explanatory variables are population density and size of the police force for each city in every year.

At a macro level, we may want to learn about the determinants of economy-wide growth rates by examining panel data—across a group of countries and over time—on their annual real per-capita GDP growth rates and a host of potential determinants like investment/GDP ratio, saving/GDP ratio, openness to international trade, average education level of the adult population, geographical location of countries in terms of longitude and latitude, common time effects affecting all countries such as world oil price in different years and finally a common time trend.

In general, panel-data analysis contains three types of explanatory variables: (a) those varying across units (like countries) and over time, (b) unit-specific effects (like geographical location) that varies across the units (e.g. countries) but not across time, and (c) time-specific effect represented by time, i.e., each year in the sample, which is common to all units.

Let there be N units of observation in the sample (like three cities in Table B.3 and different countries in growth regression example above), denoted by i, where $i = 1, 2, \ldots, N$. Likewise, let T, $t = 1, 2, \ldots, T$, be sample time period, say, from 2011 to 2021 or 2012Q1 to 2021Q3 where Q1 and Q3 denote the first and the third quarter of a year.

We write a panel regression model as:

$$Y_{it} = a_0 + b_1 X1_{it} + b_2 X2_{it} + b_3 X3_{it} + c_1 H1_i + c_2 H2_i + \gamma_1 M1_t + \gamma_2 M2_t + \eta_i + \lambda_t + u_{it}. \tag{B.44}$$

Let us understand the different terms. The X's are the variables that vary over units and time. In the cross-country growth regression models, the X's are like saving/GDP ratio and investment/GDP ratio that vary across countries within any given year and across year for a given country. The variables $H1$ and $H2$ are the *observable* unit-specific variables and $M1$ and $M2$ the *observable* time-specific variables; $H1$ could be distance from the equator and $H2$ a dummy variable representing whether a country has a political system of democracy or not; $M1$ could be time itself (capturing time trend) and $M2$ the world oil price at time t.

In addition, there may be unit-specific and time-specific determinants or effects are unknown, unavailable in the dataset or unobserved. These are represented by η_i and λ_t. There are called *fixed effects*. As examples, within-country language diversity or a measure of social cooperation for addressing drug abuse and mental health issues across countries for which the researcher may not have data on will be included in η_i. Assuming that corona virus severely afflicted nations in two years, 2020 and 2021, a dummy variable capturing these years will be a part of λ_t. Finally, u_{it} is the error term.

When a variable takes different values over time (unlike, for instance, geographical characteristics of a country), the lagged values of those variables may have significant predictive power. As an example, in a panel equation like (B.44), we may include lagged values of $X1_{it}$, $X2_{it}$ or Y_{it} as explanatory variables. In particular, if the lagged values of the dependent variable Y_{it} were included as regressors, then the panel equation would have been called a *dynamic panel model*. Suppose Y_{it} was the *level* of per-capita real GDP, not its growth rate. Then it would be reasonable to include Y_{it-1} as a regressor, because the levels of many variables that change over time exhibit a pattern.

B.15 Seemingly Unrelated Regression (SUR)

Consider state-wise GDP growth rates over time, y_{it}, where $i = 1, 2, \ldots, 50$ denotes a state and $t = 1, 2, \ldots, T$. We want to explain the agricultural output for each state by state-specific variables. Assume that these variables are exogenous like fertilizer use, rainfall, etc. In other words, we want to estimate an equation like

$$Y_{it} = a_i + \beta_{i1} X^1_{it} + \beta_{i2} X^2_{it} + u_{it}, \quad \text{Cov}(u_{it}, u_{it'}) = 0 \tag{B.45}$$

for each i. More generally, the set of X's may differ from one state to another. The problem, however, is that the error terms for any given state i may be independent over time, but that across states for a given t may not be, i.e., $\text{Cov}(u_{it}, u_{jt})$ may not be equal to zero for some pair of states i and j for some t. For instance, a group of states may be affected by massive flood situation in a given year.

As another situation, suppose we want to estimate high school graduation rates for each state separately with available data on all fifty states in the USA from a say 2000 to 2021. This generates some coefficient estimates and some error terms. However, the error terms are likely to be correlated between states for any particular year. For example, there might have been some national event in 2018 that caused graduation rates across the country to be unusually high. For that year, the error terms are likely to be correlated across the sates.

The commonality between the two examples is that the explanatory variables being exogenous, the error terms in the regressions equations may appear to be unrelated. But they are not. Put differently the regressions "seem" unrelated but they are not.

While OLS provides consistent estimates, the coefficients of the system are estimated by Generalized Least Squares (GLS). Describing GLS is, however, beyond our scope here.

B.16 Event Study Analysis

This is used in the field of finance in order to assess the impact of an "event" (e.g. *9/11* attacks) on the stock price or the stock returns. There is an *estimation period*, the time period prior or leading to the event date. This is used to calculate the estimated return predicted by the market around the date of the event. There is also an *event period*, which follows the event and is used to assesses the impact of the event. An event period would have *event windows* like 0, 5, 10, 15, and 30 days following the event.

The endeavor is to estimate the abnormal return on a stock which can be attributed to the event, where the abnormal return equals the actual return (which is observed) minus an expected return *if the event had not occurred.* The latter is a counterfactual, not observed. Depending on how we model the expected return if the event had not occurred, there are many ways to calculate the abnormal return on the date t where t is the event date + 0, event date + 5, event date + 10, and so on.

Mean-Adjusted Return (MAR): This is defined as $R_t - \bar{R}_j$, where R_t is the actual return at some point of time during the event period and $\bar{R}_j$ is the average return of the stock or the stock index during the estimation period, the implicit assumption being that nothing of significance occurred during the estimation period.

Market-Adjusted Return (MKAR): This is equal to $R_t - R_{Mt}$, where R_{Mt} is the return on the market index like say S&P500.

Risk-Adjusted Return (RAR): It is equal to $R_t - \left(\hat{\alpha} + \hat{\beta} R_{Mt}\right)$, where $\hat{\alpha}$ and $\hat{\beta}$ are the estimates of α and β of a stock from the CAPM model based on previous data (prior to the event). This is considered to be the most desirable among the three.

In the context of terrorism, event analysis is typically applied to estimate the impact of a specific major terror attack on financial markets as discussed in Chap. 6.

B.17 Regression Discontinuity Design (RDD) and Difference-in-Differences (DiD) Approach

B.17.1 RRD

Suppose we want to know if a scholarship in high school improves the students' grade in college. National scholarships in the USA are based on scoring above a

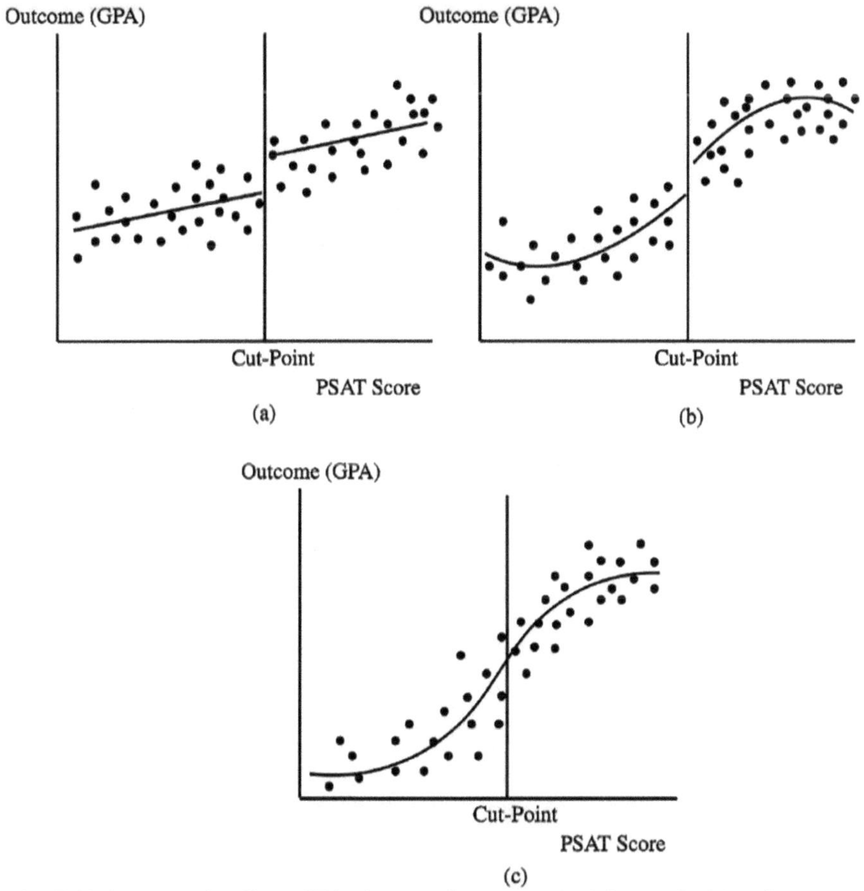

Fig. B.7: PSAT and college GPA: Scatter diagrams . (**a**) Linear. (**b**) Non-linear. (**c**) Non-linearity misconstrued as discontinuity

threshold in the standardized PSAT, which are taken by high school students in the 11th grade. It is not easy to assess the impact of such threshold clearing score in PSAT on college grade, because student score in PSAT and GPA in college may be positively correlated even in the absence of such scholarship. Personal characteristics of students like disciplinary habits, innate intelligence can contribute to such a positive relationship. The question is, how we can isolate the effect of scholarship, based on some threshold clearing, on college grade from the effects of other factors?

RDD is a regression technique to achieve this. The main idea behind RDD is that individuals with scores just below the cut-off (who did not receive the award) are likely to be good comparisons to those just above the cut-off (who did receive the award) in terms of factors like disciplinary habits and IQ, because, apart from these factors, the two groups are very alike. Those who are significantly above and below the threshold may not be very alike.

Figure B.7 illustrates three (hypothetical) examples, where the horizontal axis measures PSAT score with the scholarship threshold shown at the cut-point and the vertical axis represents college GPA. If we expect a normal, continuous, and increasing relation between PSAT score and GPA without any scholarship, we should expect a discrete jump at the threshold if the scholarship has a significant effect on its own.

Part (a) is the best scenario situation. The size of the jump is the RDD estimate of the effect of the scholarship, while the normal relationship is linear. Even if the relationship is non-linear, we can get a RDD estimate of scholarship if the scatter diagram looks like the one shown in part (b). The method should work as long as the relationship is continuous below and after the threshold but not at the threshold. The problem arises in a situation depicted in part (c), where it is a continuous and non-linear relationship with a point of inflection (at which the second derivative changes sign). Here non-linearity may be misconstrued as discontinuity—if we try to fit a linear function on either side.

How is this method implemented? If we assume a linear relation between X and Y along with the threshold at $X = X_0$ we would specify the regression equation as:

$$Y_i = a + b_1 X_i + b_2 I(X_i > X_0) + u_i, \tag{B.46}$$

where I is an indicator function that takes value 1 if $X_i > X_0$ and 0 otherwise. Note that $I(X_i > X_0)$ is a dummy variable. Here $\hat{b}_2$ is the RDD estimate of the effect of the scholarship. In general, X is called the *running variable*.

RDD approach has its limitations. There may be something else happening that has similar impact as the scholarship threshold. Or else, there are problems if there are significant number of individuals who try to manipulate to get above the threshold.

B.17.2 DiD

Suppose a state has two major cities, and a free school lunch program is introduced in city A but not in city B in period t. In other words, A and B are similar in period $t-1$ but not at time t or after. Suppose our aim is to estimate the effect of this program on the academic performance of students in terms of say scores in a standardized test, y, undertaken by students in both cities A and B in both periods $t-1$ and t. Note that the free lunch program is similar to an intervention studied in Sect. B.13.2. In the present context of comparing two units, the free lunch program is a *treatment*.

Suppose the mean scores in city A in periods $t-1$ and t are $\bar{y}_A^{t-1} = 30$ and $\bar{y}_A^t = 65$. The difference is: $D_A \equiv \bar{y}_A^t - \bar{y}_A^{t-1} = 35$. Can we say with confidence that D_A measures the effect of the free school lunch program, the treatment program? The general answer is no, because some other underlying causal factors may have changed between pre- and post-treatment or intervention dates. For instance, the state's economy may have experienced an inclusive growth of real income that might have led the parents to provide their children with better access to computers, internet, books, etc. Thus, D_A could be a result of the treatment (intervention) *and* some other factors, i.e.,

$$D_A \equiv \underbrace{\left(\bar{y}^t_{Ar} - \bar{y}^{t-1}_{Ar}\right)}_{D_{Ar}} + \underbrace{\left(\bar{y}^t_{Ao} - \bar{y}^{t-1}_{Ao}\right)}_{D_{Ao}},$$

where r and o denote intervention/treatment and other factors. We want to estimate D_{Ar}, the difference due to the intervention only. So how do we identify and eliminate D_{Ao}?

Suppose that we strongly believe that the other city B, which does not receive the treatment, has witnessed the same other effect as has city B at time t, i.e., better access to computers, books, etc. to school students in city B. Suppose that we have data on scores in the same standardized test for students in city B for periods $t-1$ and t. Let us suppose $\bar{y}^{t-1}_B = 35$ and $\bar{y}^t_B = 50$. Thus $D_B \equiv \bar{y}^t_B - \bar{y}^{t-1}_B = 15$. Further, suppose we have reasons to believe that (a) this difference is solely attributed to the other factors, i.e., $\bar{y}^t_B - \bar{y}^{t-1}_B = \bar{y}^t_{Bo} - \bar{y}^{t-1}_{Bo} = 15$ and (b) this difference is same between the cities A and B, i.e., $\bar{y}^t_{Ao} - \bar{y}^{t-1}_{Ao} = \bar{y}^t_{Bo} - \bar{y}^{t-1}_{Bo}$. Then the treatment effect is equal to

$$\begin{aligned}
\bar{y}^t_{Ar} - \bar{y}^{t-1}_{Ar} &= D_A - \left(\bar{y}^t_{Ao} - \bar{y}^{t-1}_{Ao}\right) \\
&= D_A - \left(\bar{y}^t_{Bo} - \bar{y}^{t-1}_{Bo}\right) \\
&= D_A - \left(\bar{y}^t_B - \bar{y}^{t-1}_B\right) \\
&= D_A - D_B,
\end{aligned}$$

which is a difference-in-differences, DiD.

Here is the idea. There is a *treatment group* (students in city A) and a *control group* (students in city B). The DiD estimate of the treatment is obtained by using the outcome for the treatment group as well as that of the control group. Note that

$$y^t_A - \bar{y}^{t-1}_A - \left(y^t_B - \bar{y}^{t-1}_B\right) = y^t_A - \bar{y}^t_B - \left(y^{t-1}_A - y^{t-1}_B\right).$$

That is, treatment effect = the difference between pre- and post-differences for the treatment and control groups = the difference between the post-treatment outcomes difference and the pre-treatment outcome difference.

The treatment-effect estimates are typically obtained using linear regression. In case of terrorism, an event like *9/11* can be thought—for analytical purposes—of as a treatment or intervention by nature or extraneous sources. Some periods in terms of days or week around September 11, 2001 can be considered as a treatment sample, and some periods in terms of days or week around September 11, 2000 can be considered as a control sample.

Note that difference-in-differences (DiD) is similar in spirit to regression discontinuity design (RDD). But unlike RDD, DiD relies on the existence of two groups—one that is served the treatment (after some cut-off) and one that is not. Because DiD includes a control group in the identification strategy, it is generally considered more robust.

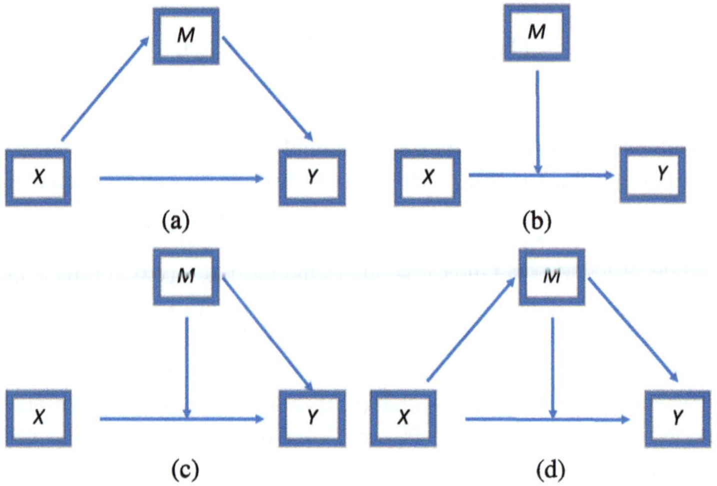

Fig. B.8: Mediator and moderator. (**a**) M is a mediator. (**b**) M is a moderator. (**c**) M a moderator. (**d**) M is a mediator-cum-moderator

B.18 Moderated Median Analysis

Chapter 15 discusses a statistical model of inclination toward adopting religious fundamentalism and supporting an organization like ISIS that uses moderated median analysis. Widely used in psychology and medical science, a moderated median analysis estimates the impact of a variable X on an outcome variable Y, where the marginal impact is influenced by another variable M or a set of other variables. Focusing on one "third" variable M, M enters the causal relation between X and Y in two generic ways, although there can be mixed or extended situations.

For instance, we may hypothesize that X is grade in school, Y is happiness and M is self-esteem—and grades affect happiness directly and through self-esteem. Here *M is a mediator.* This is exhibited in Fig. B.8c.

As another example, we may postulate that the *marginal* impact the state of being unemployed (X) on mental health (Y) depends on how socially connected an individual is, where the degree of social connectedness is M. The emphasis is on the marginal effect, while M is *not* affected by X, i.e., social connectedness is unaffected by someone being unemployed. Here M is a moderator. See panel (b) of Fig. B.8. Moderation is also known as an *interaction.* More generally, M may influence Y also, i.e., social connectedness may directly affect mental health. This is exhibited in Fig. B.8c.[16]

[16] Still another example is where negative emotions about climatic change leads to political support for the government's action and this causation may be influenced by age, the hypothesis being that the relationship between negative emotions about climate change and support for government action on climate change will be stronger among older people. There may also be other moderators, e.g., the number of young children an individual has or has to take care of (0, 1, . . .).

The same third variable M can be a mediator *and* a moderator at the same time, as shown in panel (d) of Fig. B.8. Being unemployed directly affects mental health. It affects social connectedness, which, in turn, impacts on mental health. Social connectedness also influences the marginal impact of being unemployed on mental health.

Which of the four types is the most relevant depend on the plausibility of relations. Once the cause–effect relations are decided, appropriate statistical equations are postulated to capture the relationships. Suppose the model at hand is one that is depicted in Fig. B.8c. It is a moderation model, the equations of which will be:

$$Y = a_0 + b_1 X + b_2 M + u \tag{B.47}$$

$$b_1 = a_1 + b_3 M + v. \tag{B.48}$$

where u and v are the error terms. Now substitute Eq. (B.48) into Eq. (B.47) to obtain

$$\begin{aligned} Y &= a_0 + (a_1 + b_3 M + v)X + +b_2 M + u \\ &= a_0 + a_1 X + b_3(MX) + v \cdot X + b_2 M + u \\ \text{i.e. } Y &\equiv a_0 + a_1 X + b_2 M + b_3(MX) + \epsilon, \text{ where } \epsilon \equiv v \cdot X + u. \end{aligned} \tag{B.49}$$

This is the regression equation. The statistical significance of the estimator of b_3 determines whether there is significant moderation, i.e., whether M is a significant moderator of the marginal effect of X on Y.

B.19 Count data, Poisson and negative Binomial Regression, Poisson Autoregression Models

When a variable can take values 0, 1, 2, and so on, i.e., without any fraction or decimal, it is called a *count variable* and the data itself is called *count data*. Examples are the number of accidents, the number of terror attacks, the number of crimes in a campus, etc. When the dependent variable is a count variable, linear or log-linear regression is not appropriate. First, we cannot use log if the dependent, count variable has 0 present in the same sample data. Second, these regressions can yield negative or fractional predicted values, which does not make sense. Third, typically, count data has a skewed, not symmetric distribution, so assuming normal distribution for inference purposes, as does OLS estimates, is not appropriate. Instead, two types of non-linear regression are used: negative binomial and Poisson regression.

Similar to the logit/probit model introduced in Sect. B.4.2, a probability model or probability distribution of the dependent variable Y is specified. It is a discrete probability distribution, not continuous, defined over integer values 0, 1, 2, and so on, not over any negative values. Typically, it is a negative binomial or a Poisson distribution is assumed. Some of the parameters of these two distributions are postulated such that for either distribution, the expected value of Y_i is an exponential function of a linear function of the regressors.

For example, if there are say two explanatory variables, X_1 and X_2, the parameters of negative binomial and Poisson distributions are made functions of X_1 and X_2 such that

$$E(Y_i|X_{i1}, X_{i2}) = \exp(a + b_1 X_{i1} + b_2 X_{i2}). \tag{B.50}$$

We skip negative binomial and focus on the Poisson distribution. It is given by

$$\Pr(Y_i = z) = \frac{\lambda_i^z \exp(-\lambda_i)}{z!}, \quad z = 0, 1, 2, \ldots \tag{B.51}$$

and it can be shown that the expected value of Y_i equals

$$\sum_{z=0}^{\infty} z \Pr(Y_i = z) = z\frac{\lambda_i^z e^{-\lambda_i}}{z!} = \lambda_i.$$

Thus it is postulated that $\lambda_i = \exp(a + b_1 X_{i1} + b_2 X_{i2})$.

Like logit/probit, these are non-linear regression models and the estimates are obtained by the maximum likelihood method.

Poisson Auto-Regression model refers to a time-series framework, where the outcomes $(0, 1, 2, \ldots)$, e.g., the number of hostage attacks, at different periods t, follow a Poisson distribution. That is,

$$\Pr(Y_t = z) = \frac{\lambda_t^z e^{-\lambda_t}}{z!}, \tag{B.52}$$

where λ_t is the mean of the Poisson distribution and Y_t is the number of hostage events. This is same as Eq. (B.51), except that t substitutes i. Equation (B.52), called the *measurement equation*, is analogous to Eq. (B.51).

The mean or the expected value is then related to past values of Y_t as well as what are posited as explanatory variables or covariates. This is called the *transition equation*. If we express the covariates as a vector, say $\mathbf{X}_t$, the transition equation is:

$$\lambda_t = \sum_{i=1}^{p} \rho_i Y_{t-i} + \left(1 - \sum_{i=1}^{p} \rho_i\right) e^{-\mathbf{bX}_t}, \tag{B.53}$$

This is a Poisson auto-regression model, where $\mathbf{bX}_t \equiv b_1 X_{1t} + b_2 X_{2t} + \ldots$. The vector $\mathbf{X}_t$ could include lagged effects.

This model is referred to in Chap. 12, where we analyze hostage-taking behavior. There are three covariates for each of the three hostage-taking series (kidnapping, skyjacking, and the "other"), i.e., the vector $\mathbf{X}_t$ has three elements: negotiation success, response of the target and death, each being a binary variable: negotiation success takes value 0 if some demands are met or 1 otherwise; response of the target is 0 if there is no shoot out or 1 otherwise; and death is equal to 0 if there are no deaths or 1 otherwise, the hypothesis being that deaths are anticipated to deter future incidents.

The impact of no-concession policy is measured by the estimated coefficient of the negotiation success variable, the respective b_i, together with the estimated coefficients of the Poisson auto-regression model, the ρ_i's. These variables are included contemporaneously as well as with one-period lag. The inclusion of violent ending and death permits to estimate the short-run and the long-run effects of these outcomes on future occurrences of hostage-taking.

If Eq. (B.53) is substituted into Eq. (B.52), the probability distribution of the outcome (number of hostage-taking events in that category) is a function of covariates and the dependent variable itself. The resulting equation is then estimated by the maximum likelihood method applied to the sample.

B.20 Extreme Bounds Analysis

Suppose we want to explain an outcome Y and there are several plausible explanatory variables. It does not mean that all those variables must belong to the regression equation—because some of them may turn out to be insignificant and the coefficients of some may fluctuate a lot when different combination of plausible variables are included. Extreme Bounds Analysis or testing is a way to determine which variables are robust so as to be included in the "true" regression model, not necessarily the "true" (theoretical) model itself. Thus, it deals with what we may call the variable selection uncertainty. It also addresses which way a variable should enter the regression equation: linearly, log-linearly or quadratic form, and so on?

The idea is to run numerous regressions with various combinations of variables and their functional forms in the regression equation and select those variables that are robust across these regressions. Robustness means (a) the coefficient must be statistically significant and (b) its value should not drastically fluctuate across different specifications. The number of regressions run may be in thousands or even millions (Salai-i-Martin, 1997). It depends on the pool of plausible and available explanatory variables.

B.21 Survival Models

These models aim to explain the length of spells and "survival" of entities. In Chap. 7 we discuss the factors that explain the "lifetime" of terror groups—how long a terrorist organization lasts. In Chap. 12, we study the duration of the negotiation period in a hostage situation. In labor economics, there are studies on unemployment spells. In medical science, we are interested to learn about the duration of survival of heart-attack patients. These are just a few examples.

Note that the spells (e.g. lifetime and unemployment) end with an "event," e.g., a terrorist organization cracked down or renouncing violence after a negotiation, finding a job or leaving the labor force, death of heart-attack patients and so on. The objective is to explain the duration or time-to-event in terms of days, weeks, hours or years or simply the number of uses (e.g., a machine or an equipment until it breaks down). Typically, the event of interest is termed as "death" and the waiting time is called the "survival time."

If we want to explain say the lifetime of terrorist organizations in terms of their size, political and religious orientation and environment they operate in (there are many other factors), or, unemployment spells by factors like sex, age, experience, education, etc., why not simply use linear or log-linear regression estimation? There are problems. First, in the dataset we may have observations for which the event has not occurred. If we use GTD that covers 1970 to 2019, there are groups that are still "alive" in 2019: we do not have a number for their lifetime or survival. It is not a good idea to exclude such terror groups. So the question is, how do we account for still surviving groups? Second, we want to use the estimated relation to predict, for instance, what is the probability that a heart-attack patient who has already survived for four months will die at that point of time or a terrorist organization that has been active for two years will cease to operate. These are *conditional*, not simple, probabilities. A simple linear regression, a log-linear regression or even a logit/probit model is not suitable. What is used instead is a more complicated probability model than logit or probit.

There is a wide variety of survival models depending on the statistical distribution of the "event" (death) the researcher thinks appropriate for the subject of the analysis. Regression estimates are obtained by the maximum likelihood method.

B.22 STaR (STAR) Estimation

This refers to smooth transition regression models or smooth transition autoregression model. The idea is that the marginal impact of regressors on the dependent variable may change once some or all of the regressors cross a respective threshold.[17] For example, Enders and Hoover (2012) postulate that the impact of poverty or per-capita income on the incidence of terrorism may depend on whether a country is a high-per-capita-income (lower-poverty) or a low-per-capita-income (high-poverty). On way to capture this is to exogenously specify threshold income that separates high-per-capita-income countries from the low-per-capita-income countries. World Bank follows this methodology to define lower-income, low-middle-income, upper-middle-income, and high-income countries.[18] To estimate a cause–effect relation, such a "bang-bang" classification may not be satisfactory for two reasons. (A) The critical levels are arbitrary depending on what goes inside the formula that yields which economy is of which type. (B) Given these critical values, if there is a cluster of countries in the close neighbor of the critical values, then classifying them differently can lead to serious misspecification and hence unreliable estimates.

---

[17] The change in the marginal impact may depend on the range of values for some outside variables.

[18] For the 2021 fiscal year, low-income economies are those whose per-capita gross national income does not exceed $1035 (by using a method known as World Bank Atlas method). The ranges defining lower-income, low-middle-income, upper-middle-income countries are ($1035, $4046], ($4046, $12,535], and ($12,535-higher).

An alternative approach is to postulate a process of gradual transition from state to another. Consider, for instance, the impact of income (X) on expenditure on travel (Y). It is reasonable to suppose that relatively poor will travel mostly by road, which is relatively cheap, while the relatively rich will travel mostly by air. Thus it is reasonable to postulate that the relationship between income and travel will be different for relative poor and relatively rich. In terms of regression, it may be not desirable to assume just one equation like $Y = a + bX + u$ where X spans very low and very high incomes—because the parameters a and b may depend on the level of X. At the same time, it is hard to exogenously specify a threshold level of income that differentiates the pattern of spending on travel.

Smooth transition regression adds a transition relation to a specification like $Y = a + bX + u$. An example will be

$$a + bX + \frac{1}{1 + e^{-\gamma(X-c)}}(\alpha + \beta X) + u, \quad \gamma > 0, \tag{B.54}$$

a STaR equation, where suppose that both X and Y are in log. Notice that

$$g(X) \equiv \frac{1}{1 + e^{-\gamma(X-c)}} \in (0, 1),$$

which is a "logistic function" and in Eq. (B.54), it describes transition. Hence, a function like $g(X)$ is called a *transition function*. If $X < c$ and is very small, i.e., if $X \to -\infty$, the ratio $g(x)$, approaches zero and thus $Y \simeq a + bX + u$.[19] If $X > c$ and is very large approaching ∞, then $g(x)$ approaches 1 and $Y \simeq (a + \alpha) + (b + \beta)X + u$.

The regression equation (B.54) is a STaR, which yields estimates of a, b, α, β, γ, and c. In the example of income and travel, we would expect the estimate of β to be positive.

Remarks.
[a] The transition function is non-linear and thus STaR equation is non-linear.
[b] We could postulate a non-linear relation even without the transition relation if there are grounds to believe so. That is, a STaR equation may be like

$$Y = a + b_1X + b_2X^2 + \frac{1}{1 + e^{-\gamma(X-c)}}(\alpha + \beta_1X + \beta_2X^2) + u, \quad \gamma > 0, \tag{B.55}$$

[c] There are other plausible transition functions other than the above logistic $g(X)$ function.
[d] In a multiple regression framework with say three explanatory variables X_1, X_2, and X_3, it may be reasonable to postulate a transition function based on one variable say X_1. In that case, X_1 is called a transition variable.

[e] The STaR model is often specified within an auto-regressive time-series model and the transition function is defined on lagged values of the time-series variable.

[19] At $X = c$, it is exactly $1/2$.

An example of such a STaR model will be

$$Y_t = a+b_1Y_{t-1}+b_2Y_{t-2}+b_3Y_{t-3}+\frac{1}{1+e^{-\gamma(Y_{t-1}-c)}}(\alpha+\beta_1Y_{t-1}+\beta_2Y_{t-2}+\beta_3Y_{t-3})+u_t.$$

B.23 Gravity Equation in International Trade

It refers to a regression model that explains *gross* trade flows between two countries. Typically, in many product or service groups, a country exports some to other countries and import some from other countries. For instance, US exports automobiles to Japan and imports automobiles from Japan. Hypothetically, if US exports automobiles worth \$10 billion to Japan and imports automobiles valued at \$13 billion in a given year, then the gross automobile trade flow (exports) from the USA to Japan in that year is \$10 billion and the same from Japan to the USA in \$13 billion, whereas the net exports of automobile from the USA to Japan is −\$3 billion and the same from Japan to the USA is \$3 billion. While this is an example of gross trade in a specific commodity, we can consider gross trade in a much broader categories of goods or services like manufacturing, financial services, etc.

The model was initiated by Jan Tinbergen, the first Nobel laureate in economics who shared the prize with Ragnar Frisch. He postulated that gross trade between two countries, say A and B, would increase with GDP of the exporting country, that of the importing country and the physical distance between them, i.e.,

$$T_{A,B} \propto \frac{(\mathrm{GDP}_A)^{\alpha}\cdot(\mathrm{GDP}_B)^{\beta}}{(\mathrm{Distance}_{AB})^{\gamma}}, \text{ where } \alpha, \beta, \gamma \approx 1. \tag{B.56}$$

This resembles the Newtonian gravity equation (except for the exponent of 'Distance'). This is why it came to be known that gravity equation in international trade.

Typically and more generally, however, (a) the parameters α, β, and γ are estimated from the data rather than restricted to the value 1, and (b) a more aggregative trade cost variable, say τ_{ij}, takes the place of "Distance." A classical specification of the gravity equation is in the log-linear form:

$$\ln T_{ij} = a + \alpha \ln \mathrm{GDP}_i + \beta \ln \mathrm{GDP}_j + \gamma \ln \tau_{ij} + u_{ij}, \tag{B.57}$$

where T_{ij} is the value of gross exports from the source (exporting) country i to the destination (importing) country j. There is an accompanying equation for the trade cost as a function of distance and other bilateral impediments like language difference, whether two countries share a border, etc. Typically we have cross-sectional data on bilateral trade among countries. Data on GDPs of countries, distance, language difference, etc. are readily available. Equation (B.57) is typically estimated by using cross-section data. There are panels estimations of gravity equations too.

However, a log-linear specification such as (B.57) has some well-known issues that we do not get into. In recent years, different non-linear methodologies are used to estimate the parameters of the gravity equation. But the basic ideas are the same.

Similar to international trade flows, the gravity equation is used to explain bilateral foreign direct investment flows.

References

9/11 Commission Report. (2004). *Final Report of the National Commission on Terrorist Attacks upon the United States*, Technical report, National Commission on Terrorist Attacks upon the United States. 111, 229

Abadie, A. (2006). Poverty, political freedom and the roots of terrorism. *American Economic Review Papers and Proceedings, 96*, 50–56. 567, 569, 579

Abadie, A., & Gardeazabal, J. (2003). The economic costs of conflict: A case study of the Basque Country. *American Economic Review, 93*, 113–132. 77, 273, 274, 291, 292, 310, 320

Abadie, A., & Gardeazabal, J. (2008). Terrorism and the world economy. *European Economic Review, 52*(1), 1–27. 283, 315

ABC NEWS (2021). Qatar Pledges $360 Million in Aid to Hamas-Ruled Gaza. *ABC NEWS*, January 31. 145

Abu Amer, A. (2018). Fatah and Hamas will Face Trump's Deal Disunited. *Al Jazeera* Website, December 18. https://www.aljazeera.com/indepth/opinion/fatah-hamas-face-trump-deal-disunited-181218093240784.html, accessed on January 6, 2019. 85

Acosta, N. (2020). Biden Could Help Unfreeze Colombian Peace Talks: ELN Rebel Leader. *Reuters*, November 20. 60

Adams, J. (1986). *The financing of terror: How the groups that are terrorizing the world get the money to do it.* New York: Simon and Shuster. 73, 232

Adebayo, A. A. (2014). Implications of Boko Haram terrorism on national development in Nigeria. *Mediterranean Journal of Social Sciences, 5*(16). 136, 283

Adraoui, M.-A. (2017). *Jabhat Al-Nusra in the Syrian conflict.* London: Oxford Research Group, December 20. 123

Ahern, J., Galea, S., Resnick, H., Kilpatrick, D., Bucuvalas, M., Gold, J., & Vlahov, D. (2002). Telephone images and psychological symptoms after the September 11 terrorist attacks. *Psychiatry, 65*(4), 289–300. 307

Ahmad, J., & Mehsud, S. (2018). Pakistani Taliban Appoints New Chief After Previous Leader Killed in Drone Strike. *Reuters*, June 23. 136

Äijälä, A.-L. (2016). How is ISIS Funded? Bachelor's Thesis, Tallinn University of Technology. 118, 119, 120

Aksoy, M. (2014). The effects of terrorism on Turkish stock market. *Ege Akademik Bakiş, 14*(1), 31–41. 291, 293

Aksoy, M., & Demiralay, S. (2019). The effects of terrorism on Turkish financial markets. *Defence and Peace Economics, 30*(6), 733–755. 292, 293

S. P. Das, *Economics of Terrorism and Counter-Terrorism Measures*,
https://doi.org/10.1007/978-3-030-96577-8

Al Jazeera. (2003). The Second Intifada. *Al Jazeera*, December 4. 142

Al Jazeera. (2009). The History of the Tamil Tigers. *Al Jazeera*, April. 90

Al Jazeera. (2014). Profile: The Lord's Resistance Army. *Al Jazeera*, May 6. 162

Al Jazeera. (2019). Timeline: US Military Presence in Afghanistan. *Al Jazeera*, September 8. 126

Al Jazeera. (2021). Yahya Sinwar Re-Elected as Hamas Chief in Gaza Strip. *Al Jazeera*, March 10. 143

Al Mughrabi, N. (2017). Anger as Palestinian Authority Cuts Gaza Salaries and Pays Late. *Reuters*, May 3. 146

Al Mughrabi, N., & Heller, J. (2017). Israel Reduces Power Supply to Gaza, as Abbas Pressures Hamas. *Reuters*, June 12. 146

Ali, Z. (2020). Syria: Who's in Control of Idlib? *BBC News*, February 18. https://www.bbc.com/news/world-45401474, accessed on November 26, 2021. 124

Altunbaķ, Y., & Thorton, J. (2011). Are home grown islamic terrorists different? Some UK evidence. *Southern Economic Journal, 78*(2), 262–272. 571

APEC. (2017). Strengthening Tourism Business Resilience against the Impact of Terrorist Attack. Asia-Pacific Economic Cooperation' Counter-Terrorism Working Group's Report. 294

Araz-Takay, B., Peren Arin, K., & Omay, T. (2009). The endogenous and non-linear relationship between terrorism and economic performance: Turkish evidence. *Defence and Peace Economics, 20*(1), 1–10. 277

Arin, K. P., Ciferri, D., & Spagnolo, N. (2008). The price of terror: The effects of terrorism on stock market returns and volatility. *Economics Letters, 101*(3), 164–167. 293

Asal, V., & Rethemeyer, K. R. (2008). The nature of the beast: Organizational structures and the lethality of terrorist attacks. *Journal of Politics, 70*(2), 437–449. 365

Ashour, O. (2011). From 9/11 to the Arab Spring. *Brookings OP-ED*, September 7. 153

Aslam, F., & Kang, H.-G. (2015). How different terrorist attacks affect stock markets. *Defence and Peace Economics, 26*(6), 634–648. 292

Aslam, F., Kang, H.-G., Mohti, W., Rafique, A., & Salman, A. (2018). The impact of terrorism on financial markets: Evidence from Asia. *Singapore Economic Review, 63*(5), 1183–1204. 293

Åslund, O., & Rooth, D.-O. (2005). Shifts in attitudes and labor market discrimination: Swedish experiences after 9-11. *Journal of Population Economics, 18*(4), 603–629. 287

Atikinson, S. E., Sandler, T., & Tschirhart, J. (1987). Terrorism in a bargaining framework. *Journal of Law and Economics, 30*(1), 1–21. 496, 501

Australian Transaction Report and Analysis Centre. (2014). Terrorism Financing in Australia 2014. Report. 235

Baier, S., & Bergstrand, J. H. (2009). *Bonus Vetus* OLS: A simple method for aproximating international trade-cost effects using the gravity equation. *Journal of International Economics, 77*(1), 77–85. 282, 315

Bandopadhyay, S., & Younas, J. (2011). Poverty, political freedom and the roots of terrorism in developing countries: An empirical assessment. *Economics Letters, 112*(2), 171–175. 569, 578, 579

Bandopadhyay, S., Sandler, T., & Younas, J. (2014). Foreign direct investment, aid, and terrorism. *Oxford Economic Papers, 66*(1), 25–50. 283, 316

Bandopadhyay, S., Sandler, T., & Younas, J. (2018). Trade and terrorism: A disaggregated approach. *Journal of Peace Research, 55*(5), 656–670. 282, 315

Banerjee, S. (2017). *From naxalbari to Chhattisgarh: Half-a-century of Maoist journey in India*. Belgium: Tricontinental Centre (CETRI). 64, 65

Banerjee, T., & Siebert, R. (2015). *The impact of R&D cooperations on drug variety offered on the market: Evidence from the pharmaceutical industry*. Mimeo: Auburn University and Purdue University. 325

Baumert, T., Buesa, M., & Lynch, T. (2013). The Impact of Terrorism on Stock Markets: The Boston Bombing Experience in Comparison with Previous Terrorist Events. *Documento de Trabajo*, No. 88. 289, 317

BBC News. (2003). Who Are Islamic Jihad? *BBC News*, June 9. 151

BBC News. (2012). Who Are the Kashmir Militants? *BBC News*, August 1. 175

BBC News. (2014). Profile: Popular Front for the Liberation of Palestine (PFLP). *BBC News*, November 18. 86

BBC News. (2015a). Peru Admits Shining Path Rebels Have Not Been 'Exterminated'. *BBC News*, August 6. 61

BBC News. (2015b). Profile: Ayman al-Zawahiri. *BBC News*, August 13. 154

BBC News. (2017a). Peruvian Ballet Dancer Who Hid Shining Path Rebel Is Freed. *BBC News*, September 12. 61

BBC News. (2017b). Who Are Somalia's al-Shabab? *BBC News*, October 22. 158

BBC News. (2018). Khmer Rouge: Cambodia's Years of Brutality. *BBC News*, November 16. 66

BBC News. (2019). Turkey v Syria's Kurds: The Short, Medium and long Story. *BBC News*, October 23. 81

Becker, J. (2011). Beirut Bank Seen as a Hub of Hezbollah's Financing. *New York Times*, December 13. 239

Becker, G. S., & Murphy, K. M. (2001). Prosperity Will Rise Out of the Ashes. *Wall Street Journal*, October 29. 247

Becker, G. S., & Rubinstein, Y. (2011). Fear and the Response to Terrorism: An Economic Analysis. CEP Discussion Paper No. 1079. 8, 275, 309, 310, 312

Beech, H., & Gutierrez, J. (2019). How ISIS Is Rising in the Philippines as It Dwindles in the Middle East. *New York Times*, March 9. 121

Begley, S. (2004). Afraid to Fly After 9/11, Some Took a Bigger Risk—In Cars. *Wall Street Journal*, March 23. 308

Benmelech, E., & Berrebi, C. (2007). Human capital and the productivity of suicide bombers. *Journal of Economic Perspectives, 21*(3), 223–238. 275, 285, 286, 311

Berman, E. (2000). Sect, subsidy and sacrifice: An economist's view of ultra-orthodox Jews. *Quaarterly Journal of Economics, 115*(3), 905–953. 543

Berman, E. (2009). *Radical, religious and violent: The new economics of terrorism*. Cambridge, MA: The MIT Press. 39, 508, 543

Berman, E., & Laitin, D. D. (2008). Religion, terrorism and public goods. *Journal of Public Economics, 92*, 1942–1967. 125, 140, 141, 508, 543

Bernstein, K. T., Ahern, J., Tracy, M., Boscarino, J. A., Vlahov, D. & Galea, S. (2007). Television watching and the risk of incident probable posttraumatic stress disorder: A prospective evaluation. *Journal of Nervous and Mental Disease, 195*(1), 41–47. 307

Berrebi, C. (2007). Evidence about the link between education, poverty and terrorism among palestinians. *Peace Economics, Peace Science and Public Policy, De Gruyter, 13*(1), 1–38. 559, 560, 562

Bhattacharji, P. (2010). Chechen Terrorism (Russia, Chechnya, Separatist). *Council on Foreign Relations*, April 8. 166, 167

Binder, M. K., & Ackerman, G. A. (2019). Pick your POICN: Introducing the profiles of incidents involving CBRN and Non-State Actors (POICN) database. *Studies in Conflict & Terrorism*, 1–25. 199, 201

Birkelund, G. E., Chan, T. W., Ugreninov, E., Midtbøen, A. H., & Rostad, J. (2018). Do terrorist attacks affect ethnic discrimination in the labour market? Evidence from two randomized field experiments. *British Journal of Sociology, 70*(4), 1–20. 287

Blalock, G.., Kadiyali, V., & Simon, D. H. (2009). Driving fatalities after 9/11: A hidden cost of terrorism. *Applied Economics, 41*(14), 1717–1729. 246, 308, 309, 312

Bleich, A., Gelkopf, M., & Solomon, Z. (2003). Exposure to terrorism, stress-related mental health symptoms, and coping with behaviors among a nationally representative sample in Israel. *Journal of the American Medical Association, 290*(5), 612–620. 303

Bleich, A., Gelkopf, M., Yuval, M., & Solomon, Z. (2006). Mental health and resiliency following 44 months of terrorism: A survey of an Israeli national representative sample. *BMC Medicine, 4*(Article No 21), 1–43. 303

Bleuer, C. (2020). The Exaggerated Threat of Islamist Militancy in Central Asia. World Politics Review, February 25. 170

Block, J. S. (2017). Qatar Is a Financier of Terrorism. Why Does the U.S. Tolerate It? *Los Angeles Times*, June 09. 236

Blomberg, S. B., & Hess, G. D. (2006). How much does violence tax trade? *Review of Economics and Statistics, 88*(4), 599–612. 282, 313

Blomberg, S. B., & Mody, A. (2005). How Severely Does Violence Deter International Investment? Working Paper WP 2005-01, Claremont McKenna College. 283, 315

Blomberg, S. B., Hess, G. D., & Orphanides, A. (2004a). The macroeconomic consequences of terrorism. *Journal of Monetary Economics, 51*(5), 1007–1032. 279

Blomberg, S. B., Hess, G. D., & Weerapana, A. (2004b). Economic conditions and terrorism. *European Journal of Political Economy, 20*(2), 463–478. 559

Blomberg, S. B., Engel, R. C., & Sawyer, R. (2010). On the duration and sustainability of transnational terrorist organizations. *Journal of Conflict Resolution, 54*(2), 113–131. 358, 363, 365

Blomberg, S. B., Gaibulloev, K., & Sandler, T. (2011). Terrorist group survival: Ideology, tactics and base of operations. *Public Choice, 149*(3-4), 441–463. 356, 358, 363, 365

Bonner, R. (1998). Tamil Guerrillas in Sri Lanka: Deadly and Armed to the Teeth. *New York Times*, March 7. 94

Borlini, L., & Montanaro, F. (2017). The evolution of the EU law against criminal finance: The "Hardening" of FATF standards within the EU. *Georgetown Journal of International Law, 48*(4), 1009–1062. 452

Bothen, A. (2014). An Analysis of the Basque Independence Movement and the Political Position of the Basque Country Within the Spanish State. Bachelor's Thesis, University of Maine - Main. 75

Box, M., & McCormack, G. (2004). The Red Army (1969–2001) and Aum Supreme Truth (1987–2000). *The Asia-Pacific Journal: Japan Focus, 2*(6), p. . 54

Box, G. E. P., & Tiao, G. C. (1975). Intervention analysis with applications to economic and environmental problems. *Journal of the American Statistical Association, 70*(349), 70–79. 634

Braakmann, N. (2009). The impact of September 11th, 2001 on the employment prospects of Arabs and Muslims in the German labor market. *Jahrbücher für Nationalökonomie und Statistik, 229*(1), 2–21. 287

Braakmann, N. (2010). Islamic terror and the labour market prospects of Arab men in England: Does a country's direct involvement matter? *Scottish Journal of Political Economy, 57*(4), 430–454. 287

Brackbill, R. M., Thorpe, L. E., & DiGrande, L., et. al (2006). Surveillance for world trade center disaster health effects among survivors of collapsed and damaged buildings. *Morbidity and Mortality Weekly Report: CDC Surveillance Summaries, 55*, 1–18. 297

Bradley, J. R. (2006). Iran's ethnic tinderbox. *Washington Quarterly, 30*(1), 181–190. 571

Brandt, P. T., & Sandler, T. (2009). Hostake taking: Understanding terrorism event dynamics. *Journal of Policy Modelling, 31*(5), 758–778. 494, 495, 501

Brandt, P. T., Justin, G., & Sandler, T. (2016). Why concessions should not be made to terrorist kidnappers. *European Journal of Political Economy, 44*, 41–52. 494, 495

Brockmeyer, A., Do, Q.-T., Joubert, C., Jelil, M. A., & Bhatia, K. (2018). Transnational Terrorist Recruitment: Evidence from Daesh Personnel Records. World Bank Group, Development Research Group & Middle East and North Africa Region Office of the Chief Economist. 565

Brodeur, A. (2018). The effect of terrorism on employment and consumer sentiment: Evidence from successful and failed terror attacks. *American Economic Journal: Applied Economics, 10*(4), 246–282. 284, 285, 311

Brooks, R. A. (2011). Muslim "Homegrown" Ttrrorism in the United States. *International Security, 36*(2), 7–47. 571

Brounrn, D., & Derwall, J. (2010). The impact of terrorist attacks on international stock markets. *European Financial Management, 16*(4), 585–598. 289

Bruckner, T. A., Catalano, R., & Ahern, J. (2010). Male fetal loss in the U.S. following the terrorist attacks of September 11, 2001. *BMC Public Health, 10*(Article No 273). 305

Buckley, C. (2018). China Is Detaining Muslims in Vast Numbers. The Goal: 'Transformation'. *New York Times*, September 8. 172

Bueno De Mesquita, E. (2005). The quality of terror. *American Journal of Political Science, 49*(3), 515–530. 420, 436

Buesa, M., Valiño, A., Heijs, J., Baumert, T., & Goméz, J. G. (2007). The Economic Cost of March 11: Measuring Direct Economic Cost of the Terrorist Attack on March 11, 2004 in Madrid. *Terrorism and Political Violence, 19*(4), 489–509. 245, 248, 249, 267

Burke, J. (2004). *Al-Qaeda: The true story of radical islam*. Penguine Books. 236

Byman, D. L. (2010). How to Handle Hamas. *Brookings*, August 25; originally published in *Foreign Affairs*, September/October 2010. 144

Byman, D. L. (2013). The Resurgence of al Qaeda in Iraq. Testimony Before the the Joint Hearing of the Terrorism, Nonproliferation, and Trade Subcommittee and the Middle East and North Africa Subcommittee of the House Committee on Foreign Affairs, December 12. 104

Cakaj, L., & Ronan, P. (2016). The Lord's Resistance Army is Finally Weakening in Central Africa. This Could Dismantle It. *The Washiongton Post*, December 6. 162

Callimachi, R. (2014). Paying Ransoms, Europe Bankrolls Qaeda Terror. *New York Times*, July 29. 112

Camacho, A. (2008). Stress and birth weight: Evidence from terrorist attacks. *American Economic Review Papers and Proceedings, 98*(2), 511–515. 306

Caris, C. C., & Reynolds, S. (2014). ISIS Governance in Syria. Institute for Study of War, Middle East Security Report 22. 117

Carter, D. B. (2012). A blessing or a curse? State support for terrorist groups. *International Organization, 66*(1), 129–151. 357, 359, 364, 365

Carter, S., & Cox, A. (2011). One 9/11 Tally: $3.3 Trillion. NYTimes.com, Interactive, (New York Times), September 8, accessed on September 2, 2019. 248, 266

Carter, D. A., & Simkins, B. J. (2004). The market's reaction to unexpected, catastrophic events: The case of airline stock returns and the September 11th attacks. *The Quarterly Review of Economics and Finance, 44*(4), 539–558. 288, 316

Caruso, P. (2018). Indonesia and Terrorism: Success, Failure, and an Uncertain Future. *Middle East Institute* (Washington D.C.), February 6. 172

Casey, N. (2019). Colombia's Peace Deal Promised a New Era. So Why Are These Rebels Rearming? *New York Times*, May 17. 59

Celso, A. N. (2015). The Islamic State and Boko Haram: *Fifth Wave* Jihadist Terror Groups. Foreign Policy Research Institute (FPRI), Philadelphia, Pennsylvania, Spring. 178

Chalk, P. (1999). Liberation Tigers Tamil Ealam's (LTTE) International Organization and Operations—A Preliminary Analysis. Commentary No. 77 (unclassified), Canadian Security Intelligence Service. 90, 94

Chalk, P. (2003). The Liberation Tigers of Tamil Eelam insurgency in Sri Lanka. In R. Ganguly, & I. Macduff (Eds.), *Ethnic conflict and secessionsim in South and Southeast Asia*. India: Sage Publications, Inc. 90

Chen, A. H., & Siems, T. F. (2004). The effects of terrorism on global capital markets. *European Journal of Political Economy, 20*(2), 249–266. 288, 316

Chenoweth, E. (2010). Democratic competition and terrorist activity. *Journal of Politics, 72*(1), 16–30. 575

Chenoweth, E. (2013). Terrorism and democracy. *Annual Review of Political Science, 16*(1), 355–378. 569

Chesney, M., Reshetar, G., & Karaman, M. (2011). The impact of terrorism on financial markets: An empirical study. *Journal of Banking and Finance, 35*(2), 253–267. 290

Chicago Project on Security and Threats, CPOST. (2020). Database on Suicide Attacks (October 2, 2020 Release). Retrieved from http://cpost/uchicago.edu/. 192, 193, 194

Christofis, N., Kollias, C., Papadamou, S., & Stagiannis, A. (2013). Istanbul stock market's reaction to terrorist attacks. *Doğuş Üniversitesi Dergisi, 14*(2), 153–164. 291

Chughtai, A. (2021). Syria's War: Ten Years - and Counting. *AlJazeera*, March 15. 124

Clark, A. E., Doyle, O., & Stancanelli, O. (2017). The Impact of Terrorism on Well-being: Evidence from the Boston Marathon Bombing. University College Dublin Geary Institute Working Paper WP2017/08. 300

Clarke, C. P. (2015). *Terrorism, Inc.: The Financing of Terrorism, Insurgency, and Irregular Warfare*. Praeger. 73, 90, 94, 95, 111, 130, 131, 134, 140, 145, 146, 149, 150, 151, 232, 233, 234, 235, 236, 258

Clunan, A. L. (2006). The fight against terrorist financing. *Political Science Quarterly, 121*(4), 569–596. 441, 442

CNBC. (2017). New Hamas Leader Says It is Getting Aid Again from Iran. *CNBC*, August 29. 144

CNN Library. (2018). AQAP Fast Facts. *CNN Library*, Updated on September 5. 107

Collard-Wexler, S., Pischedda, C., & Smith, M. G. (2013). Do foreign occupations cause suicide attacks? *Journal of Conflict Resolution, 58*(4), 625–657. 550, 557, 558, 575, 578

Conejo-Galindo, J., Medina, O., Fraguas, D., Sara, T., Sainz-Cortón, E., & Arango, C. (2008). Psychopathological sequelae of the 11 March terrorist attacks in Madrid: An epidemiological study of victims treated in a hospital. *European Archives of Psychiatry and Clinical Neuroscience, 258*(1), 28–34. 300

Congressional Research Service. (2021). Yemen: Civil War and Regional Intervention. Report, November 23. 106, 109

Coogan, T. P. (1995). *The Troubles: Ireland's ordeal 1966–1995 and the search for peace*: London: Hutchinson. 326

Cook, D. (2011). The rise of Boko Haram in Nigeria. *CTC Sentinel, Combating Terrorism Center at West Point, 4*(9), 3–5. 136

Council of Foreign Relations. (2020). Global Conflict Tracker, War in Afghanistan. https://www.cfr.org/global-conflict-tracker/conflict/war-afghanistan, accessed on July 17, 2020. 126

Crawford, N. C. (2021). The U.S. Budgetary Costs of the Post-9/11 Wars. Paper, Watson Institute, Brown University. 261

Crawford, N. C., & Lutz, C. (2021). Human and Budgetary Cost to Date of the U.S. War in Afghanistan. Paper, Watson Institute, Brown University, April 15. 260, 261

Crenshaw, M. (1991). How terrorism declines. *Terrorism and Political Violence, 3*(1), 69–87. 210

Cronin, A. K. (2006). How Al-Qaeda ends: The decline and demise of terrorist groups. *International Security, 31*(6), 7–48. 355

Cronin, A. K. (2009). *How terrorism ends: Understanding the decline and demise of terrorist campaigns*. Princeton, NJ: Princeton University Press. 355, 356, 360

Daily Sabah. (2017). Fighting Between FARC Dissidents, ELN Militants Leaves at Least 13 Dead. *Turkish Newpaper*, November 30. 326

Dartnell, M. Y. (1995). *Action directe: Ultra left terrorism in France 1979–1987.* Routledge. 52

Das, S. P., & Lahiri, S. (2006). A strategic analysis of terrorist activity and counter-terrorism policies. *B. E. Journals in Theoretical Economics (Topics), 6*(1), p. Article 6. 392

Das, S. P., & Lahiri, S. (2021). Why direct counter-terror measures only may fail: An analysis of direct and preventive counter-terrorism measures. *International Journal of Economic Theory, 17*(4), 416–445. 507, 513, 518

Das, S. P., & Roy Chowdhury, P. (2014). Deterrence, preemption, and panic: A common enemy problem of terrorism. *Economic Inquiry, 52*(1), 219–238. 468, 469, 472

David, S. (Ed.) (2016). *Operation thunderbolt.* Little, Brown and Company. 88

Dávila, A., & Mora, M. T. (2005). Changes in the earnings of Arab men in the US between 2000 and 2002. *Journal of Population Economics, 18*(4), 587–601. 286

de Sousa, J., Mirza, D., & Verdier, T. (2009). Trade and spillovers of transnational terrorism. *Swiss Journal of Economics and Statistics, 145*(4), 453–461. 282, 314, 315

de Sousa, J., Mirza, D., & Verdier, T. (2018). Terror networks and trade: Does the neighbor hurt? *European Economic Review, 107*(C), 27–56. 282, 314, 315

DiMaggio, C., Galea, S., & Guohua, L. (2009). Substance use and misuse in the aftermath of terrorism: A Bayesian meta-analysis. *Addiction, 104*(6), 894–904. 299

Dingji Maza, K., Koldaş, U., & Aksit, S. (2020). Challenges of combating terrorist financing in the Lake Chad region: A case of Boko Haram. *Sage Open, 10*(2), 1–17. 138, 140

Dodwell, B., Milton, D., & Rassler, D. (2016). The Caliphates Global Workforce: An Inside Look at the Islamic States Foreign Fighter Paper Trail. Technical Report, United States Military Academy Combating Terrorism Center West Point United States. 565

Dominguez, G. (2016). How the Taliban get their money. https://www.dw.com/en/how-the-taliban-get-their-money/a-18995315, accessed on September 9, 2018, January 21. 129, 131

Doosje, B., Loseman, A., & van den Bos, K. (2013). Determinants of radicalization of Islamic Youth in the Netherlands: Personal uncertainty, perceived injustice, and perceived group threat. *Journal of Social Issues, 69*(3), 586–604. 574

Drakos, K. (2004). Terrorism-induced structural shifts in financial risk: Airline stocks in the aftermath of the September 11th terror attacks. *European Journal of Political Economy, 20*(2), 435–466. 288, 316

Drakos, K. (2010). Terrorism activity, investor sentiment, and stock returns. *Review of Financial Economics, 19*(3), 128–135. 290

Drakos, K., & Gofas, A. (2006). In search of the average transnational terrorist attack venue. *Defence and Peace Economics, 17*(2), 73–93. 569, 575

Drakos, K., & Kutan, A. M. (2003). Regional effects of terrorism on tourism in three mediterrenian countries. *Journal of Conflict Resolution, 47*(5), 621–641. 294, 318

Dreher, A. (2006). Does globalization affect growth? Empirical evidence from a new index. *Applied Economics, 38*(10), 1091–1110. 576

Dreher, A., Gaston, N., & Martens, P. (2008). *Measuring globalisation: Gauging its consequence* (pp. 1091–1110). New York: Springer. 576

Dugan, L., Huang, J. Y., LaFree, G., & McCauley, C. (2008). Sudden desistance from terrorism: The armenian secret army for the liberation of armenia and the justice commandos of the armenian genocide. *Dynamics of Asymmetric Conflict, 1*(3), 231–249. 355

Eckstein, A. M. (2016). How the Weather Underground Failed at Revolution and Still Changed the World. *TIME*, November 2. 52

Eckstein, Z., & Tsiddon, D. (2004). Macroeconomic consequence of terror: Theory and the case of Israel. *Journal of Monetary Economics, 51*(5), 971–1002. 275, 276, 277

Egger, P., & Gassebner, M. (2015). International terrorism as a trade impediment? *Oxford Economic Papers, 67*(1), 42–62. 282, 315

Ehrlich, I. (1973). Participation in illegitimate activities: A theoretical and empirical investigation. *Journal of Political Economy, 81*(3), 521–565. 376

Eidelson, R. J., D'Alessio, G. R., & Eidelson, J. I. (2003). The impact of September 11 on psychologists. *Professional Psychology: Research and Practice, 34*(2), 144–150. 297

Eldor, R., & Melnick, R. (2004). Financial markets and terrorism. *European Journal of Political Economy, 20*(2), 367–386. 291

Enders, W. (2015). *Applied econometric time series* (4th edn.). New Jersey: John Wiley and Sons Inc. 635

Enders, W., & Hoover, G. A. (2012). The non-linear relationship between terrorism and poverty. *American Economic Review, 102*(3), 267–272. 564, 570, 578, 579, 648

Enders, W., & Sandler, T. (1991). Causality between transnational terrorism and tourism: The case of Spain. *Terrorism, 14*(1), 49–58. 294, 317

Enders, W., & Sandler, T. (1993). The effectiveness of anti-terrorism policies: A vector-autoregression-intervention analysis. *American Political Science Review, 87*(4), 829–844. 474, 494, 501

Enders, W., & Sandler, T. (1996). Terrorism and foreign direct investment in Spain and Greece. *Kyklos, 49*(3), 331–352. 283, 315

Enders, W., & Sandler, T. (2012). *The political economy of terrorism* (2nd edn.). Cambridge University Press. 11, 12, 40, 247, 248, 474, 481, 486, 488

Enders, W., & Su, X. (2007). Rational terrorists and optimal network structure. *Journal of Conflict Resolution, 51*(1), 33–57. 462

Enders, W., Sandler, T., & Cauly, J. (1990a). UN conventions, technology, and retaliation in the fight against terrorism: An econometric evaluation. *Terrorism and Political Violence, 2*(1), 83–105. 377, 378, 405, 493, 501

Enders, W., Sandler, T., & Cauly, J. (1990b). Assessing the impact of terrorist-thwarting policies: An intervention time series approach. *Defence and Peace Economics, 2*(1), 1–18. 494, 501

Enders, W., Sandler, T., & Parise, G. F. (1992). An econometric analysis of the impact of terrorism on tourism. *Kyklos, 45*(4), 531–554. 294, 318

Enders, W., Sachsida, A., & Sandler, T. (2006). The impact of transnational terrorism on U.S. foreign direct investment. *Political Research Quarterly, 59*(4), 517–531. 283, 316

Enders, W., Sandler, T., & Gaibulloev, K. (2011). Domestic versus transnational terrorism: Data, decomposition, and dynamics. *Journal of Peace Research, 48*(3), 319–337. 12

Enders, W., Hoover, G. A., & Sandler, T. (2016). The changing non-linear relationship between income and terrorism. *Journal of Conflict Resolution, 60*(2), 195–225. 564, 578, 579

Engene, J. O. (2007). Five decades of terrorism in Europe: The TWEED dataset. *Journal of Peace Research, 44*(1), 109–121. 186

Eruygur, A. Ç., & Omay, T. (2014). Terrorism and the stock market: A case study for turkey using STR models. *Journal of Reviews on Global Economics, 3*, 220–227. 291

Estrin, D. (2020). 'Like A Prisoner Being Let Free': Israel-Hamas Truce Lends Hope To Gaza's Jobless. *National Public Radio*. https://www.npr.org/2020/01/23/798618713/like-a-prisoner-being-let-free-israel-hamas-truce-lends-hope-to-gaza-s-jobless, accessed on August 16, 2020. 143

Eubank, W. L., & Weinberg, L. (1994). Does democracy encourage terrorism? *Terrorism and Political Science, 6*(4), 417–435. 567

Eubank, W. L., & Weinberg, L. (2001). Terrorism and democracy: Perpetrators and victims. *Terrorism and Political Science, 13*(1), 155–164. 567

European Parliament. (2016). Counter-Terrorism Funding in the EU Budget. *Briefing*, April. 257

Eyerman, J. (1998). Terrorism and democratic states: Soft targets or accessible systems? *International Interactions, 24*(2), 151–170. 568

Faber, P. G. (2017). Sources of Resilience in the Lord's Resistance Army. *CNA (Center for Naval Analyses) Analysis and Solutions*, April. 162

Faber, P. G., & Powell, A. (2017). Al-Qaeda in the Indian Subcontinent (AQIS): An Al-Qaeda Affiliate Case Study. *CNA (Center for Naval Analyses) Analysis and Solutions*, April, October. 176

Farmer, B., & Yousafzai, S. (2021). Taliban's Haqqani Network Have Considered Joint al-Qaeda Force Claims US Treasury. *The Telegraph*, January 26. 134

FATF. (2015a). Professional Money Laundering. *Financial Action Task Force, Paris-based Independent Inter-Governmental Body*, July. www.fatf-gafi.org/publications/methodsandtrends/documents/emerging-terrorist-financing-risks.html. 232

FATF. (2015b). Financing of the Terrorist Organization of the Islamic State and the Levant (ISIL). *Financial Action Task Force, Paris-based Independent Inter-Governmental Body*, www.fatf-gafi.org/publications/methodsandtrends/documents/emerging-terrorist-financing-risks.html, . 235

FATF. (2015c). Emerging Terrorist Financing Risks. *Financial Action Task Force, Paris-based Independent Inter-Governmental Body*, October. www.fatf-gafi.org/publications/methodsandtrends/documents/emerging-terrorist-financing-risks.html. 233

Fearon, J. D. (2007). Iraq's Civil War. *Foreign Affairs*, March/April. 11

Felbab-Brown, V., Trinkunas, H. A., & Hamid, S. (2018). *Militants, criminals and warlords: The challenge of local governance in an age of disorder. Brookings Institution Press*. 59

Financial Express. (2018). Who Controls Pakistan's Atomic Bomb? Hafiz Saeed says It's 'Asset of Islam', Use it for Jihad Against US. *A Financial Daily Newspaper from India*, January 2. 157

Fisher, D. G., & Dugan, L. (2019). Sociological and criminological explanations of terrorism. In E. Chenoweth, R. English, A. Gofas, & S. N. Kalyvas (Eds.) *The Oxford Handbook of Terrorism*. Oxford University Press. 34

Fleischer, A., & Buccola, S. (2002). War, terror, and the tourism market in Israel. *Applied Economics, 34*(11), 1335–1343. 294, 318

Flemming, P. A., Mickolus, E., & Sandler, T. (2008). Research note: Using the ITERATE and DOTS databases. *Journal of Strategic Security, 1*(1), p. Article 6. 187

Ford, C. A., Richard Udry, J., Gleiter, K., & Chantala, K. (2003). Reactions of young adults to September 11, 2001. *Archives of Pediatric and Adolescent Medicine, 157*(6), 572–578. 298, 299

Freedman, S. (2009). Psychological effects of terror attacks. In S. C. Shapira, J. S. Hammond, & L. A. Cole (Eds.) *Essentials of terror medicine* (Chap. 24). Springer. 300, 303

Freedman, B., & Levitt, M. (2009). Contending with the PKK's Narco-Terrorism. *The Washington Institute, Policy Analysis*. 80

Freeman, M. (2011). The sources of terrorist financing: Theory and typology. *Studies in Conflict & Terrorism, 34*, 461–475. 80, 233, 234, 236

Freeman, M., & Ruehsen, M. (2013). Terrorism financing methods: An overview. *Perspectives on Terrorism, 7*(4). 237

Frey, B. S., & Luechinger, S. (2003). How to fight terrorism: Alternatives to deterrence. *Defence and Peace Economics, 14*(4), 237–249. 28

Frey, B. S., Luechinger, S., & Stutzer, A. (2009). The life satisfaction approach to valuing public goods: The case of terrorism. *Public Choice, 138*(3-4), 317–345. 301, 302, 312, 319

Frisch, H. (2009). Strategic change in terrorist movements: Lessons from Hamas. *Studies in Conflict & Terrorism, 31*(12), 1049–1065. 144

Gaibulloev, K., & Sandler, T. (2008). Growth consequences of terrorism in Western Europe. *Kyklos, 61*(3), 411–424. 277, 278

Gaibulloev, K., & Sandler, T. (2009a). Hostage taking: Determinants of terrorist logistical and negotiation success. *Journal of Peace Research, 46*(6), 739–756. 496, 497

Gaibulloev, K., & Sandler, T. (2009b). The impact of terrorism and conflicts on growth in Asia. *Economics and Politics, 21*(3), 359–383. 278

Gaibulloev, K., & Sandler, T. (2011). The adverse effect of transnational and domestic terrorism on growth in Africa. *Journal of Peace Research, 48*(3), 355–371. 278

Gaibulloev, K., & Sandler, T. (2013). Determinants of the demise of terrorist organizations. *Southern Economic Journal, 79*(4), 774–792. 210

Gaibulloev, K., & Sandler, T. (2019). What we have learned about terrorism since 9/11. *Journal of Economic Literature, 57*(2), 275–328. 11, 566, 576

Gaibulloev, K., Sandler, T., & Sul, D. (2013). Common drivers of transnatioinal terrorism: Principal component analysis. *Economic Inquiry, 51*(1), 707–721. 356, 358, 359, 363, 365

Gaibulloev, K., Piazza, J. A., & Sandler, T. (2017). Regime types and terrorism. *International Organization, 71*(Summer), 491–522. 569, 575, 576, 579

Galea, S., Ahern, J., Resnick, H., Kilpatrick, D., Bucuvalas, M., Gold, J., & Vlahov, D. (2002). Psychological sequelae of the September 11 terror attacks in New York City. *New England Journal of Medicine, 346*(13), 982–987. 297

Gardeazabal, J., & Sandler, T. (2015). INTERPOL's surveillance network in curbing transnational terrorism. *Journal of Policy Analysis and Management, 34*(4), 761–780. 467, 468

Gassebner, M., & Luechinger, S. (2011). Lock, stock, and barrel: A comprehensive assessment of the determinants of terror. *Public Choice, 149*(3-4), 235–261. 564, 575, 576

Geis, G. (1967). The heavy electrical equipment antitrust cases in 1961. In M. B. Clinard, & R. Quinney (Eds.), *Criminal behavior systems*. New York: Holt, Rinehart & Winston. 325

Ghaddar, H. (2020). Hezbollah Has Created Parallel Financial and Welfare Systems to Manage the Current Crisis. *The Washington Institute for Near East Policy*, December 9. 151

Gigerenzer, G. (2004). Dread risk, September 11, and fatal traffic accidents. *Psychological Science, 15*(4), 286–287. 308

Gill, P. (2015). The Impact of Drone Attacks on Terrorism: The Case of Pakistan. Remote Control Project, *Oxford Research Group*. 435

Glusac, E. (2015). Russian Airplane Crash Shakes Egypt's Tourism. *New York Times*, November 15. 294

Goldbaum, C. (2021). ISIS Claims Responsibility for Mozambique Attack. *New York Times*, March 30. 122

Grattan, S. (2020). Four Years after FARC Peace Deal, Colombia Grapples with Violence. *AlJazeera*. 59

Gupta, S., Clements, B., Bhattacharya, R., & Chakravarti, S. (2004). Fiscal Consequences of armed conflict and terrorism in low- and middle-income countries. *European Journal of Political Economy, 20*(2), 403–421. 273

Haelig, C. G. (2017). The Sri Lankan civil war: Turning COIN on its head and learning to adapt. *Small Wars Journal*, Web Publication, November. 90, 91

Hakeymez, S. (2017). Turkey's Failed Peace Process with the Kurds: A Different Explanation. *Brandeis University*, Middle-East Brief, No. 111, June. 78

Halbach, U. (2018). Chechnya's Status within the Russian Federation: Ramzan Kadyrov's Private State and Vladimir Putin's Federal "Power Vertical". Stiftung Wissenschaft und Politik, German Institute for International and Security Affairs, Research Paper. 167

Halloran, R. (1987). Latin Guerrillas Joining Forces, U.S. Officers Say. *New York Times*, March 3. 361

Harper, M. (2020). Somalia Conflict: Al-Shabab 'Collects More Revenue than Government'. *BBC News*, October 26. 160

Harris, S., Nakishima, E., Mekhennet, S., & Slater, J. (2019). Sri Lankan Easter Bombings, Claimed by ISIS, How the Group Maintains Influence Even Though its Caliphate is Gone. *Washington Post*, April 24. 122

Hasan, S. (2012). Islamic jurisprudence: Sources and traditions creating diversity in human relationships. In S. Hasan (Ed.), *The Muslim world in the 21st century: Space, power and human development* (Chap. 2). Springer. 21, 36

Hegghammer, T. (2009). Jihadi-salafis or revolutionaries? On religion and politics in the study of militant islamism. In R. Meijer (Ed.) *Global Salafism: Islam's New Religious Movement*. New York: Columbia University Press. 508

Heißner, P. R., ad Neumann, S., Holland-McCowan, J., & Basra, R. (2017). Caliphate in Decline: An Estimate of Islamic State's Financial Fortunes. The International Centre for the Study of Radicalisation and Political Violence Report. 118, 121, 234

Hennigan, T. (2009). Colombian Rebel Groups Farc and ELN Agree to Unite. *Irish Times*, December 18. 326

Hewitt, C. (1984). *The effectiveness of anti-terrorist policies*. Maryland: University Press of America. 571

Hoffman, B. R. (1985). Jewish Terror Activities and the British Government in Palestine. Ph.D. dissertation, Oxford University. 47

Holman, E. A., Silver, R. C., Poulin, M., Anderson, J. P., Gil-Rivas, V., & McIntosh, D. N. (2008). Terrorism, acute stress, and cardiovascular health: A 3-year national study following the September 11th attacks. *Archives of General Psychiatry, 65*(1), 73–80. 305

Holman, E. A., Garfin, D. R., & Silver, R. C. (2014). Media's role in broadcasting acute stress following the Boston marathon bombings. *Proceedings of the National Academy of Sciences, 111*(1), 93–98. 307

Hon, M. T., Strauss, J., & Yong, S. K. (2004). Contagion in financial markets after September 11—myth or reality. *Journal of Financial Research, 27*(1), 94–114. 288, 317

Horowitz, M. C. (2010). Nonstate actors and the diffusion of innovation: The case of suicide terrorism. *International Organization, 64*(1), 33–64. 328

Horowitz, M. C., & Potter, P. B. K. (2014). Allying to kill: Terrorist intergroup cooperation and the consequences for lethality. *Journal of Conflict Resolution, 58*(2), 199–225. 328

Horton, A. (2020). Trump Orders Departure of Majority of 700 U.S. Troops in Somalia. *Washington Post*, December 4. 554

Hubbard, B. (2015). Offering Services, ISIS Digs in Deeper in Seized Terrotories. *The New York Times*, June 16. 118

Human Rights Watch. (2006). Funding the "Final War" LTTE Intimidation and Extortion in the Tamil Diaspora, vol. 18(1C). March. 94, 233

Iannaccone, L. R. (1992). Sacrifice and stigma: Reducing free-riding in cults, communes, and other collectives. *Journal of Political Economy, 100*(2), 271–292. 526, 529, 542

Iannaccone, L. R., & Berman, E. (2006). Religious extremism: The good, the bad, and the deadly. *Public Choice, 128*, 109–129. 509, 543, 544

Ibrahim, Y. (1989). Arabs Say Deadly Power Struggle Has Split Abu Nidal Terror Group. *New York Times*, November 12. 89

India Ministry of Home Affairs. (2018). Banned Terror Organizations. https://mha.gov.in/related-links/banned-organizations, accessed on December 25, 2018. 175

InSight Crime. (2020). ELN. May 4. https://www.insightcrime.org/colombia-organized-crime-news/eln-profile/, accessed on July 18, 2020. 326

Institute for Economics & Peace. (2014a). The Economic Cost of Violence Containment. 250

Institute for Economics & Peace. (2014b). Global Terrorism Index 2014: Measuring and Understanding the Impact of Terrorism. 13, 129, 138, 246, 248, 281, 283, 316

Institute for Economics & Peace. (2015). Global Terrorism Index 2015: Measuring and Understanding the Impact of Terrorism. 216, 225, 255, 257, 265, 266

Institute for Economics & Peace. (2016a). The Economic Value of Peace 2016: Measuring the Global Economic Impact of Violence and Conflict. 253

Institute for Economics & Peace. (2016b). Global Terrorism Index 2016: Measuring and Understanding the Impact of Terrorism. 16, 132, 137, 140, 233, 240, 250, 253, 255, 256, 293, 294

Institute for Economics & Peace. (2017). Global Terrorism Index 2017: Measuring and Understanding the Impact of Terrorism. 13, 16, 137, 230, 253

Institute for Economics & Peace. (2018). Global Terrorism Index 2018: Measuring the Impact of Terrorism. Available from: http://visionofhumanity.org/reports, Sydney, November. 253, 256

Institute for Economics & Peace. (2019). Global Terrorism Index 2019: Measuring the Impact of Terrorism. Available from: http://visionofhumanity.org/reports, Sydney, November. 13, 251, 253, 255

Institute for Economics & Peace. (2020a). Global Peace Index 2020: Measuring Peace in a Complex World. Available from: http://visionofhumanity.org/reports, Sydney, November. 255

Institute for Economics & Peace. (2020b). Global Terrorism Index 2020: Measuring the Impact of Terrorism. Available from: http://visionofhumanity.org/reports, Sydney, November. 137, 216, 251, 253, 256

Islam, M. Q., & Shahin, W. N. (1989). Economic methodology applied to political hostage-taking in light of the Iran-contra affair. *Southern Economic Journal, 55*(4), 1019–1024. 485

Jackson, J. (2017). The Financial Action Task Force: An Overview. U.S. Congressional Research Service. 443, 444, 448

Jackson, A. (2018). Life under the Taliban Shadow Government. Overseas Development Institute Report, June. 127

Jamieson, A. (2017). ISIS Revenue Falls 80 Percent as Militants Lose Ground in Iraq, Syria. *NBC News*, June 30, https://www.nbcnews.com/storyline/isis-terror/isis-revenue-falls-80-percent-militants-lose-ground-iraq-syria-n778071, accessed on August 13, 2020. 114

Jones, S. (2018). How ISIS Has Changed Terrorism in Indonesia. *New York Times*, May 22. 172

Jones, S. G., & Libicki, M. C. (2008). *How terrorist groups end: Lessons for countering al Qa'ida*. Santa Monica, California: RAND Corporation. 210, 353, 354, 355, 356, 357, 358, 365

Jordan, S. (2002). How IRA Bombers Trained Guerrillas. *The Guardian*, May 25. 327

Joshi, M. (1996). On the Razor's edge: The Liberation Tigers of Tamil Eelam. *Studies in Conflict & Terrorism, 19*, 19–42. 91

Jost, P. M., & Sandhu, H. S. (2000). The Hawala Alternative Remittance System and its Role in Money Laundering. Prepared by the Financial Crimes Enforcement Network in cooperation with INTERPOL/FOPAC. 238

Kagan, F. W., Kagan, K., Cafarella, J., Gambhir, H., & Zimmerman, K. (2016). U.S. Grand Strategy: Destroying ISIS and Al Qaeda, Report One Al Qaeda and ISIS: Existential Threat to the U.S. and Europe. Institute for the Study of War. 509

Kambera, G., Goh, P., Kumar, P., & Msafir, F. (2011). The finances of Lashkar-E-Taiba. *CTX, 1*(1), 6–22. 158

Kaplan, J. (2008). Terrorism's fifth wave: A theory, a conundrum and a dilemma. *Perspectives on Terrorism, 2*(2). 178

Karmon, E. (2005). *Coalitions between terrorist organizations: Revolutionaries, nationalists and islamists*. The Netherlands: Nijhoff Publishers. 327, 328

Karolyi, G. A., & Martell, R. (2010). Terrorism and the stock market. *International Review of Applied Financial Issues & Economics, 2*(2), 285–314. 289

Katzman, K. (2018). Iran's Foreign and Defense Policies. Congressional Research Service Report, January. 236

Kaushal, N., Kaestner, R., & Riemers, C. (2007). Labor market effects of September 11th on Arab and Muslim residents of the U.S. *Journal of Human Resources, 42*(2), 275–308. 287

Kiser, S. (2005). Financing Terror An Analysis and Simulation for Affecting Al Qaeda's Financial Infrastructure. Ph.D. dissertation, Pardee RAND Graduate School. 70, 73, 86, 111, 112

Knudsen, H. K., Roman, P. M., Aaron Johnson, A., & Ducharme, L. J. (2005). A changed America? The effects of September 11th on depressive symptoms and alcohol consumption. *Journal of Health and Social Behaviour, 46*(3), 260–273. 298, 299

Koëhler, D. (2014). Anglo-American networks: The internationalisation of far-right terror. In P. Jackson, & A. Shekhovtsov (Eds.), *The Post-war Anglo-American far right: A special relationship of hate*. Basingstoke: Palgrave Macmillan. 178

Kollias, C., Papadamou, S., & Stagiannis, A. (2011). Terrorism and capital markets: The effects of the Madrid and London bomb attacks. *International Review of Economics and Finance, 20*(4), 532–541. 289, 317

Krebs, V. E. (2002). Mapping network of terrorist cells. *Connections, 24*(3), 43–52. 338, 339, 340

Krieger, T., & Meierrieks, D. (2019). Income inequality, redistribution and domestic terrorism. *World Development, 116*(Not Assigned), 125–136. 570, 575, 580

Krueger, A. B. (2003). Poverty Doesn't Create Terrorists. *New York Times*, May 29. 559

Krueger, A. B. (2007). *What makes a terrorist? Economics and roots of terrorism.* Princeton, NJ: Princeton University Press. 508, 559

Krueger, A. B., & Laitin, D. D. (2008). Kto Kogo? A cross-country study of the origins and targets of terrorism. In P. Keefer, & N. Loayza (Eds.), *Terrorism, Economic Development and Political Openness* (Chap. 5, pp. 148–173). Cambridge University Press. 568

Krueger, A. B., & Malečková, J. (2002). The Economics and the Education of Suicide Bombers. *The New Republic*, pp. 27–33, June. 558, 559

Krueger, A. B., & Malečková, J. (2003). Education, poverty, and terrorism: Is there a causal connection? *Journal of Economic Perspectives, 17*(4), 119–144. 559, 561, 563, 567

Kumar, S., & Liu, J. (2013). Impact of terrorism on international stock markets. *Journal of Applied Business and Economics, 14*(4), 42–60. 290

Kunreuther, H., Michel-Kerjan, E., & Porter, B. (2003). Assessing, Managing and Financing Extreme Events: Dealing with Terrorism. NBER Working Paper No. 10179. 247

LaFree, G., & Freilich, J. D. (Eds.) (2017). *The handbook of the criminology of terrorism.* John Wiley and Sons Inc. 34

Lai, B. (2007). 'Draining the Swamp': An empirical examination of the production of international terrorism, 1968–1998. *Conflict Management and Peace Science, 24*(4), 297–310. 564, 570, 575, 578

Landes, W. M. (1978). An economic study of US aircraft hijackings, 1961–1976. *Journal of Law and Economics, 21*(1), 1–31. 370, 371, 372, 374, 405, 485, 501

Lapan, H. E., & Sandler, T. (1988). To bargain or not to bargain: That is the question. *American Economic Review: Papers and Proceedings, 78*(2), 16–20. 488

Law, R. (2009). *Terrorism: A history*. Cambridge, England: Polity Press. 39

Lee, C.-Y. (2013). Democracy, civil liberties, and hostage-taking terrorism. *Journal of Peace Research, 50*(2), 235–248. 499, 502

Leech, G. (2011). *FARC: The longest insurgency*. Zed Books. 54

Lerner, J., Gonzales, R. M., Small, D. A., & Fischhoff, B. (2003). Effects of fear and anger on perceived risk of terrorism: A national field experiment. *Psychological Science, 14*(2), 144–150. 297

Levin, D. (2018). Iran, Hamas and Palestinian Islamic Jihad. *Wilson Center*, July 9. 151, 152, 153

Levitt, S. D. (1997). Using electoral cycles in police hiring to estimate the effect of police on crime. *American Economic Review, 87*(3), 270–290. 629

Levitt, M. (2002). Charitable and Humanitarian Organizations in the Network of International Terrorist Financing. Congressional Testimony, August 1. 236

Levitt, M. (2005). Hezbollah finances: Funding the party of god. In J. K. Giraldo, & H. A. Trinkunas (Eds.), *Terrorism financing and state responses: A comparative perspective*. Monterey, California: Sponsored by the Center for Homeland Defense and Security at the Naval Postgraduate School. 149

Levitt, M. (2014). Terrorist Financing and the Islamic State. Testimony submitted to the House Committee on Financial Services, November 13. 234

Levitt, M. (2015). The P.L.O. Verdict Should Be No Surprise. *New York Times*, November 20. 85

Levitt, M. (2017). Attacking Hezbollah's Financial Network: Policy Options. Testimony submitted to the Committee on Foreign Affairs, U.S. House of Representatives, June 8. 149

Li, Q., & Schaub, D. (2004). Economic globalization and transnational terrorism: A pooled time-series analysis. *Journal of Conflict Resolution, 48*, 230–258. 567, 575

Limodio, N. (2019). Terrorism Financing, Recruitment and Attacks: Evidence from a Natural Experiment. Limodio, Nicola, Terrorism Financing, Recruitment and Attacks: Evidence from a Natural Experiment (April 2019). Chicago Booth Research Paper No. 32, 2019, Available at SSRN: https://ssrn.com/abstract=3384109 or https://dx.doi.org/10.2139/ssrn.3384109. 235

Lindelauf, R. H. A., Hamers, H. J. M., & Husslage, B. G. M. (2013). Cooperative game theoretic centrality analysis of terrorist networks: The cases of Jemaah Islamiyah and Al Qaeda. *European Journal of Operational Research, 229*(1), 230–238. 338, 341

Lipscomb, A. (2016). Culture Clash: Ethnic Unrest in Xinjiang. *US-China Today*, USC US-China Institute, September. 171

Lister, C. (2016). Profiling Jabhat al-Nusra. *Brookings Institution*, The Brookings Project on U.S. Relations with the Islamic World, Analysis Paper No. 24, July. 122, 123

Livescu, I. (2017). The Link Between Money Laundering and Corruption Is the Fight Effective? Master's thesis, Tilburg University Law School. 238

Lovelle, M. (2018). China: Xinjiang, Agriculture and the Uighur Population. Future Directions International, Strategic Analysis Paper, May 3. 170

Lynch III, T. F. (2016). India's naxalite insurgency: History, trajectory, and implications for U.S.-India security cooperation on domestic counterinsurgency. *Strategic perspectives* (vol. 22). Washigton, D.C.: Institute for National Strategic Studies. 64

Lyons-Padilla, S., Gelfand, M. J., Mirahmadi, H., Farooq, M., & van Egmond, M. (2015). Belonging nowhere: Marginalization and radicalization risk among muslim immigrants. *Behavioral Science & Policy, 1*(2), 1–12. 30, 572, 573, 574, 581

MacFarquhar, N. (2020). As Domestic Terrorists Outpace Jihadists, New U.S. Law Is Debated. *New York Times*, February 25. 571

Malik, N. (2017). Trafficking Terror. Report, The Henry Jackson Society, London. 233

Marcus, A. (2007). *Blood and belief: the PKK and the Kurdish fight for independence*. New York University Press. 39

Markoulis, S., & Katasikides, S. (2018). The effect of terrorism on stock markets: Evidence from the 21st century. *Terrorism and Political Violence*, 1–23. https://doi.org/10.1080/09546553.2018.1425207. 290

Martin, G. (2018). *Understanding terrorism: Challenges, perspectives, and issues* (6th edn.). Sage Publications, Inc. 40, 43, 60, 61, 62, 104, 137

Masood, S. (2007). Musharraf Defends Raid That Ended Red Mosque Siege. *New York Times*, July 13. 135

Matta, N., & Rojas, R. (2016). The second intifada: The dual strategy arena. *European Journal of Sociology, 57*(1), 65–113. 142

McAdams, R. H. (2010). Economic costs of inequality. *University of Chicago Legal Forum, 2010*, 23–41. 570

McCants, W. (2015). *The ISIS apocalypse: The history, strategy, and doomsday vision of the Islamic State*. New York: St. Martin's Press. 39

McCollister, K. E., French, M. T., & Fang, H. (2010). The cost of crime to society: New crime-specific estimates for policy and program evaluation. *Drug and Alcohol Dependence, 108*(1), 98–109. 250

Mckay, S. N., & Webb, D. A. (2015). Comparing counterterrorism in Indonesia and the Phillipines. *CTC Sentinel, Combating Terrorism Center at West Point, 8*(2), 18–21. 172

Meierrieks, D., & Gries, T. (2012). Causality between terrorism and economic growth. *Journal of Peace Research, 50*(1), 91–104. 280

Metcalfe, R., Powdthavee, N., & Dolan, P. (2011). Destruction and distress: Using a quasi-experiment to show the effects of the September 11 attacks on mental well-being in the United Kingdom. *Economic Journal, 121*(550), F81–F103. 299

Miguel-Tobal, J. J., Cano-Vindel, A., Gonzales-Ordi, H., Iruarrizaga, I., Rudenstine, S., Vlahov, D., & Galea, S. (2006). PTSD and depression after the Madrid March 11 train bombings. *Journal of Trauma Stress, 19*(1), 69–80. 300

Miller, E. (2014). *Patterns of terrorism in the United States, 1970–2013:* Final Report to Resilient Systems Division. DHS Science and Technology Directorate. College Park, MD: START.

Miller, E. (2016). *Patterns of terrorism in the United States* 1970–2014. College Park, MD: START. 176

Minder, R. (2018). Basque Group ETA Disbands, After Terrorist Campaign Spanning Generations. *New York Times*, May 2. 19, 209, 210, 356, 360

Mirza, D., & Verdier, T. (2014). Are lives substitute for livelihoods? Terrorism, security and US bilateral imports. *Journal of Conflict Resolution, 58*(6), 943–975. 75

Mohanty, N. (2012). *Radicalism in Islam: Resurgence and ramifications*. Maryland: University Press of America. 282, 314

Moore, J. (2015). Hawala: The Ancient Banking Practice Use to Finance Terror Groups. *Newweek*, February 24. 20

Mueller, J., & Stewart, M. G. (2011). *Terror, security and money: Balancing the risks, benefits and costs of homeland security*. New York: Oxford University Press. 238

Mueller, J., & Stewart, M. G. (2014). Evaluating counterterrorism spending. *Journal of Economic Perspectives, 28*(3), 237–247. 266

National Public Radio. (2020). Afghan Government and Taliban Reach Breakthrough To Proceed with Peace Talks. December 2, https://www.npr.org/2020/12/02/941377066/afghan-government-and-taliban-reach-breakthrough-to-restart-peace-talks, accessed on December 13, 2020. 266

Navaro, P., & Spencer, A. (2001). September 11, 2001: Assessing the Cost of Terrorism. *Milken Institute Review*, Fourth Quarter, 16–31. 133

Neria, Y., Gross, R., Olfson, M., & Gameroff, M. J. (2006). Posttraumatic stress disorder in primary care one year after the 9/11 attacks. *General Hospital Psychiatry, 28*(3), 213–222. 247

Neria, Y., Gross, R., Litz, B., & Maguen, S., et al. (2007). Prevalence and psychological correlates of complicated grief amog bereaved adults. *Journal of Trauma Stress, 20*(3), 251–262. 297

Neumayer, E., & Plümper, T. (2016). Spatial spill-overs from terrorism on tourism: Western victims in Islamic destination countries. *Public Choice, 169*(3-4), 195–206. 297

New York Times. (2012). Peace Talks With the Taliban. Editorial, New York Times, October 4. 295

Nikkinen, J., Omran, M. M., Sahlstrom, P., & Aijo, J. (2008). Stock returns and volatility following the September 11 attacks: Evidence from 53 equity markets. *International Review of Financial Analysis, 17*(1), 27–46. 132

Nitsch, V., & Schumacher, D. (2004). Terrorism and international trade: An empirical investigation. *European Journal of Political Economy, 20*(2), 423–433. 288, 317

Norland, R. (2018). Women Are Free, and Armed, in Kurdish-Controlled Northern Syria. *New York Times*, February 24. 282, 313

Novo, A. R. (2010). On All Fronts: EOKA and the Cyprus Insurgency, 1955–1959. DPhil Thesis, Oxford University. 80

Nugent, J. (2013). Lurking Not Acting, 'Real IRA' Remains a Threat. *Fortune*, August 14. 50

OECD. (2019). Money Laundering and Terrorist Financing Awareness Handbook for Tax Examiners and Tax Auditors. OECD, Paris, http://www.oecd.org/tax/crime/money-laundering-and-terrorist-financing-awareness-handbook-for-tax-examiners-and-tax-auditors.pdf. 74

Oftedal, E. (2014). The Financing of Jihadi Terrorist Cells in Europe. Norwegian Defence Research Establishment Report. 454

Omelicheva, M. Y. (2013). Terrorism in Central Asia: Dynamics, dimensions and sources. *Education about Asia, 18*(3), p. . 230, 231, 235, 243

Onuoha, F. C. (2016). Split in ISIS-Aligned Boko Haram Group. Report, Aljazeera Center for Studies. 168, 170

Onuoha, F. C., & Oyewole, S. (2018). Anatomy of Boko Haram: The Rise and Decline of a Violent Group in Nigeria. Al Jazeera Center for Studies, April 22. 137

Pape, R. A. (2005). *Dying to win: The strategic logic of suicide terrorism*. Random House. 138

Pape, R. A., & Feldman, J. K. (2010). *The explosion of global suicide terrorism: Cutting the fuse*. The University of Chicago Press. 551, 553, 556

Paybarah, A. (2021). What Is the Islamic State Khorasan, a.k.a. ISIS-K? *New York Times*, August 27. 508, 550, 551, 556

Perper, R. (2018). ISIS Made Millions from Taxes that It Then Used to Run Garbage Collections and Even a DMV. *Business Insider*, April 6. 122

Pesko, M. F. (2014). Stress and smoking: Associations with terrorism and causal impact. *Contemporary Economic Policy, 32*(2), 351–371. 118

Peters, G. (2009). How Opium Profits the Taliban. Report for the United States Institute for Peace. 298

Peters, G. (2012). Haqqani Network Financing: The Evolution of an Industry. Harmony Program, The Combating Terrorism Center at West Point, U.S. Military Academy, Department of Defense, July. 129, 130

Phillips, B. J. (2014). Terrorist group cooperation and longevity. *International Studies Quarterly, 58*(2), 336–347. 134

Phillips, B. J. (2015). Enemies with benefits? Violent rivalry nad terrorist group longevity. *Journal of Peace Research, 52*(1), 62–75. 210, 356, 358, 361, 362, 365

Phillips, B. J. (2017). Do 90 percent of terrorist groups last less than a year? Updating the conventional wisdom. *Terrorism and Political Violence* (September). http://www.tandfonline.com/doi/abstract/10.1080/09546553.2017.1361411. 325, 356, 358, 359, 360, 365

Piazza, J. A. (2008). A supply-side view of suicide terrorism: A cross-national study. *Journal of Politics, 70*(1), 28–39. 210

Piazza, J. A. (2011). Poverty, minority economic discrimination, and domestic terrorism. *Journal of Peace Research, 48*(3), 339–353. 557, 568

Pizam, A., & Fleischer, A. (2002). Severity versus frequency of acts of terrorism: Which has a larger impact on tourism demand? *Journal of Travel Research, 40*(3), 337–339. 570, 571, 580

Poe, S. (1988). Nations' responses to transnational hostage events: An empirical evaluation. *International Interactions, 14*(1), 27–40. 294, 318

Prashad, V., & Ahmet Tonak, E. (2021). Erdogan Starts a Political Earthquake in Turkey. *NEW EUROPE*, March 25. 494, 501

Prober, J. (2005). Accounting for Terror: Debunking the Paradigm of Inexpensive Terrorism. *The Washington Institute*, Policywatch 1041. 80

Prothero, M. (2005). The Money Scandal Behind the Hariri Assassination. *Time*, October 27. 230

Qiblawi, T. (2019). Iran's Revolutionary Guards, Explained. *CNN Online*, April 8, 2019, https://www.cnn.com/2019/04/08/middleeast/iran-revolutionary-guards-explainer-intl/index.html, access on July 20, 2019. 239

Rabby, F., & Rodgers III, W. M. (2010). The Impact of 9/11 and the London Bombings on the Employment and Earnings of U.K. Muslime. IZA Discussion Paper No. 4763, Bonn. 162

Rabby, F., & Rodgers III, W. M. (2011). Post 9-11 U.S. Muslim labor market outcomes. *Atlantic Economic Journal, 39*(2), 273–289. 287

Raghavan, S. (2019). With the ISIS Caliphate Defeated in Syria, an Islamist Militant Rivalry Takes Root in Yemen. *Washington Post*, April 14. 287

Raghavan, S. (2020). As Yemen's War Intensifies, an Opening for Al-Qaeda to Resurrect its Fortunes. *Washington Post*, February 25. 121

Randal, J. C. (1990). Abu Nidal Battles Dissidents. *Washington Post*, June 10. 107

Rapoport, D. C. (1992). Terrorism. In M. Hawkesworth, & M. Kogan (Eds.), *Encyclopedia of government and politics*. London: Routledge. 89

Rapoport, D. C. (2004). The four waves of modern terrorism. In A. K. Cronin, & J. M. Ludes (Eds.), *Attacking terrorism: Elements of a grand strategy.* Washington, D.C.: Georgetown University Press. 210

Rashid, A. (2010). *Taliban: Militant Islam, oil and fundamentalism in Central Asia* (2nd edn.). New Haven, CT: Yale University Press. 31, 40, 44, 52, 98, 178

Reed, A. (2015). Al Qaeda in the Indian Subcontinent: A New Frontline in the Global Jihadist Movement? International Centre for Counter-Terrorism - The Hague, Policy Brief, May. 39, 126

Reuters. (1987). Geoffrey Jackson, 72, Envoy Held 8 Months by Tupamaros. October 3. 175

Reuters. (2007). FACTBOX: The Madrid Train Bombings and What Happened Next. *World News*, February 13 15. 63

Reuters. (2011). Timeline: Key events in history of Basque separatists ETA. October 17. 230

Reuters. (2013). Saudis Will Give $100 Million to Palestinians. January 16. 75

Reuters. (2014). Kyrgyzstan says Kills 11 Uighur militants near Chinese Border. January 24. 144

Reuters. (2015). Colombia Army Raids Illegal Mines Funding FARC Rebels. May 11. 171

Reuters. (2019). Iran Strikes Opposition Positions on Border with Iraqi Kurdistan - Tasnim. July 12. 59

Richards, A. (2015). *Conceptualizing terrorism.* Oxford, England: Oxford University Press. 81

Richman, V., Santos, M. R., & Barkoulas, J. T. (2005). Short- and long-term effects of the 9/11 event: The international evidence. *International Journal of Theoretical and Applied Finance, 8*(7), 947–958. 7

Ridel, B. (2017). In Yemen, Iran Outsmarts Saudi Arabia Again. *Brookings*. 288, 317

Riedel, B. (2011). The World After 9/11—Part I. *Yale Global Online*, Setember 6, https://yaleglobal.yale.edu/content/world-after-911-part-i, accesses on August 31, 2019. 108

Robinson, G. (2018). Palestine Liberation Organization. In *The Oxford Encyclopedia of the Islamic World. Oxford Islamic Studies Online*: http://www.oxfordislamicstudies.com/article/opr/t236/e0618, accessed on November 10, 2018. 248

Rogin, J. (2017). Congress Demands Clarity on Trump Administration's Dealings with Qatar. *Washington Post*, December 20. 81

Rollins, J. (2011). Al Qaeda and Affiliates: Historical Perspective, Global Presence, and Implications for U.S. Policy. Congressional Research Service Report, January 25. 145

Romanov, D., Zussman, A., & Zussman, N. (2012). Does terrorism demoralize? Evidence from Israel. *Economica, 79*(313), 183–198. 101

Rose, A. Z., Oladosu, G., Lee, B., & Asay, G. B. (2009). The Economic Impacts of the September 11 Terrorist Attacks: A Computable General Equilibrium Analysis. *Peace Economics, Peace Science and Public Policy, 15*(2). 303, 304, 312

Rosen, A. (2015). Here's How ISIS Abuses Humanitarian Aid. *Business Insider*. https://www.businessinsider.com/how-isis-abuses-humanitarian-aid-2015-2, accessed on August 23, 2018. 248

Roth, J., Greenburg, D., & Wille, S. (2004). *Monograph on terrorist financing: Staff report to the commission*. Washington, D.C.: National Commission on Terrorist Attacks upon the United States. 118

Roul, A. (2015). Jamaat-ud Daawa: Into the Mainstream. *CTC Sentinel, Combating Terrorism Center at West Point, 8*(4), 23–26. 235

Roy, S. (2011). *Hamas and civil society in Gaza: Engaging the Islamist social sector*. Princeton, NJ: Princeton University Press. 157

Roy, N. (2018). What is the Ahl-e Hadith Movement? *Dhaka Tribune*, March 11. 144

Rubin, G. J., Brewin, C. R., Greenberg, N., Simpson, J., & Wessely, S. (2005). Psychological and behavioural reactions to the bombings in London on 7 July 2005: Cross sectional survey of a representative sample of Londoners. *BMJ, British Medical Journal (Clinical Research Ed.), 331*(7517), 606–610. 154

Rubin, G. J., Brewin, C. R., Greenberg, N., Hughes, J. H., Simpson, J., & Wessely, S. (2007). Enduring consequences of terrorism: 7-month follow-up survey of reactions to the bombings in London on 7 July 2005. *British Journal of Psychiatry, 190*, 350–356. 300
300

Russett, B. M., Oneal, J. R., & Cox, M. (2000). Clash of civilizations, or realism and liberalism déjàvu? Some evidence. *Journal of Peace Research, 37*(5), 583–608. 295

Said Aly, A. M., & Elkady, K. (2013). The Good, the Bad, and the Ugly of Egypt's Political Transition. *Brandeis University, Crown Center for Middle East Studies*, No. 70, March. 153

Salai-i-Martin, X. X. (1997). I just ran two million regressions. *American Economic Review Papers and Proceedings, 87*(2), 178–183. 647

Salith, C. (2015). Is Tal Abyad a Turning Point for Syria's Kurds? *BBC News*, June 16. 114

San-Akca, B. (2014). Democracy and vulnerability: An exploitation theory of democracies by terrorists. *Journal of Conflict Resolution, 58*(7), 1285–1310. 567

Sandler, T. (2015). Terrorism and counterterrorism: An overview. *Oxford Economic Papers, 67*(1), 1–20. 207

Sandler, T., & Scott, J. L. (1987). Terrorist success in hostage-taking incidents: An empirical study. *Journal of Conflict Resolution, 31*(1), 35–53. 496, 497

Sandler, T. & Siqueira, K. (2006). Global terrorism: deterrence versus preemption. *Canadian Journal of Economics, 39*, 1370–1387. 395, 426

Sandler, T., Arce, D. G., & Enders, W. (2011). An evaluation of INTERPOL'S cooperative-based counterterrorism linkages. *Journal of Law and Economics, 54*(1), 79–110. 468

Santifort-Jordan, C., & Sandler, T. (2014). An empirical study of suicide terrorism: A global analysis. *Southern Economic Journal, 80*(4), 981–1001. 436

Savun, B., & Phillips, B. J. (2009). Democracy, foreign policy, and terrorism. *Journal of Conflict Resolution, 53*(6), 878–904. 575

Schlenger, W. E., Caddell, J. M., Ebert, L., Jordan, K., Rourke, K., Wilson, D., Thalji, L., Michael Dennis, J., Fairbank, J. A., & Kulka, R. A. (2002). Psychological reactions to terrorist attacks. *Journal of the American Medical Association, 288*(5), 581–588. 297

Schultz, H. (2014). Nigeria's Boko Haram: Who Are They and What Do They Want? *National Geographic News*, May 8. 137

Schuster, M. A., Stein, B. D., Jaycox, L. H., Collins, R. L., Marshall, G. N., Elliot, M. N., Zhou, A. J., Kanouse, D. E., Morrison, J. L., & Berry, S. H. (2001). A national survey of stress reactions after the September 11, 2001 terrorist attacks. *New England Journal of Medicine, 345*(20), 1507–1512. 297

Science News. (2004). 9/11's Tatal Road Toll: Terror Attacks Presaged Rise in U.S. Car Deaths. January 17. 308

Sedney, D. (2015). America's Counterterrorism Policy Is Failing. *TIME*, January 21. 509

Self, K. A. (2007). Counterterrorism Policy in Colombia. M.A. Thesis in National Security, Naval Postgraduate School, Monterey, California. 59

Shahin, W. N., & Islam, M. Q. (1992). Combating political hostage-taking: An alternative approach. *Defence Economics, 3*(4), 321–327. 486

Shalev, A. Y., Rivka, T., Frenkiel-Fishman, S., Hilit, H., & Spencer, E. (2006). Psychological responses to continuous terror: A study of two communities in Israel. *American Journal of Psychiatry, 163*(4), 667–673. 303

Shane, S., & Schmit, E. (2012). Qaeda Plot to Attack Plane Foiled, U.S. Officials Say. *New York Times*, May 7. 107

Shapiro, J. N. (2013). *The terrorist's dilemma: Managing violent covert organizations*. Princeton, NJ: Princeton University Press. 6, 344, 345, 346, 348, 349, 350, 351, 363

Shay, S. (2018). The Islamic Terror Threat to the Horn of Africa. The Institute for Policy and Strategy, Lauder School of Government, Diplomacy and Strategy Inter Disciplinary Center, Israel, March. 160

Shear, M. K., Jackson, C. T., Essock, S. M., Donahue, S. A., & Felton, C. J. (2006). Screening for complicted grief among project liberty service recipients 18 months after September 11, 2001. *Psychiatry Services, 57*(9), 1291–1297. 297

Shedd, O. L., Sears Jr., S. F., Harvill, J. L., & Arshad, A., et al. (2004). The World Trade Center attack: Increased frequency of defibrillator shocks for ventricular arrhythmias in patients living remotely from New York City. *Journal of the American College of Cardiology, 44*(6), 1265–1267. 305

Shughart II, W. F. (2006). An analytical history of terrorism, 1945–2000. *Public Choice, 128*(1/2), 7–39. 41

Siddiqui, H. (2008). Ransom Claim in Ingrid Betancourt Release. *The Guardian*, July 4. 58

SIGAR. (2021). Counter Threat Finance: U.S. Agencies Do Not Know the Full Cost and Impact of Their Efforts to Disrupt Illicit Narcotics Financing in Afghanistan. Special Inspector General for Afghanistan Reconstruction Audit Report, March. 130

Silver, R. C., Alison Homan, E., McIntosh, D. N., Poulin, M., & Gil-Riva, V. (2002). Nationwide longitudinal study of psychological responses to September 11. *Journal of the American Medical Association, 288*(10), 748–766. 297

Silver, R. C., Alison Holman, E., Anderson, J. P., Poulin, M., McIntosh, D. N. & Gil-Rivas, V. (2013). Mental- and physical-health effects of acute exposure to media images of the September 11, 2001, attacks and the Iraq war. *Psychological Science, 24*(9), 1623–1634. 307

Simon, J. (2011). Technological and lone operator terrorism: Prospects for a fifth wave of global terrorism. In J. E. Rosenfeld (Ed.), *Terrorism, identity and legitimacy*. New York: Routledge. 178

Sinclair, S. J., & Antonius, D. (2012). *The psychology of terrorism fears*. Oxford University Press. 9

Singh, V. (2015). Punjab seeks Compensation for Victims of Insurgency. *The Hindu*, a daily, September 29. 173

Singh, R. (2018). India's experience with terrorism. In S. Ganguly, M. Pardesi, & N. Blarel (Eds.), *The Oxford handbook of India's national security*. Oxford: Oxford University Press. 173, 174, 175

Siqueira, K., & Sandler, T. (2007). Terrorist backlash, terrorism mitigation, and policy delegation. *Journal of Public Economics, 91*(9), 1800–1815. 435

Sivak, M., & Flannagan, M. J. (2004). Consequences for road traffic fatalities of the reduction in flying following September 11, 2001. *Transportation Research Part F, 7F*(4-5), 305–307. 308

Sloboda, B. W. (2003). Assessing the effects of terrorism on tourism by the use of time series methods. *Tourism Economics, 9*(2), 179–190. 318

Sly, L., & Haidamous, S. (2019). Trump's Sanctions on Iran are Hitting Hezbollah, and It Hurts. *Washington Post*, May 18. 151

Spencer, R. (2010). Black September Terrorist who Masterminded the Munich Massacre Dead in Syria. *The Telegraph*, July 4. 89

Stanford University. (2012). Al Jama'a Al-Islamiya. Mapping Militant Organizations, August 1. http://web.stanford.edu/group/mappingmilitants/cgi-bin/groups/view/265?highlight=al+qaeda accessed on November 28, 2018. 153

Stanford University. (2014). Caucasus Emirate. Mapping Militant Organizations, April 11. http://web.stanford.edu/group/mappingmilitants/cgi-bin/groups/view/255, accessed on December 24, 2018. 167

Stanford University. (2015a). Liberation Tigers of Tamil Eelam. Mapping Militant Organizations, July 8. http://web.stanford.edu/group/mappingmilitants/cgi-bin/groups/view/225, accessed on November 14, 2018. 90, 94, 95, 96

Stanford University. (2015b). Communist Party of the Philippines—New People's Party. Mapping Militant Organizations, August 24. http://web.stanford.edu/group/mappingmilitants/cgi-bin/groups/view/149 accessed on November 14, 2018. 67

Stanford University. (2015c). National Liberation Army (Colombia). Mapping Militant Organizations, August 17. http://web.stanford.edu/group/mappingmilitants/cgi-bin/groups/view/87. 59

Stanford University. (2015d). Revolutionary Armed Force of Colombia—People's Army. Mapping Militant Organizations. http://web.stanford.edu/group/mappingmilitants/cgi-bin/groups/view/89 accessed on November 14, 2018. 54, 59

Stanford University. (2015e). Jemaah Islamiyah. Mapping Militant Organizations. http://web.stanford.edu/group/mappingmilitants/cgi-bin/groups/view/251 accessed on December 22, 2018. 161

Stanford University. (2016a). Kata'ib Hezbollah. Mapping Militant Organizations, August 25. http://web.stanford.edu/group/mappingmilitants/cgi-bin/groups/view/361?highlight=kataib+hezbollah, accessed on November 28, 2018. 151

Stanford University. (2016b). Lashkar-e-Taiba. Mapping Militant Organizations, January 30. http://web.stanford.edu/group/mappingmilitants/cgi-bin/groups/view/79, accessed on November 30, 2018. 156, 157, 158

Stanford University. (2016c). Al Shabaab. Mapping Militant Organizations, February 20. http://web.stanford.edu/group/mappingmilitants/cgi-bin/groups/view/61, accessed on December 21, 2018. 158

Stanford University. (2017a). The Islamic State. Mapping Militant Organizations, October 23. http://web.stanford.edu/group/mappingmilitants/cgi-bin/groups/view/1 accessed on November 14, 2018. 104

Stanford University. (2017b). Haqqani Network. Mapping Militant Organizations, November 8. http://web.stanford.edu/group/mappingmilitants/cgi-bin/groups/view/363 accessed on November 17, 2018. 134

Starr, B., Browne, R., & Cohen, Z. (2020). US Announces Further Drawdown of Troops in Afghanistan and Iraq before Biden Takes Office. *CNN Politics*, November 17. 126

Stefanik, C. L. (2009). West German Terror: The Lasting Legacy of the Red Army Faction. Master's thesis, Bowling Green State University. 53

Steinberg, J. S., Arshad, A., Kowalski, M., & et al. (2004). Increased incidence of life-threatening ventricular arrhythmias in implantable defibrillator patients after the World Trade Center attack. *Journal of the American College of Cardiology, 44*(6), 1261–1264. 304

Stimson Study Group. (2018). Counterterrorism Spending: Protecting America While Promoting Efficiencies and Accountability. Report by Stimson Center. 262, 263, 264, 265, 267

Sufizada, H. (2020). The Taliban are Megarich - Here's Where They Get the Money to Wage War. *The Print*, December 14. 132

Sundquist, V. H. (2010). Political terrorism: An historial case study of the Italian Red Brigades. *Journal of Strategic Security, 3*(3), 53–67. 53

Szekely, O. (2015). Doing well by doing good: Understanding Hamas's social services as political advertising. *Studies in Conflict & Terrorism, 38*(4), 275–292. 143

Tahhan, Z. (2017). Hamas and Fatah: How are the Two Groups Different? *Al Jazeera*, October 12. 81

Tankel, S. (2009). Lashkar-e-Taiba: From 9/11 to Mumbai. Developments in Radicalisation and Political Violence working paper series. Published by The International Centre for the Study of Radicalisation and Political Violence, King's College London. 328

Tavares, J. (2004). The open society assesses its enemies: Shocks, disasters and terrorist attacks. *Journal of Monetary Economics, 51*(5), 1039–1070. 279

Taylor, M. (1988). *The terrorist*. Potomac Books, Inc. 558

The Telegraph. (2001). IRA plotted with Nazis to Invade Northern Ireland. October 19. 46

Tharoor, I. (2014a). How Israel Helped Create Hamas. *Washington Post*, July 30. 141

Tharoor, I. (2014b). How the U.S. and Five 'Terrorist Groups' Are on the Same Side in War Against the Islamic State. *Washington Post*, November 7. 326

The Economist. (1997). Bloodbath at Luxor. November 20. 153

The Guardian. (2002). Mystery Death of Abu Nidal, Once the World's Most Wanted Terrorist. August 19. 89

The Mackenzie Institute. (2015a). Abu Nidal Organization (ANO). Terrorism Profile. 89

The Mackenzie Institute. (2015b). Caucasus Emirate. Terrorism Profile. 167

The Mackenzie Institute. (2016a). Kurdistan Workers Party (PKK). Terrorism Profile. 80

The Mackenzie Institute. (2016b). Palestinian Islamic Jihad (PIJ). Terrorism Profile. 151, 152

Tsi, A. C., & Venkataramani, A. S. (2015). Communal bereavement and resilience in the aftermath of a terrorist event: Evidence from a natural experiment. *Social Science & Medicine, 146*, 155–163. 298

U.N. Security Council. (2012). First Report of the Analytical Support and Sanctions Implementation Monitoring Team Submitted Pursuant to Resolution 1988 (2011) Concerning the Taliban and Associated Individuals and Entities. 131

U.N. Security Council. (2020). Twenty-Seventh Report of the Analytical Support and Sanctions Monitoring Team Submitted Pursuant to Resolution 2368 (2017) Concerning ISIL (Da'esh), Al-Qaeda and Associated Individuals and Entities. Analytical Support and Sanctions Monitoring Team, 27th Report, December. 136

United Nations. (2021). Syria: 10 Years of War has left at least 350,000 Dead. UN News: Global Perspective Human Stories, September 24, https://news.un.org/en/story/2021/09/1101162 accessed on November 26. 124

United States Department of State. (2018). Country Reports on Terrorism 2017 - Foreign Terrorist Organizations: Indian Mujahedeen. September 19, https://www.refworld.org/docid/5bcf1f4327.html, accessed on December 25, 2018. 176

UNODC (United Nations Office on Drugs and Crime). (2019). Global Study on Homicide: Homicide Trends, Patterns and Criminal Justice Response. Report. 189, 221

van Ballegooij, W., & Bakowski, P. (2018). The Fight Against Terrorism: Cost of Non-Europe Report. RAND-Europe for the European Parliamentary Research Service, European Parliament. 252, 254, 258, 294, 318, 454

van der Merwe, T. (2017). Resource Extraction and Violent Extremism in Africa. South African Institute of International Affairs, Policy Insights #44, May. 234

van Natta Jr., D., & O'Brien, T. (2003). Flow of Saudis' Cash to Hamas Is Scrutinized. *New York Times*, September 17. 144

van Um, E. (2016). *Evaluating the political rationale of terrorist groups*: Springer VS. 326

Vittori, J. (2009). All struggles must end: The longevity of terrorist groups. *Contemporary Security Policy, 30*(3), p. . 210, 356, 357, 365

Vittori, J. (2011). *Terrorist financing and resourcing*, New York: Palgrave Macmillan. 232

Vlahov, D., Galea, S., Resnick, H., & Ahern, J., et al. (2002). Increased use of cigarette, alcohol, and Marijuana among Manhatten, New York, Residents after the September 11th terrorist attacks. *American Journal of Epidemiology, 155*(11), 988–996. 299

Volodin, S. N., & Mikhalev, A. G. (2017). Analysing the impact of terrorist attacks on stock index dynamics. *Finance and Credit, 23*(10), 575–598. 290

von Borcke, A. (1982). Violence and terror in Russian revolutionary populism: The *Narodnaya Volya*, 1879–83. In W.J. Momssen, & G. Hirschfeld (Eds.), *Social protest, violence and terror in nineteenth- and twentieth-century Europe*. London: Palgrave Macmillan. 43

Walls, E. (2017). Waves of Modern Terrorism: Examining the Past and Predicting the Future. Master's thesis, Georgetown University. 41, 42

Walsh, J. I. (2013). The Effectiveness of Drone Strikes in Counterinsurgency and Counterterrorism Campaigns. Strategic Studies Institute and U.S. Army War College Press. 435

Wash, S., & Smith, C. (2017). Authorities say Sale of Counterfeit Sneakers can Lead to Terrorist Financing. *ABC News*, abcnews.go.com, September 7. 234

Weinbaum, M. G., & Babbar, M. (2016). The Tenacious, Toxic Haqqani Network. Middle East Institute (Washington D.C.), MEI Policy Focus 2016-23, September. 134

Welshans, K. C. (2007). Nationalism and Islamic Identity in Xijiang. Ph.D. dissertation, Naval Postgraduate School, Monterey, California. 170

Wesseling, M. (2014). Evaluation of EU Measures to Combat Terrorism Financing. Document for the Committe on Civil Liberties, Justice and Home Affairs (LIBE), European Parliament. 454

White, J. (2017). *Terrorism and homeland security* (9th edn.). Belmont, California: Wadsworth Cengage Learning. 26, 44, 47, 50, 54, 60, 61, 62, 67, 68, 69, 75, 93, 101, 102, 135, 147, 172, 177, 232

Whittacker, D. J. (2001). *The terrorism reader*. New York: Routledge. 571

Wiktorowicz, Q. (2006). Anatomy of the salafi movement. *Studies in Conflict & Terrorism, 29*, 207–239. 22

Wilson Center. (2019). Timeline: The Rise, Spread, and Fall of the Islamic State. Insight and Analysis Article, October 28. 114

Windrem, R. (2015). Terror on a Shoestring: Paris Attacks Likely Cost $10,000 or Less. *NBC News*, November 19. 230

Wittig, T. (2011). *Understanding terrorist finance*. Palgrave MacMillan. 230, 232, 241

Wong, E. (2006). A Matter of Definition: What Makes a Civil War, and Who Declares It So? *New York Times*, November 26. 11

Woodruff, C. A. (2008). Political Culture and Revolution: An Analysis of the Tupamaros' Failed Attempt to Ignite a Social Revolution in Uruguay. Research Paper, Lozano Long Institute of Latin American Studies, University of Texas at Austin. 62

World Bank. (2016). Economic and Social Inclusion to Prevent Violent Extremism. World Bank Middle East and North African Region, MENA Economic Monitor. 117

World Bank. (2020). Palestinian Territories' Economic Update—April 2020. April 16, https://www.worldbank.org/en/country/westbankandgaza/publication/economic-update-april-2020 last accessed on December 13, 2020. 147

World Travel & Tourism Council. (2019). Travel & Tourism, Economic Impact 2019: World. 293

Xinhua News Agency. (2000). Sri Lanka: Sri Lanka's Rebels Involved in Trafficking Human Cargo. April. 95

Xu, J., & Chen, H. (2008). Topology of dark networks. *Communication of the ACM, 51*(10), 58–65. 337

Yaya, M. E. (2009). Terrorism and tourism: The case of Turkey. *Defence and Peace Economics, 20*(6), 477–497. 294, 318

Young, J. K., & Dugan, L. (2014). Survival of the fittest: Why terrorist groups endure. *Perspectives on Terrorism, 8*(2). http://www.terrorismanalysts.com/pt/index.php/pot/article/view/334/html, accessed on July 21, 2019. 356, 358, 359, 363, 365

Yourish, K. (2015). The Fates of 23 ISIS Hostages in Syria. *New York Times*, February 10. 488

Youssef, N. A., & Phillips, M. M. (2020). U.S. Will Move Nearly All Troops Out of Somalia, Officials Say. *Wall Street Journal*, December 4. https://www.wsj.com/articles/u-s-will-move-nearly-all-u-s-troops-out-of-somalia-11607114195, last accssed on December 13, 2020. 160

Yun, M., & Roth, M. (2008). Terrorist hostage-taking and kidnapping: Using script theory to predict the fate of a hostage. *Studies in Conflict & Terrorism, 31*(8), 736–748. 498, 503

Zehorai, I. (2014). The World's 10 Richest Terrorist Organizations. *Forbes*, December 14. 59, 74, 118, 120, 121, 132, 140, 145, 146, 151, 239, 240

Zehorai, I. (2018). The Richest Terror Organizations in the World. *Forbes*, January 1. 74, 75, 129, 132, 147, 151, 152, 153, 239, 240

Index

S. P. Das, *Economics of Terrorism and Counter-Terrorism Measures*,
https://doi.org/10.1007/978-3-030-96577-8

J

T

U

MIX
Papier aus verantwortungsvollen Quellen
Paper from responsible sources
FSC® C105338
FSC
www.fsc.org

If you have any concerns about our products,
you can contact us on
ProductSafety@springernature.com

In case Publisher is established outside the EU,
the EU authorized representative is:
Springer Nature Customer Service Center GmbH
Europaplatz 3, 69115 Heidelberg, Germany

Printed by Libri Plureos GmbH
in Hamburg, Germany